W9-DEU-222

Why Do You Need This New Edition?

If you're wondering why you should buy this new edition of *Drama: A Pocket Anthology,* here are five good reasons!

❶ A new one-act play by Latina playwright Milcha Sanchez-Scott, *The Cuban Swimmer,* reflects the struggle of a Cuban-American to find her way in American mainstream culture.

❷ A new play by Arlene Hutton, *I Dream Before I Take the Stand,* has the makings of a feminist classic, according to one reviewer.

❸ Sophocles' *Antigone* offers echoes of today's politics.

❹ Ibsen's *An Enemy of the People* appears here in an exciting adaptation by one of America's premier playwrights, Arthur Miller.

❺ And **August Wilson's *The Piano Lesson,*** is already an American classic, along with the rest of Wilson's ten-play cycle about the lives of African-Americans in Pittsburgh.

about the author

Photo by Gerry Cambridge

R.S. GWYNN has edited several other books, including *Literature: A Pocket Anthology; Poetry: A Pocket Anthology; Fiction: A Pocket Anthology; Inside Literature: Reading, Responding, Writing* (with Steven Zani); *The Art of the Short Story* (with Dana Gioia); and *Contemporary American Poetry: A Pocket Anthology* (with April Lindner). He has also authored five collections of poetry, including *No Word of Farewell: Selected Poems, 1970–2000.* He has been awarded the Michael Braude Award for verse from the American Academy of Arts and Letters. Gwynn is University Professor of English and Poet-in-Residence at Lamar University in Beaumont, Texas.

PENGUIN ACADEMICS

DRAMA
A POCKET ANTHOLOGY

FOURTH EDITION

Edited by

R. S. Gwynn
Lamar University

New York Boston San Francisco
London Toronto Sydney Tokyo Singapore Madrid
Mexico City Munich Paris Cape Town Hong Kong Montreal

Senior Sponsoring Editor: Virginia Blanford
Senior Marketing Manager: Joyce Nilsen
Senior Supplements Editor: Donna Campion
Production Manager: Denise Phillip
Project Coordination and Electronic Page Makeup: Nesbitt Graphics
Senior Cover Designer/Manager: Nancy Danahy
Cover Image: © Johannes Kroemer/Photonica/Getty Images, Inc.
Manufacturing Manager: Mary Fischer
Printer and Binder: Courier Corporation
Cover Printer: Phoenix Color Corporation

For more information about the Penguin Academics series, please contact us
by mail at Pearson Education, attn. Marketing Department, 51 Madison
Avenue, 29th Floor, New York, NY 10010, or visit us online at
www.pearsonhighered.com

For permission to use copyrighted material, grateful acknowledgment is
made to the copyright holders on p. 613, which is hereby made part of this
copyright page.

Library of Congress Cataloging-in-Publication Data

Drama: a pocket anthology / edited by R.S. Gwynn.—4th ed.
        p. cm.—(Penguin academics)
    Includes index.
    ISBN 0-205-65406-1
    1. Drama–Collections. I. Gwynn, R. S.

PN6112.D68 2009
808.2–dc22   2008024744

Copyright © 2009 by Pearson Education, Inc.

All rights reserved. No part of this publication may be reproduced, stored in
a retrieval system, or transmitted, in any form or by any means, electronic,
mechanical, photocopying, recording, or otherwise, without the prior written
permission of the publisher. Printed in the United States.

Visit us at www.pearsonhighered.com

ISBN–13: 978-0-205-65406-2
ISBN–10:   0-205-65406-1

2 3 4 5 6 7 8 9 10—CRW—11 10 09

contents

v

preface

When the *Pocket Anthology* series first appeared, our primary aim was to offer a clear alternative to the anthologies of fiction, poetry, and drama that were available at the time. *Drama: A Pocket Anthology,* now part of the Penguin Academic series from Pearson Longman, is here updated and revised for a fourth edition. Designed to be used in a wide range of courses, this brief anthology can be packaged with one or more of a rich selection of Penguin titles, which Pearson Longman offers at significantly reduced prices. Also, *Drama* is published concurrently with two companion volumes, *Fiction* and *Poetry,* as well as in a combined edition, *Literature: A Pocket Anthology,* which comprises most of the selections found in the three independent volumes, as well as introductions to all three genres. Your Pearson Longman representative can supply full details about these books and about the available Penguin titles.

What's New in This Edition

As with earlier editions of *Drama,* our goal has been to provide variety and flexibility in the selections offered. Contemporary playwrights new to this anthology include Milcha Sanchez-Scott and Arlene Hutton, each with one-acts addressing contemporary social questions: the integration of "the other" into American mainstream culture, and, in a biting play some critics have found reminiscent of Mamet but from a feminist perspective, relations between men and women. In addition, readers will find new selections from Sophocles, Ibsen, and August Wilson. While trying to balance classical and contemporary drama in a brief anthology, we have also tried to ensure the representation of women and writers of color, as well as a range of dramatic forms.

Goals of This Anthology

Drama addresses the four wishes and concerns most commonly expressed by both instructors and students. First, of course, is the variety of selections it contains. Admittedly, a pocket anthology has to be very selective in its contents, so we are especially proud that the twelve plays in this book include both established canonical writers from Sophocles and Shakespeare to Ibsen and Tennessee Williams, and contemporary playwrights such as August Wilson, David Ives, and Milcha Sanchez-Scott, who reflect the diversity that is essential to any study of contemporary theater. The range of dramatic genres in *Drama* includes a Greek tragedy, a Shakespearean tragedy, a problem play by Ibsen, and nine modern and contemporary plays ranging from one-act comedy and drama to modern tragedy to poetic realism to contemporary social drama. We strongly believe that the plays in *Drama* will provide a reading experience that is thought-provoking and enjoyable, as well as a strong introduction to drama and dramatic conventions overall.

Our second goal was flexibility. We wanted a book that could be used as both a primary and a supplemental text in a wide range of courses, from introduction to drama to advanced classes in theatre or playwriting to creative writing workshops. When combined with one of its companion volumes, *Fiction* or *Poetry*, or with novels, collections of short stories or poems by individual authors, or plays available from Penguin, *Drama* may also be used in introductory literature courses. *Drama* contains, in addition to its generous selection of plays, biographical headnotes about authors, an introduction that covers the techniques and terminology of the genre, and a concise section on writing about drama and research procedures.

Third, we wanted an affordable book. Full-size introductory literature books—and even comprehensive anthologies of drama—now cost well over $60. Pearson Education is committed to keeping the price of the *Pocket Anthology* series reasonable without compromising on design or typeface. We hope that readers will find the attractive layout of *Drama* preferable to the cramped margins and minuscule fonts found in many literature textbooks. Because of its relatively low cost, this volume may be easily supplemented in individual courses with works of criticism, handbooks of grammar and usage, or manuals of style.

Finally, we stressed portability. Many instructors have expressed concern for students who must carry literature books comprising 2,000 or more pages in backpacks already laden with books and materials for other courses. A semester is a short time, and few courses can cover more than a fraction of the material that many full-sized collections contain. Because many instructors focus on a single genre at a time, *Drama* and its companion volumes, *Fiction* and *Poetry*, remain compact yet self-contained volumes that are reasonably easy to handle and carry.

Acknowledgments

No book is ever created in a vacuum. We would like to express our gratitude to the instructors who reviewed the current edition of this volume and offered invaluable recommendations for improvement. They are Ruth Anne Baumgartner, Fairfield University; Paul Castagno, University of North Carolina/Wilmington; Thomas C. Crochunis, Shippensburg University; Laura Early, University of Louisville; and Randy Hendricks, University of West Georgia.

We are also grateful to those who reviewed earlier editions, including Melanie Abrams, California State University/San Bernardino; Francis G. Babcock, Louisiana State University; Maryam Barrie, Washtenaw Community College; Paul Bawek, Florida Southern College; Jeff Cofer, Bellevue Community College; Marla K. Dean, University of Montevallo; Verna Foster, Loyola University (Chicago); Janet Gardner, University of Massachusetts/Dartmouth; Christine Gilmore, University of Toledo; Paul Graharm, West Virginia University; Dennis G. Jerz, University of Wisconsin/Eau Claire; Kevin Kerrane, University of Delaware; Bethany Larson, Buena Vista University; Donna Long, Fairmount State University; James F. Scott, St. Louis University; Jeffrey P. Stephens, Oklahoma State University; James Stick, Des Moines Area Community College; and Karin Westman, Kansas State University.

The editor also wishes to thank Beverly Williams and Rachel Klauss for their assistance in preparing this book.

R. S. Gwynn
Lamar University

Introduction

The Play's the Thing

The theater, located in the heart of a rejuvenated downtown business district, is a relic of the silent movie era that has been restored to something approaching its former glory. While only a few members of tonight's audience can actually remember it in its prime, the expertise of the organist seated at the antique Wurlitzer instills a sense of false nostalgia in the crowd, now settling by twos and threes into red, plush-covered seats and looking around in search of familiar faces. Just as the setting is somewhat out of the ordinary, so is this group. Unlike movie audiences, they are for the most part older and less casually dressed. There are few small children present, and even the teenagers seem to be on their best behavior. Oddly, no one is eating popcorn or noisily drawing on a soda straw. A mood of seriousness and anticipation hovers over the theater, and those who have lived in the town long enough can spot the spouse or partner of one of the principal actors nervously folding a program or checking a watch.

As the organ magically descends into the recesses of the orchestra pit, the lights dim, a hush falls over the crowd, and the curtain creakily rises. There is a general murmur of approval at the ingenuity and many hours of hard work that have transformed empty space into a remarkable semblance of an upper-class drawing room in the early 1900s. Dressed as a domestic servant, a young woman, known to the audience from her frequent appearances in local television commercials, enters and begins to dust a table. She hums softly to herself. A tall young man, in everyday life a junior partner in a local law firm, wanders in carrying a tennis racket. The maid turns, sees him, and catches her breath, startled. "Why Mr. Fenton!" she exclaims. . . .

And the world begins.

The full experience of drama—whether at an amateur production like the little theater performance described here or at a huge Broadway playhouse—is much more complex than that of any other form of literature. The word **drama** itself comes from a Greek word meaning "a thing that is done," and the roots of both **theater** and **audience** call to mind the acts of seeing and hearing, respectively. Like other communal public activities—religious services, sporting events, meetings of political or fraternal organizations—drama has evolved, over many centuries, its own set of customs, rituals, and rules. The exact shape of these characteristics—**dramatic conventions**—may differ from country to country or from period to period, but they all have one aim in common, namely to define and govern an art form whose essence is to be found in public performances of written texts. No other form of literature shares this primary goal. Before we can discuss drama purely as literature, we should first ponder some aspects of its unique status as "a thing that is done."

It is worth noting that dramatists are also called playwrights. Note the spelling—a "wright" is a maker, as old family names like Cartwright or Boatwright attest. If a play is in fact *made* rather than written, then a playwright is similar to an architect who has designed a unique building. The concept may be his or hers, but the construction project requires the contributions of many other hands before the sparkling steel and glass tower alters the city's skyline. In the case of a new play, money will have to be raised by a producer, a director chosen, a cast found, a crew assembled, a set designed and built, and many hours of rehearsal completed before the curtain can be raised for the first time. Along the way, modifications to the original play may become necessary, and it is possible that the author will listen to advice from the actors, director, or stage manager and incorporate their opinions into any revisions. Professional theater is, after all, a branch of show business, and no play will survive its premiere for long if it does not attract paying crowds. The dramatists we read and study so reverently today managed to reach large popular audiences in their time. Even ancient Greek playwrights like Sophocles and Euripides must have stood by surreptitiously "counting the house" as the open-air seats slowly filled, and Shakespeare prospered as part-owner of the Globe Theatre to the extent that he was able to retire to his hometown at the ripe old age of forty-seven.

Set beside this rich communal experience, the solitary act of reading a play seems a poor substitute, contrary to the play's very nature (only a small category known as **closet drama** comprises plays intended to be read instead of acted). Yet dramatists like Shakespeare and Ibsen are counted among the giants of world literature, and their works are annually read by far more people than actually see their plays performed. In reading a play, we are forced to pay close attention to such matters as **set description,** particularly with a playwright like Ibsen, who lavishes great attention on the design of his set; references to **properties** or "props" that will figure in the action of the play; physical description of characters and costumes; **stage directions** indicating the movements and gestures made by actors in scenes; and any other **stage business,** that is, action without dialogue. Many modern dramatists are very scrupulous in detailing these matters; writers of earlier periods, however, provided little or no instruction. Reading Sophocles or Shakespeare, we are forced to concentrate on the characters' words to envision how actions and other characters were originally conceived. Reading aloud, alone or in a group, or following along in the text while listening to or watching an audio or video performance is particularly recommended for verse plays such as *Antigone* or *Othello*. Also, versions of many of the plays contained in this book are currently available on videotape or DVD. While viewing a film is an experience of a different kind from seeing a live performance, film versions obviously provide a convenient insight into the ways in which great actors have interpreted their roles. Seeing the joy in the face of Laurence Fishburne when, as Othello, he lands triumphantly in Cyprus and rejoins his bride makes his tragic fall even more poignant.

Origins of Drama

No consensus exists about the exact date of the birth of drama, but according to most authorities, it originated in Greece over 2500 years ago, an outgrowth of rites of worship of the god Dionysus, who was associated with male fertility, agriculture (especially the cultivation of vineyards), and seasonal renewal. In these Dionysian festivals a group of fifty citizens of Athens, known as a **chorus,** outfitted and trained by a leader, or *choragos,* would perform hymns of praise to the god, known as **dithyrambic poetry.** The celebration concluded with the ritual sacrifice of a goat, or *tragos.* The two main genres of drama originally took their names from these rituals; comedy comes from *kômos,* the Greek word for a festivity. These primitive revels were invariably accompanied with a union of the sexes (*gamos* in Greek, a word that survives in English words like "monogamy") celebrating fertility and continuance of the race, an ancient custom still symbolically observed in the "fade-out kiss" that concludes most comedies. Tragedy, on the other hand, literally means "song of the goat," taking its name from the animal that was killed on the altar *(thymele),* cooked, and shared by the celebrants with their god.

Around 600 B.C. certain refinements took place. In the middle of the sixth century B.C. an official springtime festival, known as the Greater or City Dionysia, was established in Athens, and prizes for the best dithyrambic poems were first awarded. At about the same time a special **orchestra,** or "dancing place," was constructed, a circular area surrounding the altar, and permanent seats, or a **theatron** ("seeing place"), arranged in a semicircle around the orchestra were added. At the back of the orchestra the façade of a temple (the **skene**) and a raised "porch" in front of it (the **proskenion,** in later theaters the **proscenium**) served as a backdrop, usually representing the palace of the ruler; walls extending to either side of the *skene,* the **parodoi,** served to conceal backstage activity from the audience. A wheeled platform, or **eccyclema,** could be pushed through the door of the *skene* to reveal the tragic consequences of a play's climax (there was no onstage "action" in Greek tragedy). Behind the *skene* a crane-like device called a **mechane** (or **deus ex machina**) could be used to lower a god from the heavens or represent a spectacular effect like the flying chariot drawn by dragons at the conclusion of Euripides' *Medea.*

In 535 B.C. a writer named Thespis won the annual competition with a startling innovation. Thespis separated one member of the chorus (called a *hypocrites,* or "actor") and had him engage in **dialogue,** spoken lines representing conversation, with the remaining members. If we define drama primarily as a story related through live action and recited dialogue, then Thespis may rightly be called the father of drama, and his name endures in "thespian," a synonym for actor.

The century after Thespis, from 500–400 B.C., saw many refinements in the way tragedies were performed and is considered the golden age of Greek drama. In this century, the careers of the three great tragic playwrights—Aeschylus (525–456 B.C.), Sophocles (496?–406 B.C.), and Euripides (c. 480–406 B.C.)—and the greatest comic playwright, Aristophanes (450?–385? B.C.) overlapped. It is no coincidence that in this remarkable period Athens, under the leadership of the general Pericles (495–429 B.C.), reached the height of its wealth, influence, and cultural development and was home to the philosophers Socrates (470–399 B.C.) and Plato (c. 427–347 B.C.). Aristotle (384–322 B.C.), the third of the great Athenian philosophers, was also a literary critic who wrote the first extended analysis of drama.

Aristotle on Tragedy

The earliest work of literary criticism in Western civilization is Aristotle's *Poetics*, an attempt to define and classify the different literary **genres** that use rhythm, language, and harmony. Aristotle identifies four genres—epic poetry, dithyrambic poetry, comedy, and tragedy—which have in common their attempts at imitation, or *mimesis*, of various types of human activity.

Aristotle comments most fully on tragedy, and his definition of the genre demands close examination:

> A tragedy, then, is the imitation of an action that is serious and also, as having magnitude, complete in itself; in language with pleasurable accessories, each kind brought in separately in the parts of the work; in a dramatic, not in a narrative form; with incidents arousing pity and fear, wherewith to accomplish its catharsis of such emotions.

First we should note that the imitation here is of *action*. Later in the passage, when Aristotle differentiates between narrative and dramatic forms of literature, it is clear that he is referring to tragedy as a type of literature written primarily for public performance. Furthermore, tragedy must be serious and must have magnitude. By this, Aristotle implies that issues of life and death must be involved and that these issues must be of public import. In many Greek tragedies, the fate of the *polis*, or city, of which the chorus is the voice, is bound up with the actions taken by the main character in the play. Despite their rudimentary form of democracy, the people of Athens would have been perplexed by a tragedy with an ordinary citizen at its center; magnitude in tragedy demands that only the affairs of persons of high rank are of sufficient importance for tragedy. Aristotle further requires that this imitated action possess a sense of completeness. At no point does he say that a tragedy has to end with a death or even in a state of unhappiness; he does require, however, that the audience sense that after the last words are spoken no further story cries out to be told.

The next part of the passage may confuse the modern reader. By "language with pleasurable accessories" Aristotle means the poetic devices of rhythm and, in the choral parts of the tragedy, music and dance as well. Reading the choral passages in a Greek tragedy, we are likely to forget that these passages were intended to be chanted or sung ("chorus" and "choir" share the same root) and danced as well ("choreography" comes from this root as well).

The rest of Aristotle's definition dwells on the emotional effects of tragedy on the audience. Pity and fear are to be evoked—pity because we must care for the characters and to some extent empathize with them, fear because we come to realize that the fate they endure involves acts—of which murder and incest are only two—that civilized men and women most abhor. Finally, Aristotle's word *catharsis* has proved controversial over the centuries. The word literally means "a purging," but readers have debated whether Aristotle is referring to a release of harmful emotions or a transformation of them. In either case, the implication is that viewing a tragedy has a beneficial effect on an audience, perhaps because the viewers' deepest fears are brought to light in a make-believe setting. How many of us, at the end of some particularly wrenching film, have turned to a companion and said, "Thank god, it was only a movie"? The sacrificial animal from whom tragedy took its name was, after all, only a stand-in whose blood was offered to the gods as a substitute for a human subject. The protagonist of a tragedy remains, in many ways, a "scapegoat" on whose head we project our own unconscious terrors.

Aristotle identifies six elements of a tragedy, and these elements are still useful in analyzing not only tragedies but other types of plays as well. In order of importance they are **plot, characterization, theme, diction, melody,** and **spectacle.** Despite the fact that the *Poetics* is over two thousand years old, Aristotle's elements still provide a useful way of understanding how plays work.

Plot

Aristotle considers plot the chief element of a play, and it is easy to see this when we consider that in discussing a film with a friend we usually give a brief summary, or **synopsis,** of the plot, stopping just short of "giving it away" by telling how the story concludes. Aristotle defines plot as "the combination of incidents, or things done in the story," and goes on to give the famous formulation that a plot "is that which has a beginning, middle, and end." Aristotle notes that the best plots are selective in their use of material and have an internal coherence and logic. Two opposite terms that Aristotle introduced are still in use, although with slightly different meanings. By a **unified plot** we generally mean one that takes place in roughly a twenty-four hour period; in a short play with a unified plot like Susan Glaspell's *Trifles,* the action is continuous. By **episodic plot** we mean one that spreads its action out over a longer period of time. A play which has a unified plot, a single setting, and no subplots is said to observe the **three unities,** which critics in some eras have virtually insisted on as ironclad rules. Although most plots are chronological, playwrights in the last half-century have experimented, sometimes radically, with such straightforward progression through time. Arthur Miller's *Death of a Salesman* effectively blends **flashbacks** to past events with his action, and David Ives's *Sure Thing* plays havoc with chronology, allowing his protagonist to "replay" his previous scenes until he has learned the way to the "sure thing" of the title.

Two other important elements of most successful plots that Aristotle mentions are **reversal** (*peripeteia* in Greek, also known as **peripety**), and **recognition** (*anagnorisis* in Greek, also known as **discovery**). By reversal he means a change "from one state of things within the play to its opposite." Aristotle cites one example from *Oedipus the King,* the tragedy he focuses on, "the Messenger, who, coming to gladden Oedipus and to remove his fears as to his mother, reveals the secret of his birth"; but an earlier reversal in the same play occurs when Jocasta, attempting to alleviate Oedipus's fears of prophecies, inadvertently mentions the "place where three roads meet" where Oedipus killed a man he took to be a stranger. Most plays have more than a single reversal; each episode or act builds on the main character's hopes that his or her problems will be solved, only to dash those expectations as the play proceeds. Recognition, the second term, is perhaps more properly an element of characterization because it involves a character's "change from ignorance to knowledge." If the events of the plot have not served to illuminate the character about his or her failings, then the audience is likely to feel that the story has lacked depth. The kind of self-knowledge that tragedies provide is invariably accompanied by suffering and won at great emotional cost. In comedy, on the other hand, reversals may bring relief to the characters, and recognition may bring about the happy conclusion of the play.

A typical plot may be broken down into several components. First comes the **exposition,** which provides the audience with essential information—who, what, when, where—that it needs to know before the play can continue. A novelist or short story writer can present information directly with some sort of variation on the "Once upon a time" opening. But dramatists have particular problems with exposition because facts must be presented in the form of dialogue and action. Greek dramatists used the first two parts of a tragedy, relying on the audience's familiarity with the myths being retold, to set up the initial situation of the play. Other types of drama use a single character to provide expository material. Medieval morality plays often use a "heavenly messenger" to deliver the opening speech, and some of Shakespeare's plays employ a single character named "Chorus" who speaks an introductory prologue and "sets the scene" for later portions of the plays as well. In *The Glass Menagerie*, Tom Wingfield fulfills this role in an unusual manner, telling the audience at the beginning, "I am the narrator of the play, and also a character in it." Occasionally, we even encounter the least elegant solution to the problem of dramatic exposition, employing minor characters whose sole function is to provide background information in the play's opening scene. Countless drawing-room comedies have raised the curtain on a pair of servants in the midst of a gossipy conversation which catches the audience up on the doings of the family members who comprise the rest of the cast.

The second part of a plot is called the **complication,** the interjection of some circumstance or event that shakes up the stable situation that has existed before the play's opening and begins the **rising action** of the play, during which the audience's tension and expectations become tightly intertwined and involved with the characters and the events they experience. Complication in a play may be both external and internal. A plague, a threatened invasion, or a conclusion of a war are typical examples of external complication, outside events which affect the characters' lives. Many other plays rely primarily on an internal complication, a single character's failure in business or love that comes from a weakness in his or her personality. Often the complication is heightened by **conflict** between two characters whom events have forced into collision with each other. Whatever the case, the complication of the plot usually introduces a problem that the characters cannot avoid. The rising action, which constitutes the body of the play, usually contains a number of moments of **crisis,** when solutions crop up momentarily but quickly disappear. These critical moments in the scenes may take the form of the kinds of reversals discussed above, and the audience's emotional involvement in the plot generally hinges on the characters' rising and falling hopes.

The central moment of crisis in the play is the **climax,** or the moment of greatest tension, which initiates the **falling action** of the plot. Perhaps "moments" of greatest tension would be a more exact phrase, for skillful playwrights know how to wring as much tension as possible from the audience. In the best plots, everything in earlier parts of the play has pointed to this scene. In tragedy, the climax is traditionally accompanied with physical action and violence—a duel, a suicide, a murder—and the play's highest pitch of emotion.

The final part of a plot is the **dénouement,** or **resolution.** The French word literally refers to the untying of a knot, and we might compare the emotional effects of climax and dénouement to a piece of cloth twisted tighter and tighter as the play progresses and then untwisted as the action winds down. The dénouement returns the play and its characters to a stable situation, although not the same one that existed at the beginning of the play, and gives some indication of what the future holds for them. A dénouement may be either closed or open. A **closed dénouement** ties up everything neatly and explains all unanswered questions the audience might have; an **open dénouement** leaves a few tantalizing loose ends.

Several other plot terms should also be noted. Aristotle mentions, not altogether favorably, plots with "double issues." The most common word for this is **subplot,** a less important story involving minor characters that may mirror the main plot of the play. Some plays may even have more than one subplot. Occasionally, a playwright finds it necessary to drop hints about coming events in the plot, perhaps to keep the audience from complaining that certain incidents have happened "out of the blue." This is called **foreshadowing.** If a climactic incident that helps to resolve the plot has not been adequately prepared for, the playwright may be accused of having resorted to a ***deus ex machina*** ending, which takes its name from the *mechane* that once literally lowered a god or goddess into the midst of the dramatic proceedings. An ending of this sort, like that of an old western movie in which the cavalry arrives out of nowhere just as the wagon train is about to be annihilated, is rarely satisfactory.

Finally, the difference between **suspense** and **dramatic irony** should be addressed. Both of these devices generate tension in the audience, although through opposite means—suspense when the audience does not know what is about to happen; dramatic irony, paradoxically, when it does. Much of our pleasure in reading a new play lies in speculating about what will happen next, but in Greek tragedy the original audience would be fully familiar with the basic outlines of the mythic story before the action even began. Thus, dramatic irony occurs at moments when the audience is more knowledgeable about events than the onstage characters are. In some plays, our foreknowledge of certain events is so strong that we may want to cry out a warning to the characters.

Characterization

The Greek word ***agon*** means "debate" and refers to the central issue or conflict of a play. From *agon* we derive two words commonly used to denote the chief characters in a play: **protagonist,** literally the "first speaker," and **antagonist,** one who speaks against him. Often the word *hero* is used as a synonym for protagonist, but we should be careful in its application; indeed, in many modern plays it may be more appropriate to speak of the protagonist as an **anti-hero** because she or he may possess few, if any, of the traditional attributes of a hero. Similarly, the word *villain* brings to mind a black-mustached, sneering character in a top hat and opera cloak from an old-fashioned **melodrama** (a play whose complications are solved happily at the last minute by the "triumph of good over evil"), and usually has little application to the complex characters one encounters in a serious play.

Aristotle, in his discussion of characterization, stresses the complexity that marks the personages in the greatest plays. Nothing grows tiresome more quickly than a perfectly virtuous man or woman at the center of a play, and nothing is more offensive to the audience than seeing absolute innocence despoiled. Although Aristotle stresses that a successful protagonist must be better than ordinary men and women, he also insists that the protagonist be somewhat less than perfect:

> There remains, then, the intermediate kind of personage, a man not preeminently virtuous and just, whose misfortune, however, is brought upon him not by vice and depravity but by some error of judgment. . . .

Aristotle's word for this error is **hamartia,** which is commonly translated as "tragic flaw" but might more properly be termed a "great error." Whether he means some innate flaw, like a psychological defect, or simply a great mistake is open to question, but writers of tragedies have traditionally created deeply flawed protagonists. In ordinary circumstances, the protagonist's strength of character may allow him to prosper, but under the pressure of events he may crack when one small chink in his armor widens and leaves him vulnerable. A typical flaw in tragedies is **hubris,** arrogance or excessive pride, which leads the protagonist into errors that might have been avoided if he or she had listened to the advice of others. Although he does not use the term himself, Aristotle touches on the concept of **poetic justice,** the audience's sense that virtue and vice have been fairly dealt with in the play and that the protagonist's punishment is to some degree deserved.

We should bear in mind that the greatest burden of characterization in drama falls on the actor or actress who undertakes a role. No matter how well written a part is, in the hands of an incompetent or inappropriate performer the character will not be credible. Vocal inflection, gesture, and even the strategic use of silence are the stock in trade of actors, for it is up to them to convince us that we are involved in the sufferings and joys of real human beings. No two actors will play the same part in the same manner. We are lucky to have two excellent film versions of Shakespeare's *Henry the Fifth* available. Comparing the cool elegance of Laurence Olivier with the rough and ready exuberance of Kenneth Branagh is a wonderful short course in the equal validity of two radically different approaches to the same role.

In reading, there are several points to keep in mind about main characters. Physical description, while it may be minimal at best, is worth paying close attention to. To cite one example from the plays contained in this edition, Shakespeare identifies Othello simply as a "Moor," a native of North Africa. Race and color are important causes of conflict in the play, to be sure, but through the years the part has been played with equal success by both black and white actors. The important issue in *Othello* is that the tragic hero is a cultural misfit in the Venetian society from which he takes a wife; he is a widely respected military leader but an outsider all the same. Shakespeare provides us with few other details of his appearance, but we can probably assume that he is a large and powerful warrior, capable of commanding men by his mere presence. Sometimes an author will give a character a name that is an indicator of his or her personality and appearance. Oedipus's name, in Greek, refers to his scarred feet. Willy Loman, the failed protagonist of Arthur Miller's *Death of a Salesman,* bears a surname ("low man") which may contain a pun on his character, a device called a **characternym.**

Character motivation is another point of characterization to ponder. Why do characters act in a certain manner? What do they hope to gain from their actions? In some cases these motives are clear enough and may be discussed openly by the characters. In other plays, motivation is more elusive, as the playwright deliberately mystifies the audience by presenting characters who perhaps are not fully aware of the reasons for their compulsions. Modern dramatists, influenced by advances in psychology, have often refused to reduce characters' actions to simple equations of cause and effect.

Two conventions that the playwright may employ in revealing motivation are **soliloquy** and **aside.** A soliloquy is a speech made by a single character on stage alone. Hamlet's soliloquies, among them some of the most famous passages in all drama, show us the process of his mind as he toys with various plans of revenge but delays putting them into action. The aside is a brief remark (traditionally delivered to the side of a raised hand) that an actor makes directly to the audience and that the other characters on stage cannot hear. Occasionally, an aside reveals a reason for a character's behavior in a scene. Neither of these devices is as widely used in today's theater as in earlier periods, but they remain part of the dramatist's collection of techniques.

Minor characters are also of great importance in a successful play, and there are several different traditional types. A **foil,** a minor character with whom a major character sharply contrasts, is used primarily as a sounding board for ideas. A **confidant** is a trusted friend or servant to whom a major character speaks frankly and openly; confidants fulfill in some respects one role that the chorus plays in Greek tragedy. **Stock characters** are stereotypes that are useful for advancing the plot and fleshing out the scenes, particularly in comedies. Hundreds of plays have employed pairs of innocent young lovers, sharp-tongued servants, and meddling mothers-in-law as part of their casts. **Allegorical characters** in morality plays like *Everyman* are clearly labeled by their names and, for the most part, are personifications of human attributes (Beauty, Good Deeds) or of theological concepts (Confession). **Comic relief** in a tragedy may be provided by minor characters like Shakespeare's fools or clowns.

Theme

Aristotle has relatively little to say about the theme of a play, simply noting, "Thought of the personages is shown in everything to be effected by their language." Because he focuses to such a large degree on the emotional side of tragedy—its stimulation of pity and fear—he seems to give less importance to the role of drama as a serious forum for the discussion of ideas, referring his readers to another of his works, *The Art of Rhetoric*, where these matters have greater prominence. Nevertheless, **theme,** the central idea or ideas that a play discusses, is important in Greek tragedy and in the subsequent history of the theater. The trilogies of early playwrights were thematically unified around an *aition*, a Greek word for the origin of a custom, just as a typical elementary school Thanksgiving pageant portrays how the holiday traditions were first established in the Plymouth Colony.

Some dramas are explicitly **didactic** in their intent, existing with the specific aim of instructing the audience in ethical, religious, or political areas. A **morality play,** a popular type of drama in the late Middle Ages, is essentially a sermon on sin and redemption rendered in dramatic terms. More subtle in its didacticism is the **problem play** of the late nineteenth century, popularized by Ibsen, which uses the theater as a forum for the serious debate of social issues like industrial pollution or women's rights. The **drama of ideas** of playwrights like George Bernard Shaw does not merely present social problems; it goes further, actually advancing programs of reform. In the United States during the Great Depression of the 1930s, Broadway theaters featured a great deal of **social drama,** in which radical social and political programs were openly propagandized. In the ensuing decades, the theater has remained a popular site for examining issues of race, class, and gender.

Keep in mind, however, that plays are not primarily religious or political forums. If we are not entertained and moved by a play's language, action, and plot, then it is unlikely that we will respond to its message. The author who has to resort to long sermons from a *raisonneur,* the French word for a character who serves primarily as the voice of reason (i.e., the mouthpiece for the playwright's opinions), is not likely to hold the audience's sympathy or attention for long. The best plays are complex enough that they cannot be reduced to simple "thesis statements" that sum up their meaning in a few words.

Diction

Aristotle was also the author of the first important manual of public speaking, *The Art of Rhetoric,* so it should come as no surprise that he devotes considerable attention in the *Poetics* to the precise words, either alone or in combinations, that playwrights use. Instead of "diction," we would probably speak today of a playwright's "style," or discuss his or her handling of various levels of idiom in the dialogue. Much of what Aristotle has to say about parts of speech and the sounds of words in Greek is of little interest to us; of chief importance is his emphasis on clarity and originality in the choice of words. For Aristotle, the language of tragedy should be "poetic" in the best sense, somehow elevated above the level of ordinary speech but not so ornate that it loses the power to communicate feelings and ideas to an audience. Realism in speech is largely a matter of illusion, and close inspection of the actual lines of modern dramatists like Miller and Williams reveals a discrepancy between the carefully chosen words that characters speak in plays, often making up lengthy **monologues,** and the halting, often inarticulate ("Ya know what I mean?") manner in which we express ourselves in everyday life. The language of the theater has always been an artificial one. The idiom of plays, whether by Shakespeare or by August Wilson, *imitates* the language of life; it does not duplicate it.

Ancient Greek is a language with a relatively small vocabulary and, even in translation, we encounter a great deal of repetition of key words. *Polis,* the Greek word for city, appears many times in Sophocles' *Antigone,* stressing the communal fate that the protagonist and the chorus, representing the citizens, share. Shakespeare's use of the full resources of the English language has been the standard against which all subsequent writers in the language can measure themselves. Shakespeare's language presents some special difficulties to the modern reader. His vocabulary is essentially the same as ours, but many words have changed in meaning or become obsolete over the last four hundred years. Shakespeare is also a master of different **levels of diction.** In the space of a few lines he can range from self-consciously flowery heights ("If after every tempest come such calms, / May the winds blow till they have waken'd death! / And let the labouring bark climb hills of seas / Olympus-high and duck again as low / As hell's to heaven!" exults Othello on being reunited with his bride in Cyprus) to the slangy level of the streets—he is a master of the off-color joke and the sarcastic put-down. We should remember that Shakespeare's poetic drama lavishly uses figurative language; his lines abound with similes, metaphors, personifications, and hyperboles, all characteristic devices of the language of poetry. Shakespeare's theater had little in the way of scenery and no "special effects," so a passage from *Hamlet* like "But, look, the morn, in russet mantle clad / Walks o'er the dew of yon high eastward hill" is not merely pretty or picturesque; it has the dramatic function of helping the audience visualize the welcome end of a long, fearful night.

It is true that playwrights since the middle of the nineteenth century have striven for more fidelity to reality, more verisimilitude, in the language their characters use, but even realistic dramatists often rise to rhetorical peaks that have little relationship to the way people actually speak. Both Ibsen and Williams began their careers as poets and, surprisingly, the first draft of Miller's "realistic" tragedy *Death of a Salesman* was largely written in verse.

Melody

Greek tragedy was accompanied by music. None of this music survives, and we cannot be certain how it was integrated into the drama. Certainly the choral parts of the play were sung and danced, and it is likely that even the dialogue involved highly rhythmical chanting, especially in passages employing **stichomythia,** rapid alternation of single lines between two actors, a device often encountered during moments of high dramatic tension. In the original language, the different poetic rhythms used in Greek tragedy are still evident, although these are for the most part lost in English translation. At any rate it is apparent that the skillful manipulation of a variety of **poetic meters,** combinations of line lengths and rhythms, for different types of scenes was an important part of the tragic poet's repertoire.

Both tragedies and comedies have been written in verse throughout the ages, often employing rhyme as well as rhythm. *Antigone* is written in a variety of poetic meters, some of which are appropriate for dialogue between actors and others for the choral odes. Shakespeare's *Othello* is composed, like all of his plays, largely in **blank verse,** that is, unrhymed lines of iambic pentameter (lines of ten syllables, alternating unstressed and stressed syllables). He also uses rhymed couplets, particularly for emphasis at the close of scenes; songs (there are three in *Othello*); and even prose passages, especially when dealing with comic or "low" characters. A study of Shakespeare's versification is beyond the scope of this discussion, but suffice it to say that a trained actor must be aware of the rhythmical patterns that Shakespeare utilized if she or he is to deliver the lines with anything approaching accuracy.

Of course, not only verse drama has rhythm. The last sentences of Tennessee Williams's prose drama *The Glass Menagerie* can be easily recast as blank verse that would not have embarrassed Shakespeare himself:

> *Then all at once my sister touches my shoulder.*
> *I turn around and look into her eyes . . .*
> *Oh, Laura, Laura, I tried to leave you behind me,*
> *but I am more faithful than I intended to be!*
> *I reach for a cigarette, I cross the street,*
> *I run into the movies or a bar,*
> *I buy a drink, I speak to the nearest stranger—*
> *anything that can blow your candles out!*
> *—for nowadays the world is lit by lightning!*
> *Blow your candles out, Laura—and so good-bye . . .*

The ancient verse heritage of tragedy lingers on in the modern theater and has proved resistant to even the prosaic rhythms of what Williams calls a "world lit by lightning."

Spectacle

Spectacle (sometimes called **mise en scène,** French for "putting on stage") is the last of Aristotle's elements of tragedy and, in his view, the least important. By spectacle we mean the purely visual dimension of a play; in ancient Greece, this meant costumes, a few props, and effects carried out by the use of the *mechane.* Costumes in Greek tragedy were simple but impressive. The tragic mask, or **persona,** and a high-heeled boot **(cothurnus)** were apparently designed to give characters a larger-than-life appearance. Historians also speculate that the mask might have additionally served as a crude megaphone to amplify the actors' voices, a necessary feature when we consider that the open-air theater in Athens could seat over 10,000 spectators.

Other elements of set decoration were kept to a minimum, although playwrights occasionally employed a few well-chosen spectacular effects like the triumphant entrance of the victorious king in Aeschylus's *Agamemnon.* Elizabethan drama likewise relied little on spectacular stage effects. Shakespeare's plays call for few props, and little attempt was made at historical accuracy in costumes, with a noble patron's cast-off clothing dressing Caesar one week, Othello the next.

Advances in technology since Shakespeare's day have obviously facilitated more elaborate effects in what we now call **staging** than patrons of earlier centuries could have envisioned. In the nineteenth century, first gas and then electric lighting not only made effects like sunrises possible but also, through the use of different combinations of color, added atmosphere to certain scenes. By Ibsen's day, realistic **box sets** were designed to resemble, in the smallest details, interiors of houses and apartments with an invisible "fourth wall" nearest the audience. Modern theater has experimented in all directions with set design, from the bare stage to barely suggested walls and furnishings, from revolving stages to scenes that "break the plane" by involving the audience in the drama. Tennessee Williams's *The Glass Menagerie* employs music, complicated lighting and sound effects, and semitransparent **scrims** onto which images are projected, all to enhance the play's dream-like atmosphere. The most impressive uses of spectacle in today's Broadway productions may represent anything from the catacombs beneath the Paris Opera House to thirty-foot-high street barricades manned by soldiers firing muskets. Modern technology can create virtually any sort of stage illusion; the only limitations in today's professional theater are imagination and budget.

Before we leave our preliminary discussion, one further element should be mentioned—**setting.** Particular locales—Thebes, Corinth, and Mycenæ—are the sites of different tragedies, and each city has its own history; in the case of Thebes, this history involves a family curse that touches the members of three generations. But for the most part, specific locales in the greatest plays are less important than the universal currents that are touched. If we are interested in the particular features of Norwegian civic government in the late nineteenth century, we would perhaps do better going to history texts than to Ibsen's *An Enemy of the People.*

Still, every play implies a larger sense of setting, a sense of history that is called the **enveloping action.** The "southern belle" youth of Amanda Wingfield, in Williams's *The Glass Menagerie,* is a fading dream as anachronistic as the "gentlemen callers" she still envisions knocking on her daughter's door. Even though a play from the past may still speak eloquently today, it also provides a "time capsule" whose contents tell us how people lived and what they most valued during the period when the play was written and first performed.

Brief History and Description of Dramatic Conventions

Greek Tragedy

By the time of Sophocles, tragedy had evolved into an art form with a complex set of conventions. Each playwright would submit a **tetralogy,** or set of four plays, to the yearly competition. The first three plays, or **trilogy,** would be tragedies, perhaps unified like those of Aeschylus's *Oresteia,* which deals with Agamemnon's tragic homecoming from the Trojan War. The fourth, called a **satyr-play,** was comic, with a chorus of goatmen engaging in bawdy revels that, oddly, mocked the serious content of the preceding tragedies. Only one complete trilogy, the *Oresteia* by Aeschylus, and one satyr-play, *The Cyclops* by Euripides, have survived. Three plays by Sophocles derived from the myths surrounding Oedipus and his family—*Oedipus the King, Oedipus at Colonus,* and *Antigone*—are still performed and read, but they were written at separate times and accompanied by other tragedies that are now lost. As tragedy developed during this period, it seems clear that playwrights thought increasingly of individual plays as complete in themselves; *Antigone* does not leave the audience with the feeling that there is more to be told, even though Creon is still alive at the end of the play.

Each tragedy was composed according to a prescribed formula, as ritualized as the order of worship in a contemporary church service. The tragedy begins with a **prologue *(prologos),*** "that which is said first." The prologue is an introductory scene that tells the audience important information about the play's setting, characters, and events immediately preceding the opening of the drama. The second part of the tragedy is called the *parodos,* the first appearance of the chorus in the play. As the members of the chorus enter the orchestra, they dance and sing more generally of the situation in which the city finds itself. Choral parts in some translations are divided into sections called **strophes** and **antistrophes,** indicating choral movements to left and right, respectively. The body of the play is made up of two types of alternating scenes. The first, an **episode** *(episodos)* is a passage of dialogue between two or more actors or between the actors and the chorus. Each of these "acts" of the tragedy is separated from the rest by a choral **ode** *(stasimon;* pl. *stasima)* during which the chorus is alone on the orchestra, commenting, as the voice of public opinion, about the course of action being taken by the main characters. Typically there are four pairs of episodes and odes in the play. The final scene of the play is called the *exodos.* During this part the climax occurs out of sight of the audience and a vivid description of this usually violent scene is sometimes delivered by a messenger or other witness. After the messenger's speech, the main character reappears and the resolution of his fate is determined. In some plays a wheeled platform called an *eccyclema* was used to move this fatal tableau into view of the spectators. A tragedy concludes with the exit of the main characters, sometimes leaving the chorus to deliver a brief speech or **epilogue,** a final summing up of the play's meaning.

While we may at first find such complicated rituals bizarre, we should keep in mind that dramatic conventions are primarily customary and artificial and have little to do with "reality" as we usually experience it. The role of the chorus (set by the time of Sophocles at fifteen members) may seem puzzling to modern readers, but in many ways, the conventions of Greek tragedy are no stranger than those of contemporary musical comedy, in which a pair of lovers burst into a duet and dance in the middle of a stroll in the park, soon to be joined by a host of other cast members. What is most remarkable about the history of drama is not how much these conventions have changed but how remarkably similar they have remained for over twenty-five centuries.

Medieval Drama

Drama flourished during Greek and Roman times, but after the fall of the Roman Empire (A.D. 476) it declined during four centuries of eclipse, and was kept alive throughout Europe only by wandering troupes of actors performing various types of **folk drama.** The "Punch and Judy" puppet show, still popular in parts of Europe, is a late survivor of this tradition, as are the ancient slapstick routines of circus clowns. Even though drama was officially discouraged by the Church for a long period, when it did reemerge it was as an outgrowth of the Roman Catholic mass, in the form of **liturgical drama.** Around the ninth century, short passages of sung dialogue between the priest and choir, called **tropes,** were added on special holidays to commemorate the event. These tropes grew more elaborate over the years until full-fledged religious pageants were being performed in front of the altar. In 1210, Pope Innocent III, wishing to restore the dignity of the services, banned such performances from the interior of the church. Moving them outside, first to the church porch and later entirely off church property, provided greater opportunity for inventiveness in action and staging.

In the fourteenth and fifteenth centuries, much of the work of putting on plays passed to the guilds, organizations of skilled craftsmen, and their productions became part of city-wide festivals in many continental and British cities. Several types of plays evolved. **Mystery plays** were derived from holy scripture. **Passion plays** (some of which survive unchanged today) focused on the crucifixion of Christ. **Miracle plays** dramatized the lives of the saints. The last and most complex, **morality plays,** were dramatized sermons with allegorical characters (e.g., Everyman, Death, Good Deeds) representing various generalized aspects of human life.

Elizabethan Drama

While the older morality plays were still performed throughout the sixteenth century, during the time of Queen Elizabeth I (b. 1533, reigned 1558–1603) a new type of drama, typical in many ways of other innovative types of literature developed during the Renaissance, began to be produced professionally by companies of actors not affiliated with any religious institutions. This **secular drama,** beginning in short pieces called **interludes** that may have been designed for entertainment during banquets or other public celebrations, eventually evolved into fulllength tragedies and comedies designed for performance in large outdoor theaters like Shakespeare's famous Globe.

A full history of this fertile period would take many pages, but a few of its dramatic conventions are worth noting. We have already mentioned blank verse, the poetic line perfected by Shakespeare's contemporary Christopher Marlowe (1564–1593). Shakespeare wrote tragedies, comedies, and historical dramas with equal success, all characterized by passages that remain the greatest examples of poetic expression in English.

The raised platform stage in an Elizabethan theater used little or no scenery, with the author's descriptive talents setting the scene and indicating lighting and weather. The stage itself had two supporting columns, which might be used to represent trees or hiding places; a raised area at the rear, which could represent a balcony or upper story of a house; a small curtained alcove at its base; and a trap door, which could serve as a grave or hiding place. In contrast to the relatively bare stage, costumes were elaborate and acting was highly stylized. Female roles were played by young boys, and the same actor might play several different minor roles in the same play. The Oscar-winning film *Shakespeare in Love* reveals a great amount of information about Elizabethan staging.

A few more brief words about Shakespeare's plays are in order. First, drama in Shakespeare's time was intended for performance, with publication being of only secondary importance. The text of many of Shakespeare's plays were published in cheap editions called **quartos** which were full of misprints and often contained different versions of the same play. Any play by Shakespeare contains words and passages that different editors have trouble agreeing on. Second, originality, in the sense that we value it, meant little to a playwright in a time before copyright laws; virtually every one of Shakespeare's plays is derived from an earlier source—Greek myth, history, another play or, in the case of *Othello,* an Italian short story of questionable literary merit. The true test of Shakespeare's genius rests in his ability to transform these raw materials into art. Finally, we should keep in mind that Shakespeare's plays were designed to appeal to a wide audience—educated aristocrats and illiterate "groundlings" filled the theater—and this fact may account for the great diversity of tones and levels of language in the plays. Purists of later eras may have been dismayed by some of Shakespeare's wheezy clowns and bad puns, but for us the mixture of "high" and "low" elements gives his plays their remarkable texture.

The Comic Genres

Shakespeare's ability to move easily between "high" and "low," between tragic and comic, should be a reminder that comedy has developed along lines parallel to tragedy and has never been wholly separate from it. Most of Aristotle's remarks on comedy are lost, but he does make the observation that comedy differs from tragedy in that comedy depicts men and women as worse than they are, whereas tragedy generally stresses their best qualities. During the great age of Greek tragedy, comedies were regularly performed at Athenian festivals. The greatest of the early comic playwrights was Aristophanes (450?–385? B.C.). The plays of Aristophanes are classified as **Old Comedy** and share many of the same structural elements as tragedy. Old Comedy was always satirical and usually obscene; in *Lysistrata,* written during the devastating Athenian wars with Sparta, the men of both sides are brought to their knees by the women of the two cities, who engage in a sex strike until the men relent. Features of Old Comedy included the use of two semichoruses (in *Lysistrata,* old men and old women); an *agon,* an extended debate between the protagonist and an authority figure; and a *parabasis,* an ode sung by the chorus at an intermission in the action which reveals the author's own views on the play's subject. **New Comedy,** which evolved in the century after Aristophanes, tended to observe more traditional moral values and stressed romance. The New Comedy of Greece greatly influenced the writings of Roman playwrights like Plautus (254–184 B.C.) and Terence (190–159 B.C.). Plautus's *Pseudolus* (combined with elements from two of his other comedies) still finds favor in its modern musical adaptation *A Funny Thing Happened on the Way to the Forum.*

Like other forms of drama, comedy virtually vanished during the early Middle Ages. Its spirit was kept alive primarily by roving companies of actors who staged improvisational dramas in the squares of towns throughout Europe. The popularity of these plays is evidenced by certain elements in the religious dramas of the same period; the *Second Shepherd's Play* (c. 1450) involves a sheep-rustler with three shepherds in an uproarious parody of the Nativity that still evokes laughter today. Even a serious play such as *Everyman* contains satirical elements in the involved excuses that gods and other characters contrive for not accompanying the protagonist on his journey with Death.

On the continent, a highly stylized form of improvisational drama appeared in sixteenth-century Italy, apparently an evolution from earlier types of folk drama. **Commedia dell'arte** involved a cast of masked stock characters (the miserly old man, the young wife, the ardent seducer) in situations involving mistaken identity and cuckoldry. *Commedia* *dell'arte,* because it is an improvisational form, does not survive, but its popularity influenced the direction that comedy would take in the following century. The great French comic playwright Molière (1622–1673) incorporated many of its elements into his own plays, which combine elements of **farce,** a type of comedy which hinges on broadly drawn characters and embarrassing situations usually involving sexual misconduct, with serious social satire. Comedy such as Molière's, which exposes the hypocrisy and pretensions of people in social situations, is called **comedy of manners;** as Molière put it, the main purpose of his plays was "the correction of mankind's vices."

Other types of comedy have also been popular in different eras. Shakespeare's comedies begin with the farcical complications of *The Comedy of Errors,* progress through romantic **pastoral** comedies such as *As You Like It,* which present an idealized view of rural life, and end with the philosophical comedies of his final period, of which *The Tempest* is the greatest example. His contemporary Ben Jonson (1572–1637) favored a type known as **comedy of humours,** a type of comedy of manners in which the conduct of the characters is determined by their underlying dominant trait (the four humours were thought to be bodily fluids whose proportions determined personality). English plays of the late seventeenth and early eighteenth centuries tended to combine the hard-edged satire of comedy of manners with varying amounts of sentimental romance. A play of this type, usually hinging on matters of inheritance and marriage, is known as a **drawing-room comedy,** and its popularity, while peaking in the mid-nineteenth century, endures today.

Modern comedy in English can be said to begin with Oscar Wilde (1854–1900) and George Bernard Shaw (1856–1950). Wilde's brilliant wit and skillful incorporation of paradoxical **epigrams,** witty sayings that have made him one of the most quoted authors of the nineteenth century, have rarely been equaled. Shaw, who began his career as a drama critic, admired both Wilde and Ibsen, and succeeded in combining the best elements of the comedy of manners and the problem play in his works. *Major Barbara* (1905), a typical **comedy of ideas,** frames serious discussion of war, religion, and poverty with a search for an heir to a millionaire's fortune and a suitable husband for one of his daughters. Most subsequent writers of comedy, from Neil Simon to Wendy Wasserstein, reveal their indebtedness to Wilde and Shaw.

One striking development of comedy in recent times lies in its deliberate harshness. So-called **black humor,** an extreme type of satire in which barriers of taste are assaulted and pain seems the constant companion of laughter, has characterized much of the work of playwrights like Samuel Beckett (1906–1989), Eugene Ionesco (1912–1994), and Edward Albee (b. 1928).

Realistic Drama, the Modern Stage, and Beyond

Realism is a term that is loosely employed as a synonym for "true to life," but in literary history it denotes a style of writing that developed in the mid-nineteenth century, first in the novels of such masters as Charles Dickens, Gustave Flaubert, and Leo Tolstoy, and later in the dramas of Ibsen and Anton Chekhov. Many of the aspects of dramatic realism have to do with staging and acting. The box set, with its invisible "fourth wall" facing the audience, could, with the added subtleties of artificial lighting, successfully mimic the interior of a typical middle-class home. Realistic prose drama dropped devices like the soliloquy in favor of more natural methods of acting such as that championed by Konstantin Stanislavsky (1863–1938), the Russian director who worked closely with Chekhov (1860–1904) to perfect a process whereby actors learned to identify with their characters' psychological problems from "inside out." This "method" acting often tries, as is the case in Chekhov's plays and, later, in those of Williams and Miller, to develop a play's **subtext,** the crucial issue in the play that no one can bear to address directly. Stanislavsky's theories have influenced several generations of actors and have become standard throughout the world of the theater. Ibsen's plays, which in fact ushered in the modern era of the theater, are often called **problem plays** because they deal with serious, even controversial or taboo, issues in society. Shaw said that Ibsen's great originality as a playwright lay in his ability to shock the members of the audience into thinking about their own lives. As the barriers of censorship have fallen over the years, the capacity of the theater to shock has perhaps been diminished, but writers still find it a forum admirably suited for debating the controversial issues which divide society.

American and world drama in the twentieth and the present centuries has gone far beyond realism to experiment with the dream-like atmosphere of **expressionism** (which, like the invisible walls in Miller's *Death of a Salesman*, employs distorted sets to mirror the troubled, perhaps even unbalanced, psyches of the play's characters) or **theater of the absurd,** which depicts a world, like that of Samuel Beckett's *Waiting* *for Godot* or the early plays of Edward Albee, without meaning in which everything seems ridiculous. Nevertheless, realism is still the dominant style of today's theater, even if our definition of it has to be modified to take into account plays as diverse as *The Glass Menagerie, Death of a Salesman,* and *The Piano Lesson.*

Film Versions: A Note

Nothing can equal the experience of an actual stage production, but the many fine film versions of the plays in this anthology offer instructors and students the opportunity to explore, in some cases, two or three different cinematic approaches to the same material. I regularly teach a course in drama and film, and I have found that the differences between print and film versions of plays offer students many challenging topics for discussion, analysis, and writing. Of course, the two media differ radically; in some cases noted below, the film versions, especially those from past decades, badly compromise the original plays. To cite one notorious instance regarding a play not in this anthology, Elia Kazan's celebrated film of Tennessee Williams's *A Streetcar Named Desire,* so wonderful in its sets, direction, and in the performances of Marlon Brando and Vivien Leigh, tampers with the play's ending (on orders from the Hollywood Production Code office) to give the impression that Stella will take her child and leave Stanley. Williams himself wrote the screenplay, and he was aware of, if not exactly happy with, the moral standards of the times.

The late O. B. Hardison, director of the Folger Shakespeare Library, once observed two important differences between plays and films. The first is that attending a play is a social function; the audience members and the performers are aware of one another's presence and respond to it. Applause can stir actors to new heights, and laughter in the wrong place can signal the beginning of a disaster. Film, on the contrary, is largely a private experience; it was with good reason that one film critic titled a collection of her reviews *A Year in the Dark.* The other chief difference, Hardison notes, is that drama is a realistic medium, whereas film is surrealistic. Watching a play, we see real persons who have a physical reality, and we see them from a uniform perspective. But film has conditioned us to its own vocabulary of close-ups, jump cuts, and panoramas, and we view a film from a variety of perspectives. These differences, as fundamental as they seem, are rarely noted by students until they are pointed out. Still, film versions provide us with a wonderful time capsule in which many treasures of the drama's past have been preserved. A reasoned list of some of these, most of them available on DVD, follows.

Antigone

Tyrone Guthrie's 1957 version of *Oedipus Rex*, available on VHS and DVD, remains the best attempt to represent Sophoclean tragedy as it was originally performed. One wishes that a similar version of *Antigone* existed. The 1961 Greek film version, directed by Yorgos Javellas and starring the formidable Irene Papas, uses English subtitles. The black-and-white film is impressive in many respects, but will probably not appeal to contemporary viewers. More useful, perhaps, is the 1974 PBS version directed by Gerald Freedman and starring Geneviève Bujold and Fritz Weaver as Antione and Creon, respectively. The script is an English-language version of Jean Anouilh's 1942 play, which is widely considered a thinly veiled protest against the German occupation of France during World War II. Anouilh reduces the chorus to a single actor (played here by Stacy Keach) and eliminates Teiresias from the plot. This modern adaptation provides a striking contrast with Sophocles's tragedy, particularly as regards the motivation for Antigone's actions in the play and Creon's reasons for condemning her.

Othello has proved to be one of Shakespeare's most popular plays on film. Orson Welles's 1952 version, thought lost for many years, was lovingly restored by his daughter Rebecca Welles and features a remastered soundtrack that remedies most of the original complaints about Welles's film. A fascinating film-noir study in Shakespeare, it features a bravura performance by Welles and an affecting one by Suzanne Cloutier as Desdemona. Less successful is Laurence Olivier's 1966 version, essentially a filmed version of his acclaimed Royal Shakespeare Company production. Olivier's controversial performance, which mimics West Indian speech patterns, as well as Maggie Smith's as Desdemona, are worth seeing, but Olivier's stage makeup, unconvincing in film close-ups, and minimal production values mar the effort. The 1980 version starring Anthony Hopkins as Othello and Bob Hoskins as Iago features interesting performances from the principals, despite Hopkins's strange hairpiece. This uncut version was part of the PBS Shakespeare series and is widely available in libraries. The 1995 film, directed by

Oliver Parker, has excellent performances by Laurence Fishburne and Kenneth Branagh and a sumptuous, erotic style. Contemporary students will probably find it the most satisfying of the four. Tim Blake Nelson's 2001 film, *O*, transposed the plot (but precious little of the language) in a contemporary version exploring rivalries between basketball teammates at a southern prep school.

An Enemy of the People

The 1978 film version, directed by George Schaefer and starring iconic action hero Steve McQueen as Thomas Stockmann, received a minimal theatrical release. Apparently the distributors quickly decided that moviegoers would not accept McQueen in the leading role, despite his finely nuanced performance. Made for under $3 milion dollars, the film captures the period accurately. Finding a copy of it, however, is very difficult. *The Henrik Ibsen Collection* (six disks) from the BBC contains a 1980 version directed by Gareth Davies and starring Robert Urquhart. Interestingly, Steven Spielberg's classic film *Jaws* is widely thought to have borrowed many plot elements from *An Enemy of the People*.

The Glass Menagerie

The 1950 version, directed by Irving Rapper, has the advantage of Gertrude Lawrence, Arthur Kennedy, and Jane Wyman in the roles of the Wingfield family, but Kirk Douglas seems oddly out of place as Jim O'Connor. The film concludes with an absurd final shot of Amanda and Laura gleefully waving as a new gentleman caller approaches their door. The 1973 version, with Katharine Hepburn and Sam Waterston, surmounts the obvious problem of Hepburn, a New Englander if ever there was one, seeming plausible as a faded southern belle. In 1987, Paul Newman directed a well-received version with Joanne Woodward and John Malkovich in the leads.

Death of a Salesman

Miller was not pleased with the 1951 film, in which Fredric March overacted badly as Willy Loman. Still, Mildred Dunnock, Kevin McCarthy, and Cameron Mitchell provided excellent support. Volker Schlöndorff's 1985 version has been widely acclaimed, although some viewers have found Dustin Hoffman ill-suited to the role that Miller wrote with the large-boned Lee J. Cobb in mind. John Malkovich and Kate Reid are very good, and Schlöndorff's impressionistic set designs and seamless handling of flashbacks are impressive. A version of the final performance of the award-winning 1999 Broadway revival, starring Brian Dennehy and Elizabeth Franz, aired on Showtime in 2000. Dennehy brought to the role of Willy Loman a magnitude that many critics found impressive.

"Master Harold". . . and the boys

A young Matthew Broderick makes a believable Hallie in the 1984 film of *"Master Harold". . . and the boys,* which was originally made for television. But Broderick, who displays ample evidence of his bright acting future, is matched step for step by the two supporting cast members, John Kani as Willie and Zakes Mokae as Sam. Mokae, as the elder of the two waiters, originated the part in 1982 and the dignity and patience he brings to the role are very moving. Essentially a photographed play, *"Master Harold". . . and the boys* succeeds on the strength of Fugard's characterizations and the actors' skills.

The Piano Lesson

This made-for-television film, which originally appeared in 1995 on Hallmark Hall of Fame, was directed by Lloyd Richards, who came to prominence as the original Broadway director of Lorraine Hansberry's *A Raisin in the Sun* in 1959. *The Piano Lesson* stars award-winning actor Alfree Woodard as Berniece Charles, and Charles S. Dutton, familiar from many television roles, as Boy Willie. The film was nominated for nine Emmys and is currently available on VHS and DVD.

Writing About Drama

WRITING ASSIGNMENTS VARY WIDELY AND YOUR TEACHER'S instructions may range from general ("Discuss any two scenes in the plays we have read") to very specific ("Write an explication, in not less than 1,000 words, on Shakespeare's use of imagery and figurative language in Othello's speech to the Venetian Senate in which he describes his courtship of Desdemona"). Such processes as choosing, limiting, and developing a topic; "brainstorming" by taking notes on random ideas and refining those ideas further through group discussion or conferences with your instructor; using the library and the Internet to locate supporting secondary sources; and revising a first draft in light of critical remarks are undoubtedly techniques you have practiced in other composition classes. Basic types of organizational schemes learned in "theme-writing" courses can also be applied to writing about drama. Formal assignments of these types should avoid contractions and jargon, and should be written in a clear, straightforward style. Most literary essays are not of the personal experience type, and you should follow common sense in avoiding the first person and slang. It goes without saying that you should carefully proofread your rough and final drafts to eliminate errors in spelling, punctuation, usage, and grammar.

Typical writing assignments on plays fall into four main categories: reviews, explication or close reading, analysis, and comparison-contrast. A review, an evaluation of an actual performance of a play, will focus less on the play itself, particularly if it is a well-known one, than on the actors' performances, the overall direction of the production, and the elements of staging. Because reviews are primarily news stories, basic information about the time and place of production should be given at the beginning of the review. A short summary of the play's plot may follow, with perhaps some remarks on its stage history, and subsequent paragraphs will evaluate the performers and the production. Remember that a review is both a *report* and a *recommendation,* either positive or negative, to readers. You should strive for accuracy in such matters as spelling the actors' names correctly, and you should also try to be fair in pointing out the strong and weak points of the production. It is essential to support any general statements about the play's successes or shortcomings with specific references to the production, so it is a good idea to take notes during the performance. Because film versions of most of the plays in this book, sometimes in several different versions, are available on VHS or DVD, you might also be asked to review one of these films, paying attention perhaps to the innovative ways in which directors like Orson Welles or Volker Schlöndorff have "opened up" the action of the plays by utilizing the more complex technical resources of motion pictures. Two good reference sources providing examples of professional drama and film reviews, respectively, are the *New York Times Theater Reviews* (available in several volumes) and the *New York Times Film Reviews;* of course, the *New York Times* and other big-city newspapers may be searched online for reviews of recent productions. Popular magazines containing drama reviews include *Time, Newsweek, The New Yorker,* and others, and these reviews are indexed in the *Readers' Guide to Periodical Literature* (now available online at many libraries). Also, yearbooks like *Theatre World* provide useful information about New York productions of plays, and official websites of recent productions can be found on the Internet.

An explication assignment, on the other hand, requires that you pay close attention to selected passages, giving a detailed account of all the nuances of a speech from a play you have read. Because Shakespeare's poetry is often full of figurative language that may not be fully understood until it has been subjected to an "unfolding" (the literal meaning of explication), individual sections of *Othello*—speeches, scenes, soliloquies— would be likely choices for writing assignments. For example, you might be asked to compare the four different accounts of Othello's courtship of Desdemona—first by Iago and Roderigo, next by her father

Brabantio, then by Othello and Desdemona themselves—that we hear in the first act of the play. Other passages that might yield more meaning under close reading include Iago's various explanations for his hatred of Othello or the several different references in the play to reputation and "good name."

Analysis assignments typically turn on definition and illustration, focusing on only one of the main elements of the play such as plot or characterization. You might be required to explain Aristotle's statements about peripety and then apply his terminology to a contemporary play like *Death of a Salesman*. Here you would attempt to locate relevant passages from the play to support Aristotle's contentions about the importance of these reversals in the best plots. Or you might be asked to provide a summary of his comments about the tragic hero and then apply this definition to a character like Willy Loman. In doing so, you might use other supporting materials such as Arthur Miller's essay "Tragedy and the Common Man," in which the author discusses the modern notion that the tragic hero need not be drawn from the upper strata of society.

Comparison and contrast assignments are also popular. You might be assigned to compare two or more characters in a single play (Willy Loman's sons Biff and Happy, for example, or male and female attitudes expressed by the two characters in David Ives's *Sure Thing*), or to contrast characters in two different plays (Antigone and Thomas Stockmann as idealists who sacrifice their personal happiness because of their beliefs). Comparison and contrast assignments require careful planning, and it is essential to find both significant similarities and differences to support your thesis. Obviously, a proposed topic about two characters who have almost nothing in common, say, Iago and Tom Wingfield, would have little discernable purpose.

Supporting your statements about a play is necessary, either by quoting directly from the play or, if you are required, to use outside sources for additional critical opinion. You may be required to use secondary sources from the library or Internet in writing your paper. A subject search through your library's books is a good starting place, especially for older playwrights who have attracted extensive critical attention. Reference books like *Twentieth Century Authors*, *Contemporary Authors*, and the *Dictionary of Literary Biography* provide compact overviews of playwrights' careers. *Contemporary Literary Criticism*, *Critical Survey of Drama*, and *Drama Criticism* contain both original evaluations and excerpts from critical pieces on published works, and the *MLA Index* will direct you to articles on drama in scholarly journals. We have already mentioned the reference books from the *New York Times* as an excellent source of drama reviews. One scholarly journal that focuses on individual passages from literary works, the *Explicator*, is also worth inspecting. In recent years, the Internet has facilitated the chores of research, and many online databases, reference works, and periodicals may be quickly located using search engines like Yahoo! (www.yahoo.com) and Google (www.google.com). The Internet also holds a wealth of information, ranging from corporate websites promoting play productions to sites on individual authors, many of which are run by universities or organizations. Navigating the Internet can be a forbidding task, and a book like Lester Faigley's *The Longman Guide to the Web* is an invaluable traveler's companion. Students should be aware, however, that websites vary widely in quality. Some are legitimate academic sources displaying sound scholarship; others are little more that "fan pages" that may contain erroneous or misleading information.

Careful documentation of your sources is essential; if you use any material other than what is termed "common knowledge," you must cite it in your paper. Common knowledge includes biographical information, an author's publications, prizes and awards received, and other information that can be found in more than one reference book. Anything else—direct quotes or material you have put in your own words by paraphrasing—requires both a parenthetical citation in the body of your paper and an entry on your works cited pages. Doing less than this is to commit an act of plagiarism, for which the penalties are usually severe. Internet materials, which are so easily cut and pasted into a manuscript, provide an easy temptation but are immediately noticeable. Nothing is easier to spot in a paper than an uncited "lift" from a source; in most cases the vocabulary and sentence structure will be radically different from the rest of the paper.

The current edition of the *MLA Handbook for Writers of Research Papers,* which is available in the reference section of almost any library and which, if you plan to write papers for other English or drama courses, is a good addition to your personal library, contains formats for bibliographies and manuscript form that most instructors consider standard; indeed, most of the handbooks of grammar and usage commonly used in college courses follow MLA style and may be sufficient for your needs. If you have doubts, ask your instructor about what format is preferred. The type of parenthetical citation used today is simple to learn and dispenses with such time-consuming and repetitive chores as footnotes and endnotes. In using parenthetical citations remember that your goal is to direct your reader from the quoted passage in the paper to its source in your bibliography and from there, if necessary, to the book or periodical from which the quote is taken. A good parenthetical citation gives only the *minimal* information needed to accomplish this. Here are a few examples from student papers on *Othello:*

> In a disarming display of modesty before the Venetian senators, Othello readily admits that his military background has not prepared him to act as an eloquent spokesman in his own defense: "[...] little of this great world can I speak / More than pertains to feats of broils and battle; / And therefore little shall I grace my cause / In speaking for myself" (1.3.86-89).

Quotations from Shakespeare's plays are cited by act, scene, and line numbers instead of by page numbers. Note that short quotes from poetic dramas require that line breaks be indicated by the virgule (/) or slash; quotes longer than five lines should be indented ten spaces and formatted to duplicate the line breaks of the original. Here, the reader knows that Shakespeare is the author, so the citation here will simply direct him or her to the anthology or the collected or single edition of Shakespeare listed in the works cited section at the end of the paper:

> Shakespeare, William. The Complete Works of Shakespeare. Ed. Hardin Craig. New York: Scott, 1961.
>
> Shakespeare, William. Othello. Ed. David Bevington. New York: Bantam, 1988.
>
> Shakespeare, William. The Tragedy of Othello, the Moor of Venice. Literature: An Introduction to Fiction, Poetry, and Drama. 10th ed. Ed. X. J. Kennedy and Dana Gioia. New York: Longman, 2007. 1368-1469.

If, on the other hand, you are quoting from a prose drama, you would probably indicate a page number.

> Unlike the mature relationship between Dr.
> and Mrs. Stockmann in <u>An Enemy of the People</u>, in <u>A</u>
> <u>Doll's House</u>, Ibsen wants to demonstrate
> immediately that Nora and Helmer share almost
> child-like attitudes toward each other. "Is that
> my little lark twittering out there?" is Helmer's
> initial line in the play (43).

The citation directs the reader to the works cited entry:

> Ibsen, Henrik. <u>Four Major Plays</u>. Trans. Rolf
>   Fjelde. New York: Signet, 1965.

Similarly, quotes from secondary critical sources should follow the same rules of common sense.

> One critic, providing a classic estimate of
> Shakespeare's skill in conceiving Othello's
> antagonist, notes, "Evil has nowhere else been
> portrayed with such mastery as in the character of
> Iago" (Bradley 173).

In this case, the critic is not named in the paper, so his name must be included in the parenthetical citation. The reader knows where to look in the works cited:

> Bradley, A. C. <u>Shakespearean Tragedy</u>. New York:
>   Fawcett, 1967.

If the writer provides the critic's name ("A. C. Bradley, providing a classic estimate . . ."), then the parentheses should contain only the page number.

Of course, different types of sources—reference book entries, articles in periodicals, newspaper reviews of plays—require different bibliographical information, so be sure to check the *MLA Handbook* if you have questions. Here are a few more of the most commonly used formats:

An Edited Collection of Essays

> Snyder, Susan, ed. <u>Othello: Critical Essays</u>. New
>   York: Garland, 1988.

A Casebook

> Dean, Leonard Fellows, ed. <u>A Casebook on Othello</u>.
>   New York: Crowell, 1961.

Play Reprinted in an Anthology or Textbook

Wilson, August. <u>Fences. Inside Literature</u>. Ed.
R. S. Gwynn and Steven J. Zani. New York:
Penguin Academics, 2007. 412–90.

Article in a Reference Book

"Othello." <u>The Oxford Companion to English
Literature</u>. Ed. Margaret Drabble. 5th ed. New
York: Oxford UP, 1985.

Article in a Scholarly Journal

Berry, Edward. "Othello's Alienation." <u>Studies in
English Literature, 1500-1900</u> 30 (1990): 315–
33.

Review in a Newspaper

Evans, Everett. "Sturdy Staging of 'Equus' Raises
Intriguing Issues." <u>Houston Chronicle</u> 19 Jan.
2008: D1+.

Play Production Website

"Sophocles's <u>Antigone</u>." 2007. 18 Dec. 2008
<http://www.washburn.edu>.

Online Article or Review

Brantley, Ben. "A 'Menagerie' Full of Stars,
Silhouettes and Weird Sounds." 23 Mar.
2005. <u>New York Times</u>. 12 Sept. 2008
<http://theater2.nytimes.com>.

Online Author Website

"Sophocles." 2008. <u>Literature Online</u>. 8 July 2008.
<http://www.online-literature.com/
sophocles/>.

Online Reference Work

"August Wilson." 2007. <u>Britannica Online</u>.
Encyclopedia Britannica. 14 June 2008.
<http://www.britannica.com>.

DRAMA

SOPHOCLES ■ (496?–406 B.C.)

Sophocles lived in Athens in the age of Pericles, during the city's greatest period of culture, power, and influence. Sophocles distinguished himself as an athlete, a musician, a military advisor, a politician and, most important, a dramatist. At sixteen, he was chosen to lead a chorus in reciting a poem on the Greek naval victory over the Persians at Salamis, and he won his first prizes as a playwright before he was thirty. Although both Aeschylus, his senior, and Euripides, his younger rival, have their champions, Sophocles, whose career spanned so long a period that he competed against both of them, is generally considered to be the most important Greek writer of tragedies; his thirty victories in the City Dionysia surpass the combined totals of his two great colleagues. Of his 123 plays, only seven survive intact, including three plays relating to Oedipus and his children, Oedipus the King, Antigone, and Oedipus at Colonus, which was produced after Sophocles' death by his grandson. He is generally credited with expanding the technical possibilities of drama by introducing a third actor in certain scenes (Aeschylus used only two) and by both reducing the number of lines given to the chorus and increasing its integration into his plays. Sophocles was intimately involved in both civic and military affairs, twice serving as a chief advisor to Pericles, and his sense of duty to the polis (Greek for "city") is apparent in many of his plays. Sophocles' importance can be judged by the many references that Aristotle makes to his works in his discussion of tragedy in the Poetics.

Antigone

Translated by Robert Fagles

Characters

Antigone, *daughter of Oedipus and Jocasta*
Ismene, *sister of Antigone*
A chorus, *of old Theban citizens and their leader*
Creon, *king of Thebes, uncle of Antigone and Ismene*
A sentry
Haemon, *son of Creon and Eurydice*
Tiresias, *a blind prophet*
A messenger

Eurydice, *wife of Creon*
Guards, attendants, and a boy

> **Time and Scene:** *The royal house of Thebes. It is still night, and the invading armies of Argos have just been driven from the city. Fighting on opposite sides, the sons of Oedipus, Eteocles and Polynices, have killed each other in combat. Their uncle, Creon, is now king of Thebes.*
>
> *Enter Antigone, slipping through the central doors of the palace. She motions to her sister, Ismene, who follows her cautiously toward an altar at the center of the stage.*[1]

ANTIGONE: My own flesh and blood—dear sister, dear Ismene,
how many griefs our father Oedipus handed down!
Do you know one, I ask you, one grief
that Zeus will not perfect for the two of us
while we still live and breathe! There's nothing,   5
no pain—our lives are pain—no private shame,
no public disgrace, nothing I haven't seen
in your griefs and mine. And now this:
an emergency decree, they say, the Commander[1]
has just declared for all of Thebes.   10
What, haven't you heard? Don't you see?
The doom reserved for enemies
marches on the ones we love the most.

ISMENE: Not I, I haven't heard a word, Antigone.
Nothing of loved ones,   15
no joy or pain has come my way, not since
the two of us were robbed of our two brothers,
both gone in a day, a double blow—
not since the armies of Argos vanished,
just this very night. I know nothing more,   20
whether our luck's improved or ruin's still to come.

ANTIGONE: I thought so. That's why I brought you out here,
past the gates, so you could hear in private.

ISMENE: What's the matter? Trouble, clearly . . .
you sound so dark, so grim.   25

ANTIGONE: Why not? Our own brothers' burial!
Hasn't Creon graced one with all the rites,

---

[1]Creon. In the original he is given a military title; Antigone will not defer to him as King.

disgraced the other? Eteocles, they say,
has been given full military honors,
rightly so—Creon has laid him in the earth 30
and he goes with glory down among the dead.
But the body of Polynices, who died miserably—
why, a city-wide proclamation, rumor has it,
forbids anyone to bury him, even mourn him.
He's to be left unwept, unburied, a lovely treasure 35
for birds that scan the field and feast to their heart's content.
Such, I hear, is the martial law our good Creon
lays down for you and me—yes, me, I tell you—
and he's coming here to alert the uninformed
in no uncertain terms, 40
and he won't treat the matter lightly. Whoever
disobeys in the least will die, his doom is sealed:
stoning to death inside the city walls!

There you have it. You'll soon show what you are,
worth your breeding, Ismene, or a coward— 45
for all your royal blood.
ISMENE: My poor sister, if things have come to this,
who am I to make or mend them, tell me,
what good am I to you?
ANTIGONE: Decide.
Will you share the labor, share the work? 50
ISMENE: What work, what's the risk? What do you mean?
ANTIGONE: [*Raising her hands.*]
Will you lift up his body with these bare hands
and lower it with me?
ISMENE: What? You'd bury him—
when a law forbids the city?
ANTIGONE: Yes!
He is my brother and—deny it as you will— 55
your brother too.
No one will ever convict me for a traitor.
ISMENE: So desperate, and Creon has expressly—
ANTIGONE: No,
he has no right to keep me from my own.
ISMENE: Oh my sister, think— 60

think how our own father died, hated,[2]
his reputation in ruins, driven on
by the crimes he brought to light himself
to gouge out his eyes with his own hands—
then mother . . . his mother and wife, both in one,   65
mutilating her life in the twisted noose—
and last, our two brothers dead in a single day,
both shedding their own blood, poor suffering boys,
battling out their common destiny hand-to-hand.
Now look at the two of us, left so alone . . .   70
think what a death we'll die, the worst of all
if we violate the laws and override
the fixed decree of the throne, its power—
we must be sensible. Remember we are women,
we're not born to contend with men. Then too,   75
we're underlings, ruled by much stronger hands,
so we must submit in this, and things still worse.

I, for one, I'll beg the dead to forgive me—
I'm forced, I have no choice—I must obey
the ones who stand in power. Why rush to extremes?   80
It's madness, madness.

ANTIGONE: I won't insist,
no, even if you should have a change of heart,
I'd never welcome you in the labor, not with me.
So, do as you like, whatever suits you best—
I will bury him myself.   85
And even if I die in the act, that death will be a glory.
I will lie with the one I love and loved by him—
an outrage sacred to the gods! I have longer
to please the dead than please the living here:
in the kingdom down below I'll lie forever.   90
Do as you like, dishonor the laws
the gods hold in honor.

ISMENE: I'd do them no dishonor . . .
but defy the city? I have no strength for that.

---

[2] This play was written before *Oedipus the King* and Oedipus at Colonnus; the latter gives us a different picture of Oedipus's end.

ANTIGONE: You have your excuses. I am on my way,
  I'll raise a mound for him, for my dear brother.   95

ISMENE: Oh Antigone, you're so rash—I'm so afraid for you!

ANTIGONE: Don't fear for me. Set your own life in order.

ISMENE: Then don't, at least, blurt this out to anyone.
  Keep it a secret. I'll join you in that, I promise.

ANTIGONE: Dear god, shout it from the rooftops. I'll hate you   100
  all the more for silence—tell the world!

ISMENE: So fiery—and it ought to chill your heart.

ANTIGONE: I know I please where I must please the most.

ISMENE: Yes, if you can, but you're in love with impossibility.

ANTIGONE: Very well then, once my strength gives out   105
  I will be done at last.

ISMENE: You're wrong from the start,
  you're off on a hopeless quest.

ANTIGONE: If you say so, you will make me hate you,
  and the hatred of the dead, by all rights,
  will haunt you night and day.   110
  But leave me to my own absurdity, leave me
  to suffer this—dreadful thing. I will suffer
  nothing as great as death without glory.

[Exit to the side.]

ISMENE: Then go if you must, but rest assured,
  wild, irrational as you are, my sister,   115
  you are truly dear to the ones who love you.

*[Withdrawing to the palace. Enter a chorus³, the old citizens of
Thebes, chanting as the sun begins to rise.]*

CHORUS: Glory!—great beam of sun, brightest of all
  that ever rose on the seven gates of Thebes,
      you burn through night at last!
        Great eye of the golden day,   120
  mounting the Dirce's⁴ banks you throw him back—
  the enemy out of Argos, the white shield⁵, the man of bronze—

---

³The chorus of old men celebrates the victory won over the Argive forces and Polynices.
⁴A river of the Theban plain.
⁵The Argive soldiers' shields were painted white.

he's flying headlong now
    the bridle of fate stampeding him with pain!

      And he had driven against our borders,   125
      launched by the warring claims of Polynices—
      like an eagle screaming, winging havoc
      over the land, wings of armor
      shielded white as snow,
      a huge army massing,   130
      crested helmets bristling for assault.

He hovered above our roofs, his vast maw gaping
closing down around our seven gates,
    his spears thirsting for the kill
      but now he's gone, look,   135
before he could glut his jaws with Theban blood
or the god of fire put our crown of towers to the torch.
He grappled the Dragon[6] none can master—Thebes—
    the clang of our arms like thunder at his back!

      Zeus hates with a vengeance all bravado,   140
      the mighty boasts of men. He watched them
      coming on in a rising flood, the pride
      of their golden armor ringing shrill—
      and brandishing his lightning
      blasted the fighter[7] just at the goal,   145
      rushing to shout his triumph from our walls.

Down from the heights he crashed, pounding down on the earth!
And a moment ago, blazing torch in hand—
    mad for attack, ecstatic
he breathed his rage, the storm   150
    of his fury hurling at our heads!
But now his high hopes have laid him low
and down the enemy ranks the iron god of war

---

[6]According to legend the Thebans sprang from the dragon's teeth sown by Cadmus.
[7]Capaneus, the most violent of the Seven against Thebes. He had almost scaled the wall when the lightning of Zeus threw him down.

deals his rewards, his stunning blows—Ares[8]
rapture of battle, our right arm in the crisis.   155

Seven captains marshaled at seven gates
seven against their equals, gave
their brazen trophies[9] up to Zeus,
god of the breaking rout of battle,
all but two: those blood brothers,   160
one father, one mother—matched in rage,
spears matched for the twin conquest—
clashed and won the common prize of death.

But now for Victory! Glorious in the morning,
joy in her eyes to meet our joy   165
she is winging[10] down to Thebes,
our fleets of chariots wheeling in her wake—
Now let us win oblivion from the wars,
thronging the temples of the gods
in singing, dancing choirs through the night!   170
Lord Dionysus,[11] god of the dance
that shakes the land of Thebes, now lead the way!

[Enter Creon from the palace, attended by his guard.]

But look, the king of the realm is coming
Creon, the new man for the new day,
whatever the gods are sending now . . .   175
what new plan will he launch?
Why this, this special session?
Why this sudden call to the old men
summoned at one command?

CREON: My countrymen,
the ship of state is safe. The gods who rocked her,   180
after a long, merciless pounding in the storm,
have righted her once more.

---

[8]Not only the god of war but also one of the patron deities of Thebes.
[9]The victors in Greek battle set up a trophy consisting of the armor of one of the enemy dead,
fixed to a post and set up at the place where the enemy turned to run away.
[10]Victory is portrayed in Greek painting and sculpture as a winged young woman.
[11]A god of the vine and of revel; his father was Zeus, and his mother, Semele, was a Theban princess.

                                    Out of the whole city
I have called you here alone. Well I know,
first, your undeviating respect
for the throne and royal power of King Laius.   185
Next, while Oedipus steered the land of Thebes,
and even after he died, your loyalty was unshakable,
you still stood by their children. Now then,
since the two sons are dead—two blows of fate
in the same day, cut down by each other's hands,   190
both killers, both brothers stained with blood—
as I am next in kin to the dead,
I now possess the throne and all its powers.

Of course you cannot know a man completely,
his character, his principles, sense of judgment,   195
not till he's shown his colors, ruling the people,
making laws. Experience, there's the test.
As I see it, whoever assumes the task,
the awesome task of setting the city's course,
and refuses to adopt the soundest policies   200
but fearing someone, keeps his lips locked tight,
he's utterly worthless. So I rate him now,
I always have. And whoever places a friend
above the good of his own country, he is nothing:
I have no use for him. Zeus my witness,   205
Zeus who sees all things, always—
I could never stand by silent, watching destruction
march against our city, putting safety to rout,
nor could I ever make that man a friend of mine
who menaces our country. Remember this: 210
our country *is* our safety.
Only while she voyages true on course
can we establish friendships, truer than blood itself.
Such are my standards. They make our city great.

Closely akin to them I have proclaimed,   215
just now, the following decree to our people
concerning the two sons of Oedipus.
Eteocles, who died fighting for Thebes,

excelling all in arms: he shall be buried,
crowned with a hero's honors, the cups we pour[12]   220
to soak the earth and reach the famous dead.

But as for his blood brother, Polynices,
who returned from exile, home to his father-city
and the gods of his race, consumed with one desire—
to burn them roof to roots—who thirsted to drink   225
his kinsmen's blood and sell the rest to slavery:
that man—a proclamation has forbidden the city
to dignify him with burial, mourn him at all.
No, he must be left unburied, his corpse
carrion for the birds and dogs to tear,   230
an obscenity for the citizens to behold!

These are my principles. Never at my hands
will the traitor be honored above the patriot.
But whoever proves his loyalty to the state—
I'll prize that man in death as well as life.   235

LEADER: If this is your pleasure, Creon, treating
   our city's enemy and our friend this way . . .
   The power is yours, I suppose, to enforce it
   with the laws, both for the dead and all of us,
   the living.

CREON: Follow my orders closely then,   240
   be on your guard.

LEADER: We're too old.
   Lay that burden on younger shoulders.

CREON: No, no,
   I don't mean the body—I've posted guards already.

LEADER: What commands for us then? What other service?

CREON: See that you never side with those who break my orders. 245

LEADER: Never. Only a fool could be in love with death.

CREON: Death is the price—you're right. But all too often
   the mere hope of money has ruined many men.

   [A sentry enters from the side.]

[12]Libations (liquid offerings—wine, honey, etc.) poured on the grave.

SENTRY: My lord,
    I can't say I'm winded from running, or set out
    with any spring in my legs either—no sir,   250
    I was lost in thought, and it made me stop, often,
    dead in my tracks, heeling, turning back,
    and all the time a voice inside me muttering,
    "Idiot, why? You're going straight to your death."
    Then muttering, "Stopped again, poor fool?   255
    If somebody gets the news to Creon first,
    what's to save your neck?"
                    And so,
    mulling it over, on I trudged, dragging my feet,
    you can make a short road take forever . . .
    but at last, look, common sense won out,   260
    I'm here, and I'm all yours,
    and even though I come empty-handed
    I'll tell my story just the same, because
    I've come with a good grip on one hope,
    what will come will come, whatever fate—   265
CREON: Come to the point!
    What's wrong—why so afraid?
SENTRY: First, myself, I've got to tell you,
    I didn't do it, didn't see who did—
    Be fair, don't take it out on me.   270
CREON: You're playing it safe, soldier,
    barricading yourself from any trouble.
    It's obvious, you've something strange to tell.
SENTRY: Dangerous too, and danger makes you delay
    for all you're worth.   275
CREON: Out with it—then dismiss!
SENTRY: All right, here it comes. The body—
    someone's just buried it, then run off . . .
    sprinkled some dry dust on the flesh,[13]
    given it proper rites.
CREON: What?   280
    What man alive would dare—
SENTRY: I've no idea, I swear it.

---

[13]A symbolic burial, all Antigone could do alone, without Ismene's help.

There was no mark of a spade, no pickaxe there,
no earth turned up, the ground packed hard and dry,
unbroken, no tracks, no wheelruts, nothing,
the workman left no trace. Just at sunup   285
the first watch of the day points it out—
it was a wonder! We were stunned . . .
a terrific burden too, for all of us, listen:
you can't see the corpse, not that it's buried,
really, just a light cover of road-dust on it,   290
as if someone meant to lay the dead to rest
and keep from getting cursed.
Not a sign in sight that dogs or wild beasts
had worried the body, even torn the skin.

But what came next! Rough talk flew thick and fast,   295
guard grilling guard—we'd have come to blows
at last, nothing to stop it; each man for himself
and each the culprit, no one caught red-handed,
all of us pleading ignorance, dodging the charges,
ready to take up red-hot iron in our fists,   300
go through fire,[14] swear oaths to the gods—
"I didn't do it, I had no hand in it either,
not in the plotting, not in the work itself!"

Finally, after all this wrangling came to nothing,
one man spoke out and made us stare at the ground,   305
hanging our heads in fear. No way to counter him,
no way to take his advice and come through
safe and sound. Here's what he said:
"Look, we've got to report the facts to Creon,
we can't keep this hidden." Well, that won out,   310
and the lot fell to me, condemned me,
unlucky as ever, I got the prize. So here I am,
against my will and yours too, well I know—
no one wants the man who brings bad news.

---

[14]Both traditional assertions of truthfulness, derived perhaps from some primitive ritual of
ordeal—only the liar would get burned.

LEADER: My king,
ever since he began I've been debating in my mind,   315
could this possibly be the work of the gods?
CREON: Stop—
before you make me choke with anger—the gods!
You, you're senile, must you be insane?
You say—why it's intolerable—say the gods
could have the slightest concern for the corpse?   320
Tell me, was it for meritorious service
they proceeded to bury him, prized him so? The hero
who came to burn their temples ringed with pillars,
their golden treasures—scorch their hallowed earth
and fling their laws to the winds.   325
Exactly when did you last see the gods
celebrating traitors? Inconceivable!
No, from the first there were certain citizens
who could hardly stand the spirit of my regime,
grumbling against me in the dark, heads together,   330
tossing wildly, never keeping their necks beneath
the yoke, loyally submitting to their king.
These are the instigators, I'm convinced—
they've perverted my own guard, bribed them
to do their work.
                Money! Nothing worse   335
in our lives, so current, rampant, so corrupting.
Money—you demolish cities, root men from their homes,
you train and twist good minds and set them on
to the most atrocious schemes. No limit,
you make them adept at every kind of outrage,   340
every godless crime—money!
                            Everyone—
the whole crew bribed to commit this crime,
they've made one thing sure at least:
sooner or later they will pay the price.

[Wheeling on the sentry.]

                                        You—
I swear to Zeus as I still believe in Zeus,   345
if you don't find the man who buried that corpse,

the very man, and produce him before my eyes,
simple death won't be enough for you,
not till we string you up alive
and wring the immorality out of you.   350
Then you can steal the rest of your days,
better informed about where to make a killing.
You'll have learned, at last, it doesn't pay
to itch for rewards from every hand that beckons.
Filthy profits wreck most men, you'll see—   355
they'll never save your life.

SENTRY: Please,
may I say a word or two, or just turn and go?

CREON: Can't you tell? Everything you say offends me.

SENTRY: Where does it hurt you, in the ears or in the heart?

CREON: And who are you to pinpoint my displeasure?   360

SENTRY: The culprit grates on your feelings,
I just annoy your ears.

CREON: Still talking?
You talk too much! A born nuisance—

SENTRY: Maybe so,
but I never did this thing, so help me!

CREON: Yes you did—
what's more, you squandered your life for silver!   365

SENTRY: Oh it's terrible when the one who does the judging
judges things all wrong.

CREON: Well now,
you just be clever about your judgments—
if you fail to produce the criminals for me,
you'll swear your dirty money brought you pain.   370

[*Turning sharply, reentering the palace.*]

SENTRY: I hope he's found. Best thing by far.
But caught or not, that's in the lap of fortune:
I'll never come back, you've seen the last of me.
I'm saved, even now, and I never thought,
I never hoped—   375
dear gods, I owe you all my thanks!

[*Rushing out.*]

Numberless wonders
terrible wonders walk the world but none the match for man—
that great wonder crossing the heaving gray sea,
    driven on by the blasts of winter
on through breakers crashing left and right,   380
    holds his steady course
and the oldest of the gods he wears away—
the Earth, the immortal, the inexhaustible—
as his plows go back and forth, year in, year out
    with the breed of stallions[15] turning up the furrows.   385

And the blithe, lightheaded race of birds he snares,
the tribes of savage beasts, the life that swarms the depths—
    with one fling of his nets
woven and coiled tight, he takes them all,
    man the skilled, the brilliant!   390
He conquers all, taming with his techniques
the prey that roams the cliffs and wild lairs,
training the stallion, clamping the yoke across
    his shaggy neck, and the tireless mountain bull.
And speech and thought, quick as the wind   395
and the mood and mind for law that rules the city—
    all these he has taught himself
and shelter from the arrows of the frost
when there's rough lodging under the cold clear sky
and the shafts of lashing rain—   400
    ready, resourceful man!
      Never without resources
never an impasse as he marches on the future—
only Death, from Death alone he will find no rescue
but from desperate plagues he has plotted his escapes.   405

Man the master, ingenious past all measure
past all dreams, the skills within his grasp—
    he forges on, now to destruction
now again to greatness. When he weaves in
the laws of the land, and the justice of the gods   410

---

[15]Mules—the working animal of a Greek farmer.

that binds his oaths together
    he and his city rise high—
       but the city casts out
that man who weds himself to inhumanity
thanks to reckless daring. Never share my hearth   415
never think my thoughts, whoever does such things.

[*Enter Antigone from the side, accompanied by the sentry.*]

Here is a dark sign from the gods—
what to make of this? I know her,
how can I deny it? That young girl's Antigone!
Wretched, child of a wretched father,   420
Oedipus. Look, is it possible?
They bring you in like a prisoner—
why? did you break the king's laws?
Did they take you in some act of mad defiance?

SENTRY: She's the one, she did it single-handed—   425
we caught her burying the body. Where's Creon?

[*Enter Creon from the palace.*]

LEADER: Back again, just in time when you need him.
CREON: In time for what? What is it?
SENTRY: My king,
there's nothing you can swear you'll never do—
second thoughts make liars of us all.   430
I could have sworn I wouldn't hurry back
(what with your threats, the buffeting I just took),
but a stroke of luck beyond our wildest hopes,
what a joy, there's nothing like it. So,
back I've come, breaking my oath, who cares?   435
I'm bringing in our prisoner—this young girl—
we took her giving the dead the last rites.
But no casting lots this time, this is *my* luck,
my prize, no one else's.
                Now, my lord,
here she is. Take her, question her,   440
cross-examine her to your heart's content.
But set me free, it's only right—
I'm rid of this dreadful business once for all.

CREON: Prisoner! Her? You took her—where, doing what?

SENTRY: Burying the man. That's the whole story.

CREON: What?   445

You mean what you say, you're telling me the truth?

SENTRY: She's the one. With my own eyes I saw her
bury the body, just what you've forbidden.
There. Is that plain and clear?

CREON: What did you see? Did you catch her in the act?   450

SENTRY: Here's what happened. We went back to our post,
those threats of yours breathing down our necks—
we brushed the corpse clean of the dust that covered it,
stripped it bare . . . it was slimy, going soft,
and we took to high ground, backs to the wind   455
so the stink of him couldn't hit us;
jostling, baiting each other to keep awake,
shouting back and forth—no napping on the job,
not this time. And so the hours dragged by
until the sun stood dead above our heads,   460
a huge white ball in the noon sky, beating,
blazing down, and then it happened—
suddenly, a whirlwind!
Twisting a great dust-storm up from the earth,
a black plague of the heavens, filling the plain,   465
ripping the leaves off every tree in sight,
choking the air and sky. We squinted hard
and took our whipping from the gods.

And after the storm passed—it seemed endless—
there, we saw the girl!   470
And she cried out a sharp, piercing cry,
like a bird come back to an empty nest,
peering into its bed, and all the babies gone . . .
Just so, when she sees the corpse bare
she bursts into a long, shattering wail   475
and calls down withering curses on the heads
of all who did the work. And she scoops up dry dust,
handfuls, quickly, and lifting a fine bronze urn,
lifting it high and pouring, she crowns the dead
with three full libations.

SOPHOCLES

we rushed her, closed on the kill like hunters,
and she, she didn't flinch. We interrogated her,
charging her with offenses past and present—
she stood up to it all, denied nothing. I tell you,
it made me ache and laugh in the same breath. 485
It's pure joy to escape the worst yourself,
it hurts a man to bring down his friends.
But all that, I'm afraid, means less to me
than my own skin. That's the way I'm made.

CREON: [*Wheeling on Antigone.*] You,
with your eyes fixed on the ground—speak up. 490
Do you deny you did this, yes or no?

ANTIGONE: I did it. I don't deny a thing.

CREON: [*To the sentry.*] You, get out, wherever you please—
you're clear of a very heavy charge.

[*He leaves; Creon turns back to Antigone.*]

You, tell me briefly, no long speeches— 495
were you aware a decree had forbidden this?

ANTIGONE: Well aware. How could I avoid it? It was public.

CREON: And still you had the gall to break this law?

ANTIGONE: Of course I did. It wasn't Zeus, not in the least,
who made this proclamation—not to me. 500
Nor did that Justice, dwelling with the gods
beneath the earth, ordain such laws for men.
Nor did I think your edict had such force
that you, a mere mortal, could override the gods,
the great unwritten, unshakable traditions. 505
They are alive, not just today or yesterday:
they live forever, from the first of time,
and no one knows when they first saw the light.

These laws—I was not about to break them,
not out of fear of some man's wounded pride, 510
and face the retribution of the gods.
Die I must, I've known it all my life—
how could I keep from knowing?—even without
your death-sentence ringing in my ears.

And if I am to die before my time 515
I consider that a gain. Who on earth,
alive in the midst of so much grief as I,
could fail to find his death a rich reward?
So for me, at least, to meet this doom of yours
is precious little pain. But if I had allowed 520
my own mother's son to rot, an unburied corpse—
that would have been an agony! This is nothing.
And if my present actions strike you as foolish,
let's just say I've been accused of folly
by a fool.

LEADER:
       Like father like daughter, 525
passionate, wild . . .
she hasn't learned to bend before adversity.

CREON: No? Believe me, the stiffest stubborn wills
fall the hardest; the toughest iron,
tempered strong in the white-hot fire, 530
you'll see it crack and shatter first of all.
And I've known spirited horses you can break
with a light bit—proud, rebellious horses.
There's no room for pride, not in a slave
not with the lord and master standing by. 535

This girl was an old hand at insolence
when she overrode the edicts we made public.
But once she had done it—the insolence,
twice over—to glory in it, laughing,
mocking us to our face with what she'd done. 540
I'm not the man, not now: she is the man
if this victory goes to her and she goes free.

Never! Sister's child or closer in blood
than all my family clustered at my altar
worshipping Guardian Zeus—she'll never escape, 545
she and her blood sister, the most barbaric death.
Yes, I accuse her sister of an equal part
in scheming this, this burial.

[*To his attendants.*]

Bring her here!
I just saw her inside, hysterical, gone to pieces.
It never fails: the mind convicts itself   550
in advance, when scoundrels are up to no good,
plotting in the dark. Oh but I hate it more
when a traitor, caught red-handed,
tries to glorify his crimes.

ANTIGONE: Creon, what more do you want   555
than my arrest and execution?

CREON: Nothing. Then I have it all.

ANTIGONE: Then why delay? Your moralizing repels me,
every word you say—pray god it always will.
So naturally all I say repels you too.

Enough.   560
Give me glory! What greater glory could I win
than to give my own brother decent burial?
These citizens here would all agree,

[*To the Chorus.*]

they would praise me too
if their lips weren't locked in fear.   565

[*Pointing to Creon.*]

Lucky tyrants—the perquisites of power!
Ruthless power to do and say whatever pleases *them.*

CREON: You alone, of all the people in Thebes,
see things that way.

ANTIGONE: They see it just that way
but defer to you and keep their tongues in leash.   570

CREON: And you, aren't you ashamed to differ so from them?
So disloyal!

ANTIGONE: Not ashamed for a moment,
not to honor my brother, my own flesh and blood.

CREON: Wasn't Eteocles a brother too—cut down, facing him?

ANTIGONE: Brother, yes, by the same mother, the same father.   575

CREON: Then how can you render his enemy such honors,
such impieties in his eyes?

ANTIGONE: He'll never testify to that,
Eteocles dead and buried.

CREON: He will—
  if you honor the traitor just as much as him.   580
ANTIGONE: But it was his brother, not some slave that died—
CREON: Ravaging our country!—
  but Eteocles died fighting in our behalf.
ANTIGONE: No matter—Death longs for the same rites for all.
CREON: Never the same for the patriot and the traitor.   585
ANTIGONE: Who, Creon, who on earth can say the ones below
  don't find this pure and uncorrupt?
CREON: Never. Once an enemy, never a friend,
  not even after death.
ANTIGONE: I was born to join in love, not hate—   590
  that is my nature.
CREON: Go down below and love,
  if love you must—love the dead! While I'm alive,
  no woman is going to lord it over me.

[*Enter Ismene from the palace, under guard.*]

CHORUS: Look,
  Ismene's coming, weeping a sister's tears,
  loving sister, under a cloud . . .   595
  her face is flushed, her cheeks streaming.
  Sorrow puts her lovely radiance in the dark.
CREON: You—
  in my own house, you viper, slinking undetected,
  sucking my life-blood! I never knew
  I was breeding twin disasters, the two of you   600
  rising up against my throne. Come, tell me,
  will you confess your part in the crime or not?
  Answer me. Swear to me.
ISMENE: I did it, yes—
  if only she consents—I share the guilt,
  the consequences too.
ANTIGONE: No,   605
  Justice will never suffer that—not you,
  you were unwilling. I never brought you in.
ISMENE: But now you face such dangers . . . I'm not ashamed
  to sail through trouble with you,
  make your troubles mine.

ANTIGONE: Who did the work?   610
   Let the dead and the god of death bear witness!
   I have no love for a friend who loves in words alone.
ISMENE: Oh no, my sister, don't reject me, please,
   let me die beside you, consecrating
   the dead together.
ANTIGONE: Never share my dying,   615
   don't lay claim to what you never touched.
   My death will be enough.
ISMENE: What do I care for life, cut off from you?
ANTIGONE: Ask Creon. Your concern is all for him.
ISMENE: Why abuse me so? It doesn't help you now.
ANTIGONE: You're right— 620
   if I mock you, I get no pleasure from it,
   only pain.
ISMENE: Tell me, dear one,
   what can I do to help you, even now?
ANTIGONE: Save yourself. I don't grudge you your survival.
ISMENE: Oh no, no, denied my portion in your death?   625
ANTIGONE: You chose to live, I chose to die.
ISMENE: Not, at least,
   without every kind of caution I could voice.
ANTIGONE: Your wisdom appealed to one world—mine, another.
ISMENE: But look, we're both guilty, both condemned to death.
ANTIGONE: Courage! Live your life. I gave myself to death,   630
   long ago, so I might serve the dead.
CREON: They're both mad, I tell you, the two of them.
   One's just shown it, the other's been that way
   since she was born.
ISMENE: True, my king,
   the sense we were born with cannot last forever ...   635
   commit cruelty on a person long enough
   and the mind begins to go.
CREON: Yours did,
   when you chose to commit your crimes with her.
ISMENE: How can I live alone, without her?
CREON: Her?
   Don't even mention her—she no longer exists.   640
ISMENE: What? You'd kill your own son's bride?

CREON: Absolutely:

there are other fields for him to plow.

ISMENE: Perhaps,

but never as true, as close a bond as theirs.

CREON: A worthless woman for my son? It repels me.

ISMENE: Dearest Haemon, your father wrongs you so!   645

CREON: Enough, enough—you and your talk of marriage!

ISMENE: Creon—you're really going to rob your son of Antigone?

CREON: Death will do it for me—break their marriage off.

LEADER: So, it's settled then? Antigone must die?

CREON: Settled, yes—we both know that.   650

[*To the guards.*]

Stop wasting time. Take them in.
From now on they'll act like women.
Tie them up, no more running loose;
even the bravest will cut and run,
once they see Death coming for their lives.   655

[*The guards escort Antigone and Ismene into the palace. Creon
remains while the old citizens form their chorus.*]

CHORUS: Blest, they are the truly blest who all their lives
have never tasted devastation. For others, once
the gods have rocked a house to its foundations
        the ruin will never cease, cresting on and on
from one generation on throughout the race—   660
like a great mounting tide
driven on by savage northern gales,
        surging over the dead black depths
rolling up from the bottom dark heaves of sand
and the headlands, taking the storm's onslaught full-force,   665
roar, and the low moaning
                                echoes on and on
                                        and now
as in ancient times I see the sorrows of the house,
the living heirs of the old ancestral kings,
piling on the sorrows of the dead
        and one generation cannot free the next—   670
some god will bring them crashing down,

the race finds no release.
And now the light, the hope
        springing up from the late last root
in the house of Oedipus, that hope's cut down in turn   675
by the long, bloody knife swung by the gods of death
by a senseless word

                by fury at the heart.

                        Zeus,
yours is the power, Zeus, what man on earth
can override it, who can hold it back?
Power that neither Sleep, the all-ensnaring   680
        no, nor the tireless months of heaven
can ever overmaster—young through all time,
mighty lord of power, you hold fast
        the dazzling crystal mansions of Olympus.
And throughout the future, late and soon   685
as through the past, your law prevails:
no towering form of greatness
        enters into the lives of mortals
                free and clear of ruin.

                        True,
our dreams, our high hopes voyaging far and wide   690
bring sheer delight to many, to many others
        delusion, blithe, mindless lusts
and the fraud steals on one slowly . . . unaware
till he trips and puts his foot into the fire.

        He was a wise old man who coined   695
the famous saying: "Sooner or later
foul is fair, fair is foul
to the man the gods will ruin"—
        He goes his way for a moment only   700
                free of blinding ruin.

[*Enter Haemon from the palace.*]

Here's Haemon now, the last of all your sons.
Does he come in tears for his bride,
his doomed bride, Antigone—
bitter at being cheated of their marriage?

CREON: We'll soon know, better than seers could tell us.   705

[Turning to Haemon.]

Son, you've heard the final verdict on your bride?
Are you coming now, raving against your father?
Or do you love me, no matter what I do?

HAEMON: Father, I'm your *son* . . . you in your wisdom
set my bearings for me—I obey you.   710
No marriage could ever mean more to me than you,
whatever good direction you may offer.

CREON: Fine, Haemon.
That's how you ought to feel within your heart,
subordinate to your father's will in every way.
That's what a man prays for: to produce good sons—   715
a household full of them, dutiful and attentive,
so they can pay his enemy back with interest
and match the respect their father shows his friend.
But the man who rears a brood of useless children,
what has he brought into the world, I ask you?   720
Nothing but trouble for himself, and mockery
from his enemies laughing in his face.
                                        Oh Haemon,
never lose your sense of judgment over a woman.
The warmth, the rush of pleasure, it all goes cold
in your arms, I warn you . . . a worthless woman   725
in your house, a misery in your bed.
What wound cuts deeper than a loved one
turned against you? Spit her out,
like a mortal enemy—let the girl go.
Let her find a husband down among the dead.   730
Imagine it: I caught her in naked rebellion,
the traitor, the only one in the whole city.
I'm not about to prove myself a liar,
not to my people, no, I'm going to kill her!
That's right—so let her cry for mercy, sing her hymns   735
to Zeus who defends all bonds of kindred blood.
Why, if I bring up my own kin to be rebels,
think what I'd suffer from the world at large.
Show me the man who rules his household well:
I'll show you someone fit to rule the state.   740

That good man, my son,
I have every confidence he and he alone
can give commands and take them too. Staunch
in the storm of spears he'll stand his ground,
a loyal, unflinching comrade at your side.   745

But whoever steps out of line, violates the laws
or presumes to hand out orders to his superiors,
he'll win no praise from me. But that man
the city places in authority, his orders
must be obeyed, large and small,   750
right and wrong.
                    Anarchy—
show me a greater crime in all the earth!
She, she destroys cities, rips up houses,
breaks the ranks of spearmen into headlong rout.
But the ones who last it out, the great mass of them   755
owe their lives to discipline. Therefore
we must defend the men who live by law,
never let some woman triumph over us.
Better to fall from power, if fall we must,
at the hands of a man—never be rated   760
inferior to a woman, never.
LEADER: To us,
unless old age has robbed us of our wits,
you seem to say what you have to say with sense.
HAEMON: Father, only the gods endow a man with reason,
the finest of all their gifts, a treasure.   765
Far be it from me—I haven't the skill,
and certainly no desire, to tell you when,
if ever, you make a slip in speech . . . though
someone else might have a good suggestion.

Of course it's not for you,   770
in the normal run of things, to watch
whatever men say or do, or find to criticize.
The man in the street, you know, dreads your glance,
he'd never say anything displeasing to your face.
But it's for me to catch the murmurs in the dark,   775

SOPHOCLES

the way the city mourns for this young girl.
"No woman," they say, "ever deserved death less,
and such a brutal death for such a glorious action.
She, with her own dear brother lying in his blood—
she couldn't bear to leave him dead, unburied,   780
food for the wild dogs or wheeling vultures.
Death? She deserves a glowing crown of gold!"
So they say, and the rumor spreads in secret,
darkly . . .

        I rejoice in your success, father—
nothing more precious to me in the world.   785
What medal of honor brighter to his children
than a father's growing glory? Or a child's
to his proud father? Now don't, please,
be quite so single-minded, self-involved,
or assume the world is wrong and you are right.   790
Whoever thinks that he alone possesses intelligence,
the gift of eloquence, he and no one else,
and character too . . . such men, I tell you,
spread them open—you will find them empty.
                                No,
it's no disgrace for a man, even a wise man,   795
to learn many things and not to be too rigid.
You've seen trees by a raging winter torrent,
how many sway with the flood and salvage every twig,
but not the stubborn—they're ripped out, roots and all.
Bend or break. The same when a man is sailing: 800
haul your sheets too taut, never give an inch,
you'll capsize, and go the rest of the voyage
keel up and the rowing-benches under.

Oh give way. Relax your anger—change!
I'm young, I know, but let me offer this: 805
it would be best by far, I admit,
if a man were born infallible, right by nature.
If not—and things don't often go that way,
it's best to learn from those with good advice.

LEADER: You'd do well, my lord, if he's speaking to the point,   810
to learn from him.

[*Turning to Haemon.*]

          and you, my boy, from him.
You both are talking sense.

CREON: So,
men our age, we're to be lectured, are we?—
schooled by a boy his age?

HAEMON: Only in what is right. But if I seem young,   815
look less to my years and more to what I do.

CREON: Do? Is admiring rebels an achievement?

HAEMON: I'd never suggest that you admire treason.

CREON: Oh?—
isn't that just the sickness that's attacked her?

HAEMON: The whole city of Thebes denies it, to a man.   820

CREON: And is Thebes about to tell me how to rule?

HAEMON: Now, you see? Who's talking like a child?

CREON: Am I to rule this land for others—or myself?

HAEMON: It's no city at all, owned by one man alone.

CREON: What? The city *is* the king's—that's the law!   825

HAEMON: What a splendid king you'd make of a desert island—
you and you alone.

CREON: [*To the chorus.*]   This boy, I do believe,
is fighting on her side, the woman's side.

HAEMON: If you are a woman, yes;
my concern is all for you.   830

CREON: Why, you degenerate—bandying accusations,
threatening me with justice, your own father!

HAEMON: I see my father offending justice—wrong.

CREON: Wrong?
To protect my royal rights?

HAEMON: Protect your rights?   835
When you trample down the honors of the gods?

CREON: You, you soul of corruption, rotten through—
woman's accomplice!

HAEMON: That may be,
but you'll never find me accomplice to a criminal.

CREON: That's what *she* is,   840
and every word you say is a blatant appeal for her—

HAEMON: And you, and me, and the gods beneath the earth.

CREON: You will never marry her, not while she's alive.

HAEMON: Then she'll die . . . but her death will kill another.

CREON: What, brazen threats? You go too far!

HAEMON: What threat?   845
Combating your empty, mindless judgments with a word?

CREON: You'll suffer for your sermons, you and your empty wisdom!

HAEMON: If you weren't my father, I'd say you were insane.

CREON: Don't flatter me with Father—you woman's slave!

HAEMON: You really expect to fling abuse at me   850
and not receive the same?

CREON: Is that so!
Now, by heaven, I promise you, you'll pay—
taunting, insulting me! Bring her out,
that hateful—she'll die now, here,
in front of his eyes, beside her groom!   855

HAEMON: No, no, she will never die beside me—
don't delude yourself. And you will never
see me, never set eyes on my face again.
Rage your heart out, rage with friends
who can stand the sight of you.   860

[*Rushing out.*]

LEADER: Gone, my king, in a burst of anger.
A temper young as his . . . hurt him once,
he may do something violent.

CREON: Let him do—
dream up something desperate, past all human limit!
Good riddance. Rest assured,   865
he'll never save those two young girls from death.

LEADER: Both of them, you really intend to kill them both?

CREON: No, not her, the one whose hands are clean—
you're quite right.

LEADER: But Antigone—
what sort of death do you have in mind for her?   870

CREON: I'll take her down some wild, desolate path
never trod by men, and wall her up alive
in a rocky vault, and set out short rations,
just the measure piety demands

to keep the entire city free of defilement.[16]   875
There let her pray to the one god she worships:
Death—who knows?—may just reprieve her from death.
Or she may learn at last, better late than never,
what a waste of breath it is to worship Death.

[*Exit to the palace.*]

CHORUS: Love, never conquered in battle
Love the plunderer laying waste the rich!   880
Love standing the night-watch
      guarding a girl's soft cheek,
you range the seas, the shepherds' steadings off in the wilds—
not even the deathless gods can flee your onset,
nothing human born for a day—   885
whoever feels your grip is driven mad.

                              Love!—
you wrench the minds of the righteous into outrage,
swerve them to their ruin—you have ignited this,
this kindred strife, father and son at war
      and Love alone the victor—   890
warm glance of the bride triumphant, burning with desire!
Throned in power, side-by-side with the mighty laws!
Irresistible Aphrodite,[17] never conquered—
Love, you mock us for your sport.   895

[*Antigone is brought from the palace under guard.*]

            But now, even I'd rebel against the king,
            I'd break all bounds when I see this—
            I fill with tears, I cannot hold them back,
            not any more . . . I see Antigone make her way
            to the bridal vault where all are laid to rest.   900
ANTIGONE: Look at me, men of my fatherland,
            setting out on the last road

---

[16]The penalty originally proclaimed was death by stoning. But this demands the participation of the citizens, and it may be that Creon, after listening to Haemon's remarks, is not as sure as he once was of popular support. Creon proposed imprisonment in a tomb with a ration of food. Since Antigone would die of starvation but not actually by anyone's hand, Creon seems to think that the city will not be "defiled," that is, will not incur blood guilt.
[17]Goddess of sexual love.

looking into the last light of day
the last I will ever see . . .
the god of death who puts us all to bed   905
takes me down to the banks of Acheron[18] alive—
   denied my part in the wedding-songs,
no wedding-song in the dusk has crowned my marriage—
I go to wed the lord of the dark waters.

CHORUS: Not crowned with glory,[19] or with a dirge,   910
   you leave for the deep pit of the dead.
   No withering illness laid you low,
   no strokes of the sword—a law to yourself,
   alone, no mortal like you, ever, you go down
   to the halls of Death alive and breathing.   915

ANTIGONE: But think of Niobe[20]—well I know her story—
think what a living death she died,
Tantalus' daughter, stranger queen from the east:
there on the mountain heights, growing stone
binding as ivy, slowly walled her round   920
and the rains will never cease, the legends say
the snows will never leave her . . .
   wasting away, under her brows the tears
showering down her breasting ridge and slopes—
a rocky death like hers puts me to sleep.   925

CHORUS: But she was a god, born of gods,
   and we are only mortals born to die.
   And yet, of course, it's a great thing
   for a dying girl to hear, just to hear
   she shares a destiny equal to the gods,   930
   during life and later, once she's dead.

---

[18]A river in the underworld.

[19]The usual version of this line is "crowned with glory." The Greek word *oukoun* can be negative or positive, depending on the accent, which determines the pronunciation; because written accents were not yet in use in Sophocles' time, no one will ever know for sure which meaning he intended. The present version is based on the belief that the chorus is expressing pity for Antigone's ignominious and abnormal death; she has no funeral at which her fame and praise are recited; she will not die by either of the usual causes—violence and disease—but by a living death. It is as they say, her own choice: she is "a law to [herself]" (line 913).

[20]A Phrygian princess married to Amphion, king of Thebes. She boasted that she had borne more children than Leto, mother of Apollo and Artemis. As vengeance, Apollo and Artemis killed all of Niobe's children. She fled to Phrygia, where she was turned into a rock on Mount Sipylus; the melting of the snow on the mountain caused "tears" to flow down the rock formation, which resembles a woman's face. See *Iliad* 24.651–69.

ANTIGONE: O you mock me!

Why, in the name of all my fathers' gods
why can't you wait till I am gone—
　　must you abuse me to my face?
O my city, all your fine rich sons!　　　　　　　　935
And you, you springs of the Dirce,
holy grove of Thebes where the chariots gather,
　　　　you at least, you'll bear me witness, look,
unmourned by friend and forced by such crude laws
I go to my rockbound prison, strange new tomb—　　940
　　always a stranger, O dear god,
　　　I have no home on earth and none below,
　　　　not with the living, not with the breathless dead.

CHORUS:　You went too far, the last limits of daring—
　　　smashing against the high throne of Justice!　　945
　　　Your life's in ruins, child—I wonder . . .
　　　do you pay for your father's terrible ordeal?

ANTIGONE:　There—at last you've touched it, the worst pain
the worst anguish! Raking up the grief for father
　　　three times over, for all the doom　　　　　950
that's struck us down, the brilliant house of Laius.
O mother, your marriage-bed
the coiling horrors, the coupling there—
　　　you with your own son, my father—doomstruck mother!
Such, such were my parents, and I their wretched child.　　955
I go to them now, cursed, unwed, to share their home—
　　　I am a stranger! O dear brother, doomed
　　　in your marriage—your marriage murders mine,[21]
　　　your dying drags me down to death alive!

[*Enter Creon.*]

CHORUS:　Reverence asks some reverence in return—　　960
　　but attacks on power never go unchecked,
　　　not by the man who holds the reins of power.
　　Your own blind will, your passion has destroyed you.

---

[21]Polynices had married the daughter of Adrastus of Argos, to seal the alliance that enabled him to
march against Thebes.

ANTIGONE: No one to weep for me, my friends,
            no wedding-song—they take me away   965
            in all my pain . . . the road lies open, waiting.
            Never again, the law forbids me to see
            the sacred eye of day. I am agony!
            No tears for the destiny that's mine,
            no loved one mourns my death.
CREON: Can't you see?   970
            If a man could wail his own dirge *before* he dies,
            he'd never finish.

            [*To the guards.*]

                            Take her away, quickly!
            Wall her up in the tomb, you have your orders.
            Abandon her there, alone, and let her choose—
            death or a buried life with a good roof for shelter. 975
            As for myself, my hands are clean. This young girl—
            dead or alive, she will be stripped of her rights,
            her stranger's rights,[22] here in the world above.
ANTIGONE: O tomb, my bridal-bed—my house, my prison
            cut in the hollow rock, my everlasting watch!   980
            I'll soon be there, soon embrace my own,
            the great growing family of our dead
            Persephone[23] has received among her ghosts.
                                                I,
            the last of them all, the most reviled by far,
            go down before my destined time's run out.   985
            But still I go, cherishing one good hope:
            my arrival may be dear to father,
            dear to you, my mother,
            dear to you, my loving brother, Eteocles—
            When you died I washed you with my hands,   990
            I dressed you all, I poured the sacred cups
            across your tombs. But now, Polynices,
            because I laid your body out as well,

---

[22]The Greek words suggest that he sees her not as a citizen but as a resident alien; by her action
she has forfeited citizenship. But now she will be deprived even of that inferior status.
[23]Queen of the underworld.

this, this is my reward. Nevertheless
I honored you—the decent will admit it—   995
well and wisely too.
                Never, I tell you,
if I had been the mother of children
or if my husband died, exposed and rotting—
I'd never have taken this ordeal upon myself,
never defied our people's will. What law,   1000
you ask, do I satisfy with what I say?
A husband dead, there might have been another.
A child by another too, if I had lost the first.
But mother and father both lost in the halls of Death,
no brother could ever spring to light again.[24]   1005
For this law alone I held you first in honor.
For this, Creon, the king, judges me a criminal
guilty of dreadful outrage, my dear brother!
And now he leads me off, a captive in his hands,
with no part in the bridal-song, the bridal-bed,
denied all joy of marriage, raising children—   1010
deserted so by loved ones, struck by fate,
I descend alive to the caverns of the dead.

What law of the mighty gods have I transgressed?
Why look to the heavens any more, tormented as I am?   1015
Whom to call, what comrades now? Just think,
my reverence only brands me for irreverence!
Very well: if this is the pleasure of the gods,
once I suffer I will know that I was wrong.
But if these men are wrong, let them suffer   1020
nothing worse than they mete out to me—
these masters of injustice!
LEADER: Still the same rough winds, the wild passion
    raging through the girl.

---

[24]This strange justification for her action has been considered unacceptable by many critics, and they have suspected that it was an interpolation by some later producer of the play. But Aristotle quotes it in the next century and appears to have no doubt of its authenticity. If genuine, it means that Antigone momentarily abandons the law she championed against Creon—that all people have a right to burial—and sees her motive as exclusive devotion to her dead brother. For someone facing the prospect of a slow and hideous death, such a self-examination and realization is not impossible. And it makes no difference to the courage and tenacity of her defiance of state power.

CREON: [*To the guards.*]   Take her away.
    You're wasting time—you'll pay for it too.   1025
ANTIGONE: Oh god, the voice of death. It's come, it's here.
CREON: True. Not a word of hope—your doom is sealed.
ANTIGONE: Land of Thebes, city of all my fathers—
    O you gods, the first gods of the race![25]
    They drag me away, now, no more delay.   1030
    Look on me, you noble sons of Thebes—
    the last of a great line of kings,
    I alone, see what I suffer now
    at the hands of what breed of men—
    all for reverence, my reverence for the gods!   1035

[*She leaves under guard; the chorus gathers.*]

CHORUS: Danaë,[26] Danaë—
    even she endured a fate like yours,
      in all her lovely strength she traded
    the light of day for the bolted brazen vault—
    buried within her tomb, her bridal-chamber,   1040
    wed to the yoke and broken.
      But she was of glorious birth
        my child, my child
    and treasured the seed of Zeus within her womb,
    the cloudburst streaming gold!   1045
      The power of fate is a wonder,
      dark, terrible wonder—
      neither wealth nor armies
      towered walls nor ships
      black hulls lashed by the salt   1050
      can save us from that force.

    The yoke tamed him too
      young Lycurgus flaming in anger

SOPHOCLES

72

---

[25]The Theban royal house traced its ancestry through Harmonia, wife of Cadmus, to Aphrodite and Ares, her parents. Cadmus's daughter was Semele.
[26]Daughter of Acrisius, king of Argos. It was prophesied that he would be killed by his daughter's son; so he shut her up in a bronze tower. But Zeus came to her in the form of a golden rain shower and she bore a son, Perseus, who did in the end accidentally kill his grandfather.

king of Edonia,[27] all for his mad taunts
Dionysus clamped him down, encased   1055
in the chain-mail of rock
        and there his rage
            his terrible flowering rage burst—
sobbing, dying away . . . at last that madman
came to know his god—   1060
        the power he mocked, the power
        he taunted in all his frenzy
        trying to stamp out
        the women strong with the god—
        the torch, the raving sacred cries—   1065
        enraging the Muses who adore the flute.

And far north[28] where the Black Rocks
        cut the sea in half
and murderous straits
split the coast of Thrace   1070
        a forbidding city stands
where once, hard by the walls
the savage Ares thrilled to watch
a king's new queen, a Fury rearing in rage
        against his two royal sons—   1075
            her bloody hands, her dagger-shuttle
stabbing out their eyes—cursed, blinding wounds—
their eyes blind sockets screaming for revenge!

They wailed in agony, cries echoing cries
        the princes doomed at birth . . .   1080
and their mother doomed to chains,
walled up in a tomb of stone[29]——

---

[27]Thrace Lycurgus opposed the introduction of Dionysiac religion into his kingdom and was imprisoned by the god.

[28]The whole story is difficult to follow, and its application to the case of Antigone is obscure. Cleopatra, the daughter of the Athenian princess Orithyia (whom Boreas, the North Wind, carried off to his home in Thrac), was married to Phineus, the Thracian king, and bore him two sons. He tired of her, abandoned her, and married Eidothea ("a king's new queen," line 1074), who put out the eyes of Cleopatra's two sons. Ares watched the savage act.

[29]Lines 1081–82 have no equivalent in the Greek text. They represent a belief that Sophocles' audience knew a version of the legend in which Cleopatra was imprisoned in a stone tomb (which is found in a later source). This would give a point of comparison to Antigone as did the imprisonment of Danaë and Lycurgus.

but she traced her own birth back
to a proud Athenian line and the high gods
and off in caverns half the world away,   1085
born of the wild North Wind
     she sprang on her father's gales,
        racing stallions up the leaping cliffs—
child of the heavens. But even on her the Fates
the gray everlasting Fates rode hard   1090
my child, my child.

[*Enter Tiresias, the blind prophet, led by a boy.*]

TIRESIAS: Lords of Thebes,
I and the boy have come together,
hand in hand. Two see with the eyes of one . . .
so the blind must go, with a guide to lead the way.
CREON: What is it, old Tiresias? What news now?
TIRESIAS: I will teach you. And you obey the seer.
CREON: I will,   1095
I've never wavered from your advice before.
TIRESIAS: And so you kept the city straight on course.
CREON: I owe you a great deal, I swear to that.
TIRESIAS: Then reflect, my son: you are poised,   1100
once more, on the razor-edge of fate.
CREON: What is it? I shudder to hear you.
TIRESIAS: You will learn
when you listen to the warnings of my craft.
As I sat on the ancient seat of augury,
in the sanctuary where every bird I know   1105
will hover at my hands[30]—suddenly I heard it,
a strange voice in the wingbeats, unintelligible,
barbaric, a mad scream! Talons flashing, ripping,
they were killing each other—that much I knew—
the murderous fury whirring in those wings   1110
made that much clear!
               I was afraid,
I turned quickly, tasted the burnt-sacrifice,
ignited the altar at all points—but no fire,

---

[30]A place where the birds gathered and Tiresias waited for omens.

the god in the fire never blazed.
Not from those offerings . . . over the embers   1115
slid a heavy ooze from the long thighbones,
smoking, sputtering out, and the bladder
puffed and burst—spraying gall into the air—
and the fat wrapping the bones slithered off
and left them glistening white. No fire!   1120
The rites failed that might have blazed the future
with a sign. So I learned from the boy here:
he is my guide, as I am guide to others.

                    And it is you—
your high resolve that sets this plague on Thebes.
The public altars and sacred hearths are fouled,   1125
one and all, by the birds and dogs with carrion
torn from the corpse, the doomstruck son of Oedipus!
and so the gods are deaf to our prayers, they spurn
the offerings in our hands, the flame of holy flesh.
No birds cry out an omen clear and true—   1130
they're gorged with the murdered victim's blood and fat.
Take these things to heart, my son, I warn you.
All men make mistakes, it is only human.
But once the wrong is done, a man
can turn his back on folly, misfortune too,   1135
if he tries to make amends, however low he's fallen,
and stops his bullnecked ways. Stubbornness
brands you for stupidity—pride is a crime.
No, yield to the dead!
Never stab the fighter when he's down.   1140

Where's the glory, killing the dead twice over?
I mean you well. I give you sound advice.
It's best to learn from a good adviser
when he speaks for your own good:
it's pure gain.
CREON: Old man—all of you! So,   1145
you shoot your arrows at my head like archers at the target—
I even have *him* loosed on me, this fortune-teller.
Oh his ilk has tried to sell me short
and ship me off for years. Well,

drive your bargains, traffic—much as you like— 1150
in the gold of India, silver-gold of Sardis.[31]
You'll never bury that body in the grave,
not even if Zeus's eagles rip the corpse
and wing their rotten pickings off to the throne of god!
Never, not even in fear of such defilement 1155
will I tolerate his burial, that traitor.
Well I know, we can't defile the gods—
no mortal has the power.
                                        No,
reverend old Tiresias, all men fall,
it's only human, but the wisest fall obscenely 1160
when they glorify obscene advice with rhetoric—
all for their own gain.

TIRESIAS: Oh god, is there a man alive
who knows, who actually believes . . .

CREON: What now?
What earth-shattering truth are you about to utter? 1165

TIRESIAS: . . . just how much a sense of judgment, wisdom
is the greatest gift we have?

CREON: Just as much, I'd say,
as a twisted mind is the worst affliction known.

TIRESIAS: You are the one who's sick, Creon, sick to death.

CREON: I am in no mood to trade insults with a seer. 1170

TIRESIAS: You have already, calling my prophecies a lie.

CREON: Why not?
You and the whole breed of seers are mad for money!

TIRESIAS: And the whole race of tyrants lusts for filthy gain.

CREON: This slander of yours—
are you aware you're speaking to the king? 1175

TIRESIAS: Well aware. Who helped you save the city?

CREON: You—
you have your skills, old seer, but you lust for injustice!

TIRESIAS: You will drive me to utter the dreadful secret in my heart.

CREON: Spit it out! Just don't speak it out for profit.

TIRESIAS: Profit? No, not a bit of profit, not for you. 1180

---

[31]In Asia Minor. Electrum, a natural alloy of gold and silver, was found in a nearby river.

CREON: Know full well, you'll never buy off my resolve.

TIRESIAS: Then know this too, learn this by heart!
          The chariot of the sun will not race through
          so many circuits more, before you have surrendered
          one born of your own loins, your own flesh and blood,   1185
          a corpse for corpses given in return, since you have thrust
          to the world below a child sprung from the world above,
          ruthlessly lodged a living soul within the grave—
          then you've robbed the gods below the earth,
          keeping a dead body here in the bright air,   1190
          unburied, unsung, unhallowed by the rites.

          You, you have no business with the dead,
          nor do the gods above—this is violence
          you have forced upon the heavens.
          And so the avengers, the dark destroyers late   1195
          but true to the mark, now lie in wait for you,
          the Furies sent by the gods and the god of death
          to strike you down with the pains that you perfected!

          There. Reflect on that, tell me I've been bribed.
          The day comes soon, no long test of time, not now,   1200
          when the mourning cries for men and women break
          throughout your halls. Great hatred rises against you—
          cities in tumult, all whose mutilated sons
          the dogs have graced with burial, or the wild beasts
          or a wheeling crow that wings the ungodly stench of carrion   1205
          back to each city, each warrior's heart and home.

          These arrows for your heart! Since you've raked me
          I loose them like an archer in my anger,
          arrows deadly true. You'll never escape
          their burning, searing force.   1210

          [*Motioning to his escort.*]

          Come, boy, take me home.
          So he can vent his rage on younger men,
          and learn to keep a gentler tongue in his head
          and better sense than what he carries now.

LEADER: The old man's gone, my king—   1215
    terrible prophecies. Well I know,
    since the hair on this old head went gray,
    he's never lied to Thebes.
CREON: I know it myself—I'm shaken, torn.
    It's a dreadful thing to yield . . . but resist now?   1220
    Lay my pride bare to the blows of ruin?
    That's dreadful too.
LEADER: But good advice,
    Creon, take it now, you must.
CREON: What should I do? Tell me . . . I'll obey.
LEADER: Go! Free the girl from the rocky vault   1225
    and raise a mound for the body you exposed.
CREON: That's your advice? You think I should give in?
LEADER: Yes, my king, quickly. Disasters sent by the gods
    cut short our follies in a flash.
CREON: Oh it's hard,
    giving up the heart's desire . . . but I will do it—   1230
    no more fighting a losing battle with necessity.
LEADER: Do it now, go, don't leave it to others.
CREON: Now—I'm on my way! Come, each of you,
    take up axes, make for the high ground,
    over there, quickly! I and my better judgment   1235
    have come round to this—I shackled her,
    I'll set her free myself. I am afraid . . .
    it's best to keep the established laws
    to the very day we die.

[*Rushing out, followed by his entourage. The chorus clusters around
the altar.*]

CHORUS: God of a hundred names!
                Great Dionysus—   1240
    Son and glory of Semele! Pride of Thebes—
    Child of Zeus whose thunder rocks the clouds—
    Lord of the famous lands of evening—
    King of the Mysteries!

King of Eleusis, Demeter's[32] plain
her breasting hills that welcome in the world—   1245
Great Dionysus!
    Bacchus, living in Thebes
the mother-city of all your frenzied women—

          Bacchus
living along the Ismenus'[33] rippling waters
standing over the field sown with the Dragons' teeth!
You—we have seen you through the flaring smoky fires,   1250
  your torches blazing over the twin peaks[34]
where nymphs of the hallowed cave climb onward
    fired with you, your sacred rage—
we have seen you at Castalia's running spring
and down from the heights of Nysa[35] crowned with ivy   1255
the greening shore rioting vines and grapes
  down you come in your storm of wild women
   ecstatic, mystic cries—
      Dionysus—
down to watch and ward the roads of Thebes!

First of all cities, Thebes you honor first   1260
you and your mother, bride of the lightning—
come, Dionysus! now your people lie
in the iron grip of plague,
come in your racing, healing stride
  down Parnassus'[36] slopes   1265
or across the moaning straits.
      Lord of the dancing—
dance, dance the constellations breathing fire!
Great master of the voices of the night!
Child of Zeus, God's offspring, come, come forth!
Lord, king, dance with your nymphs, swirling, raving   1270

---

[32]The grain and harvest goddess. Eleusis, the site of the mysteries and the worship of Demeter, is near Athens.
[33]A river at Thebes. Dionysus (or Bacchus) was among the divinities worshipped by the initiates.
[34]The two cliffs above Delphi, where Dionysus was thought to reside in the winter months.
[35]A mountain associated with Dionysiac worship; several mountains are so named, but the reference here is probably to the one on the island of Euboea, off the Attic coast.
[36]Mountain in central Greece just north of the Gulf of Corinth; an important cult of Dionysus was located there, as was Apollo's oracle at Delphi.

arm-in-arm in frenzy through the night
    they dance you, Iacchus[37]—
                       Dance, Dionysus
giver of all good things!

[*Enter a messenger from the side.*]

MESSENGER: Neighbors,
friends of the house of Cadmus and the kings,
there's not a thing in this mortal life of ours   1275
I'd praise or blame as settled once for all.
Fortune lifts and Fortune fells the lucky
and unlucky every day. No prophet on earth
can tell a man his fate. Take Creon:
there was a man to rouse your envy once,   1280
as I see it. He saved the realm from enemies;
taking power, he alone, the lord of the fatherland,
he set us true on course—flourished like a tree
with the noble line of sons he bred and reared . . .
and now it's lost, all gone.
                           Believe me,   1285
when a man has squandered his true joys,
he's good as dead, I tell you, a living corpse.
Pile up riches in your house, as much as you like—
live like a king with a huge show of pomp,
but if real delight is missing from the lot,   1290
I wouldn't give you a wisp of smoke for it,
not compared with joy.
LEADER: What now?
What new grief do you bring the house of kings?
MESSENGER: Dead, dead—and the living are guilty of their death!
LEADER: Who's the murderer? Who is dead? Tell us.   1295
MESSENGER: Haemon's gone, his blood spilled by the very hand—
LEADER: His father's or his own?
MESSENGER: His own . . .
raging mad with his father for the death—
LEADER: Oh great seer,
you saw it all, you brought your word to birth!

---

[37]Dionysus.

MESSENGER: Those are the facts. Deal with them as you will.   1300

[*As he turns to go, Eurydice enters from the palace.*]

LEADER: Look, Eurydice. Poor woman, Creon's wife,
so close at hand. By chance perhaps,
unless she's heard the news about her son.

EURYDICE: My countrymen,
all of you—I caught the sound of your words
as I was leaving to do my part,   1305
to appeal to queen Athena with my prayers.
I was just loosing the bolts, opening the doors,
when a voice filled with sorrow, family sorrow,
struck my ears, and I fell back, terrified,
into the women's arms—everything went black.   1310
Tell me the news, again, whatever it is . . .
sorrow and I are hardly strangers;
I can bear the worst.

MESSENGER: I—dear lady,
I'll speak as an eye-witness. I was there.
And I won't pass over one word of the truth.   1315
Why should I try to soothe you with a story,
only to prove a liar in a moment?
Truth is always best.

                     So,
I escorted your lord, I guided him
to the edge of the plain where the body lay,   1320
Polynices, torn by the dogs and still unmourned.
And saying a prayer to Hecate of the Crossroads,
Pluto[38] too, to hold their anger and be kind,
we washed the dead in a bath of holy water
and plucking some fresh branches, gathering . . .   1325
what was left of him, we burned them all together
and raised a high mound of native earth, and then
we turned and made for that rocky vault of hers,
the hollow, empty bed of the bride of Death.
And far off, one of us heard a voice,   1330

---

[38]Or Hades, god of the underworld. Hecate is a goddess associated with darkness and burial
grounds; offerings to her were left at crossroads.

a long wail rising, echoing
out of that unhallowed wedding-chamber,
he ran to alert the master and Creon pressed on,
closer—the strange, inscrutable cry came sharper,
throbbing around him now, and he let loose   1335
a cry of his own, enough to wrench the heart,
"Oh god, am I the prophet now? going down
the darkest road I've ever gone? My son—
it's *his* dear voice, he greets me! Go, men,
closer, quickly! Go through the gap,   1340
the rocks are dragged back—
right to the tomb's very mouth—and look,
see if it's Haemon's voice I think I hear,
or the gods have robbed me of my senses."

The king was shattered. We took his orders,   1345
went and searched, and there in the deepest,
dark recesses of the tomb we found her . . .
hanged by the neck in a fine linen noose,
strangled in her veils—and the boy,
his arms flung around her waist,   1350
clinging to her, wailing for his bride,
dead and down below, for his father's crimes
and the bed of his marriage blighted by misfortune.
When Creon saw him, he gave a deep sob,
he ran in, shouting, crying out to him,   1355
"Oh my child—what have you done? what seized you,
what insanity? what disaster drove you mad?
Come out, my son! I beg you on my knees!"
But the boy gave him a wild burning glance,
spat in his face, not a word in reply,   1360
he drew his sword—his father rushed out,
running as Haemon lunged and missed!—
and then, doomed, desperate with himself,
suddenly leaning his full weight on the blade,
he buried it in his body, halfway to the hilt.   1365
And still in his senses, pouring his arms around her,
he embraced the girl and breathing hard,
released a quick rush of blood,

bright red on her cheek glistening white.
And there he lies, body enfolding body . . .   1370
he has won his bride at last, poor boy,
not here but in the houses of the dead.

Creon shows the world that of all the ills
afflicting men the worst is lack of judgment.

[*Eurydice turns and reenters the palace.*]

LEADER: What do you make of that? The lady's gone,   1375
without a word, good or bad.
MESSENGER: I'm alarmed too
but here's my hope—faced with her son's death,
she finds it unbecoming to mourn in public.
Inside, under her roof, she'll set her women
to the task and wail the sorrow of the house.   1380
She's too discreet. She won't do something rash.
LEADER: I'm not so sure. To me, at least,
a long heavy silence promises danger,
just as much as a lot of empty outcries.
MESSENGER: We'll see if she's holding something back,   1385
hiding some passion in her heart.
I'm going in. You may be right—who knows?
Even too much silence has its dangers.

        [*Exit to the palace. Enter Creon from the side, escorted
        by attendants carrying Haemon's body on a bier.*]

LEADER: The king himself! Coming toward us,
look, holding the boy's head in his hands.   1390
Clear, damning proof, if it's right to say so—
proof of his own madness, no one else's,
        no, his own blind wrongs.
CREON: Ohhh,
so senseless, so insane . . . my crimes,
my stubborn, deadly—   1395
Look at us, the killer, the killed,
father and son, the same blood—the misery!
My plans, my mad fanatic heart,
my son, cut off so young!

Ai, dead, lost to the world, 1400
not through your stupidity, no, my own.

LEADER: Too late,
too late, you see what justice means.

CREON: Oh I've learned
through blood and tears! Then, it was then,
when the god came down and struck me—a great weight
shattering, driving me down that wild savage path, 1405
ruining, trampling down my joy. Oh the agony,
    the heartbreaking agonies of our lives.

[Enter the Messenger from the palace.]

MESSENGER: Master,
what a hoard of grief you have, and you'll have more.
The grief that lies to hand you've brought yourself—

[Pointing to Haemon's body.]

the rest, in the house, you'll see it all too soon. 1410

CREON: What now? What's worse than this?

MESSENGER: The queen is dead.
The mother of this dead boy . . . mother to the end—
poor thing, her wounds are fresh.

CREON: No, no,
harbor of Death, so choked, so hard to cleanse!—
why me? why are you killing me? 1415
Herald of pain, more words, more grief?
I died once, you kill me again and again!
What's the report, boy . . . some news for me?
My wife dead? O dear god!
Slaughter heaped on slaughter?

[The doors open; the body of Eurydice is brought out on her bier.]

MESSENGER: See for yourself: 1420
now they bring her body from the palace.

CREON: Oh no,
another, a second loss to break the heart.
What next, what fate still waits for me?
I just held my son in my arms and now,
look, a new corpse rising before my eyes— 1425
    wretched, helpless mother—O my son!

MESSENGER: She stabbed herself at the altar,
    then her eyes went dark, after she'd raised
    a cry for the noble fate of Megareus,[39] the hero
    killed in the first assault, then for Haemon,   1430
    then with her dying breath she called down
    torments on your head—you killed her sons.
CREON: Oh the dread,
    I shudder with dread! Why not kill me too?—
    run me through with a good sharp sword?
    Oh god, the misery, anguish—   1435
    I, I'm churning with it, going under.
MESSENGER: Yes, and the dead, the woman lying there,
    piles the guilt of all their deaths on you.
CREON: How did she end her life, what bloody stroke?
MESSENGER: She drove home to the heart with her own hand,   1440
    once she learned her son was dead . . . that agony.
CREON: And the guilt is all mine—
    can never be fixed on another man,
    no escape for me. I killed you,
    I, god help me, I admit it all!   1445

[To his attendants.]

    Take me away, quickly, out of sight.
    I don't even exist—I'm no one. Nothing.
LEADER: Good advice, if there's any good in suffering.
    Quickest is best when troubles block the way.
CREON: [Kneeling in prayer.]
    Come, let it come!—that best of fates for me   1450
    that brings the final day, best fate of all.
    Oh quickly, now—
    so I never have to see another sunrise.
LEADER: That will come when it comes;
    we must deal with all that lies before us.   1455
    The future rests with the ones who tend the future.
CREON: That prayer—I poured my heart into that prayer!

[39]Another son of Creon and Eurydice; he was killed during the siege of the city. Tiresias had prophesied that his death would save Thebes.

LEADER: No more prayers now. For mortal men
           there is no escape from the doom we must endure.

CREON: Take me away, I beg you, out of sight.   1460
          A rash, indiscriminate fool!
          I murdered you, my son, against my will—
          you too, my wife . . .

                              Wailing wreck of a man,
          whom to look to? where to lean for support?

[*Desperately turning from Haemon to Eurydice on their biers.*]

          Whatever I touch goes wrong—once more   1465
          a crushing fate's come down upon my head.

[*The messenger and attendants lead Creon into the palace.*]

CHORUS: Wisdom is by far the greatest part of joy,
           and reverence toward the gods must be safeguarded.
           The mighty words of the proud are paid in full
           with mighty blows of fate, and at long last   1470
           those blows will teach us wisdom.

                         [*The old citizens exit to the side.*]

William Shakespeare, the supreme writer of English, was born, baptized, and buried in the market town of Stratford-on-Avon, eighty miles from London. Son of a glove maker and merchant who was high bailiff (or mayor) of the town, he probably attended grammar school and learned to read Latin authors in the original. At eighteen he married Anne Hathaway, twenty-six, by whom he had three children, including twins. By 1592 he had become well known and envied as an actor and playwright in London. From 1594 until he retired, he belonged to the same theatrical company, the Lord Chamberlain's Men (later renamed the King's Men in honor of their patron, James I), for whom he wrote thirty-six plays—some of them, such as Hamlet and King Lear, profound reworkings of old plays. As an actor, Shakespeare is believed to have played supporting roles, such as Hamlet's father's ghost. The company prospered, moved into the Globe Theatre in 1599, and in 1608 bought the fashionable Blackfriars as well; Shakespeare owned an interest in both theaters. When plagues shut down the theaters from 1592 to 1594, Shakespeare turned to story poems; his great sonnets (published only in 1609) probably also date from the 1590s. Plays were regarded as entertainments of little literary merit and Shakespeare did not bother to supervise their publication. After The Tempest (1611), the last play entirely from his hand, he retired to Stratford, where since 1597 he had owned the second largest house in town. Most critics agree that when he wrote Othello (c. 1604), Shakespeare was at the height of his literary powers.

The Tragedy of Othello, The Moor of Venice

Edited by David Bevington

Characters

Othello, *the Moor*
Brabantio [*a senator*], *father to Desdemona*

NOTE ON THE TEXT: This text of *Othello* is based on that of the First Folio, or large collection, of Shakespeare's plays (1623). But there are many differences between the Folio text and that of the play's first printing in the Quarto, or small volume, of 1621 (eighteen or nineteen years after the play's first performance). Some readings from the Quarto are included. For the reader's convenience, some material has been added by the editor, David Bevington (some indications of scene, some stage directions). Such additions are enclosed in brackets. Bevington's text and notes were prepared for his book *The Complete Works of Shakespeare*, 4th ed. (New York: HarperCollins, 1992).

Cassio, *an honorable lieutenant* [*to Othello*]
Iago [*Othello's ancient*], *a villain*
Roderigo, *a gulled gentleman*
Duke of Venice
Senators [*of Venice*]
Montano, *governor of Cyprus*
Gentlemen of Cyprus
Lodovico and Gratiano [*kinsmen to Brabantio*], *two noble Venetians*
Sailors
Clown
Desdemona [*daughter to Brabantio and*], *wife to Othello*
Emilia, *wife to Iago*
Bianca, *a courtesan* [*and mistress to Cassio*]
A Messenger
A Herald
A Musician
Servants, Attendants, Officers, Senators, Musicians, Gentlemen]

[Scene: *Venice; a seaport in Cyprus*]

Act I

Scene I. Venice. A street

Enter Roderigo and Iago.

RODERIGO: Tush, never tell me!° I take it much unkindly
  That thou, Iago, who hast had my purse
  As if the strings were thine, shouldst know of this.°
IAGO: 'Sblood,° but you'll not hear me.
  If ever I did dream of such a matter,   5
  Abhor me.
RODERIGO: Thou toldst me thou didst hold him in thy hate.
IAGO: Despise me
  If I do not. Three great ones of the city,
  In personal suit to make me his lieutenant,   10
  Off-capped to him;° and by the faith of man,
  I know my price, I am worth no worse a place.
  But he, as loving his own pride and purposes,

---

1 **never tell me** (An expression of incredulity, like "tell me another one.")   3 **this** i.e., Desdemona's elopement   4 **'Sblood** by His (Christ's) blood   11 **him** i.e., Othello

Evades them with a bombast circumstance°
Horribly stuffed with epithets of war,° 15
And, in conclusion,
Nonsuits° my mediators. For, "Certes,"° says he,
"I have already chose my officer."
And what was he?
Forsooth, a great arithmetician,° 20
One Michael Cassio, a Florentine,
A fellow almost damned in a fair wife,°
That never set a squadron in the field
Nor the division of a battle° knows
More than a spinster°—unless the bookish theoric,° 25
Wherein the togaed° consuls° can propose°
As masterly as he. Mere prattle without practice
Is all his soldiership. But he, sir, had th' election;
And I, of whom his° eyes had seen the proof
At Rhodes, at Cyprus, and on other grounds 30
Christened° and heathen, must be beeled and calmed°
By debitor and creditor.° This countercaster,°
He, in good time,° must his lieutenant be,
And I—God bless the mark!°—his Moorship's ancient.°
RODERIGO: By heaven, I rather would have been his hangman.° 35
IAGO: Why, there's no remedy. 'Tis the curse of service;
Preferment° goes by letter and affection,°
And not by old gradation,° where each second
Stood heir to th' first. Now, sir, be judge yourself
Whether I in any just term° am affined° 40
To love the Moor.

---

14 **bombast circumstance** wordy evasion. (Bombast is cotton padding.)   15 **epithets of war** military
expressions   17 **Nonsuits** rejects the petition of.   **Certes** certainly   20 **arithmetician** i.e., a man
whose military knowledge is merely theoretical, based on books of tactics   22 **A . . . wife** (Cassio
does not seem to be married, but his counterpart in Shakespeare's source does have a woman in
his house. See also Act IV, Scene i, line 127.)   24 **division of a battle** disposition of a military unit
25 **a spinster** i.e., a housewife, one whose regular occupation is spinning.   **theoric** theory
26 **togaed** wearing the toga.   **consuls** counselors, senators.   **propose** discuss   29 **his** i.e.,
Othello's   31 **Christened** Christian.   **beeled and calmed** left to leeward without wind, becalmed.
(A sailing metaphor.)   32 **debitor and creditor** (A name for a system of bookkeeping, here used as
a contemptuous nickname for Cassio.)   **countercaster** i.e., bookkeeper, one who tallies with
counters, or "metal disks." (Said contemptuously.)   33 **in good time** opportunely, i.e., forsooth
34 **God bless the mark** (Perhaps originally a formula to ward off evil; here an expression of
impatience.)   **ancient** standard-bearer, ensign   35 **his hangman** the executioner of him
37 **Preferment** promotion.   **letter and affection** personal influence and favoritism   38 **old gradation**
step-by-step seniority, the traditional way   40 **term** respect   **affined** bound

RODERIGO: I would not follow him then.

IAGO: O sir, content you.°
I follow him to serve my turn upon him.
We cannot all be masters, nor all masters   45
Cannot be truly° followed. You shall mark
Many a duteous and knee-crooking knave
That, doting on his own obsequious bondage,
Wears out his time, much like his master's ass,
For naught but provender, and when he's old, cashiered.°   50
Whip me° such honest knaves. Others there are
Who, trimmed in forms and visages of duty,°
Keep yet their hearts attending on themselves,
And, throwing but shows of service on their lords,
Do well thrive by them, and when they have lined their coats,°   55
Do themselves homage.° These fellows have some soul,
And such a one do I profess myself. For, sir,
It is as sure as you are Roderigo,
Were I the Moor I would not be Iago.°
In following him, I follow but myself—   60
Heaven is my judge, not I for love and duty,
But seeming so for my peculiar° end.
For when my outward action doth demonstrate
The native° act and figure° of my heart
In compliment extern,° 'tis not long after   65
But I will wear my heart upon my sleeve
For daws° to peck at. I am not what I am.°

RODERIGO: What a full° fortune does the thick-lips° owe°
If he can carry 't thus!°

IAGO: Call up her father.
Rouse him, make after him, poison his delight,   70
Proclaim him in the streets; incense her kinsmen,

---

43 **content you** don't you worry about that   46 **truly** faithfully   50 **cashiered** dismissed from service   51 **Whip me** whip, as far as I'm concerned   52 **trimmed . . . duty** dressed up in the mere form and show of dutifulness   55 **lined their coats** i.e., stuffed their purses   56 **Do themselves homage** i.e., attend to self-interest solely   59 **Were . . . Iago** i.e., if I were able to assume command, I certainly would not choose to remain a subordinate, or, I would keep a suspicious eye on a flattering subordinate   62 **peculiar** particular, personal   64 **native** innate.   **figure** shape, intent   65 **compliment extern** outward show. (Conforming in this case to the inner workings and intention of the heart.)   67 **daws** small crowlike birds, proverbially stupid and avaricious.   **I am not what I am** i.e., I am not one who wears his heart on his sleeve   68 **full** swelling.   **thick-lips** (Elizabethans often applied the term "Moor" to Negroes.)   **owe** own   69 **carry 't thus** carry this off

And, though he in a fertile climate dwell,
Plague him with flies.° Though that his joy be joy,°
Yet throw such changes of vexation° on 't
As it may° lose some color.° 75

RODERIGO: Here is her father's house. I'll call aloud.

IAGO: Do, with like timorous° accent and dire yell
As when, by night and negligence,° the fire
Is spied in populous cities.

RODERIGO: What ho, Brabantio! Signor Brabantio, ho! 80

IAGO: Awake! What ho, Brabantio! Thieves, thieves, thieves!
Look to your house, your daughter, and your bags!
Thieves, thieves!

Brabantio [enters] above [at a window].°

BRABANTIO: What is the reason of this terrible summons?
What is the matter° there? 85

RODERIGO: Signor, is all your family within?

IAGO: Are your doors locked?

BRABANTIO: Why, wherefore ask you this?

IAGO: Zounds,° sir, you're robbed. For shame, put on your gown!
Your heart is burst; you have lost half your soul.
Even now, now, very now, an old black ram 90
Is tupping° your white ewe. Arise, arise!
Awake the snorting° citizens with the bell,
Or else the devil° will make a grandsire of you.
Arise, I say!

BRABANTIO: What, have you lost your wits?

RODERIGO: Most reverend signor, do you know my voice? 95

BRABANTIO: Not I. What are you?

RODERIGO: My name is Roderigo.

BRABANTIO: The worser welcome.
I have charged thee not to haunt about my doors.
In honest plainness thou hast heard me say 100

72–73 **though ... flies** though he seems prosperous and happy now, vex him with misery
73 **Though ... be joy** although he seems fortunate and happy. (Repeats the idea of line 72.)
74 **changes of vexation** vexing changes   75 **As it may** that may cause it to.   **some color** some of its
fresh gloss   77 **timorous** frightening   78 **and negligence** i.e., by negligence   83 **[s.d.] at a window**
(This stage direction, from the Quarto, probably calls for an appearance on the gallery above and
rearstage.)   85 **the matter** your business   88 **Zounds** by His (Christ's) wounds   91 **tupping**
covering, copulating with. (Said of sheep.)   92 **snorting** snoring   93 **the devil** (The devil was
conventionally pictured as black.)

My daughter is not for thee; and now, in madness,
Being full of supper and distempering° drafts,
Upon malicious bravery° dost thou come
To start° my quiet.

RODERIGO: Sir, sir, sir—

BRABANTIO: But thou must needs be sure   105
My spirits and my place° have in their power
To make this bitter to thee.

RODERIGO: Patience, good sir.

BRABANTIO: What tell'st thou me of robbing? This is Venice;
My house is not a grange.°

RODERIGO: Most grave Brabantio,
In simple° and pure soul I come to you.   110

IAGO: Zounds, sir, you are one of those that will not serve God if
the devil bid you. Because we come to do you service and you
think we are ruffians, you'll have your daughter covered with a
Barbary° horse; you'll have your nephews° neigh to you; you'll
have coursers° for cousins° and jennets° for germans.°   115

BRABANTIO: What profane wretch art thou?

IAGO: I am one, sir, that comes to tell you your daughter and the
Moor are now making the beast with two backs.

BRABANTIO: Thou art a villain.

IAGO: You are—a senator.°

BRABANTIO: This thou shalt answer.° I know thee, Roderigo.

RODERIGO: Sir, I will answer anything. But I beseech you,   120
If't be your pleasure and most wise° consent—
As partly I find it is—that your fair daughter,
At this odd-even° and dull watch o' the night,
Transported with° no worse nor better guard
But with a knave° of common hire, a gondolier,   125
To the gross clasps of a lascivious Moor—
If this be known to you and your allowance°

---

102 **distempering** intoxicating   103 **Upon malicious bravery** with hostile intent to defy me   104 **start** startle, disrupt   106 **My spirits and my place** my temperament and my authority of office.   **have in** have it in   109 **grange** isolated country house   110 **simple** sincere   114 **Barbary** from northern Africa (and hence associated with Othello).   **nephews** i.e., grandsons   115 **coursers** powerful horses. **cousins** kinsmen.   **jennets** small Spanish horses.   **germans** near relatives   118 **a senator** (Said with mock politeness, as though the word itself were an insult.)   119 **answer** be held accountable for   121 **wise** well-informed   123 **odd-even** between one day and the next, i.e., about midnight   124 **with** by   125 **But with a knave** than by a low fellow, a servant   127 **allowance** permission

We then have done you bold and saucy° wrongs.
But if you know not this, my manners tell me
We have your wrong rebuke. Do not believe   130
That, from° the sense of all civility,°
I thus would play and trifle with your reverence.°
Your daughter, if you have not given her leave,
I say again, hath made a gross revolt,
Tying her duty, beauty, wit,° and fortunes   135
In an extravagant° and wheeling° stranger°
Of here and everywhere. Straight° satisfy yourself.
If she be in her chamber or your house,
Let loose on me the justice of the state
For thus deluding you.   140

BRABANTIO: Strike on the tinder,° ho!
Give me a taper! Call up all my people!
This accident° is not unlike my dream.
Belief of it oppresses me already.
Light, I say, light!   *Exit [above].*

IAGO: Farewell, for I must leave you.   145
It seems not meet° nor wholesome to my place°
To be producted°—as, if I stay, I shall—
Against the Moor. For I do know the state,
However this may gall° him with some check,°
Cannot with safety cast° him, for he's embarked°   150
With such loud reason° to the Cyprus wars,
Which even now stands in act,° that, for their souls,°
Another of his fathom° they have none
To lead their business; in which regard,°
Though I do hate him as I do hell pains,   155
Yet for necessity of present life°

---

128 saucy insolent   **131 from** contrary to.   **civility** good manners, decency   **132 your reverence**
the respect due to you   **135 wit** intelligence   **136 extravagant** expatriate, wandering far from
home.   **wheeling** roving about, vagabond.   **stranger** foreigner   **137 Straight** straightway
141 tinder charred linen ignited by a spark from flint and steel, used to light torches or tapers
(lines 142, 167)   **143 accident** occurrence, event   **146 meet** fitting.   **place** position (as ensign)
147 producted produced (as a witness)   **149 gall** rub; oppress.   **check** rebuke   **150 cast** dismiss.
embarked engaged   **151 loud reason** unanimous shout of confirmation (in the Senate)
152 stands in act are going on.   **for their souls** to save themselves   **153 fathom** i.e., ability, depth
of experience   **154 in which regard** out of regard for which   **156 life** livelihood

I must show out a flag and sign of love,
Which is indeed but sign. That you shall surely find him,
Lead to the Sagittary° the raisèd search,°
And there will I be with him. So farewell. [*Exit.*] 160

Enter [below] Brabantio [in his nightgown°] with servants and
torches.

BRABANTIO: It is too true an evil. Gone she is;
And what's to come of my despisèd time°
Is naught but bitterness. Now, Roderigo,
Where didst thou see her?—O unhappy girl!—
With the Moor, sayst thou?—Who would be a father!— 165
How didst thou know 'twas she?—O, she deceives me
Past thought!—What said she to you?—Get more tapers.
Raise all my kindred.—Are they married, think you?

RODERIGO: Truly, I think they are.

BRABANTIO: O heaven! How got she out? O treason of the blood! 170
Fathers, from hence trust not your daughters' minds
By what you see them act. Is there not charms°
By which the property° of youth and maidhood
May be abused?° Have you not read, Roderigo,
Of some such thing?

RODERIGO: Yes, sir, I have indeed. 175

BRABANTIO: Call up my brother.—O, would you had had her!—
Some one way, some another.—Do you know
Where we may apprehend her and the Moor?

RODERIGO: I think I can discover° him, if you please
To get good guard and go along with me. 180

BRABANTIO: Pray you, lead on. At every house I'll call;
I may command° at most.—Get weapons, ho!
And raise some special officers of night.—
On, good Roderigo. I will deserve° your pains.

[*Exeunt.*]

---

159 **Sagittary** (An inn or house where Othello and Desdemona are staying, named for its sign of
Sagittarius, or Centaur.)   **raisèd search** search party roused out of sleep   160 **[s.d.] nightgown**
dressing gown. (This costuming is specified in the Quarto text.)   162 **time** i.e., remainder of life
172 **charms** spells   173 **property** special quality, nature   174 **abused** deceived   179 **discover** reveal,
uncover   182 **command** demand assistance   184 **deserve** show gratitude for

Scene II. Venice. Another street, before Othello's lodgings

Enter Othello, Iago, attendants with torches.

IAGO: Though in the trade of war I have slain men,
    Yet do I hold it very stuff° o' the conscience
    To do no contrived° murder. I lack iniquity
    Sometimes to do me service. Nine or ten times
    I had thought t' have yerked° him° here under the ribs.   5
OTHELLO: 'Tis better as it is.
IAGO: Nay, but he prated,
    And spoke such scurvy and provoking terms
    Against your honor
    That, with the little godliness I have,
    I did full hard forbear him.° But, I pray you, sir,   10
    Are you fast married? Be assured of this,
    That the magnifico° is much beloved,
    And hath in his effect° a voice potential°
    As double as the Duke's. He will divorce you,
    Or put upon you what restraint or grievance   15
    The law, with all his might to enforce it on,
    Will give him cable.°
OTHELLO: Let him do his spite.
    My services which I have done the seigniory°
    Shall out-tongue his complaints. 'Tis yet to know°—
    Which, when I know that boasting is an honor,   20
    I shall promulgate—I fetch my life and being
    From men of royal siege,° and my demerits°
    May speak unbonneted° to as proud a fortune
    As this that I have reached. For know, Iago,
    But that I love the gentle Desdemona,   25
    I would not my unhousèd° free condition
    Put into circumscription and confine°
    For the sea's worth.° But look, what lights come yond?

---

2 very stuff essence, basic material (continuing the metaphor of *trade* from line 1)   **3 contrived** premeditated   **5 yerked** stabbed.   **him** i.e., Roderigo   **10 I . . . him** I restrained myself with great difficulty from assaulting him   **12 magnifico** Venetian grandee, i.e., Brabantio   **13 in his effect** at his command.   **potential** powerful   **17 cable** i.e., scope   **18 seigniory** Venetian government   **19 yet to know** not yet widely known   **22 siege** i.e., rank. (Literally, a seat used by a person of distinction.)   **demerits** deserts   **23 unbonneted** without removing the hat, i.e., on equal terms (? Or "with hat off," "in all due modesty.")   **26 unhousèd** unconfined, undomesticated   **27 circumscription and confine** restriction and confinement   **28 the sea's worth** all the riches at the bottom of the sea.

Enter Cassio [and certain officers°] with torches.

IAGO: Those are the raisèd father and his friends.
          You were best go in.

OTHELLO: Not I. I must be found.   30
          My parts, my title, and my perfect soul°
          Shall manifest me rightly. Is it they?

IAGO: By Janus,° I think no.

OTHELLO: The servants of the Duke? And my lieutenant?
          The goodness of the night upon you, friends!   35
          What is the news?

CASSIO: The Duke does greet you, General,
          And he requires your haste-post-haste appearance
          Even on the instant.

OTHELLO: What is the matter,° think you?

CASSIO: Something from Cyprus, as I may divine.°
          It is a business of some heat.° The galleys   40
          Have sent a dozen sequent° messengers
          This very night at one another's heels,
          And many of the consuls,° raised and met,
          Are at the Duke's already. You have been hotly called for;
          When, being not at your lodging to be found,   45
          The Senate hath sent about° three several° quests
          To search you out.

OTHELLO: 'Tis well I am found by you.
          I will but spend a word here in the house
          And go with you.   [*Exit.*]

CASSIO: Ancient, what makes° he here?

IAGO: Faith, he tonight hath boarded° a land carrack.°   50
          If it prove lawful prize,° he's made forever.

CASSIO: I do not understand.

IAGO: He's married.

CASSIO: To who?

[s.d.] officers (The Quarto text calls for "Cassio with lights, officers with torches.")   **31 My . . . soul** my natural gifts, my position or reputation, and my unflawed conscience   **33 Janus** Roman two-faced god of beginnings   **38 matter** business   **39 divine** guess   **40 heat** urgency   **41 sequent** successive   **43 consuls** senators   **46 about** all over the city.   **several** separate   **49 makes** does   **50 boarded** gone aboard and seized as an act of piracy (with sexual suggestion).   **carrack** large merchant ship   **51 prize** booty

[*Enter Othello.*]

IAGO: Marry,° to—Come, Captain, will you go?

OTHELLO: Have with you.°

CASSIO: Here comes another troop to seek for you.   55

[*Enter Brabantio, Roderigo, with officers and torches.*°]

IAGO: It is Brabantio. General, be advised.°
He comes to bad intent.

OTHELLO: Holla! Stand there!

RODERIGO: Signor, it is the Moor.

BRABANTIO: Down with him, thief!

[*They draw on both sides.*]

IAGO: You, Roderigo! Come, sir, I am for you.

OTHELLO: Keep up° your bright swords, for the dew will rust
them.   60
Good signor, you shall more command with years
Than with your weapons.

BRABANTIO: O thou foul thief, where hast thou stowed my
daughter?
Damned as thou art, thou hast enchanted her!
For I'll refer me° to all things of sense,°   65
If she in chains of magic were not bound
Whether a maid so tender, fair, and happy,
So opposite to marriage that she shunned
The wealthy curlèd darlings of our nation,
Would ever have, t' incur a general mock,   70
Run from her guardage° to the sooty bosom
Of such a thing as thou—to fear, not to delight.
Judge me the world if 'tis not gross in sense°
That thou hast practiced on her with foul charms,
Abused her delicate youth with drugs or minerals°   75

---

53 **Marry** (An oath, originally "by the Virgin Mary"; here used with wordplay on *married*.)   54 **Have with you** i.e., let's go   55 **[s.d.] officers and torches** (The Quarto text calls for "others with lights and weapons.")   56 **be advised** be on your guard   60 **Keep up** keep in the sheath   65 **refer me** submit my case.   **things of sense** commonsense understandings, or, creatures possessing common sense   71 **her guardage** my guardianship of her   73 **gross in sense** obvious   75 **minerals** i.e., poisons

WILLIAM SHAKESPEARE

That weakens motion.° I'll have 't disputed on;°
'Tis probable and palpable to thinking.
I therefore apprehend and do attach° thee
For an abuser of the world, a practicer
Of arts inhibited° and out of warrant.°—   80
Lay hold upon him! If he do resist,
Subdue him at his peril.

OTHELLO: Hold your hands,
Both you of my inclining° and the rest.
Were it my cue to fight, I should have known it
Without a prompter.—Whither will you that I go   85
To answer this your charge?

BRABANTIO: To prison, till fit time
Of law and course of direct session°
Call thee to answer.

OTHELLO: What if I do obey?
How may the Duke be therewith satisfied,   90
Whose messengers are here about my side
Upon some present business of the state
To bring me to him?

OFFICER: 'Tis true, most worthy signor.
The Duke's in council, and your noble self,
I am sure, is sent for.

BRABANTIO: How? The Duke in council?   95
In this time of the night? Bring him away.°
Mine's not an idle° cause. The Duke himself,
Or any of my brothers of the state,
Cannot but feel this wrong as 'twere their own;
For if such actions may have passage free,°   100
Bondslaves and pagans shall our statesmen be.

                                            [*Exeunt.*]

---

76 weakens motion impair the vital faculties.   **disputed on** argued in court by professional counsel, debated by experts   **78 attach** arrest   **80 arts inhibited** prohibited arts, black magic.   **out of warrant** illegal   **83 inclining** following, party   **88 course of direct session** regular or specially convened legal proceedings   **96 away** right along   **97 idle** trifling   **100 have passage free** are allowed to go unchecked

Scene III. Venice. A council chamber

Enter Duke [and] Senators [and sit at a table, with lights], and
Officers.° [The Duke and Senators are reading dispatches.]

DUKE: There is no composition° in these news
    That gives them credit.
FIRST SENATOR: Indeed, they are disproportioned.°
    My letters say a hundred and seven galleys.
DUKE: And mine, a hundred forty.
SECOND SENATOR: And mine, two hundred.   5
    But though they jump° not on a just° account—
    As in these cases, where the aim° reports
    'Tis oft with difference—yet do they all confirm
    A Turkish fleet, and bearing up to Cyprus.
DUKE: Nay, it is possible enough to judgment.   10
    I do not so secure me in the error
    But the main article I do approve°
    In fearful sense.
SAILOR [*within*]:   What ho, what ho, what ho!

    [*Enter Sailor.*]

OFFICER: A messenger from the galleys.
DUKE: Now, what's the business?   15
SAILOR: The Turkish preparation° makes for Rhodes.
    So was I bid report here to the state
    By Signor Angelo.
DUKE: How say you by° this change?
FIRST SENATOR: This cannot be
    By no assay° of reason. 'Tis a pageant°   20
    To keep us in false gaze.° When we consider
    Th' importancy of Cyprus to the Turk,
    And let ourselves again but understand
    That, as it more concerns the Turk than Rhodes,
    So may he with more facile question bear it,°   25

[s.d.] Enter . . . Officers (The Quarto text calls for the Duke and senators to "sit at a table with lights and attendants.")
1 composition consistency   **3 disproportioned** inconsistent   **6 jump** agree.   **just** exact   **7 the aim** conjecture   **11–12 I do not . . . approve** I do not take such (false) comfort in the discrepancies that I fail to perceive the main point, i.e., that the Turkish fleet is threatening   **16 preparation** fleet prepared for battle   **19 by** about   **20 assay** test.   **pageant** mere show   **21 in false gaze** looking the wrong way   **25 So may . . . it** so also he (the Turk) can more easily capture it (Cyprus)

For that° it stands not in such warlike brace,
But altogether lacks th' abilities°
That Rhodes is dressed in°—if we make thought of this,
We must not think the Turk is so unskillful°
To leave that latest° which concerns him first,   30
Neglecting an attempt of ease and gain
To wake° and wage° a danger profitless.

DUKE: Nay, in all confidence, he's not for Rhodes.

OFFICER: Here is more news.

[*Enter a Messenger.*]

MESSENGER: The Ottomites, reverend and gracious,   35
Steering with due course toward the isle of Rhodes,
Have there injointed them° with an after° fleet.

FIRST SENATOR: Ay, so I thought. How many, as you guess?

MESSENGER: Of thirty sail; and now they do restem
Their backward course,° bearing with frank appearance°   40
Their purposes toward Cyprus. Signor Montano,
Your trusty and most valiant servitor,°
With his free duty° recommends° you thus,
And prays you to believe him.

DUKE: 'Tis certain then for Cyprus.   45
Marcus Luccicos, is not he in town?

FIRST SENATOR: He's now in Florence.

DUKE: Write from us to him, post-post-haste. Dispatch.

FIRST SENATOR: Here comes Brabantio and the valiant Moor.

[*Enter Brabantio, Othello, Cassio, Iago, Roderigo, and officers.*]

DUKE: Valiant Othello, we must straight° employ you   50
Against the general enemy° Ottoman.
[*To Brabantio.*] I did not see you; welcome, gentle° signor.
We lacked your counsel and your help tonight.

BRABANTIO: So did I yours. Good Your Grace, pardon me;
Neither my place° nor aught I heard of business   55

---

26 **For that** since. **brace** state of defense   27 **abilities** means of self-defense   28 **dressed in**
equipped with   29 **unskillful** deficient in judgment   30 **latest** last   32 **wake** stir up.   **wage** risk
37 **injointed them** joined themselves.   **after** second, following   39–40 **restem . . . course** retrace
their original course   40 **frank appearance** undisguised intent   42 **servitor** officer under your
command   43 **free duty** freely given and loyal service.   **recommends** commends himself and
reports to   50 **. . . straight** straightway.   51 **general enemy** universal enemy to all Christendom
52 **gentle** noble   55 **place** official position

Hath raised me from my bed, nor doth the general care
Take hold on me, for my particular° grief
Is of so floodgate° and o'erbearing nature
That it engluts° and swallows other sorrows
And it is still itself.°

DUKE: Why, what's the matter?   60
BRABANTIO: My daughter! O, my daughter!
DUKE AND SENATORS: Dead?
BRABANTIO: Ay, to me.
She is abused,° stol'n from me, and corrupted
By spells and medicines bought of mountebanks;
For nature so preposterously to err,
Being not deficient,° blind, or lame of sense,°   65
Sans° witchcraft could not.
DUKE: Whoe'er he be that in this foul proceeding
Hath thus beguiled your daughter of herself,
And you of her, the bloody book of law
You shall yourself read in the bitter letter   70
After your own sense°—yea, though our proper° son
Stood in your action.°
BRABANTIO: Humbly I thank Your Grace.
Here is the man, this Moor, whom now it seems
Your special mandate for the state affairs
Hath hither brought.
ALL: We are very sorry for 't.   75
DUKE [to Othello]:   What, in your own part, can you say to this?
BRABANTIO: Nothing, but this is so.
OTHELLO: Most potent, grave, and reverend signors,
My very noble and approved° good masters:
That I have ta'en away this old man's daughter,   80
It is most true; true, I have married her.
The very head and front° of my offending
Hath this extent, no more. Rude° am I in my speech,
And little blessed with the soft phrase of peace;

57 **particular** personal   58 **floodgate** i.e., overwhelming (as when floodgates are opened)
59 **engluts** engulfs   60 **is still itself** remains undiminished   62 **abused** deceived   65 **deficient**
defective.   **fame of sense** deficient in sensory perception   66 **Sans** without   71 **After . . . sense**
according to your own interpretation.   **our proper** my own   72 **Stood . . . action** were under your
accusation   79 **approved** proved, esteemed   82 **head and front** height and breadth, entire extent
83 **Rude** unpolished

For since these arms of mine had seven years' pith,°   85
Till now some nine moons wasted,° they have used
Their dearest° action in the tented field;
And little of this great world can I speak
More than pertains to feats of broils and battle,
And therefore little shall I grace my cause   90
In speaking for myself. Yet, by your gracious patience,
I will a round° unvarnished tale deliver
Of my whole course of love—what drugs, what charms,
What conjuration, and what mighty magic,
For such proceeding I am charged withal,°   95
I won his daughter.

BRABANTIO: A maiden never bold;
Of spirit so still and quiet that her motion
Blushed at herself;° and she, in spite of nature,
Of years,° of country, credit,° everything,
To fall in love with what she feared to look on!   100
It is a judgment maimed and most imperfect
That will confess° perfection so could err
Against all rules of nature, and must be driven
To find out practices° of cunning hell
Why this should be. I therefore vouch° again   105
That with some mixtures powerful o'er the blood,°
Or with some dram conjured to this effect,°
He wrought upon her.

DUKE: To vouch this is no proof,
Without more wider° and more overt test°
Than these thin habits° and poor likelihoods°   110
Of modern seeming° do prefer° against him.

---

85 since . . . pith i.e., since I was seven. **pith** strength, vigor   **86 Till . . . wasted** until some nine months ago (since when Othello has evidently not been on active duty, but in Venice); alternately, Othello may be revealing his age in saying that his life is nine-twelfths over (making him in his early 50s).   **87 dearest** most valuable   **92 round** plain   **95 withal** with   **97–98 her . . . herself** i.e., she blushed easily at herself. (*Motion* can suggest the impulse of the soul or of the emotions, or physical movement.)   **99 years** i.e., difference in age.   **credit** virtuous reputation   **102 confess** concede (that)   **104 practices** plots   **105 vouch** assert   **106 blood** passions   **107 dram . . . effect** dose made by magical spells to have this effect   **109 more wider** fuller.   **test** testimony   **110 habits** garments, i.e., appearances.   **poor likelihoods** weak inferences   **111 modern seeming** commonplace assumption.   **prefer** bring forth

FIRST SENATOR: But Othello, speak.
Did you by indirect and forcèd courses°
Subdue and poison this young maid's affections?
Or came it by request and such fair question°   115
As soul to soul affordeth?

OTHELLO: I do beseech you,
Send for the lady to the Sagittary
And let her speak of me before her father.
If you do find me foul in her report,
The trust, the office I do hold of you   120
Not only take away, but let your sentence
Even fall upon my life.

DUKE: Fetch Desdemona hither.

OTHELLO: Ancient, conduct them. You best know the place.

[Exeunt Iago and attendants.]

And, till she come, as truly as to heaven
I do confess the vices of my blood,°   125
So justly° to your grave ears I'll present
How I did thrive in this fair lady's love,
And she in mine.

DUKE: Say it, Othello.

OTHELLO: Her father loved me, oft invited me,   130
Still° questioned me the story of my life
From year to year—the battles, sieges, fortunes
That I have passed.
I ran it through, even from my boyish days
To th' very moment that he bade me tell it,   135
Wherein I spoke of most disastrous chances,
Of moving accidents° by flood and field,
Of hairbreadth scapes i' th' imminent deadly breach,°
Of being taken by the insolent foe
And sold to slavery, of my redemption thence,   140
And portance° in my travels' history,

---

113 **forcèd courses** means used against her will   115 **question** conversation   125 **blood** passions, human nature   126 **justly** truthfully, accurately   131 **Still** continually   137 **moving accidents** stirring happenings   138 **imminent . . . breach** death-threatening gaps made in a fortification   141 **portance** conduct

Wherein of antres° vast and deserts idle,°
Rough quarries,° rocks, and hills whose heads touch heaven,
It was my hint° to speak—such was my process—
And of the Cannibals that each other eat,   145
The Anthropophagi,° and men whose heads
Do grow beneath their shoulders. These things to hear
Would Desdemona seriously incline;
But still the house affairs would draw her thence,
Which ever as she could with haste dispatch   150
She'd come again, and with a greedy ear
Devour up my discourse. Which I, observing,
Took once a pliant° hour, and found good means
To draw from her a prayer of earnest heart
That I would all my pilgrimage dilate,°   155
Whereof by parcels° she had something heard,
But not intentively.° I did consent,
And often did beguile her of her tears,
When I did speak of some distressful stroke
That my youth suffered. My story being done,   160
She gave me for my pains a world of sighs.
She swore, in faith, 'twas strange, 'twas passing° strange,
'Twas pitiful, 'twas wondrous pitiful.
She wished she had not heard it, yet she wished
That heaven had made her° such a man. She thanked me,   165
And bade me, if I had a friend that loved her,
I should but teach him how to tell my story,
And that would woo her. Upon this hint° I spake.
She loved me for the dangers I had passed,
And I loved her that she did pity them.   170
This only is the witchcraft I have used.
Here comes the lady. Let her witness it.

[*Enter Desdemona, Iago, [and] attendants.*]

---

142 antres caverns. **idle** barren, desolate **143 Rough quarries** rugged rock formations **144 hint**
occasion, opportunity **146 Anthropophagi** man-eaters. (A term from Pliny's *Natural History*.)
153 pliant well-suiting **155 dilate** relate in detail **156 by parcels** piecemeal **157 intentively** with
full attention, continuously **162 passing** exceedingly **165 made her** created her to be **168 hint**
opportunity. (Othello does not mean that she was dropping hints.)

DUKE: I think this tale would win my daughter too.
Good Brabantio,
Take up this mangled matter at the best.°   175
Men do their broken weapons rather use
Than their bare hands.
BRABANTIO: I pray you, hear her speak.
If she confess that she was half the wooer,
Destruction on my head if my bad blame
Light on the man!—Come hither, gentle mistress.   180
Do you perceive in all this noble company
Where most you owe obedience?
DESDEMONA: My noble Father,
I do perceive here a divided duty.
To you I am bound for life and education;°
My life and education both do learn° me   185
How to respect you. You are the lord of duty;°
I am hitherto your daughter. But here's my husband,
And so much duty as my mother showed
To you, preferring you before her father,
So much I challenge° that I may profess   190
Due to the Moor my lord.
BRABANTIO: God be with you! I have done.
Please it Your Grace, on to the state affairs.
I had rather to adopt a child than get° it.
Come hither, Moor.   195

[*He joins the hands of Othello and Desdemona.*]

I here do give thee that with all my heart°
Which, but thou hast already, with all my heart°
I would keep from thee.—For your sake,° jewel,
I am glad at soul I have no other child,
For thy escape° would teach me tyranny,   200
To hang clogs° on them.—I have done, my lord.

---

175 Take . . . best make the best of a bad bargain   **184 education** upbringing   **185 learn** teach
186 of duty to whom duty is due   **190 challenge** claim   **194 get** beget   **196 with all my heart**
wherein my whole affection has been engaged   **197 with all my heart** willingly, gladly   **198 For
your sake** on your account   **200 escape** elopement   **201 clogs** (Literally, blocks of wood fastened
to the legs of criminals or convicts to inhibit escape.)

DUKE: Let me speak like yourself,° and lay a sentence°
Which, as a grece° or step, may help these lovers
Into your favor.
When remedies° are past, the griefs are ended   205
By seeing the worst, which late on hopes depended.°
To mourn a mischief° that is past and gone
Is the next° way to draw new mischief on.
What° cannot be preserved when fortune takes,
Patience her injury a mockery makes.°   210
The robbed that smiles steals something from the thief;
He robs himself that spends a bootless grief.°
BRABANTIO: So let the Turk of Cyprus us beguile,
We lose it not, so long as we can smile.
He bears the sentence well that nothing bears   215
But the free comfort which from thence he hears,
But he bears both the sentence and the sorrow
That, to pay grief, must of poor patience borrow.°
These sentences, to sugar or to gall,
Being strong on both sides, are equivocal.   220°
But words are words. I never yet did hear
That the bruisèd heart was piercèd through the ear.°
I humbly beseech you, proceed to th' affairs of state.
DUKE: The Turk with a most mighty preparation makes for
Cyprus. Othello, the fortitude° of the place is best known to 225
you; and though we have there a substitute° of most allowed°
sufficiency, yet opinion, a sovereign mistress of effects, throws
a more safer voice on you.° You must therefore be content
to slubber° the gloss of your new fortunes with this more
stubborn° and boisterous expedition.

WILLIAM SHAKESPEARE

106

202 like yourself i.e., as you would, in your proper temper. lay a sentence apply a maxim
203 grece step   205 remedies hopes of remedy   206 which . . . depended which griefs were
sustained until recently by hopeful anticipation   207 mischief misfortune, injury   208 next
nearest   209 What whatever   210 Patience . . . makes patience laughs at the injury inflicted by
fortune (and thus eases the pain)   212 spends a bootless grief indulges in unavailing grief
215–218 He bears . . . borrow a person well bears out your maxim who can enjoy its platitudinous
comfort, free of all genuine sorrow, but anyone whose grief bankrupts his poor patience is left
with your saying and his sorrow, too. (Bears the sentence also plays on the meaning, "receives
judicial sentence.")   219–220 These . . . equivocal these fine maxims are equivocal, either sweet or
bitter in their application   222 piercèd . . . ear i.e., surgically lanced and cured by mere words of
advice   225 fortitude strength   226 substitute deputy. allowed acknowledged   226–227 opinion
. . . on you general opinion, an important determiner of affairs, chooses you as the best man
228 slubber soil, sully. stubborn harsh, rough

OTHELLO: The tyrant custom, most grave senators,   230
    Hath made the flinty and steel couch of war
    My thrice-driven° bed of down. I do agnize°
    A natural and prompt alacrity
    I find in hardness,° and do undertake
    These present wars against the Ottomites.   235
    Most humbly therefore bending to your state,°
    I crave fit disposition for my wife,
    Due reference of place and exhibition,°
    With such accommodation° and besort°
    As levels° with her breeding.°   240
DUKE: Why, at her father's.
BRABANTIO: I will not have it so.
OTHELLO: Nor I.
DESDEMONA: Nor I. I would not there reside,
    To put my father in impatient thoughts
    By being in his eye. Most gracious Duke,
    To my unfolding° lend your prosperous° ear,   245
    And let me find a charter° in your voice,
    T' assist my simpleness.
DUKE: What would you, Desdemona?
DESDEMONA: That I did love the Moor to live with him,
    My downright violence and storm of fortunes°   250
    May trumpet to the world. My heart's subdued
    Even to the very quality of my lord.°
    I saw Othello's visage in his mind,
    And to his honors and his valiant parts°
    Did I my soul and fortunes consecrate.   255
    So that, dear lords, if I be left behind
    A moth° of peace, and he go to the war,
    The rites° for why I love him are bereft me,

---

232 **thrice-driven** thrice sifted, winnowed.   **agnize** know in myself, acknowledge   234 **hardness** hardship   236 **bending . . . state** bowing or kneeling to your authority   238 **reference . . . exhibition** provision of appropriate place to live and allowance of money   239 **accommodation** suitable provision.   **besort** attendance   240 **levels** equals, suits.   **breeding** social position, upbringing   245 **unfolding** explanation, proposal.   **prosperous** propitious   246 **charter** privilege, authorization   250 **My . . . fortunes** my plain and total breach of social custom, taking my future by storm and disrupting my whole life   251–252 **My heart's . . . lord** my heart is brought wholly into accord with Othello's virtues; I love him for his virtues   254 **parts** qualities   257 **moth** i.e., one who consumes merely   258 **rites** rites of love (with a suggestion, too, of "rights," sharing)

WILLIAM SHAKESPEARE

And I a heavy interim shall support
By his dear° absence. Let me go with him.   260

OTHELLO: Let her have your voice.°
Vouch with me, heaven, I therefor beg it not
To please the palate of my appetite,
Nor to comply with heat°—the young affects°
In me defunct—and proper° satisfaction,   265
But to be free° and bounteous to her mind.
And heaven defend° your good souls that you think°
I will your serious and great business scant
When she is with me. No, when light-winged toys
Of feathered Cupid seel° with wanton dullness   270
My speculative and officed instruments,°
That° my disports° corrupt and taint° my business,
Let huswives make a skillet of my helm,
And all indign° and base adversities
Make head° against my estimation!°   275

DUKE: Be it as you shall privately determine,
Either for her stay or going. Th' affair cries haste,
And speed must answer it.

A SENATOR: You must away tonight.

DESDEMONA: Tonight, my lord?

DUKE: This night.

OTHELLO: With all my heart.

DUKE: At nine i' the morning here we'll meet again.   280
Othello, leave some officer behind,
And he shall our commission bring to you,
With such things else of quality and respect°
As doth import° you.

OTHELLO: So please Your Grace, my ancient;
A man he is of honesty and trust.   285
To his conveyance I assign my wife,

---

260 **dear** (1) heartfelt (2) costly   261 **voice** consent   264 **heat** sexual passion.   **young affects**
passions of youth, desires   265 **proper** personal   266 **free** generous   267 **defend** forbid.   **think**
should think   270 **seel** i.e., make blind (as in falconry, by sewing up the eyes of the hawk during
training)   271 **speculative ... instruments** eyes and other faculties used in the performance of
duty   272 **That** so that.   **disports** sexual pastimes.   **taint** impair   274 **indign** unworthy, shameful
275 **Make head** raise an army.   **estimation** reputation   283 **of quality and respect** of importance
and relevance   284 **import** concern

With what else needful Your Good Grace shall think
To be sent after me.
DUKE: Let it be so.
Good night to everyone. [*To Brabantio.*] And, noble signor,
If virtue no delighted° beauty lack,   290
Your son-in-law is far more fair than black.
FIRST SENATOR: Adieu, brave Moor. Use Desdemona well.
BRABANTIO: Look to her, Moor, if thou hast eyes to see.
She has deceived her father, and may thee.

[*Exeunt [Duke, Brabantio, Cassio, Senators, and officers].*]

OTHELLO: My life upon her faith! Honest Iago,   295
My Desdemona must I leave to thee.
I prithee, let thy wife attend on her,
And bring them after in the best advantage.°
Come, Desdemona. I have but an hour
Of love, of worldly matters and direction,°   300
To spend with thee. We must obey the time.°

Exit [with Desdemona].

RODERIGO: Iago—
IAGO: What sayst thou, noble heart?
RODERIGO: What will I do, think'st thou?
IAGO: Why, go to bed and sleep.   305
RODERIGO: I will incontinently° drown myself.
IAGO: If thou dost, I shall never love thee after. Why, thou silly
gentleman?
RODERIGO: It is silliness to live when to live is torment; and then
have we a prescription° to die when death is our physician.
IAGO: O villainous!° I have looked upon the world for four times
times seven years, and, since I could distinguish betwixt a ben-   310
efit and an injury, I never found man that knew how to love
himself. Ere I would say I would drown myself for the love of a
guinea hen,° I would change my humanity with a baboon.

---

290 **delighted** capable of delighting   298 **in . . . advantage** at the most favorable opportunity
300 **direction** instructions   301 **the time** the urgency of the present crisis   306 **incontinently**
immediately, without self-restraint   308–309 **prescription** (1) right based on long-established
custom (2) doctor's prescription   310 **villainous** i.e., what perfect nonsense   313 **guinea hen** (A
slang term for a prostitute.)

RODERIGO: What should I do? I confess it is my shame to be so fond,° but it is not in my virtue° to amend it. 315

IAGO: Virtue? A fig!° 'Tis in ourselves that we are thus or thus. Our bodies are our gardens, to the which our wills are gardeners; so that if we will plant nettles or sow lettuce, set hyssop° and weed up thyme, supply it with one gender° of herbs or distract it with° many, either to have it sterile with idleness° or manured with industry—why, the power and corrigible authority° of this lies in our wills. If the beam° of our lives had not one scale of reason to poise° another of sensuality, the 320 blood° and baseness of our natures would conduct us to most preposterous conclusions. But we have reason to cool our raging motions,° our carnal stings, our unbitted° lusts, whereof I take this that you call love to be a sect or scion.° 325

RODERIGO: It cannot be.

IAGO: It is merely a lust of the blood and a permission of the will. Come, be a man. Drown thyself? Drown cats and blind puppies. I have professed me thy friend, and I confess me knit to thy deserving with cables of perdurable° toughness. I could never better stead° thee than now. Put money in thy purse. Follow thou the wars; defeat thy favor° with an usurped° beard. I 330 say, put money in thy purse. It cannot be long that Desdemona should continue her love to the Moor—put money in thy purse—nor he his to her. It was a violent commencement in her, and thou shalt see an answerable sequestration°—put but money in thy purse. These Moors are changeable in their wills°—fill thy purse with money. The food that to him now is 335 as luscious as locusts° shall be to him shortly as bitter as coloquintida.° She must change for youth; when she is sated with his body, she will find the error of her choice. She must have change, she must. Therefore put money in thy purse. If thou

---

314 fond infatuated   **315 virtue** strength, nature   **316 fig** (To give a fig is to thrust the thumb between the first and second fingers in a vulgar and insulting gesture.)   **318 hyssop** an herb of the mint family   **319 gender** kind.   **distract it with** divide it among.   **320 idleness** want of cultivation.   **corrigible authority** power to correct   **321 beam** balance.   **322 poise** counterbalance. **blood** natural passions   324 **motions** appetites.   **unbitted** unbridled, uncontrolled   **325 sect or scion** cutting or offshoot   **329 perdurable** very durable   **330 stead** assist   **331 defeat thy favor** disguise your face.   **usurped** (The suggestion is that Roderigo is not man enough to have a beard of his own.)   **334–335 an answerable sequestration** a corresponding separation or estrangement **336 wills** carnal appetites   **337 locusts** fruit of the carob tree (see Matthew 3:4), or perhaps honeysuckle.   **coloquintida** colocynth or bitter apple, a purgative

WILLIAM SHAKESPEARE

wilt needs damn thyself, do it a more delicate way than drowning. Make° all the money thou canst. If sanctimony° and a frail vow betwixt an erring° barbarian and a supersubtle Venetian be not too hard for my wits and all the tribe of hell, thou shalt enjoy her. Therefore make money. A pox of drowning thyself! It is clean out of the way.° Seek thou rather to be hanged in compassing° thy joy than to be drowned and go without her.

RODERIGO: Wilt thou be fast° to my hopes if I depend on the issue?°

IAGO: Thou art sure of me. Go, make money. I have told thee often, and I retell thee again and again, I hate the Moor. My cause is hearted;° thine hath no less reason. Let us be conjunctive° in our revenge against him. If thou canst cuckold him, thou dost thyself a pleasure, me a sport. There are many events in the womb of time which will be delivered. Traverse,° go, provide thy money. We will have more of this tomorrow. Adieu.

RODERIGO: Where shall we meet i' the morning?

IAGO: At my lodging.

RODERIGO: I'll be with thee betimes.° [*He starts to leave.*]

IAGO: Go to, farewell.—Do you hear, Roderigo?

RODERIGO: What say you?

IAGO: No more of drowning, do you hear?

RODERIGO: I am changed.

IAGO: Go to, farewell. Put money enough in your purse.

RODERIGO: I'll sell all my land.   *Exit.*

IAGO: Thus do I ever make my fool my purse;
For I mine own gained knowledge should profane
If I would time expend with such a snipe°
But for my sport and profit. I hate the Moor;
And it is thought abroad° that twixt my sheets
He's done my office.° I know not if 't be true;
But I, for mere suspicion in that kind,
Will do as if for surety.° He holds me well;°

340

345

350

355

360

365

---

341 Make raise, collect. **sanctimony** sacred ceremony **342 erring** wandering, vagabond, unsteady **344 clean . . . way** entirely unsuitable as a course of action. **compassing** encompassing, embracing **346 fast** true. **issue** (successful) outcome **348 hearted** fixed in the heart, heartfelt **349 conjunctive** united **351 Traverse** (A military marching term.) **355 betimes** early **364 snipe** woodcock, i.e., fool **366 it is thought abroad** it is rumored **367 my office** i.e., my sexual function as husband **369 do . . . surety** act as if on certain knowledge. **holds me well** regards me favorably

The better shall my purpose work on him. 370
Cassio's a proper° man. Let me see now:
To get his place and to plume up° my will
In double knavery—How, how?—Let's see:
After some time, to abuse° Othello's ear
That he° is too familiar with his wife. 375
He hath a person and a smooth dispose°
To be suspected, framed to make women false.
The Moor is of a free° and open° nature,
That thinks men honest that but seem to be so,
And will as tenderly° be led by the nose 380
As asses are.
I have 't. It is engendered. Hell and night
Must bring this monstrous birth to the world's light.

[Exit.]

Act II

Scene I. A seaport in Cyprus. An open place near the quay

Enter Montano and two Gentlemen

MONTANO: What from the cape can you discern at sea?

FIRST GENTLEMAN: Nothing at all. It is a high-wrought flood.°
I cannot, twixt the heaven and the main,°
Descry a sail.

MONTANO: Methinks the wind hath spoke aloud at land; 5
A fuller blast ne'er shook our battlements.
If it hath ruffianed° so upon the sea,
What ribs of oak, when mountains° melt on them,
Can hold the mortise?° What shall we hear of this?

SECOND GENTLEMAN: A segregation° of the Turkish fleet. 10
For do but stand upon the foaming shore,
The chidden° billow seems to pelt the clouds;

---

371 **proper** handsome   372 **plume up** put a feather in the cap of, i.e., glorify, gratify   374 **abuse**
deceive   375 **he** i.e., Cassio   376 **dispose** disposition   378 **free** frank, generous.   **open**
unsuspicious   380 **tenderly** readily
2 **high-wrought flood** very agitated sea   3 **main** ocean (also at line 41)   7 **ruffianed** raged
8 **mountains** i.e., of water   9 **hold the mortise** hold their joints together. (A *mortise* is the socket
hollowed out in fitting timbers.)   10 **segregation** dispersal   12 **chidden** i.e., rebuked, repelled (by
the shore), and thus shot into the air

The wind-shaked surge, with high and monstrous mane,°
Seems to cast water on the burning Bear°
And quench the guards of th' ever-fixèd pole.   15
I never did like molestation° view
On the enchafèd° flood.
MONTANO: If that° the Turkish fleet
Be not ensheltered and embayed,° they are drowned;
It is impossible to bear it out.°   20

Enter a [Third] Gentleman.

THIRD GENTLEMAN: News, lads! Our wars are done.
The desperate tempest hath so banged the Turks
That their designment° halts.° A noble ship of Venice
Hath seen a grievous wreck° and sufferance°
On most part of their fleet.   25
MONTANO: How? Is this true?
THIRD GENTLEMAN: The ship is here put in,
A Veronesa;° Michael Cassio,
Lieutenant to the warlike Moor Othello,
Is come on shore; the Moor himself at sea,   30
And is in full commission here for Cyprus.
MONTANO: I am glad on 't. 'Tis a worthy governor.
THIRD GENTLEMAN: But this same Cassio, though he speak of comfort
Touching the Turkish loss, yet he looks sadly°
And prays the Moor be safe, for they were parted   35
With foul and violent tempest.
MONTANO: Pray heaven he be,
For I have served him, and the man commands
Like a full° soldier. Let's to the seaside, ho!
As well to see the vessel that's come in
As to throw out our eyes for brave Othello,   40

---

13 monstrous mane (The surf is like the mane of a wild beast.)   **14 the burning Bear** i.e., the constellation Ursa Minor or the Little Bear, which includes the polestar (and hence regarded as the guards of *th' ever-fixèd pole* in the next line; sometimes the term *guards* is applied to the two "pointers" of the Big Bear or Dipper, which may be intended here.)   **16 like molestation** comparable disturbance   **17 enchafèd** angry   **18 If that** if   **19 embayed** sheltered by a bay   **20 bear it out** survive, weather the storm   **23 designment** design, enterprise.   **halts** is lame   **24 wreck** shipwreck.   **sufferance** damage, disaster   **28 Veronesa** i.e., fitted out in Verona for Venetian service, or possibly *Verennessa* (the Folio spelling), i.e., *verrinessa*, a cutter (from *verrinare*, "to cut through")   **34 sadly** gravely   **38 full** perfect

Even till we make the main and th' aerial blue°
An indistinct regard.°
THIRD GENTLEMAN: Come, let's do so,
    For every minute is expectancy°
    Of more arrivance.°

[*Enter Cassio.*]

CASSIO: Thanks, you the valiant of this warlike isle,   45
    That so approve° the Moor! O, let the heavens
    Give him defense against the elements,
    For I have lost him on a dangerous sea.
MONTANO: Is he well shipped?
CASSIO: His bark is stoutly timbered, and his pilot   50
    Of very expert and approved allowance;°
    Therefore my hopes, not surfeited to death,°
    Stand in bold cure.°

[*A cry*] *within:* "A sail, a sail, a sail!"

CASSIO: What noise?
A GENTLEMAN: The town is empty. On the brow o' the sea°   55
    Stand ranks of people, and they cry "A sail!"
CASSIO: My hopes do shape him for° the governor.

[*A shot within.*]

SECOND GENTLEMAN: They do discharge their shot of courtesy;°
    Our friends at least.
CASSIO: I pray you, sir, go forth,
    And give us truth who 'tis that is arrived.   60
SECOND GENTLEMAN: I shall.   *Exit.*
MONTANO: But, good Lieutenant, is your general wived?
CASSIO: Most fortunately. He hath achieved a maid
    That paragons° description and wild fame,°
    One that excels the quirks° of blazoning° pens,   65

---

41 **the main . . . blue** the sea and the sky   42 **An indistinct regard** indistinguishable in our view
43 **is expectancy** gives expectation   44 **arrivance** arrival   46 **approve** admire, honor   51 **approved
allowance** tested reputation   52 **surfeited to death** i.e., overextended, worn thin through repeated
application or delayed fulfillment   53 **in bold cure** in strong hopes of fulfillment   55 **brow o' the
sea** cliff-edge   57 **My . . . for** I hope it is   58 **discharge . . . courtesy** fire a salute in token of
respect and courtesy   64 **paragons** surpasses.   **wild fame** extravagant report   65 **quirks** witty
conceits.   **blazoning** setting forth as though in heraldic language

And in th' essential vesture of creation
Does tire the enginer.°

[*Enter [Second] Gentleman.*°]

      How now? Who has put in?°
SECOND GENTLEMAN: 'Tis one Iago, ancient to the General.
CASSIO: He's had most favorable and happy speed.
    Tempests themselves, high seas, and howling winds,   70
    The guttered° rocks and congregated sands—
    Traitors ensteeped° to clog the guiltless keel—
    As° having sense of beauty, do omit°
    Their mortal° natures, letting go safely by
    The divine Desdemona.
MONTANO: What is she?   75
CASSIO: She that I spake of, our great captain's captain,
    Left in the conduct of the bold Iago,
    Whose footing° here anticipates our thoughts
    A sennight's° speed. Great Jove, Othello guard,
    And swell his sail with thine own powerful breath,   80
    That he may bless this bay with his tall° ship,
    Make love's quick pants in Desdemona's arms,
    Give renewed fire to our extincted spirits,
    And bring all Cyprus comfort!

[*Enter Desdemona, Iago, Roderigo, and Emilia.*]

              O, behold,
    The riches of the ship is come on shore!   85
    You men of Cyprus, let her have your knees.

[*The gentlemen make curtsy to Desdemona.*]

    Hail to thee, lady! And the grace of heaven
    Before, behind thee, and on every hand
    Enwheel thee round!
DESDEMONA: I thank you, valiant Cassio.
    What tidings can you tell me of my lord?   90

66–67 **in . . . enginer** in her real, God-given, beauty, (she) defeats any attempt to praise her. **enginer** engineer, i.e., poet, one who devises. **[s.d.] Second Gentleman** (So identified in the Quarto text here and in lines 58, 61, 68, and 96; the Folio calls him a gentleman.) **67 put in** i.e., to harbor **71 guttered** jagged, trenched **72 ensteeped** lying under water **73 As** as if. **omit** forbear to exercise **74 mortal** deadly **78 footing** landing **79 sennight's** week's **81 tall** splendid, gallant

CASSIO: He is not yet arrived, nor know I aught
But that he's well and will be shortly here.

DESDEMONA: O, but I fear—How lost you company?

CASSIO: The great contention of the sea and skies
Parted our fellowship.

                    (Within) "A sail, a sail!" [A shot.]
                    But hark. A sail!   95

SECOND GENTLEMAN: They give their greeting to the citadel.
This likewise is a friend.

CASSIO: See for the news.

                              [Exit Second Gentleman.]

Good Ancient, you are welcome. [Kissing Emilia.] Welcome,
    mistress.
Let it not gall your patience, good Iago,
That I extend° my manners; 'tis my breeding°   100
That gives me this bold show of courtesy.

IAGO: Sir, would she give you so much of her lips
As of her tongue she oft bestows on me,
You would have enough.

DESDEMONA: Alas, she has no speech!°   105

IAGO: In faith, too much.
I find it still,° when I have list° to sleep.
Marry, before your ladyship, I grant,
She puts her tongue a little in her heart
And chides with thinking.°

EMILIA: You have little cause to say so.   110

IAGO: Come on, come on. You are pictures out of doors,°
Bells° in your parlors, wildcats in your kitchens,°
Saints° in your injuries, devils being offended,
Players° in your huswifery,° and huswives° in your beds.

DESDEMONA: O, fie upon thee, slanderer!   115

WILLIAM SHAKESPEARE

116

---

100 **extend** give scope to.   **breeding** training in the niceties of etiquette   105 **she has no speech** i.e., she's not a chatterbox, as you allege   107 **still** always.   **list** desire   110 **with thinking** i.e., in her thoughts only   111 **pictures out of doors** i.e., silent and well-behaved in public   112 **Bells** i.e., jangling, noisy, and brazen.   **in your kitchens** i.e., in domestic affairs. (Ladies would not do the cooking.)   113 **Saints** martyrs   114 **Players** idlers, triflers, or deceivers.   **huswifery** housekeeping. **huswives** hussies (i.e., women are "busy" in bed, or unduly thrifty in dispensing sexual favors)

IAGO: Nay, it is true, or else I am a Turk.°
You rise to play, and go to bed to work.

EMILIA: You shall not write my praise.

IAGO: No, let me not.

DESDEMONA: What wouldst write of me, if thou shouldst
praise me?

IAGO: O gentle lady, do not put me to 't,   120
For I am nothing if not critical.°

DESDEMONA: Come on, essay.°—There's one gone to the harbor?

IAGO: Ay, madam.

DESDEMONA: I am not merry, but I do beguile
The thing I am° by seeming otherwise.   125
Come, how wouldst thou praise me?

IAGO: I am about it, but indeed my invention
Comes from my pate as birdlime° does from frieze°—
It plucks out brains and all. But my Muse labors,°
And thus she is delivered: 130
If she be fair and wise, fairness and wit,
The one's for use, the other useth it.°

DESDEMONA: Well praised! How if she be black° and witty?

IAGO: If she be black, and thereto have a wit,
She'll find a white° that shall her blackness fit.°   135

DESDEMONA: Worse and worse.

EMILIA: How if fair and foolish?

IAGO: She never yet was foolish that was fair,
For even her folly° helped her to an heir.°

DESDEMONA: These are old fond° paradoxes to make fools
laugh i' th' alehouse.
What miserable praise hast thou for her that's foul and foolish?   140

IAGO: There's none so foul° and foolish thereunto,°
But does foul° pranks which fair and wise ones do.

DESDEMONA: O heavy ignorance! Thou praisest the worst best.
But what praise couldst thou bestow on a deserving woman

---

116 a Turk an infidel, not to be believed   **121 critical** censorious   **122 essay** try   **125 The thing I am**
i.e., my anxious self   **128 birdlime** sticky substance used to catch small birds.   **frieze** coarse woolen
cloth   **129 labors** (1) exerts herself (2) prepares to deliver a child (with a following pun on *delivered*
in line 130)   **132 The one's . . . it** i.e., her cleverness will make use of her beauty   **133 black** dark-
complexioned, brunette   **135 a white** a fair person (with word-play on "wight," a person)   **fit** (with
sexual suggestion of mating)   **138 folly** (with added meaning of "lechery, wantonness")   **to an heir**
i.e., to bear a child   **139 fond** foolish   **141 foul** ugly.   **thereunto** in addition   **142 foul** sluttish

indeed, one that, in the authority of her merit, did justly put
on the vouch° of very malice itself?   145

IAGO: She that was ever fair, and never proud,
    Had tongue at will, and yet was never loud,
    Never lacked gold and yet went never gay,°
    Fled from her wish, and yet said, "Now I may,"°
    She that being angered, her revenge being nigh,   150
    Bade her wrong stay° and her displeasure fly,
    She that in wisdom never was so frail
    To change the cod's head for the salmon's tail,°
    She that could think and ne'er disclose her mind,
    See suitors following and not look behind,   155
    She was a wight, if ever such wight were—

DESDEMONA: To do what?

IAGO: To suckle fools° and chronicle small beer.°

DESDEMONA: O most lame and impotent conclusion! Do not
learn of him, Emilia, though he be thy husband. How say you,   160
Cassio? Is he not a most profane° and liberal° counselor?

CASSIO: He speaks home,° madam. You may relish° him more
in° the soldier than in the scholar.

[Cassio and Desdemona stand together, conversing intimately.]

IAGO *[aside]:*   He takes her by the palm. Ay, well said,° whisper.
With as little a web as this will I ensnare as great a fly as Cas-   165
sio. Ay, smile upon her, do; I will gyve° thee in thine own
courtship.° You say true;° 'tis so, indeed. If such tricks as these
strip you out of your lieutenantry, it had been better you had
not kissed your three fingers so oft, which now again you are
most apt to play the sir° in. Very good; well kissed! An excellent courtesy! 'Tis so, indeed. Yet again your fingers to your
lips? Would they were clyster pipes° for your sake! *[Trumpet*   170
within.] The Moor! I know his trumpet.

---

145 **put . . . vouch** compel the approval   148 **gay** extravagantly clothed   149 **Fled . . . may** avoided
temptation where the choice was hers   151 **Bade . . . stay** i.e., resolved to put up with her injury
patiently   153 **To . . . tail** i.e., to exchange a lackluster husband for a sexy lover (?) (**Cod's head** is
slang for "penis," and tail, for "pudendum.")   158 **suckle fools** breastfeed babies   **chronicle small
beer** i.e., keep petty household accounts; keep track of trivial matters   161 **profane** irreverent,
ribald   **liberal** licentious free-spoken   162 **home** right to the target (a term from fencing)   **relish**
appreciate   **in** in the character of   164 **well said** well done   166 **gyve** fetter, shackle.   **courtship**
courtesy, show of courtly manners.   **You say true** i.e., that's right, go ahead   169 **the sir** i.e., the
fine gentleman   170 **clyster pipes** tubes used for enemas and douches

WILLIAM SHAKESPEARE

CASSIO: 'Tis truly so.

DESDEMONA: Let's meet him and receive him.

CASSIO: Lo, where he comes!

[*Enter Othello and attendants.*]

OTHELLO: O my fair warrior!

DESDEMONA: My dear Othello!   175

OTHELLO: It gives me wonder great as my content
To see you here before me. O my soul's joy,
If after every tempest come such calms,
May the winds blow till they have wakened death,
And let the laboring bark climb hills of seas   180
Olympus-high, and duck again as low
As hell's from heaven! If it were now to die,
'Twere now to be most happy, for I fear
My soul hath her content so absolute
That not another comfort like to this   185
Succeeds in unknown fate.°

DESDEMONA: The heavens forbid
But that our loves and comforts should increase
Even as our days do grow!

OTHELLO: Amen to that, sweet powers!
I cannot speak enough of this content.   190
It stops me here; it is too much of joy.
And this, and this, the greatest discords be

[*They kiss.*]°

That e'er our hearts shall make!

IAGO [*aside*]: O, you are well tuned now!
But I'll set down° the pegs that make this music,   195
As honest as I am.°

OTHELLO: Come, let us to the castle.
News, friends! Our wars are done, the Turks are drowned.
How does my old acquaintance of this isle?—
Honey, you shall be well desired° in Cyprus;   200

---

186 Succeeds . . . fate i.e., can follow in the unknown future **192 [s.d.] They kiss** (The direction is from the Quarto.) **195 set down** loosen (and hence untune the instrument) **196 As . . . I am** for all my supposed honesty **200 desired** welcomed

I have found great love amongst them. O my sweet,
I prattle out of fashion,° and I dote
In mine own comforts.—I prithee, good Iago,
Go to the bay and disembark my coffers.°
Bring thou the master° to the citadel;   205
He is a good one, and his worthiness
Does challenge° much respect.—Come, Desdemona.—
Once more, well met at Cyprus!

> [*Exeunt Othello and Desdemona [and all
> but Iago and Roderigo].*]

IAGO [*to an attendant*]:   Do thou meet me presently at the harbor.
[*To Roderigo.*] Come hither. If thou be'st valiant—as, they say,
base men° being in love have then a nobility in their natures   210
more than is native to them—list° me. The Lieutenant tonight
watches on the court of guard.° First, I must tell thee this:
Desdemona is directly in love with him.

RODERIGO: With him? Why, 'tis not possible.

IAGO: Lay thy finger thus,° and let thy soul be instructed. Mark   215
me with what violence she first loved the Moor, but° for brag-
ging and telling her fantastical lies. To love him still for prat-
ing? Let not thy discreet heart think it. Her eye must be fed;
and what delight shall she have to look on the devil? When
the blood is made dull with the act of sport,° there should be,
again to inflame it and to give satiety a fresh appetite, loveli-
ness in favor,° sympathy° in years, manners, and beauties—all   220
which the Moor is defective in. Now, for want of these required conveniences,° her delicate tenderness will find itself
abused,° begin to heave the gorge,° disrelish and abhor the
Moor. Very nature° will instruct her in it and compel her to
some second choice. Now, sir, this granted—as it is a most
pregnant° and unforced position—who stands so eminent in   225

---

202 **out of fashion** irrelevantly, incoherently (?)   204 **coffers** chests, baggage   205 **master** ship's
captain   207 **challenge** lay claim to, deserve   210 **base men** even lowly born men   211 **list** listen
to   212 **court of guard** guardhouse. (Cassio is in charge of the watch.)   215 **thus** i.e., on your lips
216 **but** only   219 **the act of sport** sex   220 **favor** appearance.   **sympathy** correspondence,
similarity   222 **required conveniences** things conducive to sexual compatibility   223 **abused**
cheated, revolted.   **heave the gorge** experience nausea   224 **Very nature** her very instincts
225 **pregnant** evident, cogent

the degree of° this fortune as Cassio does? A knave very voluble,° no further conscionable° than in putting on the mere
form of civil and humane° seeming for the better compassing
of his salt° and most hidden loose affection.° Why, none, why,
none. A slipper° and subtle knave, a finder out of occasions,
that has an eye can stamp° and counterfeit advantages,°   230
though true advantage never present itself; a devilish knave.
Besides, the knave is handsome, young, and hath all those req-
uisites in him that folly° and green° minds look after. A pesti-
lent complete knave, and the woman hath found him° already.

RODERIGO: I cannot believe that in her. She's full of most blessed
condition.°   235

IAGO: Blessed fig's end!° The wine she drinks is made of grapes.
If she had been blessed, she would never have loved the Moor.
Blessed pudding!° Didst thou not see her paddle with the
palm of his hand? Didst not mark that?

RODERIGO: Yes, that I did; but that was but courtesy.

IAGO: Lechery, by this hand. An index° and obscure° prologue to   240
the history of lust and foul thoughts. They met so near with their
lips that their breaths embraced together. Villainous thoughts,
Roderigo! When these mutualities° so marshal the way, hard at
hand° comes the master and main exercise, th' incorporate° conclusion. Pish! But, sir, be you ruled by me. I have brought you
from Venice. Watch you° tonight; for the command, I'll lay 't   245
upon you.° Cassio knows you not. I'll not be far from you. Do
you find some occasion to anger Cassio, either by speaking too
loud, or tainting° his discipline, or from what other course you
please, which the time shall more favorably minister.°

RODERIGO: Well.   250

IAGO: Sir, he's rash and very sudden in choler,° and haply° may
strike at you. Provoke him that he may, for even out of that

---

226 in . . . of as next in line for   **227 voluble** facile, glib.   **conscionable** conscientious, conscience-
bound   **228 humane** polite, courteous.   **salt** licentious   **229 affection** passion.   **slipper** slippery
230 an eye can stamp an eye that can coin, create   **231 advantages** favorable opportunities
233 folly wantonness.   **green** immature   **234 found him** sized him up, perceived his intent
235 condition disposition   **236 fig's end** (See Act I, Scene iii, line 316 for the vulgar gesture of the
fig.)   **237 pudding** sausage   **240 index** table of contents.   **obscure** (i.e., the *lust and foul thoughts*
in line 241 are secret, hidden from view)   **243 mutualities** exchanges, intimacies.   **hard at hand**
closely following   **244 incorporate** carnal   **245 Watch you** stand watch   **245–246 for the
command . . . you** I'll arrange for you to be appointed, given orders   **247 tainting** disparaging
249 minister provide   **251 choler** wrath   **haply** perhaps

will I cause these of Cyprus to mutiny,° whose qualification°
shall come into no true taste° again but by the displanting of
Cassio. So shall you have a shorter journey to your desires by
the means I shall then have to prefer° them, and the impedi-   255
ment most profitably removed, without the which there were
no expectation of our prosperity.

RODERIGO: I will do this, if you can bring it to any opportunity.

IAGO: I warrant° thee. Meet me by and by° at the citadel. I must
fetch his necessaries ashore. Farewell.   260

RODERIGO: Adieu.   [*Exit.*]

IAGO: That Cassio loves her, I do well believe 't;
That she loves him, 'tis apt° and of great credit.°
The Moor, howbeit that I endure him not,
Is of a constant, loving, noble nature,   265
And I dare think he'll prove to Desdemona
A most dear husband. Now, I do love her too,
Not out of absolute lust—though peradventure
I stand accountant° for as great a sin—
But partly led to diet° my revenge   270
For that I do suspect the lusty Moor
Hath leaped into my seat, the thought whereof
Doth, like a poisonous mineral, gnaw my innards;
And nothing can or shall content my soul
Till I am evened with him, wife for wife,   275
Or failing so, yet that I put the Moor
At least into a jealousy so strong
That judgment cannot cure. Which thing to do,
If this poor trash of Venice, whom I trace°
For° his quick hunting, stand the putting on,°   280
I'll have our Michael Cassio on the hip,°
Abuse° him to the Moor in the rank garb—°

---

253 mutiny riot.   **qualification** appeasement.   **true taste** i.e., acceptable state   **255 prefer** advance
259 warrant assure.   **by and by** immediately   **263 apt** probable.   **credit** credibility
269 accountant accountable   **270 diet** feed   **279 trace** i.e., train, or follow (?), or perhaps *trash*, a
hunting term, meaning to put weights on a hunting dog in order to slow him down   **280 For** to
make more eager.   **stand ... on** respond properly when I incite him to quarrel   **281 on the hip** at
my mercy, where I can throw him. (A wrestling term.)   **282 Abuse** slander.   **rank garb** coarse
manner, gross fashion

WILLIAM SHAKESPEARE

For I fear Cassio with my nightcap° too—
Make the Moor thank me, love me, and reward me
For making him egregiously an ass   285
And practicing upon° his peace and quiet
Even to madness. 'Tis here, but yet confused.
Knavery's plain face is never seen till used.

[*Exit.*]

Scene II. Cyprus. A street

Enter Othello's Herald with a proclamation.

HERALD: It is Othello's pleasure, our noble and valiant general,
that, upon certain tidings now arrived, importing the mere
perdition° of the Turkish fleet, every man put himself into triumph:° some to dance, some to make bonfires, each man to
what sport and revels his addiction° leads him. For, besides
these beneficial news, it is the celebration of his nuptial. So   5
much was his pleasure should be proclaimed. All offices° are
open, and there is full liberty of feasting from this present
hour of five till the bell have told eleven. Heaven bless the isle
of Cyprus and our noble general Othello!

[*Exit.*]

Scene III. Cyprus. The Citadel

Enter Othello, Desdemona, Cassio, and attendants.

OTHELLO: Good Michael, look you to the guard tonight.
Let's teach ourselves that honorable stop°
Not to outsport° discretion.
CASSIO: Iago hath direction what to do,
But notwithstanding, with my personal eye   5
Will I look to 't.
OTHELLO: Iago is most honest.
Michael, good night. Tomorrow with your earliest°

---

283 with my nightcap i.e., as a rival in my bed, as one who gives me cuckold's horns   **286 practicing
upon** plotting against
2 mere perdition complete destruction   **3 triumph** public celebration   **4 addiction** inclination
6 offices rooms where food and drink are kept   **2 stop** restraint
3 outsport celebrate beyond the bounds of   **7 with your earliest** at your earliest convenience

Let me have speech with you. [*To Desdemona.*]
     Come, my dear love,
The purchase made, the fruits are to ensue;
That profit's yet to come 'tween me and you.°—   10
Good night.

     [*Exit [Othello, with Desdemona and attendants].*]
[*Enter Iago.*]

CASSIO: Welcome, Iago. We must to the watch.

IAGO: Not this hour,° Lieutenant; 'tis not yet ten o' the clock. Our general cast° us thus early for the love of his Desdemona; who° let us not therefore blame. He hath not yet made wanton the night with her, and she is sport for Jove.   15

CASSIO: She's a most exquisite lady.

IAGO: And, I'll warrant her, full of game.

CASSIO: Indeed, she's a most fresh and delicate creature.

IAGO: What an eye she has! Methinks it sounds a parley° to provocation.

CASSIO: An inviting eye, and yet methinks right modest.   20

IAGO: And when she speaks, is it not an alarum° to love?

CASSIO: She is indeed perfection.

IAGO: Well, happiness to their sheets! Come, Lieutenant, I have a stoup° of wine, and here without° are a brace° of Cyprus gallants that would fain have a measure° to the health of black Othello.   25

CASSIO: Not tonight, good Iago. I have very poor and unhappy brains for drinking. I could well wish courtesy would invent some other custom of entertainment.

IAGO: O, they are our friends. But one cup! I'll drink for you.°

CASSIO: I have drunk but one cup tonight, and that was craftily   30 qualified° too, and behold what innovation° it makes here.° I am unfortunate in the infirmity and dare not task my weakness with any more.

IAGO: What, man? 'Tis a night of revels. The gallants desire it.

9–10 **The purchase . . . you** i.e., though married, we haven't yet consummated our love   13 **Not this hour** not for an hour yet.   **cast** dismissed   14 **who** i.e., Othello   19 **sounds a parley** calls for a conference, issues an invitation   21 **alarum** signal calling men to arms (continuing the military metaphor of *parley*, line 19)   23 **stoup** measure of liquor, two quarts   24 **without** outside.   **brace** pair   24–25 **fain have a measure** gladly drink a toast   28 **for you** in your place. (Iago will do the steady drinking to keep the gallants company while Cassio has only one cup.)   29 **qualified** diluted   30 **innovation** disturbance, insurrection.   **here** i.e., in my head

CASSIO: Where are they?

IAGO: Here at the door. I pray you, call them in.

CASSIO: I'll do 't, but it dislikes me.°   _Exit._   35

IAGO: If I can fasten but one cup upon him,
With that which he hath drunk tonight already,
He'll be as full of quarrel and offense°
As my young mistress' dog. Now, my sick fool Roderigo,
Whom love hath turned almost the wrong side out,   40
To Desdemona hath tonight caroused°
Potations pottle-deep;° and he's to watch.°
Three lads of Cyprus—noble swelling° spirits,
That hold their honors in a wary distance,°
The very elements° of this warlike isle—   45
Have I tonight flustered with flowing cups,
And they watch° too. Now, 'mongst this flock of drunkards
Am I to put our Cassio in some action
That may offend the isle.—But here they come.

[_Enter Cassio, Montano, and gentlemen; [servants following_
with wine].]

If consequence do but approve my dream,°   50
My boat sails freely both with wind and stream.°

CASSIO: 'Fore God, they have given me a rouse° already.

MONTANO: Good faith, a little one; not past a pint, as I am a
soldier.

IAGO: Some wine, ho! [He _sings._]
"And let me the cannikin° clink, clink,   55
And let me the cannikin clink.
A soldier's a man,
O, man's life's but a span;°
Why, then, let a soldier drink."
Some wine, boys!   60

CASSIO: 'Fore God, an excellent song.

---

35 it dislikes me i.e., I'm reluctant   **38 offense** readiness to take offense   **41 caroused** drunk off
42 pottle-deep to the bottom of the tankard.   **watch** stand watch   **43 swelling** proud   **44 hold . . .
distance** i.e., are extremely sensitive of their honor   **45 very elements** typical sort   **47 watch** are
members of the guard   **50 If . . . dream** if subsequent events will only substantiate my scheme
51 stream current   **52 rouse** full draft of liquor   **55 cannikin** small drinking vessel   **58 span** brief
span of time. (Compare Psalm 39:6 as rendered in the 1928 _Book of Common Prayer:_ "Thou hast
made my days as it were a span long.")

IAGO: I learned it in England, where indeed they are most potent in potting.° Your Dane, your German, and your swag-bellied Hollander—drink, ho!—are nothing to your English.

CASSIO: Is your Englishman so exquisite in his drinking? 65

IAGO: Why, he drinks you,° with facility, your Dane° dead drunk; he sweats not° to overthrow your Almain;° he gives your Hollander a vomit ere the next pottle can be filled.

CASSIO: To the health of our general!

MONTANO: I am for it, Lieutenant, and I'll do you justice.° 70

IAGO: O sweet England! [*He sings.*]

> "King Stephen was and—a worthy peer,
>> His breeches cost him but a crown;
> He held them sixpence all too dear,
>> With that he called the tailor lown.° 75
> He was a wight of high renown,
>> And thou art but of low degree.
> 'Tis pride° that pulls the country down;
>> Then take thy auld° cloak about thee."

Some wine, ho! 80

CASSIO: 'Fore God, this is a more exquisite song than the other.

IAGO: Will you hear 't again?

CASSIO: No, for I hold him to be unworthy of his place that does those things. Well, God's above all; and there be souls must be saved, and there be souls must not be saved. 85

IAGO: It's true, good Lieutenant.

CASSIO: For mine own part—no offense to the General, nor any man of quality°—I hope to be saved.

IAGO: And so do I too, Lieutenant.

CASSIO: Ay, but, by your leave, not before me; the lieutenant is to be saved before the ancient. Let's have no more of this; 90 let's to our affairs.—God forgive us our sins!—Gentlemen, let's look to our business. Do not think, gentlemen, I am drunk. This is my ancient; this is my right hand, and this is my left. I am not drunk now. I can stand well enough, and speak well enough.

---

62 potting drinking **66 drinks you** drinks. **your Dane** your typical Dane. **sweats not** i.e., need not exert himself **67 Almain** German **70 I'll . . . justice** i.e., I'll drink as much as you **75 lown** lout, rascal **78 pride** i.e., extravagance in dress **79 auld** old **88 quality** rank

GENTLEMEN: Excellent well.   95

CASSIO: Why, very well then; you must not think then that I am
    drunk.   *Exit.*

MONTANO: To th' platform, masters. Come, let's set the watch.°

                             [Exeunt Gentlemen.]

IAGO: You see this fellow that is gone before.
    He's a soldier fit to stand by Caesar
    And give direction; and do but see his vice.   100
    'Tis to his virtue a just equinox,°
    The one as long as th' other. 'Tis pity of him.
    I fear the trust Othello puts him in,
    On some odd time of his infirmity,
    Will shake this island.

MONTANO: But is he often thus?   105

IAGO: 'Tis evermore the prologue to his sleep.
    He'll watch the horologe a double set,°
    If drink rock not his cradle.

MONTANO: It were well
    The General were put in mind of it.
    Perhaps he sees it not, or his good nature   110
    Prizes the virtue that appears in Cassio
    And looks not on his evils. Is not this true?

    [Enter Roderigo.]

IAGO [aside to him]:   How now, Roderigo?
    I pray you, after the Lieutenant; go.   *[Exit Roderigo.]*

MONTANO: And 'tis great pity that the noble Moor   115
    Should hazard such a place as his own second
    With° one of an engraffed° infirmity.
    It were an honest action to say so
    To the Moor.

IAGO: Not I, for this fair island.
    I do love Cassio well and would do much   120

127

---

97 set the watch mount the guard   **101 just equinox** exact counterpart. (*Equinox* is a day on which daylight and nighttime hours are equal.)   **107 watch . . . set** stay awake twice around the clock or *horologe*   **116–117 hazard . . . With** risk giving such an important position as his second in command to   **117 engraffed** engrafted, inveterate

To cure him of this evil.   [*Cry within:* "Help! Help!"]
But, hark! What noise?

[*Enter Cassio, pursuing° Roderigo.*]

CASSIO: Zounds, you rogue! You rascal!

MONTANO: What's the matter, Lieutenant?

CASSIO: A knave teach me my duty? I'll beat the knave into a twiggen° bottle.

RODERIGO: Beat me?   125

CASSIO: Dost thou prate, rogue? [*He strikes Roderigo.*]

MONTANO: Nay, good Lieutenant. [*Restraining him.*] I pray you, sir, hold your hand.

CASSIO: Let me go, sir, or I'll knock you o'er the mazard.°

MONTANO: Come, come, you're drunk.

CASSIO: Drunk?   [*They fight.*]   130

IAGO [*aside to Roderigo*]: Away, I say. Go out and cry a mutiny.°

[*Exit Roderigo.*]

Nay, good Lieutenant—God's will, gentlemen—
Help, ho!—Lieutenant—sir—Montano—sir—
Help, masters!°—Here's a goodly watch indeed!

[*A bell rings.*]°

Who's that which rings the bell?—Diablo,° ho!   135
The town will rise.° God's will, Lieutenant, hold!
You'll be ashamed forever.

Enter Othello and attendants [with weapons].

OTHELLO: What is the matter here?

MONTANO: Zounds, I bleed still.
I am hurt to th' death. He dies! [*He thrusts at Cassio.*]

OTHELLO: Hold, for your lives!

IAGO: Hold, ho! Lieutenant—sir—Montano—gentlemen—   140
Have you forgot all sense of place and duty?
Hold! The General speaks to you. Hold, for shame!

---

121 [s.d.] pursuing (The Quarto text reads, "driving in.")   **124 twiggen** wicker-covered. (Cassio vows to assail Roderigo until his skin resembles wickerwork or until he has driven Roderigo through the holes in a wickerwork.)   **128 mazard** i.e., head (literally, a drinking vessel)   **131 mutiny** riot
134 masters sirs   **[s.d.] A bell rings** (This direction is from the Quarto, as are *Exit Roderigo* at line 114, *They fight* at line 130, and *with weapons* at line 137.)   **135 Diablo** the devil   **136 rise** grow riotous

OTHELLO: Why, how now, ho! From whence ariseth this?
     Are we turned Turks, and to ourselves do that
     Which heaven hath forbid the Ottomites?°   145
     For Christian shame, put by this barbarous brawl!
     He that stirs next to carve for° his own rage
     Holds his soul light;° he dies upon his motion.°
     Silence that dreadful bell. It frights the isle
     From her propriety.° What is the matter, masters?   150
     Honest Iago, that looks dead with grieving,
     Speak. Who began this? On thy love, I charge thee.
IAGO: I do not know. Friends all but now, even now,
     In quarter° and in terms° like bride and groom
     Devesting them° for bed; and then, but now—   155
     As if some planet had unwitted men—
     Swords out, and tilting one at others' breasts
     In opposition bloody. I cannot speak°
     Any beginning to this peevish odds;°
     And would in action glorious I had lost   160
     Those legs that brought me to a part of it!
OTHELLO: How comes it, Michael, you are thus forgot?°
CASSIO: I pray you, pardon me. I cannot speak.
OTHELLO: Worthy Montano, you were wont be° civil;
     The gravity and stillness° of your youth   165
     The world hath noted, and your name is great
     In mouths of wisest censure.° What's the matter
     That you unlace° your reputation thus
     And spend your rich opinion° for the name
     Of a night-brawler? Give me answer to it.   170
MONTANO: Worthy Othello, I am hurt to danger.
     Your officer, Iago, can inform you—
     While I spare speech, which something° now offends° me—
     Of all that I do know; nor know I aught

144–145 to ourselves . . . Ottomites inflict on ourselves the harm that heaven has prevented the
Turks from doing (by destroying their fleet)   **147 carve for** i.e., indulge, satisfy with his sword
148 Holds . . . light i.e., places little value on his life   **upon his motion** if he moves   **150 propriety**
proper state or condition   **154 In quarter** in friendly conduct, within bounds.   **in terms** on good
terms   **155 Devesting them** undressing themselves   **158 speak** explain   **159 peevish odds** childish
quarrel   **162 are thus forgot** have forgotten yourself thus   **164 wont be** accustomed to be
165 stillness sobriety   **167 censure** judgment   **168 unlace** undo, lay open (as one might loose the
strings of a purse containing reputation)   **169 opinion** reputation   **173 something** somewhat
offends pains

By me that's said or done amiss this night,   175
Unless self-charity be sometimes a vice,
And to defend ourselves it be a sin
When violence assails us.

OTHELLO: Now, by heaven,
My blood° begins my safer guides° to rule,
And passion, having my best judgment collied,°   180
Essays° to lead the way. Zounds, if I stir,
Or do but lift this arm, the best of you
Shall sink in my rebuke. Give me to know
How this foul rout° began, who set it on;
And he that is approved in° this offense,   185
Though he had twinned with me, both at a birth,
Shall lose me. What? In a town of° war
Yet wild, the people's hearts brim full of fear,
To manage° private and domestic quarrel?
In night, and on the court and guard of safety?°   190
'Tis monstrous. Iago, who began 't?

MONTANO [to Iago]:   If partially affined,° or leagued in office,°
Thou dost deliver more or less than truth,
Thou art no soldier.

IAGO: Touch me not so near.
I had rather have this tongue cut from my mouth   195
Than it should do offense to Michael Cassio;
Yet, I persuade myself, to speak the truth
Shall nothing wrong him. Thus it is, General.
Montano and myself being in speech,
There comes a fellow crying out for help,   200
And Cassio following him with determined sword
To execute° upon him. Sir, this gentleman

[indicating Montano]

Steps in to Cassio and entreats his pause.°
Myself the crying fellow did pursue,

179 **blood** passion (of anger)   **guides** i.e., reason   180 **collied** darkened   181 **Essays** undertakes
184 **rout** riot   185 **approved in** found guilty of   187 **town of** town garrisoned for   189 **manage**
undertake   190 **on . . . safety** at the main guardhouse or headquarters and on watch   192 **partially**
affined made partial by some personal relationship   **leagued in office** in league as fellow officers
202 **execute** give effect to (his anger)   203 **his pause** him to stop

Lest by his clamor—as it so fell out—   205
The town might fall in fright. He, swift of foot,
Outran my purpose, and I returned, the rather°
For that I heard the clink and fall of swords
And Cassio high in oath, which till tonight
I ne'er might say before. When I came back—   210
For this was brief—I found them close together
At blow and thrust, even as again they were
When you yourself did part them.
More of this matter cannot I report.
But men are men; the best sometimes forget.°   215
Though Cassio did some little wrong to him,
As men in rage strike those that wish them best,°
Yet surely Cassio, I believe, received
From him that fled some strange indignity,
Which patience could not pass.°

OTHELLO: I know, Iago,   220
Thy honesty and love doth mince this matter,
Making it light to Cassio. Cassio, I love thee,
But nevermore be officer of mine.

[*Enter Desdemona, attended.*]

Look if my gentle love be not raised up.
I'll make thee an example.   225

DESDEMONA: What is the matter, dear?

OTHELLO: All's well now, sweeting;
Come away to bed. [*To Montano.*] Sir, for your hurts,
Myself will be your surgeon.°—Lead him off.

[*Montano is led off.*]

Iago, look with care about the town
And silence those whom this vile brawl distracted.   230
Come, Desdemona. 'Tis the soldiers' life
To have their balmy slumbers waked with strife.

                        Exit [*with all but Iago and Cassio*].

IAGO: What, are you hurt, Lieutenant?

---

207 **rather** sooner   215 **forget** forget themselves   217 **those . . . best** i.e., even those who are well
disposed   220 **pass** pass over, overlook   228 **be your surgeon** i.e., make sure you receive medical
attention

CASSIO: Ay, past all surgery.

IAGO: Marry, God forbid!   235

CASSIO: Reputation, reputation, reputation! O, I have lost my
reputation! I have lost the immortal part of myself, and what
remains is bestial. My reputation, Iago, my reputation!

IAGO: As I am an honest man, I thought you had received some
bodily wound; there is more sense in that than in reputation.   240
Reputation is an idle and most false imposition,° oft got without merit and lost without deserving. You have lost no reputation at all, unless you repute yourself such a loser. What, man,
there are more ways to recover° the General again. You are but
now cast in his mood°—a punishment more in policy° than in
malice, even so as one would beat his offenseless dog to af-
fright an imperious lion.° Sue° to him again and he's yours.   245

CASSIO: I will rather sue to be despised than to deceive so good
a commander with so slight,° so drunken, and so indiscreet an
officer. Drunk? And speak parrot?° And squabble? Swagger?
Swear? And discourse fustian with one's own shadow? O thou
invisible spirit of wine, if thou hast no name to be known by,   250
let us call thee devil!

IAGO: What was he that you followed with your sword? What had
he done to you?

CASSIO: I know not.

IAGO: Is 't possible?

CASSIO: I remember a mass of things, but nothing distinctly; a   255
quarrel, but nothing wherefore.° O God, that men should put
an enemy in their mouths to steal away their brains! That we
should, with joy, pleasance, revel, and applause° transform
ourselves into beasts!

IAGO: Why, but you are now well enough. How came you thus
recovered?

CASSIO: It hath pleased the devil drunkenness to give place to
the devil wrath. One unperfectness shows me another, to
make me frankly despise myself.   260

---

241 **false imposition** thing artificially imposed and of no real value   243 **recover** regain favor with
244 **cast in his mood** dismissed in a moment of anger.   **in policy** done for expediency's sake and
as a public gesture   245 **would . . . lion** i.e., would make an example of a minor offender in order
to deter more important and dangerous offenders   246 **Sue** petition   248 **slight** worthless
248–249 **speak parrot** talk nonsense, rant   256 **wherefore** why   258 **applause** desire for applause

IAGO: Come, you are too severe a moraler.° As the time, the
place, and the condition of this country stands, I could heartily
wish this had not befallen; but since it is as it is, mend it for
your own good.

CASSIO: I will ask him for my place again; he shall tell me I am a   265
drunkard. Had I as many mouths as Hydra,° such an answer
would stop them all. To be now a sensible man, by and by a
fool, and presently a beast! O, strange! Every inordinate cup is
unblessed, and the ingredient is a devil.

IAGO: Come, come, good wine is a good familiar creature, if it be
well used. Exclaim no more against it. And, good Lieutenant, I   270
think you think I love you

CASSIO: I have well approved° it, sir. I drunk!

IAGO: You or any man living may be drunk at a time,° man. I'll
tell you what you shall do. Our general's wife is now the general—I may say so in this respect, for that° he hath devoted   275
and given up himself to the contemplation, mark, and denote-
ment° of her parts° and graces. Confess yourself freely to her;
importune her help to put you in your place again. She is of so
free,° so kind, so apt, so blessed a disposition, she holds it a
vice in her goodness not to do more than she is requested.
This broken joint between you and her husband entreat her to
splinter;° and, my fortunes against any lay° worth naming, this   280
crack of your love shall grow stronger than it was before.

CASSIO: You advise me well.

IAGO: I protest,° in the sincerity of love and honest kindness.

CASSIO: I think it freely;° and betimes in the morning I will beseech the virtuous Desdemona to undertake for me. I am des-   285
perate of my fortunes if they check° me here.

IAGO: You are in the right. Good night, Lieutenant. I must to the
watch.

CASSIO: Good night, honest Iago.   [*Exit Cassio.*]

---

262 **moraler** moralizer   266 **Hydra** the Lernaean Hydra, a monster with many heads and the
ability to grow two heads when one was cut off, slain by Hercules as the second of his twelve
labors   272 **approved** proved   273 **at a time** at one time or another   274–275 **in . . . that** in view of
this fact, that   275–276 **mark, and denotement** (Both words mean "observation.")   276 **parts**
qualities   277 **free** generous   280 **splinter** bind with splints   **lay** stake, wager   283 **protest** insist,
declare   284 **freely** unreservedly   286 **check** repulse

IAGO: And what's he then that says I play the villain,
When this advice is free° I give, and honest,   290
Probal° to thinking, and indeed the course
To win the Moor again? For 'tis most easy
Th' inclining° Desdemona to subdue°
In any honest suit; she's framed as fruitful°
As the free elements.° And then for her   295
To win the Moor—were 't to renounce his baptism,
All seals and symbols of redeemèd sin—
His soul is so enfettered to her love
That she may make, unmake, do what she list,
Even as her appetite° shall play the god   300
With his weak function.° How am I then a villain,
To counsel Cassio to this parallel° course
Directly to his good? Divinity of hell!°
When devils will the blackest sins put on,°
They do suggest° at first with heavenly shows,   305
As I do now. For whiles this honest fool
Plies Desdemona to repair his fortune,
And she for him pleads strongly to the Moor,
I'll pour this pestilence into his ear,
That she repeals him° for her body's lust;   310
And by how much she strives to do him good,
She shall undo her credit with the Moor.
So will I turn her virtue into pitch,°
And out of her own goodness make the net
That shall enmesh them all.

[*Enter Roderigo.*]

                      How now, Roderigo?   315
RODERIGO: I do follow here in the chase, not like a hound that
hunts, but one that fills up the cry.° My money is almost spent;

---

290 free (1) free from guile (2) freely given   **291 Probal** probable, reasonable   **293 inclining** favorably disposed.   **subdue** persuade   **294 framed as fruitful** created as generous   **295 free elements** i.e., earth, air, fire, and water, unrestrained and spontaneous   **300 her appetite** her desire, or, perhaps, his desire for her   **301 function** exercise of faculties (weakened by his fondness for her)   **302 parallel** corresponding to these facts and to his best interests   **303 Divinity of hell** inverted theology of hell (which seduces the soul to its damnation)   **304 put on** further, instigate   **305 suggest** tempt   **310 repeals him** attempts to get him restored   **313 pitch** i.e., (1) foul blackness (2) a snaring substance   **317 fills up the cry** merely takes part as one of the pack

I have been tonight exceedingly well cudgeled; and I think the issue will be I shall have so much° experience for my pains, and so, with no money at all and a little more wit, return again to Venice.   320

IAGO: How poor are they that have not patience!
What wound did ever heal but by degrees?
Thou know'st we work by wit, and not by witchcraft,
And wit depends on dilatory time.
Does 't not go well? Cassio hath beaten thee,   325
And thou, by that small hurt, hast cashiered° Cassio.
Though other things grow fair against the sun,
Yet fruits that blossom first will first be ripe.°
Content thyself awhile. By the Mass, 'tis morning!
Pleasure and action make the hours seem short.   330
Retire thee; go where thou art billeted.
Away, I say! Thou shalt know more hereafter.
Nay, get thee gone.   [*Exit Roderigo.*]
                        Two things are to be done.
My wife must move° for Cassio to her mistress;
I'll set her on;   335
Myself the while to draw the Moor apart
And bring him jump° when he may Cassio find
Soliciting his wife. Ay, that's the way.
Dull not device° by coldness and delay.   *Exit.*

Act III

Scene I. Before the chamber of Othello and Desdemona

Enter Cassio [and] Musicians.

CASSIO: Masters, play here—I will content your pains°—
Something that's brief, and bid "Good morrow, General."

[*They play.*]

[*Enter*] Clown.

---

318 so much just so much and no more   **326 cashiered** dismissed from service   **327–328 Though . . . ripe** i.e., plans that are well-prepared and set expeditiously in motion will soonest ripen into success   **334 move** plead   **337 jump** precisely   **339 device** plot   **coldness** lack of zeal   **1 content your pains** reward your efforts

CLOWN: Why, masters, have your instruments been in Naples, that they speak i' the nose° thus?

A MUSICIAN: How, sir, how? 5

CLOWN: Are these, I pray you, wind instruments?

A MUSICIAN: Ay, marry, are they, sir.

CLOWN: O, thereby hangs a tail.

A MUSICIAN: Whereby hangs a tale, sir?

CLOWN: Marry, sir, by many a wind instrument° that I know. 10 But, masters, here's money for you. [*He gives money.*] And the General so likes your music that he desires you, for love's sake,° to make no more noise with it.

A MUSICIAN: Well, sir, we will not.

CLOWN: If you have any music that may not° be heard, to 't again; but, as they say, to hear music the General does not greatly care. 15

A MUSICIAN: We have none such, sir.

CLOWN: Then put up your pipes in your bag, for I'll away.° Go, vanish into air, away! [*Exeunt Musicians.*]

CASSIO: Dost thou hear, mine honest friend?

CLOWN: No, I hear not your honest friend; I hear you. 20

CASSIO: Prithee, keep up° thy quillets.° There's a poor piece of gold for thee. [*He gives money.*] If the gentle-woman that attends the General's wife be stirring, tell her there's one Cassio entreats her a little favor of speech.° Wilt thou do this?

CLOWN: She is stirring, sir. If she will stir° hither, I shall seem° to notify unto her. 25

CASSIO: Do, good my friend. [*Exit Clown.*]

[*Enter Iago.*]

In happy time,° Iago.

IAGO: You have not been abed, then?

CASSIO: Why, no. The day had broke
Before we parted. I have made bold, Iago,

3–4 speak i' the nose (1) sound nasal (2) sound like one whose nose has been attacked by syphilis. (Naples was popularly supposed to have a high incidence of venereal disease.) **10 wind instrument** (With a joke on flatulence. The *tail*, line 8, that hangs nearby the *wind instrument* suggests the penis.) **12 for love's sake** (1) out of friendship and affection (2) for the sake of lovemaking in Othello's marriage **14 may not** cannot **17 I'll away** (Possibly a misprint, or a snatch of song?) **21 keep up** do not bring out, do not use. **quillets** quibbles, puns **23 a little . . . speech** the favor of a brief talk **25 stir** bestir herself (with a play on *stirring*, "rousing herself from rest") **seem** deem it good, think fit **26 In happy time** i.e., well-met

To send in to your wife. My suit to her   30
Is that she will to virtuous Desdemona
Procure me some access.

IAGO: I'll send her to you presently;
And I'll devise a means to draw the Moor
Out of the way, that your converse and business   35
May be more free.

CASSIO: I humbly thank you for 't.   *Exit [Iago].*

                                        I never knew
A Florentine° more kind and honest.

Enter Emilia.

EMILIA: Good morrow, good Lieutenant. I am sorry
For your displeasure;° but all will sure be well.   40
The General and his wife are talking of it,
And she speaks for you stoutly.° The Moor replies
That he you hurt is of great fame° in Cyprus
And great affinity,° and that in wholesome wisdom
He might not but refuse you; but he protests° he loves you   45
And needs no other suitor but his likings
To take the safest occasion by the front°
To bring you in again.

CASSIO: Yet I beseech you,
If you think fit, or that it may be done,
Give me advantage of some brief discourse   50
With Desdemona alone.

EMILIA: Pray you, come in.
I will bestow you where you shall have time
To speak your bosom° freely.

CASSIO: I am much bound to you.   *[Exeunt.]*

Scene II. The Citadel

Enter Othello, Iago, and Gentlemen.

OTHELLO *[giving letters]*:   These letters give, Iago, to the pilot.
And by him do my duties° to the Senate.

---

38 **Florentine** i.e., even a fellow Florentine. (Iago is a Venetian; Cassio is a Florentine.)
40 **displeasure** fall from favor   42 **stoutly** spiritedly   43 **fame** reputation, importance   44 **affinity**
kindred, family connection   45 **protests** insists   47 **occasion . . . front** opportunity by the forelock
53 **bosom** inmost thoughts
2 **do my duties** convey my respects

That done, I will be walking on the works;°
Repair° there to me.

IAGO: Well, my good lord, I'll do 't.

OTHELLO: This fortification, gentlemen, shall we see 't?   5

GENTLEMEN: We'll wait upon° your lordship.   [*Exeunt.*]

Scene III. The garden of the Citadel

Enter Desdemona, Cassio, and Emilia.

DESDEMONA: Be thou assured, good Cassio, I will do
All my abilities in thy behalf.

EMILIA: Good madam, do. I warrant it grieves my husband
As if the cause were his.

DESDEMONA: O, that's an honest fellow. Do not doubt, Cassio,   5
But I will have my lord and you again
As friendly as you were.

CASSIO: Bounteous madam,
Whatever shall become of Michael Cassio,
He's never anything but your true servant.

DESDEMONA: I know 't. I thank you. You do love my lord;   10
You have known him long, and be you well assured
He shall in strangeness° stand no farther off
Than in a politic° distance.

CASSIO: Ay, but, lady,
That policy may either last so long,
Or feed upon such nice and waterish diet,°   15
Or breed itself so out of circumstance,°
That, I being absent and my place supplied,°
My general will forget my love and service.

DESDEMONA: Do not doubt° that. Before Emilia here
I give thee warrant° of thy place. Assure thee,   20
If I do vow a friendship I'll perform it
To the last article. My lord shall never rest.

---

3 works breastworks, fortifications   **4 Repair** return, come   **6 wait upon** attend
12 strangeness aloofness   **13 politic** required by wise policy   **15 Or . . . diet** or sustain itself at
length upon such trivial and meager technicalities   **16 breed . . . circumstance** continually renew
itself so out of chance events, or yield so few chances for my being pardoned   **17 supplied** filled
by another person   **19 doubt** fear   **20 warrant** guarantee

WILLIAM SHAKESPEARE

I'll watch him tame° and talk him out of patience;°
His bed shall seem a school, his board° a shrift;°
I'll intermingle everything he does   25
With Cassio's suit. Therefore be merry, Cassio,
For thy solicitor° shall rather die
Than give thy cause away.°

Enter Othello and Iago [at a distance].

EMILIA: Madam, here comes my lord.
CASSIO: Madam, I'll take my leave.   30
DESDEMONA: Why, stay, and hear me speak.
CASSIO: Madam, not now. I am very ill at ease,
Unfit for mine own purposes.
DESDEMONA: Well, do your discretion.°   *[Exit Cassio.]*
IAGO: Ha? I like not that.   35
OTHELLO: What dost thou say?
IAGO: Nothing, my lord; or if—I know not what.
OTHELLO: Was not that Cassio parted from my wife?
IAGO: Cassio, my lord? No, sure, I cannot think it,
That he would steal away so guiltylike,   40
Seeing you coming.
OTHELLO: I do believe 'twas he.
DESDEMONA: How now, my lord?
I have been talking with a suitor here,
A man that languishes in your displeasure.   45
OTHELLO: Who is 't you mean?
DESDEMONA: Why, your lieutenant, Cassio. Good my lord,
If I have any grace or power to move you,
His present reconciliation take;°
For if he be not one that truly loves you,   50
That errs in ignorance and not in cunning,°
I have no judgment in an honest face.
I prithee, call him back.
OTHELLO: Went he hence now?

---

23 **watch him tame** tame him by keeping him from sleeping (a term from falconry)   **out of patience** past his endurance   24 **board** dining table.   **shrift** confessional   27 **solicitor** advocate   28 **away** up   34 **do your discretion** act according to your own discretion   49 **His ... take** let him be reconciled to you right away   51 **in cunning** wittingly

DESDEMONA: Yes, faith, so humbled   55
That he hath left part of his grief with me
To suffer with him. Good love, call him back.

OTHELLO: Not now, sweet Desdemon. Some other time.

DESDEMONA: But shall 't be shortly?

OTHELLO: The sooner, sweet, for you.   60

DESDEMONA: Shall 't be tonight at supper?

OTHELLO: No, not tonight.

DESDEMONA: Tomorrow dinner,° then?

OTHELLO: I shall not dine at home.
I meet the captains at the citadel.   65

DESDEMONA: Why, then, tomorrow night, or Tuesday morn,
On Tuesday noon, or night, on Wednesday morn.
I prithee, name the time, but let it not
Exceed three days. In faith, he's penitent;
And yet his trespass, in our common reason°—   70
Save that, they say, the wars must make example
Out of her best°—is not almost° a fault
T' incur a private check.° When shall he come?
Tell me, Othello. I wonder in my soul
What you would ask me that I should deny,   75
Or stand so mammering on.° What? Michael Cassio,
That came a-wooing with you, and so many a time,
When I have spoke of you dispraisingly,
Hath ta'en your part—to have so much to do
To bring him in!° By 'r Lady, I could do much—   80

OTHELLO: Prithee, no more. Let him come when he will;
I will deny thee nothing.

DESDEMONA: Why, this is not a boon.
'Tis as I should entreat you wear your gloves,
Or feed on nourishing dishes, or keep you warm,   85
Or sue to you to do a peculiar° profit
To your own person. Nay, when I have a suit
Wherein I mean to touch° your love indeed,

---

63 dinner (The noontime meal.)   **70 common reason** everyday judgments   **71–72 Save . . . best**
were it not that, as the saying goes, military discipline requires making an example of the very best
men. (*Her* refers to wars as a singular concept.)   **72 not almost** scarcely   **73 private check** even a
private reprimand   **76 mammering on** wavering about   **80 bring him in** restore him to favor
86 peculiar particular, personal   **88 touch** test

It shall be full of poise° and difficult weight,
And fearful to be granted. 90

OTHELLO: I will deny thee nothing.
Whereon,° I do beseech thee, grant me this,
To leave me but a little to myself.

DESDEMONA: Shall I deny you? No. Farewell, my lord.

OTHELLO: Farewell, my Desdemona. I'll come to thee straight.° 95

DESDEMONA: Emilia, come.—Be as your fancies° teach you;
Whate'er you be, I am obedient. *Exit [with Emilia].*

OTHELLO: Excellent wretch!° Perdition catch my soul
But I do love thee! And when I love thee not,
Chaos is come again.° 100

IAGO: My noble lord—

OTHELLO: What dost thou say, Iago?

IAGO: Did Michael Cassio, when you wooed my lady,
Know of your love?

OTHELLO: He did, from first to last. Why dost thou ask? 105

IAGO: But for a satisfaction of my thought;
No further harm.

OTHELLO: Why of thy thought, Iago?

IAGO: I did not think he had been acquainted with her.

OTHELLO: O, yes, and went between us very oft.

IAGO: Indeed? 110

OTHELLO: Indeed? Ay, indeed. Discern'st thou aught in that?
Is he not honest?

IAGO: Honest, my lord?

OTHELLO: Honest. Ay, honest.

IAGO: My lord, for aught I know. 115

OTHELLO: What dost thou think?

IAGO: Think, my lord?

OTHELLO: "Think, my lord?" By heaven, thou echo'st me,
As if there were some monster in thy thought
Too hideous to be shown. Thou dost mean something. 120
I heard thee say even now, thou lik'st not that,

---

89 poise weight, heaviness; or equipoise, delicate balance involving hard choice   **92 Whereon** in return for which   **95 straight** straightway   **96 fancies** inclinations   **98 wretch** (A term of affectionate endearment.)   **99–100 And . . . again** i.e., my love for you will last forever, until the end of time when chaos will return. (But with an unconscious, ironic suggestion that, if anything should induce Othello to cease loving Desdemona, the result would be chaos.)

When Cassio left my wife. What didst not like?
And when I told thee he was of my counsel°
In my whole course of wooing, thou criedst "Indeed?"
And didst contract and purse° thy brow together   125
As if thou then hadst shut up in thy brain
Some horrible conceit.° If thou dost love me,
Show me thy thought.

IAGO: My lord, you know I love you.

OTHELLO: I think thou dost;   130
And, for° I know thou'rt full of love and honesty,
And weigh'st thy words before thou giv'st them breath,
Therefore these stops° of thine fright me the more;
For such things in a false disloyal knave
Are tricks of custom,° but in a man that's just   135
They're close dilations,° working from the heart
That passion cannot rule.°

IAGO: For° Michael Cassio,
I dare be sworn I think that he is honest.

OTHELLO: I think so too.

IAGO: Men should be what they seem;
Or those that be not, would they might seem none!°   140

OTHELLO: Certain, men should be what they seem.

IAGO: Why, then, I think Cassio's an honest man.

OTHELLO: Nay, yet there's more in this.
I prithee, speak to me as to thy thinkings,
As thou dost ruminate, and give thy worst of thoughts   145
The worst of words.

IAGO: Good my lord, pardon me.
Though I am bound to every act of duty,
I am not bound to that° all slaves are free to.°
Utter my thoughts? Why, say they are vile and false,
As where's the palace whereinto foul things   150
Sometimes intrude not? Who has that breast so pure

---

123 **of my counsel** in my confidence   125 **purse** knit   127 **conceit** fancy   131 **for** because
133 **stops** pauses   135 **of custom** customary   136 **close dilations** secret or involuntary expressions
or delays   137 **That passion cannot rule** i.e., that are too passionately strong to be restrained
(referring to the workings), or . . . that cannot rule its own passions (referring to the heart).
137 **For** as for   140 **none** i.e., not to be men, or not seem to be honest   148 **that** that which.
free to free with respect to

But some uncleanly apprehensions
Keep leets and law days,° and in sessions sit
With° meditations lawful?°

OTHELLO: Thou dost conspire against thy friend,° Iago,   155
If thou but think'st him wronged and mak'st his ear
A stranger to thy thoughts.

IAGO: I do beseech you,
Though I perchance am vicious° in my guess—
As I confess it is my nature's plague
To spy into abuses, and oft my jealousy°   160
Shapes faults that are not—that your wisdom then,°
From one° that so imperfectly conceits,°
Would take no notice, nor build yourself a trouble
Out of his scattering° and unsure observance.
It were not for your quiet nor your good,   165
Nor for my manhood, honesty, and wisdom,
To let you know my thoughts.

OTHELLO: What dost thou mean?

IAGO: Good name in man and woman, dear my lord,
Is the immediate° jewel of their souls.
Who steals my purse steals trash; 'tis something, nothing;   170
'Twas mine, 'tis his, and has been slave to thousands;
But he that filches from me my good name
Robs me of that which not enriches him
And makes me poor indeed.

OTHELLO: By heaven, I'll know thy thoughts.   175

IAGO: You cannot, if° my heart were in your hand,
Nor shall not, whilst 'tis in my custody.

OTHELLO: Ha?

IAGO: O, beware, my lord, of jealousy.
It is the green-eyed monster which doth mock
The meat it feeds on.° That cuckold lives in bliss   180

---

153 **Keep leets and law days** i.e., hold court, set up their authority in one's heart. (*Leets* are a kind of manor court; *law days* are the days courts sit in session, or those sessions.) 154 **With** along with. **lawful** innocent   155 **thy friend** i.e., Othello   158 **vicious** wrong   160 **jealousy** suspicious nature 161 **then** on that account   162 **one** i.e., myself, iago.   **conceits** judges, conjectures   164 **scattering** random   169 **immediate** essential, most precious   176 **if** even if   179–180 **doth mock . . . on** mocks and torments the heart of its victim, the man who suffers jealousy

Who, certain of his fate, loves not his wronger;°
But O, what damnèd minutes tells° he o'er
Who dotes, yet doubts, suspects, yet fondly loves!

OTHELLO: O misery!

IAGO: Poor and content is rich, and rich enough,°   185
But riches fineless° is as poor as winter
To him that ever fears he shall be poor.
Good God, the souls of all my tribe defend
From jealousy!

OTHELLO: Why, why is this?   190
Think'st thou I'd make a life of jealousy,
To follow still the changes of the moon
With fresh suspicions?° No! To be once in doubt
Is once° to be resolved.° Exchange me for a goat
When I shall turn the business of my soul   195
To such exsufflicate and blown° surmises
Matching thy inference.° 'Tis not to make me jealous
To say my wife is fair, feeds well, loves company,
Is free of speech, sings, plays, and dances well;
Where virtue is, these are more virtuous.   200
Nor from mine own weak merits will I draw
The smallest fear or doubt of her revolt,°
For she had eyes, and chose me. No, Iago,
I'll see before I doubt; when I doubt, prove;
And on the proof, there is no more but this—   205
Away at once with love or jealousy.

IAGO: I am glad of this, for now I shall have reason
To show the love and duty that I bear you
With franker spirit. Therefore, as I am bound,
Receive it from me. I speak not yet of proof.   210
Look to your wife; observe her well with Cassio.

WILLIAM SHAKESPEARE

144

---

181 his wronger i.e., his faithless wife. (The unsuspecting cuckold is spared the misery of loving his wife only to discover she is cheating on him.) **182 tells** counts **185 Poor . . . enough** to be content with what little one has is the greatest wealth of all. (Proverbial.) **186 fineless** boundless **192–193 To follow . . . suspicions** to be constantly imagining new causes for suspicion, changing incessantly like the moon **194 once** once and for all. **resolved** free of doubt, having settled the matter **196 exsufflicate and blown** inflated and blown up, rumored about, or, spat out and flyblown, hence, loathsome, disgusting **197 inference** description or allegation **202 doubt . . . revolt** fear of her unfaithfulness

Wear your eyes thus, not° jealous nor secure.°
I would not have your free and noble nature,
Out of self-bounty,° be abused.° Look to 't.
I know our country disposition well;   215
In Venice they do let God see the pranks
They dare not show their husbands; their best conscience
Is not to leave 't undone, but keep 't unknown.
OTHELLO: Dost thou say so?
IAGO: She did deceive her father, marrying you;   220
And when she seemed to shake and fear your looks,
She loved them most.
OTHELLO: And so she did.
IAGO: Why, go to,° then!
She that, so young, could give out such a seeming,°
To seel° her father's eyes up close as oak,°
He thought 'twas witchcraft! But I am much to blame.   225
I humbly do beseech you of your pardon
For too much loving you.
OTHELLO: I am bound° to thee forever.
IAGO: I see this hath a little dashed your spirits.
OTHELLO: Not a jot, not a jot.
IAGO: I' faith, I fear it has.   230
I hope you will consider what is spoke
Comes from my love. But I do see you're moved.
I am to pray you not to strain my speech
To grosser issues° nor to larger reach°
Than to suspicion.   235
OTHELLO: I will not.
IAGO: Should you do so, my lord,
My speech should fall into such vile success°
Which my thoughts aimed not. Cassio's my worthy friend.
My lord, I see you're moved.
OTHELLO: No, not much moved.   240
I do not think but Desdemona's honest.°

---

212 not neither.   **secure** free from uncertainty   **214 self-bounty** inherent or natural goodness
and generosity.   **abused** deceived   **222 go to** (An expression of impatience.)   **223 seeming** false
appearance   **224 seel** blind (a term from falconry)   **oak** (A close-grained wood.)   **228 bound**
indebted (but perhaps with ironic sense of "tied")   **234 issues** significances.   **reach** meaning,
scope   **238 success** effect, result   **241 honest** chaste

IAGO: Long live she so! And long live you to think so!

OTHELLO: And yet, how nature erring from itself—

IAGO: Ay, there's the point! As—to be bold with you—
Not to affect° many proposèd matches   245
Of her own clime, complexion, and degree,°
Whereto we see in all things nature tends—
Foh! One may smell in such a will° most rank,
Foul disproportion,° thoughts unnatural.
But pardon me. I do not in position°   250
Distinctly speak of her, though I may fear
Her will, recoiling° to her better° judgment,
May fall to match you with her country forms°
And happily repent.°

OTHELLO: Farewell, farewell!
If more thou dost perceive, let me know more.   255
Set on thy wife to observe. Leave me, Iago.

IAGO [*going*]: My lord, I take my leave.

OTHELLO: Why did I marry? This honest creature doubtless
Sees and knows more, much more, than he unfolds.

IAGO [*returning*]: My Lord, I would I might entreat your honor   260
To scan° this thing no farther. Leave it to time.
Although 'tis fit that Cassio have his place—
For, sure, he fills it up with great ability—
Yet, if you please to hold him off awhile,
You shall by that perceive him and his means.°   265
Note if your lady strain his entertainment°
With any strong or vehement importunity;
Much will be seen in that. In the meantime,
Let me be thought too busy° in my fears—
As worthy cause I have to fear I am—   270
And hold her free,° I do beseech your honor.

OTHELLO: Fear not my government.°

IAGO: I once more take my leave.   [*Exit.*]

---

245 affect prefer, desire   **246 clime . . . degree** country, color, and social position   **248 will** sensuality, appetite   **249 disproportion** abnormality   **250 position** argument, proposition   **252 recoiling** reverting.   **better** i.e., more natural and reconsidered   **253 fall . . . forms** undertake to compare you with Venetian norms of handsomeness   **254 happily repent** haply repent her marriage   **261 scan** scrutinize   **265 his means** the method he uses (to regain his post)   **266 strain his entertainment** urge his reinstatement   **269 busy** interfering   **271 hold her free** regard her as innocent   **272 government** self-control, conduct

OTHELLO: This fellow's of exceeding honesty,
     And knows all qualities,° with a learnèd spirit,   275
     Of human dealings. If I do prove her haggard,°
     Though that her jesses° were my dear heartstrings,
     I'd whistle her off and let her down the wind°
     To prey at fortune.° Haply, for° I am black
     And have not those soft parts of conversation°   280
     That chamberers° have, or for I am declined
     Into the vale of years—yet that's not much—
     She's gone. I am abused,° and my relief
     Must be to loathe her. O curse of marriage,
     That we can call these delicate creatures ours   285
     And not their appetites! I had rather be a toad
     And live upon the vapor of a dungeon
     Than keep a corner in the thing I love
     For others' uses. Yet, 'tis the plague of great ones;
     Prerogatived° are they less than the base.°   290
     'Tis destiny unshunnable, like death.
     Even then this forkèd° plague is fated to us
     When we do quicken.° Look where she comes.

[*Enter Desdemona and Emilia.*]

     If she be false, O, then heaven mocks itself!
     I'll not believe 't.
DESDEMONA: How now, my dear Othello?   295
     Your dinner, and the generous° islanders
     By you invited, do attend° your presence.
OTHELLO: I am to blame.
DESDEMONA: Why do you speak so faintly?
     Are you not well?
OTHELLO: I have a pain upon my forehead here.   300

---

275 **qualities** natures, types   276 **haggard** wild (like a wild female hawk)   277 **jesses** straps fastened
around the legs of a trained hawk   278 **I'd . . . wind** i.e., I'd let her go forever. (To release a hawk
downwind was to invite it not to return.)   279 **prey at fortune** fend for herself in the wild.
Haply, for perhaps because   280 **soft . . . conversation** pleasing graces of social behavior
281 **chamberers** gallants   283 **abused** deceived   290 **Prerogatived** privileged (to have honest wives).
the base ordinary citizens. (Socially prominent men are especially prone to the unavoidable
destiny of being cuckolded and to the public shame that goes with it.)   292 **forkèd** (An allusion
to the horns of the cuckold.)   293 **quicken** receive life. (Quicken may also mean to swarm with
maggots as the body festers, as in Act IV, Scene ii, line 69, in which case lines 292–293 suggest that
even then, in death, we are cuckolded by *forkèd* worms.)   296 **generous** noble   297 **attend** await

DESDEMONA: Faith, that's with watching.° 'Twill away again.

[*She offers her handkerchief.*]

Let me but bind it hard, within this hour
It will be well.

OTHELLO: Your napkin° is too little.
Let it alone.° Come, I'll go in with you.

[*He puts the handkerchief from him, and it drops.*]

DESDEMONA: I am very sorry that you are not well.   305

Exit [*with Othello*].

EMILIA [*picking up the handkerchief*]:   I am glad I have found this
napkin.
This was her first remembrance from the Moor.
My wayward° husband hath a hundred times
Wooed me to steal it, but she so loves the token—
For he conjured her she should ever keep it—   310
That she reserves it evermore about her
To kiss and talk to. I'll have the work ta'en out,°
And give 't Iago. What he will do with it
Heaven knows, not I;
I nothing but to please his fantasy.°   315

[*Enter Iago.*]

IAGO: How now? What do you here alone?

EMILIA: Do not you chide. I have a thing for you.

IAGO: You have a thing for me? It is a common thing°—

EMILIA: Ha?

IAGO: To have a foolish wife.   320

EMILIA: O, is that all? What will you give me now
For that same handkerchief?

IAGO: What handkerchief?

EMILIA: What handkerchief?
Why, that the Moor first gave to Desdemona;   325
That which so often you did bid me steal.

301 **watching** too little sleep   303 **napkin** handkerchief   304 **Let it alone** i.e., never mind
308 **wayward** capricious   312 **work ta'en out** design of the embroidery copied   315 **fantasy** whim
318 **common thing** (With bawdy suggestion; *common* suggests coarseness and availability to all
comers, and *thing* is a slang term for the pudendum.)

IAGO: Hast stolen it from her?

EMILIA: No, faith. She let it drop by negligence,
And to th' advantage° I, being here, took 't up.
Look, here 'tis.

IAGO: A good wench! Give it me.   330

EMILIA: What will you do with 't, that you have been so earnest
To have me filch it?

IAGO [snatching it]:   Why, what is that to you?

EMILIA: If it be not for some purpose of import,
Give 't me again. Poor lady, she'll run mad
When she shall lack° it.

IAGO: Be not acknown on't.°   335
I have use for it. Go, leave me.   [Exit Emilia.]
I will in Cassio's lodging lose° this napkin
And let him find it. Trifles light as air
Are to the jealous confirmations strong
As proofs of Holy Writ. This may do something.   340
The Moor already changes with my poison.
Dangerous conceits° are in their natures poisons,
Which at the first are scarce found to distaste,°
But with a little act° upon the blood
Burn like the mines of sulfur.

[Enter Othello.]

                    I did say so.   345
Look where he comes! Not poppy nor mandragora°
Nor all the drowsy syrups of the world
Shall ever medicine thee to that sweet sleep
Which thou owedst° yesterday.

OTHELLO: Ha, ha, false to me?

IAGO: Why, how now, General? No more of that.   350

OTHELLO: Avaunt! Begone! Thou hast set me on the rack.
I swear 'tis better to be much abused
Than but to know 't a little.

IAGO: How now, my lord?

---

329 to th' advantage taking the opportunity   **335 lack** miss.   **Be . . . on't** do not confess knowledge of it   **337 lose** (The Folio spelling, *loose*, is a normal spelling for "lose," but it may also contain the idea of "let go," "release.")   **342 conceits** fancies, ideas   **343 distaste** be distasteful   **344 act** action, working   **346 mandragora** an opiate made of the mandrake root   **349 thou owedst** you did own

OTHELLO: What sense had I of her stolen hours of lust?
　　　　I saw 't not, thought it not, it harmed not me.　　　　　355
　　　　I slept the next night well, fed well, was free° and merry;
　　　　I found not Cassio's kisses on her lips.
　　　　He that is robbed, not wanting° what is stolen,
　　　　Let him not know 't and he's not robbed at all.

IAGO: I am sorry to hear this.　　　　　　　　　　　　360

OTHELLO: I had been happy if the general camp,
　　　　Pioners° and all, had tasted her sweet body,
　　　　So° I had nothing known. O, now, forever
　　　　Farewell the tranquil mind! Farewell content!
　　　　Farewell the plumèd troops and the big° wars　　　　365
　　　　That makes ambition virtue! O, farewell!
　　　　Farewell the neighing steed and the shrill trump,
　　　　The spirit-stirring drum, th' ear-piercing fife,
　　　　The royal banner, and all quality,°
　　　　Pride,° pomp, and circumstance° of glorious war!　　　370
　　　　And O, you mortal engines,° whose rude throats
　　　　Th' immortal Jove's dread clamors° counterfeit,
　　　　Farewell! Othello's occupation's gone.

IAGO: Is 't possible, my lord?

OTHELLO: Villain, be sure thou prove my love a whore!　　　375
　　　　Be sure of it. Give me the ocular proof,
　　　　Or, by the worth of mine eternal soul,
　　　　Thou hadst been better have been born a dog
　　　　Than answer my waked wrath!

IAGO:　　　　　　　　　　　　Is 't come to this?

OTHELLO: Make me to see 't, or at the least so prove it　　　380
　　　　That the probation° bear no hinge nor loop
　　　　To hang a doubt on, or woe upon thy life!

IAGO: My noble lord—

OTHELLO: If thou dost slander her and torture me,
　　　　Never pray more; abandon all remorse;°　　　　　　385
　　　　On horror's head horrors accumulate;°

---

356 **free** carefree   358 **wanting** missing   362 **Pioners** diggers of mines, the lowest grade of soldiers   363 **So** provided   365 **big** stately   369 **quality** character, essential nature   370 **Pride** rich display.   **circumstance** pageantry   371 **mortal engines** i.e., cannon. (*Mortal* means "deadly.")   372 **Jove's dread clamors** i.e., thunder   381 **probation** proof   385 **remorse** pity, penitent hope for salvation   386 **horrors accumulate** add still more horrors

Do deeds to make heaven weep, all earth amazed;°
For nothing canst thou to damnation add
Greater than that.

IAGO: O grace! O heaven forgive me!
Are you a man? Have you a soul or sense?   390
God b' wi' you; take mine office. O wretched fool,°
That lov'st to make thine honesty a vice!°
O monstrous world! Take note, take note, O world,
To be direct and honest is not safe.
I thank you for this profit,° and from hence°   395
I'll love no friend, sith° love breeds such offense.°

OTHELLO: Nay, stay. Thou shouldst be° honest.

IAGO: I should be wise, for honesty's a fool
And loses that° it works for.

OTHELLO: By the world,
I think my wife be honest and think she is not;   400
I think that thou art just and think thou art not.
I'll have some proof. My name, that was as fresh
As Dian's° visage, is now begrimed and black
As mine own face. If there be cords, or knives,
Poison, or fire, or suffocating streams,   405
I'll not endure it. Would I were satisfied!

IAGO: I see, sir, you are eaten up with passion.
I do repent me that I put it to you.
You would be satisfied?

OTHELLO: Would? Nay, and I will.

IAGO: And may; but how? How satisfied, my lord?   410
Would you, the supervisor,° grossly gape on?
Behold her topped?

OTHELLO: Death and damnation! O!

IAGO: It were a tedious difficulty, I think,
To bring them to that prospect. Damn them then,°
If ever mortal eyes do see them bolster°   415

---

387 amazed confounded with horror   **391 O wretched fool** (Iago addresses himself as a fool for
having carried honesty too far.)   **392 vice** failing, something overdone   **395 profit** profitable
instruction.   **hence** henceforth   **396 sith** since.   **offense** i.e., harm to the one who offers help
and friendship   **397 Thou shouldst be** it appears that you are. (But Iago replies in the sense of
"ought to be.")   **399 that** what   **403 Dian** Diana, goddess of the moon and of chastity
411 supervisor onlooker   **414 Damn them then** i.e., they would have to be really incorrigible
415 bolster go to bed together, share a bolster

More° than their own.° What then? How then?
What shall I say? Where's satisfaction?
It is impossible you should see this,
Were they as prime° as goats, as hot as monkeys,
As salt° as wolves in pride,° and fools as gross   420
As ignorance made drunk. But yet I say,
If imputation and strong circumstances°
Which lead directly to the door of truth
Will give you satisfaction, you might have 't.

OTHELLO: Give me a living reason she's disloyal.   425

IAGO: I do not like the office.
But sith° I am entered in this cause so far,
Pricked° to 't by foolish honesty and love,
I will go on. I lay with Cassio lately,
And being troubled with a raging tooth   430
I could not sleep. There are a kind of men
So loose of soul that in their sleeps will mutter
Their affairs. One of this kind is Cassio.
In sleep I heard him say, "Sweet Desdemona,
Let us be wary, let us hide our loves!"   435
And then, sir, would he grip and wring my hand,
Cry "O sweet creature!", then kiss me hard,
As if he plucked up kisses by the roots
That grew upon my lips; then laid his leg
Over my thigh, and sighed, and kissed, and then   440
Cried, "Cursèd fate that gave thee to the Moor!"

OTHELLO: O monstrous! Monstrous!

IAGO: Nay, this was but his dream.

OTHELLO: But this denoted a foregone conclusion.°
'Tis a shrewd doubt,° though it be but a dream.

IAGO: And this may help to thicken other proofs   445
That do demonstrate thinly.

OTHELLO: I'll tear her all to pieces.

---

416 More other.   **own** own eyes   **419 prime** lustful   **420 salt** wanton, sensual.   **pride** heat
422 imputation . . . circumstances strong circumstantial evidence   **427 sith** since   **428 Pricked**
spurred   **443 foregone conclusion** concluded experience or action   **444 shrewd doubt** suspicious
circumstance

IAGO: Nay, but be wise. Yet we see nothing done;
        She may be honest yet. Tell me but this:
        Have you not sometimes seen a handkerchief
        Spotted with strawberries° in your wife's hand?   450
OTHELLO: I gave her such a one. 'Twas my first gift.
IAGO: I know not that; but such a handkerchief—
        I am sure it was your wife's—did I today
        See Cassio wipe his beard with.
OTHELLO: If it be that—
IAGO: If it be that, or any that was hers,   455
        It speaks against her with the other proofs.
OTHELLO: O, that the slave° had forty thousand lives!
        One is too poor, too weak for my revenge.
        Now do I see 'tis true. Look here, Iago,
        All my fond° love thus do I blow to heaven.   460
        'Tis gone.
        Arise, black vengeance, from the hollow hell!
        Yield up, O love, thy crown and hearted° throne
        To tyrannous hate! Swell, bosom, with thy freight°,
        For 'tis of aspics'° tongues!   465
IAGO: Yet be content.°
OTHELLO: O, blood, blood, blood!
IAGO: Patience, I say. Your mind perhaps may change.
OTHELLO: Never, Iago. Like to the Pontic Sea,°
        Whose icy current and compulsive course   470
        Ne'er feels retiring ebb, but keeps due on
        To the Propontic° and the Hellespont,°
        Even so my bloody thoughts with violent pace
        Shall ne'er look back, ne'er ebb to humble love,
        I that a capable° and wide revenge   475
        Swallow them up. Now, by yond marble° heaven,
        [Kneeling] In the due reverence of a sacred vow
        I here engage my words.

---

450 **Spotted with strawberries** embroidered with a strawberry pattern   457 **the slave** i.e., Cassio
460 **fond** foolish (but also suggesting "affectionate")   463 **hearted** fixed in the heart   464 **freight**
burden   465 **aspics'** venomous serpents'   466 **content** calm   469 **Pontic Sea** Black Sea
472 **Propontic** Sea of Marmara, between the Black Sea and the Aegean.   **Hellespont** Dardanelles,
straits where the Sea of Marmara joins with the Aegean   475 **capable** ample, comprehensive
476 **marble** i.e., gleaming like marble and unrelenting

IAGO: Do not rise yet.

[*He kneels.*]° Witness, you ever-burning lights above,
You elements that clip° us round about,   480
Witness that here Iago doth give up
The execution° of his wit,° hands, heart,
To wronged Othello's service. Let him command,
And to obey shall be in me remorse,°
What bloody business ever.° [*They rise.*]

OTHELLO: I greet thy love,   485
Not with vain thanks, but with acceptance bounteous,
And will upon the instant put thee to 't.°
Within these three days let me hear thee say
That Cassio's not alive.

IAGO: My friend is dead;
'Tis done at your request. But let her live.   490

OTHELLO: Damn her, lewd minx!° O, damn her, damn her!
Come, go with me apart. I will withdraw
To furnish me with some swift means of death
For the fair devil. Now art thou my lieutenant.

IAGO: I am your own forever.   [*Exeunt.*]   495

Scene IV. Before the Citadel

Enter Desdemona, Emilia, and Clown.

DESDEMONA: Do you know, sirrah,° where Lieutenant Cassio lies?°

CLOWN: I dare not say he lies anywhere.

DESDEMONA: Why, man?

CLOWN: He's a soldier, and for me to say a soldier lies, 'tis
stabbing.

DESDEMONA: Go to. Where lodges he?   5

CLOWN: To tell you where he lodges is to tell you where I lie.

DESDEMONA: Can anything be made of this?

CLOWN: I know not where he lodges, and for me to devise a
lodging and say he lies here, or he lies there, were to lie in
mine own throat.°

---

479 [s.d.] He kneels (In the Quarto text, Iago kneels here after Othello has knelt at line 477.)
480 clip encompass   **482 execution** exercise, action.   **wit** mind   **484 remorse** pity (for Othello's wrongs)   **485 ever** soever   **487 to 't** to the proof   **491 minx** wanton
1 sirrah (A form of address to an inferior.)   **lies** lodges. (But the Clown makes the obvious pun.)
9 lie . . . throat (1) lie egregiously and deliberately (2) use the windpipe to speak a lie

DESDEMONA: Can you inquire him out, and be edified by report?   10

CLOWN: I will catechize the world for him; that is, make questions, and by them answer.

DESDEMONA: Seek him, bid him come hither. Tell him I have moved° my lord on his behalf and hope all will be well.

CLOWN: To do this is within the compass of man's wit, and therefore I will attempt the doing it.   15

[*Exit Clown.*]

DESDEMONA: Where should I lose that handkerchief, Emilia?

EMILIA: I know not, madam.

DESDEMONA: Believe me, I had rather have lost my purse
Full of crusadoes;° and but my noble Moor   20
Is true of mind and made of no such baseness
As jealous creatures are, it were enough
To put him to ill thinking.

EMILIA: Is he not jealous?

DESDEMONA: Who, he? I think the sun where he was born
Drew all such humors° from him.

EMILIA: Look where he comes.   25

[*Enter Othello.*]

DESDEMONA: I will not leave him now till Cassio
Be called to him.—How is 't with you, my lord?

OTHELLO: Well, my good lady. [*Aside.*] O, hardness to dissemble!—
How do you, Desdemona?

DESDEMONA: Well, my good lord.

OTHELLO: Give me your hand. [*She gives her hand.*] This hand is moist, my lady.

DESDEMONA: It yet hath felt no age nor known no sorrow.

OTHELLO: This argues° fruitfulness° and liberal° heart.   30
Hot, hot, and moist. This hand of yours requires
A sequester° from liberty, fasting and prayer,
Much castigation,° exercise devout;°   35
For here's a young and sweating devil here

___

13 **moved** petitioned   20 **crusadoes** Portuguese gold coins   25 **humors** (Refers to the four bodily fluids thought to determine temperament.)   32 **argues** gives evidence of.   **fruitfulness** generosity, amorousness, and fecundity.   **liberal** generous and sexually free   34 **sequester** separation, sequestration   35 **castigation** corrective discipline.   **exercise devout** i.e., prayer, religious meditation, etc.

WILLIAM SHAKESPEARE

That commonly rebels. 'Tis a good hand,
A frank° one.

DESDEMONA: You may indeed say so,
For 'twas that hand that gave away my heart.

OTHELLO: A liberal hand. The hearts of old gave hands,°   40
But our new heraldry is hands, not hearts.°

DESDEMONA: I cannot speak of this. Come now, your promise.

OTHELLO: What promise, chuck?°

DESDEMONA: I have sent to bid Cassio come speak with you.

OTHELLO: I have a salt and sorry rheum° offends me;   45
Lend me thy handkerchief.

DESDEMONA: Here, my lord. [*She offers a handkerchief.*]

OTHELLO: That which I gave you.

DESDEMONA: I have it not about me.

OTHELLO: Not?

DESDEMONA: No, faith, my lord.   50

OTHELLO: That's a fault. That handkerchief
Did an Egyptian to my mother give.
She was a charmer,° and could almost read
The thoughts of people. She told her, while she kept it
'Twould make her amiable° and subdue my father   55
Entirely to her love, but if she lost it
Or made a gift of it, my father's eye
Should hold her loathèd and his spirits should hunt
After new fancies.° She, dying, gave it me,
And bid me, when my fate would have me wived,   60
To give it her.° I did so; and take heed on 't;
Make it a darling like your precious eye.
To lose 't or give 't away were such perdition°
As nothing else could match.

DESDEMONA: Is 't possible?

OTHELLO: 'Tis true. There's magic in the web° of it.   65
A sibyl, that had numbered in the world

---

38 frank generous, open (with sexual suggestion)   **40 The hearts . . . hands** i.e., in former times, people would give their hearts when they gave their hands to something   **41 But . . . hearts** i.e., in our decadent times, the joining of hands is no longer a badge to signify the giving of hearts   **43 chuck** (A term of endearment.)   **45 salt . . . rheum** distressful head cold or watering of the eyes   **53 charmer** sorceress   **55 amiable** desirable   **59 fancies** loves   **61 her** i.e., to my wife   **63 perdition** loss   **65 web** fabric, weaving

The sun to course two hundred compasses,°
In her prophetic fury° sewed the work;°
The worms were hallowed that did breed the silk,
And it was dyed in mummy° which the skillful   70
Conserved of° maidens' hearts.

DESDEMONA: I' faith! Is 't true?

OTHELLO: Most veritable. Therefore look to 't well.

DESDEMONA: Then would to God that I had never seen 't!

OTHELLO: Ha? Wherefore?

DESDEMONA: Why do you speak so startingly and rash?°   75

OTHELLO: Is 't lost? Is 't gone? Speak, is 't out o' the way?°

DESDEMONA: Heaven bless us!

OTHELLO: Say you?

DESDEMONA: It is not lost; but what an if° it were?

OTHELLO: How?   80

DESDEMONA: I say it is not lost.

OTHELLO: Fetch 't, let me see 't.

DESDEMONA: Why, so I can, sir, but I will not now.
    This is a trick to put me from my suit.
    Pray you, let Cassio be received again.

OTHELLO: Fetch me the handkerchief! My mind misgives.   85

DESDEMONA: Come, come,
    You'll never meet a more sufficient° man.

OTHELLO: The handkerchief!

DESDEMONA: I pray, talk° me of Cassio.

OTHELLO: The handkerchief!

DESDEMONA: A man that all his time°
    Hath founded his good fortunes on your love,   90
    Shared dangers with you—

OTHELLO: The handkerchief!

DESDEMONA: I' faith, you are to blame.

OTHELLO: Zounds!   [Exit Othello.]

EMILIA: Is not this man jealous?   95

---

67 **compasses** annual circlings. (The *sibyl*, or prophetess, was two-hundred years old.)
68 **prophetic fury** frenzy of prophetic inspiration. **work** embroidered pattern 70 **mummy**
medicinal or magical preparation drained from mummified bodies 71 **Conserved of** prepared or
preserved out of 75 **startingly and rash** disjointedly and impetuously excitedly 76 **out o' the way**
lost, misplaced 79 **an if** if 87 **sufficient** able, complete 88 **talk** talk to 89 **all his time**
throughout his career

DESDEMONA: I ne'er saw this before.
Sure, there's some wonder in this handkerchief.
I am most unhappy in the loss of it.

EMILIA: 'Tis not a year or two shows us a man.°
They are all but stomachs, and we all but° food;   100
They eat us hungerly,° and when they are full
They belch us.

[*Enter Iago and Cassio.*]

Look you, Cassio and my husband.

IAGO [*to Cassio*]:   There is no other way; 'tis she must do 't.
And, lo, the happiness!° Go and importune her.

DESDEMONA: How now, good Cassio? What's the news with
you?   105

CASSIO: Madam, my former suit. I do beseech you
That by your virtuous° means I may again
Exist and be a member of his love
Whom I, with all the office° of my heart,
Entirely honor. I would not be delayed.   110
If my offense be of such mortal° kind
That nor my service past, nor° present sorrows,
Nor purposed merit in futurity
Can ransom me into his love again,
But to know so must be my benefit;°   115
So shall I clothe me in a forced content,
And shut myself up in° some other course,
To fortune's alms.°

DESDEMONA: Alas, thrice-gentle Cassio,
My advocation° is not now in tune.
My lord is not my lord; nor should I know him,   120
Were he in favor° as in humor° altered.
So help me every spirit sanctified
As I have spoken for you all my best
And stood within the blank° of his displeasure

---

99 'Tis . . . man i.e., you can't really know a man even in a year or two of experience (?), or, real men come along seldom (?)   **100 but** nothing but   **101 hungerly** hungrily   **104 the happiness** in happy time, fortunately met   **107 virtuous** efficacious   **109 office** loyal service   **111 mortal** fatal   **112 nor . . . nor** neither . . . nor   **115 But . . . benefit** merely to know that my case is hopeless will have to content me (and will be better than uncertainty)   **117 shut . . . in** confine myself to   **118 To fortune's alms** throwing myself on the mercy of fortune   **119 advocation** advocacy   **121 favor** appearance.   **humor** mood   **124 within the blank** within point-blank range. (The *blank* is the center of the target.)

For my free speech! You must awhile be patient.   125
What I can do I will, and more I will
Than for myself I dare. Let that suffice you.

IAGO: Is my lord angry?

EMILIA: He went hence but now,
And certainly in strange unquietness.

IAGO: Can he be angry? I have seen the cannon   130
When it hath blown his ranks into the air,
And like the devil from his very arm
Puffed his own brother—and is he angry?
Something of moment° then. I will go meet him.
There's matter in 't indeed, if he be angry.   135

DESDEMONA: I prithee, do so.   *Exit [Iago].*
                         Something, sure, of state,°
Either from Venice, or some unhatched practice°
Made demonstrable here in Cyprus to him,
Hath puddled° his clear spirit; and in such cases
Men's natures wrangle with inferior things,   140
Though great ones are their object. 'Tis even so;
For let our finger ache, and it indues°
Our other, healthful members even to a sense
Of pain. Nay, we must think men are not gods,
Nor of them look for such observancy°   145
As fits the bridal.° Beshrew me° much, Emilia,
I was, unhandsome° warrior as I am,
Arraigning his unkindness with° my soul;
But now I find I had suborned the witness,°
And he's indicted falsely.

EMILIA: Pray heaven it be   150
State matters, as you think, and no conception
Nor no jealous toy° concerning you.

DESDEMONA: Alas the day! I never gave him cause.

---

134 **of moment** of immediate importance, momentous   136 **of state** concerning state affairs
137 **unhatched practice** as yet unexecuted or undiscovered plot   139 **puddled** muddied   142 **indues**
brings to the same condition   145 **observancy** attentiveness   146 **bridal** wedding (when a
bridegroom is newly attentive to his bride).   **Beshrew me** (A mild oath.)   147 **unhandsome**
insufficient, unskillful   148 **with** before the bar of   149 **suborned the witness** induced the witness
to give false testimony   152 **toy** fancy

EMILIA: But jealous souls will not be answered so;
They are not ever jealous for the cause,   155
But jealous for° they're jealous. It is a monster
Begot upon itself,° born on itself.
DESDEMONA: Heaven keep that monster from Othello's mind!
EMILIA: Lady, amen.
DESDEMONA: I will go seek him. Cassio, walk hereabout.   160
If I do find him fit, I'll move your suit
And seek to effect it to my uttermost.
CASSIO: I humbly thank your ladyship.

                                        Exit [*Desdemona with Emilia*].
[*Enter Bianca.*]

BIANCA: Save° you, friend Cassio!
CASSIO: What make° you from home?
How is 't with you, my most fair Bianca?   165
I' faith, sweet love, I was coming to your house.
BIANCA: And I was going to your lodging, Cassio.
What, keep a week away? Seven days and nights?
Eightscore-eight° hours? And lovers' absent hours
More tedious than the dial° eightscore times?   170
O weary reckoning!
CASSIO: Pardon me, Bianca.
I have this while with leaden thoughts been pressed;
But I shall, in a more continuate° time,
Strike off this score° of absence. Sweet Bianca,

[*giving her Desdemona's handkerchief*]

Take me this work out.°
BIANCA: O Cassio, whence came this?   175
This is some token from a newer friend.°
To the felt absence now I feel a cause.
Is 't come to this? Well, well.
CASSIO: Go to, woman!
Throw your vile guesses in the devil's teeth,
From whence you have them. You are jealous now   180

---

156 for because   157 Begot upon itself generated solely from itself   164 Save God save.   make do
169 Eightscore-eight one hundred sixty-eight, the number of hours in a week   170 the dial a
complete revolution of the clock   173 continuate uninterrupted   174 Strike . . . score settle this
account   175 Take . . . out copy this embroidery for me   176 friend mistress

That this is from some mistress, some remembrance.
No, by my faith, Bianca.
BIANCA: Why, whose is it?
CASSIO: I know not, neither. I found it in my chamber.
I like the work well. Ere it be demanded°—
As like° enough it will—I would have it copied. 185
Take it and do 't, and leave me for this time.
BIANCA: Leave you? Wherefore?
CASSIO: I do attend here on the General,
And think it no addition,° nor my wish,
To have him see me womaned. 190
BIANCA: Why, I pray you?
CASSIO: Not that I love you not.
BIANCA: But that you do not love me.
I pray you, bring° me on the way a little,
And say if I shall see you soon at night. 195
CASSIO: 'Tis but a little way that I can bring you,
For I attend here; but I'll see you soon.
BIANCA: 'Tis very good. I must be circumstanced.°

[*Exeunt omnes.*]

Act IV

Scene I. Before the Citadel

Enter Othello and Iago.

IAGO: Will you think so?
OTHELLO: Think so, Iago?
IAGO: What,
To kiss in private?
OTHELLO: An unauthorized kiss!
IAGO: Or to be naked with her friend in bed
An hour or more, not meaning any harm?
OTHELLO: Naked in bed, Iago, and not mean harm? 5
It is hypocrisy against the devil.
They that mean virtuously and yet do so,
The devil their virtue tempts, and they tempt heaven.

---

184 demanded inquired for   **185 like** likely   **189 addition** i.e., addition to my reputation   **194 bring** accompany   **198 be circumstanced** be governed by circumstance, yield to your conditions

IAGO: If they do nothing, 'tis a venial° slip.
  But if I give my wife a handkerchief—   10
OTHELLO: What then?
IAGO: Why then, 'tis hers, my lord, and being hers,
  She may, I think, bestow 't on any man.
OTHELLO: She is protectress of her honor too.
  May she give that?   15
IAGO: Her honor is an essence that's not seen;
  They have it° very oft that have it not.
  But, for the handkerchief—
OTHELLO: By heaven, I would most gladly have forgot it.
  Thou saidst—O, it comes o'er my memory   20
  As doth the raven o'er the infectious house,°
  Boding to all—he had my handkerchief.
IAGO: Ay, what of that?
OTHELLO: That's not so good now.
IAGO: What
  If I had said I had seen him do you wrong?
  Or heard him say—as knaves be such abroad,°   25
  Who having, by their own importunate suit,
  Or voluntary dotage° of some mistress,
  Convincèd or supplied° them, cannot choose
  But they must blab—
OTHELLO: Hath he said anything?
IAGO: He hath, my lord; but, be you well assured,   30
  No more than he'll unswear.
OTHELLO: What hath he said?
IAGO: Faith, that he did—I know not what he did.
OTHELLO: What? What?
IAGO: Lie—
OTHELLO: With her?
IAGO: With her, on her; what you will.
OTHELLO: Lie with her? Lie on her? We say "lie on her" when
  they belie° her. Lie with her? Zounds, that's fulsome.°—   35

---

9 **venial** pardonable   17 **They have it** i.e., they enjoy a reputation for it   21 **raven . . . house**
(Allusion to the belief that the raven hovered over a house of sickness or infection, such as one
visited by the plague.)   25 **abroad** around about   27 **voluntary dotage** willing infatuation
28 **Convincèd or supplied** seduced or sexually gratified   35 **belie** slander   36 **fulsome** foul

Handkerchief—confessions—handkerchief!—To confess and be
hanged for his labor—first to be hanged and then to confess.°—
I tremble at it. Nature would not invest herself in such shad-
owing passion without some instruction.° It is not words° that
shakes me thus. Pish! Noses, ears, and lips.—Is 't possible?—
Confess—handkerchief!—O devil!   40

[*Falls in a trance.*]

IAGO: Work on,
My medicine, work! Thus credulous fools are caught,
And many worthy and chaste dames even thus,
All guiltless, meet reproach.—What, ho! My lord!   45
My lord, I say! Othello!

Enter Cassio.

                              How now, Cassio?
CASSIO: What's the matter?
IAGO: My lord is fall'n into an epilepsy.
This is his second fit. He had one yesterday.
CASSIO: Rub him about the temples.
IAGO: No, forbear.   50
The lethargy° must have his° quiet course.
If not, he foams at mouth, and by and by
Breaks out to savage madness. Look, he stirs.
Do you withdraw yourself a little while.
He will recover straight. When he is gone,   55
I would on great occasion° speak with you.

                                    [*Exit Cassio.*]

How is it, General? Have you not hurt your head?
OTHELLO: Dost thou mock me?°
IAGO: I mock you not, by heaven.
Would you would bear your fortune like a man!
OTHELLO: A hornèd man's a monster and a beast.   60

37–38 first . . . to confess (Othello reverses the proverbial *confess* and be *hanged*; Cassio is to be
given no time to confess before he dies.)   **38–39 Nature . . . instruction** i.e., without some
foundation in fact, nature would not have dressed herself in such an overwhelming passion that
comes over me now and fills my mind with images, or in such a lifelike fantasy as Cassio had in
his dream of lying with Desdemona   **39 words** mere words   **51 lethargy** coma.   **his** its   **56 on
great occasion** on a matter of great importance   **58 mock me** (Othello takes Iago's question about
hurting his head to be a mocking reference to the cuckold's horns.)

IAGO: There's many a beast then in a populous city,
        And many a civil° monster.
OTHELLO: Did he confess it?
IAGO: Good sir, be a man.
        Think every bearded fellow that's but yoked°   65
        May draw with you.° There's millions now alive
        That nightly lie in those unproper° beds
        Which they dare swear peculiar.° Your case is better.°
        O, 'tis the spite of hell, the fiend's arch-mock,
        To lip° a wanton in a secure° couch   70
        And to suppose her chaste! No, let me know,
        And knowing what I am,° I know what she shall be.°
OTHELLO: O, thou art wise. 'Tis certain.
IAGO: Stand you awhile apart;
        Confine yourself but in a patient list.°   75
        Whilst you were here o'erwhelmèd with your grief—
        A passion most unsuiting such a man—
        Cassio came hither. I shifted him away,°
        And laid good 'scuse upon your ecstasy,°
        Bade him anon return and here speak with me,   80
        The which he promised. Do but encave° yourself
        And mark the fleers,° the gibes, and notable° scorns
        That dwell in every region of his face;
        For I will make him tell the tale anew,
        Where, how, how oft, how long ago, and when   85
        He hath and is again to cope° your wife.
        I say, but mark his gesture. Marry, patience!
        Or I shall say you're all-in-all in spleen,°
        And nothing of a man.
OTHELLO: Dost thou hear, Iago?
        I will be found most cunning in my patience;   90
        But—dost thou hear?—most bloody.

---

62 civil i.e., dwelling in a city   **65 yoked** (1) married (2) put into the yoke of infamy and cuckoldry
66 draw with you pull as you do, like oxen who are yoked, i.e., share your fate as cuckold
67 unproper not exclusively their own   **68 peculiar** private, their own.   **better** i.e., because you
know the truth   **70 lip** kiss.   **secure** free from suspicion   **72 what I am** i.e., a cuckold.   **she shall
be** will happen to her   **75 in . . . list** within the bounds of patience   **78 shifted him away** used a
dodge to get rid of him   **79 ecstasy** trance   **81 encave** conceal   **82 fleers** sneers.   **notable**
obvious   **86 cope** encounter with, have sex with   **88 all-in-all in spleen** utterly governed by
passionate impulses

IAGO: That's not amiss;
But yet keep time° in all. Will you withdraw?

[*Othello stands apart.*]

Now will I question Cassio of Bianca,
A huswife° that by selling her desires
Buys herself bread and clothes. It is a creature   95
That dotes on Cassio—as 'tis the strumpet's plague
To beguile many and be beguiled by one.
He, when he hears of her, cannot restrain°
From the excess of laughter. Here he comes.

[*Enter Cassio.*]

As he shall smile, Othello shall go mad;   100
And his unbookish° jealousy must conster°
Poor Cassio's smiles, gestures, and light behaviors
Quite in the wrong.—How do you now, Lieutenant?

CASSIO: The worser that you give me the addition°
Whose want° even kills me.   105

IAGO: Ply Desdemona well and you are sure on 't.
[*Speaking lower.*] Now, if this suit lay in Bianca's power,
How quickly should you speed!

CASSIO [*laughing*]:   Alas, poor caitiff!°

OTHELLO [*aside*]:   Look how he laughs already!   110

IAGO: I never knew a woman love man so.

CASSIO: Alas, poor rogue! I think, i' faith, she loves me.

OTHELLO: Now he denies it faintly, and laughs it out.

IAGO: Do you hear, Cassio?

OTHELLO: Now he importunes him
To tell it o'er. Go to!° Well said,° well said.   115

IAGO: She gives it out that you shall marry her.
Do you intend it?

CASSIO: Ha, ha, ha!

OTHELLO: Do you triumph, Roman?° Do you triumph?

---

92 keep time keep yourself steady (as in music)   **94 huswife** hussy   **98 restrain** refrain
101 unbookish uninstructed.   **conster** construe   **104 addition** title   **105 Whose want** the lack of
which   **109 caitiff** wretch   **115 Go to** (An expression of remonstrance.)   **Well said** well done
119 Roman (The Romans were noted for their *triumphs* or triumphal processions.)

CASSIO: I marry her? What? A customer?° Prithee, bear some   120
charity to my wit;° do not think it so unwholesome. Ha, ha, ha!

OTHELLO: So, so, so, so! They laugh that win.°

IAGO: Faith, the cry° goes that you shall marry her.

CASSIO: Prithee, say true.

IAGO: I am a very villain else.°   125

OTHELLO: Have you scored me?° Well.

CASSIO: This is the monkey's own giving out. She is persuaded I
will marry her out of her own love and flattery,° not out of my
promise.

OTHELLO: Iago beckons me.° Now he begins the story.

CASSIO: She was here even now; she haunts me in every place. I   130
was the other day talking on the seabank° with certain Venetians, and thither comes the bauble,° and, by this hand,° she
falls me thus about my neck—

[He embraces Iago.]

OTHELLO: Crying, "O dear Cassio!" as it were; his gesture
imports it.

CASSIO: So hangs and lolls and weep upon me, so shakes and
pulls me. Ha, ha, ha!

OTHELLO: Now he tells how she plucked him to my chamber. O,   135
I see that nose of yours, but not that dog I shall throw it to.°

CASSIO: Well, I must leave her company.

IAGO: Before me,° look where she comes.

Enter Bianca [with Othello's handkerchief].

CASSIO: 'Tis such another fitchew!° Marry, a perfumed one.—
What do you mean by this haunting of me?

BIANCA: Let the devil and his dam° haunt you! What did you   140
mean by that same handkerchief you gave me even now? I
was a fine fool to take it. I must take out the work? A likely

---

120 **customer** i.e., prostitute.   **bear . . . wit** be more charitable to my judgment   122 **They . . . win**
i.e., they that laugh last laugh best   123 **cry** rumor   125 **I . . . else** call me a complete rogue if I'm
not telling the truth   126 **scored me** scored off me, beaten me, made up my reckoning, branded
me   128 **flattery** self-flattery, self-deception   129 **beckons** signals   131 **seabank** seashore
132 **bauble** plaything   **by this hand** I make my vow   136 **not . . . to** (Othello imagines himself
cutting off Cassio's nose and throwing it to a dog.)   138 **Before** me i.e., on my soul   139 **'Tis . . .**
fitchew what a polecat she is! Just like all the others. (Polecats were often compared with prostitutes
because of their rank smell and presumed lechery.)   141 **dam** mother

piece of work,° that you should find it in your chamber and know not who left it there! This is some minx's token, and I must take out the work? There; give it your hobbyhorse.° [*She* 145 *gives him the handkerchief.*] Wheresoever you had it, I'll take out no work on 't.

CASSIO: How now, my sweet Bianca? How now? How now?

OTHELLO: By heaven, that should be° my handkerchief!

BIANCA: If you'll come to supper tonight, you may; if you will not, come when you are next prepared for.° 150

[*Exit.*]

IAGO: After her, after her.

CASSIO: Faith, I must. She'll rail in the streets else.

IAGO: Will you sup there?

CASSIO: Faith, I intend so.

IAGO: Well, I may chance to see you, for I would very fain speak with you. 155

CASSIO: Prithee, come. Will you?

IAGO: Go to.° Say no more.

[*Exit Cassio.*]

OTHELLO [*advancing*]:   How shall I murder him, Iago?

IAGO: Did you perceive how he laughed at his vice?

OTHELLO: O, Iago! 160

IAGO: And did you see the handkerchief?

OTHELLO: Was that mine?

IAGO: Yours, by this hand. And to see how he prizes the foolish woman your wife! She gave it him, and he hath given it his whore.

OTHELLO: I would have him nine years a-killing. A fine woman! A fair woman! A sweet woman! 165

IAGO: Nay, you must forget that.

OTHELLO: Ay, let her rot and perish, and be damned tonight, for she shall not live. No, my heart is turned to stone; I strike it, and it hurts my hand. O, the world hath not a sweeter creature! She might lie by an emperor's side and command him tasks. 170

---

143 **A likely . . . work** a fine story   145 **hobbyhorse** harlot   148 **should be** must be   149–150 **when . . . for** when I'm ready for you (i.e., never)   157 **Go to** (an expression of remonstrance)

IAGO: Nay, that's not your way.°

OTHELLO: Hang her! I do but say what she is. So delicate with
her needle! An admirable musician! O, she will sing the savage-
ness out of a bear. Of so high and plenteous wit and invention!° 175

IAGO: She's the worse for all this.

OTHELLO: O, a thousand, a thousand times! And then, of so gentle a condition!°

IAGO: Ay, too gentle.°

OTHELLO: Nay, that's certain. But yet the pity of it, Iago! O, Iago,
the pity of it, Iago!   180

IAGO: If you are so fond° over her iniquity, give her patent° to offend, for if it touch not you it comes near nobody.

OTHELLO: I will chop her into messes.° Cuckold me?

IAGO: O, 'tis foul in her.

OTHELLO: With mine officer?   185

IAGO: That's fouler.

OTHELLO: Get me some poison, Iago, this night. I'll not ex-
postulate with her, lest her body and beauty unprovide° my
mind again. This night, Iago.

IAGO: Do it not with poison. Strangle her in her bed, even the
bed she hath contaminated.   190

OTHELLO: Good, good! The justice of it pleases. Very good.

IAGO: And for Cassio, let me be his undertaker.° You shall hear
more by midnight.

OTHELLO: Excellent good. [A trumpet within.] What trumpet is
that same?

IAGO: I warrant, something from Venice.

[Enter Lodovico, Desdemona, and attendants.]

'Tis Lodovico. This comes from the Duke.   195
See, your wife's with him.

LODOVICO: God save you, worthy General!

OTHELLO: With all my heart,° sir.

LODOVICO [giving him a letter]:   The Duke and the senators of
Venice greet you.

172 your way i.e., the way you should think of her   175 invention imagination   177 gentle a
condition well-born and well-bred   178 gentle generous, yielding (to other men)   181 fond foolish.
patent license   183 messes portions of meat, i.e., bits   188 unprovide weaken, render unfit
192 be his undertaker undertake to dispatch him   197 With all my heart i.e., I thank you most heartily

OTHELLO: I kiss the instrument of their pleasures.

[*He opens the letter, and reads.*]

DESDEMONA: And what's the news, good cousin Lodovico? 200

IAGO: I am very glad to see you, signor.
  Welcome to Cyprus.

LODOVICO: I thank you. How does Lieutenant Cassio?

IAGO: Lives, sir.

DESDEMONA: Cousin, there's fall'n between him and my lord 205
  An unkind° breach; but you shall make all well.

OTHELLO: Are you sure of that?

DESDEMONA: My lord?

OTHELLO [*reads*]: "This fail you not to do, as you will—"

LODOVICO: He did not call; he's busy in the paper. 210
  Is there division twixt my lord and Cassio?

DESDEMONA: A most unhappy one. I would do much
  T' atone° them, for the love I bear to Cassio.

OTHELLO: Fire and brimstone!

DESDEMONA: My lord? 215

OTHELLO: Are you wise?

DESDEMONA: What, is he angry?

LODOVICO: Maybe the letter moved him;
  For, as I think, they do command him home,
  Deputing Cassio in his government.°

DESDEMONA: By my troth, I am glad on 't.° 220

OTHELLO: Indeed?

DESDEMONA: My lord?

OTHELLO: I am glad to see you mad.°

DESDEMONA: Why, sweet Othello—

OTHELLO [*striking her*]: Devil! 225

DESDEMONA: I have not deserved this.

LODOVICO: My lord, this would not be believed in Venice,
  Though I should swear I saw 't. 'Tis very much.°
  Make her amends; she weeps.

---

206 unkind unnatural, contrary to their natures; hurtful **213 atone** reconcile **219 government** office **220 on 't** of it **223 I am . . . mad** i.e., I am glad to see that you are insane enough to rejoice in Cassio's promotion (? Othello bitterly plays on Desdemona's *I am glad.*) **228 very much** too much, outrageous

OTHELLO: O devil, devil!
　　If that the earth could teem° with woman's tears,　　　230
　　Each drop she falls would prove a crocodile.°
　　Out of my sight!
DESDEMONA: I will not stay to offend you. [*Going.*]
LODOVICO: Truly, an obedient lady.
　　I do beseech your lordship, call her back.
OTHELLO: Mistress!　　　235
DESDEMONA [*returning*]: My lord?
OTHELLO: What would you with her, sir?°
LODOVICO: Who, I, my lord?
OTHELLO: Ay, you did wish that I would make her turn.
　　Sir, she can turn, and turn, and yet go on　　　240
　　And turn again; and she can weep, sir, weep;
　　And she's obedient,° as you say, obedient,
　　Very obedient.—Proceed you in your tears.—
　　Concerning this, sir—O well-painted passion!°—
　　I am commanded home.—Get you away;　　　245
　　I'll send for you anon.—Sir, I obey the mandate
　　And will return to Venice.—Hence, avaunt!

　　　　　　　　　　　　　　　　[*Exit Desdemona.*]

　　Cassio shall have my place. And, sir, tonight
　　I do entreat that we may sup together.
　　You are welcome, sir, to Cyprus.—Goats and monkeys!°　[*Exit.*] 250
LODOVICO: Is this the noble Moor whom our full Senate
　　Call all in all sufficient? Is this the nature
　　Whom passion could not shake? Whose solid virtue
　　The shot of accident nor dart of chance
　　Could neither graze nor pierce?
IAGO: 　　　　　　　　　　　　He is much changed.　　　255
LODOVICO: Are his wits safe? Is he not light of brain?
IAGO: He's that he is. I may not breathe my censure

---

230 teem breed, be impregnated　　**231 falls ... crocodile** (Crocodiles were supposed to weep hypocritical tears for their victims.)　　**237 What ... sir** (Othello implies that Desdemona is pliant and will do a *turn*, lines 239–241, for any man.)　　**242 obedient** (with much the same sexual connotation as *turn* in lines 239–241)　　**244 passion** i.e., grief　　**250 Goats and monkeys** (See Act III, Scene iii, line 419.)

What he might be. If what he might he is not,
I would to heaven he were!°

LODOVICO: What, strike his wife?

IAGO: Faith, that was not so well; yet would I knew   260
That stroke would prove the worst!

LODOVICO: Is it his use?°
Or did the letters work upon his blood°
And new-create his fault?

IAGO: Alas, alas!
It is not honesty in me to speak
What I have seen and known. You shall observe him,   265
And his own courses will denote° him so
That I may save my speech. Do but go after,
And mark how he continues.

LODOVICO: I am sorry that I am deceived in him.   *Exeunt.*

Scene II. The Citadel

Enter Othello and Emilia.

OTHELLO: You have seen nothing then?

EMILIA: Nor ever heard, nor ever did suspect.

OTHELLO: Yes, you have seen Cassio and she together.

EMILIA: But then I saw no harm, and then I heard
Each syllable that breath made up between them.   5

OTHELLO: What, did they never whisper?

EMILIA: Never, my lord.

OTHELLO: Nor send you out o' the way?

EMILIA: Never.

OTHELLO: To fetch her fan, her gloves, her mask, nor nothing?   10

EMILIA: Never, my lord.

OTHELLO: That's strange.

EMILIA: I durst, my lord, to wager she is honest,
Lay down my soul at stake.° If you think other,
Remove your thought; it doth abuse your bosom.°   15

257–259 I may . . . were i.e., I dare not venture an opinion as to whether he's of unsound mind, as
you suggest, but, if he isn't, then it might be better to wish he were in fact insane, since only that
could excuse his wild behavior   **261 use** custom   **262 blood** passions   **266 courses will denote**
actions will reveal
14 at stake as the wager   **15 abuse your bosom** deceive you

If any wretch have put this in your head,
Let heaven requite it with the serpent's curse!°
For if she be not honest, chaste, and true,
There's no man happy; the purest of their wives
Is foul as slander.

OTHELLO: Bid her come hither. Go.   20

[Exit Emilia.]

She says enough; yet she's a simple bawd
That cannot say as much.° This° is a subtle whore,
A closet lock and key° of villainous secrets.
And yet she'll kneel and pray; I have seen her do 't.

[Enter Desdemona and Emilia.]

DESDEMONA: My lord, what is your will?   25
OTHELLO: Pray you, chuck, come hither.
DESDEMONA: What is your pleasure?
OTHELLO: Let me see your eyes.
Look in my face.
DESDEMONA: What horrible fancy's this?
OTHELLO [to Emilia]:   Some of your function,° mistress.
Leave procreants° alone and shut the door;   30
Cough or cry "hem" if anybody come.
Your mystery, your mystery!° Nay, dispatch.

[Exit Emilia.]

DESDEMONA [kneeling]:   Upon my knees, what doth your
speech import?
I understand a fury in your words,
But not the words.   35
OTHELLO: Why, what art thou?
DESDEMONA: Your wife, my lord, your true
And loyal wife.
OTHELLO: Come, swear it, damn thyself,

WILLIAM SHAKESPEARE

172

---

17 **the serpent's curse** the curse pronounced by God on the serpent for deceiving Eve, just as some
man has done to Othello and Desdemona. (See Genesis 3:14.)   **21-22 she's . . . much** i.e., any
procuress or go-between who couldn't make up as plausible a story as Emilia's would have to be
pretty stupid   **22 This** i.e., Desdemona   **23 closet lock and key** i.e., concealer   **29 Some . . .
function** i.e., practice your chosen profession, that of bawd (by guarding the door)   **30 procreants**
mating couples   **32 mystery** trade, occupation

Lest, being like one of heaven,° the devils themselves
Should fear to seize thee. Therefore be double damned:
Swear thou art honest.

DESDEMONA: Heaven doth truly know it.   40

OTHELLO: Heaven truly knows that thou art false as hell.

DESDEMONA: To whom, my lord? With whom? How am I false?

OTHELLO [*weeping*]:   Ah, Desdemon! Away, away, away!

DESDEMONA: Alas the heavy day! Why do you weep?
Am I the motive° of these tears, my lord?   45
If haply you my father do suspect
An instrument of this your calling back,
Lay not your blame on me. If you have lost him,
I have lost him too.

OTHELLO: Had it pleased heaven
To try me with affliction, had they° rained   50
All kinds of sores and shames on my bare head,
Steeped me in poverty to the very lips,
Given to captivity me and my utmost hopes,
I should have found in some place of my soul
A drop of patience. But, alas, to make me   55
A fixèd figure for the time of scorn°
To point his° slow and moving finger° at!
Yet could I bear that too, well, very well.
But there where I have garnered° up my heart,
Where either I must live or bear no life,   60
The fountain° from the which my current runs
Or else dries up—to be discarded thence!
Or keep it as a cistern° for foul toads
To knot° and gender° in! Turn thy complexion there,°
Patience, thou young and rose-lipped cherubin—   65
Ay, there look grim as hell!°

DESDEMONA: I hope my noble lord esteems me honest.°

---

38 being . . . heaven looking like an angel   **45 motive** cause   **50 they** i.e., heavenly powers
56 time of scorn i.e., scornful world   **57 his** its.   **slow and moving finger** i.e., hour hand of the
clock, moving so slowly it seems hardly to move at all. (Othello envisages himself as being eternally
pointed at by the scornful world as the numbers on a clock are pointed at by the hour hand.)
59 garnered stored   **61 fountain** spring   **63 cistern** cesspool   **64 knot** couple.   **gender** engender.
Turn . . . there change your color, grow pale, at such a sight   **65–66 Patience . . . hell** (Even
Patience, that rose-lipped cherub, will look grim and pale at this spectacle.)   **67 honest** chaste

OTHELLO: O, ay, as summer flies are in the shambles,°
    That quicken° even with blowing.° O thou weed,
    Who art so lovely fair and smell'st so sweet   70
    That the sense aches at thee, would thou hadst ne'er been born!
DESDEMONA: Alas, what ignorant° sin have I committed?
OTHELLO: Was this fair paper, this most goodly book,
    Made to write "whore" upon? What committed?
    Committed? O thou public commoner!°   75
    I should make very forges of my cheeks,
    That would to cinders burn up modesty,
    Did I but speak thy deeds. What committed?
    Heaven stops the nose at it and the moon winks;°
    The bawdy° wind, that kisses all it meets,   80
    Is hushed within the hollow mine° of earth
    And will not hear 't. What committed?
    Impudent strumpet!
DESDEMONA: By heaven, you do me wrong.
OTHELLO: Are not you a strumpet?
DESDEMONA: No, as I am a Christian.   85
    If to preserve this vessel° for my lord
    From any other foul unlawful touch
    Be not to be a strumpet, I am none.
OTHELLO: What, not a whore?
DESDEMONA: No, as I shall be saved.   90
OTHELLO: Is 't possible?
DESDEMONA: O, heaven forgive us!
OTHELLO: I cry you mercy,° then.
    I took you for that cunning whore of Venice
    That married with Othello. [*Calling out.*] You, mistress,
    That have the office opposite to Saint Peter   95
    And keep the gate of hell!

    [*Enter Emilia.*]

            You, you, ay, you!

---

68 shambles slaughterhouse   **69 quicken** come to life.   **with blowing** i.e., with the puffing up of something rotten in which maggots are breeding   **72 ignorant sin** sin in ignorance
75 commoner prostitute   **79 winks** closes her eyes. (The moon symbolizes chastity.)   **80 bawdy** kissing one and all   **81 mine** cave (where the winds were thought to dwell)   **86 vessel** body
92 cry you mercy beg your pardon

We have done our course.° There's money for your pains.
[*He gives money.*]
I pray you, turn the key and keep our counsel.   [*Exit.*]
EMILIA: Alas, what does this gentleman conceive?°
How do you, madam? How do you, my good lady?   100
DESDEMONA: Faith, half asleep.°
EMILIA: Good madam, what's the matter with my lord?
DESDEMONA: With who?
EMILIA: Why, with my lord, madam.
DESDEMONA: Who is thy lord?
EMILIA: He that is yours, sweet lady.   105
DESDEMONA: I have none. Do not talk to me, Emilia.
I cannot weep, nor answers have I none
But what should go by water.° Prithee, tonight
Lay on my bed my wedding sheets, remember;
And call thy husband hither.   110
EMILIA: Here's a change indeed!   [*Exit.*]
DESDEMONA: 'Tis meet I should be used so, very meet.°
How have I been behaved, that he might stick°
The small'st opinion° on my least misuse?°

[*Enter Iago and Emilia.*]

IAGO: What is your pleasure, madam? How is 't with you?   115
DESDEMONA: I cannot tell. Those that do teach young babes
Do it with gentle means and easy tasks.
He might have chid me so, for, in good faith,
I am a child to chiding.
IAGO: What is the matter, lady?   120
EMILIA: Alas, Iago, my lord hath so bewhored her,
Thrown such despite and heavy terms upon her,
That true hearts cannot bear it.
DESDEMONA: Am I that name, Iago?
IAGO: What name, fair lady?   125
DESDEMONA: Such as she said my lord did say I was.
EMILIA: He called her whore. A beggar in his drink
Could not have laid such terms upon his callet.°

---

97 **course** business (with an indecent suggestion of "trick," turn at sex)   99 **conceive** suppose, think
101 **half asleep** i.e., dazed   108 **go by water** be expressed by tears   112 **meet** fitting   113 **stick**
attach   114 **opinion** censure.   **least misuse** slightest misconduct   128 **callet** whore

IAGO: Why did he so?

DESDEMONA [*weeping*]:   I do not know. I am sure I am none
    such.   130

IAGO: Do not weep, do not weep. Alas the day!

EMILIA: Hath she forsook so many noble matches,
    Her father and her country and her friends,
    To be called whore? Would it not make one weep?

DESDEMONA: It is my wretched fortune.

IAGO: Beshrew° him for 't!   135
    How comes this trick° upon him?

DESDEMONA: Nay, heaven doth know.

EMILIA: I will be hanged if some eternal° villain,
    Some busy and insinuating° rogue,
    Some cogging,° cozening° slave, to get some office,
    Have not devised this slander. I will be hanged else.   140

IAGO: Fie, there is no such man. It is impossible.

DESDEMONA: If any such there be, heaven pardon him!

EMILIA: A halter° pardon him! And hell gnaw his bones!
    Why should he call her whore? Who keeps her company?
    What place? What time? What form?° What likelihood?   145
    The Moor's abused by some most villainous knave,
    Some base notorious knave, some scurvy fellow.
    O heaven, that° such companions° thou'dst unfold,°
    And put in every honest hand a whip
    To lash the rascals naked through the world   150
    Even from the east to th' west!

IAGO: Speak within door.°

EMILIA: O, fie upon them! Some such squire° he was
    That turned your wit the seamy side without°
    And made you to suspect me with the Moor.

IAGO: You are a fool. Go to.°

DESDEMONA: Alas, Iago,   155
    What shall I do to win my lord again?
    Good friend, go to him; for, by this light of heaven,

WILLIAM SHAKESPEARE

176

---

135 Beshrew curse **136 trick** strange behavior, delusion **137 eternal** inveterate **138 insinuating** ingratiating, fawning, wheedling **139 cogging** cheating. **cozening** defrauding **143 halter** hangman's noose **145 form** appearance, circumstance **148 that** would that **companions** fellows **unfold** expose **151 within door** i.e., not so loud **152 squire** fellow **153 seamy side without** wrong side out **155 Go to** i.e., that's enough

I know not how I lost him. Here I kneel. [*She kneels.*]
If e'er my will did trespass 'gainst his love,
Either in discourse° of thought or actual deed,   160
Or that° mine eyes, mine ears, or any sense
Delighted them° in any other form;
Or that I do not yet,° and ever did,
And ever will—though he do shake me off
To beggarly divorcement—love him dearly,   165
Comfort forswear° me! Unkindness may do much,
And his unkindness may defeat° my life,
But never taint my love. I cannot say "whore."
It does abhor° me now I speak the word;
To do the act that might the addition° earn   170
Not the world's mass of vanity° could make me.

[*She rises.*]

IAGO: I pray you, be content. 'Tis but his humor.°
The business of the state does him offense,
And he does chide with you.
DESDEMONA: If 'twere no other—   175
IAGO: It is but so, I warrant. [*Trumpets within.*]
Hark, how these instruments summon you to supper!
The messengers of Venice stays the meat.°
Go in, and weep not. All things shall be well.

[*Exeunt Desdemona and Emilia.*]
[*Enter Roderigo.*]

How now, Roderigo?   180
RODERIGO: I do not find that thou deal'st justly with me.
IAGO: What in the contrary?
RODERIGO: Every day thou daff'st me° with some device,° Iago,
and rather, as it seems to me now, keep'st from me all conve-
niency° than suppliest me with the least advantage° of hope. I   185

---

160 **discourse of thought** process of thinking   161 **that** if (also in line 163)   162 **Delighted them**
took delight   163 **yet** still   166 **Comfort forswear** may heavenly comfort forsake   167 **defeat**
destroy   169 **abhor** (1) fill me with abhorrence (2) make me whorelike   170 **addition** title
171 **vanity** showy splendor   172 **humor** mood   178 **stays the meat** are waiting to dine   183 **thou
daff'st me** you put me off.   **device** excuse, trick   184 **conveniency** advantage, opportunity
185 **advantage** increase

will indeed no longer endure it, nor am I yet persuaded to put up° in peace what already I have foolishly suffered.

IAGO: Will you hear me, Roderigo?

RODERIGO: Faith, I have heard too much, for your words and performances are no kin together.

IAGO: You charge me most unjustly. 190

RODERIGO: With naught but truth. I have wasted myself out of my means. The jewels you have had from me to deliver° Desdemona would half have corrupted a votarist.° You have told me she hath received them and returned me expectations and comforts of sudden respect° and acquaintance, but I find none. 195

IAGO: Well, go to, very well.

RODERIGO: "Very well"! "Go to"! I cannot go to,° man, nor 'tis not very well. By this hand, I think it is scurvy, and begin to find myself fopped° in it.

IAGO: Very well.

RODERIGO: I tell you 'tis not very well.° I will make myself 200 known to Desdemona. If she will return me my jewels, I will give over my suit and repent my unlawful solicitation; if not, assure yourself I will seek satisfaction° of you.

IAGO: You have said now?°

RODERIGO: Ay, and said nothing but what I protest intendment° of doing.

IAGO: Why, now I see there's mettle in thee, and even from this 205 instant do build on thee a better opinion than ever before. Give me thy hand, Roderigo. Thou hast taken against me a most just exception; but yet I protest I have dealt most directly in thy affair.

RODERIGO: It hath not appeared.

IAGO: I grant indeed it hath not appeared, and your suspicion is 210 not without wit and judgment. But, Roderigo, if thou hast that in thee indeed which I have greater reason to believe now than ever—I mean purpose, courage, and valor—this night

---

186 **put up** submit to, tolerate   192 **deliver** deliver to   193 **votarist** nun   194 **sudden respect** immediate consideration   197 **I cannot go to** (Roderigo changes Iago's *go to*, an expression urging patience, to *I cannot go to*, "I have no opportunity for success in wooing.")   198 **fopped** fooled, duped   200 **not very well** (Roderigo changes Iago's *very well*, "all right, then," to *not very well*, "not at all good.")   202 **satisfaction** repayment. (The term normally means settling of accounts in a duel.)   203 **You . . . now** have you finished?   204 **intendment** intention

show it. If thou the next night following enjoy not Desdemona, take me from this world with treachery and devise engines for° my life.   215

RODERIGO: Well, what is it? Is it within reason and compass?

IAGO: Sir, there is especial commission come from Venice to de-
pute Cassio in Othello's place.

RODERIGO: Is that true? Why, then Othello and Desdemona return again to Venice.   220

IAGO: O, no; he goes into Mauritania and takes away with him
the fair Desdemona, unless his abode be lingered here by
some accident; wherein none can be so determinate° as the
removing of Cassio.

RODERIGO: How do you mean, removing of him?

IAGO: Why, by making him uncapable of Othello's place—knocking   225
out his brains.

RODERIGO: And that you would have me to do?

IAGO: Ay, if you dare do yourself a profit and a right. He sups
tonight with a harlotry,° and thither will I go to him. He
knows not yet of his honorable fortune. If you will watch his
going thence, which I will fashion to fall out° between twelve   230
and one, you may take him at your pleasure. I will be near to
second your attempt, and he shall fall between us. Come,
stand not amazed at it, but go along with me. I will show you
such a necessity in his death that you shall think yourself
bound to put it on him. It is now high° suppertime, and the
night grows to waste.° About it.   235

RODERIGO: I will hear further reason for this.

IAGO: And you shall be satisfied.   [*Exeunt.*]

Scene III. The Citadel

Enter Othello, Lodovico, Desdemona, Emilia, and attendants.

LODOVICO: I do beseech you, sir, trouble yourself no further.

OTHELLO: O, pardon me; 'twill do me good to walk.

LODOVICO: Madam, good night. I humbly thank your ladyship.

DESDEMONA: Your honor is most welcome.

---

214 engines for plots against   **223 determinate** conclusive   **229 harlotry** slut   **230 fall out** occur
234 high fully   **235 grows to waste** wastes away

OTHELLO: Will you walk, sir? 5

O, Desdemona!

DESDEMONA: My lord?

OTHELLO: Get you to bed on th' instant.
I will be returned forthwith. Dismiss your attendant there.
Look 't be done.

DESDEMONA: I will, my lord. 10

Exit [Othello, with Lodovico and attendants].

EMILIA: How goes it now? He looks gentler than he did.

DESDEMONA: He says he will return incontinent,°
And hath commanded me to go to bed,
And bid me to dismiss you.

EMILIA: Dismiss me? 15

DESDEMONA: It was his bidding. Therefore, good Emilia,
Give me my nightly wearing, and adieu.
We must not now displease him.

EMILIA: I would you had never seen him!

DESDEMONA: So would not I. My love doth so approve him 20
That even his stubbornness,° his checks,° his frowns—
Prithee, unpin me—have grace and favor in them.

[Emilia prepares Desdemona for bed.]

EMILIA: I have laid those sheets you bade me on the bed.

DESDEMONA: All's one.° Good faith, how foolish are our minds!
If I do die before thee, prithee shroud me 25
In one of these same sheets.

EMILIA: Come, come, you talk.°

DESDEMONA: My mother had a maid called Barbary.
She was in love, and he she loved proved mad°
And did forsake her. She had a song of "Willow."
An old thing 'twas, but it expressed her fortune, 30
And she died singing it. That song tonight
Will not go from my mind; I have much to do
But to go hang° my head all at one side
And sing it like poor Barbary. Prithee, dispatch.

---

12 incontinent immediately   **21 stubbornness** roughness   **checks** rebukes   **24 All's one** all right.
It doesn't really matter   **26 talk** i.e., prattle   **28 mad** wild, i.e., faithless   **32–33 I . . . hang** I can
scarcely keep myself from hanging

WILLIAM SHAKESPEARE

EMILIA: Shall I go fetch your nightgown?° 35
DESDEMONA: No, unpin me here.
   This Lodovico is a proper° man.
EMILIA: A very handsome man.
DESDEMONA: He speaks well.
EMILIA: I know a lady in Venice would have walked barefoot to 40
   Palestine for a touch of his nether lip.
DESDEMONA [singing]:
    "The poor soul sat sighing by a sycamore tree,
    Sing all a green willow;°
    Her hand on her bosom, her head on her knee,
    Sing willow, willow, willow. 45
    The fresh streams ran by her and murmured her moans;
    Sing willow, willow, willow;
    Her salt tears fell from her, and softened the stones—"
   Lay by these.
     [*Singing.*] "Sing willow, willow, willow—" 50
   Prithee, hie thee.° He'll come anon.°
   [*Singing.*] "Sing all a green willow must be my garland.
   Let nobody blame him; his scorn I approve—"
   Nay, that's not next.—Hark! Who is 't that knocks?
EMILIA: It's the wind.
DESDEMONA [singing]:
    "I called my love false love; but what said he then? 55
    Sing willow, willow, willow;
    If I court more women, you'll couch with more men."
   So, get thee gone. Good night. Mine eyes do itch;
   Doth that bode weeping?
EMILIA: 'Tis neither here nor there. 60
DESDEMONA: I have heard it said so. O, these men, these men!
   Dost thou in conscience think—tell me, Emilia—
   That there be women do abuse° their husbands
   In such gross kind?
EMILIA: There be some such, no question.
DESDEMONA: Wouldst thou do such a deed for all the world? 65
EMILIA: Why, would not you?

35 **nightgown** dressing gown   37 **proper** handsome   43 **willow** (A conventional emblem of disappointed love.)   51 **hie thee** hurry.   **anon** right away   63 **abuse** deceive

DESDEMONA: No, by this heavenly light!

EMILIA: Nor I neither by this heavenly light;
I might do 't as well i' the dark.

DESDEMONA: Wouldst thou do such a deed for all the world?

EMILIA: The world's a huge thing. It is a great price   70
For a small vice.

DESDEMONA: Good troth, I think thou wouldst not.

EMILIA: By my troth, I think I should, and undo 't when I had
done. Marry, I would not do such a thing for a joint ring,° nor
for measures of lawn,° nor for gowns, petticoats, nor caps, nor
any petty exhibition.° But for all the whole world! Uds° pity,   75
who would not make her husband a cuckold to make him a
monarch? I should venture purgatory for 't.

DESDEMONA: Beshrew me if I would do such a wrong
For the whole world.

EMILIA: Why, the wrong is but a wrong i' the world, and having
the world for your labor, 'tis a wrong in your own world, and
you might quickly make it right.   80

DESDEMONA: I do not think there is any such woman.

EMILIA: Yes, a dozen, and as many
To th' vantage° as would store° the world they played° for.   85
But I do think it is their husbands' faults
If wives do fall. Say that they slack their duties°
And pour our treasures into foreign laps,°
Or else break out in peevish jealousies,
Throwing restraint upon us? Or say they strike us,°   90
Or scant our former having in despite?°
Why, we have galls,° and though we have some grace,
Yet have we some revenge. Let husbands know
Their wives have sense° like them. They see, and smell,
And have their palates both for sweet and sour,   95
As husbands have. What is it that they do
When they change us for others? Is it sport?°
I think it is. And doth affection° breed it?

---

74 **joint ring** a ring made in separate halves.   **lawn** fine linen   75 **exhibition** gift   76 **Uds** God's
85 **To th' vantage** in addition, to boot   **store** populate   **played** (1) gambled (2) sported sexually
87 **duties** marital duties   88 **pour . . . laps** i.e., are unfaithful, give what is rightfully ours (semen)
to other women   90 **Throwing . . . us** i.e., jealously restricting our freedom to see other men
91 **scant . . . despite** reduce our allowance to spite us   92 **have galls** i.e., are capable of resenting
injury and insult   94 **sense** physical sense   97 **sport** sexual pastime   98 **affection** passion

I think it doth. Is 't frailty that thus errs?
It is so, too. And have not we affections,   100
Desires for sport, and frailty, as men have?
Then let them use us well; else let them know,
The ills we do, their ills instruct us so.
DESDEMONA: Good night, good night. God me such uses° send
Not to pick bad from bad, but by bad mend!°   105

[*Exeunt.*]

Act V

Scene I. A Street in Cyprus

Enter Iago and Roderigo.

IAGO: Here stand behind this bulk.° Straight will he come.
Wear thy good rapier bare,° and put it home.
Quick, quick! Fear nothing. I'll be at thy elbow.
It makes us or it mars us. Think on that,
And fix most firm thy resolution.   5
RODERIGO: Be near at hand. I may miscarry in 't.
IAGO: Here, at thy hand. Be bold, and take thy stand.

[*Iago stands aside. Roderigo conceals himself.*]

RODERIGO: I have no great devotion to the deed;
And yet he hath given me satisfying reasons.
'Tis but a man gone. Forth, my sword! He dies.   10

[*He draws.*]

IAGO: I have rubbed this young quat° almost to the sense,°
And he grows angry. Now, whether he kill Cassio
Or Cassio him, or each do kill the other,
Every way makes my gain. Live Roderigo,°
He calls me to a restitution large   15
Of gold and jewels that I bobbed° from him
As gifts to Desdemona.

---

104 **uses** habit, practice   105 **Not . . . mend** i.e., not to learn bad conduct from others' badness (as Emilia has suggested women learn from men), but to mend my ways by perceiving what badness is, making spiritual benefit out of evil and adversity
1 **bulk** framework projecting from the front of a shop   2 **bare** unsheathed   11 **quat** pimple, pustule.   **to the sense** to the quick   14 **Live Roderigo** if Roderigo lives   16 **bobbed** swindled

It must not be. If Cassio do remain,
He hath a daily beauty in his life
That makes me ugly; and besides, the Moor   20
May unfold° me to him; there stand I in much peril.
No, he must die. Be 't so. I hear him coming.

[*Enter Cassio.*]

RODERIGO [*coming forth*]:   I know his gait, 'tis he.—Villain, thou
diest!

[*He attacks Cassio.*]

CASSIO: That thrust had been mine enemy indeed,
But that my coat° is better than thou know'st.   25
I will make proof° of thine.

[*He draws, and wounds Roderigo.*]

RODERIGO: O, I am slain! [*He falls.*]

[*Iago, from behind, wounds Cassio in the leg, and exits.*]

CASSIO: I am maimed forever. Help, ho! Murder! Murder!

[*Enter Othello.*]

OTHELLO: The voice of Cassio! Iago keeps his word.
RODERIGO: O, villain that I am!
OTHELLO: It is even so.   30
CASSIO: O, help, ho! Light! A surgeon!
OTHELLO: 'Tis he. O brave Iago, honest and just,
That hast such noble sense of thy friend's wrong!
Thou teachest me. Minion,° your dear lies dead,
And your unblest fate hies.° Strumpet, I come.   35
Forth of° my heart those charms, thine eyes, are blotted;
Thy bed, lust-stained, shall with lust's blood be spotted.

[*Exit Othello.*]

[*Enter Lodovico and Gratiano.*]

CASSIO: What ho! No watch? No passage?° Murder! Murder!

---

21 unfold expose   **25 coat** (Possibly a garment of mail under the outer clothing, or simply a
tougher coat than Roderigo expected.)   **26 proof** a test   **34 Minion** hussy (i.e., Desdemona)
35 hies hastens on   **36 Forth of** from out   **38 passage** people passing by

GRATIANO: 'Tis some mischance. The voice is very direful.
CASSIO: O, help! 40
LODOVICO: Hark!
RODERIGO: O wretched villain!
LODOVICO: Two or three groan. 'Tis heavy° night;
These may be counterfeits. Let's think 't unsafe
To come in to° the cry without more help. 45

[*They remain near the entrance.*]

RODERIGO: Nobody come? Then shall I bleed to death.

Enter Iago [in his shirtsleeves, with a light].

LODOVICO: Hark!
GRATIANO: Here's one comes in his shirt, with light and weapons.
IAGO: Who's there? Whose noise is this that cries on° murder?
LODOVICO: We do not know.
IAGO: Did not you hear a cry? 50
CASSIO: Here, here! For heaven's sake, help me!
IAGO: What's the matter?

[*He moves toward Cassio.*]

GRATIANO [*to Lodovico*]: This is Othello's ancient, as I take it.
LODOVICO [*to Gratiano*]: The same indeed, a very valiant fellow.
IAGO [*to Cassio*]: What° are you here that cry so grievously?
CASSIO: Iago? O, I am spoiled,° undone by villains! 55
Give me some help.
IAGO: O me, Lieutenant! What villains have done this?
CASSIO: I think that one of them is hereabout,
And cannot make° away.
IAGO: O treacherous villains!

[*To Lodovico and Gratiano.*]

What are you there? Come in, and give some help. [*They
advance.*] 60
RODERIGO: O, help me there!
CASSIO: That's one of them.

---

43 **heavy** thick, dark   45 **come in to** approach   49 **cries on** cries out   54 **What** who (also at lines
60 and 66)   55 **spoiled** ruined, done for   59 **make** get

IAGO: O murderous slave! O villain!

[*He stabs Roderigo.*]

RODERIGO: O damned Iago! O inhuman dog!

IAGO: Kill men i' the dark?—Where be these bloody thieves?—
How silent is this town!—Ho! Murder, murder!—   65
[*To Lodovico and Gratiano.*] What may you be? Are you of
good or evil?

LODOVICO: As you shall prove us, praise° us.

IAGO: Signor Lodovico?

LODOVICO: He, sir.

IAGO: I cry you mercy.° Here's Cassio hurt by villains.   70

GRATIANO: Cassio?

IAGO: How is 't, brother?

CASSIO: My leg is cut in two.

IAGO: Marry, heaven forbid!
Light, gentlemen! I'll bind it with my shirt.   75

[*He hands them the light, and tends to Cassio's wound.*]

[*Enter Bianca.*]

BIANCA: What is the matter, ho? Who is 't that cried?

IAGO: Who is 't that cried?

BIANCA: O my dear Cassio!
My sweet Cassio! O Cassio, Cassio, Cassio!

IAGO: O notable strumpet! Cassio, may you suspect
Who they should be that have thus mangled you?   80

CASSIO: No.

GRATIANO: I am sorry to find you thus. I have been to seek you.

IAGO: Lend me a garter. [*He applies a tourniquet.*] So.—O, for a
chair,°
To bear him easily hence!

BIANCA: Alas, he faints! O Cassio, Cassio, Cassio!   85

IAGO: Gentlemen all, I do suspect this trash
To be a party in this injury.—
Patience awhile, good Cassio.—Come, come;
Lend me a light. [*He shines the light on Roderigo.*] Know
we this face or no?

---

67 **praise** appraise   70 **I cry you mercy** I beg your pardon   83 **chair** litter

Alas, my friend and my dear countryman
Roderigo! No.—Yes, sure.—O heaven! Roderigo!
GRATIANO: What, of Venice?
IAGO: Even he, sir. Did you know him?
GRATIANO: Know him? Ay.
IAGO: Signor Gratiano? I cry your gentle° pardon.
These bloody accidents° must excuse my manners
That so neglected you.
GRATIANO: I am glad to see you.
IAGO: How do you, Cassio? O, a chair, a chair!
GRATIANO: Roderigo!
IAGO: He, he, 'tis he. [*A litter is brought in.*] O, that's well
said;° the chair.
Some good man bear him carefully from hence;
I'll fetch the General's surgeon. [*To Bianca.*] For you, mistress,
Save you your labor.°—He that lies slain here, Cassio,
Was my dear friend. What malice° was between you?
CASSIO: None in the world, nor do I know the man.
IAGO [*to Bianca*]:   What, look you pale?—O, bear him out
o' th' air.°

[*Cassio and Roderigo are borne off.*]

Stay you,° good gentlemen.—Look you pale, mistress?—
Do you perceive the gastness° of her eye?—
Nay, if you stare,° we shall hear more anon.—
Behold her well; I pray you, look upon her.
Do you see, gentlemen? Nay, guiltiness
Will speak, though tongues were out of use.

[*Enter Emilia.*]

EMILIA: 'Las, what's the matter? What's the matter, husband?
IAGO: Cassio hath here been set on in the dark
By Roderigo and fellows that are scaped.
He's almost slain, and Roderigo dead.
EMILIA: Alas, good gentleman! Alas, good Cassio!

90

95

100

105

110

115

---

95 gentle noble   **96 accidents** sudden events   **100 well said** well done   **103 Save . . . labor** i.e.,
never you mind tending Cassio   **104 malice** enmity   **106 bear . . . air** (Fresh air was thought to be
dangerous for a wound.)   **107 Stay you** (Lodovico and Gratiano are evidently about to leave.)
108 gastness terror   **109 stare** (Iago pretends to interpret Bianca's wild looks as an involuntary
confession of guilt.)

IAGO: This is the fruits of whoring. Prithee, Emilia,
Go know° of Cassio where he supped tonight.
[*To Bianca.*] What, do you shake at that?   120
BIANCA: He supped at my house, but I therefore shake not.
IAGO: O, did he so? I charge you go with me.
EMILIA: O, fie upon thee, strumpet!
BIANCA: I am no strumpet, but of life as honest°
As you that thus abuse me.   125
EMILIA: As I? Faugh! Fie upon thee!
IAGO: Kind gentlemen, let's go see poor Cassio dressed.°—
Come, mistress, you must tell's another tale.
Emilia, run you to the citadel
And tell my lord and lady what hath happed.—   130
Will you go on afore? [*Aside.*] This is the night
That either makes me or fordoes° me quite.   *Exeunt.*

Scene II. A bedchamber in the Citadel

Enter Othello [with a light], and Desdemona in her bed.°

OTHELLO: It is the cause,° it is the cause, my soul.
Let me not name it to you, you chaste stars!
It is the cause. Yet I'll not shed her blood,
Nor scar that whiter skin of hers than snow,
And smooth as monumental° alabaster.   5
Yet she must die, else she'll betray more men.
Put out the light, and then put out the light.°
If I quench thee, thou flaming minister,°
I can again thy former light restore,
Should I repent me;° but once put out thy light,   10
Thou cunning'st pattern° of excelling nature,
I know not where is that Promethean heat°
That can thy light relume.° When I have plucked thy rose,

---

119 know learn   **124 honest** chaste   **127 Cassio dressed** Cassio's wounds dressed   **132 fordoes**
undoes, ruins   **[s.d.] in her bed** (Either the curtains are drawn back to reveal the bed in a recessed
area backstage, or the bed is "thrust out" onstage as the scene begins.)
1 cause i.e., cause of justice, the offense itself, which Othello must correct as an agent of justice
5 monumental i.e., used in making tombs and funeral monuments   **7 the light . . . light** the torch
or lamp . . . Desdemona's life   **8 flaming minister** torch or lamp that serves me   **10 repent me**
change my mind   **11 Thou . . . pattern** you skillfully wrought perfect example   **12 Promethean
heat** divine fire (alluding to the theft of fire from heaven by Prometheus)   **13 relume** rekindle

WILLIAM SHAKESPEARE

I cannot give it vital growth again;
It needs must wither. I'll smell thee on the tree.   15

[*He kisses her.*]

O balmy breath, that dost almost persuade
Justice to break her sword! One more, one more.
Be thus when thou art dead, and I will kill thee,
And love thee after. One more, and that's the last.

[*He kisses her.*]

So sweet was ne'er so fatal. I must weep,   20
But they are cruel° tears. This sorrow's heavenly;
It strikes where it doth love.° She wakes.
DESDEMONA: Who's there? Othello?
OTHELLO: Ay, Desdemona.
DESDEMONA: Will you come to bed, my lord?   25
OTHELLO: Have you prayed tonight, Desdemon?
DESDEMONA: Ay, my lord.
OTHELLO: If you bethink yourself of any crime°
Unreconciled as yet to heaven and grace,
Solicit° for it straight.°   30
DESDEMONA: Alack, my lord, what may you mean by that?
OTHELLO: Well, do it, and be brief. I will walk by.
I would not kill thy unprepared spirit.
No, heaven forfend!° I would not kill thy soul.
DESDEMONA: Talk you of killing?
OTHELLO: Ay, I do.
DESDEMONA: Then heaven   35
Have mercy on me!
OTHELLO: Amen, with all my heart!
DESDEMONA: If you say so, I hope you will not kill me.
OTHELLO: Humh!
DESDEMONA: And yet I fear you; for you're fatal then
When your eyes roll so. Why I should fear I know not,   40
Since guiltiness I know not; but yet I feel I fear.
OTHELLO: Think on thy sins.

---

21 **cruel** unrelenting   22 **It . . . love** (Compare Hebrews 12:6: "For whom the Lord loveth he
chasteneth.")   28 **crime** sin   30 **Solicit** petition, pray.   **straight** immediately   34 **forfend** forbid

DESDEMONA: They are loves I bear to you.°

OTHELLO: Ay, and for that thou diest.

DESDEMONA: That death's unnatural that kills for loving.
Alas, why gnaw you so your nether lip?   45
Some bloody passion shakes your very frame.
These are portents; but yet I hope, I hope,
They do not point on° me.

OTHELLO: Peace, and be still!

DESDEMONA: I will so. What's the matter?   50

OTHELLO: That handkerchief which I so loved and gave thee
Thou gav'st to Cassio.

DESDEMONA: No, by my life and soul!
Send for the man and ask him.

OTHELLO: Sweet soul, take heed, take heed of perjury.
Thou art on thy deathbed.   55

DESDEMONA: Ay, but not yet to die.

OTHELLO: Yes, presently.°
Therefore confess thee freely of thy sin;
For to deny each article with oath
Cannot remove nor choke the strong conception°
That I do groan withal.° Thou art to die.   60

DESDEMONA: Then Lord have mercy on me!

OTHELLO: I say, amen.

DESDEMONA: And have you mercy too! I never did
Offend° you in my life; never loved Cassio
But with such general warranty° of heaven
As I might love. I never gave him token.   65

OTHELLO: By heaven, I saw my handkerchief in 's hand.
O perjured woman! Thou dost stone° my heart,
And makes me call what I intend to do
A murder, which I thought a sacrifice.
I saw the handkerchief.

DESDEMONA: He found it, then.   70
I never gave it him. Send for him hither;
Let him confess a truth.

---

42 **They are . . . you** i.e., if I sinned, it was in loving you more than my father or more than God
48 **point on** point at, predict what is to happen to   56 **presently** immediately   59 **conception**
(1) belief in your guilt (2) plan in my mind   60 **groan withal** (1) groan at in sorrow (2) as in giving
birth   63 **Offend** wrong   64 **warranty** sanction   67 **stone** turn to stone, harden

OTHELLO: He hath confessed.

DESDEMONA: What, my lord?

OTHELLO: That he hath used thee.

DESDEMONA: How? Unlawfully?

OTHELLO: Ay.

DESDEMONA: He will not say so.

OTHELLO: No, his mouth is stopped;   75
   Honest Iago hath ta'en order° for 't.

DESDEMONA: O, my fear interprets. What, is he dead?

OTHELLO: Had all his hairs been lives, my great revenge
   Had stomach for them all.

DESDEMONA: Alas, he is betrayed and I undone! [*She weeps.*]   80

OTHELLO: Out, strumpet! Weep'st thou for him to my face?

DESDEMONA: O, banish me, my lord, but kill me not!

OTHELLO: Down, strumpet!

DESDEMONA: Kill me tomorrow; let me live tonight!

OTHELLO: Nay, if you strive—   85

DESDEMONA: But half an hour!

OTHELLO: Being done,° there is no pause.

DESDEMONA: But while I say one prayer!

OTHELLO: It is too late.

[*Smothers her.*]

EMILIA [*at the door*]:   My lord, my lord! What, ho! My lord, my lord!

OTHELLO: What noise is this? Not dead? Not yet quite dead?
   I that am cruel am yet merciful;   90
   I would not have thee linger in thy pain.

[*He dispatches her.*]

                                   So, so.

EMILIA [*within*]:   What, ho! My lord, my lord!

OTHELLO: Who's there?

EMILIA [*within*]:   O, good my lord, I would speak a word with you!

OTHELLO: Yes, 'tis Emilia.—By and by.—She's dead.
   'Tis like° she comes to speak of Cassio's death.—   95
   The noise was here.° Ha! No more moving?

---

76 ta'en order taken measures   **86 Being done** i.e., since justice has begun its relentless course   **95 like** likely that   **96 here** (The Folio's *high* is possible, suggesting that the commotion of the attack on Cassio was loud.)

WILLIAM SHAKESPEARE

Still as the grave. Shall she come in? Were 't good?—
I think she stirs again. No. What's best to do?
If she come in, she'll sure speak to my wife.
My wife! My wife! What wife? I have no wife.   100
O, insupportable! O heavy hour!
Methinks it should be now a huge eclipse
Of sun and moon, and that th' affrighted globe
Should yawn° at alteration.°
EMILIA [*within*]:   I do beseech you
That I may speak with you, O, good my lord!   105
OTHELLO: I had forgot thee. O, come in, Emilia.—
Soft,° by and by. Let me the curtains draw.—

[*He closes the bed-curtains and opens the door.*]

Where art thou?

[*Enter Emilia.*]

                    What's the matter with thee now?
EMILIA: O, my good lord, yonder's foul murders done!
OTHELLO: What, now?   110
EMILIA: But now, my lord.
OTHELLO: It is the very error° of the moon;
She comes more nearer earth than she was wont,
And makes men mad.
EMILIA: Cassio, my lord, hath killed a young Venetian   115
Called Roderigo.
OTHELLO: Roderigo killed?
And Cassio killed?
EMILIA: No, Cassio is not killed.
OTHELLO: Not Cassio killed? Then murder's out of tune,
And sweet revenge grows harsh.
DESDEMONA: O, falsely, falsely murdered!   120
EMILIA: O Lord, what cry is that?
OTHELLO: That? What?
EMILIA: Out° and alas, that was my lady's voice.

[*She opens the bed-curtains.*]

---

104 yawn gape in amazement, i.e., move in an earthquake. (According to Pliny, earthquakes often happen during eclipses.)   **at alteration** at these cataclysmic events in nature, well-suited to express the horror of Desdemona's death   **107 Soft** wait a minute   **112 error** aberration, irregularity
123 Out (A cry of dismay, intensifying *alas*.)

Help, help, ho, help! O lady, speak again!
Sweet Desdemona! O sweet mistress, speak! 125
DESDEMONA: A guiltless death I die.
EMILIA: O, who hath done this deed?
DESDEMONA: Nobody; I myself. Farewell.
Commend me to my kind lord. O, farewell! [*She dies.*]
OTHELLO: Why, how should she be murdered?
EMILIA: Alas, who knows? 130
OTHELLO: You heard her say herself it was not I.
EMILIA: She said so. I must needs report the truth.
OTHELLO: She's like a liar gone to burning hell!
'Twas I that killed her.
EMILIA: O, the more angel she,
And you the blacker devil! 135
OTHELLO: She turned to folly,° and she was a whore.
EMILIA: Thou dost belie° her, and thou art a devil.
OTHELLO: She was false as water.
EMILIA: Thou art rash as fire to say
That she was false. O, she was heavenly true! 140
OTHELLO: Cassio did top her. Ask thy husband else.°
O, I were damned beneath all depth in hell
But that I did proceed upon just grounds
To this extremity. Thy husband knew it all.
EMILIA: My husband? 145
OTHELLO: Thy husband.
EMILIA: That she was false to wedlock?
OTHELLO: Ay, with Cassio. Nay, had she been true,
If heaven would make me such another world
Of one entire and perfect chrysolite,° 150
I'd not have sold her for it.
EMILIA: My husband?
OTHELLO: Ay, 'twas he that told me on her first.
An honest man he is, and hates the slime
That sticks on filthy deeds. 155
EMILIA: My husband?
OTHELLO: What needs this iterance,° woman? I say thy husband.

---

136 folly i.e., wantonness, fleshly sin **137 belie** slander **141 else** i.e., if you don't believe me
150 chrysolite precious topaz **157 iterance** iteration, repetition

EMILIA: O mistress, villainy hath made mocks with° love!
    My husband say she was false?

OTHELLO: He, woman;
    I say thy husband. Dost understand the word?   160
    My friend, thy husband, honest, honest Iago.

EMILIA: If he say so, may his pernicious soul
    Rot half a grain a day! He lies to th' heart.
    She was too fond of her most filthy bargain.

OTHELLO: Ha?   [*He draws.*]   165

EMILIA: Do thy worst!
    This deed of thine is no more worthy heaven
    Than thou wast worthy her.

OTHELLO: Peace, you were best.°

EMILIA: Thou hast not half that power to do me harm
    As I have to be hurt.° O gull!° O dolt!   170
    As ignorant as dirt! Thou hast done a deed—
    I care not for thy sword; I'll make thee known,
    Though I lost twenty lives.—Help! Help, ho, help!
    The Moor hath killed my mistress! Murder, murder!

[*Enter Montano, Gratiano, and Iago.*]

MONTANO: What is the matter? How now, General?   175

EMILIA: O, are you come, Iago? You have done well,
    That men must lay their murders on your neck.

GRATIANO: What is the matter?

EMILIA [*to Iago*]:   Disprove this villain, if thou be'st a man.
    He says thou toldst him that his wife was false.   180
    I know thou didst not; thou'rt not such a villain.
    Speak, for my heart is full.

IAGO: I told him what I thought, and told no more
    Than what he found himself was apt° and true.

EMILIA: But did you ever tell him she was false?   185

IAGO: I did.

EMILIA: You told a lie, an odious, damnèd lie!
    Upon my soul, a lie, a wicked lie.
    She false with Cassio? Did you say with Cassio?

---

158 made mocks with derided, made sport of   **168 you were best** it would be best for you   **170 to be hurt** i.e., to endure hurt.   **gull** dupe   **184 apt** plausible

IAGO: With Cassio, mistress. Go to, charm° your tongue.   190

EMILIA: I will not charm my tongue; I am bound to speak.

My mistress here lies murdered in her bed—

ALL: O heavens forfend!

EMILIA: And your reports have set the murder on.

OTHELLO: Nay, stare not, masters. It is true indeed.   195

GRATIANO: 'Tis a strange truth.

MONTANO: O monstrous act!

EMILIA: Villainy, villainy, villainy!

I think upon 't—I think I smell 't! O villainy!

I thought so then°—I'll kill myself for grief—

O villainy, villainy!   200

IAGO: What, are you mad? I charge you, get you home.

EMILIA: Good gentlemen, let me have leave to speak.

'Tis proper I obey him, but not now.

Perchance, Iago, I will ne'er go home.

OTHELLO: O! O! O!   [*Othello falls on the bed.*°]

EMILIA: Nay, lay thee down and roar,   205

For thou hast killed the sweetest innocent

That e'er did lift up eye.°

OTHELLO [*rising*]:   O, she was foul!

I scarce did know you, uncle. There lies your niece,

Whose breath indeed these hands have newly stopped.

I know this act shows° horrible and grim.   210

GRATIANO: Poor Desdemona! I am glad thy father's dead.

Thy match was mortal to him, and pure grief

Shore his old thread° in twain. Did he live now,

This sight would make him do a desperate turn,°

Yea, curse his better angel from his side,   215

And fall to reprobance.°

OTHELLO: 'Tis pitiful. But yet Iago knows

That she with Cassio hath the act of shame

A thousand times committed. Cassio confessed it;

---

190 charm keep silent (as though by a magic spell)   **199 then** (Perhaps at Act III, Scene iii, lines 331–332 and Act IV, Scene ii, lines 137–154.)   **205 [s.d.] Othello ... bed** (This direction is from the Quarto, as also *He kisses her* at line 19 and *She dies* at line 129.)   **207 lift up eye** i.e., lift her eyes to heaven   **210 shows** looks   **213 Shore ... thread** sheared the thread of his old age (as Atropos, one of the three Fates, was thought to do)   **214 turn** deed   **216 reprobance** damnation, i.e., suicide

And she did gratify° his amorous works   220
With that recognizance° and pledge of love
Which I first gave her. I saw it in his hand;
It was a handkerchief, an antique token
My father gave my mother.

EMILIA: O God! O heavenly God!   225

IAGO: Zounds, hold your peace.

EMILIA: 'Twill out, 'twill out! I peace?
No, I will speak as liberal as the north.°
Let heaven and men and devils, let them all,
All, all, cry shame against me, yet I'll speak.

IAGO: Be wise, and get you home.

EMILIA: I will not.

[*Iago threatens Emilia.*]

GRATIANO: Fie   230
Your sword upon a woman?

EMILIA: O thou dull Moor! That handkerchief thou speak'st of
I found by fortune and did give my husband;
For often, with a solemn earnestness,
More than indeed belonged° to such a trifle,   235
He begged of me to steal 't.

IAGO: Villainous whore!

EMILIA: She give it Cassio? No, alas! I found it,
And I did give 't my husband.

IAGO: Filth, thou liest!

EMILIA: By heaven, I do not, I do not, gentlemen.
O murderous coxcomb!° What should such a fool   240
Do with so good a wife?

OTHELLO: Are there no stones° in heaven
But what serves for the thunder?—Precious° villain!

[*He runs at Iago; Montano disarms Othello. Iago, from behind,
stabs Emilia.*°]

GRATIANO: The woman falls! Sure he hath killed his wife.

---

220 **gratify** reward   221 **recognizance** token   227 **liberal as the north** freely as the north wind
(blows)   235 **belonged** was appropriate   240 **coxcomb** fool. (Addressed to Othello.)   242 **stones**
bolts, such as those used for thunderbolts   243 **Precious** i.e., arrant, utter.   [**s.d.**] **He . . . Emilia**
(The Quarto text reads, "The Moor runs at Iago. Iago kills his wife." The Quarto also specifies the
exit of Iago at line 245 and the death of Emilia at line 260.)

WILLIAM SHAKESPEARE

EMILIA: Ay, ay. O, lay me by my mistress' side.   245

Exit [Iago.]

GRATIANO: He's gone, but his wife's killed.
MONTANO: 'Tis a notorious villain. Take you this weapon,
    Which I have here recovered from the Moor.
    Come, guard the door without. Let him not pass,
    But kill him rather. I'll after that same villain,   250
    For 'tis a damnèd slave.

Exit [with all but Othello and Emilia, who has been laid by
Desdemona's side].

OTHELLO: I am not valiant neither,
    But every puny whipster° gets my sword.
    But why should honor° outlive honesty?°
    Let it go all.
EMILIA: What did thy song bode, lady?   255
    Hark, canst thou hear me? I will play the swan,
    And die in music. [*She sings.*] "Willow, willow, willow."
    Moor, she was chaste. She loved thee, cruel Moor.
    So come my soul to bliss as I speak true.
    So speaking as I think, alas, I die.   [*She dies.*]   260
OTHELLO: I have another weapon in this chamber;
    It was a sword of Spain, the ice-brook's temper°—
    O, here it is. [*He finds a sword.*] Uncle, I must come forth.
GRATIANO [*within*]:   If thou attempt it, it will cost thee dear.
    Thou hast no weapon, and perforce must suffer.   265
OTHELLO: Look in upon me then and speak with me,
    Or, naked° as I am, I will assault thee.

[*Enter Gratiano.*]

GRATIANO: What is the matter?
OTHELLO: Behold, I have a weapon;
    A better never did itself sustain
    Upon a soldier's thigh. I have seen the day   270
    That, with this little arm and this good sword,

---

253 **whipster** contemptible fellow (one who is always ready to whip out his sword)   254 **honor** i.e.,
the bravery for which one enjoys a soldier's reputation.   **honesty** true integrity   262 **the ice-
brook's temper** tempered in ice-cold water   267 **naked** unarmed

I have made my way through more impediments
Than twenty times your stop.° But O, vain boast!
Who can control his fate? 'Tis not so now.
Be not afraid, though you do see me weaponed;   275
Here is my journey's end, here is my butt°
And very seamark° of my utmost sail.

[*Gratiano steps back.*]

Do you go back dismayed? 'Tis a lost° fear;
Man but a rush° against Othello's breast
And he retires. Where should Othello go?   280

[*He turns to Desdemona.*]

Now, how dost thou look now? O ill-starred wench!
Pale as thy smock! When we shall meet at compt,°
This look of thine will hurl my soul from heaven,
And fiends will snatch at it. Cold, cold, my girl?
Even like thy chastity. O cursèd, cursèd slave!°   285
Whip me, ye devils,
From the possession of this heavenly sight!
Blow me about in winds! Roast me in sulfur!
Wash me in steep-down gulfs of liquid fire!
O Desdemon! Dead, Desdemon! Dead! O! O!   290

Enter Lodovico, Cassio [*carried in a litter*°], Montano, and Iago
[*prisoner*], with officers.

LODOVICO: Where is this rash and most unfortunate man?
OTHELLO: That's he that was Othello. Here I am.
LODOVICO: Where is that viper? Bring the villain forth.

[*Iago is led forward.*]

OTHELLO: I look down towards his feet;° but that's a fable.
If that thou be'st a devil, I cannot kill thee.   295

[*He wounds Iago.*]

---

273 **stop** power (to stop)   276 **butt** goal, limit (an archery term)   277 **seamark** beacon (marking his
destination or limit)   278 **lost** wasted, unneeded   279 **Man . . . rush** wield no more than a reed
282 **compt** account, judgment day   285 **slave** i.e., Othello himself   290 **[s.d.] in a litter** (The
Quarto specifies that Cassio is "in a chair.")   294 **towards his feet** i.e., to see if they are cloven, as
the devil's are fabled to be

LODOVICO: Wrench his sword from him.

[*Othello is disarmed.*]

IAGO: I bleed, sir, but not killed.

OTHELLO: I am not sorry neither. I'd have thee live,
For in my sense° 'tis happiness to die.

LODOVICO: O thou Othello, that was once so good,
Fall'n in the practice° of a cursèd slave,°   300
What shall be said to thee?

OTHELLO: Why, anything.
An honorable murderer, if you will,
For naught I did in hate, but all in honor.

LODOVICO: This wretch hath part confessed his villainy.
Did you and he consent° in Cassio's death?   305

OTHELLO: Ay.

CASSIO: Dear General, I never gave you cause.

OTHELLO: I do believe it, and I ask your pardon.
Will you, I pray, demand that demi-devil
Why he hath thus ensnared my soul and body?   310

IAGO: Demand me nothing. What you know, you know.
From this time forth I never will speak word.

LODOVICO: What, not to pray?

GRATIANO: Torments° will ope your lips.

OTHELLO: Well, thou dost best.   315

LODOVICO: Sir, you shall understand what hath befall'n,
Which, as I think, you know not. Here is a letter
Found in the pocket of the slain Roderigo;
And here another. [*He produces letters.*] The one of them
imports
The death of Cassio, to be undertook   320
By Roderigo.

OTHELLO: O villain!

CASSIO: Most heathenish and most gross!°

LODOVICO [*showing another paper*]:   Now here's another
discontented° paper
Found in his pocket too. And this, it seems,

---

298 in my sense to one who feels as I do   **300 in the practice** through the plotting, into the snare.
slave villain   **305 consent** agree   **314 Torments** torture   **322 gross** monstrous   **323 discontented**
full of discontent

Roderigo meant t' have sent this damnèd villain; 325
But that belike° Iago in the interim
Came in and satisfied him.°

OTHELLO: O thou pernicious caitiff!—
How came you, Cassio, by that handkerchief
That was my wife's?

CASSIO: I found it in my chamber; 330
And he himself confessed but even now
That there he dropped it for a special purpose
Which wrought to his desire.°

OTHELLO: O fool, fool, fool!

CASSIO: There is besides in Roderigo's letter
How he upbraids Iago, that he made him 335
Brave° me upon the watch, whereon it came°
That I was cast;° and even but now he spake,
After long seeming dead, Iago hurt him,
Iago set him on.

LODOVICO [to Othello]: You must forsake this room and go 340
with us.
Your power and your command is taken off,°
And Cassio rules in Cyprus. For this slave,
If there be any cunning cruelty
That can torment him much and hold him long,°
It shall be his. You shall close prisoner rest° 345
Till that the nature of your fault be known
To the Venetian state.—Come, bring away.

OTHELLO: Soft you;° a word or two before you go.
I have done the state some service, and they know 't.
No more of that. I pray you, in your letters, 350
When you shall these unlucky° deeds relate,
Speak of me as I am; nothing extenuate,
Nor set down aught in malice. Then must you speak
Of one that loved not wisely but too well;
Of one not easily jealous but, being wrought,° 355

---

326 belike most likely   **327 Came . . . him** interposed and gave him satisfactory explanation
333 wrought . . . desire worked out as he wished, fitted in with his plan   **336 Brave** defy.   **whereon
it came** whereof it came about   **337 cast** dismissed   **341 taken off** taken away   **344 hold him long**
keep him alive a long time (during his torture)   **345 rest** remain   **348 Soft you** one moment
351 unlucky unfortunate   **355 wrought** worked upon, worked into a frenzy

Perplexed° in the extreme; of one whose hand,
Like the base Indian,° threw a pearl away
Richer than all his tribe; of one whose subdued° eyes,
Albeit unusèd to the melting mood,
Drops tears as fast as the Arabian trees   360
Their medicinable gum.° Set you down this;
And say besides that in Aleppo once,
Where a malignant and a turbaned Turk
Beat a Venetian and traduced the state,
I took by th' throat the circumcisèd dog   365
And smote him, thus.   [*He stabs himself.*°]

LODOVICO: O bloody period!°

GRATIANO: All that is spoke is marred.

OTHELLO: I kissed thee ere I killed thee. No way but this,
Killing myself, to die upon a kiss.   370

[*He kisses Desdemona and*] *dies.*

CASSIO: This did I fear, but thought he had no weapon;
For he was great of heart.

LODOVICO [*to Iago*]:   O Spartan dog,°
More fell° than anguish, hunger, or the sea!
Look on the tragic loading of this bed.
This is thy work. The object poisons sight;   375
Let it be hid.° Gratiano, keep° the house,
[*The bed curtains are drawn*]
And seize upon° the fortunes of the Moor,
For they succeed on° you. [*To Cassio.*] To you, Lord Governor,
Remains the censure° of this hellish villain,
The time, the place, the torture. O, enforce it!   380
Myself will straight aboard, and to the state
This heavy act with heavy heart relate.   *Exeunt.*

—1604?

---

356 **Perplexed** distraught   357 **Indian** (This reading from the Quarto pictures an ignorant savage who cannot recognize the value of a precious jewel. The Folio reading, *Iudean* or *Judean*, i.e., infidel or disbeliever, may refer to Herod, who slew Mariamne in a fit of jealousy, or to Judas Iscariot, the betrayer of Christ.)   358 **subdued** i.e., overcome by grief   361 **gum** i.e., myrrh 366 **[s.d.] He stabs himself** (This direction is in the Quarto text.)   367 **period** termination, conclusion 372 **Spartan dog** (Spartan dogs were noted for their savagery and silence.)   373 **fell** cruel   376 **Let it be hid** i.e., draw the bed curtains. (No stage direction specifies that the dead are to be carried offstage at the end of the play.)   **keep** remain in   377 **seize upon** take legal possession of 378 **succeed on** pass as though by inheritance to   379 **censure** sentencing

Henrik Ibsen, universally acknowledged as the first of the great modern playwrights, was born in Skien, a small town in Norway, the son of a merchant who went bankrupt during Ibsen's childhood. Ibsen first trained for a medical career, but drifted into the theater, gaining, like Shakespeare and Molière, important dramatic training through a decade's service as a stage manager and director. Ibsen was unsuccessful in establishing a theater in Oslo, and he spent almost thirty years living and writing in Germany and Italy. The fame he won through early poetic dramas like Peer Gynt *(1867), which is considered the supreme exploration of the Norwegian national character, was overshadowed by the realistic prose plays he began writing, starting with* Pillars of Society *(1877).* A Doll's House *(1879) and* Ghosts *(1881), which deal, respectively, with a woman's struggle for independence and self-respect and with the taboo subject of venereal disease, made Ibsen an internationally famous, if controversial, figure. In fact, Ibsen wrote* An Enemy of the People *as a response to the public outcry over* Ghosts, *whose subject was considered so controversial that it could not be performed in London until 1891, and then for only a single performance in a private subscription theater. Although Ibsen's type of realism, displayed in "problem plays" such as these and later psychological dramas like* The Wild Duck *(1885) and* Hedda Gabler *(1890), has become so fully assimilated into our literary heritage that now it is difficult to think of him as an innovator, his marriage of the tightly constructed plots of the conventional "well-made play" to serious discussion of social issues was one of the most significant developments in the history of drama. His most influential advocate in English-speaking countries was George Bernard Shaw, whose* The Quintessence of Ibsenism *(1891) is one of the earliest and most influential studies of Ibsen's dramatic methods and ideas.*

An Enemy of the People

Adapted by Arthur Miller

Characters

Morten Kiil
Billing
Mrs. Stockmann
Peter Stockmann

Hovstad
Dr. Stockmann
Morten
Ejlif
Captain Horster
Petra
Aslaksen
The drunk

Synopsis of Scenes

The Action Takes Place in a Norwegian Town

Throughout, in the stage directions, right and left mean stage right and stage left.

Act I

Scene I. Dr. Stockmann's living room

It is evening. Dr. Stockmann's living room is simply but cheerfully furnished. A doorway, upstage right, leads into the entrance hall, which extends from the front door to the dining room, running unseen behind the living room. At the left is another door, which leads to the Doctor's study and other rooms. In the upstage left corner is a stove. Toward the left foreground is a sofa with a table behind it. In the right foreground are two chairs, a small table between them, on which stand a lamp and a bowl of apples. At the back, to the left, an open doorway leads to the dining room, part of which is seen. The windows are in the right wall, a bench in front of them.

As the curtain rises, Billing and Morten Kiil are eating in the dining room. Billing is junior editor of the People's Daily Messenger. *Kiil is a slovenly old man who is feeding himself in a great hurry. He gulps his last bite and comes into the living room, where he puts on his coat and ratty fur hat. Billing comes in to help him.*

BILLING: You sure eat fast, Mr. Kiil. [*Billing is an enthusiast to the point of foolishness.*]

KIIL: Eating don't get you anywhere, boy. Tell my daughter I went home.

Kiil starts across to the front door. Billing returns to his food in the dining room. Kiil halts at the bowl of apples; he takes one, tastes it, likes it, takes another and puts it in his pocket, then continues on toward the door. Again he stops, returns, and takes another apple for his pocket. Then he sees a tobacco can on the table. He covers his action from Billing's possible glance, opens the can, smells it, pours some into his side pocket. He is just closing the can when Catherine Stockman enters from the dining room.

MRS. STOCKMANN: Father! You're not going, are you?

KIIL: Got business to tend to.

MRS. STOCKMANN: Oh, you're only going back to your room and you know it. Stay! Mr. Billing's here, and Hovstad's coming. It'll be interesting for you.

KIIL: Got all kinds of business. The only reason I came over was the butcher told me you bought roast beef today. Very tasty, dear.

MRS. STOCKMANN: Why don't you wait for Tom? He only went for a little walk.

KIIL [*taking out his pipe*]:   You think he'd mind if I filled my pipe?

MRS. STOCKMANN: No, go ahead. And here—take some apples. You should always have some fruit in your room.

KIIL: No, no, wouldn't think of it.

The doorbell rings.

MRS. STOCKMANN: That must be Hovstad. [*She goes to the door and opens it.*]

Peter Stockmann, the Mayor, enters. He is a bachelor, nearing sixty. He has always been one of those men who make it their life work to stand in the center of the ship to keep it from overturning. He probably envies the family life and warmth of this house, but when he comes he never wants to admit he came and often sits with his coat on.

MRS. STOCKMANN: Peter! Well, this is a surprise!

PETER STOCKMANN: I was just passing by . . . [*He sees Kiil and smiles, amused.*] Mr. Kiil!

KIIL [*sarcastically*]:   Your Honor! [*He bites into his apple and exits.*]

MRS. STOCKMANN: You musn't mind him, Peter, he's getting terribly old. Would you like a bite to eat?

PETER STOCKMANN: No, no thanks. [*He sees Billing now, and Billing nods to him from the dining room.*]

MRS. STOCKMANN [*embarrassed*]:   He just happened to drop in.

PETER STOCKMANN: That's all right. I can't take hot food in the evening. Not with my stomach.

MRS. STOCKMANN: Can't I ever get you to eat anything in this house?

PETER STOCKMANN: Bless you, I stick to my tea and toast. Much healthier and more economical.

MRS. STOCKMANN [*smiling*]:   You sound as though Tom and I throw money out the window.

PETER STOCKMANN: Not you, Catherine. He wouldn't be home, would he?

MRS. STOCKMANN: He went for a little walk with the boys.

PETER STOCKMANN: You don't think that's dangerous, right after dinner? [*There is a loud knocking on the front door.*] That sounds like my brother.

MRS. STOCKMANN: I doubt it, so soon. Come in, please.

Hovstad enters. He is in his early thirties, a graduate of the peasantry struggling with a terrible conflict. For while he hates authority and wealth, he cannot bring himself to cast off a certain desire to partake of them. Perhaps he is dangerous because he wants more than anything to belong, and in a radical that is a withering wish, not easily to be borne.

MRS. STOCKMANN: Mr. Hovstad—

HOVSTAD: Sorry I'm late. I was held up at the printing shop. [*Surprised*]:   Good evening, Your Honor.

PETER STOCKMANN [*rather stiffly*]:   Hovstad. On business, no doubt.

HOVSTAD: Partly. It's about an article for the paper—

PETER STOCKMANN [*sarcastically*]: Ha! I don't doubt it. I understand my brother has become a prolific contributor to—what do you call it?—the *People's Daily Liberator*?

HOVSTAD [*laughing, but holding his ground*]:   The *People's Daily Messenger*, sir. The Doctor sometimes honors the *Messenger* when he wants to uncover the real truth of some subject.

PETER STOCKMANN: The truth! Oh, yes, I see.

MRS. STOCKMANN [*nervously to Hovstad*]:   Would you like to . . . [*She points to dining room.*]

PETER STOCKMANN: I don't want you to think I blame the Doctor for using your paper. After all, every performer goes for the audience that applauds him most. It's really not your paper I have anything against, Mr. Hovstad.

HOVSTAD: I really didn't think so, Your Honor.

PETER STOCKMANN: As a matter of fact, I happen to admire the spirit of tolerance in our town. It's magnificent. Just don't forget that we have it because we all believe in the same thing; it brings us together.

HOVSTAD: Kirsten Springs, you mean.

PETER STOCKMANN: The springs, Mr. Hovstad, our wonderful new springs. They've changed the soul of this town. Mark my words, Kirsten Springs are going to put us on the map, and there is no question about it.

MRS. STOCKMANN: That's what Tom says too.

PETER STOCKMANN: Everything is shooting ahead—real estate going up, money changing hands every hour, business humming—

HOVSTAD: And no more unemployment.

PETER STOCKMANN: Right. Give us a really good summer, and sick people will be coming here in carloads. The springs will turn into a regular fad, a new Carlsbad. And for once the well-to-do people won't be the only ones paying taxes in this town.

HOVSTAD: I hear reservations are really starting to come in?

PETER STOCKMANN: Coming in every day. Looks very promising, very promising.

HOVSTAD: That's fine. [*To Mrs. Stockmann*]: Then the Doctor's article will come in handy.

PETER STOCKMANN: He's written something again?

HOVSTAD: No, it's a piece he wrote at the beginning of the winter, recommending the water. But at the time I let the article lie.

PETER STOCKMANN: Why, some hitch in it?

HOVSTAD: Oh, no, I just thought it would have a bigger effect in the spring, when people start planning for the summer.

PETER STOCKMANN: That's smart, Mr. Hovstad, very smart.

MRS. STOCKMANN: Tom is always so full of ideas about the springs; every day he—

PETER STOCKMANN: Well, he ought to be, he gets his salary from the springs, my dear.

HOVSTAD: Oh, I think it's more than that, don't you? After all, Doctor Stockmann *created* Kirsten Springs.

PETER STOCKMANN: You don't say! I've been hearing that lately, but I did think I had a certain modest part—

MRS. STOCKMANN: Oh, Tom always says—

HOVSTAD: I only meant the original idea was—

PETER STOCKMANN: My good brother is never at a loss for ideas. All sorts of ideas. But when it comes to putting them into action you need another kind of man, and I did think that at least people in this house would—

MRS. STOCKMANN: But Peter, dear—we didn't mean to— Go get yourself a bite, Mr. Hovstad, my husband will be here any minute.

HOVSTAD: Thank you, maybe just a little something. [*He goes into the dining room and joins Billing at the table*].

PETER STOCKMANN, [*lowering his voice*]:   Isn't it remarkable? Why is it that people without background can never learn tact?

MRS. STOCKMANN: Why let it bother you? Can't you and Thomas share the honor like good brothers?

PETER STOCKMANN: The trouble is that certain men are never satisfied to share, Catherine.

MRS. STOCKMANN: Nonsense. You've always gotten along beautifully with Tom— That must be him now.

She goes to the front door, opens it. Dr. Stockmann is laughing and talking outside. He is in the prime of his life. He might be called the eternal amateur—a lover of things, of people, of sheer living, a man for whom the days are too short, and the future fabulous with discoverable joys. And for all this most people will not like him—he will not compromise for less than God's own share of the world while they have settled for less than Man's.

DR. STOCKMANN [*in the entrance hall*]:   Hey, Catherine! Here's another guest for you! Here's a hanger for your coat, Captain. Oh, that's right, you don't wear overcoats! Go on in, boys. You kids must be hungry all over again. Come here, Captain Horster, I want you to get a look at this roast. [*He pushes Captain Horster along the hallway to the dining room. Ejlif and Morten also go to the dining room*].

MRS. STOCKMANN: Tom, dear . . . [*She motions toward Peter in the living room*].

DR. STOCKMANN [*turns around in the doorway to the living room and sees Peter*]: Oh, Peter . . . [*He walks across and stretches out his hand.*] Say now, this is really nice.

PETER STOCKMANN: I'll have to go in a minute.

DR. STOCKMANN: Oh, nonsense, not with the toddy on the table. You haven't forgotten the toddy, have you, Catherine?

MRS. STOCKMANN: Of course not, I've got the water boiling. [*She goes into the dining room*].

PETER STOCKMANN: Toddy too?

DR. STOCKMANN: Sure, just sit down and make yourself at home.

PETER STOCKMANN: No, thanks, I don't go in for drinking parties.

DR. STOCKMANN: But this is no party.

PETER STOCKMANN: What else do you call it? [*He looks toward the dining room*]. It's extraordinary how you people can consume all this food and live.

DR. STOCKMANN [*rubbing his hands*]: Why? What's finer than to watch young people eat? Peter, those are the fellows who are going to stir up the whole future.

PETER STOCKMANN [*a little alarmed*]: Is that so! What's there to stir up? *He sits in a chair to the left.*

DR. STOCKMANN [*walking around*]: Don't worry, they'll let us know when the time comes. Old idiots like you and me, we'll be left behind like—

PETER STOCKMANN: I've never been called *that* before.

DR. STOCKMANN: Oh, Peter, don't jump on me every minute! You know your trouble, Peter? Your impressions are blunted. You ought to sit up there in that crooked corner of the north for five years, the way I did, and then come back here. It's like watching the first seven days of creation!

PETER STOCKMANN: Here!

DR. STOCKMANN: Things to work and fight for, Peter! Without that you're dead. Catherine, you sure the mailman came today?

MRS. STOCKMANN, [*from the dining room*]: There wasn't any mail today.

DR. STOCKMANN: And another thing, Peter—a good income; *that's* something you learn to value after you've lived on a starvation diet.

PETER STOCKMANN: When did you starve?

DR. STOCKMANN: Damned near! It was pretty tough going a lot of the time up there. And now, to be able to live like a prince! Tonight, for instance, we had roast beef for dinner, and, by God, there was enough left for supper too. Please have a piece—come here.

PETER STOCKMANN: Oh, no, no—please, certainly not.

DR. STOCKMANN: At least let me show it to you! Come in here—we even have a tablecloth. [*He pulls his brother toward the dining room.*]

PETER STOCKMANN: I saw it.

DR. STOCKMANN: Live to the hilt! that's my motto. Anyway, Catherine says I'm earning almost as much as we spend.

PETER STOCKMANN [*refusing an apple*]: Well, you are improving.

DR. STOCKMANN: Peter, that was a joke! You're supposed to laugh! [*He sits in the other chair to the left*].

PETER STOCKMANN: Roast beef twice a day is no joke.

DR. STOCKMANN: Why can't I give myself the pleasure of having people around me? It's a necessity for me to see young, lively, happy people, free people burning with a desire to do something. You'll see. When Hovstad comes in we'll talk and—

PETER STOCKMANN: Oh, yes, Hovstad. That reminds me. He told me he was going to print one of your articles.

DR. STOCKMANN: One of my articles?

PETER STOCKMANN: Yes, about the springs—an article you wrote during the winter?

DR. STOCKMANN: Oh, that one! In the first place, I don't want that one printed right now.

PETER STOCKMANN: No? It sounded to me like it would be very timely.

DR. STOCKMANN: Under normal conditions, maybe so. [*He gets up and walks across the floor*].

PETER STOCKMANN [*looking after him*]: Well, what is abnormal about the conditions now?

DR. STOCKMANN [*stopping*]: I can't say for the moment, Peter—at least not tonight. There could be a great deal abnormal about conditions; then again, there could be nothing at all.

PETER STOCKMANN: Well, you've managed to sound mysterious. Is there anything wrong? Something you're keeping from me? Because I wish once in a while you'd remind yourself that I am chairman of the board for the springs.

DR. STOCKMANN: And I would like *you* to remember that, Peter. Look, let's not get into each other's hair.

PETER STOCKMANN: I don't make a habit of getting into people's hair! But I'd like to underline that everything concerning Kirsten Springs must be treated in a businesslike manner, through the proper channels, and dealt with by the legally constituted authorities. I can't allow anything done behind my back in a roundabout way.

DR. STOCKMANN: When did I ever go behind your back, Peter?

PETER STOCKMANN: You have an ingrained tendency to go your own way, Thomas, and that simply can't go on in a well-organized society. The individual really must subordinate himself to the over-all, or [*groping for words, he points to himself*] to the authorities who are in charge of the general welfare. *He gets up.*

DR. STOCKMANN: Well, that's probably so. But how the hell does that concern me, Peter?

PETER STOCKMANN: My dear Thomas, this is exactly what you will never learn. But you had better watch out because someday you might pay dearly for it. Now I've said it. Good-bye.

DR. STOCKMANN: Are you out of your mind? You're absolutely on the wrong track.

PETER STOCKMANN: I am usually not. Anyway, may I be excused? [*He nods toward the dining room.*] Good-by, Catherine. Good evening, gentlemen. [*He leaves*].

MRS. STOCKMANN, [*entering the living room*]: He left?

DR. STOCKMANN: And burned up!

MRS. STOCKMANN: What did you do to him now?

DR. STOCKMANN: What does he want from me? He can't expect me to give him an accounting of every move I make, every thought I think, until I am ready to do it.

MRS. STOCKMANN: Why? What should you give him an accounting of?

DR. STOCKMANN [*hesitantly*]: Just leave that to me, Catherine. Peculiar the mailman didn't come today.

Hovstad, Billing, and Captain Horster have gotten up from the dining-room table and enter the living room. Ejlif and Morten come in a little later. Catherine exits.

BILLING [*stretching out his arms*]: After a meal like that, by God, I feel like a new man. This house is so—

HOVSTAD [*cutting him off*]: The Mayor certainly wasn't in a glowing mood tonight.

DR. STOCKMANN: It's his stomach. He has a lousy digestion.

HOVSTAD: I think two editors from the *People's Daily Messenger* didn't help either.

DR. STOCKMANN: No, it's just that Peter is a lonely man. Poor fellow, all he knows is official business and duties, and then all that damn weak tea that he pours into himself. Catherine, may we have the toddy?

MRS. STOCKMANN [*calling from the dining room*]:   I'm just getting it.

DR. STOCKMANN: Sit down here on the couch with me, Captain Horster—a rare guest like you—sit here. Sit down, friends.

HORSTER: This used to be such an ugly house. Suddenly it's beautiful!

Billing and Hovstad sit down at the right. Mrs. Stockmann brings a tray with pot, glasses, bottles, etc. on it, and puts it on the table behind the couch.

BILLING [*to Horster, intimately, indicating Stockmann*]:   Great man!

MRS. STOCKMANN: Here you are. Help yourselves.

DR. STOCKMANN [*taking a glass*]:   We sure will. [*He mixes the toddy.*] And the cigars, Ejlif—you know where the box is. And Morten, get my pipe. [*The boys go out to the left.*] I have a sneaking suspicion that Ejlif is snitching a cigar now and then, but I don't pay any attention. Catherine, you know where I put it? Oh, he's got it. Good boys! [*The boys bring the various things in.*] Help yourselves, fellows. I'll stick to the pipe. This one's gone through plenty of blizzards with me up in the north. Skol! [*He looks around.*] Home! What an invention, heh?

The boys sit down on the bench near the windows.

MRS. STOCKMANN [*who has sat down and is now knitting*]:   Are you sailing soon, Captain Horster?

HORSTER: I expect to be ready next week.

MRS. STOCKMANN: And then to America, Captain?

HORSTER: Yes, that's the plan.

BILLING: Oh, then you won't be home for the new election?

HORSTER: Is there going to be another election?

BILLING: Didn't you know?

HORSTER: No, I don't get mixed up in those things.

BILLING: But you are interested in public affairs, aren't you?

HORSTER: Frankly, I don't understand a thing about it.

He does, really, although not very much. Captain Horster is one of the longest silent roles in dramatic literature, but he is not to be thought of as characterless. It is not a bad thing to have a courageous, quiet man for a friend, even if it has gone out of fashion.

MRS. STOCKMANN [*sympathetically*]:   Neither do I, Captain. Maybe that's why I'm always so glad to see you.

BILLING: Just the same, you ought to vote, Captain.

HORSTER: Even if I don't understand anything about it?

BILLING: Understand! What do you mean by that? Society, Captain, is like a ship—every man should do something to help navigate the ship.

HORSTER: That may be all right on shore, but on board a ship it doesn't work out so well.

Petra in hat and coat and with textbooks and notebooks under her arm comes into the entrance hall. She is Ibsen's clear-eyed hope for the future—and probably ours. She is forthright, determined, and knows the meaning of work, which to her is the creation of good on the earth.

PETRA [*from the hall*]:   Good evening.

DR. STOCKMANN, *warmly*:   Good evening, Petra!

BILLING [*to Horster*]:   Great young woman!

There are mutual greetings. Petra removes her coat and hat and places the books on a chair in the entrance hall.

PETRA [*entering the living room*]:   And here you are, lying around like lizards while I'm out slaving.

DR. STOCKMANN: Well, you come and be a lizard too. Come here, Petra, sit with me. I look at her and say to myself, "How did I do it?"

Petra goes over to her father and kisses him.

BILLING: Shall I mix a toddy for you?

PETRA [*coming up to the table*]:   No, thanks, I had better do it myself— you always mix it too strong. Oh, Father, I forgot—I have a letter for you. [*She goes to the chair where her books are.*]

DR. STOCKMANN [*alerted*]:   Who's it from?

PETRA: I met the mailman on the way to school this morning and he gave me your mail too, and I just didn't have time to run back.

DR. STOCKMANN [*getting up and walking toward her*]: And you don't give it to me until now!

PETRA: I really didn't have time to run back, Father.

MRS. STOCKMANN: If she didn't have time . . .

DR. STOCKMANN: Let's see it—come on, child! [*He takes the letter and looks at the envelope.*] Yes, indeed.

MRS. STOCKMANN: Is that the one you've been waiting for?

DR. STOCKMANN: I'll be right back. There wouldn't be a light on in my room, would there?

MRS. STOCKMANN: The lamp is on the desk, burning away.

DR. STOCKMANN: Please excuse me for a moment. [*He goes into his study and quickly returns. Mrs. Stockmann hands him his glasses. He goes out again.*]

PETRA: What is that, Mother?

MRS. STOCKMANN: I don't know. The last couple of days he's been asking again and again about the mailman.

BILLING: Probably an out-of-town patient of his.

PETRA: Poor Father, he's got much too much to do. [*She mixes her drink.*] This ought to taste good.

HOVSTAD: By the way, what happened to that English novel you were going to translate for us?

PETRA: I started it, but I've gotten so busy—

HOVSTAD: Oh, teaching evening school again?

PETRA: Two hours a night.

BILLING: Plus the high school every day?

PETRA [*sitting down on the couch*]: Yes, five hours, and every night a pile of lessons to correct!

MRS. STOCKMANN: She never stops going.

HOVSTAD: Maybe that's why I always think of you as kind of breathless and—well, breathless.

PETRA: I love it. I get so wonderfully tired.

BILLING [*to Horster*]: She looks tired.

MORTEN: You must be a wicked woman, Petra.

PETRA [*laughing*]: Wicked?

MORTEN: You work so much. My teacher says that work is a punishment for our sins.

EJLIF: And you believe that?

MRS. STOCKMANN: Ejlif! Of course he believes his teacher!

BILLING [*smiling*]:   Don't stop him . . .

HOVSTAD: Don't you like to work, Morten?

MORTEN: Work? No.

HOVSTAD: Then what will you ever amount to in this world?

MORTEN: Me? I'm going to be a Viking.

EJLIF: You can't! You'd have to be a heathen!

MORTEN: So I'll be a heathen.

MRS. STOCKMANN: I think it's getting late, boys.

BILLING: I agree with you, Morten. I think—

MRS. STOCKMANN [*making signs to Billing*]:   You certainly don't, Mr. Billing.

BILLING: Yes, by God, I do. I am a real heathen and proud of it. You'll see, pretty soon we're all going to be heathens!

MORTEN: And then we can do anything we want!

BILLING: Right! You see, Morten—

MRS. STOCKMANN, [*interrupting*]:   Don't you have any homework for tomorrow, boys? Better go in and do it.

EJLIF: Oh, can't we stay in here a while?

MRS. STOCKMANN: No, neither of you. Now run along.

The boys say good night and go off at the left.

HOVSTAD: You really think it hurts them to listen to such talk?

MRS. STOCKMANN: I don't know, but I don't like it.

Dr. Stockmann enters from his study, an open letter in his hand. He is like a sleepwalker, astonished, engrossed. He walks toward the front door.

MRS. STOCKMANN: Tom!

He turns, suddenly aware of them.

DR. STOCKMANN: Boys, there is going to be news in this town!

BILLING: News?

MRS. STOCKMANN: What kind of news?

DR. STOCKMANN: A terrific discovery, Catherine.

HOVSTAD: Really?

MRS. STOCKMANN: That you made?

DR. STOCKMANN: That I made. *He walks back and forth.* Now let the baboons running this town call me a lunatic! Now they'd better watch out. Oh, how the mighty have fallen!

PETRA: What is it, Father?

DR. STOCKMANN: Oh, if Peter were only here! Now you'll see how human beings can walk around and make judgments like blind rats.

HOVSTAD: What in the world's happened, Doctor?

DR. STOCKMANN [*stopping at the table*]: It's the general opinion, isn't it, that our town is a sound and healthy spot?

HOVSTAD: Of course.

MRS. STOCKMANN: What happened?

DR. STOCKMANN: Even a rather unusually healthy spot! Oh, God, a place that can be recommended not only to all people but to sick people!

MRS. STOCKMANN: But, Tom, what are you—

DR. STOCKMANN: And we certainly have recommended it. I myself have written and written, in the *People's Messenger*, pamphlets—

HOVSTAD: Yes, yes, but—

DR. STOCKMANN: The miraculous springs that cost such a fortune to build, the whole Health Institute, is a pesthole!

PETRA: Father! The springs?

MRS. STOCKMANN [*simultaneously*]: Our springs?

BILLING: That's unbelievable!

DR. STOCKMANN: You know the filth up in Windmill Valley? That stuff that has such a stinking smell? It comes down from the tannery up there, and the same damn poisonous mess comes right out into the blessed, miraculous water we're supposed to *cure* people with!

HORSTER: You mean actually where our beaches are?

DR. STOCKMANN: Exactly.

HOVSTAD: How are you so sure about this, Doctor?

DR. STOCKMANN: I had a suspicion about it a long time ago—last year there were too many sick cases among the visitors, typhoid and gastric disturbances.

MRS. STOCKMANN: That did happen. I remember Mrs. Svensen's niece—

DR. STOCKMANN: Yes, dear. At the time we thought that the visitors brought the bug, but later this winter I got a new idea and I started investigating the water.

MRS. STOCKMANN: So that's what you've been working on!

DR. STOCKMANN: I sent samples of the water to the University for an exact chemical analysis.

HOVSTAD: And that's what you have just received?

DR. STOCKMANN [*waving the letter again*]:   This is it. It proves the existence of infectious organic matter in the water.

MRS. STOCKMANN: Well, thank God you discovered it in time.

DR. STOCKMANN: I think we can say that, Catherine.

MRS. STOCKMANN: Isn't it wonderful!

HOVSTAD: And what do you intend to do now, Doctor?

DR. STOCKMANN: Put the thing right, of course.

HOVSTAD: Do you think that can be done?

DR. STOCKMANN: Maybe. If not, the whole Institute is useless. But there's nothing to worry about—I am quite clear on what has to be done.

MRS. STOCKMANN: But, Tom, why did you keep it so secret?

DR. STOCKMANN: What did you want me to do? Go out and shoot my mouth off before I really knew? [*He walks around, rubbing his hands.*] You don't realize what this means, Catherine—the whole water system has got to be changed.

MRS. STOCKMANN: The *whole* water system?

DR. STOCKMANN: The whole water system. The intake is too low, it's got to be raised to a much higher spot. The whole construction's got to be ripped out!

PETRA: Well, Father, at last you can prove they should have listened to you!

DR. STOCKMANN: Ha, she remembers!

MRS. STOCKMANN: That's right, you did warn them—

DR. STOCKMANN: Of course I warned them. When they started the damned thing I told them not to build it down there! But who am I, a mere scientist, to tell politicians where to build a health institute! Well, now they're going to get it, both barrels!

BILLING: This is tremendous! (*To Horster*):   He's a great man!

DR. STOCKMANN: It's bigger than tremendous. [*He starts toward his study.*] Wait'll they see this! (*He stops.*) Petra, my report is on my desk . . . [*Petra goes into his study.*] An envelope, Catherine! [*She goes for it.*] Gentlemen, this final proof from the University [*Petra comes out with the report, which he takes*] and my report [*he flicks the pages*] five solid, explosive pages . . .

MRS. STOCKMANN [*handing him an envelope*]:   Is this big enough?

DR. STOCKMANN: Fine. Right to the Board of Directors! [*He inserts the report, seals the envelope, and hands it to Catherine.*] Will you give this to the maid—what's her name again?

MRS. STOCKMANN: Randine, dear, Randine.

DR. STOCKMANN: Tell our darling Randine to wipe her nose and run over to the Mayor right now.

Mrs. Stockmann just stands there looking at him.

DR. STOCKMANN: What's the matter, dear?

MRS. STOCKMANN: I don't know . . .

PETRA: What's Uncle Peter going to say about this?

MRS. STOCKMANN: That's what I'm wondering.

DR. STOCKMANN: What can he say! He ought to be damn glad that such an important fact is brought out before we start an epidemic! Hurry, dear!

Catherine exits at the left.

HOVSTAD: I would like to put a brief item about this discovery in the *Messenger*.

DR. STOCKMANN: Go ahead. I'd really be grateful for that now.

HOVSTAD: Because the public ought to know soon.

DR. STOCKMANN: Right away.

BILLING: By God, you'll be the leading man in this town, Doctor.

DR. STOCKMANN [*walking around with an air of satisfaction*]:   Oh, there was nothing to it. Every detective gets a lucky break once in his life. But just the same I—

BILLING: Hovstad, don't you think the town ought to pay Dr. Stockmann some tribute?

DR. STOCKMANN: Oh, no, no . . .

HOVSTAD: Sure, let's all put in a word for—

BILLING: I'll talk to Aslaksen about it!

Catherine enters.

DR. STOCKMANN: No, no, fellows, no fooling around! I won't put up with any commotion. Even if the Board of Directors wants to give me an increase I won't take it—I just won't take it, Catherine.

MRS. STOCKMANN [*dutifully*]:   That's right, Tom.

PETRA [*lifting her glass*]:   Skol, Father!

EVERYBODY: Skol, Doctor!

HORSTER: Doctor, I hope this will bring you great honor and pleasure.

DR. STOCKMANN: Thanks, friends, thanks. There's one blessing above all others. To have earned the respect of one's neighbors is—is— Catherine, I'm going to dance!

He grabs his wife and whirls her around. There are shouts and struggles, general commotion. The boys in nightgowns stick their heads through the doorway at the right, wondering what is going on. Mrs. Stockmann, seeing them, breaks away and chases them upstairs as the curtain falls.

Scene II. The same, the following morning

Dr. Stockmann's living room the following morning. As the curtain rises, Mrs. Stockmann comes in from the dining room, a sealed letter in her hand. She goes to the study door and peeks in.

MRS. STOCKMANN: Are you there, Tom?

DR. STOCKMANN, [*from within*]:   I just got in. [*He enters the living room.*] What's up?

MRS. STOCKMANN: From Peter. It just came. [*She hands him the envelope.*]

DR. STOCKMANN: Oh, let's see. [*He opens the letter and reads*]: "I am returning herewith the report you submitted . . ." [*He continues to read, mumbling to himself.*]

MRS. STOCKMANN: Well, what does he say? Don't stand there!

DR. STOCKMANN [*putting the letter in his pocket*]:   He just says he'll come around this afternoon.

MRS. STOCKMANN: Oh. Well, maybe you ought to try to remember to be home then.

DR. STOCKMANN: Oh, I sure will. I'm through with my morning visits anyway.

MRS. STOCKMANN: I'm dying to see how he's going to take it.

DR. STOCKMANN: Why, is there any doubt? He'll probably make it look like he made the discovery, not I.

MRS. STOCKMANN: But aren't you a little bit afraid of that?

DR. STOCKMANN: Oh, underneath he'll be happy, Catherine. It's just that Peter is so afraid that somebody else is going to do something good for this town.

MRS. STOCKMANN: I wish you'd go out of your way and share the honors with him. Couldn't we say that he put you on the right track or something?

DR. STOCKMANN: Oh, I don't mind—as long as it makes everybody happy.

Morten Kiil sticks his head through the doorway. He looks around searchingly and chuckles. He will continue chuckling until he leaves the house. He is the archetype of the little twinkle-eyed man who sneaks into so much of Ibsen's work. He will chuckle you right over the precipice. He is the dealer, the man with the rat's finely tuned brain. But he is sometimes likable because he is without morals and announces the fact by laughing.

KIIL [*slyly*]: Is it really true?

MRS. STOCKMANN [*walking toward him*]: Father!

DR. STOCKMANN: Well, good morning!

MRS. STOCKMANN: Come on in.

KIIL: It better be true or I'm going.

DR. STOCKMANN: What had better be true?

KIIL: This crazy story about the water system. Is it true?

MRS. STOCKMANN: Of course it's true! How did you find out about it?

KIIL: Petra came flying by on her way to school this morning.

DR. STOCKMANN: Oh, she did?

KIIL: Ya. I thought she was trying to make a fool out of me—

MRS. STOCKMANN: Now why would she do that?

KIIL: Nothing gives more pleasure to young people than to make fools out of old people. But this is true, eh?

DR. STOCKMANN: Of course it's true. Sit down here. It's pretty lucky for the town, eh?

KIIL [*fighting his laughter*]: Lucky for the town!

DR. STOCKMANN: I mean, that I made the discovery before it was too late.

KIIL: Tom, I never thought you had the imagination to pull your own brother's leg like this.

DR. STOCKMANN: Pull his leg?

MRS. STOCKMANN: But, Father, he's not—

KIIL: How does it go now, let me get it straight. There's some kind of—like cockroaches in the waterpipes—

DR. STOCKMANN [*laughing*]:   No, not cockroaches.

KIIL: Well, some kind of little animals.

MRS. STOCKMANN: Bacteria, Father.

KIIL [*who can barely speak through his laughter*]:   Ah, but a whole mess of them, eh?

DR. STOCKMANN: Oh, there'd be millions and millions.

KIIL: And nobody can see them but you, is that it?

DR. STOCKMANN: Yes, that's—well, of course anybody with a micro— [*He breaks off.*] What are you laughing at?

MRS. STOCKMANN [*smiling at Kiil*]:   You don't understand, Father. Nobody can actually see bacteria, but that doesn't mean they're not there.

KIIL: Good girl, you stick with him! By God, this is the best thing I ever heard in my life!

DR. STOCKMANN [*smiling*]:   What do you mean?

KIIL: But tell me, you think you are actually going to get your brother to believe this?

DR. STOCKMANN: Well, we'll see soon enough!

KIIL: You really think he's that crazy?

DR. STOCKMANN: I hope the whole town will be that crazy, Morten.

KIIL: Ya, they probably are, and it'll serve them right too—they think they're so much smarter than us old-timers. Your good brother ordered them to bounce me out of the council, so they chased me out like a dog! Make jackasses out of all of them, Stockmann!

DR. STOCKMANN: Yes, but, Morten—

KIIL: Long-eared, short-tailed jackasses! [*He gets up.*] Stockmann, if you can make the Mayor and his elegant friends grab at this bait, I will give a couple of hundred crowns to charity, and right now, right on the spot.

DR. STOCKMANN: Well, that would be very kind of you, but I'm—

KIIL: I haven't got much to play around with, but if you can pull the rug out from under him with this cockroach business, I'll give at least fifty crowns to some poor people on Christmas Eve. Maybe this'll teach them to put some brains back in Town Hall!

Hovstad enters from the hall.

HOVSTAD: Good morning! Oh, pardon me . . .

KIIL [*enjoying this proof immensely*]:   Oh, this one is in on it, too?

HOVSTAD: What's that, sir?

DR. STOCKMANN: Of course he's in on it.

KIIL: Couldn't I have guessed that! And it's going to be in the papers, I suppose. You're sure tying down the corners, aren't you? Well, lay it on thick. I've got to go.

DR. STOCKMANN: Oh, no, stay a while, let me explain it to you!

KIIL: Oh, I get it, don't worry! Only you can see them, heh? That's the best idea I've ever—damn it, you shouldn't do this for nothing! [*He goes toward the hall.*]

MRS. STOCKMANN [*following him out, laughing*]:   But, Father, you don't understand about bacteria.

DR. STOCKMANN [*laughing*]:   The old badger doesn't believe a word of it.

HOVSTAD: What does he think you're doing?

DR. STOCKMANN: Making an idiot out of my brother—imagine that?

HOVSTAD: You got a few minutes?

DR. STOCKMANN: Sure, as long as you like.

HOVSTAD: Have you heard from the Mayor?

DR. STOCKMANN: Only that he's coming over later.

HOVSTAD: I've been thinking about this since last night—

DR. STOCKMANN: Don't say?

HOVSTAD: For you as a medical man, a scientist, this is a really rare opportunity. But I've been wondering if you realize that it ties in with a lot of other things.

DR. STOCKMANN: How do you mean? Sit down. [*They sit at the right*]. What are you driving at?

HOVSTAD: You said last night that the pollution comes from impurities in the ground—

DR. STOCKMANN: It comes from the poisonous dump up in Windmill Valley.

HOVSTAD: Doctor, I think it comes from an entirely different dump.

DR. STOCKMANN: What do you mean?

HOVSTAD [*with growing zeal*]:   The same dump that is poisoning and polluting our whole social life in this town.

DR. STOCKMANN: For God's sake, Hovstad, what are you babbling about?

HOVSTAD: Everything that matters in this town has fallen into the hands of a few bureaucrats.

DR. STOCKMANN: Well, they're not all bureaucrats—

HOVSTAD: They're all rich, all with old reputable names, and they've got everything in the palm of their hands.

DR. STOCKMANN: Yes, but they happen to have ability and knowledge.

HOVSTAD: Did they show ability and knowledge when they built the water system where they did?

DR. STOCKMANN: No, of course not, but that happened to be a blunder, and we'll clear it up now.

HOVSTAD: You really imagine it's going to be as easy as all that?

DR. STOCKMANN: Easy or not easy, it's got to be done.

HOVSTAD: Doctor, I've made up my mind to give this whole scandal very special treatment.

DR. STOCKMANN: Now wait. You can't call it a scandal yet.

HOVSTAD: Doctor, when I took over the *People's Messenger* I swore I'd blow that smug cabal of old, stubborn, self-satisfied fogies to bits. This is the story that can do it.

DR. STOCKMANN: But I still think we owe them a deep debt of gratitude for building the springs.

HOVSTAD: The Mayor being your brother, I wouldn't ordinarily want to touch it, but I know you'd never let that kind of thing obstruct the truth.

DR. STOCKMANN: Of course not, but . . .

HOVSTAD: I want you to understand me. I don't have to tell you I come from a simple family. I know in my bones what the underdog needs—he's got to have a say in the government of society. That's what brings out ability, intelligence, and self-respect in people.

DR. STOCKMANN: I understand that, but . . .

HOVSTAD: I think a newspaperman who turns down any chance to give the underdog a lift is taking on a responsibility that I don't want. I know perfectly well that in fancy circles they call it agitation, and they can call it anything they like if it makes them happy, but I have my own conscience—

DR. STOCKMANN [*interrupting*]: I agree with you, Hovstad, but this is just the water supply and— [*There is a knock on the door.*] Damn it! Come in!

Mr. Aslaksen, the publisher, enters from the hall. He is simply but neatly dressed. He wears gloves and carries a hat and an umbrella in his hand. He is so utterly drawn it is unnecessary to say anything at all about him.

ASLAKSEN: I beg your pardon, Doctor, if I intrude . . .

HOVSTAD [*standing up*]: Are you looking for me, Aslaksen?

ASLAKSEN: No, I didn't know you were here. I want to see the Doctor.

DR. STOCKMANN: What can I do for you?

ASLAKSEN: Is it true, Doctor, what I hear from Mr. Billing, that you intend to campaign for a better water system?

DR. STOCKMANN: Yes, for the Institute. But it's not a campaign.

ASLAKSEN: I just wanted to call and tell you that we are behind you a hundred percent.

HOVSTAD [*to Dr. Stockmann*]: There, you see!

DR. STOCKMANN: Mr. Aslaksen, I thank you with all my heart. But you see—

ASLAKSEN: We can be important, Doctor. When the little business-man wants to push something through, he turns out to be the majority, you know, and it's always good to have the majority on your side.

DR. STOCKMANN: That's certainly true, but I don't understand what this is all about. It seems to me it's a simple straightforward business. The water—

ASLAKSEN: Of course we intend to behave with moderation, Doctor. I always try to be a moderate and careful man.

DR. STOCKMANN: You are known for that, Mr. Aslaksen, but—

ASLAKSEN: The water system is very important to us little business-men, Doctor. Kirsten Springs are becoming a gold mine for this town, especially for the property owners, and that is why, in my capacity as chairman of the Property Owners Association—

DR. STOCKMANN: Yes.

ASLAKSEN: And furthermore, as a representative of the Temperance Society—You probably know, Doctor, that I am active for prohibition.

DR. STOCKMANN: So I have heard.

ASLAKSEN: As a result, I come into contact with all kinds of people, and since I am known to be a law-abiding and solid citizen, I have a certain influence in this town—you might even call it a little power.

DR. STOCKMANN: I know that very well, Mr. Aslaksen.

ASLAKSEN: That's why you can see that it would be practically nothing for me to arrange a demonstration.

DR. STOCKMANN: Demonstration! What are you going to demonstrate about?

ASLAKSEN: The citizens of the town complimenting you for bringing this important matter to everybody's attention. Obviously it would have to be done with the utmost moderation so as not to hurt the authorities.

HOVSTAD: This could knock the big-bellies right into the garbage can!

ASLAKSEN: No indiscretion or extreme aggressiveness toward the authorities, Mr. Hovstad! I don't want any wild-eyed radicalism on this thing. I've had enough of that in my time, and no good ever comes of it. But for a good solid citizen to express his calm, frank, and free opinion is something nobody can deny.

DR. STOCKMANN [*shaking the publisher's hand*]: My dear Aslaksen, I can't tell you how it heartens me to hear this kind of support. I am happy—I really am—I'm happy. Listen! Wouldn't you like a glass of sherry?

ASLAKSEN: I am a member of the Temperance Society. I—

DR. STOCKMANN: Well, how about a glass of beer?

ASLAKSEN [*considers, then*]: I don't think I can go quite that far, Doctor. I never take anything. Well, good day, and I want you to remember that the little man is behind you like a wall.

DR. STOCKMANN: Thank you.

ASLAKSEN: You have the solid majority on your side, because when the little—

DR. STOCKMANN [*trying to stop Aslaksen's talk*]: Thanks for that, Mr. Aslaksen, and good day.

ASLAKSEN: Are you going back to the printing shop, Mr. Hovstad?

HOVSTAD: I just have a thing or two to attend to here.

ASLAKSEN: Very well. (*He leaves.*)

HOVSTAD: Well, what do you say to a little hypodermic for these fence-sitting deadheads?

DR. STOCKMANN [*surprised*]: Why? I think Aslaksen is a very sincere man.

HOVSTAD: Isn't it time we pumped some guts into these well-intentioned men of good will? Under all their liberal talk they still idolize authority, and that's got to be rooted out of this town. This blunder of the water system has to be made clear to every voter. Let me print your report.

DR. STOCKMANN: Not until I talk to my brother.

HOVSTAD: I'll write an editorial in the meantime, and if the Mayor won't go along with us—

DR. STOCKMANN: I don't see how you can imagine such a thing!

HOVSTAD: Believe me, Doctor, it's possible, and then—

DR. STOCKMANN: Listen, I promise you: he will go along, and then you can print my report, every word of it.

HOVSTAD: On your word of honor?

DR. STOCKMANN [*giving Hovstad the manuscript*]:   Here it is. Take it. It can't do any harm for you to read it. Return it to me later.

HOVSTAD: Good day, Doctor.

DR. STOCKMANN: Good day. You'll see, it's going to be easier than you think, Hovstad!

HOVSTAD: I hope so, Doctor. Sincerely. Let me know as soon as you hear from His Honor. *He leaves.*

DR. STOCKMANN [*goes to the dining room and looks in*]:   Catherine! Oh, you're home already, Petra!

PETRA [*coming in*]:   I just got back from school.

MRS. STOCKMANN [*entering*]:   Hasn't he been here yet?

DR. STOCKMANN: Peter? No, but I just had a long chat with Hovstad. He's really fascinated with my discovery, and you know, it has more implications that I thought at first. Do you know what I have backing me up?

MRS. STOCKMANN: What in heaven's name have you got backing you up?

DR. STOCKMANN: The solid majority.

MRS. STOCKMANN: Is that good?

DR. STOCKMANN: Good? It's wonderful. You can't imagine the feeling, Catherine, to know that your own town feels like a brother to you. I have never felt so at home in this town since I was a boy. *A noise is heard.*

MRS. STOCKMANN: That must be the front door.

DR. STOCKMANN: Oh, it's Peter then. Come in.

PETER STOCKMANN [*entering from the hall*]:   Good morning!

DR. STOCKMANN: It's nice to see you, Peter.

MRS. STOCKMANN: Good morning. How are you today?

PETER STOCKMANN: Well, so so. [*To Dr. Stockmann.*]   I received your thesis about the condition of the springs yesterday.

DR. STOCKMANN: I got your note. Did you read it?

PETER STOCKMANN: I read it.

DR. STOCKMANN: Well, what do you have to say?

Peter Stockmann clears his throat and glances at the women.

MRS. STOCKMANN: Come on, Petra. [*She and Petra leave the room at the left.*]

PETER STOCKMANN [*after a moment*]:   Thomas, was it really necessary to go into this investigation behind my back?

DR. STOCKMANN: Yes. Until I was convinced myself, there was no point in—

PETER STOCKMANN: And now you are convinced?

DR. STOCKMANN: Well, certainly. Aren't you too, Peter? *Pause.* The University chemists corroborated . . .

PETER STOCKMANN: You intend to present this document to the Board of Directors, officially, as the medical officer of the springs?

DR. STOCKMANN: Of course, something's got to be done, and quick.

PETER STOCKMANN: You always use such strong expressions, Thomas. Among other things, in your report you say that we *guarantee* our guests and visitors a permanent case of poisoning.

DR. STOCKMANN: But, Peter, how can you describe it any other way? Imagine! Poisoned internally and externally!

PETER STOCKMANN: So you merrily conclude that we must build a waste-disposal plant—and reconstruct a brand-new water system from the bottom up!

DR. STOCKMANN: Well, do you know some other way out? I don't.

PETER STOCKMANN: I took a little walk over to the city engineer this morning and in the course of conversation I sort of jokingly mentioned these changes—as something we might consider for the future, you know.

DR. STOCKMANN: The future won't be soon enough, Peter.

PETER STOCKMANN: The engineer kind of smiled at my extravagance and gave me a few facts. I don't suppose you have taken the trouble to consider what your proposed changes would cost?

DR. STOCKMANN: No, I never thought of that.

PETER STOCKMANN: Naturally. Your little project would come to at least three hundred thousand crowns.

DR. STOCKMANN [*astonished*]:   That expensive!

PETER STOCKMANN: Oh, don't look so upset—it's only money. The worst thing is that it would take some two years.

DR. STOCKMANN: Two years?

PETER STOCKMANN: At the least. And what do you propose we do about the springs in the meantime? Shut them up, no doubt! Because we would have to, you know. As soon as the rumor gets around that the water is dangerous, we won't have a visitor left. So that's the picture, Thomas. You have it in your power literally to ruin your own town.

DR. STOCKMANN: Now look, Peter! I don't want to ruin anything.

PETER STOCKMANN: Kirsten Springs are the blood supply of this town, Thomas—the only future we've got here. Now will you stop and think?

DR. STOCKMANN: Good God! Well, what do you think we ought to do?

PETER STOCKMANN: Your report has not convinced me that the conditions are as dangerous as you try to make them.

DR. STOCKMANN: Now listen; they are even worse than the report makes them out to be. Remember, summer is coming, and the warm weather!

PETER STOCKMANN: I think you're exaggerating. A capable physician ought to know what precautions to take.

DR. STOCKMANN: And what then?

PETER STOCKMANN: The existing water supply for the springs is a fact, Thomas, and has got to be treated as a fact. If you are reasonable and act with discretion, the directors of the Institute will be inclined to take under consideration any means to make possible improvements, reasonably and without financial sacrifices.

DR. STOCKMANN: Peter, do you imagine that I would ever agree to such trickery?

PETER STOCKMANN: Trickery?

DR. STOCKMANN: Yes, a trick, a fraud, a lie! A treachery, a downright crime, against the public and against the whole community!

PETER STOCKMANN: I said before that I am not convinced that there is any actual danger.

DR. STOCKMANN: Oh, you aren't? Anything else is impossible! My report is an absolute fact. The only trouble is that you and your administration were the ones who insisted that the water supply be built where it is, and now you're afraid to admit the blunder you committed. Damn it! Don't you think I can see through it all?

PETER STOCKMANN: All right, let's suppose that's true. Maybe I do care a little about my reputation. I still say I do it for the good of the town—without moral authority there can be no government. And that is why, Thomas, it is my duty to prevent your report from reaching the Board. Some time later I will bring up the matter for discussion. In the meantime, not a single word is to reach the public.

DR. STOCKMANN: Oh, my dear Peter, do you imagine you can prevent that!

PETER STOCKMANN: It will be prevented.

DR. STOCKMANN: It can't be. There are too many people who already know about it.

PETER STOCKMANN, *angered:*   Who? It can't possibly be those people from the *Daily Messenger* who—

DR. STOCKMANN: Exactly. The liberal, free, and independent press will stand up and do its duty!

PETER STOCKMANN: You are an unbelievably irresponsible man, Thomas! Can't you imagine what consequences that is going to have for you?

DR. STOCKMANN: For me?

PETER STOCKMANN: Yes, for you and your family.

DR. STOCKMANN: What the hell are you saying now!

PETER STOCKMANN: I believe I have the right to think of myself as a helpful brother, Thomas.

DR. STOCKMANN: You have been, and I thank you deeply for it.

PETER STOCKMANN: Don't mention it. I often couldn't help myself. I had hoped that by improving your finances I would be able to keep you from running completely hog wild.

DR. STOCKMANN: You mean it was only for your own sake?

PETER STOCKMANN: Partly, yes. What do you imagine people think of an official whose closest relatives get themselves into trouble time and time again?

DR. STOCKMANN: And that's what I have done?

PETER STOCKMANN: You do it without knowing it. You're like a man with an automatic brain—as soon as an idea breaks into your head, no matter how idiotic it may be, you get up like a sleepwalker and start writing a pamphlet about it.

DR. STOCKMANN: Peter, don't you think it's a citizen's duty to share a new idea with the public?

PETER STOCKMANN: The public doesn't need new ideas—the public is much better off with old ideas.

DR. STOCKMANN: You're not even embarrassed to say that?

PETER STOCKMANN: Now look, I'm going to lay this out once and for all. You're always barking about authority. If a man gives you an order he's persecuting you. Nothing is important enough to respect once you decide to revolt against your superiors. All right then, I give up. I'm not going to try to change you any more. I told you the stakes you are playing for here, and now I am going to give you an order. And I warn you, you had better obey it if you value your career.

DR. STOCKMANN: What kind of an order?

PETER STOCKMANN: You are going to deny these rumors officially.

DR. STOCKMANN: How?

PETER STOCKMANN: You simply say that you went into the examination of the water more thoroughly and you find that you overestimated the danger.

DR. STOCKMANN: I see.

PETER STOCKMANN: And that you have complete confidence that whatever improvements are needed, the management will certainly take care of them.

DR. STOCKMANN [after a pause]: My convictions come from the condition of the water. My convictions will change when the water changes, and for no other reason.

PETER STOCKMANN: What are you talking about convictions? You're an official, you keep your convictions to yourself!

DR. STOCKMANN: To myself?

PETER STOCKMANN: As an official, I said. God knows, as a private person that's something else, but as a subordinate employee of the Institute, you have no right to express any convictions or personal opinions about anything connected with policy.

DR. STOCKMANN: Now you listen to me. I am a doctor and a scientist—

PETER STOCKMANN: This has nothing to do with science!

DR. STOCKMANN: Peter, I have the right to express my opinion on anything in the world!

PETER STOCKMANN: Not about the Institute—that I forbid.

DR. STOCKMANN: You forbid!

PETER STOCKMANN: I forbid you as your superior, and when I give orders you obey.

DR. STOCKMANN: Peter, if you weren't my brother—

PETRA [throwing the door at the left open]: Father! You aren't going to stand for this! [She enters.]

MRS. STOCKMANN [coming in after her]: Petra, Petra!

PETER STOCKMANN: What have you two been doing, eavesdropping?

MRS. STOCKMANN: You were talking so loud we couldn't help . . .

PETRA: Yes, I was eavesdropping!

PETER STOCKMANN: That makes me very happy.

DR. STOCKMANN [*approaching his brother*]:   You said something to me about forbidding—

PETER STOCKMANN: You forced me to.

DR. STOCKMANN: So you want me to spit in my own face officially— is that it?

PETER STOCKMANN: Why must you always be so colorful?

DR. STOCKMANN: And if I don't obey?

PETER STOCKMANN: Then we will publish our own statement, to calm the public.

DR. STOCKMANN: Good enough! And I will write against you. I will stick to what I said, and I will prove that I am right and that you are wrong, and what will you do then?

PETER STOCKMANN: Then I simply won't be able to prevent your dismissal.

DR. STOCKMANN: What!

PETRA: Father!

PETER STOCKMANN: Dismissed from the Institute is what I said. If you want to make war on Kirsten Springs, you have no right to be on the Board of Directors.

DR. STOCKMANN (*after a pause*):   You'd dare to do that?

PETER STOCKMANN: Oh, no, you're the daring man.

PETRA: Uncle, this is a rotten way to treat a man like Father!

MRS. STOCKMANN: Will you be quiet, Petra!

PETER STOCKMANN: So young and you've got opinions already—but that's natural. (*To Mrs. Stockmann.*) Catherine dear, you're probably the only sane person in this house. Knock some sense into his head, will you? Make him realize what he's driving his whole family into.

DR. STOCKMANN: My family concerns nobody but myself.

PETER STOCKMANN: His family and his own town.

DR. STOCKMANN: I'm going to show you who loves his town. The people are going to get the full stink of this corruption, Peter, and then we will see who loves his town!

PETER STOCKMANN: You love your town when you blindly, spitefully, stubbornly go ahead trying to cut off our most important industry?

DR. STOCKMANN: That source is poisoned, man. We are getting fat by peddling filth and corruption to innocent people!

PETER STOCKMANN: I think this has gone beyond opinions and convictions, Thomas. A man who can throw that kind of insinuation around is nothing but a traitor to society!

DR. STOCKMANN [*starting toward his brother in a fury*]:   How dare you to—

MRS. STOCKMANN [*stepping between them*]:   Tom!

PETRA [*grabbing her father's arm*]:   Be careful, Father!

PETER STOCKMANN [*with dignity*]:   I won't expose myself to violence. You have been warned. Consider what you owe yourself and your family! Good day! [*He exits.*]

DR. STOCKMANN [*walking up and down*]:   He's insulted. *He's* insulted!

MRS. STOCKMANN: It's shameful, Tom.

PETRA: Oh, I would love to give him a piece of my mind!

DR. STOCKMANN: It was my own fault! I should have shown my teeth right from the beginning. He called me a traitor to society. Me! Damn it all, that's not going to stick!

MRS. STOCKMANN: Please, think! He's got all the power on his side.

DR. STOCKMANN: Yes, but I have the truth on mine.

MRS. STOCKMANN: Without power, what good is the truth?

PETRA: Mother, how can you say such a thing?

DR. STOCKMANN: That's ridiculous, Catherine. I have the liberal press with me, and the majority. If that isn't power, what is?

MRS. STOCKMANN: But, for heaven's sake, Tom, you aren't going to—

DR. STOCKMANN: What am I not going to do?

MRS. STOCKMANN: You aren't going to fight it out in public with your brother!

DR. STOCKMANN: What the hell else do you want me to do?

MRS. STOCKMANN: But it won't do you any earthly good. If they won't do it, they won't. All you'll get out of it is a notice that you're fired.

DR. STOCKMANN: I am going to do my duty, Catherine. Me, the man he calls a traitor to society!

MRS. STOCKMANN: And how about your duty toward your family— the people you're supposed to provide for?

PETRA: Don't always think of us first, Mother.

MRS. STOCKMANN [*to Petra*]:   You can talk! If worst comes to worst, you can manage for yourself. But what about the boys, Tom, and you and me?

DR. STOCKMANN: What about you? You want me to be the miserable animal who'd crawl up the boots of that damn gang? Will you be happy if I can't face myself the rest of my life?

MRS. STOCKMANN: Tom, Tom, there's so much injustice in the world! You've simply got to learn to live with it. If you go on this way, God help us, we'll have no money again. Is it so long since the north that you've forgotten what it was to live like we lived? Haven't we had enough of that for one lifetime? [*The boys enter.*] What will happen to them? We've got nothing if you're fired!

DR. STOCKMANN: Stop it! [*He looks at the boys.*] Well, boys, did you learn anything in school today?

MORTEN [*looking at them, puzzled*]:   We learned what an insect is.

DR. STOCKMANN: You don't say!

MORTEN: What happened here? Why is everybody—

DR. STOCKMANN: Nothing, nothing. You know what I'm going to do, boys? From now on I'm going to teach you what a man is. [*He looks at Mrs. Stockmann. She cries as the curtain falls.*]

Act II

Scene I. Editorial offices of the *People's Daily Messenger*

The editorial office of the People's Daily Messenger. At the back of the room, to the left, is a door leading to the printing room. Near it, in the left wall, is another door. At the right of the stage is the entrance door. In the middle of the room there is a large table covered with papers, newspapers, and books. Around it are a few chairs. A writing desk stands against the right wall. The room is dingy and cheerless, the furniture shabby.

As the curtain rises, Billing is sitting at the desk, reading the manuscript. Hovstad comes in after a moment from the printing room. Billing looks up.

BILLING: The Doctor not come yet?

HOVSTAD: No, not yet. You finish it?

Billing holds up a hand to signal "just a moment." He reads on, the last paragraph of the manuscript. Hovstad comes and stands over him, reading with him. Now Billing closes the manuscript, glances up at Hovstad with some trepidation, then looks off. Hovstad, looking at Billing, walks a few steps away.

HOVSTAD: Well? What do you think of it?

BILLING [*with some hesitation*]:   It's devastating. The Doctor is a brilliant man. I swear, I myself never really understood how incompetent those fat fellows are, on top. [*He picks up the manuscript and waves it a little.*] I hear the rumble of revolution in this.

HOVSTAD [*looking toward the door*]:   Sssh! Aslaksen's inside.

BILLING: Aslaksen's a coward. With all that moderation talk, all he's saying is, he's yellow. You're going to print this, aren't you?

HOVSTAD: Sure, I'm just waiting for the Doctor to give the word. If his brother hasn't given in, we put it on the press anyway.

BILLING: Yes, but if the Mayor's against this it's going to get pretty rough. You know that, don't you?

HOVSTAD: Just let him try to block the reconstruction—the little businessmen and the whole town'll be screaming for his head. Aslaksen'll see to that.

BILLING [*ecstatically*]:   The stockholders'll have to lay out a fortune of money if this goes through!

HOVSTAD: My boy, I think it's going to bust them. And when the springs go busted, the people are finally going to understand the level of genius that's been running this town. Those five sheets of paper are going to put in a liberal administration once and for all.

BILLING: It's a revolution. You know that? [*With hope and fear.*] I mean it, we're on the edge of a real revolution!

DR. STOCKMANN (*entering*):   Put it on the press!

HOVSTAD (*excited*):   Wonderful! What did the Mayor say?

DR. STOCKMANN: The Mayor has declared war, so war is what it's going to be! [*He takes the manuscript from Billing.*] And this is only the beginning! You know what he tried to do?

BILLING [*calling into the printing room*]:   Mr. Aslaksen, the Doctor's here!

DR. STOCKMANN [*continuing*]:   He actually tried to blackmail me! He's got the nerve to tell me that I'm not allowed to speak my mind without his permission! Imagine the shameless effrontery!

HOVSTAD: He actually said it right out?

DR. STOCKMANN: Right to my face! The trouble with me was I kept giving them credit for being our kind of people, but they're dictators!

They're people who'll try to hold power even if they have to poison the town to do it.

Toward the last part of Dr. Stockmann's speech Aslaksen enters.

ASLAKSEN: Now take it easy, Doctor, you—you mustn't always be throwing accusations. I'm with you, you understand, but moderation—

DR. STOCKMANN [*cutting him off*]:   What'd you think of the article, Hovstad?

HOVSTAD: It's a masterpiece. In one blow you've managed to prove beyond any doubt what kind of men are running us.

ASLAKSEN: May we print it now, then?

DR. STOCKMANN: I should say *so!*

HOVSTAD: We'll have it ready for tomorrow's paper.

DR. STOCKMANN: And listen, Mr. Aslaksen, do me a favor, will you? You run a fine paper, but supervise the printing personally, eh? I'd hate to see the weather report stuck into the middle of my article.

ASLAKSEN (*laughing*):   Don't worry, that won't happen this time!

DR. STOCKMANN: Make it perfect, eh? Like you were printing money. You can't imagine how I'm dying to see it in print. After all the lies in the papers, the half-lies, the quarter-lies—to finally see the absolute, unvarnished truth about something important. And this is only the beginning. We'll go on to other subjects and blow up every lie we live by! What do you say, Aslaksen?

ASLAKSEN (*nodding in agreement*):   But just remember . . .

BILLING and HOVSTAD *together with* ASLAKSEN: Moderation!

ASLAKSEN [*to Billing and Hovstad*]:   I don't know what's so funny about that!

BILLING (*enthralled*):   Doctor Stockmann, I feel as though I were standing in some historic painting. Goddammit, this is a historic day! Someday this scene'll be in a museum, entitled, "The Day the Truth Was Born."

DR. STOCKMANN [*suddenly*]:   Oh! I've got a patient half-bandaged down the street. [*He leaves.*]

HOVSTAD [*to Aslaksen*]:   I hope you realize how useful he could be to us.

ASLAKSEN: I don't like that business about "this is only the beginning." Let him stick to the springs.

BILLING: What makes you so scared all the time?

ASLAKSEN: I have to live here. It'd be different if he were attacking the national government or something, but if he thinks I'm going to start going after the whole town administration—

BILLING: What's the difference? Bad is bad!

ASLAKSEN: Yes, but there is a difference. You attack the national government, what's going to happen? Nothing. They go right on. But a town administration—they're liable to be overthrown or something! I represent the small property owners in this town—

BILLING: Ha! It's always the same. Give a man a little property and the truth can go to hell!

ASLAKSEN: Mr. Billing, I'm older than you are. I've seen fireeaters before. You know who used to work at that desk before you? Councilman Stensford—*councilman!*

BILLING: Just because I work at a renegade's desk, does that mean—

ASLAKSEN: You're a politician. A politician never knows where he's going to end up. And besides you applied for a job as secretary to the Magistrate, didn't you?

HOVSTAD [*surprised, laughs*]:   Billing!

BILLING [*to Hovstad*]:   Well, why not? If I get it I'll have a chance to put across some good things. I could put plenty of big boys on the spot with a job like that!

ASLAKSEN: All right, I'm just saying. [*He goes to the printing-room door.*] People change. Just remember when you call me a coward—I may not have made the hot speeches, but I never went back on my beliefs either. Unlike some of the big radicals around here, I didn't change. Of course, I *am* a little more moderate, but moderation is—

HOVSTAD: Oh, God!

ASLAKSEN: I don't see what's so funny about that! [*He glares at Hovstad and goes out.*]

BILLING: If we could get rid of him we—

HOVSTAD: Take it easy—he pays the printing bill, he's not that bad. [*He picks up the manuscript.*] I'll get the printer on this. [*He starts out.*]

BILLING: Say, Hovstad, how about asking Stockmann to back us? Then we could really put out a paper!

HOVSTAD: What would he do for money?

BILLING: His father-in-law.

HOVSTAD: Kiil? Since when has he got money?

BILLING: I think he's loaded with it.

HOVSTAD: No! Why, as long as I've known him he's worn the same overcoat, the same suit—

BILLING: Yeah, and the same ring on his right hand. You ever get a look at that boulder? [*He points to his finger.*]

HOVSTAD: No, I never—

BILLING: All year he wears the diamond inside, but on New Year's Eve he turns it around. Figure it out—when a man has no visible means of support, what is he living on? Money, right?

Petra enters, carrying a book.

PETRA: Hello.

HOVSTAD: Well, fancy seeing you here. Sit down. What—

PETRA [*walking slowly up to Hovstad*]:   I want to ask you a question. [*She starts to open the book.*]

BILLING: What's that?

PETRA: The English novel you wanted translated.

HOVSTAD: Aren't you going to do it?

PETRA [*with deadly seriousness and curiosity*]:   I don't get this.

HOVSTAD: You don't get what?

PETRA: This book is absolutely against everything you people believe.

HOVSTAD: Oh, it isn't that bad.

PETRA: But, Mr. Hovstad, it says if you're good there's a supernatural force that'll fix it so you end up happy. And if you're bad you'll be punished. Since when does the world work that way?

HOVSTAD: Yes, Petra, but this is a newspaper, people like to read that kind of thing. They buy the paper for that and then we slip in our political stuff. A newspaper can't buck the public—

PETRA [*astonished, beginning to be angry*]:   You don't say! [*She starts to go.*]

HOVSTAD [*hurrying after her*]:   Now, wait a minute, I don't want you to go feeling that way. [*He holds the manuscript out to Billing.*] Here, take this to the printer, will you?

BILLING [*taking the manuscript*]:   Sure. (*He goes.*)

HOVSTAD: I just want you to understand something: I never even read that book. It was Billing's idea.

PETRA [*trying to penetrate his eyes*]:   I thought he was a radical.

HOVSTAD: He is. But he's also a—

PETRA [*testily*]:   A newspaperman.

HOVSTAD: Well, that too, but I was going to say that Billing is trying to get the job as secretary to the Magistrate.

PETRA: What?

HOVSTAD: People are—people, Miss Stockmann.

PETRA: But the Magistrate! He's been fighting everything progressive in this town for thirty years.

HOVSTAD: Let's not argue about it, I just didn't want you to go out of here with a wrong idea of me. I guess you know that I—I happen to admire women like you. I've never had a chance to tell you, but I—well, I want you to know it. Do you mind? [*He smiles.*]

PETRA: No, I don't mind, but—reading that book upset me. I really don't understand. Will you tell me why you're supporting my father?

HOVSTAD: What's the mystery? It's a matter of principle.

PETRA: But a paper that'll print a book like this has no principle.

HOVSTAD: Why do you jump to such extremes? You're just like . . .

PETRA: Like what?

HOVSTAD: I simply mean that . . .

PETRA [*moving away from him*]:   Like my father, you mean. You really have no use for him, do you?

HOVSTAD: Now wait a minute!

PETRA: What's behind this? Are you just trying to hold my hand or something?

HOVSTAD: I happen to agree with your father, and that's why I'm printing his stuff.

PETRA: You're trying to put something over, I think. Why are you in this?

HOVSTAD: Who're you accusing? Billing gave you that book, not me!

PETRA: But you don't mind printing it, do you? What are you trying to do with my father? You have no principles—what are you up to here?

Aslaksen hurriedly enters from the printing shop, Stockmann's manuscript in his hand.

ASLAKSEN: My God! Hovstad! (*He sees Petra*). Miss Stockmann.

PETRA [*looking at Hovstad*]:   I don't think I've been so frightened in my life. [*She goes out.*]

HOVSTAD [*starting after her*]:   Please, you mustn't think I—

ASLAKSEN [*stopping him*]:   Where are you going? The Mayor's out there.

HOVSTAD: The Mayor!

ASLAKSEN: He wants to speak to you. He came in the back door. He doesn't want to be seen.

HOVSTAD: What does he want? [*He goes to the printing-room door, opens it, calls out with a certain edge of servility.*] Come in, Your Honor!

PETER STOCKMANN [*entering*]:   Thank you.

Hovstad carefully closes the door.

PETER STOCKMANN [*walking around*]:   It's clean! I always imagined this place would look dirty. But it's clean. [*Commendingly.*] Very nice, Mr. Aslaksen. [*He puts his hat on the desk.*]

ASLAKSEN: Not at all, Your Honor—I mean to say, I always . . .

HOVSTAD: What can I do for you, Your Honor? Sit down?

PETER STOCKMANN [*sits, placing his cane on the table*]:   I had a very annoying thing happen today, Mr. Hovstad.

HOVSTAD: That so?

PETER STOCKMANN: It seems my brother has written some sort of—memorandum. About the springs.

HOVSTAD: You don't say.

PETER STOCKMANN [*looking at Hovstad now*]:   He mentioned it . . . to you?

HOVSTAD: Yes. I think he said something about it.

ASLAKSEN [*nervously starts to go out, attempting to hide the manuscript*]:   Will you excuse me, gentlemen . . .

PETER STOCKMANN [*pointing to the manuscript*]:   That's it, isn't it?

ASLAKSEN: This? I don't know, I haven't had a chance to look at it, the printer just handed it to me . . .

HOVSTAD: Isn't that the thing the printer wanted the spelling checked?

ASLAKSEN: That's it. it's only a question of spelling. I'll be right back.

PETER STOCKMANN: I'm very good at spelling. [*He holds out his hand.*] Maybe I can help you.

HOVSTAD: No, Your Honor, there's some Latin in it. You wouldn't know Latin, would you?

PETER STOCKMANN: Oh, yes. I used to help my brother with his Latin all the time. Let me have it.

Aslaksen gives him the manuscript. Peter Stockmann looks at the title on the first page, then glances up sarcastically at Hovstad, who avoids his eyes.

PETER STOCKMANN: You're going to print this?

HOVSTAD: I can't very well refuse a signed article. A signed article is the author's responsibility.

PETER STOCKMANN: Mr. Aslaksen, you're going to allow this?

ASLAKSEN: I'm the publisher, not the editor, Your Honor. My policy is freedom for the editor.

PETER STOCKMANN: You have a point—I can see that.

ASLAKSEN [*reaching for the manuscript*]:   So if you don't mind . . .

PETER STOCKMANN: Not at all. [*But he holds on to the manuscript. After a pause.*] This reconstruction of the springs—

ASLAKSEN: I realize, Your Honor—it does mean tremendous sacrifices for the stockholders.

PETER STOCKMANN: Don't upset yourself. The first thing a Mayor learns is that the less wealthy can always be prevailed upon to demand a spirit of sacrifice for the public good.

ASLAKSEN: I'm glad you see that.

PETER STOCKMANN: Oh, yes. Especially when it's the wealthy who are going to do the sacrificing. What you don't seem to understand, Mr. Aslaksen, is that so long as I am Mayor, any changes in those springs are going to be paid for by a municipal loan.

ASLAKSEN: A municipal—you mean you're going to tax the people for this?

PETER STOCKMANN: Exactly.

HOVSTAD: But the springs are a private corporation!

PETER STOCKMANN: The corporation built Kirsten Springs out of its own money. If the people want them changed, the people naturally must pay the bill. The corporation is in no position to put out any more money. It simply can't do it.

ASLAKSEN [*to Hovstad*]:   That's impossible! People will never stand for a new tax. [*To the Mayor.*] Is this a fact or your opinion?

PETER STOCKMANN: It happens to be a fact. Plus another fact— you'll forgive me for talking about facts in a newspaper office—but don't forget that the springs will take two years to make over. Two years without income for your small businessmen, Mr. Aslaksen, and a heavy new tax besides. And all because [*his private emotion comes to the surface; he throttles the manuscript in his hand*] because of this dream, this hallucination, that we live in a pesthole!

HOVSTAD: That's based on science.

PETER STOCKMANN [*raising the manuscript and throwing it down on the table.*]   This is based on vindictiveness, on his hatred of authority and nothing else. [*He pounds on the manuscript.*] This is the mad dream of a man who is trying to blow up our way of life! It has nothing to do with reform or science or anything else, but pure and simple destruction! And I intend to see to it that the people understand it exactly so!

ASLAKSEN [*hit by this*]:   My God! [*To Hovstad.*]   Maybe . . . You sure you want to support this thing, Hovstad?

HOVSTAD [*nervously*]:   Frankly I'd never thought of it in quite that way. I mean . . . [*To the Mayor.*] When you think of it psychologically it's completely possible, of course, that the man is simply out to—I don't know what to say, Your Honor. I'd hate to hurt the town in any way. I never imagined we'd have to have a new tax.

PETER STOCKMANN: You should have imagined it because you're going to have to advocate it. Unless, of course, liberal and radical newspaper readers enjoy high taxes. But you'd know that better than I. I happen to have here a brief story of the actual facts. It proves that, with a little care, nobody need be harmed at all by the water. [*He takes out a long envelope.*] Of course, in time we'd have to make a few minor structural changes and we'd pay for those.

HOVSTAD: May I see that?

PETER STOCKMANN: I want you to *study* it, Mr. Hovstad, and see if you don't agree that—

BILLING [*entering quickly*]:   Are you expecting the Doctor?

PETER STOCKMANN [*alarmed*]:   He's here?

BILLING: Just coming across the street.

PETER STOCKMANN: I'd rather not run into him here. How can I . . .

BILLING: Right this way, sir, hurry up!

ASLAKSEN, [*at the entrance door, peeking*]:   Hurry up!

PETER STOCKMANN, [*going with Billing through the door at the left*]: Get him out of here right away! [*They exit.*]

HOVSTAD: Do something, do something!

Aslaksen pokes among some papers on the table. Hovstad sits at the desk, starts to "write." Dr. Stockmann enters.

DR. STOCKMANN: Any proofs yet? [*He sees they hardly turn to him.*] I guess not, eh?

ASLAKSEN [*without turning*]:   No, you can't expect them for some time.

DR. STOCKMANN: You mind if I wait?

HOVSTAD: No sense in that, Doctor, it'll be quite a while yet.

DR. STOCKMANN [*laughing, places his hand on Hovstad's back*]:   Bear with me, Hovstad, I just can't wait to see it in print.

HOVSTAD: We're pretty busy, Doctor, so . . .

DR. STOCKMANN [*starting toward the door*]:   Don't let me hold you up. That's the way to be, busy, busy. We'll make this town shine like a jewel! [*He has opened the door, now he comes back.*] Just one thing. I—

HOVSTAD: Couldn't we talk some other time? We're very—

DR. STOCKMANN: Two words. Just walking down the street now, I looked at the people, in the stores, driving the wagons, and suddenly I was—well, touched, you know? By their innocence, I mean. What I'm driving at is, when this exposé breaks they're liable to start making a saint out of me or something, and I—Aslaksen, I want you to promise me that you're not going to try to get up any dinner for me or—

ASLAKSEN [turning toward the Doctor]: Doctor, there's no use concealing—

DR. STOCKMANN: I knew it. Now look, I will simply not attend a dinner in my honor.

HOVSTAD [getting up]: Doctor, I think it's time we—

Mrs. Stockmann enters.

MRS. STOCKMANN: I thought so. Thomas, I want you home. Now come. I want you to talk to Petra.

DR. STOCKMANN: What happened? What are you doing here?

HOVSTAD: Something wrong, Mrs. Stockmann?

MRS. STOCKMANN [leveling a look of accusation at Hovstad]: Doctor Stockmann is the father of three children, Mr. Hovstad.

DR. STOCKMANN: Now look, dear, everybody knows that. What's the—

MRS. STOCKMANN [restraining an outburst at her husband]: Nobody would believe it from the way you're dragging us into this disaster!

DR. STOCKMANN: What disaster?

MRS. STOCKMANN [to Hovstad]: He treated you like a son, now you make a fool of him?

HOVSTAD: I'm not making a—

DR. STOCKMANN: Catherine! (He indicates Hovstad.) How can you accuse—

MRS. STOCKMANN [to Hovstad]: He'll lose his job at the springs, do you realize that? You print the article, and they'll grind him up like a piece of flesh!

DR. STOCKMANN: Catherine, you're embarrassing me! I beg your pardon, gentlemen . . .

MRS. STOCKMANN: Mr. Hovstad, what are you up to?

DR. STOCKMANN: I won't have you jumping at Hovstad, Catherine!

MRS. STOCKMANN: I want you home! This man is not your friend!

DR. STOCKMANN: He is my friend! Any man who shares my risk is my friend! You simply don't understand that as soon as this breaks everybody in this town is going to come out in the streets and drive that gang of— [*He picks up the Mayor's cane from the table, notices what it is, and stops. He looks from it to Hovstad and Aslaksen.*] What's this? [*They don't reply. Now he notices the hat on the desk and picks it up with the tip of the cane. He looks at them again. He is angry, incredulous.*]   What the hell is he doing here?

ASLAKSEN: All right, Doctor, now let's be calm and—

DR. STOCKMANN [*starting to move*]:   Where is he? What'd he do, talk you out of it? Hovstad! [*Hovstad remains immobile.*] He won't get away with it! Where'd you hide him? [*He opens the door at the left.*]

ASLAKSEN: Be careful, Doctor!

Peter Stockmann enters with Billing through the door Dr. Stockmann opened. Peter Stockmann tries to hide his embarrassment.

DR. STOCKMANN: Well, Peter, poisoning the water was not enough! You're working on the press now, eh? [*He crosses to the entrance door.*]

PETER STOCKMANN: My hat, please. And my stick. [*Dr. Stockmann puts on the Mayor's hat.*] Now what's *this* nonsense! Take that off, that's official insignia!

DR. STOCKMANN: I just wanted you to realize, Peter, [*he takes off the hat and looks at it*] that anyone may wear this hat in a democracy, and that a free citizen is not afraid to touch it. [*He hands him the hat.*] And as for the baton of command, Your Honor, it can pass from hand to hand. [*He hands the cane to Peter Stockmann.*] So don't gloat yet. The people haven't spoken. [*He turns to Hovstad and Aslaksen.*] And I have the people because I have the truth, my friends!

ASLAKSEN: Doctor, we're not scientists. We can't judge whether your article is really true.

DR. STOCKMANN: Then print it under my name. Let *me* defend it!

HOVSTAD: I'm not printing it. I'm not going to sacrifice this newspaper. When the whole story gets out the public is not going to stand for any changes in the springs.

ASLAKSEN: His Honor just told us, Doctor—you see, there will have to be a new tax—

DR. STOCKMANN: Ahhhhh! Yes. I see. That's why you're not scientists suddenly and can't decide if I'm telling the truth. Well. So!

HOVSTAD: Don't take that attitude. The point is—

DR. STOCKMANN: The point, the point, oh, the point is going to fly through this town like an arrow, and I am going to fire it! *To Aslaksen:* Will you print this article as a pamphlet? I'll pay for it.

ASLAKSEN: I'm not going to ruin this paper and this town. Doctor, for the sake of your family—

MRS. STOCKMANN: You can leave his family out of this, Mr. Aslaksen. God help me, I think you people are horrible!

DR. STOCKMANN: My article, if you don't mind.

ASLAKSEN [*giving it to him*]:   Doctor, you won't get it printed in this town.

PETER STOCKMANN: Can't you forget it? [*He indicates Hovstad and Aslaksen.*] Can't you see now that everybody—

DR. STOCKMANN: Your Honor, I can't forget it, and you will never forget it as long as you live. I am going to call a mass meeting, and I—

PETER STOCKMANN: And who is going to rent you a hall?

DR. STOCKMANN: Then I will take a drum and go from street to street, proclaiming that the springs are befouled and poison is rotting the body politic! [*He starts for the door.*]

PETER STOCKMANN: And I believe you really are that mad!

DR. STOCKMANN: Mad? Oh, my brother, you haven't even heard me raise my voice yet. Catherine? [*He holds out his hand, she gives him her elbow. They go stiffly out.*]

Peter Stockmann looks regretfully toward the exit, then takes out his manuscript and hands it to Hovstad, who in turn gives it to Billing, who hands it to Aslaksen, who takes it and exits. Peter Stockmann puts his hat on and moves toward the door. Blackout. The curtain falls.

Act II

Scene II. A room in Captain Horster's house

A room in Captain Horster's house. The room is bare, as though unused for a long time. A large doorway is at the left, two shuttered windows at the back, and another door at the right. Upstage right, packing cases have been set together, forming a platform, on which are a chair and a small table.

There are two chairs next to the platform at the right. One chair stands downstage left.

The room is angled, thus making possible the illusion of a large crowd off in the wing to the left. The platform faces the audience at an angle, thus giving the speakers the chance to speak straight out front and creating the illusion of a large crowd by addressing "people" in the audience.

As the curtain rises the room is empty. Captain Horster enters, carrying a pitcher of water, a glass, and a bell. He is putting these on the table when Billing enters. A crowd is heard talking outside in the street.

BILLING: Captain Horster?

HORSTER [*turning*]:   Oh, come in. I don't have enough chairs for a lot of people so I decided not to have chairs at all.

BILLING: My name is Billing. Don't you remember, at the Doctor's house?

HORSTER [*a little coldly*]:   Oh, yes, sure. I've been so busy I didn't recognize you. [*He goes to a window and looks out.*] Why don't those people come inside?

BILLING: I don't know, I guess they're waiting for the Mayor or somebody important so they can be sure it's respectable in here. I wanted to ask you a question before it begins, Captain. Why are you lending your house for this? I never heard of you connected with anything political.

HORSTER [*standing still*]:   I'll answer that. I travel most of the year and—did you ever travel?

BILLING: Not abroad, no.

HORSTER: Well, I've been in a lot of places where people aren't allowed to say unpopular things. Did you know that?

BILLING: Sure, I've read about it.

HORSTER [*simply*]:   Well, I don't like it. [*He starts to go out.*]

BILLING: One more question. What's your opinion about the Doctor's proposition to rebuild the springs?

HORSTER [*turning, thinks, then*]:   Don't understand a thing about it.

Three citizens enter.

HORSTER: Come in, come in. I don't have enough chairs so you'll just have to stand. [*He goes out.*]

FIRST CITIZEN: Try the horn.

SECOND CITIZEN: No, let him start to talk first.

THIRD CITIZEN [*a big beef of a man, takes out a horn*]:   Wait'll they hear this! I could blow your mustache off with this!

Horster returns. He sees the horn and stops abruptly.

HORSTER: I don't want any roughhouse, you hear me?

Mrs. Stockmann and Petra enter.

HORSTER: Come in. I've got chairs just for you.

MRS. STOCKMANN [*nervously*]:   There's quite a crowd on the sidewalk. Why don't they come in?

HORSTER: I suppose they're waiting for the Mayor.

PETRA: Are all those people on his side?

HORSTER: Who knows? People are bashful, and it's so unusual to come to a meeting like this, I suppose they—

BILLING [*going over to this group*]:   Good evening, ladies. *They simply look at him.* I don't blame you for not speaking. I just wanted to say I don't think this is going to be a place for ladies tonight.

MRS. STOCKMANN: I don't remember asking your advice, Mr. Billing.

BILLING: I'm not as bad as you think, Mrs. Stockmann.

MRS. STOCKMANN: Then why did you print the Mayor's statement and not a word about my husband's report? Nobody's had a chance to find out what he really stands for. Why, everybody on the street there is against him already!

BILLING: If we printed his report it only would have hurt your husband.

MRS. STOCKMANN: Mr. Billing, I've never said this to anyone in my life, but I think you're a liar.

Suddenly the third citizen lets out a blast on his horn. The women jump, Billing and Horster turn around quickly.

HORSTER: You do that once more and I'll throw you out of here!

Peter Stockmann enters. Behind him comes the crowd. He pretends to be unconnected with them. He goes straight to Mrs. Stockmann, bows.

PETER STOCKMANN: Catherine? Petra?

PETRA: Good evening.

PETER STOCKMANN: Why so coldly? He wanted a meeting and he's got it. [*To Horster.*]   Isn't he here?

HORSTER: The Doctor is going around town to be sure there's a good attendance.

PETER STOCKMANN: Fair enough. By the way, Petra, did you paint that poster? The one somebody stuck on the Town Hall?

PETRA: If you can call it painting, yes.

PETER STOCKMANN: You know I could arrest you? It's against the law to deface the Town Hall.

PETRA: Well, here I am. [*She holds out her hands for the handcuffs.*]

MRS. STOCKMANN [*taking it seriously*]:   If you arrest her, Peter, I'll never speak to you!

PETER STOCKMANN [*laughing*]:   Catherine, you have no sense of humor!

He crosses and sits down at the left. They sit right. A drunk comes out of the crowd.

DRUNK: Say, Billy, who's runnin'? Who's the candidate?

HORSTER: You're drunk, Mister, now get out of here!

DRUNK: There's no law says a man who's drunk can't vote!

HORSTER [*pushing the drunk toward the door as the crowd laughs*]:   Get out of here! Get out!

DRUNK: I wanna vote! I got a right to vote!

Aslaksen enters hurriedly, sees Peter Stockmann, and rushes to him.

ASLAKSEN: Your Honor . . . [*He points to the door.*] He's . . .

DR. STOCKMANN [*offstage*]:   Right this way, gentlemen! In you go, come on, fellows!

Hovstad enters, glances at Peter Stockmann and Aslaksen, then at Dr. Stockmann and another crowd behind him, who enter.

DR. STOCKMANN: Sorry, no chairs, gentlemen, but we couldn't get a hall, y'know, so just relax. It won't take long anyway. [*He goes to the platform, sees Peter Stockmann.*] Glad you're here, Peter!

PETER STOCKMANN: Wouldn't miss it for the world.

DR. STOCKMANN: How do you feel, Catherine?

MRS. STOCKMANN (*nervously*):   Just promise me, don't lose your temper . . .

HORSTER [*seeing the drunk pop in through the door*]:   Did I tell you to get out of here!

DRUNK: Look, if you ain't votin', what the hell's going on here? [*Horster starts after him.*] Don't push!

HENRIK IBSEN

246

PETER STOCKMANN [*to the drunk*]:   I order you to get out of here and stay out!

DRUNK: I don't like the tone of your voice! And if you don't watch your step I'm gonna tell the Mayor right now, and he'll throw yiz all in the jug! [*To all*]:   What're you, a revolution here?

The crowd bursts out laughing; the drunk laughs with them, and they push him out. Dr. Stockmann mounts the platform.

DR. STOCKMANN [*quieting the crowd*]:   All right, gentlemen, we might as well begin. Quiet down, please. [*He clears his throat.*] The issue is very simple—

ASLAKSEN: We haven't elected a chairman, Doctor.

DR. STOCKMANN: I'm sorry, Mr. Aslaksen, this isn't a meeting. I advertised a lecture and I—

A CITIZEN: I came to a meeting, Doctor. There's got to be some kind of control here.

DR. STOCKMANN: What do you mean, control? What is there to control?

SECOND CITIZEN: Sure, let him speak, this is no meeting!

THIRD CITIZEN: Your Honor, why don't you take charge of this—

DR. STOCKMANN: Just a minute now!

THIRD CITIZEN: Somebody responsible has got to take charge. There's a big difference of opinion here—

DR. STOCKMANN: What makes you so sure? You don't even know yet what I'm going to say.

THIRD CITIZEN: I've got a pretty good idea what you're going to say, and I don't like it! If a man doesn't like it here, let him go where it suits him better. We don't want any troublemakers here!

There is assent from much of the crowd. Dr. Stockmann looks at them with new surprise.

DR. STOCKMANN: Now look, friend, you don't know anything about me—

FOURTH CITIZEN: We know plenty about you, Stockmann!

DR. STOCKMANN: From what? From the newspapers? How do you know I don't like this town? [*He picks up his manuscript.*] I'm here to save the life of this town!

PETER STOCKMANN [*quickly*]:   Now just a minute, Doctor, I think the democratic thing to do is to elect a chairman.

FIFTH CITIZEN: I nominate the Mayor!

Seconds are heard.

PETER STOCKMANN: No, no, no! That wouldn't be fair. We want a neutral person. I suggest Mr. Aslaksen—

SECOND CITIZEN: I came to a lecture, I didn't—

THIRD CITIZEN [*to second citizen*]:   What're you afraid of, a fair fight? [*To the Mayor*]:   Second Mr. Aslaksen!

The crowd assents.

DR. STOCKMANN: All right, if that's your pleasure. I just want to remind you that the reason I called this meeting was that I have a very important message for you people and I couldn't get it into the press, and nobody would rent me a hall. [*To Peter Stockmann:*] I just hope I'll be given time to speak here. Mr. Aslaksen?

As Aslaksen mounts the platform and Dr. Stockmann steps down, Kiil enters, looks shrewdly around.

ASLAKSEN: I just have one word before we start. Whatever is said tonight, please remember, the highest civic virtue is moderation. [*He can't help turning to Dr. Stockmann, then back to the crowd.*] Now if anybody wants to speak—

The drunk enters suddenly.

DRUNK, *pointing at Aslaksen*:   I heard that! Since when you allowed to electioneer at the poles? [*Citizens push him toward the door amid laughter.*] I'm gonna report this to the Mayor, goddammit! [*They push him out and close the door.*]

ASLAKSEN: Quiet, please, quiet. Does anybody want the floor?

Dr. Stockmann starts to come forward, raising his hand, but Peter Stockmann also has his hand raised.

PETER STOCKMANN: Mr. Chairman!

ASLAKSEN [*quickly recognizing Peter Stockmann*]:   His Honor the Mayor will address the meeting.

Dr. Stockmann stops, looks at Peter Stockmann, and, suppressing a remark, returns to his place. The Mayor mounts the platform.

PETER STOCKMANN: Gentlemen, there's no reason to take very long to settle this tonight and return to our ordinary, calm, and peaceful life. Here's the issue: Doctor Stockmann, my brother—and believe me, it is not easy to say this—has decided to destroy Kirsten Springs, our Health Institute—

DR. STOCKMANN: Peter!

ASLAKSEN [*ringing his bell*]: Let the Mayor continue, please. There mustn't be any interruptions.

PETER STOCKMANN: He has a long and very involved way of going about it, but that's the brunt of it, believe me.

THIRD CITIZEN: Then what're we wasting time for? Run him out of town!

Others join in the cry.

PETER STOCKMANN: Now wait a minute. I want no violence here. I want you to understand his motives. He is a man, always has been, who is never happy unless he is badgering authority, ridiculing authority, destroying authority. He wants to attack the springs so he can prove that the administration blundered in the construction.

DR. STOCKMANN [*to Aslaksen*]: May I speak? I—

ASLAKSEN: The Mayor's not finished.

PETER STOCKMANN: Thank you. Now there are a number of people here who seem to feel that the Doctor has a right to say anything he pleases. After all, we are a democratic country. Now, God knows, in ordinary times I'd agree a hundred per cent with anybody's right to say anything. But these are not ordinary times. Nations have crises, and so do towns. There are ruins of nations, and there are ruins of towns all over the world, and they were wrecked by people who, in the guise of reform, and pleading for justice, and so on, broke down all authority and left only revolution and chaos.

DR. STOCKMANN: What the hell are you talking about!

ASLAKSEN: I'll have to insist, Doctor—

DR. STOCKMANN: I called a lecture! I didn't invite him to attack me. He's got the press and every hall in town to attack me, and I've got nothing but this room tonight!

ASLAKSEN: I don't think you're making a very good impression, Doctor.

Assenting laughter and catcalls. Again Dr. Stockmann is taken aback by this reaction.

ASLAKSEN: Please continue, Your Honor.

PETER STOCKMANN: Now this is our crisis. We know what this town was without our Institute. We could barely afford to keep the streets in condition. It was a dead, third-rate hamlet. Today we're just on the verge of becoming internationally known as a resort. I predict that within five years the income of every man in this room will be immensely greater. I predict that our schools will be bigger and better. And in time this town will be crowded with fine carriages; great homes will be built here; first-class stores will open all along Main Street. I predict that if we are not defamed and maliciously attacked we will someday be one of the richest and most beautiful resort towns in the world. There are your choices. Now all you've got to do is ask yourselves a simple question: Has any one of us the right, the "democratic right," as they like to call it, to pick at minor flaws in the springs, to exaggerate the most picayune faults? [*Cries of No, No!*] And to attempt to publish these defamations for the whole world to see? We live or die on what the outside world thinks of us. I believe there is a line that must be drawn, and if a man decides to cross that line, we the people must finally take him by the collar and declare, "You cannot say that!"

There is an uproar of assent. Aslaksen rings the bell.

PETER STOCKMANN [*continuing*]:   All right then. I think we all understand each other. Mr. Aslaksen, I move that Doctor Stockmann be prohibited from reading his report at this meeting! [*He goes back to his chair, which meanwhile Kiil has occupied.*]

Aslaksen rings the bell to quiet the enthusiasm. Dr. Stockmann is jumping to get up on the platform, the report in his hand.

ASLAKSEN: Quiet, please. Please now. I think we can proceed to the vote.

DR. STOCKMANN: Well, aren't you going to let me speak at all?

ASLAKSEN: Doctor, we are just about to vote on that question.

DR. STOCKMANN: But damn it, man, I've got a right to—

PETRA, *standing up*:   Point of order, Father!

DR. STOCKMANN [*picking up the cue*]:   Yes, point of order!

ASLAKSEN [*turning to him now*]:   Yes, Doctor.

Dr. Stockmann, at a loss, turns to Petra for further instructions.

PETRA: You want to discuss the motion.

DR. STOCKMANN: That's right, damn it, I want to discuss the motion!

ASLAKSEN: Ah . . . [*He glances at Peter Stockmann.*] All right, go ahead.

DR. STOCKMANN, *to the crowd:* Now, listen. [*He points at Peter Stock-mann.*] He talks and he talks and he talks, but not a word about the facts! [*He holds up the manuscript.*]

THIRD CITIZEN: We don't want to hear any more about the water!

FOURTH CITIZEN: You're just trying to blow up everything!

DR. STOCKMANN: Well, judge for yourselves, let me read—

Cries of No, No, No! The man with the horn blows it. Aslaksen rings the bell. Dr. Stockmann is utterly shaken. Astonished, he looks at the maddened faces. He lowers the hand holding the manuscript and steps back, defeated.

ASLAKSEN: Please, please now, quiet. We can't have this uproar! [*Quiet returns.*] I think, Doctor, that the majority wants to take the vote before you start to speak. If they so will, you can speak. Otherwise, majority rules. You won't deny that.

DR. STOCKMANN [*turns, tosses the manuscript on the floor, turns back to Aslaksen*]: Don't bother voting. I understand everything now. Can I have a few minutes—

PETER STOCKMANN: Mr. Chairman!

DR. STOCKMANN [*to his brother*]: I won't mention the Institute. I have a new discovery that's a thousand times more important than all the Institutes in the world. [*To Aslaksen*]: May I have the platform.

ASLAKSEN [*to the crowd*]: I don't see how we can deny him that, as long as he confines himself to—

DR. STOCKMANN: The springs are not the subject. [*He mounts the plat-form, looks at the crowd.*] Before I go into my subject I want to con-gratulate the liberals and radicals among us, like Mr. Hovstad—

HOVSTAD: What do you mean, radical! Where's your evidence to call me a radical!

DR. STOCKMANN: You've got me there. There isn't any evidence. I guess there never really was. I just wanted to congratulate you on your self-control tonight—you who have fought in every parlor for the principle of free speech these many years.

HOVSTAD: I believe in democracy. When my readers are overwhelm-ingly against something, I'm not going to impose my will on the majority.

DR. STOCKMANN: You have begun my remarks, Mr. Hovstad. [*He turns to the crowd.*] Gentlemen, Mrs. Stockmann, Miss Stockmann. Tonight

I was struck by a sudden flash of light, a discovery second to none. But before I tell it to you—a little story. I put in a good many years in the north of our country. Up there the rulers of the world are the great seal and the gigantic squadrons of duck. Man lives on ice, huddled together in little piles of stones. His whole life consists of grubbing for food. Nothing more. He can barely speak his own language. And it came to me one day that it was romantic and sentimental for a man of my education to be tending these people. They had not yet reached the stage where they needed a doctor. If the truth were to be told, a veterinary would be more in order.

BILLING: Is that the way you refer to decent hard-working people!

DR. STOCKMANN: I expected that, my friend, but don't think you can fog up my brain with that magic word—the People! Not any more! Just because there is a mass of organisms with the human shape, they do not automatically become a People. That honor has to be earned! Nor does one automatically become a Man by having human shape, and living in a house, and feeding one's face—and agreeing with one's neighbors. That name *also* has to be earned. Now, when I came to my conclusions about the springs—

PETER STOCKMANN: You have no right to—

DR. STOCKMANN: That's a picayune thing, to catch me on a word, Peter. I am not going into the springs. *To the crowd:* When I became convinced of my theory about the water, the authorities moved in at once, and I said to myself, I will fight them to the death, because—

THIRD CITIZEN: What're you trying to do, make a revolution here? He's a revolutionist!

DR. STOCKMANN: Let me finish. I thought to myself: The majority, I have the majority! And let me tell you, friends, it was a grand feeling. Because that's the reason I came back to this place of my birth. I wanted to give my education to this town. I loved it so, I spent months without pay or encouragement and dreamed up the whole project of the springs. And why? Not as my brother says, so that fine carriages could crowd our streets, but so that we might cure the sick, so that we might meet people from all over the world and learn from them, and become broader and more civilized. In other words, more like Men, more like A People.

A CITIZEN: You don't like anything about this town, do you?

ANOTHER CITIZEN: Admit it, you're a revolutionist, aren't you? Admit it!

DR. STOCKMANN: I don't admit it! I proclaim it now! I am a revolutionist! I am in revolt against the age-old lie that the majority is always right!

HOVSTAD: He's an aristocrat all of a sudden!

DR. STOCKMANN: And more! I tell you now that the majority is always wrong, and in this way!

PETER STOCKMANN: Have you lost your mind! Stop talking before—

DR. STOCKMANN: Was the majority right when they stood by while Jesus was crucified? [*Silence.*] Was the majority right when they refused to believe that the earth moved around the sun and let Galileo be driven to his knees like a dog? It takes fifty years for the majority to be right. The majority is never right until it *does* right.

HOVSTAD: I want to state right now, that although I've been this man's friend, and I've eaten at his table many times, I now cut myself off from him absolutely.

DR. STOCKMANN: Answer me this! Please, one more moment! A platoon of soldiers is walking down a road toward the enemy. Every one of them is convinced he is on the right road, the safe road. But two miles ahead stands one lonely man, the outpost. He sees that this road is dangerous, that his comrades are walking into a trap. He runs back, he finds the platoon. Isn't it clear that this man must have the right to warn the majority, to argue with the majority, to fight with the majority if he believes he has the truth? Before many can know something, *one* must know it! [*His passion has silenced the crowd.*] It's always the same. Rights are sacred until it hurts for somebody to use them. I beg you now—I realize the cost is great, the inconvenience is great, the risk is great that other towns will get the jump on us while we're rebuilding—

PETER STOCKMANN: Aslaksen, he's not allowed to—

DR. STOCKMANN: Let me prove it to you! The water is poisoned!

THIRD CITIZEN [*steps up on the platform, waves his fist in Dr. Stockmann's face*]:   One more word about poison and I'm gonna take you outside!

The crowd is roaring; some try to charge the platform. The horn is blowing. Aslaksen rings his bell. Peter Stockmann steps forward, raising his hands. Kiil quietly exits.

PETER STOCKMANN: That's enough. Now stop it! Quiet! There is not going to be any violence here! [*There is silence. He turns to Dr. Stockmann*] Doctor, come down and give Mr. Aslaksen the platform.

DR. STOCKMANN [*staring down at the crowd with new eyes*]: I'm not through yet.

PETER STOCKMANN: Come down or I will not be responsible for what happens.

MRS. STOCKMANN: I'd like to go home. Come on, Tom.

PETER STOCKMANN: I move the chairman order the speaker to leave the platform.

VOICES: Sit down! Get off that platform!

DR. STOCKMANN: All right. Then I'll take this to out-of-town newspapers until the whole country is warned!

PETER STOCKMANN: You wouldn't dare!

HOVSTAD: You're trying to ruin this town—that's all; trying to ruin it.

DR. STOCKMANN: You're trying to build a town on a morality so rotten that it will infect the country and the world! If the only way you can prosper is this murder of freedom and truth, then I say with all my heart, "Let it be destroyed! Let the people perish!"

He leaves the platform.

FIRST CITIZEN [*to the Mayor*]: Arrest him! Arrest him!

SECOND CITIZEN: He's a traitor!

Cries of "Enemy! Traitor! Revolution!"

ASLAKSEN [*ringing for quiet*]: I would like to submit the following resolution: The people assembled here tonight, decent and patriotic citizens, in defense of their town and their country, declare that Doctor Stockmann, medical officer of Kirsten Springs, is an enemy of the people and of his community.

An uproar of assent starts.

MRS. STOCKMANN [*getting up*]: That's not true! He loves this town!

DR. STOCKMANN: You damned fools, you fools!

The Doctor and his family are all standing together, at the right, in a close group.

ASLAKSEN [*shouting over the din*]: Is there anyone against this motion! Anyone against!

HORSTER [*raising his hand*]: I am.

ASLAKSEN: One? [*He looks around.*]

DRUNK [*who has returned, raising his hand*]: Me too! You can't do without a doctor! Anybody'll . . . tell you . . .

ASLAKSEN: Anyone else? With all votes against two, this assembly formally declares Doctor Thomas Stockmann to be the people's enemy. In the future, all dealings with him by decent, patriotic citizens will be on that basis. The meeting is adjourned.

Shouts and applause. People start leaving. Dr. Stockmann goes over to Horster.

DR. STOCKMANN: Captain, do you have room for us on your ship to America?

HORSTER: Any time you say, Doctor.

DR. STOCKMANN: Catherine? Petra?

The three start for the door, but a gantlet has formed, dangerous and silent, except for

THIRD CITIZEN: You'd better get aboard soon, Doctor!

MRS. STOCKMANN: Let's go out the back door.

HORSTER: Right this way.

DR. STOCKMANN: No, no. No back doors. *To the crowd:* I don't want to mislead anybody—the enemy of the people is not finished in this town—not quite yet. And if anybody thinks—

The horn blasts, cutting him off. The crowd starts yelling hysterically: "Enemy! Traitor! Throw him in the river! Come on, throw him in the river! Enemy! Enemy! Enemy!" The Stockmanns, erect, move out through the crowd, with Horster. Some of the crowd follow them out, yelling.

Downstage, watching, are Peter Stockmann, Billing, Aslaksen, and Hovstad. The stage is throbbing with the chant, "Enemy, Enemy, Enemy!" as the curtain falls.

Act III

Dr. Stockmann's living room the following morning. The windows are broken. There is great disorder. As the curtain rises, Dr. Stockmann enters, a robe over shirt and trousers—it's cold in the house. He picks up a stone from the floor, lays it on the table.

DR. STOCKMANN: Catherine! Tell what's-her-name there are still some rocks to pick up in here.

MRS. STOCKMANN [*from inside*]:   She's not finished sweeping up the glass.

As Dr. Stockmann bends down to get at another stone under a chair a rock comes through one of the last remaining panes. He rushes to the window, looks out. Mrs. Stockmann rushes in.

MRS. STOCKMANN [*frightened*]:   You all right?

DR. STOCKMANN [*looking out*]:   A little boy. Look at him run! [*He picks up the stone.*] How fast the poison spreads—even to the children!

MRS. STOCKMANN [*looking out the window*]:   It's hard to believe this is the same town.

DR. STOCKMANN [*adding this rock to the pile on the table*]:   I'm going to keep these like sacred relics. I'll put them in my will. I want the boys to have them in their homes to look at every day. [*He shudders.*] Cold in here. Why hasn't what's-her-name got the glazier here?

MRS. STOCKMANN: She's getting him . . .

DR. STOCKMANN: She's been getting him for two hours! We'll freeze to death in here.

MRS. STOCKMANN [*unwillingly*]: He won't come here, Tom.

DR. STOCKMANN [*stops moving*]: No! The glazier's afraid to fix my windows?

MRS. STOCKMANN: You don't realize—people don't like to be pointed out. He's got neighbors, I suppose, and—[*She hears something.*] Is that someone at the door, Randine?

She goes to the front door. He continues picking up stones. She comes back.

MRS. STOCKMANN: Letter for you.

DR. STOCKMANN [*taking and opening it*]:   What's this now?

MRS. STOCKMANN [*continuing his pick-up for him*]:   I don't know how we're going to do any shopping with everybody ready to bite my head off and—

DR. STOCKMANN: Well, what do you know? We're evicted.

MRS. STOCKMANN: Oh, no!

DR. STOCKMANN: He hates to do it, but with public opinion what it is . . .

MRS. STOCKMANN [*frightened*]:   Maybe we shouldn't have let the boys go to school today.

DR. STOCKMANN: Now don't get all frazzled again.

MRS. STOCKMANN: But the landlord is such a nice man. If he's got to throw us out, the town must be ready to murder us!

DR. STOCKMANN: Just calm down, will you? We'll go to America, and the whole thing'll be like a dream.

MRS. STOCKMANN: But I don't want to go to America— [*She notices his pants.*] When did this get torn?

DR. STOCKMANN [*examining the tear*]: Must've been last night.

MRS. STOCKMANN: Your best pants!

DR. STOCKMANN: Well, it just shows you, that's all—when a man goes out to fight for the truth he should never wear his best pants. [*He calms her*]. Stop worrying, will you? You'll sew them up, and in no time at all we'll be three thousand miles away.

MRS. STOCKMANN: But how do you know it'll be any different there?

DR. STOCKMANN: I don't know. It just seems to me, in a big country like that, the spirit must be bigger. Still, I suppose they must have the solid majority there too. I don't know, at least there must be more room to hide there.

MRS. STOCKMANN: Think about it more, will you? I'd hate to go half around the world and find out we're in the same place.

DR. STOCKMANN: You know, Catherine, I don't think I'm ever going to forget the face of that crowd last night.

MRS. STOCKMANN: Don't think about it.

DR. STOCKMANN: Some of them had their teeth bared, like animals in a pack. And who leads them? Men who call themselves liberals! Radicals! [*She starts looking around at the furniture, figuring.*] The crowd lets out one roar, and where are they, my liberal friends? I bet if I walked down the street now not one of them would admit he ever met me! Are you listening to me?

MRS. STOCKMANN: I was just wondering what we'll ever do with this furniture if we go to America.

DR. STOCKMANN: Don't you ever listen when I talk, dear?

MRS. STOCKMANN: Why must I listen? I know you're right.

Petra enters.

MRS. STOCKMANN: Petra! Why aren't you in school?

DR. STOCKMANN: What's the matter?

PETRA [*with deep emotion, looks at Dr. Stockmann, goes up and kisses him*]: I'm fired.

MRS. STOCKMANN: They wouldn't!

PETRA: As of two weeks from now. But I couldn't bear to stay there.

DR. STOCKMANN [*shocked*]: Mrs. Busk fired you?

MRS. STOCKMANN: Who'd ever imagine she could do such a thing!

PETRA: It hurt her. I could see it, because we've always agreed so about things. But she didn't dare do anything else.

DR. STOCKMANN: The glazier doesn't dare fix the windows, the landlord doesn't dare let us stay on—

PETRA: The landlord!

DR. STOCKMANN: Evicted, darling! Oh, God, on the wreckage of all the civilizations in the world there ought to be a big sign: "They Didn't Dare!"

PETRA: I really can't blame her, Father. She showed me three letters she got this morning—

DR. STOCKMANN: From whom?

PETRA: They weren't signed.

DR. STOCKMANN: Oh, naturally. The big patriots with their anonymous indignation, scrawling out the darkness of their minds onto dirty little slips of paper—that's morality, and *I'm* the traitor! What did the letters say?

PETRA: Well, one of them was from somebody who said that he'd heard at the club that somebody who visits this house said that I had radical opinions about certain things.

DR. STOCKMANN: Oh, wonderful! Somebody heard that somebody heard that she heard, that he heard . . . ! Catherine, pack as soon as you can. I feel as though vermin were crawling all over me.

Horster enters.

HORSTER: Good morning.

DR. STOCKMANN: Captain! You're just the man I want to see.

HORSTER: I thought I'd see how you all were.

MRS. STOCKMANN: That's awfully nice of you, Captain, and I want to thank you for seeing us through the crowd last night.

PETRA: Did you get home all right? We hated to leave you alone with that mob.

HORSTER: Oh, nothing to it. In a storm there's just one thing to remember: it will pass.

DR. STOCKMANN: Unless it kills you.

HORSTER: You mustn't let yourself get too bitter.

DR. STOCKMANN: I'm trying, I'm trying. But I don't guarantee how I'll feel when I try to walk down the street with "Traitor" branded on my forehead.

MRS. STOCKMANN: Don't think about it.

HORSTER: Ah, what's a word?

DR. STOCKMANN: A word can be like a needle sticking in your heart, Captain. It can dig and corrode like an acid, until you become what they want you to be—really an enemy of the people.

HORSTER: You mustn't ever let that happen, Doctor.

DR. STOCKMANN: Frankly, I don't give a damn any more. Let summer come, let an epidemic break out, then they'll know whom they drove into exile. When are you sailing?

PETRA: You really decided to go, Father?

DR. STOCKMANN: Absolutely. When do you sail, Captain?

HORSTER: That's really what I came to talk to you about.

DR. STOCKMANN: Why? Something happen to the ship?

MRS. STOCKMANN [*happily, to Dr. Stockmann*]:   You see! We can't go!

HORSTER: No, the ship will sail. But I won't be aboard.

DR. STOCKMANN: No!

PETRA: You fired too? 'Cause I was this morning.

MRS. STOCKMANN: Oh, Captain, you shouldn't have given us your house.

HORSTER: Oh, I'll get another ship. It's just that the owner, Mr. Vik, happens to belong to the same party as the Mayor, and I suppose when you belong to a party, and the party takes a certain position . . . Because Mr. Vik himself is a very decent man.

DR. STOCKMANN: Oh, they're all decent men!

HORSTER: No, really, he's not like the others.

DR. STOCKMANN: He doesn't have to be. A party is like a sausage grinder: it mashes up clearheads, longheads, fatheads, blockheads—and what comes out? Meatheads!

There is a knock on the hall door. Petra goes to answer.

MRS. STOCKMANN: Maybe that's the glazier!

DR. STOCKMANN: Imagine, Captain! [*He points to the window.*] Refused to come all morning!

Peter Stockmann enters, his hat in his hand. Silence.

PETER STOCKMANN: If you're busy . . .

DR. STOCKMANN: Just picking up broken glass. Come in, Peter. What can I do for you this fine, brisk morning? [*He demonstratively pulls his robe tighter around his throat.*]

MRS. STOCKMANN: Come inside, won't you, Captain?

HENRIK IBSEN

HORSTER: Yes, I'd like to finish our talk, Doctor.

DR. STOCKMANN: Be with you in a minute, Captain.

Horster follows Petra and Catherine out through the dining-room doorway. Peter Stockmann says nothing, looking at the damage.

DR. STOCKMANN: Keep your hat on if you like, it's a little drafty in here today.

PETER STOCKMANN: Thanks, I believe I will. *He puts his hat on.* I think I caught cold last night—that house was freezing.

DR. STOCKMANN: I thought it was kind of warm—suffocating, as a matter of fact. What do you want?

PETER STOCKMANN: May I sit down? *He indicates a chair near the window.*

DR. STOCKMANN: Not there. A piece of the solid majority is liable to open your skull. Here.

They sit on the couch. Peter Stockmann takes out a large envelope.

DR. STOCKMANN: Now don't tell me.

PETER STOCKMANN: Yes. [*He hands the Doctor the envelope.*]

DR. STOCKMANN: I'm fired.

PETER STOCKMANN: The Board met this morning. There was nothing else to do, considering the state of public opinion.

DR. STOCKMANN [*after a pause*]: You look scared, Peter.

PETER STOCKMANN: I—I haven't completely forgotten that you're still my brother.

DR. STOCKMANN: I doubt that.

PETER STOCKMANN: You have no practice left in this town, Thomas.

DR. STOCKMANN: Oh, people always need a doctor.

PETER STOCKMANN: A petition is going from house to house. Everybody is signing it. A pledge not to call you any more. I don't think a single family will dare refuse to sign it.

DR. STOCKMANN: You started that, didn't you?

PETER STOCKMANN: No. As a matter of fact, I think it's all gone a little too far. I never wanted to see you ruined, Thomas. This will ruin you.

DR. STOCKMANN: No, it won't.

PETER STOCKMANN: For once in your life, will you act like a responsible man?

DR. STOCKMANN: Why don't you say it, Peter? You're afraid I'm going out of town to start publishing about the springs, aren't you?

PETER STOCKMANN: I don't deny that. Thomas, if you really have the good of the town at heart, you can accomplish everything without damaging anybody, including yourself.

DR. STOCKMANN: What's this now?

PETER STOCKMANN: Let me have a signed statement saying that in your zeal to help the town you went overboard and exaggerated. Put it any way you like, just so you calm anybody who might feel nervous about the water. If you'll give me that, you've got your job. And I give you my word, you can gradually make all the improvements you feel are necessary. Now, that gives you what you want . . .

DR. STOCKMANN: You're nervous, Peter.

PETER STOCKMANN [*nervously*]:   I am not nervous!

DR. STOCKMANN: You expect me to remain in charge while people are being poisoned? [*He gets up*].

PETER STOCKMANN: In time you can make your changes.

DR. STOCKMANN: When, five years, ten years? You know your trouble, Peter? You just don't grasp—even now—that there are certain men you can't buy.

PETER STOCKMANN: I'm quite capable of understanding that. But you don't happen to be one of those men.

DR. STOCKMANN [*after a slight pause*]:   What do you mean by that now?

PETER STOCKMANN: You know damned well what I mean by that. Morten Kiil is what I mean by that.

DR. STOCKMANN: Morten Kiil?

PETER STOCKMANN: Your father-in-law, Morten Kiil.

DR. STOCKMANN: I swear, Peter, one of us is out of his mind! What are you talking about?

PETER STOCKMANN: Now don't try to charm me with that professional innocence!

DR. STOCKMANN: What are you talking about?

PETER STOCKMANN: You don't know that your father-in-law has been running around all morning buying up stock in Kirsten Springs?

DR. STOCKMANN [*perplexed*]:   Buying up stock?

PETER STOCKMANN: Buying up stock, every share he can lay his hands on!

DR. STOCKMANN: Well, I don't understand, Peter. What's that got to do with—

PETER STOCKMANN [*walking around agitatedly*]:   Oh, come now, come now, come now!

DR. STOCKMANN: I hate you when you do that! Don't just walk around gabbling "Come now, come now!" What the hell are you talking about?

PETER STOCKMANN: Very well, if you insist on being dense. A man wages a relentless campaign to destroy confidence in a corporation. He even goes so far as to call a mass meeting against it. The very next morning, when people are still in a state of shock about it all, his father-in-law runs all over town, picking up shares at half their value.

DR. STOCKMANN [*realizing, turns away*]:   My God!

PETER STOCKMANN: And you have the nerve to speak to me about principles!

DR. STOCKMANN: You mean you actually believe that I . . . ?

PETER STOCKMANN: I'm not interested in psychology! I believe what I see! And what I see is nothing but a man doing a dirty, filthy job for Morten Kiil. And let me tell you—by tonight every man in this town'll see the same thing!

DR. STOCKMANN: Peter, you, you . . .

PETER STOCKMANN: Now go to your desk and write me a statement denying everything you've been saying, or . . .

DR. STOCKMANN: Peter, you're a low creature!

PETER STOCKMANN: All right then, you'd better get this one straight, Thomas. If you're figuring on opening another attack from out of town, keep this in mind: the morning it's published I'll send out a subpoena for you and begin a prosecution for conspiracy. I've been trying to make you respectable all my life; now if you want to make the big jump there'll be nobody there to hold you back. Now do we understand each other?

DR. STOCKMANN: Oh, we do, Peter! [*Peter Stockmann starts for the door.*] Get the girl—what the hell is her name—scrub the floors, wash down the walls, a pestilence has been here!

Kiil enters. Peter Stockmann almost runs into him. Peter turns to his brother.

PETER STOCKMANN, *pointing to Kiil*:   Ha! [*He turns and goes out.*]

Kiil, humming quietly, goes to a chair.

DR. STOCKMANN: Morten! What have you done? What's the matter with you? Do you realize what this makes me look like?

Kiil has started taking some papers out of his pocket. Dr. Stockmann breaks off on seeing them. Kiil places them on the table.

DR. STOCKMANN: Is that—them?

KIIL: That's them, yes. Kirsten Springs shares. And very easy to get this morning.

DR. STOCKMANN: Morten, don't play with me—what is this all about?

KIIL: What are you so nervous about? Can't a man buy some stock without . . . ?

DR. STOCKMANN: I want an explanation, Morten.

KIIL [*Nodding*]:   Thomas, they hated you last night—

DR. STOCKMANN: You don't have to tell me that.

KIIL: But they also believed you. They'd love to murder you, but they believe you. [*Slight pause*]. The way they say it, the pollution is coming down the river from Windmill Valley.

DR. STOCKMANN: That's exactly where it's coming from.

KIIL: Yes. And that's exactly where my tannery is.

Pause. Dr. Stockmann sits down slowly.

DR. STOCKMANN: Well, Morten, I never made a secret to you that the pollution was tannery waste.

KIIL: I'm not blaming you. It's my fault. I didn't take you seriously. But it's very serious now. Thomas, I got that tannery from my father; he got it from his father; and his father got it from my great-grandfather. I do not intend to allow my family's name to stand for the three generations of murdering angels who poisoned this town.

DR. STOCKMANN: I've waited a long time for this talk, Morten. I don't think you can stop that from happening.

KIIL: No, but you can.

DR. STOCKMANN: I?

KIIL [*nudging the shares*]:   I've bought these shares because—

DR. STOCKMANN: Morten, you've thrown your money away. The springs are doomed.

KIIL: I never throw my money away, Thomas. These were bought with your money.

DR. STOCKMANN: My money? What . . . ?

KIIL: You've probably suspected that I might leave a little something for Catherine and the boys?

DR. STOCKMANN: Well, naturally, I'd hoped you'd . . .

KIIL [*touching the shares*]:   I decided this morning to invest that money in some stock.

DR. STOCKMANN [*slowly getting up*]:   You bought that junk with Catherine's money!

KIIL: People call me "badger," and that's an animal that roots out things, but it's also some kind of a pig, I understand. I've lived a clean man and I'm going to die clean. You're going to clean my name for me.

DR. STOCKMANN: Morten . . .

KIIL: Now I want to see if you really belong in a strait jacket.

DR. STOCKMANN: How could you do such a thing? What's the matter with you!

KIIL: Now don't get excited, it's very simple. If you should make another investigation of the water—

DR. STOCKMANN: I don't *need* another investigation, I—

KIIL: If you think it over and decide that you ought to change your opinion about the water—

DR. STOCKMANN: But the water is poisoned! It is poisoned!

KIIL: If you simply go on insisting the water is poisoned [*he holds up the shares*] with these in your house, then there's only one explanation for you—you're absolutely crazy. [*He puts the shares down on the table again.*]

DR. STOCKMANN: You're right! I'm mad! I'm insane!

KIIL [*with more force*]:   You're stripping the skin off your family's back! Only a madman would do a thing like that!

DR. STOCKMANN: Morten, Morten, I'm a penniless man! Why didn't you tell me before you bought this junk?

KIIL: Because you would understand it better if I told you after. [*He goes up to Dr. Stockmann, holds him by the lapels. With terrific force, and the twinkle still in his eye*]: And, goddammit, I think you do understand it now, don't you? Millions of tons of water come down that river. How do you know the day you made your tests there wasn't something unusual about the water?

DR. STOCKMANN [*not looking at Kiil*]:   Yes, but I . . .

KIIL: How do you know? Why couldn't those little animals have clotted up only the patch of water you souped out of the river? How do you know the rest of it wasn't pure?

DR. STOCKMANN: It's not probable. People were getting sick last summer . . .

KIIL: They were sick when they came here or they wouldn't have come!

DR. STOCKMANN [*breaking away*]: Not intestinal diseases, skin diseases . . .

KIIL [*following him*]: The only place anybody gets a bellyache is here! There are no carbuncles in Norway? Maybe the food was bad. Did you ever think of the food?

DR. STOCKMANN [*with the desire to agree with him*]: No, I didn't look into the food . . .

KIIL: Then what makes you so sure it's the water?

DR. STOCKMANN: Because I tested the water and—

KIIL [*taking hold of him again*]: Admit it! We're all alone here. You have some doubt.

DR. STOCKMANN: Well, there's always a possible . . .

KIIL: Then part of it's imaginary.

DR. STOCKMANN: Well, nothing is a hundred per cent on this earth, but—

KIIL: Then you have a perfect right to doubt the other way! You have a scientific right! And did you ever think of some disinfectant? I bet you never even thought of that.

DR. STOCKMANN: Not for a mass of water like that, you can't . . .

KIIL: Everything can be killed. That's science! Thomas, I never liked your brother either, you have a perfect right to hate him.

DR. STOCKMANN: I didn't do it because I hate my brother.

KIIL: Part of it, part of it, don't deny it! You admit there's some doubt in your mind about the water, you admit there may be ways to disinfect it, and yet you went after your brother as though these doubts didn't exist; as though the only way to cure the thing was to blow up the whole Institute! There's hatred in that, boy, don't forget it. [*He points to the shares*]. These can belong to you now, so be sure, be sure! Tear the hatred out of your heart, stand naked in front of yourself—*are you sure?*

DR. STOCKMANN: What right have you to gamble my family's future on the strength of my convictions?

KIIL: Aha! Then the convictions are not really that strong!

DR. STOCKMANN: I am ready to hang for my convictions! But no man has a right to make martyrs of others; my family is innocent.

Sell back those shares, give her what belongs to her. I'm a penniless man!

KIIL: Nobody is going to say Morten Kiil wrecked this town.

[*He gathers up the shares.*] You retract your convictions—or these go to my charity.

DR. STOCKMANN: Everything?

KIIL: There'll be a little something for Catherine, but not much. I want my good name. It's exceedingly important to me.

DR. STOCKMANN [*bitterly*]: And charity . . .

KIIL: Charity will do it, or you will do it. It's a serious thing to destroy a town.

DR. STOCKMANN: Morten, when I look at you, I swear to God I see the devil!

The door opens, and before we see who is there . . .

DR. STOCKMANN: You!

Aslaksen enters, holding up his hand defensively.

ASLAKSEN: Now don't get excited! Please!

Hovstad enters. He and Aslaksen stop short and smile on seeing Kiil.

KIIL: Too many intellectuals here: I'd better go.

ASLAKSEN [*apologetically*]: Doctor, can we have five minutes of—

DR. STOCKMANN: I've got nothing to say to you.

KIIL [*going to the door*]: I want an answer right away. You hear? I'm waiting. [*He leaves.*]

DR. STOCKMANN: All right, say it quick, what do you want?

HOVSTAD: We don't expect you to forgive our attitude at the meeting, but . . .

DR. STOCKMANN [*groping for the word*]: Your attitude was prone . . . prostrated . . . prostituted!

HOVSTAD: All right, call it whatever you—

DR. STOCKMANN: I've got a lot on my mind, so get to the point. What do you want?

ASLAKSEN: Doctor, you should have told us what was in back of it all. You could have had the *Messenger* behind you all the way.

HOVSTAD: You'd have had public opinion with you now. Why didn't you tell us?

DR. STOCKMANN: Look, I'm very tired, let's not beat around the bush!

HOVSTAD [*gesturing toward the door where Kiil went out*]:   He's been all over town buying up stock in the springs. It's no secret any more.

DR. STOCKMANN [*after a slight pause*]:   Well, what about it?

HOVSTAD [*in a friendly way*]:   You don't want me to spell it out, do you?

DR. STOCKMANN: I certainly wish you would. I—

HOVSTAD: All right, let's lay it on the table. Aslaksen, you want to . . . ?

ASLAKSEN: No, no, go ahead.

HOVSTAD: Doctor, in the beginning we supported you. But it quickly became clear that if we kept on supporting you in the face of public hysteria—

DR. STOCKMANN: Your paper created the hysteria.

HOVSTAD: One thing at a time, all right? [*Slowly, to drive it into Dr. Stockmann's head*]: We couldn't go on supporting you because, in simple language, we didn't have the money to withstand the loss in circulation. You're boycotted now? Well, the paper would have been boycotted too, if we'd stuck with you.

ASLAKSEN: You can see that, Doctor.

DR. STOCKMANN: Oh, yes. But what do you want?

HOVSTAD: *The People's Messenger* can put on such a campaign that in two months you will be hailed as a hero in this town.

ASLAKSEN: We're ready to go.

HOVSTAD: We will prove to the public that you had to buy up the stock because the management would not make the changes required for public health. In other words, you did it for absolutely scientific, public-spirited reasons. Now what do you say, Doctor?

DR. STOCKMANN: You want money from me, is that it?

ASLAKSEN: Well, now, Doctor . . .

HOVSTAD [*to Aslaksen*]:   No, don't walk around it. [*To Dr. Stockmann.*] If we started to support you again, Doctor, we'd lose circulation for a while. We'd like you—or Mr. Kiil rather—to make up the deficit. [*Quickly.*]   Now that's open and aboveboard, and I don't see anything wrong with it. Do you?

Pause. Dr. Stockmann looks at him, then turns and walks to the windows, deep in thought.

ASLAKSEN: Remember, Doctor, you need the paper, you need it desperately.

DR. STOCKMANN [*returning*]:   No, there's nothing wrong with it at all. I—I'm not at all averse to cleaning up my name—although for myself it never was dirty. But I don't *enjoy* being hated, if you know what I mean.

ASLAKSEN: Exactly.

HOVSTAD: Aslaksen, will you show him the budget . . .

Aslaksen reaches into his pocket.

DR. STOCKMANN: Just a minute. There is one point. I hate to keep repeating the same thing, but the water is poisoned.

HOVSTAD: Now, Doctor . . .

DR. STOCKMANN: Just a minute. The Mayor says that he will levy a tax on everybody to pay for the reconstruction. I assume you are ready to support that tax at the same time you're supporting me.

ASLAKSEN: That tax would be extremely unpopular.

HOVSTAD: Doctor, with you back in charge of the baths, I have absolutely no fear that anything can go wrong.

DR. STOCKMANN: In other words, you will clean up my name—so that I can be in charge of the corruption.

HOVSTAD: But we can't tackle everything at once. A new tax—there'd be an uproar!

ASLAKSEN: It would ruin the paper!

DR. STOCKMANN: Then you don't intend to do anything about the water?

HOVSTAD: We have faith you won't let anyone get sick.

DR. STOCKMANN: In other words, gentlemen, you are looking for someone to blackmail into paying your printing bill.

HOVSTAD [*indignantly*]: We are trying to clear your name, Doctor Stockmann! And if you refuse to cooperate, if that's going to be your attitude . . .

DR. STOCKMANN: Yes? Go on. What will you do?

HOVSTAD [*to Aslaksen*]:   I think we'd better go.

DR. STOCKMANN [*stepping in their way*]:   What will you do? I would like you to tell me. Me, the man two minutes ago you were going to make into a hero—what will you do now that I won't pay you?

ASLAKSEN: Doctor, the public is almost hysterical . . .

DR. STOCKMANN: To my face, tell me what you are going to do!

HOVSTAD: The Mayor will prosecute you for conspiracy to destroy a corporation, and without a paper behind you, you will end up in prison.

DR. STOCKMANN: And you'll support him, won't you? I want it from your mouth, Hovstad. This little victory you will not deny me. [*Hovstad starts for the door. Dr. Stockmann steps into his way*]. Tell the hero, Hovstad. You're going to go on crucifying the hero, are you not? Say it to me! You will not leave here until I get this from your mouth!

HOVSTAD [*looking directly at Dr. Stockmann*]:   You are a madman. You are insane with egotism. And don't excuse it with humanitarian slogans, because a man who'll drag his family through a lifetime of disgrace is a demon in his heart! [*He advances on Dr. Stockmann.*] You hear me? A demon who cares more for the purity of a public bath than the lives of his wife and children. Doctor Stockmann, you deserve everything you're going to get!

Dr. Stockmann is struck by Hovstad's ferocious conviction. Aslaksen comes toward him, taking the budget out of his pocket.

ASLAKSEN [*nervously*]:   Doctor, please consider it. It won't take much money, and in two months' time I promise you your whole life will change and . . .

Offstage Mrs. Stockmann is heard calling in a frightened voice, "What happened? My God, what's the matter?" She runs to the front door. Dr. Stockmann, alarmed, goes quickly to the hallway. Ejlif and Morten enter. Morten's head is bruised. Petra and Captain Horster enter from the left.

MRS. STOCKMANN: Something happened! Look at him!

MORTEN: I'm all right, they just . . .

DR. STOCKMANN [*looking at the bruise*]:   What happened here?

MORTEN: Nothing, Papa, I swear . . .

DR. STOCKMANN [*to Ejlif*]:   What happened? Why aren't you in school?

EJLIF: The teacher said we better stay home the rest of the week.

DR. STOCKMANN: The boys hit him?

EJLIF: They started calling you names, so he got sore and began to fight with one kid, and all of a sudden the whole bunch of them . . .

MRS. STOCKMANN [*to Morten*]:   Why did you answer!

MORTEN [*indignantly*]:   They called him a traitor! My father is no traitor!

EJLIF: But you didn't have to answer!

MRS. STOCKMANN: You should've known they'd all jump on you! They could have killed you!

MORTEN: I don't care!

DR. STOCKMANN [*to quiet him—and his own heart*]:   Morten . . .

MORTEN [*pulling away from his father*]:   I'll kill them! I'll take a rock and the next time I see one of them I'll kill him!

Dr. Stockmann reaches for Morten, who, thinking his father will chastise him, starts to run. Dr. Stockmann catches him and grips him by the arm.

MORTEN: Let me go! Let me . . . !

DR. STOCKMANN: Morten . . . Morten . . .

MORTEN [*crying in his father's arms*]:   They called you traitor, an enemy . . . [*He sobs.*]

DR. STOCKMANN: Sssh. That's all. Wash your face.

Mrs. Stockmann takes Morten. Dr. Stockmann stands erect, faces Aslaksen and Hovstad.

DR. STOCKMANN: Good day, gentlemen.

HOVSTAD: Let us know what you decide and we'll—

DR. STOCKMANN: I've decided. I am an enemy of the people.

MRS. STOCKMANN: Tom, what are you . . . ?

DR. STOCKMANN: To such people, who teach their own children to think with their fists—to them I'm an enemy! And my boy . . . my boys . . . my family . . . I think you can count us all enemies.

ASLAKSEN: Doctor, you could have everything you want!

DR. STOCKMANN: Except the truth. I could have everything but that—that the water is poisoned!

HOVSTAD: But you'll be in charge.

DR. STOCKMANN: But the children are poisoned, the people are poisoned! If the only way I can be a friend of the people is to take charge of that corruption, then I am an enemy! The water is poisoned, poisoned, poisoned! That's the beginning of it and that's the end of it! Now get out of here!

HOVSTAD: You know where you're going to end?

DR. STOCKMANN: I said get out of here! [*He grabs Aslaksen's umbrella out of his hand.*]

MRS. STOCKMANN: What are you doing?

Aslaksen and Hovstad back toward the door as Dr. Stockmann starts to swing.

ASLAKSEN: You're a fanatic, you're out of your mind!

MRS. STOCKMANN: [grabbing Dr. Stockmann to take the umbrella]   What are you doing?

DR. STOCKMANN: They want me to buy the paper, the public, the pollution of the springs, buy the whole pollution of this town! They'll make a hero out of me for that! [Furiously, to Aslaksen and Hovstad:] But I'm not a hero, I'm the enemy—and now you're first going to find out what kind of enemy I am! I will sharpen my pen like a dagger—you, all you friends of the people, are going to bleed before I'm done! Go, tell them to sign the petitions! Warn them not to call me when they're sick! Beat up my children! And never let her [he points to Petra] in the school again or she'll destroy the immaculate purity of the vacuum there! See to all the barricades—the truth is coming! Ring the bells, sound the alarm! The truth, the truth is out, and soon it will be prowling like a lion in the streets!

HOVSTAD: Doctor, you're out of your mind.

He and Aslaksen turn to go. They are in the doorway.

EJLIF, *rushing at them:*   Don't you say that to him!

DR. STOCKMANN [*as Mrs. Stockmann cries out, rushes them with the umbrella*]:   Out of here!

They rush out. Dr. Stockmann throws the umbrella after them, then slams the door. Silence. He has his back pressed against the door, facing his family.

DR. STOCKMANN: I've had all the ambassadors of hell today, but there'll be no more. Now, now listen, Catherine! Children, listen. Now we're besieged. They'll call for blood now, they'll whip the people like oxen— [*A rock comes through a remaining pane. The boys start for the window.*] Stay away from there!

MRS. STOCKMANN: The Captain knows where we can get a ship.

DR. STOCKMANN: No ships.

PETRA: We're staying?

MRS. STOCKMANN: But they can't go back to school! I won't let them out of the house!

DR. STOCKMANN: We're staying.

PETRA: Good!

DR. STOCKMANN: We must be careful now. We must live through this. Boys, no more school. I'm going to teach you, and Petra will. Do you know any kids, street louts, hookey-players—

EJLIF: Oh, sure, we—

DR. STOCKMANN: We'll want about twelve of them to start. But I want them good and ignorant, absolutely uncivilized. Can we use your house, Captain?

HORSTER: Sure, I'm never there.

DR. STOCKMANN: Fine. We'll begin, Petra, and we'll turn out not tax-payers and newspaper subscribers, but free and independent people, hungry for the truth. Oh, I forgot! Petra, run to Grandpa and tell him—tell him as follows: No!

MRS. STOCKMANN [*puzzled*]: What do you mean?

DR. STOCKMANN [*going over to Mrs. Stockmann*]: It means, my dear, that we are all alone. And there'll be a long night before it's day—

A rock comes through a paneless window. Horster goes to the window. A crowd is heard approaching.

HORSTER: Half the town is out!

MRS. STOCKMANN: What's going to happen? Tom! What's going to happen?

DR. STOCKMANN [*holding his hands up to quiet her, and with a trembling mixture of trepidation and courageous insistence*]: I don't know. But remember now, everybody. You are fighting for the truth, and that's why you're alone. And that makes you strong. We're the strongest people in the world . . .

The crowd is heard angrily calling outside. Another rock comes through a window.

DR. STOCKMANN: . . . and the strong must learn to be lonely!

The crowd noise gets louder. He walks upstage toward the windows as a wind rises and the curtains start to billow out toward him. the curtain falls.

—1882

SUSAN GLASPELL ▪ [1882–1948]

Susan Glaspell was born in Iowa and educated at Drake University. Glaspell was one of the founders, with her husband George Cram Cook, of the Provincetown Players. This company, founded in the Cape Cod resort village, was committed to producing experimental drama, an alternative to the standard fare playing in Broadway theaters. Eventually it was relocated to New York. Along with Glaspell, Eugene O'Neill, America's only Nobel Prize–winning dramatist, wrote plays for this group. Trained as a journalist and the author of short stories and novels, Glaspell wrote Trifles *[1916], her first play, shortly after the founding of the Players, basing her plot on an Iowa murder case she had covered. The one-act play, with both Glaspell and her husband in the cast, premiered during the Players' second season and also exists in a short-story version. Glaspell won the Pulitzer Prize for Drama in 1930 for* Alison's House, *basing the title character on poet Emily Dickinson. A socialist and feminist, Glaspell lived in Provincetown in her last years, writing* The Road to the Temple, *a memoir of her husband's life, and novels.*

Trifles

Characters

George Henderson, *County Attorney*
Mrs. Peters
Henry Peters, *Sheriff*
Lewis Hale, *a neighbor*
Mrs. Hale

The kitchen in the now abandoned farmhouse of John Wright, a gloomy kitchen, and left without having been put in order—unwashed pans under the sink, a loaf of bread outside the breadbox, a dish towel on the table— other signs of incompleted work. At the rear the outer door opens, and the Sheriff comes in, followed by the County Attorney and Hale. The Sheriff and Hale are men in middle life, the County Attorney is a young man; all are much bundled up and go at once to the stove. They are followed by the two women—the Sheriff's Wife first; she is a slight wiry woman, a thin nervous face. Mrs. Hale is larger and would ordinarily be called more comfortable looking, but she is disturbed now and looks fearfully about as she enters. The women have come in slowly and stand close together near the door.

COUNTY ATTORNEY [*rubbing his hands*]:   This feels good. Come up to the fire, ladies.

MRS. PETERS [*after taking a step forward*]:   I'm not—cold.

SHERIFF [*unbuttoning his overcoat and stepping away from the stove as if to the beginning of official business*]:   Now, Mr. Hale, before we move things about, you explain to Mr. Henderson just what you saw when you came here yesterday morning.

COUNTY ATTORNEY: By the way, has anything been moved? Are things just as you left them yesterday?

SHERIFF [*looking about*]:   It's just the same. When it dropped below zero last night, I thought I'd better send Frank out this morning to make a fire for us—no use getting pneumonia with a big case on; but I told him not to touch anything except the stove—and you know Frank.

COUNTY ATTORNEY: Somebody should have been left here yesterday.

SHERIFF: Oh—yesterday. When I had to send Frank to Morris Center for that man who went crazy—I want you to know I had my hands full yesterday. I knew you could get back from Omaha by today, and as long as I went over everything here myself—

COUNTY ATTORNEY: Well, Mr. Hale, tell just what happened when you came here yesterday morning.

HALE: Harry and I had started to town with a load of potatoes. We came along the road from my place; and as I got here, I said, "I'm going to see if I can't get John Wright to go in with me on a party telephone." I spoke to Wright about it once before, and he put me off, saying folks talked too much anyway, and all he asked was peace and quiet—I guess you know about how much he talked himself; but I thought maybe if I went to the house and talked about it before his wife, though I said to Harry that I didn't know as what his wife wanted made much difference to John—

COUNTY ATTORNEY: Let's talk about that later, Mr. Hale. I do want to talk about that, but tell now just what happened when you got to the house.

HALE: I didn't hear or see anything; I knocked at the door, and still it was all quiet inside. I knew they must be up, it was past eight o'clock. So I knocked again, and I thought I heard somebody say, "Come in." I wasn't sure, I'm not sure yet, but I opened the door—this door [*indicating the door by which the two women are still standing*], and there in that rocker—[*pointing to it*] sat Mrs. Wright. [*They all look at the rocker.*]

COUNTY ATTORNEY: What—was she doing?

HALE: She was rockin' back and forth. She had her apron in her hand and was kind of—pleating it.

COUNTY ATTORNEY: And how did she—look?

HALE: Well, she looked queer.

COUNTY ATTORNEY: How do you mean—queer?

HALE: Well, as if she didn't know what she was going to do next. And kind of done up.

COUNTY ATTORNEY: How did she seem to feel about your coming?

HALE: Why, I don't think she minded—one way or other. She didn't pay much attention. I said, "How do, Mrs. Wright, it's cold, ain't it?" And she said, "Is it?"—and went on kind of pleating at her apron. Well, I was surprised; she didn't ask me to come up to the stove, or to set down, but just sat there, not even looking at me, so I said, "I want to see John." And then she—laughed. I guess you would call it a laugh. I thought of Harry and the team outside, so I said a little sharp: "Can't I see John?" "No," she says, kind o' dull like. "Ain't he home?" says I. "Yes," says she, "he's home." "Then why can't I see him?" I asked her, out of patience. "'Cause he's dead," says she. *"Dead?"* says I. She just nodded her head, not getting a bit excited, but rockin' back and forth. "Why—where is he?" says I, not knowing what to say. She just pointed upstairs—like that [*himself pointing to the room above*]. I got up, with the idea of going up there. I walked from there to here—then I says, "Why, what did he die of?" "He died of a rope around his neck," says she, and just went on pleatin' at her apron. Well, I went out and called Harry. I thought I might—need help. We went upstairs, and there he was lyin'—

COUNTY ATTORNEY: I think I'd rather have you go into that upstairs, where you can point it all out. Just go on now with the rest of the story.

HALE: Well, my first thought was to get that rope off. I looked . . . [*Stops, his face twitches.*] . . . but Harry, he went up to him, and he said, "No, he's dead all right, and we'd better not touch anything." So we went back downstairs. She was still sitting that same way.

"Has anybody been notified?" I asked. "No," says she, unconcerned. "Who did this, Mrs. Wright?" said Harry. He said it businesslike—and she stopped pleatin' of her apron. "I don't know," she says. "You don't *know*?" says Harry. "No," says she, "Weren't you sleepin' in the bed with him?" says Harry. "Yes," says she, "but I was on the inside." "Somebody slipped a rope round his neck and strangled him, and you didn't wake up?" says Harry. "I didn't wake up," she said after him. We must 'a looked as if we didn't see how that could be, for after a minute she said, "I sleep sound." Harry was going to ask her more questions, but I said maybe we ought to let her tell her story first to the coroner, or the sheriff, so Harry went fast as he could to Rivers' place, where there's a telephone.

COUNTY ATTORNEY: And what did Mrs. Wright do when she knew that you had gone for the coroner?

HALE: She moved from that chair to this over here . . . [*Pointing to a small chair in the corner.*] . . . and just sat there with her hands held together and looking down. I got a feeling that I ought to make some conversation, so I said I had come in to see if John wanted to put in a telephone, and at that she started to laugh, and then she stopped and looked at me—scared. [*The County Attorney, who has had his notebook out, makes a note.*] I dunno, maybe it wasn't scared. I wouldn't like to say it was. Soon Harry got back, and then Dr. Lloyd came, and you, Mr. Peters, and so I guess that's all I know that you don't.

COUNTY ATTORNEY [*looking around*]: I guess we'll go upstairs first—and then out to the barn and around there. [*To the Sheriff.*] You're convinced that there was nothing important here—nothing that would point to any motive?

SHERIFF: Nothing here but kitchen things.

[*The County Attorney, after again looking around the kitchen, opens the door of a cupboard closet. He gets up on a chair and looks on a shelf. Pulls his hand away, sticky.*]

COUNTY ATTORNEY: Here's a nice mess.

[*The women draw nearer.*]

MRS. PETERS [*to the other woman*]: Oh, her fruit; it did freeze. [*To the Lawyer.*] She worried about that when it turned so cold. She said the fir'd go out and her jars would break.

SHERIFF: Well, can you beat the women! Held for murder and wor-ryin' about her preserves.

COUNTY ATTORNEY: I guess before we're through she may have something more serious than preserves to worry about.

HALE: Well, women are used to worrying over trifles.

[*The two women move a little closer together.*]

COUNTY ATTORNEY [*with the gallantry of a young politician*]:   And yet, for all their worries, what would we do without the ladies? [*The women do not unbend. He goes to the sink, takes a dipperful of water from the pail and, pouring it into a basin, washes his hands. Starts to wipe them on the roller towel, turns it for a cleaner place.*] Dirty towels! [*Kicks his foot against the pans under the sink.*] Not much of a house-keeper, would you say, ladies?

MRS. HALE [*stiffly*]:   There's a great deal of work to be done on a farm.

COUNTY ATTORNEY: To be sure. And yet . . . [*With a little bow to her.*] . . . I know there are some Dickson county farmhouses which do not have such roller towels. [*He gives it a pull to expose its full length again.*]

MRS. HALE: Those towels get dirty awful quick. Men's hands aren't always as clean as they might be.

COUNTY ATTORNEY: Ah, loyal to your sex, I see. But you and Mrs. Wright were neighbors. I suppose you were friends, too.

MRS. HALE [*shaking her head*]:   I've not seen much of her of late years. I've not been in this house—it's more than a year.

COUNTY ATTORNEY: And why was that? You didn't like her?

MRS. HALE: I liked her all well enough. Farmers' wives have their hands full, Mr. Henderson. And then—

COUNTY ATTORNEY: Yes—?

MRS. HALE [*looking about*]:   It never seemed a very cheerful place.

COUNTY ATTORNEY: No—it's not cheerful. I shouldn't say she had the homemaking instinct.

MRS. HALE: Well, I don't know as Wright had, either.

COUNTY ATTORNEY: You mean that they didn't get on very well?

MRS. HALE: No, I don't mean anything. But I don't think a place'd be any cheerfuler for John Wright's being in it.

COUNTY ATTORNEY: I'd like to talk more of that a little later. I want to get the lay of things upstairs now. [*He goes to the left, where three steps lead to a stair door.*]

SHERIFF: I suppose anything Mrs. Peters does'll be all right. She was to take in some clothes for her, you know, and a few little things. We left in such a hurry yesterday.

COUNTY ATTORNEY: Yes, but I would like to see what you take, Mrs. Peters, and keep an eye out for anything that might be of use to us.

MRS. PETERS: Yes, Mr. Henderson.

[The women listen to the men's steps on the stairs, then look about the kitchen.]

MRS. HALE: I'd hate to have men coming into my kitchen, snooping around and criticizing. [She arranges the pans under the sink which the Lawyer had shoved out of place.]

MRS. PETERS: Of course it's no more than their duty.

MRS. HALE: Duty's all right, but I guess that deputy sheriff that came out to make the fire might have got a little of this on. [Gives the roller towel a pull.] Wish I'd thought of that sooner. Seems mean to talk about her for not having things slicked up when she had to come away in such a hurry.

MRS. PETERS [who has gone to a small table in the left rear corner of the room, and lifted one end of a towel that covers a pan]:   She had bread set. [Stands still.]

MRS. HALE [eyes fixed on a loaf of bread beside the breadbox, which is on a low shelf at the other side of the room. Moves slowly toward it]:   She was going to put this in there. [Picks up loaf, then abruptly drops it. In a manner of returning to familiar things.] It's a shame about her fruit. I wonder if it's all gone. [Gets up on the chair and looks.] I think there's some here that's all right, Mrs. Peters. Yes—here; [Holding it toward the window.] this is cherries, too. [Looking again.] I declare I believe that's the only one. [Gets down, bottle in her hand. Goes to the sink and wipes it off on the outside.] She'll feel awful bad after all her hard work in the hot weather. I remember the afternoon I put up my cherries last summer. [She puts the bottle on the big kitchen table, center of the room, front table. With a sigh, is about to sit down in the rocking chair. Before she is seated realizes what chair it is; with a slow look at it, steps back. The chair, which she has touched, rocks back and forth.]

MRS. PETERS: Well, I must get those things from the front room closet. [She goes to the door at the right, but after looking into the other room steps back.] You coming with me, Mrs. Hale? You could help

SUSAN GLASPELL

me carry them. [*They go into the other room; reappear, Mrs. Peters carrying a dress and skirt, Mrs. Hale following with a pair of shoes.*]

MRS. PETERS: My, it's cold in there. [*She puts the cloth on the big table, and hurries to the stove.*]

MRS. HALE [*examining the skirt*]:   Wright was close. I think maybe that's why she kept so much to herself. She didn't even belong to the Ladies' Aid. I suppose she felt she couldn't do her part, and then you don't enjoy things when you feel shabby. She used to wear pretty clothes and be lively, when she was Minnie Foster, one of the town girls singing in the choir. But that—oh, that was thirty years ago. This all you was to take in?

MRS. PETERS: She said she wanted an apron. Funny thing to want, for there isn't much to get you dirty in jail, goodness knows. But I suppose just to make her feel more natural. She said they was in the top drawer in this cupboard. Yes, here. And then her little shawl that always hung behind the door. [*Opens stair door and looks.*] Yes, here it is. [*Quickly shuts door leading upstairs.*]

MRS. HALE [*abruptly moving toward her*]:   Mrs. Peters?

MRS. PETERS: Yes, Mrs. Hale?

MRS. HALE: Do you think she did it?

MRS. PETERS [*in a frightened voice*]:   Oh, I don't know.

MRS. HALE: Well, I don't think she did. Asking for an apron and her little shawl. Worrying about her fruit.

MRS. PETERS [*starts to speak, glances up, where footsteps are heard in the room above. In a low voice*]:   Mr. Peters says it looks bad for her. Mr. Henderson is awful sarcastic in speech, and he'll make fun of her sayin' she didn't wake up.

MRS. HALE: Well, I guess John Wright didn't wake when they was slipping that rope under his neck.

MRS. PETERS: No, it's strange. It must have been done awful crafty and still. They say it was such a—funny way to kill a man, rigging it all up like that.

MRS. HALE: That's just what Mr. Hale said. There was a gun in the house. He says that's what he can't understand.

MRS. PETERS: Mr. Henderson said coming out that what was needed for the case was a motive; something to show anger, or— sudden feeling.

MRS. HALE [*who is standing by the table*]:   Well, I don't see any signs of anger around here. [*She puts her hand on the dish towel which lies on the table, stands looking down at the table, one half of which is clean, the other half messy.*] It's wiped here. [*Makes a move as if to finish work, then turns and looks at loaf of bread outside the breadbox. Drops towel. In that voice of coming back to familiar things.*] Wonder how they are finding things upstairs? I hope she had it a little more red-up there. You know, it seems kind of *sneaking*. Locking her up in town and then coming out here and trying to get her own house to turn against her!

MRS. PETERS: But, Mrs. Hale, the law is the law.

MRS. HALE: I s'pose 'tis. [*Unbuttoning her coat.*] Better loosen up your things, Mrs. Peters. You won't feel them when you go out.

[*Mrs. Peters takes off her fur tippet, goes to hang it on a hook at the back of room, stands looking at the under part of the small corner table.*]

MRS. PETERS: She was piecing a quilt. [*She brings the large sewing basket, and they look at the bright pieces.*]

MRS. HALE: It's log cabin pattern. Pretty, isn't it? I wonder if she was goin' to quilt or just knot it?

[*Footsteps have been heard coming down the stairs. The Sheriff enters, followed by Hale and the County Attorney.*]

SHERIFF: They wonder if she was going to quilt it or just knot it. [*The men laugh, the women look abashed.*]

COUNTY ATTORNEY [*rubbing his hands over the stove*]:   Frank's fire didn't do much up there, did it? Well, let's go out to the barn and get that cleared up.

[*The men go outside.*]

MRS. HALE [*resentfully*]:   I don't know as there's anything so strange, our takin' up our time with little things while we're waiting for them to get the evidence. [*She sits down at the big table, smoothing out a block with decision.*] I don't see as it's anything to laugh about.

MRS. PETERS [*apologetically*]:   Of course they've got awful important things on their minds. [*Pulls up a chair and joins Mrs. Hale at the table.*]

MRS. HALE [*examining another block*]:   Mrs. Peters, look at this one. Here, this is the one she was working on, and look at the sewing! All the rest of it has been so nice and even. And look at this! It's all over the place! Why, it looks as if she didn't know what she was about! [*After she has said this, they look at each other, then started to glance back at the door. After an instant Mrs. Hale has pulled at a knot and ripped the sewing.*]

MRS. PETERS: Oh, what are you doing, Mrs. Hale?

MRS. HALE [*mildly*]:   Just pulling out a stitch or two that's not sewed very good. [*Threading a needle.*] Bad sewing always made me fidgety.

MRS. PETERS [*nervously*]:   I don't think we ought to touch things.

MRS. HALE: I'll just finish up this end. [*Suddenly stopping and leaning forward.*] Mrs. Peters?

MRS. PETERS: Yes, Mrs. Hale?

MRS. HALE: What do you suppose she was so nervous about?

MRS. PETERS: Oh—I don't know. I don't know as she was nervous. I sometimes sew awful queer when I'm just tired. [*Mrs. Hale starts to say something, looks at Mrs. Peters, then goes on sewing.*] Well, I must get these things wrapped up. They may be through sooner than we think. [*Putting apron and other things together.*] I wonder where I can find a piece of paper, and string.

MRS. HALE: In that cupboard, maybe.

MRS. PETERS [*looking in cupboard*]:   Why, here's a birdcage. [*Holds it up.*] Did she have a bird, Mrs. Hale?

MRS. HALE: Why, I don't know whether she did or not—I've not been here for so long. There was a man around last year selling canaries cheap, but I don't know as she took one; maybe she did. She used to sing real pretty herself.

MRS. PETERS [*glancing around*]:   Seems funny to think of a bird here. But she must have had one, or why should she have a cage? I wonder what happened to it?

MRS. HALE: I s'pose maybe the cat got it.

MRS. PETERS: No, she didn't have a cat. She's got that feeling some people have about cats—being afraid of them. My cat got in her room, and she was real upset and asked me to take it out.

MRS. HALE: My sister Bessie was like that. Queer, ain't it?

MRS. PETERS [*examining the cage*]:   Why, look at this door. It's broke. One hinge is pulled apart.

MRS. HALE [*looking, too*]:   Looks as if someone must have been rough with it.

MRS. PETERS: Why, yes. [*She brings the cage forward and puts it on the table.*]

SUSAN GLASPELL

MRS. HALE: I wish if they're going to find any evidence they'd be about it. I don't like this place.

MRS. PETERS: But I'm awful glad you came with me, Mrs. Hale. It would be lonesome for me sitting here alone.

MRS. HALE: It would, wouldn't it? [*Dropping her sewing.*] But I tell you what I do wish, Mrs. Peters. I wish I had come over sometimes when *she* was here. I—[*Looking around the room.*]—wish I had.

MRS. PETERS: But of course you were awful busy, Mrs. Hale—your house and your children.

MRS. HALE: I could've come. I stayed away because it weren't cheerful—and that's why I ought to have come. I—I've never liked this place. Maybe because it's down in a hollow, and you don't see the road. I dunno what it is, but it's a lonesome place and always was. I wish I had come over to see Minnie Foster sometimes. I can see now—[*Shakes her head.*]

MRS. PETERS: Well, you mustn't reproach yourself, Mrs. Hale. Somehow we just don't see how it is with other folks until—something comes up.

MRS. HALE: Not having children makes less work—but it makes a quiet house, and Wright out to work all day, and no company when he did come in. Did you know John Wright, Mrs. Peters?

MRS. PETERS: Not to know him; I've seen him in town. They say he was a good man.

MRS. HALE: Yes—good; he didn't drink, and kept his word as well as most, I guess, and paid his debts. But he was a hard man, Mrs. Peters. Just to pass the time of day with him. [*Shivers.*] Like a raw wind that gets to the bone. [*Pauses, her eye falling on the cage.*] I should think she would 'a wanted a bird. But what do you suppose went with it?

MRS. PETERS: I don't know, unless it got sick and died. [*She reaches over and swings the broken door, swings it again; both women watch it.*]

MRS. HALE: You weren't raised round here, were you? [*Mrs. Peters shakes her head.*] You didn't know—her?

MRS. PETERS: Not till they brought her yesterday.

MRS. HALE: She—come to think of it, she was kind of like a bird herself—real sweet and pretty, but kind of timid and—fluttery. How—she—did—change. [*Silence; then as if struck by a happy thought and relieved to get back to everyday things.*] Tell you what,

Mrs. Peters, why don't you take the quilt in with you? It might take up her mind.

MRS. PETERS: Why, I think that's a real nice idea, Mrs. Hale. There couldn't possibly be any objection to it, could there? Now, just what would I take? I wonder if her patches are in here—and her things. [*They look in the sewing basket.*]

MRS. HALE: Here's some red. I expect this has got sewing things in it [*Brings out a fancy box.*] What a pretty box. Looks like something somebody would give you. Maybe her scissors are in here. [*Opens box. Suddenly puts her hand to her nose.*] Why—[*Mrs. Peters bends nearer, then turns her face away.*] There's something wrapped up in this piece of silk.

MRS. PETERS: Why, this isn't her scissors.

MRS. HALE [*lifting the silk*]: Oh, Mrs. Peters—it's—[*Mrs. Peters bends closer.*]

MRS. PETERS: It's the bird.

MRS. HALE [*jumping up*]: But, Mrs. Peters—look at it. Its neck! Look at its neck! It's all—other side *to.*

MRS. PETERS: Somebody—wrung—its neck.

[*Their eyes meet. A look of growing comprehension of horror. Steps are heard outside. Mrs. Hale slips box under quilt pieces, and sinks into her chair. Enter Sheriff and County Attorney. Mrs. Peters rises.*]

COUNTY ATTORNEY [*as one turning from serious things to little pleasantries*]: Well, ladies, have you decided whether she was going to quilt it or knot it?

MRS. PETERS: We think she was going to—knot it.

COUNTY ATTORNEY: Well, that's interesting, I'm sure. [*Seeing the birdcage.*] Has the bird flown?

MRS. HALE [*putting more quilt pieces over the box*]: We think the—cat got it.

COUNTY ATTORNEY [*preoccupied*]: Is there a cat?

[*Mrs. Hale glances in a quick covert way at Mrs. Peters.*]

MRS. PETERS: Well, not now. They're superstitious, you know. They leave.

COUNTY ATTORNEY [*to Sheriff Peters, continuing an interrupted conversation*]: No sign at all of anyone having come from the outside.

Their own rope. Now let's go up again and go over it piece by piece. [*They start upstairs.*] It would have to have been someone who knew just the—

[*Mrs. Peters sits down. The two women sit there not looking at one another, but as if peering into something and at the same time holding back. When they talk now, it is the manner of feeling their way over strange ground, as if afraid of what they are saying, but as if they cannot help saying it.*]

MRS. HALE: She liked the bird. She was going to bury it in that pretty box.

MRS. PETERS [*in a whisper*]:   When I was a girl—my kitten—there was a boy took a hatchet, and before my eyes—and before I could get there—[*Covers her face an instant.*] If they hadn't held me back, I would have—[*Catches herself, looks upstairs where steps are heard, falters weakly.*]—hurt him.

MRS. HALE [*with a slow look around her*]:   I wonder how it would seem never to have had any children around. [*Pause.*] No, Wright wouldn't like the bird—a thing that sang. She used to sing. He killed that, too.

MRS. PETERS [*moving uneasily*]:   We don't know who killed the bird.

MRS. HALE: I knew John Wright.

MRS. PETERS: It was an awful thing was done in this house that night, Mrs. Hale. Killing a man while he slept, slipping a rope around his neck that choked the life out of him.

MRS. HALE: His neck. Choked the life out of him.

[*Her hand goes out and rests on the birdcage.*]

MRS. PETERS [*with a rising voice*]:   We don't know who killed him. We don't *know*.

MRS. HALE [*her own feeling not interrupted*]:   If there'd been years and years of nothing, then a bird to sing to you, it would be awful—still, after the bird was still.

MRS. PETERS [*something within her speaking*]:   I know what stillness is. When we homesteaded in Dakota, and my first baby died—after he was two years old, and me with no other then—

MRS. HALE [*moving*]:   How soon do you suppose they'll be through, looking for evidence?

MRS. PETERS: I know what stillness is. [*Pulling herself back.*] The law has got to punish crime, Mrs. Hale.

SUSAN GLASPELL

MRS. HALE [*not as if answering that*]:   I wish you'd seen Minnie Foster when she wore a white dress with blue ribbons and stood up there in the choir and sang. [*A look around the room.*] Oh, I *wish* I'd come over here once in a while! That was a crime! That was a crime! Who's going to punish that?

MRS. PETERS [*looking upstairs*]:   We mustn't—take on.

MRS. HALE: I might have known she needed help! I know how things can be—for women. I tell you, it's queer, Mrs. Peters. We live close together and we live far apart. We all go through the same things—it's all just a different kind of the same thing. [*Brushes her eyes, noticing the bottle of fruit, reaches out for it.*] If I was you, I wouldn't tell her her fruit was gone. Tell her it *ain't*. Tell her it's all right. Take this in to prove it to her. She—she may never know whether it was broke or not.

MRS. PETERS [*takes the bottle, looks about for something to wrap it in; takes petticoat from the clothes brought from the other room, very nervously begins winding this around the bottle. In a false voice*]:   My, it's a good thing the men couldn't hear us. Wouldn't they just laugh! Getting all stirred up over a little thing like a—dead canary. As if that could have anything to do with—with—wouldn't they *laugh*!

[*The men are heard coming downstairs.*]

MRS. HALE [*under her breath*]:   Maybe they would—maybe they wouldn't.

COUNTY ATTORNEY: No, Peters, it's all perfectly clear except a reason for doing it. But you know juries when it comes to women. If there was some definite thing. Something to show—something to make a story about—a thing that would connect up with this strange way of doing it.

[*The women's eyes meet for an instant. Enter Hale from outer door.*]

HALE: Well, I've got the team around. Pretty cold out there.

COUNTY ATTORNEY: I'm going to stay here awhile by myself. [*To the Sheriff.*] You can send Frank out for me, can't you? I want to go over everything. I'm not satisfied that we can't do better.

SHERIFF: Do you want to see what Mrs. Peters is going to take in?

[*The Lawyer goes to the table, picks up the apron, laughs.*]

COUNTY ATTORNEY: Oh I guess they're not very dangerous things the ladies have picked up. [*Moves a few things about, disturbing the quilt pieces which cover the box. Steps back.*] No, Mrs. Peters doesn't need supervising. For that matter, a sheriff's wife is married to the law. Ever think of it that way, Mrs. Peters?

MRS. PETERS: Not—just that way.

SHERIFF [*chuckling*]: Married to the law. [*Moves toward the other room.*] I just want you to come in here a minute, George. We ought to take a look at these windows.

COUNTY ATTORNEY [*scoffingly*]: Oh, windows!

SHERIFF: We'll be right out, Mr. Hale.

[*Hale goes outside. The Sheriff follows the County Attorney into the other room. Then Mrs. Hale rises, hands tight together, looking intensely at Mrs. Peters, whose eyes take a slow turn, finally meeting, Mrs. Hale's. A moment Mrs. Hale holds her, then her own eyes point the way to where the box is concealed. Suddenly Mrs. Peters throws back quilt pieces and tries to put the box in the bag she is wearing. It is too big. She opens box, starts to take the bird out, cannot touch it, goes to pieces, stands there helpless. Sound of a knob turning in the other room. Mrs. Hale snatches the box and puts it in the pocket of her big coat. Enter County Attorney and Sheriff.*]

COUNTY ATTORNEY [*facetiously*]: Well, Henry, at least we found out that she was not going to quilt it. She was going to—what is it you call it, ladies?

MRS. HALE [*her hand against her pocket*]: We call it—knot it, Mr. Henderson.

CURTAIN

—1917

SUSAN GLASPELL

Tennessee Williams was the first important American playwright to emerge in the post–World War II period. Born Thomas Lanier Williams and raised in St. Louis, he took his professional name from his mother's southern forebears. Williams studied at the University of Missouri and Washington University, ultimately completing a degree in drama at the University of Iowa. After staging some of his early one-act plays with the Group Theater (later known as the Actors Studio), Williams first came to larger public attention with The Glass Menagerie, *which won a Drama Critics Circle award in 1945.* The Glass Menagerie *is clearly autobiographical, drawing on Williams's memories of life with his faded southern belle mother and his tragically disturbed sister, Rose, who ultimately had to be institutionalized. Subsequent plays draw on Williams's life and his southern roots. In 1947* A Streetcar Named Desire *received the Pulitzer Prize, the first of two Williams would win in a forty-year career.* A Streetcar Named Desire, *which starred the young Marlon Brando on stage and film, is, in contrast to* The Glass Menagerie, *a brutally naturalistic tragedy in which no romantic illusions are allowed to survive. Both Jessica Tandy, who originated the stage role, and Vivien Leigh, who starred in the film, were acclaimed for their portrayals of Blanche DuBois. Williams's plays are constantly revived in little theaters and on Broadway. In the last decade both* A Streetcar Named Desire, *with Alec Baldwin, and* Cat on a Hot Tin Roof, *starring Kathleen Turner, completed successful New York engagements, and 2005 saw yet another Broadway revival of* The Glass Menagerie, *starring Jessica Lange. Some of the film adaptations of Williams's plays, several of which have screenplays written by the author, remain classics, especially Elia Kazan's version of* A Streetcar Named Desire. *Williams published his autobiography in 1975. A fascinating collection of his correspondence, which gives insight into both his concerns as a writer and his intensely troubled personal life, appeared in 2000.*

The Glass Menagerie

> nobody, not even the rain, has such small hands.
>
> e. e. cummings

Characters

Amanda Wingfield, *the mother.—A little woman of great but confused vitality clinging frantically to another time and place. Her characterization* must be carefully created, not copied from type. She is not paranoiac, but her life is paranoia. There is much to admire in Amanda, and as much to love and pity as there is to laugh at. Certainly she has endurance and a kind of heroism, and though her foolishness makes her unwittingly cruel at times, there is tenderness in her slight person.

Laura Wingfield, her daughter.—Amanda, having failed to establish contact with reality, continues to live vitally in her illusions, but Laura's situation is even graver. A childhood illness has left her crippled, one leg slightly shorter than the other, and held in a brace. This defect need not be more than suggested on the stage. Stemming from this, Laura's separation increases till she is like a piece of her own glass collection, too exquisitely fragile to move from the shelf.

Tom Wingfield, her son.—And the narrator of the play. A poet with a job in a warehouse. His nature is not remorseless, but to escape from a trap he has to act without pity.

Jim O'Connor, the gentleman caller.—A nice, ordinary young man.

Scene: An alley in St. Louis.

Part 1. Preparation for a Gentleman Caller.

Part 2. The Gentleman Calls.

Part 3. Now and the Past.

Scene I

The Wingfield apartment is in the rear of the building, one of those vast hive-like conglomerations of cellular living-units that flower as warty growths in overcrowded urban centers of lower middle-class population and are symptomatic of the impulse of this largest and fundamentally enslaved section of American society to avoid fluidity and differentiation and to exist and function as one interfused mass of automatism.

The apartment faces an alley and is entered by a fire-escape, a structure whose name is a touch of accidental poetic truth, for all of these huge buildings are always burning with the slow and implacable fires of human desperation. The fire escape is included in the set—that is, the landing of it and steps descending from it.

The scene is memory and is therefore non-realistic. Memory takes a lot of poetic license. It omits some details; others are exaggerated, according to the

*emotional value of the articles it touches, for memory is seated predomi-
nantly in the heart. The interior is therefore rather dim and poetic.*

*At the rise of the curtain, the audience is faced with the dark, grim rear wall
of the Wingfield tenement. This building, which runs parallel to the footlights, is flanked on both sides by dark, narrow alleys which run into murky
canyons of tangled clotheslines, garbage cans and the sinister latticework of
neighboring fire-escapes. It is up and down these side alleys that exterior en-
trances and exits are made, during the play. At the end of Tom's opening
commentary, the dark tenement wall slowly reveals (by means of a trans-
parency) the interior of the ground floor Wingfield apartment.*

*Downstage is the living room, which also serves as a sleeping room for
Laura, the sofa unfolding to make her bed. Upstage, center, and divided by a
wide arch or second proscenium with transparent faded portieres (or second
curtain), is the dining room. In an old-fashioned what-not in the living
room are seen scores of transparent glass animals. A blown-up photograph
of the father hangs on the wall of the living room, facing the audience, to the
left of the archway. It is the face of a very handsome young man in a dough-
boy's First World War cap. He is gallantly smiling, ineluctably smiling, as if
to say, "I will be smiling forever."*

*The audience hears and sees the opening scene in the dining room through
both the transparent wall of the building and the transparent gauze
portieres of the diningroom arch. It is during this revealing scene that the
fourth wall slowly ascends, out of sight.*

*This transparent exterior wall is not brought down again until the very end
of the play, during Tom's final speech.*

*The narrator is an undisguised convention of the play. He takes whatever
license with dramatic convention as is convenient to his purposes.*

*Tom enters dressed as a merchant sailor from alley, stage left, and strolls
across the front of the stage to the fire-escape. There he stops and lights a
cigarette. He addresses the audience.*

TOM: Yes, I have tricks in my pocket, I have things up my sleeve. But I
       am the opposite of a stage magician. He gives you the illusion that
       has the appearance of truth. I give you truth in the pleasant dis-
       guise of illusion. To begin with, I turn back time. I reverse it to that
       quaint period, the thirties, when the huge middle class of America
       was matriculating in a school for the blind. Their eyes had failed

them, or they had failed their eyes, and so they were having their fingers pressed forcibly down on the fiery Braille alphabet of a dissolving economy. In Spain there was revolution. Here there was only shouting and confusion. In Spain there was Guernica. Here there were disturbances of labor, sometimes pretty violent, in otherwise peaceful cities such as Chicago, Cleveland, Saint Louis . . . . This is the social background of the play.

[Music.]

The play is memory. Being a memory play, it is dimly lighted, it is sentimental, it is not realistic. In memory everything seems to happen to music. That explains the fiddle in the wings. I am the narrator of the play, and also a character in it. The other characters are my mother, Amanda, my sister, Laura, and a gentleman caller who appears in the final scenes. He is the most realistic character in the play, being an emissary from a world of reality that we were somehow set apart from. But since I have a poet's weakness for symbols, I am using this character also as a symbol; he is the long delayed but always expected something that we live for. There is a fifth character in the play who doesn't appear except in this larger-than-life photograph over the mantel. This is our father who left us a long time ago. He was a telephone man who fell in love with long distances; he gave up his job with the telephone company and skipped the light fantastic out of town . . . . The last we heard of him was a picture post-card from Mazatlan, on the Pacific coast of Mexico, containing a message of two words—"Hello—Good-bye!" and no address. I think the rest of the play will explain itself . . . .

Amanda's voice becomes audible through the portieres.

[Legend on Screen: "Où Sont Les Neiges?"]°

He divides the portieres and enters the upstage area. Amanda and Laura are seated at a drop-leaf table. Eating is indicated by gestures without food or utensils. Amanda faces the audience. Tom and Laura are seated in profile. The interior has lit up softly and through the scrim we see Amanda and Laura seated at the table in the upstage area.

Où Sont Les Neiges refrain from a poem by François Villion [1431–1463?]: "Where are the snows of yesteryear?"

AMANDA [calling]: Tom?

TOM: Yes, Mother.

AMANDA: We can't say grace until you come to the table!

TOM: Coming, Mother. [He bows slightly and withdraws, reappearing a few moments later in his place at the table.]

AMANDA [to her son]: Honey, don't push with your fingers. If you have to push with something, the thing to push with is a crust of bread. And chew—chew! Animals have sections in their stomachs which enable them to digest food without mastication, but human beings are supposed to chew their food before they swallow it down. Eat food leisurely, son, and really enjoy it. A well-cooked meal has lots of delicate flavors that have to be held in the mouth for appreciation. So chew your food and give your salivary glands a chance to function!

[Tom deliberately lays his imaginary fork down and pushes his chair back from the table.]

TOM: I haven't enjoyed one bite of this dinner because of your constant directions on how to eat it. It's you that makes me rush through meals with your hawk-like attention to every bite I take. Sickening—spoils my appetite—all this discussion of animals' secretion—salivary glands—mastication!

AMANDA [lightly]: Temperament like a Metropolitan star! [He rises and crosses downstage.] You're not excused from the table.

TOM: I am getting a cigarette.

AMANDA: You smoke too much. [Laura rises.]

LAURA: I'll bring in the blanc mange.

[He remains standing with cigarette by the portieres during the following.]

AMANDA [rising]: No, sister, no, sister—you be the lady this time and I'll be the darky.

LAURA: I'm already up.

AMANDA: Resume your seat, little sister—I want you to stay fresh and pretty—for gentlemen callers!

LAURA: I'm not expecting any gentlemen callers.

AMANDA [crossing out to kitchenette. Airily.]: Sometimes they come when they are least expected! Why, I remember one Sunday afternoon in the Blue Mountain—[Enters kitchenette.]

TOM: I know what's coming!

LAURA: Yes. But let her tell it.

TOM: Again?

LAURA: She loves to tell it.

[*Amanda returns with bowl of dessert.*]

AMANDA: One Sunday afternoon in Blue Mountain—your mother received—*seventeen!*—gentlemen callers! Why sometimes there weren't chairs enough to accommodate them all. We had to send the nigger over to bring in folding chairs from the parish house.

TOM [*remaining at portieres*]: How did you entertain those gentlemen callers?

AMANDA: I understood the art of conversation!

TOM: I bet you could talk.

AMANDA: Girls in those days *knew* how to talk, I can tell you.

TOM: Yes?

[*Image: Amanda as a Girl on a Porch Greeting Callers.*]

AMANDA: They knew how to entertain their gentlemen callers. It wasn't enough for a girl to be possessed of a pretty face and a graceful figure—although I wasn't slighted in either respect. She also needed to have a nimble wit and a tongue to meet all occasions.

TOM: What did you talk about?

AMANDA: Things of importance going on in the world! Never anything coarse or common or vulgar. [*She addresses Tom as though he were seated in the vacant chair at the table though he remains by portieres. He plays this scene as though he held the book.*] My callers were gentlemen—all! Among my callers were some of the most prominent young planters of the Mississippi Delta—planters and sons of planters!

[*Tom motions for music and a spot of light on Amanda. Her eyes lift, her face glows, her voice becomes rich and elegiac.*]

[Screen Legend: "Où Sont Les Neiges?"]

There was young Champ Laughlin who later became vice-president of the Delta Planters Bank. Hadley Stevenson who was drowned in Moon Lake and left his widow one hundred and fifty thousand in Government bonds. There were the Cutrere brothers, Wesley and Bates. Bates was one of my bright particular beaux!

He got in a quarrel with that wild Wainright boy. They shot it out on the floor of Moon Lake Casino. Bates was shot through the stomach. Died in the ambulance on his way to Memphis. His widow was also well provided for, came into eight or ten thousand acres, that's all. She married him on the rebound— never loved her—carried my picture on him the night he died! And there was that boy that every girl in the Delta had set her cap for! That beautiful, brilliant young Fitzhugh boy from Green County!

TOM: What did he leave his widow?

AMANDA: He never married! Gracious, you talk as though all of my old admirers had turned up their toes to the daisies!

TOM: Isn't this the first you mentioned that still survives?

AMANDA: That Fitzhugh boy went North and made a fortune—came to be known as the Wolf of Wall Street! He had the Midas touch, whatever he touched turned to gold! And I could have been Mrs. Duncan J. Fitzhugh, mind you! But—I picked your *father!*

LAURA [*rising*]: Mother, let me clear the table.

AMANDA: No dear, you go in front and study your typewriter chart. Or practice your shorthand a little. Stay fresh and pretty!—It's almost time for our gentlemen callers to start arriving. [*She flounces girlishly toward the kitchenette.*] How many do you suppose we're going to entertain this afternoon?

[*Tom throws down the paper and jumps up with a groan.*]

LAURA [*alone in the dining room*]: I don't believe we're going to receive any, Mother.

AMANDA [*reappearing, airily*]: What? No one—not one? You must be joking! [*Laura nervously echoes her laugh. She slips in a fugitive manner through the half-open portieres and draws them gently behind her. A shaft of very clear light is thrown on her face against the faded tapestry of the curtain.*] [*Music: "The Glass Menagerie" Under Faintly.*] [*Lightly*] Not one gentleman caller? It can't be true! There must be a flood, there must have been a tornado!

LAURA: It isn't a flood, it's not a tornado, Mother. I'm just not popular like you were in Blue Mountain . . . . [*Tom utters another groan. Laura glances at him with a faint, apologetic smile. Her voice catching a little*] Mother's afraid I'm going to be an old maid.

[The Scene Dims Out with "Glass Menagerie" Music.]

On the dark stage the screen is lighted with the image of blue roses. Gradually Laura's figure becomes apparent and the screen goes out. The music subsides. Laura is seated in the delicate ivory chair at the small clawfoot table. She wears a dress of soft violet material for a kimono—her hair tied back from her forehead with a ribbon. She is washing and polishing her collection of glass.

Amanda appears on the fire-escape steps. At the sound of her ascent, Laura catches her breath, thrusts the bowl of ornaments away and seats herself stiffly before the diagram of the typewriter keyboard as though it held her spellbound. Something has happened to Amanda. It is written in her face as she climbs to the landing: a look that is grim and hopeless and a little absurd.

She has one of those cheap or imitation velvety-looking cloth coats with imitation fur collar. Her hat is five or six years old, one of those dreadful cloche hats that were worn in the late twenties, and she is clasping an enormous black patent-leather pocketbook with nickel clasp and initials. This is her full-dress outfit, the one she usually wears to the D.A.R.

Before entering she looks through the door. She purses her lips, opens her eyes wide, rolls them upward and shakes her head. Then she slowly lets herself in the door. Seeing her mother's expression Laura touches her lips with a nervous gesture.

LAURA: Hello, Mother, I was—[*She makes a nervous gesture toward the chart on the wall. Amanda leans against the shut door and stares at Laura with a martyred look.*]

AMANDA: Deception? Deception? [*She slowly removes her hat and gloves, continuing the swift suffering stare. She lets the hat and gloves fall on the floor—a bit of acting.*]

LAURA [*shakily*]:   How was the D.A.R. meeting? [*Amanda slowly opens her purse and removes a dainty white handkerchief which she shakes out delicately and delicately touches to her lips and nostrils.*] Didn't you go to the D.A.R. meeting, Mother?

AMANDA [*faintly, almost inaudibly*]:   —No.—No. [*Then more forcibly*] I did not have the strength—to go to the D.A.R. In fact, I did not have the courage. I waited to find a hole in the ground and hide myself in it forever! [*She crosses slowly to the wall and removes the diagram of the typewriter keyboard. She holds it in front of her for a* second, *staring at it sweetly and sorrowfully—then bites her lips and tears it in two pieces.*]

LAURA [*faintly*]:   Why did you do that, Mother? [*Amanda repeats the same procedure with the chart of the Gregg Alphabet.*] Why are you—

AMANDA: Why? Why? How old are you, Laura?

LAURA: Mother, you know my age.

AMANDA: I thought that you were an adult; it seems that I was mistaken. [*She crosses slowly to the sofa and sinks down and stares at Laura.*]

LAURA: Please don't stare at me, Mother.

[*Amanda closes her eyes and lowers her head. Count ten.*]

AMANDA: What are we going to do, what is going to become of us, what is the future?

[*Count ten.*]

LAURA: Has something happened, Mother? [*Amanda draws a long breath and takes out the handkerchief again. Dabbing process.*] Mother, has—something happened?

AMANDA: I'll be right in a minute. I'm just bewildered—[*count five*] — by life . . . .

LAURA: Mother, I wish you would tell me what's happened.

AMANDA: As you know, I was supposed to be inducted into my office at the D.A.R. this afternoon. [*Image: A Swarm of Typewriters.*] But I stopped off at Rubicam's Business College to speak to your teachers about your having a cold and ask them what progress they thought you were making down there.

LAURA: Oh . . . .

AMANDA: I went to the typing instructor and introduced myself as your mother. She didn't know who you were. Wingfield, she said. We don't have any such student enrolled at the school! I assured her she did, that you had been going to classes since early in January. "I wonder," she said, "if you could be talking about that terribly shy little girl who dropped out of school after only a few days' attendance?" "No," I said, "Laura, my daughter, has been going to school every day for the past six weeks!" "Excuse me," she said. She took the attendance book out and there was your name, unmistakably printed, and all the dates you were absent until they decided that you had dropped out of school. I still said, "No, there must have been some mistake! There must have been some mix-up in the records!" And she said, "No—I remember her perfectly now. Her hand shook so that she couldn't hit the right keys! The first time we gave a speed-test, she broke down completely—was sick at the stomach and almost had to be carried into the washroom! After that morning she never showed up any more. We phoned the house but never got any answer"—while I was working at Famous and Barr, I suppose demonstrating those—Oh! I felt so weak I could barely keep on my feet. I had to sit down while they got me a glass of water! Fifty dollars' tuition, all of our plans—my hopes and ambitions for you—just gone up the spout, just gone up the spout like that. [*Laura draws a long breath and gets awkwardly to her feet. She crosses to the victrola and winds it up.*] What are you doing?

LAURA: Oh! [*She releases the handle and returns to her seat.*]

AMANDA: Laura, where have you been going when you've gone out pretending that you were going to business college?

LAURA: I've just been going out walking.

AMANDA: That's not true.

LAURA: It is. I just went walking.

AMANDA: Walking? Walking? In winter? Deliberately courting pneumonia in that light coat? Where did you walk to, Laura?

LAURA: It was the lesser of two evils, Mother. [*Image: Winter Scene in Park.*] I couldn't go back up. I—threw up—on the floor!

AMANDA: From half past seven till after five thirty every day you mean to tell me you walked around in the park, because you wanted to make me think that you were still going to Rubicam's Business College?

LAURA: It wasn't as bad as it sounds. I went inside places to get warmed up.

AMANDA: Inside where?

LAURA: I went in the art museum and the birdhouses at the Zoo. I visited the penguins every day! Sometimes I did without lunch and went to the movies. Lately I've been spending most of my afternoons in the Jewel-box, that big glass house where they raise the tropical flowers.

AMANDA: You did all this to deceive me, just for the deception? [*Laura looks down.*] Why?

TENNESSEE WILLIAMS

296

LAURA: Mother, when you're disappointed, you get that awful suffering look on your face. Like the picture of Jesus' mother in the museum!

AMANDA: Hush!

LAURA: I couldn't face it.

[*Pause: A whisper of strings.*]

[Legend: "The Crust of Humility."]

AMANDA [*hopelessly fingering the huge pocketbook*]:   So what are we going to do the rest of our lives? Stay home and watch the parades go by? Amuse ourselves with the glass menagerie, darling? Eternally play those worn-out phonograph records your father left as a painful reminder of him? We won't have a business career—we've given that up because it gave us nervous indigestion! [*Laughs wearily.*] What is there left but dependency all our lives? I know so well what becomes of unmarried women who aren't prepared to occupy a position. I've seen such pitiful cases in the South—barely tolerated spinsters living upon the grudging patronage of sister's husband or brother's wife!—stuck away in some little mousetrap of a room—encouraged by one inlaw to visit another—little birdlike women without any nest—eating the crust of humility all their life! Is that the future that we've mapped out for ourselves? I swear it's the only alternative I can think of! It isn't a very pleasant alternative, is it? Of course—some girls *do* marry. [*Laura twists her hands nervously.*] Haven't you ever liked some boy?

LAURA: Yes, I liked one once. [*Rises.*] I came across his picture a while ago.

AMANDA [*with some interest*]:   He gave you his picture?

LAURA: No, it's in the year-book.

AMANDA [*disappointed*]:   Oh—a high-school boy.

[Screen Image: Jim as a High-School Hero Bearing a Silver Cup.]

LAURA: Yes. His name was Jim. [*Laura lifts the heavy annual from the clawfoot table.*] Here he is in *The Pirates of Penzance*.

AMANDA [*absently*]:   The what?

LAURA: The operetta the senior class put on. He had a wonderful voice and we sat across the aisle from each other Mondays, Wednesdays, and Fridays in the Aud. Here he is with the silver cup for debating! See his grin?

AMANDA [*absently*]:   He must have had a jolly disposition.

LAURA: He used to call me—Blue Roses.

[Image: Blue Roses.]

AMANDA: Why did he call you such a name as that?

LAURA: When I had that attack of pleurosis—he asked me what was the matter when I came back. I said pleurosis—he thought I said Blue Roses! So that's what he always called me after that. Whenever he saw me, he'd holler, "Hello, Blue Roses!" I didn't care for the girl that he went out with. Emily Meisenbach. Emily was the best-dressed girl at Soldan. She never struck me, though, as being sincere . . . . It says in the Personal Section—they're engaged. That's—six years ago! They must be married by now.

AMANDA: Girls that aren't cut out for business careers usually wind up married to some nice man. [*Gets up with a spark of revival.*] Sister, that's what you'll do!

[*Laura utters a startled, doubtful laugh. She reaches quickly for a piece of glass.*]

LAURA: But, Mother—

AMANDA: Yes? [*Crossing to photograph.*]

LAURA [*in a tone of frightened apology*]: I'm—crippled!

[Image: Screen.]

AMANDA: Nonsense! Laura, I've told you never, never to use that word. Why, you're not crippled, you just have a little defect—hardly noticeable, even! When people have some slight disadvantage like that, they cultivate other things to make up for it—develop charm—and vivacity—and—*charm!* That's all you have to do! [*She turns again to the photograph.*] One thing your father had *plenty of*—was *charm!*

[*Tom motions to the fiddle in the wings.*]

[The Scene Fades Out with Music.]

Scene III
(Legend on the Screen: "After the Fiasco—")

[*Tom speaks from the fire-escape landing.*]

TOM: After the fiasco at Rubicam's Business College, the idea of getting a gentleman caller for Laura began to play a more important part in Mother's calculations. It became an obsession.

Like some archetype of the universal unconscious, the image of the gentleman caller haunted our small apartment . . . . [*Image: Young Man at Door with Flowers.*] An evening at home rarely passed without some allusion to this image, this specter, this hope . . . . Even when he wasn't mentioned, his presence hung in Mother's preoccupied look and in my sister's frightened, apologetic manner—hung like a sentence passed upon the Wingfields! Mother was a woman of action as well as words. She began to take logical steps in the planned direction. Late that winter and in the early spring—realizing that extra money would be needed to properly feather the nest and plume the bird—she conducted a vigorous campaign on the telephone, roping in subscribers to one of those magazines for matrons called *The Home-maker's Companion*, the type of journal that features the serialized sublimation of ladies of letters who think in terms of delicate cup-like breasts, slim, tapering waists, rich, creamy thighs, eyes like wood-smoke in autumn, fingers that soothe and caress like strains of music, bodies as powerful as Etruscan sculpture.

[Screen Image: Glamour Magazine Cover.]

[*Amanda enters with phone on long extension cord. She is spotted in the dim stage.*]

AMANDA: Ida Scott? This is Amanda Wingfield! We *missed* you at the D.A.R. last Monday! I said to myself: She's probably suffering with that sinus condition! How is that sinus condition? Horrors! Heaven have mercy!—You're a Christian martyr, yes, that's what you are, a Christian martyr! Well, I just now happened to notice that your subscription to the *Companion's* about to expire! Yes, it expires with the next issue, honey!—just when that wonderful new serial by Bessie Mae Hopper is getting off to such an exciting start. Oh, honey, it's something that you can't miss! You remember how *Gone With the Wind* took everybody by storm! You simply couldn't go out if you hadn't read it. All everybody *talked* was Scarlett O'Hara. Well, this is a book that critics already compare to *Gone With the Wind*. It's the *Gone With the Wind* of the post-World War generation!—What?—Burning? Oh, honey, don't let them burn, go take a look in the oven and I'll hold the wire! Heavens—I think she's hung up!

[Dim Out.]

[Legend on Screen: "You Think I'm in Love with Continental Shoemakers?"]

[Before the stage is lighted, the violent voices of Tom and Amanda are heard. They are quarreling behind the portieres. In front of them stands Laura with clenched hands and panicky expression. A clear pool of light on her figure throughout this scene.]

TOM: What in Christ's name am I—

AMANDA [*shrilly*]: Don't you use that—

TOM: Supposed to do!

AMANDA: Expression! Not in my—

TOM: Ohhh!

AMANDA: Presence! Have you gone out of your senses?

TOM: I have, that's true, *driven* out!

AMANDA: What is the mater with you, you—big—big—IDIOT!

TOM: Look—I've got *no thing*, no single thing—

AMANDA: Lower your voice?

TOM: In my life here that I can call my OWN! Everything is—

AMANDA: Stop that shouting!

TOM: Yesterday you confiscated my books! You had the nerve to—

AMANDA: I took that horrible novel back to the library—yes! That hideous book by that insane Mr. Lawrence. [*Tom laughs wildly.*] I cannot control the output of diseased minds or people who cater to them—[*Tom laughs still more wildly.*] BUT I WON'T ALLOW SUCH FILTH BROUGHT INTO MY HOUSE! No, no, no, no, no!

TOM: House, house! Who pays rent on it, who makes a slave of himself to—

AMANDA [*fairly screeching*]: Don't you DARE to—

TOM: No, no, I musn't say things! *I've* got to just—

AMANDA: Let me tell you—

TOM: I don't want to hear any more! [*He tears the portieres open. The upstage area is lit with a turgid smoky red glow.*]

Amanda's hair is in metal curlers and she wears a very old bathrobe, much too large for her slight figure, a relic of the faithless Mr. Wingfield. An upright typewriter and a mild disarray of manuscripts are on the drop-leaf table. The quarrel was probably precipitated by Amanda's interruption of his creative labor. A chair lying overthrown on the floor. Their gesticulating shadows are cast on the ceiling by the fiery glow.

AMANDA: You *will* hear more, you—

TOM: No, I won't hear more, I'm going out!

AMANDA: You come right back in—

TOM: Out, out out! Because I'm—

AMANDA: Come back here, Tom Wingfield! I'm not through talking to you!

TOM: Oh, go—

LAURA [*desperately*]:   Tom!

AMANDA: You're going to listen, and no more insolence from you! I'm at the end of my patience! [*He comes back toward her.*]

TOM: What do you think I'm at? Aren't I supposed to have any patience to reach the end of, Mother? I know, I know. It seems unimportant to you, what I'm *doing*—what I *want* to do—having a little *difference* between them! You don't think that—

AMANDA: I think you've been doing things that you're ashamed of. That's why you act like this. I don't believe that you go every night to movies. Nobody goes to the movies night after night. Nobody in their right minds goes to movies as often as you pretend to. People don't go to the movies at nearly midnight, and movies don't let out at two A.M. Come in stumbling. Muttering to yourself like a maniac! You get three hours' sleep and then go to work. Oh, I can picture the way you're doing down there. Moping, doping, because you're in no condition.

TOM [*wildly*]:   No, I'm in no condition!

AMANDA: What right have you got to jeopardize your job? Jeopardize the security of us all? How do you think we'd manage if you were—

TOM: Listen! You think I'm crazy *about the warehouse?* [*He bends fiercely toward her slight figure.*] You think I'm in love with the Continental Shoemakers? You think I want to spend fifty-five *years* down there in that—*celotex interior!* with—*fluorescent—tubes!* Look! I'd rather somebody picked up a crowbar and battered out my brains than go back mornings! I *go!* Every time you come in yelling that God damn *"Rise and Shine!" "Rise and Shine!"* I say to myself "How *lucky dead* people are!" But I get up. I *go!* For sixty-five dollars a month I gave up all that I dream of doing and being *ever!* And you say self—*self's* all I ever think of. Why, listen, if self is what I thought of, Mother, I'd be where he is—GONE! [*Pointing to father's picture.*] As far as the system of transportation reaches! [*He starts past her. She grabs his arm.*] Don't grab at me, Mother!

AMANDA: Where are you going?

TOM: I'm going to the *movies!*

AMANDA: I don't believe that lie!

TOM [*crouching toward her, overtowering her tiny figure. She backs away, gasping*]: I'm going to opium dens! Yes, opium dens, dens of vice and criminals' hang-outs, Mother. I've joined the Hogan gang, I'm a hired assassin, I carry a tommy-gun in a violin case! I run a string of cat-houses in the Valley. They call me Killer, Killer Wingfield, I'm leading a double-life, a simple, honest warehouse worker by day, by night a dynamic *czar* of the *underworld, Mother.* I go to gambling casinos, I spin away fortunes on the roulette table! I wear a patch over one eye and a false mustache, sometimes I put on green whiskers. On those occasions they call me—*El Diablo!* Oh, I could tell you things to make you sleepless! My enemies plan to dynamite this place. They're going to blow us all sky-high some night! I'll be glad, very happy, and so will you! You'll go up, up on a broomstick, over Blue Mountain with seventeen gentlemen callers! You ugly—babbling old—*witch* . . . . [*He goes through a series of violent, clumsy movements, seizing his overcoat, lunging to the door, pulling it fiercely open. The women watch him, aghast. His arm catches in the sleeve of the coat as he struggles to pull it on. For a moment he is pinioned by the bulky garment. With an outraged groan he tears the coat off again, splitting the shoulders of it, and hurls it across the room. It strikes against the shelf of Laura's glass collection, there is a tinkle of shattering glass. Laura cries out as if wounded.*]

[Music Legend: "The Glass Menagerie."]

LAURA [*shrilly*]: My glass! —menagerie . . . . [*She covers her face and turns away.*]

[*But Amanda is still stunned and stupefied by the "ugly witch" so that she barely notices this occurrence. Now she recovers her speech.*]

AMANDA [*in an awful voice*]: I won't speak to you—until you apologize! [*She crosses through the portieres and draws them together behind her. Tom is left with Laura. Laura clings weakly to the mantel with her face averted. Tom stares at her stupidly for a moment. Then he crosses to shelf. Drops awkwardly to his knees to collect the fallen glass, glancing at Laura as if he would speak but couldn't.*]

["The Glass Menagerie" steals in as the Scene Dims Out.]

Scene IV

The interior is dark. Faint light in the alley. A deep-voiced bell in a church is tolling the hour by five as the scene commences.

Tom appears at the top of the alley. After each solemn boom of the bell in the tower, he shakes a little noise-maker or rattle as if to express the tiny spasm of man in contrast to the sustained power and dignity of the Almighty. This and the unsteadiness of his advance make it evident that he has been drinking.

As he climbs the few steps to the fire-escape landing light steals up inside. Laura appears in night-dress, observing Tom's empty bed in the front room.

Tom fishes in his pockets for the door-key, removing a motley assortment of articles in the search, including a perfect shower of movie-ticket stubs and an empty bottle. At last he finds the key, but just as he is about to insert it, it slips from his fingers. He strikes a match and crouches below the door.

TOM [*bitterly*]:   One crack—and it falls through!

[*Laura opens the door.*]

LAURA: Tom! Tom, what are you doing?

TOM: Looking for a door-key.

LAURA: Where have you been all this time?

TOM: I have been to the movies.

LAURA: All this time at the movies?

TOM: There was a very long program. There was a Garbo picture and a Mickey Mouse and a travelogue and a newsreel and a preview of coming attractions. And there was an organ solo and a collection for the milk-fund—simultaneously—which ended up in a terrible fight between a fat lady and an usher!

LAURA [*innocently*]:   Did you have to stay through everything?

TOM: Of course! And, oh, I forgot! There was a big stage show! The headliner on this stage show was Malvolio the Magician. He performed wonderful tricks, many of them, such as pouring water back and forth between pitchers. First it turned to wine and then it turned to beer and then it turned to whiskey. I know it was whiskey it finally turned into because he needed somebody to come up out of the audience to help him, and I came up—both shows! It was Kentucky Straight Bourbon. A very generous fellow, he gave souvenirs. [*He pulls from his back pocket a shimmering rainbow-colored scarf.*] He gave me this. This is his magic scarf. You can have it, Laura. You wave it over a canary cage and you get a bowl of gold-fish. You wave it over the goldfish bowl and they fly away canaries . . . . But the wonderfulest trick of all was the coffin trick. We nailed him into a coffin and he got out of the coffin without removing one nail. [*He has come inside.*] There is a trick that would come in handy for me—get me out of this 2 by 4 situation! [*Flops onto bed and starts removing shoes.*]

LAURA: Tom—Shhh!

TOM: What you shushing me for?

LAURA: You'll wake up Mother.

TOM: Goody, goody! Pay 'er back for those "Rise an' Shines." [*Lies down, groaning.*] You know it don't take much intelligence to get yourself into a nailed-up coffin, Laura. But who in hell ever got himself out of one without removing one nail?

[*As if in answer, the father's grinning photograph lights up.*]

[Scene Dims Out.]

Immediately following: The church bell is heard striking six. At the sixth stroke the alarm clock goes off in Amanda's room, and after a few moments we hear her calling: "Rise and Shine! Rise and Shine! Laura, go tell your brother to rise and shine!"

TOM [*sitting up slowly*]:   I'll rise—but I won't shine.

[*The light increases.*]

AMANDA: Laura, tell your brother his coffee is ready.

[*Laura slips into the front room.*]

LAURA: Tom! it's nearly seven. Don't make Mother nervous. [*He stares at her stupidly. Beseechingly.*] Tom, speak to Mother this morning. Make up with her, apologize, speak to her!

TOM: She won't to me. It's her that started not speaking.

LAURA: If you just say you're sorry she'll start speaking.

TOM: Her not speaking—is that such a tragedy?

LAURA: Please—please!

AMANDA [*calling from kitchenette*]:   Laura, are you going to do what I asked you to do, or do I have to get dressed and go out myself?

LAURA: Going, going—soon as I get on my coat! [*She pulls on a shapeless felt hat with nervous, jerky movement, pleadingly glancing at Tom. Rushes awkwardly for coat. The coat is one of Amanda's, inaccurately made-over, the sleeves too short for Laura.*] Butter and what else?

AMANDA [*entering upstage*]:   Just butter. Tell them to charge it.

LAURA: Mother, they make such faces when I do that.

AMANDA: Sticks and stones may break my bones, but the expression of Mr. Garfinkel's face won't harm me! Tell your brother his coffee is getting cold.

LAURA [*at door*]:   Do what I asked you, will you, will you, Tom?

[*He looks sullenly away.*]

AMANDA: Laura, go now or just don't go at all!

LAURA [*rushing out*]:   Going—going! [*A second later she cries out. Tom springs up and crosses to the door. Amanda rushes anxiously in. Tom opens the door.*]

TOM: Laura?

LAURA: I'm all right. I slipped, but I'm all right.

AMANDA [*peering anxiously after her*]:   If anyone breaks a leg on those fire-escape steps, the landlord ought to be sued for every cent he possesses! [*She shuts the door. Remembers she isn't speaking and returns to the other room.*]

[*As Tom enters listlessly for his coffee, she turns her back to him and stands rigidly facing the widow on the gloomy gray vault of the areaway. Its light on her face with its aged but childish features is cruelly sharp, satirical as a Daumier print.*]

[Music Under: "Ave Maria."]

[*Tom glances sheepishly but sullenly at her averted figure and slumps at the table. The coffee is scalding hot; he sips it and gasps and spits it back in the cup. At his gasp, Amanda catches her breath and half turns. Then catches herself and turns back to the window.*]

Tom blows on his coffee, glancing sidewise at his mother. She clears her throat. Tom clears his. He starts to rise. Sinks back down again, scratches his head, clears his throat again. Amanda coughs. Tom raises his cup in both hands to blow on it, his eyes

staring over the rim of it at his mother for several moments. Then
he slowly sets the cup down and awkwardly and hesitantly rises
from the chair.]

TOM [*hoarsely*]:   Mother. I—I apologize. Mother. [*Amanda draws a*
quick, shuddering breath. Her face works grotesquely. She breaks into
childlike tears.] I'm sorry for what I said, for everything that I said, I
didn't mean it.

AMANDA [*sobbingly*]:   My devotion has made me a witch and so I
make myself hateful to my children!

TOM: No, you *don't.*

AMANDA: I worry so much, don't sleep, it makes me nervous!

TOM [*gently*]:   I understand that.

AMANDA: I've had to put up a solitary battle all these years. But you're
my right-hand bower! Don't fall down, don't fail!

TOM [*gently*]:   I try, Mother.

AMANDA [*with great enthusiasm*]:   Try and you will succeed! [*The*
notion makes her breathless.] Why, you—you're just *full* of natural
endowments! Both of my children—they're *unusual* children! Don't
you think I know it? I'm so—*proud!* Happy and—feel I've—so
much to be thankful for but—Promise me one thing, son!

TOM: What, Mother?

AMANDA: Promise, son, you'll—never be a drunkard!

TOM [*turns to her grinning*]:   I will never be a drunkard!

AMANDA: That's what frightened me so, that you'd be drinking! Eat a
bowl of Purina!

TOM: Just coffee, Mother.

AMANDA: Shredded wheat biscuit?

TOM: No. No, Mother, just coffee.

AMANDA: You can't put in a day's work on an empty stomach. You've
got ten minutes—don't gulp! Drinking too-hot liquids makes can-
cer of the stomach . . . . Put cream in.

TOM: No, thank you.

AMANDA: To cool it.

TOM: No! No, thank you, I want it black.

AMANDA: I know, but it's not good for you. We have to do all that we
can to build ourselves up. In these trying times we live in, all that we
have to cling to is each other . . . . That's why it's so important to—
Tom, I—I sent out your sister so I could discuss something with
you. If you hadn't spoken I would have spoken to you. [*Sits down.*]

TOM [*gently*]:   What is it, Mother, that you want to discuss?
AMANDA: Laura!

[*Tom puts his cup down slowly.*]

> [Legend on Screen: "Laura."]
> [Music: "The Glass Menagerie."]

TOM: —Oh.—Laura . . .
AMANDA [*touching his sleeve*]:   You know how Laura is. So quiet but—
still water runs deep! She notices things and I think she—broods
about them. [*Tom looks up.*] A few days ago I came in and she was
crying.
TOM: What about?
AMANDA: You.
TOM: Me?
AMANDA: She has an idea that you're not happy here.
TOM: What gave her that idea?
AMANDA: What gives her any idea? However, you do act strangely.
I—I'm not criticizing, understand *that*! I know your ambitions do
not lie in the warehouse, that like everybody in the whole wide
world—you've had to—make sacrifices, but—Tom—Tom—life's
not easy, it calls for—Spartan endurance! There's so many things
in my heart that I cannot describe to you! I've never told you but
I—*loved* your father . . . .
TOM [*gently*]:   I know that, Mother.
AMANDA: And you—when I see you taking after his ways! Staying
out late—and—well, you *had* been drinking the night you were
in that—terrifying condition! Laura says that you hate the apartment and that you go out nights to get away from it! Is that true,
Tom?
TOM: No. You say there's so much in your heart that you can't de-
scribe to me. That's true of me, too. There's so much in my heart
that I can't describe to *you*! So let's respect each other's—
AMANDA: But, why—*why*, Tom—are you always so *restless?* Where do
you go to, nights?
TOM: I—go to the movies.
AMANDA: Why do you go to the movies so much, Tom?
TOM: I go to the movies because—I like adventure. Adventure is
something I don't have much of at work, so I go to the movies.
AMANDA: But, Tom, you go to the movies *entirely too much!*

TOM: I like a lot of adventure.

[*Amanda looks baffled, then hurt. As the familiar inquisition re-sumes he becomes hard and impatient again. Amanda slips back into her querulous attitude toward him.*]

[Image on Screen: Sailing Vessel with Jolly Roger.]

AMANDA: Most young men find adventure in their careers.

TOM: Then most young men are not employed in a warehouse.

AMANDA: The world is full of young men employed in warehouses and offices and factories.

TOM: Do all of them find adventure in their careers?

AMANDA: They do or they do without it! Not everybody has a craze for adventure.

TOM: Man is by instinct a lover, a hunter, a fighter, and none of these instincts are given much play at the warehouse!

ARMANDA: Man is by instinct! Don't quote instinct to me! Instinct is something that people have got away from! It belongs to animals! Christian adults don't want it!

TOM: What do Christian adults want, then, Mother?

AMANDA: Superior things! Things of the mind and the spirit! Only animals have to satisfy instincts! Surely your aims are somewhat higher than theirs! Than monkeys—pigs—

TOM: I reckon they're not.

AMANDA: You're joking. However, that isn't what I wanted to discuss.

TOM [*rising*]:   I haven't much time.

AMANDA [*pushing his shoulders*]:   Sit down.

TOM: You want me to punch in red at the warehouse, Mother?

AMANDA: You have five minutes. I want to talk about Laura.

[Legend: "Plans and Provisions."]

TOM: All right! What about Laura?

AMANDA: We have to be making plans and provisions for her. She's older than you, two years, and nothing has happened. She just drifts along doing nothing. It frightens me terribly how she just drifts along.

TOM: I guess she's the type that people call home girls.

AMANDA: There's no such type, and if there is, it's a pity! That is un-less the home is hers, with a husband!

TOM: What?

AMANDA: Oh, I can see the handwriting on the wall as plain as I see the nose in front of my face! It's terrifying! More and more you remind me of your father! He was out all hours without explanation— Then *left!* *Good-bye!* And me with the bag to hold. I saw that letter you got from the Merchant Marine. I know what you're dreaming of. I'm not standing here blindfolded. Very well, then. Then *do* it! But not till there's somebody to take your place.

TOM: What do you mean?

AMANDA: I mean that as soon as Laura has got somebody to take care of her, married, a home of her own, independent—why, then you'll be free to go wherever you please, on land, on sea, whichever way the wind blows! But until that time you've got to look out for your sister. I don't say me because I'm old and don't matter! I say for your sister because she's young and dependent. I put her in business college—a dismal failure! Frightened her so it made her sick to her stomach. I took her over to the Young People's League at the church. Another fiasco. She spoke to nobody, nobody spoke to her. Now all she does is fool with those pieces of glass and play those worn-out records. What kind of life is that for a girl to lead!

TOM: What can I do about it?

AMANDA: Overcome selfishness! Self, self, self is all that you ever think of! [*Tom springs up and crosses to get his coat. It is ugly and bulky. He pulls on a cap with earmuffs.*] Where is your muffler? Put your wool muffler on! [*He snatches it angrily from the closet and tosses it around his neck and pulls both ends tight.*] Tom! I haven't said what I had in mind to ask you.

TOM: I'm too late to—

AMANDA [*catching his arms very importunately. Then shyly.*]: Down the warehouse, aren't there some—nice young men?

TOM: No!

AMANDA: There *must* be—*some.*

TOM: Mother—

[*Gesture.*]

AMANDA: Find out one that's clean-living—doesn't drink and—ask him out for sister?

TOM: What?

AMANDA: For *sister!* To *meet!* Get acquainted!

TOM [*stamping to door*]:   Oh, my *go-osh!*

AMANDA: Will you? [*He opens door. Imploringly*] Will you? [*He starts down.*] Will you? *Will* you, dear?

TOM [*calling back*]: YES!

[*Amanda closes the door hesitantly and with a troubled but faintly hopeful expression.*]

[Screen Image: Glamour Magazine Cover.]

[*Spot Amanda at phone.*]

AMANDA: Ella Cartwright? This is Amanda Wingfield! How are you, honey? How is that kidney condition? [*Count five.*] Horrors! [*Count five.*] You're a Christian martyr, yes, honey, that's what you are, a Christian martyr! Well, I just happened to notice in my little red book that your subscription to the *Companion* has just run out! I knew that you wouldn't want to miss out on the wonderful serial starting in this new issue. It's by Bessie Mae Hopper, the first thing she's written since *Honeymoon for Three*. Wasn't that a strange and interesting story? Well, this one is even lovelier, I believe. It has a sophisticated society background. It's all about the horsey set on Long Island!

[Fade Out.]

Scene V

[Legend on Screen: "Annunciation."] Fade With Music.

It is early dusk of a spring evening. Supper has just been finished in the Wingfield apartment. Amanda and Laura in light-colored dresses are removing dishes from the table, in the upstage area, which is shadowy, their movements formalized almost as a dance or ritual, their moving forms as pale and silent as moths. Tom, in white shirt and trousers, rises from the table and crosses toward the fire-escape.

AMANDA [*as he passes her*]: Son, will you do me a favor?

TOM: What?

AMANDA: Comb your hair! You look so pretty when your hair is combed! [*Tom slouches on the sofa with the evening paper. Enormous caption "Franco Triumphs."*] There is only one respect in which I would like you to emulate your father.

TOM: What respect is that?

TENNESSEE WILLIAMS

AMANDA: The care he always took of his appearance. He never allowed himself to look untidy. [*He throws down the paper and crosses to the fire-escape.*] Where are you going?

TOM: I'm going out to smoke.

AMANDA: You smoke too much. A pack a day at fifteen cents a pack. How much would that amount to in a month? Thirty times fifteen is how much, Tom? Figure it out and you will be astounded at what you could save. Enough to give you a night-school course in accounting at Washington U! Just think what a wonderful thing that would be for you, son!

[*Tom is unmoved by the thought.*]

TOM: I'd rather smoke. [*He steps out on the landing, letting the screen door slam.*]

AMANDA [*sharply*]: I know! That's the tragedy of it . . . . [*Alone, she turns to look at her husband's picture.*]

[Dance Music: "All the World Is Waiting for the Sunrise!"]

TOM [*to the audience*]: Across the alley from us was the Paradise Dance Hall. On evenings in spring the windows and doors were open and the music came outdoors. Sometimes the lights were turned out except for a large glass sphere that hung from the ceiling. It would turn slowly about and filter the dusk with delicate rainbow colors. Then the orchestra played a waltz or a tango, something that had a slow and sensuous rhythm. Couples would come outside, to the relative privacy of the alley. You could see them kissing behind ashpits and telephone poles. This was the compensation for lives that passed like mine, without any change or adventure. Adventure and change were imminent in this year. They were waiting around the corner for all these kinds. Suspended in the mist over Berchtesgaden, caught in the folds of Chamberlain's umbrella—In Spain there was Guernica! But here there was only hot swing music and liquor, dance halls, bars, and movies, and sex that hung in the gloom like a chandelier and flooded the world with brief, deceptive rainbows . . . . All the world was waiting for bombardments!

[*Amanda turns from the picture and comes outside.*]

AMANDA [*sighing*]: A fire-escape landing's a poor excuse for a porch. [*She spreads a newspaper on a step and sits down, gracefully and*

demurely as if she were settling into a swing on a Mississippi veranda.]
What are you looking at?

TOM: The moon.

AMANDA: Is there a moon this evening?

TOM: It's rising over Garfinkel's Delicatessen.

AMANDA: So it is! A little silver slipper of a moon. Have you made a wish on it yet?

TOM: Um-hum.

AMANDA: What did you wish for.

TOM: That's a secret.

AMANDA: A secret, huh? Well, I won't tell you mine either. I will be just as mysterious as you.

TOM: I bet I can guess what yours is.

AMANDA: Is my head so transparent?

TOM: You're not a sphinx.

AMANDA: No, I don't have secrets. I'll tell you what I wished for on the moon. Success and happiness for my precious children! I wish for that whenever there's a moon, and when there isn't a moon, I wish for it, too.

TOM: I thought perhaps you wished for a gentleman caller.

AMANDA: Why do you say that?

TOM: Don't you remember asking me to fetch one?

AMANDA: I remember suggesting that it would be nice for your sister if you brought home some nice young man from the warehouse. I think I've made that suggestion more than once.

TOM: Yes, you have made it repeatedly.

AMANDA: Well?

TOM: We are going to have one.

AMANDA: What?

TOM: A gentleman caller!

[The Annunciation Is Celebrated with Music.]

[*Amanda rises.*]

[Image on Screen: Caller with Bouquet.]

AMANDA: You mean you have asked some nice young man to come over?

TOM: Yep. I've asked him to dinner.

AMANDA: You really did?

TOM: I did!

AMANDA: You did, and did he—*accept?*

TOM: He did!

AMANDA: Well, well—well, well! That's—lovely!

TOM: I thought that you would be pleased.

AMANDA: It's definite, then?

TOM: Very definite.

AMANDA: Soon?

TOM: Very soon.

AMANDA: For heaven's sake, stop putting on and tell me some things, will you?

TOM: What things do you want me to tell you?

AMANDA: Naturally I would like to know when he's *coming!*

TOM: He's coming tomorrow.

AMANDA: Tomorrow?

TOM: Yep. Tomorrow.

AMANDA: But, Tom!

TOM: Yes, Mother?

AMANDA: Tomorrow gives me no time!

TOM: Time for what?

AMANDA: Preparations! Why didn't you phone me at once, as soon as you asked him, the minute that he accepted? Then, don't you see, I could have been getting ready!

TOM: You don't have to make any fuss.

AMANDA: Oh, Tom, Tom, Tom, of course I have to make a fuss! I want things nice, not sloppy! Not thrown together. I'll certainly have to do some fast thinking, won't I?

TOM: I don't see why you have to think at all.

AMANDA: You just don't know. We can't have a gentleman caller in a pig-sty! All my wedding silver has to be polished, the monogrammed table linen ought to be laundered! The windows have to be washed and fresh curtains put up. And how about clothes? We have to *wear* something, don't we?

TOM: Mother, this boy is no one to make a fuss over!

AMANDA: Do you realize he's the first young man we've had introduced to your sister? It's terrible, dreadful, disgraceful that poor little sister has never received a single gentleman caller! Tom, come inside! [*She opens the screen door.*]

TOM: What for?

AMANDA: I want to ask you some things.

TENNESSEE WILLIAMS

TOM: If you're going to make such a fuss, I'll call it off, I'll tell him not to come.

AMANDA: You certainly won't do anything of the kind. Nothing offends people worse than broken engagements. It simply means I'll have to work like a Turk! We won't be brilliant, but we'll pass inspection. Come on inside. [*Tom follows, groaning.*] Sit down.

TOM: Any particular place you would like me to sit?

AMANDA: Thank heavens I've got that new sofa! I'm also making payments on a floor lamp I'll have sent out! And put the chintz covers on, they'll brighten things up! Of course I'd hoped to have these walls re-papered . . . . What is the young man's name?

TOM: His name is O'Connor.

AMANDA: That, of course, means fish—tomorrow is Friday! I'll have that salmon loaf—with Durkee's dressing! What does he do? He works at the warehouse?

TOM: Of course! How else would I—

AMANDA: Tom, he—doesn't drink?

TOM: Why do you ask me that?

AMANDA: Your father *did*!

TOM: Don't get started on that!

AMANDA: He *does* drink, then?

TOM: Not that I know of!

AMANDA: Make sure, be certain! The last thing I want for my daughter's a boy who drinks?

TOM: Aren't you being a little premature? Mr. O'Connor has not yet appeared on the scene!

AMANDA: But will tomorrow. To meet your sister, and what do I know about his character? Nothing! Old maids are better off than wives of drunkards!

TOM: Oh, my God.

AMANDA: Be still!

TOM [*leaning forward to whisper*]:   Lots of fellows meet girls whom they don't marry!

AMANDA: Oh, talk sensibly, Tom—and don't be sarcastic! [*She has gotten a hairbrush.*]

TOM: What are you doing?

AMANDA: I'm brushing that cow-lick down! What is this young man's position at the warehouse?

TOM [*submitting grimly to the brush and the interrogation*]:   This young man's position is that of a shipping clerk, Mother.

AMANDA: Sounds to me like a fairly responsible job, the sort of a job *you* would be in if you just had more *get-up*. What is his salary? Have you got any idea?

TOM: I would judge it to be approximately eighty-five dollars a month.

AMANDA: Well—not princely, but—

TOM: Twenty more than I make.

AMANDA: Yes, how well I know! But for a family man, eighty-five dollars a month is not much more than you can just get by on . . . .

TOM: Yes, but Mr. O'Connor is not a family man.

AMANDA: He might be, mightn't he? Some time in the future?

TOM: I see. Plans and provisions.

AMANDA: You are the only young man that I know of who ignores the fact that the future becomes the present, the present the past, and the past turns into everlasting regret if you don't plan for it!

TOM: I will think that over and see what I can make of it.

AMANDA: Don't be supercilious with your mother! Tell me some more about this—what do you call him?

TOM: James D. O'Connor. The D. is for Delaney.

AMANDA: Irish on *both* sides! *Gracious!* And doesn't drink?

TOM: Shall I call him up and ask him right this minute?

AMANDA: The only way to find out about those things is to make discreet inquiries at the proper moment. When I was a girl in Blue Mountain and it was suspected that a young man drank, the girl whose attentions he had been receiving, if any girl *was*, would sometimes speak to the minister of his church, or rather her father would if her father was living, and sort of feel him out on the young man's character. That is the way such things are discreetly handled to keep a young woman from making a tragic mistake!

TOM: Then how did you happen to make a tragic mistake?

AMANDA: That innocent look of your father's had everyone fooled! He *smiled*—the world was *enchanted!* No girl can do worse than put herself at the mercy of a handsome appearance! I hope that Mr. O'Connor is not too good-looking.

TOM: No, he's not too good-looking. He's covered with freckles and hasn't too much of a nose.

AMANDA: He's not right-down homely, though?

TOM: Not right-down homely. Just medium homely, I'd say.

AMANDA: Character's what to look for in a man.

TOM: That's what I've always said, Mother.

AMANDA: You've never said anything of the kind and I suspect you would never give it a thought.

TOM: Don't be suspicious of me.

AMANDA: At least I hope he's the type that's up and coming.

TOM: I think he really goes in for self-improvement.

AMANDA: What reason have you to think so?

TOM: He goes to night school.

AMANDA [beaming]: Splendid! What does he do, I mean study?

TOM: Radio engineering and public speaking!

AMANDA: Then he has visions of being advanced in the world! Any young man who studies public speaking is aiming to have an executive job some day! And radio engineering? A thing for the future! Both of these facts are very illuminating. Those are the sort of things that a mother should know concerning any young man who comes to call on her daughter. Seriously or—not.

TOM: One little warning. He doesn't know about Laura. I didn't let on that we had dark ulterior motives. I just said, why don't you come have dinner with us? He said okay and that was the whole conversation.

AMANDA: I bet it was! You're eloquent as an oyster. However, he'll know about Laura when he gets here. When we sees how lovely and sweet and pretty she is, he'll thank his lucky stars he was asked to dinner.

TOM: Mother, you mustn't expect too much of Laura.

AMANDA: What do you mean?

TOM: Laura seems all those things to you and me because she's ours and we love her. We don't even notice she's crippled any more.

AMANDA: Don't say crippled! You know that I never allow that word to be used!

TOM: But face facts, Mother. She is and—that's not all—

AMANDA: What do you mean "not all"?

TOM: Laura is very different from other girls.

AMANDA: I think the difference is all to her advantage.

TOM: Not quite all—in the eyes of others—strangers—she's terribly shy and lives in a world of her own and those things make her seem a little peculiar to people outside the house.

AMANDA: Don't say peculiar.

TOM: Face the facts. She is.

[*The Dance-Hall Music Changes to a Tango That Has a Minor and Somewhat Ominous Tone.*]

AMANDA: In what way is she peculiar—may I ask?

TOM [*gently*]:   She lives in a world of her own—a world of—little glass ornaments, Mother . . . . [*Gets up, Amanda remains holding the brush, looking at him, troubled.*] She plays old phonograph records and—that's about all—[*He glances at himself in the mirror and crosses to the door.*]

AMANDA [sharply]:   Where are you going?

TOM: I'm going to the movies. [*Out screen door.*]

AMANDA: Not to the movies, every night to the movies! [*Follows quickly to screen door.*] I don't believe you always go to the movies! [*He is gone. Amanda looks worriedly after him for a moment. Then vitality and optimism return and she turns from the door. Crossing to portieres.*] Laura! Laura! [*Laura answers from kitchenette.*]

LAURA: Yes, Mother.

AMANDA: Let those dishes go and come in front! [*Laura appears with dish towel. Gaily*] Laura, come here and make a wish on the moon!

LAURA [*entering*]:   Moon—moon?

AMANDA: A little silver slipper of a moon. Look over your left shoulder, Laura, and make a wish! [*Laura looks faintly puzzled as if called out of sleep. Amanda seizes her shoulders and turns her at angle by the door.*] Now! Now, darling, *wish!*

LAURA: What shall I wish for, Mother?

AMANDA [*her voice trembling and her eyes suddenly filling with tears*]: Happiness! Good Fortune!

[*The violin rises and the stage dims out.*]

Scene VI

[Image: High School Hero.]

TOM: And so the following evening I brought Jim home to dinner. I had known Jim slightly in high school. In high school Jim was a hero. He had tremendous Irish good nature and vitality with the scrubbed and polished look of white chinaware. He seemed to move in a continual spotlight. He was a star in basketball, captain of the debating club, president of the senior class and the glee club and he sang the male lead in the annual light operas. He was always running or bounding, never just walking. He seemed always at the point of defeating the law of gravity. He was shooting with such velocity through his adolescence that you would logically expect him to arrive at nothing short of the White House by the time he was thirty. But Jim apparently ran into more interference after his graduation from Soldan. His speed had definitely slowed. Six years after he left high school he was holding a job that wasn't much better than mine.

[Image: Clerk.]

He was the only one at the warehouse with whom I was on friendly terms. I was valuable to him as someone who could remember his former glory, who had seen him win basketball games and the silver cup in debating. He knew of my secret practice of retiring to a cabinet of the washroom to work on poems when business was slack in the warehouse. He called me Shakespeare. And while the other boys in the warehouse regarded me with suspicious hostility, Jim took a humorous attitude toward me. Gradually his attitude affected the others, their hostility wore off and they also began to smile at me as people smile at an oddly fashioned dog who trots across their path at some distance.

I knew that Jim and Laura had known each other at Soldan, and I had heard Laura speak admiringly of his voice. I didn't know if Jim remembered her or not. In high school Laura had been as unobtrusive as Jim had been astonishing. If he did remember Laura, it was not as my sister for when I asked him to dinner, he grinned and said, "You know, Shakespeare, I never thought of you as having folks!" He was about to discover that I did . . . .

[Light upstage.]
[Legend on Screen: "The Accent of a Coming Foot."]

[*Friday evening. It is about five o'clock of a late spring evening which comes "scattering poems in the sky." A delicate lemony light is in the Wingfield apartment. Amanda has worked like a Turk in preparation for the gentleman caller. The results are astonishing. The new floor lamp with its rose-silk shade is in place, a colored paper lantern conceals the broken light fixture in the ceiling, new billowing white curtains are at the windows, chintz covers are on chairs, and sofa, a pair of new sofa pillows make their initial appearance.*

Open boxes and tissue paper are scattered on the floor.

Laura stands in the middle with lifted arms while Amanda crouches before her, adjusting the hem of the new dress, devout and ritualistic. The dress is colored and designed by memory. The arrangement of Laura's hair is changed; it is softer and more becoming. A fragile, unearthly prettiness has come out in Laura: she is like a piece of translucent glass touched by light, given a momentary radiance, not actual, not lasting.]

AMANDA [*impatiently*]:   Why are you trembling?

LAURA: Mother, you've made me so nervous!

AMANDA: How have I made you nervous?

LAURA: By all this fuss! You make it seem so important?

AMANDA: I don't understand you, Laura. You couldn't be satisfied with just sitting home, and yet whenever I try to arrange something for you, you seem to resist it. [*She gets up.*] Now take a look at yourself. No, wait! Wait just a moment—I have an idea!

LAURA: What is it now?

[*Amanda produces two powder puffs which she wraps in handkerchiefs and stuffs in Laura's bosom.*]

LAURA: Mother, what are you doing?

AMANDA: They call them "Gay Deceivers"!

LAURA: I won't wear them!

AMANDA: You will!

LAURA: Why should I?

AMANDA: Because, to be painfully honest, your chest is flat.

LAURA: You make it seem like we were setting a trap.

AMANDA: All pretty girls are a trap, a pretty trap, and men expect them to be.

[Legend: "A Pretty Trap."]

Now look at yourself, young lady. This is the prettiest you will ever be! I've got to fix myself now! You're going to be surprised by your mother's appearance.

[*She crosses through portieres, humming gaily.*]

[*Laura moves slowly to the long mirror and stares solemnly at herself. A wind blows the white curtains inward in a slow, graceful motion and with a faint, sorrowful sighing.*]

AMANDA [*offstage*]:   It isn't dark enough yet. [*She turns slowly before the mirror with a troubled look.*]

[Legend on Screen: "This Is My Sister: Celebrate Her with Strings!" Music.]

AMANDA [*laughing, off*]:   I'm going to show you something. I'm going to make a spectacular appearance!

LAURA: What is it, Mother?

AMANDA: Possess your soul in patience—you will see! Something I've resurrected from that old trunk! Styles haven't changed so terribly much after all . . . . [*She parts the portieres.*] Now just look at your mother! [*She wears a girlish frock of yellowed voile with a blue silk sash. She carries a bunch of jonquils—the legend of her youth is nearly revived. Feverishly*] This is the dress in which I led the cotillion. Won the cakewalk twice at Sunset Hill, wore one spring to the Governor's ball in Jackson! See how I sashayed around the ballroom, Laura? [*She raises her skirt and does a mincing step around the room.*] I wore it on Sundays for my gentleman callers! I had it on the day I met your father—I had malaria fever all that spring. The change of climate from East Tennessee to the Delta—weakened resistance—I had a little temperature all the time—not enough to be serious—just enough to make me restless and giddy! Invitations poured in parties all over the Delta!—"Stay in bed," said Mother, "you have fever!"—but I just wouldn't.—I took quinine but kept on going, going!—Evenings, dances!—Afternoon, long, long rides! Picnics—lovely!—So lovely, that country in May.—All lacy with dogwood, literally flooded with jonquils.—That was the spring I had the craze for jonquils. Jonquils became an absolute obsession. Mother said, "Honey, there's no more room for jonquils." And still I kept bringing in more jonquils. Whenever, wherever I saw them, I'd say, "Stop! Stop! I see jonquils!" I made the young men help me gather the jonquils! It was a joke, Amanda and her jonquils! Finally there were no more vases to hold them, every available space was filled with jonquils. No vases to hold them? All right, I'll hold them myself! And then I—[*She stops in front of the picture.*] [*Music.*] met your father! Malaria fever and jonquils and then—this—boy . . . . [*She switches on the rose-colored lamp.*] I hope they get here before it starts to rain. [*She crosses upstage and places the jonquils in a bowl on the table.*] I gave your brother a little extra change so he and Mr. O'Connor could take the service car home.

LAURA [*with altered look*]: What did you say his name was?

AMANDA: O'Connor.

LAURA: What is his first name?

AMANDA: I don't remember. Oh, yes, I do. It was—Jim!

[*Laura sways slightly and catches hold of a chair.*]

[Legend on Screen: "Not Jim!"]

LAURA [*faintly*]: Not—Jim!

AMANDA: Yes, that was it, it was Jim! I've never know a Jim that wasn't nice!

[Music: Ominous.]

LAURA: Are you sure his name is Jim O'Connor?

AMANDA: Yes. Why?

LAURA: Is he the one that Tom used to know in high school?

AMANDA: He didn't say so. I think he just got to know him at the warehouse.

LAURA: There was a Jim O'Connor we both knew in high school— [*Then, with effort.*] If that is the one that Tom is bringing to dinner— you'll have to excuse me, I won't come to the table.

AMANDA: What sort of nonsense is this?

LAURA: You asked me once if I'd ever liked a boy. Don't you remember I showed you this boy's picture?

AMANDA: You mean the boy you showed me in the year book?

LAURA: Yes, that boy.

AMANDA: Laura, Laura, were you in love with that boy?

LAURA: I don't know, Mother. All I know is I couldn't sit at the table if it was him!

AMANDA: It won't be him! It isn't the least bit likely. But whether it is or not, you will come to the table. You will not be excused.

LAURA: I'll have to be, Mother.

AMANDA: I don't intend to humor your silliness, Laura. I've had too much from you and your brother, both! So just sit down and compose yourself till they come. Tom has forgotten his key so you'll have to let them in, when they arrive.

LAURA [*panicky*]: Oh, Mother—*you* answer the door!

AMANDA [*lightly*]:   I'll be in the kitchen—busy!

LAURA: Oh, Mother, please answer the door, don't make me do it!

AMANDA [*crossing into kitchenette*]:   I've got to fix the dressing for the salmon. Fuss, fuss—silliness!—over a gentleman caller!

[*Door swings shut. Laura is left alone.*]

[Legend: "Terror!"]

[*She utters a low moan and turns off the lamp—sits stiffly on the edge of the sofa, knotting her fingers together.*]

[Legend on Screen: "The Opening of a Door!"]

[*Tom and Jim appear on the fire-escape steps and climb to the landing. Hearing their approach, Laura rises with a panicky gesture. She retreats to the portieres.*

The doorbell. Laura catches her breath and touches her throat. Low drums.]

AMANDA [*calling*]:   Laura, sweetheart! The door!

[*Laura stares at it without moving.*]

JIM: I think we just beat the rain.

TOM: Uh-huh. [*He rings again, nervously, Jim whistles and fishes for a cigarette.*]

AMANDA [*very, very gaily*]:   Laura, that is your brother and Mr. O'Connor! Will you let them in, darling?

[*Laura crosses toward kitchenette door*].

LAURA [*breathlessly*]:   Mother—you go to the door!

[*Amanda steps out of the kitchenette and stares furiously at Laura. She points imperiously at the door.*]

LAURA: Please, please!

AMANDA [*in a fierce whisper*]:   What is the matter with you, you silly thing?

LAURA [*desperately*]:   Please, you answer it, *please!*

AMANDA: I told you I wasn't going to humor you, Laura. Why have you chosen this time to lose your mind?

LAURA: Please, please, please, you go!

AMANDA: You'll have to go to the door because I can't.

LAURA [*despairingly*]:   I can't either!

AMANDA: Why?

LAURA: I'm *sick?*

AMANDA: I'm sick, too—of your nonsense! Why can't you and your brother be normal people? Fantastic whims and behavior! [*Tom gives a long ring.*] Preposterous goings on! Can you give me one reason—[*Calls out lyrically.*] COMING! JUST ONE SECOND!—why should you be afraid to open a door? Now you answer it, Laura!

LAURA: Oh, oh, oh . . . [*She returns through the portieres. Darts to the victrola and winds it frantically and turns it on.*]

AMANDA: Laura Wingfield, you march right to that door!

LAURA: Yes—yes, Mother.

[*A faraway, scratchy rendition of "Dardanella" softens the air and gives her strength to move through it. She slips to the door and draws it cautiously open. Tom enters with the caller, Jim O'Connor.*]

TOM: Laura, this is Jim. Jim, this is my sister, Laura.

JIM [*stepping inside*]:   I didn't know that Shakespeare had a sister!

LAURA [*retreating stiff and trembling from the door*]:   How—how do you do?

JIM [*heartily extending his hand*]:   Okay!

[*Laura touches it hesitantly with hers.*]

JIM: Your hand's *cold,* Laura!

LAURA: Yes, well—I've been playing the victrola . . . .

JIM: Must have been playing classical music on it! You ought to play a little hot swing music to warm you up!

LAURA: Excuse me—I haven't finished playing the victrola . . . .

[*She turns awkwardly and hurries onto the front room. She pauses a second by the victrola. Then catches her breath and darts through the portieres like a frightened deer.*]

JIM [*grinning*]:   What was the matter?

TOM: Oh—with Laura? Laura is—terribly shy.

JIM: Shy, huh? It's unusual to meet a shy girl nowadays. I don't believe you ever mentioned you had a sister.

TOM: Well, now you know. I have one. Here is the *Post Dispatch.* You want a piece of it?

JIM: Uh-huh.

TOM: What piece? The comics?

JIM: Sports! [*Glances at it.*] Ole Dizzy Dean is on his bad behavior.

TOM [*disinterest*]:   Yeah? [*Lights cigarette and crosses back to fire-escape door.*]

JIM: Where are *you* going?

TOM: I'm going out on the terrace.

JIM [*goes after him*]:   You know, Shakespeare—I'm going to sell you a bill of goods!

TOM: What goods?

JIM: A course I'm taking.

TOM: Huh?

JIM: In public speaking! You and me, we're not the warehouse type.

TOM: Thanks—that's good news. But what has public speaking got to do with it?

JIM: It fits you for—executive positions!

TOM: Awww.

JIM: I tell you it's done a helluva lot for me.

[Image: Executive at Desk.]

TOM: In what respect?

JIM: In every! Ask yourself what is the difference between you an' me in the office down front? Brains?—No!—Ability?—No! Then what? Just one little thing—

TOM: What is that one little thing?

JIM: Primarily it amounts to—social poise! Being able to square up to people and hold your own on any social level!

AMANDA [*off stage*]:   Tom?

TOM: Yes, Mother?

AMANDA: Is that you and Mr. O'Connor?

TOM: Yes, Mother.

AMANDA: Well, you just make yourselves comfortable in there.

TOM: Yes, Mother.

AMANDA: Ask Mr. O'Connor if he would like to wash his hands.

JIM: Aw—no—no—thank you—I took care of that at the warehouse. Tom—

TOM: Yes?

JIM: Mr. Mendoza was speaking to me about you.

TOM: Favorably?

JIM: What do you think?

TOM: Well—

JIM: You're going to be out of a job if you don't wake up.

TOM: I am waking up—

JIM: You show no signs.

TOM: The signs are interior.

[Image on Screen: The Sailing Vessel with Jolly Roger Again.]

TOM: I'm planning to change. [*He leans over the rail speaking with quiet exhilaration. The incandescent marquees and signs of the first-run movie houses light his face from across the alley. He looks like a voyager.*] I'm right at the point of committing myself to a future that doesn't include the warehouse and Mr. Mendoza or even a night-school course in public speaking.

JIM: What are you gassing about?

TOM: I'm tired of the movies.

JIM: Movies!

TOM: Yes, movies! Look at them—[*A wave toward the marvels of Grand Avenue.*] All of those glamorous people—having adventures—hogging it all, gobbling the whole thing up! You know what happens? People go to the *movies* instead of *moving*! Hollywood characters are supposed to have all the adventures for everybody in America, while everybody in America sits in a dark room and watches them have them! Yes, until there's a war. That's when adventure becomes available to the masses! *Everyone's* dish, not only Gable's! Then the people in the dark room come out of the dark room to have some adventures themselves—Goody, goody—It's our turn now, to go to the South Sea Island—to make a safari—to be exotic, far-off—But I'm not patient. I don't want to wait till then. I'm tired of the *movies* and I am *about* to move!

JIM [*incredulously*]: Move?

TOM: Yes.

JIM: When?

TOM: Soon!

JIM: Where? Where?

[*Theme Three: Music Seems to Answer the Question, While Tom Thinks It Over. He Searches Among His Pockets.*]

TOM: I'm starting to boil inside. I know I seem dreamy, but inside—well, I'm boiling! Whenever I pick up a shoe, I shudder a little thinking how short life is and what I am doing!—Whatever that means. I know it doesn't mean shoes—except as something to wear on a traveler's feet! [*Finds paper.*] Look—

JIM: What?

TOM: I'm a member.

JIM [*reading*]:   The Union of Merchant Seamen.

TOM: I paid my dues this month, instead of the light bill.

JIM: You will regret it when they turn the lights off.

TOM: I won't be here.

JIM: How about your mother?

TOM: I'm like my father. The bastard son of a bastard! See how he grins? And he's been absent going on sixteen years!

JIM: You're just talking, you drip. How does you mother feel about it?

TOM: Shhh—Here comes Mother! Mother is not acquainted with my plans.

AMANDA [*enters portiere*]:   Where are you all?

TOM: On the terrace, Mother.

[*They start inside. She advances to them. Tom is distinctly shocked at her appearance. Even Jim blinks a little. He is making his first contact with girlish Southern vivacity and in spite of the night-school course in public speaking is somewhat thrown off the beam by the unexpected outlay of social charm. Certain responses are attempted by Jim but are swept aside by Amanda's gay laughter and chatter. Tom is embarrassed but after the first shock Jim reacts very warmly. Grins and chuckles, is altogether won over.*]

[Image: Amanda as a Girl.]

AMANDA [*coyly smiling, shaking her girlish ringlets*]:   Well, well, well, so this is Mr. O'Connor. Introductions entirely unnecessary. I've heard so much about you from my boy. I finally said to him, Tom—good gracious!—why don't you bring this paragon to supper? I'd like to meet this nice young man at the warehouse!—Instead of just hearing him sing your praises so much! I don't know why my son is so stand-offish—that's not Southern behavior! Let's sit down and—I think we could stand a little more air in here! Tom, leave the door open. I felt a nice fresh breeze a moment ago. Where has it gone? Mmm, so warm already! And not quite summer, even. We're going to burn up when summer really gets started. However, we're having—we're having a very light supper. I think light things are better fo' this time of year. The same as light clothes are. Light clothes an' light food are what warm weather calls fo'. You know our blood gets so thick during th' winter—it takes a while fo' us to *adjust* ou'selves!—when the season changes . . . It's come so quick this year. I wasn't prepared. All of a sudden— heavens! Already summer!—I ran to the trunk an' pulled out this light dress—Terribly old! Historical almost! But feels so good—so good an' co-ol, y'know . . . .

TOM: Mother—

AMANDA: Yes, honey?

TOM: How about—supper?

AMANDA: Honey, you go ask Sister if supper is ready! You know that Sister is in full charge of supper! Tell her you hungry boys are waiting for it. [*To Jim*] Have you met Laura?

JIM: She—

AMANDA: Let you in? Oh, good, you've met already! It's rare for a girl as sweet an' pretty as Laura to be domestic! But Laura is, thank heavens, not only pretty but also very domestic. I'm not at all. I never was a bit. I never could make a thing but angel-food cake. Well, in the South we had so many servants. Gone, gone, gone. All vestiges of gracious living! Gone completely! I wasn't prepared for what the future brought me. All of my gentleman callers were sons of planters and so of course I assumed that I would be married to one and raise my family on a large piece of land with plenty of servants. But man proposes—and woman accepts the proposal!—To vary that old, old saying a little bit—I married no planter! I married a man who worked for the telephone company!—that gallantly smiling gentleman over there! [*Points to the picture.*] A telephone man who—fell in love with long distance!—Now he travels and I don't even know where!—But what am I going on for about my—tribulations! Tell me yours—I hope you don't have any! Tom?

TOM [*returning*]: Yes, Mother?

AMANDA: Is supper nearly ready?

TOM: It looks to me like supper is on the table.

AMANDA: Let me look—[*She rises prettily and looks through portieres.*] Oh, lovely—but where is Sister?

TOM: Laura is not feeling well and she says that she thinks she'd better not come to the table.

TENNESSEE WILLIAMS

AMANDA: What?—Nonsense!—Laura? Oh, Laura!

LAURA [*off stage, faintly*]: Yes, Mother.

AMANDA: You really must come to the table. We won't be seated until you come to the table! Come in, Mr. O'Connor. You sit over there and I'll—Laura? Laura Wingfield! You're keeping us waiting, honey! We can't say grace until you come to the table!

[*The back door is pushed weakly open and Laura comes in. She is obviously quite faint, her lips trembling, her eyes wide and staring. She moves unsteadily toward the table.*]

[Legend: "Terror!"]

[*Outside a summer storm is coming abruptly. The white curtains billow inward at the windows and there is a sorrowful murmur and deep blue dusk. Laura suddenly stumbles—She catches at a chair with a faint moan.*]

TOM: Laura!

AMANDA: Laura! [*There's a clap of thunder*]. [*Legend: "Ah!"*] [*Despairingly*] Why, Laura, you *are* sick, darling! Tom, help your sister into the living room, dear! Sit in the living room, Laura—rest on the sofa. Well! [*To the gentleman caller*] Standing over the hot stove made her ill! I told her that it was just too warm this evening, but—[*Tom comes back in. Laura is on the sofa.*] Is Laura all right now?

TOM: Yes.

AMANDA: What is that? Rain? A nice cool rain has come up? [*She gives the gentleman caller a frightened look.*] I think we may—have grace—now . . . [*Tom looks at her stupidly.*] Tom, honey—you say grace!

TOM: Oh . . . "For these and all thy mercies—" [*They bow their heads. Amanda stealing a nervous glance at Jim. In the living room Laura, stretched on the sofa, clenches her hands to her lips, to hold back a shuddering sob.*] God's Holy Name be praised—

[The Scene Dims Out.]

Scene VII. A souvenir

Half an hour later. Dinner is just being finished in the upstage area which is concealed by the drawn portieres.

As the curtain rises Laura is still huddled upon the sofa, her feet drawn un-
der her, her head resting on a pale blue pillow, her eyes wide and mysteri-
ously watchful. The new floor lamp with its shade of rose-colored silk gives a
soft, becoming light to her face, bringing out the fragile, unearthly prettiness
which usually escapes attention. There is a steady murmur of rain, but it is
slackening and stops soon after the scene begins; the air outside becomes pale
and luminous as the moon breaks out.

A moment after the curtain rises, the lights in both rooms flicker and go
out.

JIM: Hey, there, Mr. Light Bulb!

[*Amanda laughs nervously.*]

[Legend: "Suspension of a Public Service."]

AMANDA: Where was Moses when the lights went out? Ha-ha. Do
you know the answer to that one, Mr. O'Connor?

JIM: No, Ma'am, what's the answer?

AMANDA: In the dark! [*Jim laughs appreciatively.*] Everybody sit still.
I'll light the candles. Isn't it lucky we have them on the table?
Where's a match. Which of you gentlemen can provide a match?

JIM: Here.

AMANDA: Thank you, sir.

JIM: Not at all, Ma'am!

AMANDA: I guess the fuse has burnt out. Mr. O'Connor, can you tell a
burnt-out fuse? I know I can't and Tom is a total loss when it
comes to mechanics. [*Sound: Getting Up: Voices Recede a Little to
Kitchenette.*] Oh, be careful, you don't bump into something. We
don't want our gentleman caller to break his neck. Now wouldn't
that be a fine howdy-do?

JIM: Ha-ha! Where is the fuse-box?

AMANDA: Right there next to the stove. Can you see anything?

JIM: Just a minute.

AMANDA: Isn't electricity a mysterious thing? Wasn't it Benjamin
Franklin who tied a key to a kite? We live in such a mysterious universe, don't we? Some people say that science clears up all the
mysteries for us. In my opinion it only creates more! Have you
found it yet?

JIM: No, Ma'am. All these fuses look okay to me.

AMANDA: Tom!

TOM: Yes, Mother?

AMANDA: That light bill I gave you several days ago. The one I told you we got the notices about?

TOM: Oh.—Yeah.

[Legend: "Ha!"]

AMANDA: You didn't neglect to pay it by any chance.

TOM: Why, I—

AMANDA: Didn't! I might have known it!

JIM: Shakespeare probably wrote a poem on the light bill, Mrs. Wingfield.

AMANDA: I might have known better than to trust him with it! There's such a high price for negligence in this world!

JIM: Maybe the poem will win a ten-dollar prize.

AMANDA: We'll just have to spend the remainder of the evening in the nineteenth century, before Mr. Edison made the Mazda lamp!

JIM: Candlelight is my favorite kind of light.

AMANDA: That shows you're romantic! But that's no excuse for Tom. Well, we got through dinner. Very considerate of them to let us get through dinner before they plunged us into everlasting darkness, wasn't it, Mr. O'Connor?

JIM: Ha-ha!

AMANDA: Tom, as a penalty for your carelessness you can help me with the dishes.

JIM: Let me give you a hand.

AMANDA: Indeed you will not!

JIM: I ought to be good for something.

AMANDA: Good for something? [*Her tone is rhapsodic.*] *You?* Why, Mr. O'Connor, nobody, *nobody's* given me this much entertainment in years—as you have!

JIM: Aw, now, Mrs. Wingfield!

AMANDA: I'm not exaggerating, not one bit! But Sister is all by her lonesome. You go keep her company in the parlor! I'll give you this lovely old candelabrum that used to be on the altar at the church of the Heavenly Rest. It was melted a little out of shape when the church burnt down. Lightning struck it one spring. Gypsy Jones was holding a revival at the time and he estimated that the church was destroyed because the Episcopalians gave card parties.

JIM: Ha-ha.

AMANDA: And how about coaxing Sister to drink a little wine? I think it would be good for her! Can you carry both at once?

JIM: Sure, I'm Superman!

AMANDA: Now, Thomas, get into this apron!

[*The door of the kitchenette swings closed on Amanda's gay laughter; the flickering light approaches the portieres. Laura sits up nervously as he enters. Her speech at first is low and breathless from the almost intolerable strain of being alone with a stranger.*]

[Legend: "I Don't Suppose You Remember Me at All!"]

[*In her first speeches in this scene, before Jim's warmth overcomes her paralyzing shyness, Laura's voice is thin and breathless as though she has run up a steep flight of stairs. Jim's attitude is gently humorous. In playing this scene it should be stressed that while the incident is apparently unimportant, it is to Laura the climax of her secret life.*]

JIM: Hello, there, Laura.

LAURA [*faintly*]:   Hello. [*She clears her throat.*]

JIM: How are you feeling now? Better?

LAURA: Yes. Yes, thank you.

JIM: This is for you. A little dandelion wine. [*He extends it toward her with extravagant gallantry.*]

LAURA: Thank you.

JIM: Drink it—but don't get drunk! [*He laughs heartily. Laura takes the glass uncertainly; laughs shyly.*] Where shall I set the candles?

LAURA: Oh—oh, anywhere . . .

JIM: How about here on the floor? Any objections?

LAURA: No.

JIM: I'll spread a newspaper under to catch the drippings. I like to sit on the floor. Mind if I do?

LAURA: Oh, no.

JIM: Give me a pillow?

LAURA: What?

JIM: A pillow!

LAURA: Oh . . . [*Hands him one quickly.*]

JIM: How about you? Don't you like to sit on the floor?

LAURA: Oh—yes.

JIM: Why don't you, then?

LAURA: I—will.

JIM: Take a pillow! [*Laura does. Sits on the other side of the cande-labrum. Jim crosses his legs and smiles engagingly at her.*] I can't hardly see you sitting way over there.

LAURA: I can—see you.

JIM: I know, but that's not fair, I'm in the limelight. [*Laura moves her pillow closer.*] Good! Now I can see you! Comfortable?

LAURA: Yes.

JIM: So am I. Comfortable as a cow. Will you have some gum?

LAURA: No, thank you.

JIM: I think that I will indulge, with your permission. [*Musingly unwraps it and holds it up.*] Think of the fortune made by the guy that invented the first piece of chewing gum. Amazing, huh? The Wrigley Building is one of the sights of Chicago.—I saw it summer before last when I went up to the Century of Progress. Did you take in the Century of Progress?

LAURA: No, I didn't.

JIM: Well, it was quite a wonderful exposition. What impressed me most was the Hall of Science. Gives you an idea of what the future will be in America, even more wonderful than the present time is! [*Pause. Smiling at her*] Your brother tells me you're shy. Is that right, Laura?

LAURA: I—don't know.

JIM: I judge you to be an old-fashioned type of girl. Well, I think that's a pretty good type to be. Hope you don't think I'm being too personal—do you?

LAURA [*hastily, out of embarrassment*]:   I believe I *will* take a piece of gum, if you—don't mind. [*Clearing her throat*] Mr. O'Connor, have you—kept up with your singing?

JIM: Singing? Me?

LAURA: Yes. I remember what a beautiful voice you had.

JIM: When did you hear me sing?

[Voice Offstage in the Pause.]

VOICE [*offstage*]:   O blow, ye winds, heigh-ho,
A-roving I will go!
I'm off to my love

TENNESSEE WILLIAMS

> With a boxing glove—
>
> Ten thousand miles away!

JIM: You say you've heard me sing?

LAURA: Oh, yes! Yes, very often . . . I—don't suppose you remember me—at all?

JIM [*smiling doubtfully*]: You know I have an idea I've seen you before. I had that idea soon as you opened the door. It seemed almost like I was about to remember your name. But the name that I started to call you—wasn't a name! And so I stopped myself before I said it.

LAURA: Wasn't it—Blue Roses?

JIM [*springs up, grinning*]: Blue Roses! My gosh, yes—Blue Roses! That's what I had on my tongue when you opened the door! Isn't it funny what tricks your memory plays? I didn't connect you with the high school somehow or other. But that's where it was; it was high school. I didn't even know you were Shakespeare's sister! Gosh, I'm sorry.

LAURA: I didn't expect you to. You—barely knew me!

JIM: But we did have a speaking acquaintance, huh?

LAURA: Yes, we—spoke to each other.

JIM: When did you recognize me?

LAURA: Oh, right away!

JIM: Soon as I came in the door?

LAURA: When I heard your name I thought it was probably you. I knew that Tom used to know you a little in high school. So when you came in the door—Well, then I was—sure.

JIM: Why didn't you say something, then?

LAURA [*breathlessly*]: I didn't know what to say, I was—too surprised!

JIM: For goodness' sakes! You know, this sure is funny!

LAURA: Yes! Yes, isn't it, though . . .

JIM: Didn't we have a class in something together?

LAURA: Yes, we did.

JIM: What class was that?

LAURA: It was—singing—Chorus!

JIM: Aw!

LAURA: I sat across the aisle from you in the Aud.

JIM: Aw.

LAURA: Mondays, Wednesdays and Fridays.

JIM: Now I remember—you always came in late.

LAURA: Yes, it was so hard for me, getting upstairs. I had that brace on my leg—it clumped so loud!

TENNESSEE WILLIAMS

JIM: I never heard any clumping.

LAURA [*wincing at the recollection*]:   To me it sounded like—thunder!

JIM: Well, well, well. I never even noticed.

LAURA: And everybody was seated before I came in. I had to walk in front of all those people. My seat was in the back row. I had to go clumping all the way up the aisle with everyone watching!

JIM: You shouldn't have been self-conscious.

LAURA: I know, but I was. It was always such a relief when the singing started.

JIM: Aw, yes. I've placed you now! I used to call you Blue Roses. How was it that I got started calling you that?

LAURA: I was out of school a little while with pleurosis. When I came back you asked me what was the matter. I said I had pleurosis—you thought I said Blue Roses. That's what you always called me after that!

JIM: I hope you didn't mind.

LAURA: Oh, no—I liked it. You see, I wasn't acquainted with many—people . . . .

JIM: As I remember you sort of stuck by yourself.

LAURA: I—I—never had much luck at—making friends.

JIM: I don't see why you wouldn't.

LAURA: Well, I—started out badly.

JIM: You mean being—

LAURA: Yes, it sort of—stood between me—

JIM: You shouldn't have let it!

LAURA: I know but it did, and—

JIM: You were shy with people!

LAURA: I tried not to be but never could—

JIM: Overcome it?

LAURA: No, I—I never could!

JIM: I guess being shy is something you have to work out of kind of gradually.

LAURA [*sorrowfully*]:   Yes—I guess it—

JIM: Takes time!

LAURA: Yes.

JIM: People are not so dreadful when you know them. That's what you have to remember! And everybody has problems, not just you, but practically everybody has got some problems. You think of yourself as having the only problems, as being the only one who is disappointed. But just look around you and you will see lots of people as disappointed as you are. For instance, I hoped when I was going to high school that I would be further along at this time, six years later, than I am now—You remember that wonderful write-up I had in *The Torch?*

LAURA: Yes! [*She rises and crosses to the table.*]

JIM: It said I was bound to succeed in anything I went into! [*Laura returns with the annual.*] Holy Jeez! *The Torch!* [*He accepts it reverently. They smiled across it with mutual wonder. Laura crouches beside him and they begin to turn through it. Laura's shyness is dissolving in his warmth.*]

LAURA: Here you are in *Pirates of Penzance!*

JIM [*wistfully*]:   I sang the baritone lead in that operatta.

LAURA [*rapidly*]:   So—*beautifully!*

JIM [*protesting*]:   Aw—

LAURA: Yes, yes—beautifully—beautifully!

JIM: You heard me?

LAURA: All three times!

JIM: No!

LAURA: Yes!

JIM: All three performances?

LAURA [*looking down*]:   Yes.

JIM: Why?

LAURA: I—wanted to ask you to—autograph my program.

JIM: Why didn't you ask me to?

LAURA: You were always surrounded by your own friends so much that I never had a chance to.

JIM: You should have just—

LAURA: Well, I—thought you might think I was—

JIM: Thought I might think you was—what?

LAURA: Oh—

JIM [*with reflective relish*]:   I was beleaguered by females in those days.

LAURA: You were terribly popular!

JIM: Yeah—

LAURA: You had such a—friendly way—

JIM: I was spoiled in high school.

LAURA: Everybody—liked you!

JIM: Including you?

LAURA: I—yes, I—I did, too—[*She gently closes the book in her lap.*]

JIM: Well, well, well!—Give me that program, Laura. [*She hands it to him. He signs it with a flourish.*] There you are—better late then never!

LAURA: Oh, I—what a—surprise!

JIM: My signature isn't worth very much right now. But some day—maybe—it will increase in value! Being disappointed is one thing and being discouraged is something else. I am disappointed but I'm not discouraged. I'm twenty-three years old. How old are you?

LAURA: I'll be twenty-four in June.

JIM: That's not old age!

LAURA: No, but—

JIM: You finished high school?

LAURA [*with difficulty*]: I didn't go back.

JIM: You mean you dropped out?

LAURA: I made bad grades in my final examinations. [*She rises and replaces the book and the program. Her voice strained.*] How is—Emily Meisenbach getting along?

JIM: Oh, that kraut-head!

LAURA: Why do you call her that?

JIM: That's what she was.

LAURA: You're not still—going with her?

JIM: I never see her.

LAURA: It said in the Personal Section that you were—engaged!

JIM: I know, but I wasn't impressed by that—propaganda!

LAURA: It wasn't—the truth?

JIM: Only in Emily's optimistic opinion!

LAURA: Oh—

[Legend: "What Have You Done Since High School?"]

[*Jim lights a cigarette and leans indolently back on his elbows smiling at Laura with a warmth and charm which light her inwardly with altar candles. She remains by the table and turns in her hands a piece of glass to cover her tumult.*]

JIM [*after several reflective puffs on a cigarette*]: What have you done since high school? [*She seems not to hear him.*] Huh? [*Laura looks up.*] I said what have you done since high school, Laura?

LAURA: Nothing much.

JIM: You must have been doing something these six long years.

LAURA: Yes.

JIM: Well, then, such as what?

LAURA: I took a business course at business college—

JIM: How did that work out?

LAURA: Well, not very—well—I had to drop out, it gave me— indigestion—

[*Jim laughs gently.*]

JIM: What are you doing now?

LAURA: I don't do anything—much. Oh, please don't think I sit around doing nothing! My glass collection takes up a good deal of my time. Glass is something you have to take good care of.

JIM: What did you say—about glass?

LAURA: Collection I said—I have one—[*She clears her throat and turns away again, acutely shy.*]

JIM [*abruptly*]: You know what I judge to be the trouble with you? Inferiority complex! Know what that is? That's what they call it when someone low-rates himself? I understand it because I had it, too. Although my case was not so aggravated as yours seems to be. I had it until I took up public speaking, developed my voice, and learned that I had an aptitude for science. Before that time I never thought of myself as being outstanding in any way whatsoever! Now I've never made a regular study of it, but I have a friend who says I can analyze people better than doctors that make a profession of it. I don't claim that to be necessarily true, but I can sure guess a person's psychology, Laura. [*Takes out his gum.*] Excuse me, Laura. I always take it out when the flavor is gone. I'll use this scrap of paper to wrap it in. I know how it is to get it stuck on a shoe. Yep—that's what I judge to be your principal trouble. A lack of confidence in yourself as a person. You don't have the proper amount of faith in yourself. I'm basing that fact on a number of your remarks and also on certain observations I've made. For instance that clumping you thought was so awful in high school. You say that you even dreaded to walk into class. You see what you did? You dropped out of school, you gave up an education because of a clump, which as far as I know was practically nonexistent! A little physical defect is what you have? Hardly noticeable even! Magnified thousands of times by imagination! You know what my strong advice to you is? Think of yourself as superior in some way!

LAURA: In what way would I think?

JIM: Why, man alive, Laura! Just look about you a little. What do you see? A world full of common people! All of 'em born and all of 'em going to die! Which of them has one-tenth of your good points! Or mine! Or anyone else's, as far as that goes—Gosh! Everybody excels in some one thing. Some in many! [*Unconsciously glances at himself in the mirror.*] All you've got to do is discover in what! Take me, for instance. [*He adjusts his tie at the mirror.*] My interest happens to lie in electrodynamics. I'm taking a course in radio engineering at night school, Laura, on top of a fairly responsible job at the warehouse. I'm taking that course and studying public speaking.

LAURA: Ohhhh.

JIM: Because I believe in the future of television! [*Turning back to her.*] I wish to be ready to go up right along with it. Therefore I'm planning to get in on the ground floor. In fact, I've already made the right connections and all that remains is for the industry itself to get under way! Full steam—[*His eyes are starry.*] Knowledge—Zzzzzp! Money—Zzzzzzp! Power! That's the cycle democracy is built on! [*His attitude is convincingly dynamic. Laura stares at him, even her shyness eclipsed in her absolute wonder. He suddenly grins.*] I guess you think I think a lot of myself!

LAURA: No—o-o-o, I—

JIM: Now how about you? Isn't there something you take more interest in than anything else?

LAURA: Well, I do—as I said—have my—glass collection—

[*A peal of girlish laughter from the kitchen.*]

JIM: I'm not right sure I know what you're talking about. What kind of glass is it?

LAURA: Little articles of it, they're ornaments mostly! Most of them are little animals made out of glass, the tiniest little animals in the world. Mother calls them a glass menagerie! Here's an example of one, if you'd like to see it! This one is one of the oldest. It's nearly thirteen. [*He stretches out his hand.*] [*Music: "The Glass Menagerie."*] Oh, be careful—if you breathe, it breaks!

JIM: I'd better not take it. I'm pretty clumsy with things.

LAURA: Go on. I trust you with him! [*Places it in his palm.*] There now—you're holding him gently! Hold him over the light, he loves the light! You see how the light shines through him?

JIM: It sure does shine!

TENNESSEE WILLIAMS

338

LAURA: I shouldn't be partial, but he is my favorite one.

JIM: What kind of thing is this one supposed to be?

LAURA: Haven't you noticed the single horn on his forehead?

JIM: A unicorn, huh?

LAURA: Mmm-hmmm!

JIM: Unicorns, aren't they extinct in the modern world?

LAURA: I know!

JIM: Poor little fellow, he must feel sort of lonesome.

LAURA [smiling]: Well, if he does he doesn't complain about it. He stays on a shelf with some horses that don't have horns and all of them seem to get along nicely together.

JIM: How do you know?

LAURA [lightly]: I haven't heard any arguments among them!

JIM [grinning]: No arguments, huh? Well, that's a pretty good sign! Where shall I set him?

LAURA: Put him on the table. They all like a change of scenery once in a while!

JIM [stretching]: Well, well, well, well—Look how big my shadow is when I stretch!

LAURA: Oh, oh, yes—it stretches across the ceiling!

JIM [crossing to door]: I think it's stopped raining. [Opens fire-escape door] Where does the music come from?

LAURA: From the Paradise Dance Hall across the alley.

JIM: How about cutting the rug a little, Miss Wingfield?

LAURA: Oh, I—

JIM: Or is your program filled up? Let me have a look at it. [Grasps imaginary card.] Why, every dance is taken! I'll just have to scratch some out. [Waltz Music: "La Golondrina."] Ahhh, a waltz! [He executes some sweeping turns by himself then holds his arms toward Laura.]

LAURA [breathlessly]: I—can't dance!

JIM: There you go, that inferiority stuff!

LAURA: I've never danced in my life!

JIM: Come on, try!

LAURA: Oh, but I'd step on you!

JIM: I'm not made out of glass.

LAURA: How—how—how do we start?

JIM: Just leave it to me. You hold your arms out a little.

LAURA: Like this?

JIM: A little bit higher. Right. Now don't tighten up, that's the main thing about it—relax.

LAURA [*laughing breathlessly*]:   It's hard not to.

JIM: Okay.

LAURA: I'm afraid you can't budge me.

JIM: What do you bet I can't? [*He swings her into motion.*]

LAURA: Goodness, yes, you can!

JIM: Let yourself go, now, Laura, just let yourself go.

LAURA: I'm—

JIM: Come on!

LAURA: Trying!

JIM: Not so stiff—Easy does it!

LAURA: I know but I'm—

JIM: Loosen th' backbone! There now, that's a lot better.

LAURA: Am I?

JIM: Lots, lots better! [*He moves her about the room in a clumsy waltz.*]

LAURA: Oh, my!

JIM: Ha-ha!

LAURA: Goodness, yes you can!

JIM: Ha-ha-ha! [*They suddenly bump into the table, Jim stops.*] What did we hit on?

LAURA: Table.

JIM: Did something fall off it? I think—

LAURA: Yes.

JIM: I hope that it wasn't the little glass horse with the horn!

LAURA: Yes.

JIM: Aw, aw, aw. Is it broken?

LAURA: Now it is just like all the other horses.

JIM: It's lost its—

LAURA: Horn! It doesn't matter. Maybe it's a blessing in disguise.

JIM: You'll never forgive me. I bet that was your favorite piece of glass.

LAURA: I don't have favorites much. It's no tragedy, Freckles. Glass breaks so easily. No matter how careful you are. The traffic jars the shelves and things fall off them.

JIM: Still I'm awfully sorry that I was the cause.

LAURA [*smiling*]:   I'll just imagine he had an operation. The horn was removed to make him feel less—freakish! [*They both laugh.*] Now he will feel more at home with the other horses, the ones that don't have horns . . .

JIM: Ha-ha, that's very funny! [*Suddenly serious.*] I'm glad to see that you have a sense of humor. You know—you're—well—very different! Surprisingly different from anyone else I know! [*His voice becomes soft and hesitant with a genuine feeling.*] Do you mind me telling you that? [*Laura is abashed beyond speech.*] You make me feel sort of—I don't know how to put it! I'm usually pretty good at expressing things, but—This is something that I don't know how to say! [*Laura touches her throat, clears it—turns the broken unicorn in her hands.*] [*Even softer.*] Has anyone ever told you that you were pretty? [*Pause: Music.*] [*Laura looks up slowly, with wonder, and shakes her head.*] Well, you are! In a very different way from anyone else. And all the nicer because of the difference, too. [*His voice becomes low and husky. Laura turns away, nearly faint with the novelty of her emotions.*] I wish that you were my sister. I'd teach you to have some confidence in yourself. The different people are not like other people, but being different is nothing to be ashamed of. Because other people are not such wonderful people. They're one hundred times one thousand. You're one times one! They walk all over the earth. You just stay here. They're common as—weeds, but—you—well, you're—Blue Roses!

[Image on Screen: Blue Roses.]
[Music Changes.]

LAURA: But blue is wrong for—roses . . .

JIM: It's right for you—You're—pretty!

LAURA: In what respect am I pretty?

JIM: In all respects—believe me! Your eyes—your hair—are pretty! Your hands are pretty! [*He catches hold of her hand.*] You think I'm making this up because I'm invited to dinner and have to be nice. Oh, I could do that! I could put on an act for you, Laura, and say lots of things without being very sincere. But this time I am. I'm talking to you sincerely. I happened to notice you had this inferiority complex that keeps you from feeling comfortable with people. Somebody needs to build your confidence up and make you proud instead of shy and turning away and—blushing—Somebody ought to—ought to—*kiss* you, Laura!

[*His hand slips slowly up her arm to her shoulder.*] [*Music Swells Tumultuously.*] [*He suddenly turns her about and kisses her on the* lips. *When he releases her Laura sinks on the sofa with a bright, dazed look. Jim backs away and fishes in his pocket for a cigarette.*] [*Legend on Screen: "Souvenir."*] Stumble- john! [*He lights the cigarette, avoiding her look. There is a peal of girlish laughter from Amanda in the kitchen. Laura slowly raises and opens her hand. It still contains the little broken glass animal. She looks at it with a tender, bewildered expression.*] Stumble-john! I shouldn't have done that—That was way off the beam. You don't smoke, do you? [*She looks up, smiling, not hearing the question. He sits besides her a little gingerly. She looks at him speechlessly—waiting. He coughs decorously and moves a little farther aside as he considers the situation and senses her feelings, dimly, with perturbation. Gently.*] Would you—care for a—mint? [*She doesn't seem to hear him but her look grows brighter even.*] Peppermint—Life Saver? My pocket's a regular drug store—wherever I go . . . [*He pops a mint in his mouth. Then gulps and decides to make a clean breast of it. He speaks slowly and gingerly.*] Laura, you know, if I had a sister like you, I'd do the same thing as Tom. I'd bring out fellows—introduce her to them. The right type of boys of a type to—appreciate her. Only—well—he made a mistake about me. Maybe I've got no call to be saying this. This may not have been the idea in having me over. But what if it was? There's nothing wrong about that. The only trouble is that in my case—I'm not in a situation to—do the right thing. I can't take down your number and say I'll phone. I can't call up next week and—ask for a date. I thought I had better explain the situation in case you misunderstood it and—hurt your feelings . . . . [*Pause. Slowly, very slowly, Laura's look changes, her eyes returning slowly from his to the ornament in her palm.*]

[*Amanda utters another gay laugh in the kitchen.*]

LAURA [*faintly*]: You—won't—call again?

JIM: No, Laura. I can't. [*He rises from the sofa.*] As I was just explaining, I've—got strings on me, Laura, I've—been going steady! I go out all the time with a girl named Betty. She's a home-girl like you, and Catholic, and Irish, and in a great many ways we—get along fine. I met her last summer on a moonlight boat trip up the river to Alton, on the Majestic. Well—right away from the start it was—

love! [Legend: "Love!"] [Laura sways slightly forward and grips the arm of the sofa. He fails to notice, now enrapt in his own comfortable being.] Being in love has made a new man of me! [Leaning stiffly forward, clutching the arm of the sofa, Laura struggles visibly with her storm. But Jim is oblivious, she is a long way off.] The power of love is really pretty tremendous! Love is something that—changes the whole world, Laura! [The storm abates a little and Laura leans back. He notices her again.] It happened that Betty's aunt took sick, she got a wire and had to go to Centralia. So Tom—when he asked me to dinner—I naturally just accepted the invitation, not knowing that you—that he—that I—[He stops awkwardly.] Huh—I'm a stumble-john! [He flops back on the sofa. The holy candles in the altar of Laura's face have been snuffed out! There is a look of almost infinite desolation. Jim glances at her uneasily.] I wish that you would—say something. [She bites her lip which was trembling and then bravely smiles. She opens her hand again on the broken glass ornament. Then she gently takes his hand and raises it level to her own. She carefully places the unicorn in the palm of his hand, then pushes his fingers closed upon it.] What are you—doing that for? You want me to have him?—Laura? [She nods.] What for?

LAURA: A—souvenir . . .

[She rises unsteadily and crouches beside the victrola to wind it up.]

[Legend on Screen: "Things Have a Way of Turning Out So Badly."]
    [Or Image: "Gentleman Caller Waving Good-Bye—Gaily."]

[At this moment Amanda rushes brightly back in the front room. She bears a pitcher of fruit punch in an old-fashioned cut-glass pitcher and a plate of macaroons. The plate has a gold border and poppies painted on it.]

AMANDA: Well, well, well! Isn't the air delightful after the shower? I've made you children a little liquid refreshment. [Turns gaily to the gentleman caller.] Jim, do you know that song about lemonade?
"Lemonade, lemonade
Made in the shade and stirred with a spade—
Good enough for any old maid!"
JIM [uneasily]:   Ha-ha! No—I never heard it.
AMANDA: Why, Laura! You look so serious!
JIM: We were having a serious conversation.

AMANDA: Good! Now you're better acquainted!

JIM [*uncertainly*]:   Ha-ha! Yes.

AMANDA: You modern young people are much more serious-minded than my generation. I was so gay as a girl!

JIM: You haven't changed, Mrs. Wingfield.

AMANDA: Tonight I'm rejuvenated! The gaiety of the occasion, Mr. O'Connor! [*She tosses her head with a peal of laughter. Spills lemonade.*] Oooo! I'm baptizing myself!

JIM: Here—let me—

AMANDA [*setting the pitcher down.*]:   There now. I discovered we had some maraschino cherries. I dumped them in, juice and all!

JIM: You shouldn't have gone to that trouble, Mrs. Wingfield.

AMANDA: Trouble, trouble? Why it was loads of fun! Didn't you hear me cutting up in the kitchen? I bet your ears were burning! I told Tom how outdone with him I was for keeping you to himself so long a time! He should have brought you over much, much sooner! Well, now that you've found your way, I want you to be a very frequent caller! Not just occasional but all the time. Oh, we're going to have a lot of gay times together! I see them coming! Mmm, just breathe that air! So fresh, and the moon's so pretty! I'll skip back out—I know where my place is when young folks are having a—serious conversation!

JIM: Oh, don't go out, Mrs. Wingfield. The fact of the matter is I've got to be going.

AMANDA: Going, now? You're joking! Why, it's only the shank of the evening, Mr. O'Connor.

JIM: Well, you now how it is.

AMANDA: You mean you're a young workingman and have to keep workingmen's hours. We'll let you off early tonight. But only on the condition that next time you stay later. What's the best night for you? Isn't Saturday night the best night for you workingmen?

JIM: I have a couple of time-clocks to punch, Mrs. Wingfield. One at morning, another one at night.

AMANDA: My, but you are ambitious! You work at night, too?

JIM: No, Ma'am, not work but—Betty! [*He crosses deliberately to pick up his hat. The band at the Paradise Dance Hall goes into a tender waltz.*]

AMANDA: Betty? Betty? Who's—Betty! [*There is an ominous cracking sound in the sky.*]

JIM: Oh, just a girl. The girl I go steady with! [*He smiles charmingly. The sky falls.*]

[Legend: "The Sky Falls"]

AMANDA [*a long-drawn exhalation*]:   Ohhhh . . . Is it a serious romance, Mr. O'Connor?

JIM: We're going to be married the second Sunday in June.

AMANDA: Ohhhh—how nice! Tom didn't mention that you were engaged to be married.

JIM: The cat's not out of the bag at the warehouse yet. You know how they are. They call you Romeo and stuff like that. [*He stops at the oval mirror to put on his hat. He carefully shapes the brim and the crown to give a discreetly dashing effect.*] It's been a wonderful evening, Mrs. Wingfield. I guess this is what they mean by Southern hospitality.

AMANDA: It really wasn't anything at all.

JIM: I hope it don't seem like I'm rushing off. But I promised Betty I'd pick her up at the Wabash depot, an' by the time I get my jalopy down there her train'll be in. Some women are pretty upset if you keep 'em waiting.

AMANDA: Yes, I know—The tyranny of women! [*Extends her hand.*] Goodbye, Mr. O'Connor. I wish you luck—and happiness—and success! All three of them, and so does Laura!—Don't you, Laura?

LAURA: Yes!

JIM [*taking her hand*]:   Goodbye, Laura. I'm certainly going to treasure that souvenir. And don't you forget the good advice I gave you. [*Raises his voice to a cheery shout.*] So long, Shakespeare! Thanks again, ladies—Good night!

[*He grins and ducks jauntily out. Still bravely grimacing, Amanda closes the door on the gentleman caller. Then she turns back to the room with a puzzled expression. She and Laura don't dare to face each other. Laura crouches beside the victrola to wind it.*]

AMANDA [*faintly*]:   Things have a way of turning out so badly. I don't believe that I would play the victrola. Well, well—well—Our gentleman caller was engaged to be married! Tom!

TOM [*from back*]:   Yes, Mother?

AMANDA: Come in here a minute. I want to tell you something awfully funny.

TOM [*enters with macaroon and a glass of the lemonade*]:   Has the gentleman caller gotten away already?

AMANDA: The gentleman caller has made an early departure. What a
wonderful joke you played on us!

TOM: How do you mean?

AMANDA: You didn't mention that he was engaged to be married.

TOM: Jim? Engaged?

AMANDA: That's what he just informed us.

TOM: I'll be jiggered! I didn't know about that.

AMANDA: That seems very peculiar.

TOM: What's peculiar about it?

AMANDA: Didn't you call him your best friend down at the warehouse?

TOM: He is, but how did I know?

AMANDA: It seems extremely peculiar that you wouldn't know your
best friend was going to be married!

TOM: The warehouse is where I work, not where I know things about
people!

AMANDA: You don't know things anywhere! You live in a dream; you
manufacture illusions! [*He crosses to door.*] Where are you going?

TOM: I'm going to the movies.

AMANDA: That's right, now that you've had us make such fools of
ourselves. The effort, the preparations, all the expense! The new
floor lamp, the rug, the clothes for Laura! All for what? To entertain
some other girl's fiancé! Go to the movies, go! Don't think about
us, a mother deserted, an unmarried sister who's crippled and has
no job! Don't let anything interfere with your selfish pleasure! Just
go, go, go—to the movies!

TOM: All right, I will! The more you shout about my selfishness to me
the quicker I'll go, and I won't go to the movies!

AMANDA: Go, then! Then go to the moon—you selfish dreamer!

*Tom smashes his glass on the floor. He plunges out on the fire-
escape, slamming the door. Laura screams—cut by door.*

*Dance-hall music up. Tom goes to the rail and grips it desper-
ately, lifting his face in the chill white moonlight penetrating the
narrow abyss of the alley.*

[Legend on Screen: "And So Good-Bye . . ."]

[*Tom's closing speech is timed with the interior pantomime. The interior scene is played as though viewed through sound-proof glass. Amanda appears to be making a comforting speech to Laura who is huddled upon the sofa. Now that we cannot hear the mother's speech, her silliness is gone and she has dignity and tragic beauty. Laura's dark hair hides her face until at the end of the speech she lifts it to smile at her mother. Amanda's gestures are slow and graceful, almost dancelike, as she comforts her daughter. At the end of her speech she glances a moment at the father's picture—then withdraws through the portieres. At close of Tom's speech, Laura blows out the candles, ending the play.*]

TOM: I didn't go to the moon, I went much further—for time is the longest distance between two places—Not long after that I was fired for writing a poem on the lid of a shoe-box. I left Saint Louis. I descended the steps of this fire-escape for a last time and followed, from then on, in my father's footsteps, attempting to find in motion what was lost in space—I traveled around a great deal. The cities swept about me like dead leaves, leaves that were brightly colored but torn away from the branches. I would have stopped, but I was pursued by something. It always came upon me unawares, taking me altogether by surprise. Perhaps it was a familiar bit of music. Perhaps it was only a piece of transparent glass— Perhaps I am walking along a street at night, in some strange city, before I have found companions. I pass the lighted window of a shop where perfume is sold. The window is filled with pieces of colored glass, tiny transparent bottles in delicate colors, like bits of a shattered rainbow. Then all at once my sister touches my shoulder. I turn around and look into her eyes . . . Oh, Laura, Laura, I tried to leave you behind me, but I am more faithful than I intended to be! I reach for a cigarette, I cross the street, I run into the movies or a bar, I buy a drink, I speak to the nearest stranger— anything that can blow your candles out! [*Laura bends over the candles.*]—for nowadays the world is lit by lightning! Blow out your candles, Laura—and so goodbye . . .

[*She blows the candles out.*]

[The Scene Dissolves.]

—1944

Arthur Miller gained a reputation as a major American dramatist with his second play and continued to be productive in his mid-80s. Miller was born in Harlem, the son of prosperous Jewish immigrants who suffered badly during the depression. He studied drama at the University of Michigan and was for a time employed by the Federal Theatre Project, a Roosevelt-era government program dedicated to bringing drama with social themes to audiences in areas outside New York. His first success was All My Sons *(1947), an Ibsen-esque problem play about a manufacturer who profits during World War II by knowingly supplying defective parts that caused airplanes to crash.* All My Sons, *following closely on the heels of investigations of wartime profiteering, easily found appreciative audiences.* Death of a Salesman *(1949) won Miller a Pulitzer Prize. Originally a short story based to some degree on one of Miller's uncles,* Death of a Salesman *evolved into its final form over many years. When Miller finally sat down at the typewriter to write the play, he said, "All I had was the first two lines and a death." During the height of the play's success, Miller wrote a famous essay titled "Tragedy and the Common Man," in which he dismisses the ancient "rule" that true tragedy can concern only the lives and fates of the famous. "I believe," he said, "that the common man is as apt a subject for tragedy in its highest sense as kings were. . . . If the exaltation of tragic action were truly a property of the high-bred character alone, it is inconceivable that the mass of mankind should cherish tragedy above all other forms, let alone be capable of understanding it." Miller's fame was further increased by* The Crucible *(1953), a play about the Salem witch trials that had obvious contemporary political overtones, drawing on Miller's own McCarthy-era investigations by the House Un-Amerian Activities Committee into his past political affiliations. Miller risked a jail term for his refusal to cooperate with the committee. His marriage to Marilyn Monroe, which is in part the subject of* After the Fall *(1964), ended unhappily shortly after Miller completed work on the screenplay of* The Misfits, *which proved to be Monroe's final film. Other important plays include* A View from the Bridge *(1955), which has been revived several times on Broadway and also exists in an operatic version;* Incident at Vichy *(1964), a play about the Holocaust;* The Price *(1968);* Broken Glass, *another play about anti-Semiticism; and* Ride Down Mount Morgan *(1998), which starred Patrick Stewart in its Broadway production. Miller's autobiography,* Timebends, *was published in 1987. In it he proudly recounts his experiences in 1983 directing a Chinese production of* Death of a Salesman *in Beijing, the first contemporary American play produced in China. Like Tennessee Williams's plays, Miller's are frequently revived; the final performance of the 1999 award-winning production of* Death of a Salesman *was televised on Showtime. Miller's last play,* Finishing the Picture, *enjoyed a successful run in Chicago in the fall of 2004, only months before the playwright's death at 89 in February 2005.*

Death of a Salesman

Characters

Willy Loman
Linda
Biff
Happy
Bernard
The Woman
Charley
Uncle Ben
Howard Wagner
Jenny
Stanley
Miss Forsythe
Letta

Scene: *The action takes place in Willy Loman's house and yard and in various places he visits in the New York and Boston of today.*

Act I

A melody is heard, played upon a flute. It is small and fine, telling of grass and trees and the horizon. The curtain rises.

Before us is the Salesman's house. We are aware of towering, angular shapes behind it, surrounding it on all sides. Only the blue light of the sky falls upon the house and forestage; the surrounding area shows an angry glow of orange. As more light appears, we see a solid vault of apartment houses around the small, fragile-seeming home. An air of the dream clings to the place, a dream rising out of reality. The kitchen at center seems actual enough, for there is a kitchen table with three chairs, and a refrigerator. But no other fixtures are seen. At the back of the kitchen there is a draped entrance, which leads to the living room. *To the right of the kitchen, on a level raised two feet, is a bedroom furnished only with a brass bedstead and a straight chair. On a shelf over the bed a silver athletic trophy stands. A window opens onto the apartment house at the side.*

Behind the kitchen, on a level raised six and a half feet, is the boys' bedroom, at present barely visible. Two beds are dimly seen, and at the back of the room a dormer window. (This bedroom is above the unseen living room.) At the left a stairway curves up to it from the kitchen.

The entire setting is wholly or, in some places, partially transparent. The roof-line of the house is one-dimensional; under and over it we see the apartment buildings. Before the house lies an apron, curving beyond the forestage into the orchestra. This forward area serves as the back yard as well as the locale of all Willy's imaginings and of his city scenes. Whenever the action is in the present the actors observe the imaginary wall-lines, entering the house only through its door at the left. But in the scenes of the past these boundaries are broken, and characters enter or leave a room by stepping "through" a wall onto the forestage.

From the right, Willy Loman, the Salesman, enters, carrying two large sample cases. The flute plays on. He hears but is not aware of it. He is past sixty years of age, dressed quietly. Even as he crosses the stage to the doorway of the house, his exhaustion is apparent. He unlocks the door, comes into the kitchen, and thankfully lets his burden down, feeling the soreness of his palms. A word-sigh escapes his lips—it might be "Oh, boy, oh, boy." He closes the door, then carries his cases out into the living room, through the draped kitchen doorway.

Linda, his wife, has stirred in her bed at the right. She gets out and puts on a robe, listening. Most often jovial, she has developed an iron repression of her exceptions to Willy's behavior—she more than loves him, she admires him, as though his mercurial nature, his temper, his massive dreams and little cruelties, served her only as sharp reminders of the turbulent longings within him, longings which she shares but lacks the temperament to utter and follow to their end.

LINDA [*hearing Willy outside the bedroom, calls with some trepidation*]: Willy!

WILLY: It's all right. I came back.

LINDA: Why? What happened? [*Slight pause.*] Did something happen, Willy?

WILLY: No, nothing happened.

LINDA: You didn't smash the car, did you?

WILLY [with casual irritation]: I said nothing happened. Didn't you hear me?

LINDA: Don't you feel well?

WILLY: I'm tired to the death. [The flute has faded away. He sits on the bed beside her, a little numb.] I couldn't make it. I just couldn't make it, Linda.

LINDA [very carefully, delicately]: Where were you all day? You look terrible.

WILLY: I got as far as a little above Yonkers. I stopped for a cup of coffee. Maybe it was the coffee.

LINDA: What?

WILLY [after a pause]: I suddenly couldn't drive any more. The car kept going off onto the shoulder, y'know?

LINDA [helpfully]: Oh. Maybe it was the steering again. I don't think Angelo knows the Studebaker.

WILLY: No, it's me, it's me. Suddenly I realize I'm goin' sixty miles an hour and I don't remember the last five minutes. I'm—I can't seem to—keep my mind to it.

LINDA: Maybe it's your glasses. You never went for your new glasses.

WILLY: No, I see everything. I came back ten miles an hour. It took me nearly four hours from Yonkers.

LINDA [resigned]: Well, you'll just have to take a rest, Willy, you can't continue this way.

WILLY: I just got back from Florida.

LINDA: But you didn't rest your mind. Your mind is overactive, and the mind is what counts, dear.

WILLY: I'll start out in the morning. Maybe I'll feel better in the morning. [She is taking off his shoes.] These goddam arch supports are killing me.

LINDA: Take an aspirin. Should I get you an aspirin? It'll soothe you.

WILLY [with wonder]: I was driving along, you understand? And I was fine. I was even observing the scenery. You can imagine, me looking at scenery, on the road every week of my life. But it's so beautiful up there, Linda, the trees are so thick, and the sun is warm. I opened the windshield and just let the warm air bathe over me. And then all of a sudden I'm goin' off the road! I'm tellin' ya, I absolutely forgot I was driving. If I'd've gone the other way over the white line I might've killed somebody. So I went on again—and five minutes later I'm dreamin' again, and I nearly . . . [*He presses two fingers against his eyes.*] I have such thoughts, I have such strange thoughts.

LINDA: Willy, dear. Talk to them again. There's no reason why you can't work in New York.

WILLY: They don't need me in New York. I'm the New England man. I'm vital in New England.

LINDA: But you're sixty years old. They can't expect you to keep traveling every week.

WILLY: I'll have to send a wire to Portland. I'm supposed to see Brown and Morrison tomorrow morning at ten o'clock to show the line. Goddammit, I could sell them! [*He starts putting on his jacket.*]

LINDA [*taking the jacket from him*]: Why don't you go down to the place tomorrow and tell Howard you've simply got to work in New York? You're too accommodating, dear.

WILLY: If old man Wagner was alive I'd a been in charge of New York now! That man was a prince, he was a masterful man. But that boy of his, that Howard, he don't appreciate. When I went north the first time, the Wagner Company didn't know where New England was!

LINDA: Why don't you tell those things to Howard, dear?

WILLY [*encouraged*]: I will, I definitely will. Is there any cheese?

LINDA: I'll make you a sandwich.

WILLY: No, go to sleep. I'll take some milk. I'll be up right away. The boys in?

LINDA: They're sleeping. Happy took Biff on a date tonight.

WILLY [*interested*]: That so?

LINDA: It was so nice to see them shaving together, one behind the other, in the bathroom. And going out together. You notice? The whole house smells of shaving lotion.

WILLY: Figure it out. Work a lifetime to pay off a house. You finally own it, and there's nobody to live in it.

LINDA: Well, dear, life is a casting off. It's always that way.

WILLY: No, no, some people—some people accomplish something. Did Biff say anything after I went this morning?

LINDA: You shouldn't have criticized him, Willy, especially after he just got off the train. You mustn't lose your temper with him.

WILLY: When the hell did I lose my temper? I simply asked him if he was making any money. Is that a criticism?

LINDA: But, dear, how could he make any money?

WILLY [*worried and angered*]: There's such an undercurrent in him. He became a moody man. Did he apologize when I left this morning?

LINDA: He was crestfallen, Willy. You know how he admires you. I think if he finds himself, then you'll both be happier and not fight any more.

WILLY: How can he find himself on a farm? Is that a life? A farm hand? In the beginning, when he was young, I thought, well, a young man, it's good for him to tramp around, take a lot of different jobs. But it's more than ten years now and he has yet to make thirty-five dollars a week!

LINDA: He's finding himself, Willy.

WILLY: Not finding yourself at the age of thirty-four is a disgrace!

LINDA: Shh!

WILLY: The trouble is he's lazy, goddammit!

LINDA: Willy, please!

WILLY: Biff is a lazy bum!

LINDA: They're sleeping. Get something to eat. Go on down.

WILLY: Why did he come home? I would like to know what brought him home.

LINDA: I don't know. I think he's still lost, Willy. I think he's very lost.

WILLY: Biff Loman is lost. In the greatest country in the world a young man with such—personal attractiveness, gets lost. And such a hard worker. There's one thing about Biff—he's not lazy.

LINDA: Never.

WILLY [*with pity and resolve*]: I'll see him in the morning; I'll have a nice talk with him. I'll get him a job selling. He could be big in no time. My God! Remember how they used to follow him around in high school? When he smiled at one of them their faces lit up. When he walked down the street . . . [*He loses himself in reminiscences.*]

LINDA [*trying to bring him out of it*]: Willy, dear, I got a new kind of American-type cheese today. It's whipped.

WILLY: Why do you get American when I like Swiss?

LINDA: I just thought you'd like a change . . .

WILLY: I don't want a change! I want Swiss cheese. Why am I always being contradicted?

LINDA [*with a covering laugh*]: I thought it would be a surprise.

WILLY: Why don't you open a window in here, for God's sake?

LINDA [*with infinite patience*]: They're all open, dear.

WILLY: The way they boxed us in here. Bricks and windows, windows and bricks.

LINDA: We should've bought the land next door.

WILLY: The street is lined with cars. There's not a breath of fresh air in the neighborhood. The grass don't grow any more, you can't raise a carrot in the back yard. They should've had a law against apartment houses. Remember those two beautiful elm trees out there? When I and Biff hung the swing between them?

LINDA: Yeah, like being a million miles from the city.

WILLY: They should've arrested the builder for cutting those down. They massacred the neighborhood. [*Lost.*] More and more I think of those days, Linda. This time of year it was lilac and wisteria. And then the peonies would come out, and the daffodils. What fragrance in this room!

LINDA: Well, after all, people had to move somewhere.

WILLY: No, there's more people now.

LINDA: I don't think there's more people. I think . . .

WILLY: There's more people! That's what's ruining this country! Population is getting out of control. The competition is maddening! Smell the stink from that apartment house! And another one on the other side . . . How can they whip cheese?

On Willy's last line, Biff and Happy raise themselves up in their beds, listening.

LINDA: Go down, try it. And be quiet.

WILLY [*turning to Linda, guiltily*]: You're not worried about me, are you, sweetheart?

BIFF: What's the matter?

HAPPY: Listen!

LINDA: You've got too much on the ball to worry about.

WILLY: You're my foundation and my support, Linda.

LINDA: Just try to relax, dear. You make mountains out of molehills.

WILLY: I won't fight with him any more. If he wants to go back to Texas, let him go.

LINDA: He'll find his way.

WILLY: Sure. Certain men just don't get started till later in life. Like Thomas Edison, I think. Or B. F. Goodrich. One of them was deaf. [*He starts for the bedroom doorway.*] I'll put my money on Biff.

LINDA: And Willy—if it's warm Sunday we'll drive in the country. And we'll open the windshield, and take lunch.

WILLY: No, the windshields don't open on the new cars.

LINDA: But you opened it today.

WILLY: Me? I didn't. [*He stops.*] Now isn't that peculiar! Isn't that a remarkable . . . [*He breaks off in amazement and fright as the flute is heard distantly.*]

LINDA: What, darling?

WILLY: That is the most remarkable thing.

LINDA: What, dear?

WILLY: I was thinking of the Chevvy. [*Slight pause.*] Nineteen twenty-eight . . . when I had that red Chevvy . . . [*Breaks off:*] That funny? I coulda sworn I was driving that Chevvy today.

LINDA: Well, that's nothing. Something must've reminded you.

WILLY: Remarkable. Ts. Remember those days? The way Biff used to simonize that car? The dealer refused to believe there was eighty thousand miles on it. [*He shakes his head.*] Heh! [*To Linda.*] Close your eyes, I'll be right up. [*He walks out of the bedroom.*]

HAPPY [*to Biff*]: Jesus, maybe he smashed up the car again!

LINDA [*calling after Willy*]: Be careful on the stairs, dear! The cheese is on the middle shelf. [*She turns, goes over to the bed, takes his jacket, and goes out of the bedroom.*]

Light has risen on the boys' room. Unseen, Willy is heard talking to himself; "Eighty thousand miles," and a little laugh. Biff gets out of bed, comes downstage a bit, and stands attentively. Biff is two years older than his brother Happy, well built, but in these days bears a worn air and seems less self-assured. He has succeeded less, and his dreams are stronger and less acceptable than Happy's. Happy is tall, powerfully made. Sexuality is like a visible color on him, or a scent that many women have discovered. He, like his brother, is lost, but in a different way, for he has never allowed himself to turn his face toward defeat and is thus more confused and hard-skinned, although seemingly more content.

HAPPY [*getting out of bed*]: He's going to get his license taken away if he keeps that up. I'm getting nervous about him, y'know, Biff?

BIFF: His eyes are going.

HAPPY: No, I've driven with him. He sees all right. He just doesn't keep his mind on it. I drove into the city with him last week.

He stops at a green light and then it turns red and he goes. [*He laughs.*]

BIFF: Maybe he's color-blind.

HAPPY: Pop? Why he's got the finest eye for color in the business. You know that.

BIFF [*sitting down on his bed*]: I'm going to sleep.

HAPPY: You're not still sour on Dad, are you, Biff?

BIFF: He's all right, I guess.

WILLY [*underneath them, in the living room*]: Yes, sir, eighty thousand miles—eighty-two thousand!

BIFF: You smoking?

HAPPY [*holding out a pack of cigarettes*]: Want one?

BIFF [*taking a cigarette*]: I can never sleep when I smell it.

WILLY: What a simonizing job, heh!

HAPPY [*with deep sentiment*]: Funny, Biff, y'know? Us sleeping in here again? The old beds. [*He pats his bed affectionately.*] All the talk that went across those beds, huh? Our whole lives.

BIFF: Yeah. Lotta dreams and plans.

HAPPY [*with a deep and masculine laugh*]: About five hundred women would like to know what was said in this room. [*They share a soft laugh.*]

BIFF: Remember that big Betsy something—what the hell was her name—over on Bushwick Avenue?

HAPPY [*combing his hair*]: With the collie dog!

BIFF: That's the one. I got you in there, remember?

HAPPY: Yeah, that was my first time—I think. Boy, there was a pig. [*They laugh, almost crudely.*] You taught me everything I know about women. Don't forget that.

BIFF: I bet you forgot how bashful you used to be. Especially with girls.

HAPPY: Oh, I still am, Biff.

BIFF: Oh, go on.

HAPPY: I just control it, that's all. I think I got less bashful and you got more so. What happened, Biff? Where's the old humor, the old confidence? [*He shakes Biff's knee. Biff gets up and moves restlessly about the room.*] What's the matter?

BIFF: Why does Dad mock me all the time?

HAPPY: He's not mocking you, he . . .

BIFF: Everything I say there's a twist of mockery on his face. I can't get near him.

HAPPY: He just wants you to make good, that's all. I wanted to talk to you about Dad for a long time, Biff. Something's—happening to him. He—talks to himself.

BIFF: I noticed that this morning. But he always mumbled.

HAPPY: But not so noticeable. It got so embarrassing I sent him to Florida. And you know something? Most of the time he's talking to you.

BIFF: What's he say about me?

HAPPY: I can't make it out.

BIFF: What's he say about me?

HAPPY: I think the fact that you're not settled, that you're still kind of up in the air . . .

BIFF: There's one or two other things depressing him, Happy.

HAPPY: What do you mean?

BIFF: Never mind. Just don't lay it all to me.

HAPPY: But I think if you just got started—I mean—is there any future for you out there?

BIFF: I tell ya, Hap, I don't know what the future is. I don't know— what I'm supposed to want.

HAPPY: What do you mean?

BIFF: Well, I spent six or seven years after high school trying to work myself up. Shipping clerk, salesman, business of one kind or another. And it's a measly manner of existence. To get on that subway on the hot mornings in summer. To devote your whole life to keeping stock, or making phone calls, or selling or buying. To suffer fifty weeks of the year for the sake of a two-week vacation, when all you really desire is to be outdoors, with your shirt off. And always to have to get ahead of the next fella. And still—that's how you build a future.

HAPPY: Well, you really enjoy it on a farm? Are you content out there?

BIFF [*with rising agitation*]: Hap, I've had twenty or thirty different kinds of jobs since I left home before the war, and it always turns out the same. I just realized it lately. In Nebraska when I herded cattle, and the Dakotas, and Arizona, and now in Texas. It's why I came home now, I guess, because I realized it. This farm I work on, it's spring there now, see? And they've got about fifteen new colts. There's nothing more inspiring or—beautiful than the sight of a mare and a new colt. And it's cool there now, see? Texas is cool now, and it's spring. And whenever spring comes to where I am, I suddenly get the feeling, my God, I'm not gettin' anywhere! What the hell am I doing, playing around with horses, twenty-eight dollars a week! I'm thirty-four years old, I oughta be makin' my future. That's when I come running home. And now, I get here, and I don't know what to do with myself. [*After a pause.*] I've always made a point of not wasting my life, and everytime I come back here I know that all I've done is to waste my life.

HAPPY: You're a poet, you know that, Biff? You're a—you're an idealist!

BIFF: No, I'm mixed up very bad. Maybe I oughta get married. Maybe I oughta get stuck into something. Maybe that's my trouble. I'm like a boy. I'm not married, I'm not in business, I just—I'm like a boy. Are you content, Hap? You're a success, aren't you? Are you content?

HAPPY: Hell, no!

BIFF: Why? You're making money, aren't you?

HAPPY [*moving about with energy, expressiveness*]: All I can do now is wait for the merchandise manager to die. And suppose I get to be merchandise manager? He's a good friend of mine, and he just built a terrific estate on Long Island. And he lived there about two months and sold it, and now he's building another one. He can't enjoy it once it's finished. And I know that's just what I would do. I don't know what the hell I'm workin' for. Sometimes I sit in my apartment—all alone. And I think of the rent I'm paying. And it's crazy. But then, it's what I always wanted. My own apartment, a car, and plenty of women. And still, goddammit, I'm lonely.

BIFF [*with enthusiasm*]: Listen, why don't you come out West with me?

HAPPY: You and I, heh?

BIFF: Sure, maybe we could buy a ranch. Raise cattle, use our muscles. Men built like we are should be working out in the open.

HAPPY [*avidly*]: The Loman Brothers, heh?

BIFF [*with vast affection*]: Sure, we'd be known all over the counties!

HAPPY [*enthralled*]: That's what I dream about, Biff. Sometimes I want to just rip my clothes off in the middle of the store and outbox that goddam merchandise manager. I mean I can outbox, outrun, and outlift anybody in that store, and I have to take orders from those common, petty sons-of-bitches till I can't stand it any more.

BIFF: I'm tellin' you, kid, if you were with me I'd be happy out there.

HAPPY [*enthused*]: See, Biff, everybody around me is so false that I'm constantly lowering my ideals . . .

BIFF: Baby, together we'd stand up for one another, we'd have someone to trust.

HAPPY: If I were around you . . .

BIFF: Hap, the trouble is we weren't brought up to grub for money. I don't know how to do it.

HAPPY: Neither can I!

BIFF: Then let's go!

HAPPY: The only thing is—what can you make out there?

BIFF: But look at your friend. Builds an estate and then hasn't the peace of mind to live in it.

HAPPY: Yeah, but when he walks into the store the waves part in front of him. That's fifty-two thousand dollars a year coming through the revolving door, and I got more in my pinky finger than he's got in his head.

BIFF: Yeah, but you just said . . .

HAPPY: I gotta show some of those pompous, self-important executives over there that Hap Loman can make the grade. I want to walk into the store the way he walks in. Then I'll go with you, Biff. We'll be together yet, I swear. But take those two we had tonight. Now weren't they gorgeous creatures?

BIFF: Yeah, yeah, most gorgeous I've had in years.

HAPPY: I get that any time I want, Biff. Whenever I feel disgusted. The only trouble is, it gets like bowling or something. I just keep knockin' them over and it doesn't mean anything. You still run around a lot?

BIFF: Naa. I'd like to find a girl—steady, somebody with substance.

HAPPY: That's what I long for.

BIFF: Go on! You'd never come home.

HAPPY: I would! Somebody with character, with resistance! Like Mom, y'know? You're gonna call me a bastard when I tell you this. That girl Charlotte I was with tonight is engaged to be married in five weeks. [*He tries on his new hat.*]

BIFF: No kiddin'!

HAPPY: Sure, the guy's in line for the vice-presidency of the store. I don't know what gets into me, maybe I just have an over-developed sense of competition or something, but I went and ruined her, and furthermore I can't get rid of her. And he's the third executive I've done that to. Isn't that a crummy characteristic? And to top it all, I go to their weddings! [*Indignantly, but laughing.*] Like I'm not supposed to take bribes. Manufacturers offer me a hundred-dollar bill now and then to throw an order their way. You know how honest I am, but it's like this girl, see. I hate myself for it. Because I don't want the girl, and, still, I take it and—I love it!

BIFF: Let's go to sleep.

HAPPY: I guess we didn't settle anything, heh?

BIFF: I just got one idea that I think I'm going to try.

HAPPY: What's that?

BIFF: Remember Bill Oliver?

HAPPY: Sure, Oliver is very big now. You want to work for him again?

BIFF: No, but when I quit he said something to me. He put his arm on my shoulder, and he said, "Biff, if you ever need anything, come to me."

HAPPY: I remember that. That sounds good.

BIFF: I think I'll go to see him. If I could get ten thousand or even seven or eight thousand dollars I could buy a beautiful ranch.

HAPPY: I bet he'd back you. 'Cause he thought highly of you, Biff. I mean, they all do. You're well liked, Biff. That's why I say to come back here, and we both have the apartment. And I'm tellin' you, Biff, any babe you want . . .

BIFF: No, with a ranch I could do the work I like and still be something. I just wonder though. I wonder if Oliver still thinks I stole that carton of basketballs.

HAPPY: Oh, he probably forgot that long ago. It's almost ten years. You're too sensitive. Anyway, he didn't really fire you.

BIFF: Well, I think he was going to. I think that's why I quit. I was never sure whether he knew or not. I know he thought the world of me, though. I was the only one he'd let lock up the place.

WILLY [*below*]: You gonna wash the engine, Biff?

HAPPY: Shh!

Biff looks at Happy, who is gazing down, listening. Willy is mumbling in the parlor.

HAPPY: You hear that?

They listen. Willy laughs warmly.

BIFF [*growing angry*]: Doesn't he know Mom can hear that?

WILLY: Don't get your sweater dirty, Biff!

A look of pain crosses Biff's face.

HAPPY: Isn't that terrible? Don't leave again, will you? You'll find a job here. You gotta stick around. I don't know what to do about him, it's getting embarrassing.

WILLY: What a simonizing job!

BIFF: Mom's hearing that!

WILLY: No kiddin', Biff, you got a date? Wonderful!

HAPPY: Go on to sleep. But talk to him in the morning, will you?

BIFF [*reluctantly getting into bed*]: With her in the house. Brother!

HAPPY [*getting into bed*]: I wish you'd have a good talk with him.

The light on their room begins to fade.

BIFF [*to himself in bed*]: That selfish, stupid . . .

HAPPY: Sh . . . Sleep, Biff.

Their light is out. Well before they have finished speaking, Willy's form is dimly seen below in the darkened kitchen. He opens the refrigerator, searches in there, and takes out a bottle of milk. The apartment houses are fading out, and the entire house and surroundings become covered with leaves. Music insinuates itself as the leaves appear.

WILLY: Just wanna be careful with those girls, Biff, that's all. Don't make any promises. No promises of any kind. Because a girl, y'know, they always believe what you tell 'em, and you're very young, Biff, you're too young to be talking seriously to girls.

Light rises on the kitchen. Willy, talking, shuts the refrigerator door and comes downstage to the kitchen table. He pours milk into a glass. He is totally immersed in himself, smiling faintly.

WILLY: Too young entirely, Biff. You want to watch your schooling first. Then when you're all set, there'll be plenty of girls for a boy like you. [*He smiles broadly at a kitchen chair.*] That so? The girls pay for you? [*He laughs.*] Boy, you must really be makin' a hit.

Willy is gradually addressing—physically—a point offstage, speaking through the wall of the kitchen, and his voice has been rising in volume to that of a normal conversation.

WILLY: I been wondering why you polish the car so careful. Ha! Don't leave the hubcaps, boys. Get the chamois to the hubcaps. Happy, use newspaper on the windows, it's the easiest thing. Show him how to do it, Biff! You see, Happy? Pad it up, use it like a pad. That's it, that's it, good work. You're doin' all right, Hap. [*He pauses, then nods in approbation for a few seconds, then looks upward.*] Biff, first thing we gotta do when we get time is clip that big branch over the house. Afraid it's gonna fall in a storm and hit the roof. Tell you what. We get a rope and sling her around, and then we climb up there with a couple of saws and take her down. Soon as you finish the car, boys, I wanna see ya. I got a surprise for you, boys.

BIFF [*offstage*]:   Whatta ya got, Dad?

WILLY: No, you finish first. Never leave a job till you're finished— remember that. [*Looking toward the "big trees."*] Biff, up in Albany I saw a beautiful hammock. I think I'll buy it next trip, and we'll hang it right between those two elms. Wouldn't that be something? Just swingin' there under those branches. Boy, that would be . . .

Young Biff and Young Happy appear from the direction Willy was addressing. Happy carries rags and a pail of water. Biff, wearing a sweater with a block "S," carries a football.

BIFF [*pointing in the direction of the car offstage*]:   How's that, Pop, professional?

WILLY: Terrific. Terrific job, boys. Good work, Biff.

HAPPY: Where's the surprise, Pop?

WILLY: In the back seat of the car.

HAPPY: Boy! [*He runs off.*]

BIFF: What is it, Dad? Tell me, what'd you buy?

WILLY [*laughing, cuffs him*]:   Never mind, something I want you to have.

BIFF [*turns and starts off*]:   What is it, Hap?

HAPPY [*offstage*]:   It's a punching bag!

BIFF: Oh, Pop!

WILLY: It's got Gene Tunney's signature on it!

Happy runs onstage with a punching bag.

BIFF: Gee, how'd you know we wanted a punching bag?

WILLY: Well, it's the finest thing for the timing.

HAPPY [*lies down on his back and pedals with his feet*]:   I'm losing weight, you notice, Pop?

WILLY [*to Happy*]:   Jumping rope is good too.

BIFF: Did you see the new football I got?

WILLY [*examining the ball*]:   Where'd you get a new ball?

BIFF: The coach told me to practice my passing.

WILLY: That so? And he gave you the ball, heh?

BIFF: Well, I borrowed it from the locker room. [*He laughs confidentially.*]

WILLY [*laughing with him at the theft*]:   I want you to return that.

HAPPY: I told you he wouldn't like it!

BIFF [*angrily*]:   Well, I'm bringing it back!

WILLY [*stopping the incipient argument, to Happy*]:   Sure, he's gotta practice with a regulation ball, doesn't he? [*To Biff.*] Coach'll probably congratulate you on your initiative!

BIFF: Oh, he keeps congratulating my initiative all the time, Pop.

WILLY: That's because he likes you. If somebody else took that ball there'd be an uproar. So what's the report, boys, what's the report?

BIFF: Where'd you go this time, Dad? Gee we were lonesome for you.

WILLY [*pleased, puts an arm around each boy and they come down to the apron*]:   Lonesome, heh?

BIFF: Missed you every minute.

WILLY: Don't say? Tell you a secret, boys. Don't breathe it to a soul. Someday I'll have my own business, and I'll never have to leave home any more.

HAPPY: Like Uncle Charley, heh?

WILLY: Bigger than Uncle Charley! Because Charley is not—liked. He's liked, but he's not—well liked.

BIFF: Where'd you go this time, Dad?

WILLY: Well, I got on the road, and I went north to Providence. Met the Mayor.

BIFF: The Mayor of Providence!

WILLY: He was sitting in the hotel lobby.

BIFF: What'd he say?

WILLY: He said, "Morning!" And I said, "Morning!" And I said, "You got a fine city here, Mayor." And then he had coffee with me. And then I went to Waterbury. Waterbury is a fine city. Big clock city, the famous Waterbury clock. Sold a nice bill there. And then Boston—Boston is the cradle of the Revolution. A fine city. And a couple of other towns in Mass., and on to Portland and Bangor and straight home!

BIFF: Gee, I'd love to go with you sometime, Dad.

WILLY: Soon as summer comes.

HAPPY: Promise?

WILLY: You and Hap and I, and I'll show you all the towns. America is full of beautiful towns and fine, upstanding people. And they know me, boys, they know me up and down New England. The finest people. And when I bring you fellas up, there'll be open sesame for all of us, 'cause one thing, boys: I have friends. I can park my car in any street in New England, and the cops protect it like their own. This summer, heh?

BIFF AND HAPPY [*together*]: Yeah! You bet!

WILLY: We'll take our bathing suits.

HAPPY: We'll carry your bags, Pop!

WILLY: Oh, won't that be something! Me comin' into the Boston stores with you boys carryin' my bags. What a sensation!

Biff is prancing around, practicing passing the ball.

WILLY: You nervous, Biff, about the game?

BIFF: Not if you're gonna be there.

WILLY: What do they say about you in school, now that they made you captain?

HAPPY: There's a crowd of girls behind him everytime the classes change.

BIFF [*taking Willy's hand*]: This Saturday, Pop, this Saturday—just for you, I'm going to break through for a touchdown.

HAPPY: You're supposed to pass.

BIFF: I'm takin' one play for Pop. You watch me, Pop, and when I take off my helmet, that means I'm breakin' out. Then you watch me crash through that line!

WILLY [*kisses Biff*]: Oh, wait'll I tell this in Boston!

Bernard enters in knickers. He is younger than Biff, earnest and loyal, a worried boy.

BERNARD: Biff, where are you? You're supposed to study with me today.

WILLY: Hey, looka Bernard. What're you lookin' so anemic about, Bernard?

BERNARD: He's gotta study, Uncle Willy. He's got Regents next week.

HAPPY [*tauntingly, spinning Bernard around*]: Let's box, Bernard!

BERNARD: Biff! [*He gets away from Happy.*] Listen, Biff, I heard Mr. Birnbaum say that if you don't start studyin' math he's gonna flunk you, and you won't graduate. I heard him!

WILLY: You better study with him, Biff. Go ahead now.

BERNARD: I heard him!

BIFF: Oh, Pop, you didn't see my sneakers! [*He holds up a foot for Willy to look at.*]

WILLY: Hey, that's a beautiful job of printing!

BERNARD [*wiping his glasses*]: Just because he printed University of Virginia on his sneakers doesn't mean they've got to graduate him, Uncle Willy!

WILLY [*angrily*]: What're you talking about? With scholarships to three universities they're gonna flunk him?

BERNARD: But I heard Mr. Birnbaum say . . .

WILLY: Don't be a pest, Bernard! [*To his boys.*] What an anemic!

BERNARD: Okay, I'm waiting for you in my house, Biff.

Bernard goes off. The Lomans laugh.

WILLY: Bernard is not well liked, is he?

BIFF: He's liked, but he's not well liked.

HAPPY: That's right, Pop.

WILLY: That's just what I mean. Bernard can get the best marks in school, y'understand, but when he gets out in the business world, y'understand, you are going to be five times ahead of him. That's why I thank Almighty God you're both built like Adonises. Because the man who makes an appearance in the business world, the man who creates personal interest, is the man who gets ahead. Be liked and you will never want. You take me, for instance. I never have to wait in line to see a buyer. "Willy Loman is here!" That's all they have to know, and I go right through.

BIFF: Did you knock them dead, Pop?

WILLY: Knocked 'em cold in Providence, slaughtered 'em in Boston.

HAPPY [*on his back, pedaling again*]: I'm losing weight, you notice, Pop?

Linda enters as of old, a ribbon in her hair, carrying a basket of washing.

LINDA [*with youthful energy*]: Hello, dear!

WILLY: Sweetheart!

LINDA: How'd the Chevvy run?

WILLY: Chevrolet, Linda, is the greatest car ever built. [*To the boys.*] Since when do you let your mother carry wash up the stairs?

BIFF: Grab hold there, boy!

HAPPY: Where to, Mom?

LINDA: Hang them up on the line. And you better go down to your friends, Biff. The cellar is full of boys. They don't know what to do with themselves.

BIFF: Ah, when Pop comes home they can wait!

WILLY [*laughs appreciatively*]: You better go down and tell them what to do. Biff.

BIFF: I think I'll have them sweep out the furnace room.

WILLY: Good work, Biff.

BIFF [*goes through wall-line of kitchen to doorway at back and calls down*]: Fellas! Everybody sweep out the furnace room! I'll be right down!

VOICES: All right! Okay, Biff.

BIFF: George and Sam and Frank, come out back! We're hangin' up the wash! Come on, Hap, on the double! [*He and Happy carry out the basket.*]

LINDA: The way they obey him!

WILLY: Well, that's training, the training. I'm tellin' you, I was sellin' thousands and thousands, but I had to come home.

LINDA: Oh, the whole block'll be at that game. Did you sell anything?

WILLY: I did five hundred gross in Providence and seven hundred gross in Boston.

LINDA: No! Wait a minute. I've got a pencil. [*She pulls pencil and paper out of her apron pocket.*] That makes your commission . . . Two hundred—my God! Two hundred and twelve dollars!

WILLY: Well, I didn't figure it yet, but . . .

LINDA: How much did you do?

WILLY: Well, I—I did—about a hundred and eighty gross in Providence. Well, no—it came to—roughly two hundred gross on the whole trip.

LINDA [*without hesitation*]: Two hundred gross. That's . . . [*She figures.*]

WILLY: The trouble was that three of the stores were half-closed for inventory in Boston. Otherwise I woulda broke records.

LINDA: Well, it makes seventy dollars and some pennies. That's very good.

WILLY: What do we owe?

LINDA: Well, on the first there's sixteen dollars on the refrigerator . . .

WILLY: Why sixteen?

LINDA: Well, the fan belt broke, so it was a dollar eighty.

WILLY: But it's brand new.

LINDA: Well, the man said that's the way it is. Till they work themselves in, y'know.

They move through the wall-line into the kitchen.

WILLY: I hope we didn't get stuck on that machine.

LINDA: They got the biggest ads of any of them!

WILLY: I know, it's a fine machine. What else?

LINDA: Well, there's nine-sixty for the washing machine. And for the
vacuum cleaner there's three and a half due on the fifteenth. Then
the roof, you got twenty-one dollars remaining.

WILLY: It don't leak, does it?

LINDA: No, they did a wonderful job. Then you owe Frank for the
carburetor.

WILLY: I'm not going to pay that man! That goddam Chevrolet, they
ought to prohibit the manufacture of that car!

LINDA: Well, you owe him three and a half. And odds and ends,
comes to around a hundred and twenty dollars by the fifteenth.

WILLY: A hundred and twenty dollars! My God, if business don't pick
up I don't know what I'm gonna do!

LINDA: Well, next week you'll do better.

WILLY: Oh, I'll knock 'em dead next week. I'll go to Hartford. I'm very
well liked in Hartford. You know, the trouble is, Linda, people don't
seem to take to me.

They move onto the forestage.

LINDA: Oh, don't be foolish.

WILLY: I know it when I walk in. They seem to laugh at me.

LINDA: Why? Why would they laugh at you? Don't talk that way, Willy.

*Willy moves to the edge of the stage. Linda goes into the kitchen
and starts to darn stockings.*

WILLY: I don't know the reason for it, but they just pass me by. I'm not
noticed.

LINDA: But you're doing wonderful, dear. You're making seventy to a
hundred dollars a week.

WILLY: But I gotta be at it ten, twelve hours a day. Other men—I don't
know—they do it easier. I don't know why—I can't stop myself—I
talk too much. A man oughta come in with a few words. One thing
about Charley. He's a man of few words, and they respect him.

LINDA: You don't talk too much, you're just lively.

WILLY [*smiling*]: Well, I figure, what the hell, life is short, a couple of jokes. [*To himself:*] I joke too much! [*The smile goes.*]

LINDA: Why? You're . . .

WILLY: I'm fat. I'm very—foolish to look at, Linda. I didn't tell you, but Christmas time I happened to be calling on F. H. Stewarts, and a salesman I know, as I was going in to see the buyer I heard him say something about—walrus. And I—I cracked him right across the face. I won't take that. I simply will not take that. But they do laugh at me. I know that.

LINDA: Darling . . .

WILLY: I gotta overcome it. I know I gotta overcome it. I'm not dressing to advantage, maybe.

LINDA: Willy, darling, you're the handsomest man in the world . . .

WILLY: Oh, no, Linda.

LINDA: To me you are. [*Slight pause.*] The handsomest.

From the darkness is heard the laughter of a woman. Willy doesn't turn to it, but it continues through Linda's lines.

LINDA: And the boys, Willy. Few men are idolized by their children the way you are.

Music is heard as behind a scrim, to the left of the house; The Woman, dimly seen, is dressing.

WILLY [*with great feeling*]: You're the best there is. Linda, you're a pal, you know that? On the road—on the road I want to grab you sometimes and just kiss the life outa you.

The laughter is loud now, and he moves into a brightening area at the left, where The Woman has come from behind the scrim and is standing, putting on her hat, looking into a "mirror" and laughing.

WILLY: 'Cause I get so lonely—especially when business is bad and there's nobody to talk to. I get the feeling that I'll never sell anything again, that I won't make a living for you, or a business, a business for the boys. [*He talks through The Woman's subsiding laughter; The Woman primps at the "mirror."*] There's so much I want to make for . . .

THE WOMAN: Me? You didn't make me, Willy. I picked you.

WILLY [*pleased*]: You picked me?

THE WOMAN [*who is quite proper-looking, Willy's age*]: I did. I've been sitting at that desk watching all the salesmen go by, day in, day out.

But you've got such a sense of humor, and we do have such a good time together, don't we?

WILLY: Sure, sure. [*He takes her in his arms.*] Why do you have to go now?

THE WOMAN: It's two o'clock . . .

WILLY: No, come on in! [*He pulls her.*]

THE WOMAN: . . . my sisters'll be scandalized. When'll you be back?

WILLY: Oh, two weeks about. Will you come up again?

THE WOMAN: Sure thing. You do make me laugh. It's good for me. [*She squeezes his arm, kisses him.*] And I think you're a wonderful man.

WILLY: You picked me, heh?

THE WOMAN: Sure. Because you're so sweet. And such a kidder.

WILLY: Well, I'll see you next time I'm in Boston.

THE WOMAN: I'll put you right through to the buyers.

WILLY [*slapping her bottom*]: Right. Well, bottoms up!

THE WOMAN [*slaps him gently and laughs*]: You just kill me, Willy. [*He suddenly grabs her and kisses her roughly.*] You kill me. And thanks for the stockings. I love a lot of stockings. Well, good night.

WILLY: Good night. And keep your pores open!

THE WOMAN: Oh, Willy!

The Woman bursts out laughing, and Linda's laughter blends in. The Woman disappears into the dark. Now the area at the kitchen table brightens. Linda is sitting where she was at the kitchen table, but now is mending a pair of her silk stockings.

LINDA: You are, Willy. The handsomest man. You've got no reason to feel that . . .

WILLY [*coming out of The Woman's dimming area and going over to Linda*]: I'll make it all up to you, Linda, I'll . . .

LINDA: There's nothing to make up, dear. You're doing fine, better than . . .

WILLY [*noticing her mending*]: What's that?

LINDA: Just mending my stockings. They're so expensive . . .

WILLY [*angrily, taking them from her*]: I won't have you mending stockings in this house! Now throw them out!

Linda puts the stockings in her pocket.

BERNARD [*entering on the run*]: Where is he? If he doesn't study!

WILLY [*moving to the forestage, with great agitation*]: You'll give him the answers!

BERNARD: I do, but I can't on a Regents! That's a state exam! They're liable to arrest me!

WILLY: Where is he? I'll whip him, I'll whip him!

LINDA: And he'd better give back that football, Willy, it's not nice.

WILLY: Biff! Where is he? Why is he taking everything?

LINDA: He's too rough with the girls, Willy. All the mothers are afraid of him!

WILLY: I'll whip him!

BERNARD: He's driving the car without a license!

The Woman's laugh is heard.

WILLY: Shut up!

LINDA: All the mothers . . .

WILLY: Shut up!

BERNARD [*backing quietly away and out*]:   Mr. Birnbaum says he's stuck up.

WILLY: Get outa here!

BERNARD: If he doesn't buckle down he'll flunk math! [*He goes off.*]

LINDA: He's right, Willy, you've gotta . . .

WILLY [*exploding at her*]:   There's nothing the matter with him! You want him to be a worm like Bernard? He's got spirit, personality . . .

As he speaks, Linda, almost in tears, exits into the living room. Willy is alone in the kitchen, wilting and staring. The leaves are gone. It is night again, and the apartment houses look down from behind.

WILLY: Loaded with it. Loaded! What is he stealing? He's giving it back, isn't he? Why is he stealing? What did I tell him? I never in my life told him anything but decent things.

Happy in pajamas has come down the stairs; Willy suddenly becomes aware of Happy's presence.

HAPPY: Let's go now, come on.

WILLY [*sitting down at the kitchen table*]:   Huh! Why did she have to wax the floors herself? Everytime she waxes the floors she keels over. She knows that!

HAPPY: Shh! Take it easy. What brought you back tonight?

WILLY: I got an awful scare. Nearly hit a kid in Yonkers. God! Why didn't I go to Alaska with my brother Ben that time! Ben! That man was a genius, that man was success incarnate! What a mistake! He begged me to go.

HAPPY: Well, there's no use in . . .

WILLY: You guys! There was a man started with the clothes on his back and ended up with diamond mines!

HAPPY: Boy, someday I'd like to know how he did it.

WILLY: What's the mystery? The man knew what he wanted and went out and got it! Walked into a jungle, and comes out, the age of twenty-one, and he's rich! The world is an oyster, but you don't crack it open on a mattress!

HAPPY: Pop, I told you I'm gonna retire you for life.

WILLY: You'll retire me for life on seventy goddam dollars a week? And your women and your car and your apartment, and you'll retire me for life! Christ's sake, I couldn't get past Yonkers today! Where are you guys, where are you? The woods are burning! I can't drive a car!

Charley has appeared in the doorway. He is a large man, slow of speech, laconic, immovable. In all he says, despite what he says, there is pity, and, now, trepidation. He has a robe over pajamas, slippers on his feet. He enters the kitchen.

CHARLEY: Everything all right?

HAPPY: Yeah, Charley, everything's . . .

WILLY: What's the matter?

CHARLEY: I heard some noise. I thought something happened. Can't we do something about the walls? You sneeze in here, and in my house hats blow off.

HAPPY: Let's go to bed, Dad. Come on.

Charley signals to Happy to go.

WILLY: You go ahead, I'm not tired at the moment.

HAPPY [*to Willy*]:   Take it easy, huh? [*He exits.*]

WILLY: What're you doin' up?

CHARLEY [*sitting down at the kitchen table opposite Willy*]:   Couldn't sleep good. I had a heartburn.

WILLY: Well, you don't know how to eat.

CHARLEY: I eat with my mouth.

WILLY: No, you're ignorant. You gotta know about vitamins and things like that.

CHARLEY: Come on, let's shoot. Tire you out a little.

WILLY [*hesitantly*]:   All right. You got cards?

CHARLEY [*taking a deck from his pocket*]:   Yeah, I got them. Someplace. What is it with those vitamins?

WILLY [*dealing*]:   They build up your bones. Chemistry.

CHARLEY: Yeah, but there's no bones in a heartburn.

WILLY: What are you talkin' about? Do you know the first thing about it?

CHARLEY: Don't get insulted.

WILLY: Don't talk about something you don't know anything about.

They are playing. Pause.

CHARLEY: What're you doin' home?

WILLY: A little trouble with the car.

CHARLEY: Oh. [*Pause.*] I'd like to take a trip to California.

WILLY: Don't say.

CHARLEY: You want a job?

WILLY: I got a job, I told you that. [*After a slight pause.*] What the hell are you offering me a job for?

CHARLEY: Don't get insulted.

WILLY: Don't insult me.

CHARLEY: I don't see no sense in it. You don't have to go on this way.

WILLY: I got a good job. [*Slight pause.*] What do you keep comin' in here for?

CHARLEY: You want me to go?

WILLY [*after a pause, withering*]:   I can't understand it. He's going back to Texas again. What the hell is that?

CHARLEY: Let him go.

WILLY: I got nothin' to give him, Charley, I'm clean, I'm clean.

CHARLEY: He won't starve. None a them starve. Forget about him.

WILLY: Then what have I got to remember?

CHARLEY: You take it too hard. To hell with it. When a deposit bottle is broken you don't get your nickel back.

WILLY: That's easy enough for you to say.

CHARLEY: That ain't easy for me to say.

WILLY: Did you see the ceiling I put up in the living room?

CHARLEY: Yeah, that's a piece of work. To put up a ceiling is a mystery to me. How do you do it?

WILLY: What's the difference?

CHARLEY: Well, talk about it.

WILLY: You gonna put up a ceiling?

CHARLEY: How could I put up a ceiling?

WILLY: Then what the hell are you bothering me for?

CHARLEY: You're insulted again.

WILLY: A man who can't handle tools is not a man. You're disgusting.

CHARLEY: Don't call me disgusting, Willy.

Uncle Ben, carrying a valise and an umbrella, enters the forestage from around the right corner of the house. He is a stolid man, in his sixties, with a mustache and an authoritative air. He is utterly certain of his destiny, and there is an aura of far places about him. He enters exactly as Willy speaks.

WILLY: I'm getting awfully tired, Ben.

Ben's music is heard. Ben looks around at everything.

CHARLEY: Good, keep playing; you'll sleep better. Did you call me Ben?

Ben looks at his watch.

WILLY: That's funny. For a second there you reminded me of my brother Ben.

BEN: I only have a few minutes. [*He strolls, inspecting the place. Willy and Charley continue playing.*]

CHARLEY: You never heard from him again, heh? Since that time?

WILLY: Didn't Linda tell you? Couple of weeks ago we got a letter from his wife in Africa. He died.

CHARLEY: That so.

BEN [*chuckling*]:   So this is Brooklyn, eh?

CHARLEY: Maybe you're in for some of his money.

WILLY: Naa, he had seven sons. There's just one opportunity I had with that man . . .

BEN: I must make a train, William. There are several properties I'm looking at in Alaska.

WILLY: Sure, sure! If I'd gone with him to Alaska that time, everything would've been totally different.

CHARLEY: Go on, you'd froze to death up there.

WILLY: What're you talking about?

BEN: Opportunity is tremendous in Alaska, William. Surprised you're not up there.

WILLY: Sure, tremendous.

CHARLEY: Heh?

WILLY: There was the only man I ever met who knew the answers.

CHARLEY: Who?

BEN: How are you all?

WILLY [*taking a pot, smiling*]:   Fine, fine.

CHARLEY: Pretty sharp tonight.

BEN: Is Mother living with you?

WILLY: No, she died a long time ago.

CHARLEY: Who?

BEN: That's too bad. Fine specimen of a lady, Mother.

WILLY [to Charley]: Heh?

BEN: I'd hoped to see the old girl.

CHARLEY: Who died?

BEN: Heard anything from Father, have you?

WILLY [unnerved]: What do you mean, who died?

CHARLEY [taking a pot]: What're you talkin' about?

BEN [looking at his watch]: William, it's half-past eight!

WILLY [as though to dispel his confusion he angrily stops Charley's hand]: That's my build!

CHARLEY: I put the ace . . .

WILLY: If you don't know how to play the game I'm not gonna throw my money away on you!

CHARLEY [rising]: It was my ace, for God's sake!

WILLY: I'm through, I'm through!

BEN: When did Mother die?

WILLY: Long ago. Since the beginning you never knew how to play cards.

CHARLEY [picks up the cards and goes to the door]: All right! Next time I'll bring a deck with five aces.

WILLY: I don't play that kind of game!

CHARLEY [turning to him]: You ought to be ashamed of yourself!

WILLY: Yeah?

CHARLEY: Yeah! [He goes out.]

WILLY [slamming the door after him]: Ignoramus!

BEN [as Willy comes toward him through the wall-line of the kitchen]: So you're William.

WILLY [shaking Ben's hand]: Ben! I've been waiting for you so long! What's the answer? How did you do it?

BEN: Oh, there's a story in that.

Linda enters the forestage, as of old, carrying the wash basket.

LINDA: Is this Ben?

BEN [gallantly]: How do you do, my dear.

LINDA: Where've you been all these years? Willy's always wondered why you . . .

WILLY [*pulling Ben away from her impatiently*]:   Where is Dad? Didn't you follow him? How did you get started?

BEN: Well, I don't know how much you remember.

WILLY: Well, I was just a baby, of course, only three or four years old . . .

BEN: Three years and eleven months.

WILLY: What a memory, Ben!

BEN: I have many enterprises, William, and I have never kept books.

WILLY: I remember I was sitting under the wagon in—was it Nebraska?

BEN: It was South Dakota, and I gave you a bunch of wild flowers.

WILLY: I remember you walking away down some open road.

BEN [*laughing*]:   I was going to find Father in Alaska.

WILLY: Where is he?

BEN: At that age I had a very faulty view of geography, William. I discovered after a few days that I was heading due south, so instead of Alaska, I ended up in Africa.

LINDA: Africa!

WILLY: The Gold Coast!

BEN: Principally diamond mines.

LINDA: Diamond mines!

BEN: Yes, my dear. But I've only a few minutes . . .

WILLY: No! Boys! Boys! [*Young Biff and Happy appear.*] Listen to this. This is your Uncle Ben, a great man! Tell my boys, Ben!

BEN: Why, boys, when I was seventeen I walked into the jungle, and when I was twenty-one I walked out. [*He laughs.*] And by God I was rich.

WILLY [*to the boys*]:   You see what I been talking about? The greatest things can happen!

BEN [*glancing at his watch*]:   I have an appointment in Ketchikan Tuesday week.

WILLY: No, Ben! Please tell about Dad. I want my boys to hear. I want them to know the kind of stock they spring from. All I remember is a man with a big beard, and I was in Mamma's lap, sitting around a fire, and some kind of high music.

BEN: His flute. He played the flute.

WILLY: Sure, the flute, that's right!

New music is heard, a high, rollicking tune.

BEN: Father was a very great and a very wild-hearted man. We would start in Boston, and he'd toss the whole family into the wagon, and then he'd drive the team right across the country; through Ohio, and Indiana, Michigan, Illinois, and all the Western states. And we'd stop in the towns and sell the flutes that he'd made on the way. Great inventor, Father. With one gadget he made more in a week than a man like you could make in a lifetime.

WILLY: That's just the way I'm bringing them up, Ben—rugged, well liked, all-around.

BEN: Yeah? [*To Biff.*] Hit that, boy—hard as you can. [*He pounds his stomach.*]

BIFF: Oh, no, sir!

BEN [*taking boxing stance*]:   Come on, get to me! [*He laughs.*]

WILLY: Go to it. Biff! Go ahead, show him!

BIFF: Okay! [*He cocks his fists and starts in.*]

LINDA [*to Willy*]:   Why must he fight, dear?

BEN [*sparring with Biff*]:   Good boy! Good boy!

WILLY: How's that, Ben, heh?

HAPPY: Give him the left, Biff!

LINDA: Why are you fighting?

BEN: Good boy! [*Suddenly comes in, trips Biff, and stands over him, the point of his umbrella poised over Biff's eye.*]

LINDA: Look out, Biff!

BIFF: Gee!

BEN [*patting Biff's knee*]:   Never fight fair with a stranger, boy. You'll never get out of the jungle that way. [*Taking Linda's hand and bowing.*] It was an honor and a pleasure to meet you, Linda.

LINDA [*withdrawing her hand coldly, frightened*]:   Have a nice—trip.

BEN [*to Willy*]:   And good luck with your—what do you do?

WILLY: Selling.

BEN: Yes. Well . . . [*He raises his hand in farewell to all.*]

WILLY: No, Ben, I don't want you to think . . . [*He takes Ben's arm to show him.*] It's Brooklyn, I know, but we hunt too.

BEN: Really, now.

WILLY: Oh, sure, there's snakes and rabbits and—that's why I moved out here. Why, Biff can fell any one of these trees in no time! Boys! Go right over to where they're building the apartment house and get some sand. We're gonna rebuild the entire front stoop right now! Watch this, Ben!

BIFF: Yes, sir! On the double, Hap!

HAPPY [*as he and Biff run off*]:   I lost weight, Pop, you notice?

Charley enters in knickers, even before the boys are gone.

CHARLEY: Listen, if they steal any more from that building the watchman'll put the cops on them!

LINDA [*to Willy*]: Don't let Biff . . .

Ben laughs lustily.

WILLY: You shoulda seen the lumber they brought home last week. At least a dozen six-by-tens worth all kinds a money.

CHARLEY: Listen, if that watchman . . .

WILLY: I gave them hell, understand. But I got a couple of fearless characters there.

CHARLEY: Willy, the jails are full of fearless characters.

BEN [*clapping Willy on the back, with a laugh at Charley*]: And the stock exchange, friend!

WILLY [*joining in Ben's laughter*]: Where are the rest of your pants?

CHARLEY: My wife bought them.

WILLY: Now all you need is a golf club and you can go upstairs and go to sleep. [*To Ben.*] Great athlete! Between him and his son Bernard they can't hammer a nail!

BERNARD [*rushing in*]: The watchman's chasing Biff!

WILLY [*angrily*]: Shut up! He's not stealing anything!

LINDA [*alarmed, hurrying off left*]: Where is he? Biff, dear! [*She exits.*]

WILLY [*moving toward the left, away from Ben*]: There's nothing wrong. What's the matter with you?

BEN: Nervy boy. Good!

WILLY [*laughing*]: Oh, nerves of iron, that Biff!

CHARLEY: Don't know what it is. My New England man comes back and he's bleedin', they murdered him up there.

WILLY: It's contacts, Charley, I got important contacts!

CHARLEY [*sarcastically*]: Glad to hear it, Willy. Come in later, we'll shoot a little casino. I'll take some of your Portland money. [*He laughs at Willy and exits.*]

WILLY [*turning to Ben*]: Business is bad, it's murderous. But not for me, of course.

BEN: I'll stop by on my way back to Africa.

WILLY [*longingly*]: Can't you stay a few days? You're just what I need, Ben, because I—I have a fine position here, but I—well, Dad left when I was such a baby and I never had a chance to talk to him and I still feel—kind of temporary about myself.

BEN: I'll be late for my train.

They are at opposite ends of the stage.

WILLY: Ben, my boys—can't we talk? They'd go into the jaws of hell for me, see, but I . . .

BEN: William, you're being first-rate with your boys. Outstanding, manly chaps!

WILLY [hanging on to his words]:   Oh, Ben, that's good to hear! Because sometimes I'm afraid that I'm not teaching them the right kind of—Ben, how should I teach them?

BEN [giving great weight to each word, and with a certain vicious audacity]: William, when I walked into the jungle, I was seventeen. When I walked out I was twenty-one. And, by God, I was rich! [He goes off into darkness around the right corner of the house.]

WILLY: . . . was rich! That's just the spirit I want to imbue them with! To walk into a jungle! I was right! I was right! I was right!

Ben is gone, but Willy is still speaking to him as Linda, in night-gown and robe, enters the kitchen, glances around for Willy, then goes to the door of the house, looks out and sees him. Comes down to his left. He looks at her.

LINDA: Willy, dear? Willy?

WILLY: I was right!

LINDA: Did you have some cheese? [He can't answer.] It's very late, darling. Come to bed, heh?

WILLY [looking straight up]:   Gotta break your neck to see a star in this yard.

LINDA: You coming in?

WILLY: Whatever happened to that diamond watch fob? Remember? When Ben came from Africa that time? Didn't he give me a watch fob with a diamond in it?

LINDA: You pawned it, dear. Twelve, thirteen years ago. For Biff's radio correspondence course.

WILLY: Gee, that was a beautiful thing. I'll take a walk.

LINDA: But you're in your slippers.

WILLY [starting to go around the house at the left]:   I was right! I was! [Half to Linda, as he goes, shaking his head.] What a man! There was a man worth talking to. I was right!

LINDA [calling after Willy]:   But in your slippers, Willy!

Willy is almost gone when Biff, in his pajamas, comes down the stairs and enters the kitchen.

BIFF: What is he doing out there?

LINDA: Sh!

BIFF: God Almighty, Mom, how long has he been doing this?

LINDA: Don't, he'll hear you.

BIFF: What the hell is the matter with him?

LINDA: It'll pass by morning.

BIFF: Shouldn't we do anything?

LINDA: Oh, my dear, you should do a lot of things, but there's nothing to do, so go to sleep.

Happy comes down the stair and sits on the steps.

HAPPY: I never heard him so loud, Mom.

LINDA: Well, come around more often; you'll hear him. [*She sits down at the table and mends the lining of Willy's jacket.*]

BIFF: Why didn't you ever write me about this, Mom?

LINDA: How would I write to you? For over three months you had no address.

BIFF: I was on the move. But you know I thought of you all the time. You know that, don't you, pal?

LINDA: I know, dear, I know. But he likes to have a letter. Just to know that there's still a possibility for better things.

BIFF: He's not like this all the time, is he?

LINDA: It's when you come home he's always the worst.

BIFF: When I come home?

LINDA: When you write you're coming, he's all smiles, and talks about the future, and—he's just wonderful. And then the closer you seem to come, the more shaky he gets, and then, by the time you get here, he's arguing, and he seems angry at you. I think it's just that maybe he can't bring himself to—to open up to you. Why are you so hateful to each other? Why is that?

BIFF [*evasively*]: I'm not hateful, Mom.

LINDA: But you no sooner come in the door than you're fighting!

BIFF: I don't know why. I mean to change. I'm tryin', Mom, you understand?

LINDA: Are you home to stay now?

BIFF: I don't know. I want to look around, see what's doin'.

LINDA: Biff, you can't look around all your life, can you?

BIFF: I just can't take hold, Mom. I can't take hold of some kind of a life.

LINDA: Biff, a man is not a bird, to come and go with the spring time.

BIFF: Your hair . . . [*He touches her hair.*] Your hair got so gray.

LINDA: Oh, it's been gray since you were in high school. I just stopped dyeing it, that's all.

BIFF: Dye it again, will ya? I don't want my pal looking old.

[*He smiles.*]

LINDA: You're such a boy! You think you can go away for a year and . . . You've got to get it into your head now that one day you'll knock on this door and there'll be strange people here . . .

BIFF: What are you talking about? You're not even sixty, Mom.

LINDA: But what about your father?

BIFF [*lamely*]: Well, I meant him too.

HAPPY: He admires Pop.

LINDA: Biff, dear, if you don't have any feeling for him, then you can't have any feeling for me.

BIFF: Sure I can, Mom.

LINDA: No. You can't just come to see me, because I love him. [*With a threat, but only a threat, of tears.*] He's the dearest man in the world to me, and I won't have anyone making him feel unwanted and low and blue. You've got to make up your mind now, darling, there's no leeway any more. Either he's your father and you pay him that respect, or else you're not to come here. I know he's not easy to get along with—nobody knows that better than me but . . .

WILLY [*from the left, with a laugh*]: Hey, hey, Biffo!

BIFF [*starting to go out after Willy*]: What the hell is the matter with him? [*Happy stops him.*]

LINDA: Don't—don't go near him!

BIFF: Stop making excuses for him! He always, always wiped the floor with you. Never had an ounce of respect for you.

HAPPY: He's always had respect for . . .

BIFF: What the hell do you know about it?

HAPPY [*surlily*]: Just don't call him crazy!

BIFF: He's got no character—Charley wouldn't do this. Not in his own house—spewing out that vomit from his mind.

HAPPY: Charley never had to cope with what he's got to.

BIFF: People are worse off than Willy Loman. Believe me, I've seen them!

LINDA: Then make Charley your father, Biff. You can't do that, can you? I don't say he's a great man. Willy Loman never made a lot of money. His name was never in the paper. He's not the finest character that ever lived. But he's a human being, and a terrible thing is happening to him. So attention must be paid. He's not to be allowed to fall into his grave like an old dog. Attention, attention must be finally paid to such a person. You called him crazy . . .

BIFF: I didn't mean . . .

LINDA: No, a lot of people think he's lost his—balance. But you don't have to be very smart to know what his trouble is. The man is exhausted.

HAPPY: Sure!

LINDA: A small man can be just as exhausted as a great man. He works for a company thirty-six years this March, opens up unheard-of territories to their trademark, and now in his old age they take his salary away.

HAPPY [indignantly]: I didn't know that, Mom.

LINDA: You never asked, my dear! Now that you get your spending money someplace else you don't trouble your mind with him.

HAPPY: But I gave you money last . . .

LINDA: Christmas time, fifty dollars! To fix the hot water it cost ninety-seven fifty! For five weeks he's been on straight commission, like a beginner, an unknown!

BIFF: Those ungrateful bastards!

LINDA: Are they any worse than his sons? When he brought them business, when he was young, they were glad to see him. But now his old friends, the old buyers that loved him so and always found some order to hand him in a pinch—they're all dead, retired. He used to be able to make six, seven calls a day in Boston. Now he takes his valises out of the car and puts them back and takes them out again and he's exhausted. Instead of walking he talks now. He drives seven hundred miles, and when he gets there no one knows him any more, no one welcomes him. And what goes through a man's mind, driving seven hundred miles home without having earned a cent? Why shouldn't he talk to himself? Why? When he has to go to Charley and borrow fifty dollars a week and pretend to me that it's his pay? How long can that go on? How long? You see what I'm sitting here and waiting for? And you tell me he has no character? The man who never worked a day but for your benefit? When does he get the medal for that? Is this

his reward—to turn around at the age of sixty-three and find his sons, who he loved better than his life, one a philandering bum . . .

HAPPY: Mom!

LINDA: That's all you are, my baby! [*To Biff.*] And you! What happened to the love you had for him? You were such pals! How you used to talk to him on the phone every night! How lonely he was till he could come home to you!

BIFF: All right, Mom. I'll live here in my room, and I'll get a job. I'll keep away from him, that's all.

LINDA: No, Biff. You can't stay here and fight all the time.

BIFF: He threw me out of this house, remember that.

LINDA: Why did he do that? I never knew why.

BIFF: Because I know he's a fake and he doesn't like anybody around who knows!

LINDA: Why a fake? In what way? What do you mean?

BIFF: Just don't lay it all at my feet. It's between me and him—that's all I have to say. I'll chip in from now on. He'll settle for half my paycheck. He'll be all right. I'm going to bed. [*He starts for the stairs.*]

LINDA: He won't be all right.

BIFF [*turning on the stairs, furiously*]: I hate this city and I'll stay here. Now what do you want?

LINDA: He's dying, Biff.

Happy turns quickly to her, shocked.

BIFF [*after a pause*]: Why is he dying?

LINDA: He's been trying to kill himself.

BIFF [*with great horror*]: How?

LINDA: I live from day to day.

BIFF: What're you talking about?

LINDA: Remember I wrote you that he smashed up the car again? In February?

BIFF: Well?

LINDA: The insurance inspector came. He said that they have evidence. That all these accidents in the last year—weren't—weren't—accidents.

HAPPY: How can they tell that? That's a lie.

LINDA: It seems there's a woman . . . [*She takes a breath as:*]

BIFF [*sharply but contained*]: What woman?

LINDA [*simultaneously*]: . . . and this woman . . .

ARTHUR MILLER

LINDA: What?

BIFF: Nothing. Go ahead.

LINDA: What did you say?

BIFF: Nothing. I just said what woman?

HAPPY: What about her?

LINDA: Well, it seems she was walking down the road and saw his car. She says that he wasn't driving fast at all, and that he didn't skid. She says he came to that little bridge, and then deliberately smashed into the railing, and it was only the shallowness of the water that saved him.

BIFF: Oh, no, he probably just fell asleep again.

LINDA: I don't think he fell asleep.

BIFF: Why not?

LINDA: Last month . . . [*With great difficulty.*] Oh, boys, it's so hard to say a thing like this! He's just a big stupid man to you, but I tell you there's more good in him than in many other people. [*She chokes, wipes her eyes.*] I was looking for a fuse. The lights blew out, and I went down the cellar. And behind the fuse box—it happened to fall out—was a length of rubber pipe—just short.

HAPPY: No kidding!

LINDA: There's a little attachment on the end of it. I knew right away. And sure enough, on the bottom of the water heater there's a new little nipple on the gas pipe.

HAPPY [*angrily*]: That—jerk.

BIFF: Did you have it taken off?

LINDA: I'm—I'm ashamed to. How can I mention it to him? Every day I go down and take away that little rubber pipe. But, when he comes home, I put it back where it was. How can I insult him that way? I don't know what to do. I live from day to day, boys. I tell you, I know every thought in his mind. It sounds so old-fashioned and silly, but I tell you he put his whole life into you and you've turned your backs on him. [*She is bent over in the chair, weeping, her face in her hands.*] Biff, I swear to God! Biff, his life is in your hands!

HAPPY [*to Biff*]: How do you like that damned fool!

BIFF [*kissing her*]: All right, pal, all right. It's all settled now. I've been remiss. I know that, Mom. But now I'll stay, and I swear to you, I'll apply myself. [*Kneeling in front of her, in a fever of self-reproach.*] It's just—you see, Mom, I don't fit in business. Not that I won't try. I'll try, and I'll make good.

HAPPY: Sure you will. The trouble with you in business was you never tried to please people.

BIFF: I know, I . . .

HAPPY: Like when you worked for Harrison's. Bob Harrison said you were tops, and then you go and do some damn fool thing like whistling whole songs in the elevator like a comedian.

BIFF [*against Happy*]: So what? I like to whistle sometimes.

HAPPY: You don't raise a guy to a responsible job who whistles in the elevator!

LINDA: Well, don't argue about it now.

HAPPY: Like when you'd go off and swim in the middle of the day instead of taking the line around.

BIFF [*his resentment rising*]: Well, don't you run off? You take off sometimes, don't you? On a nice summer day?

HAPPY: Yeah, but I cover myself!

LINDA: Boys!

HAPPY: If I'm going to take a fade the boss can call any number where I'm supposed to be and they'll swear to him that I just left. I'll tell you something that I hate to say, Biff, but in the business world some of them think you're crazy.

BIFF [*angered*]: Screw the business world!

HAPPY: All right, screw it! Great, but cover yourself!

LINDA: Hap, Hap!

BIFF: I don't care what they think! They've laughed at Dad for years, and you know why? Because we don't belong in this nuthouse of a city! We should be mixing cement on some open plain or—or carpenters. A carpenter is allowed to whistle!

Willy walks in from the entrance of the house, at left.

WILLY: Even your grandfather was better than a carpenter. [*Pause. They watch him.*] You never grew up. Bernard does not whistle in the elevator, I assure you.

BIFF [*as though to laugh Willy out of it*]: Yeah, but you do, Pop.

WILLY: I never in my life whistled in an elevator! And who in the business world thinks I'm crazy?

BIFF: I didn't mean it like that, Pop. Now don't make a whole thing out of it, will ya?

WILLY: Go back to the West! Be a carpenter, a cowboy, enjoy yourself!

LINDA: Willy, he was just saying . . .

WILLY: I heard what he said!

HAPPY [*trying to quiet Willy*]: Hey, Pop, come on now . . .

WILLY [*continuing over Happy's line*]: They laugh at me, heh? Go to Fi-lene's, go to the Hub, go to Slattery's, Boston. Call out the name Willy Loman and see what happens! Big shot!

BIFF: All right, Pop.

WILLY: Big!

BIFF: All right!

WILLY: Why do you always insult me?

BIFF: I didn't say a word. [*To Linda.*] Did I say a word?

LINDA: He didn't say anything, Willy.

WILLY [*going to the doorway of the living room*]: All right, good night, good night.

LINDA: Willy, dear, he just decided . . .

WILLY [*to Biff*]: If you get tired hanging around tomorrow, paint the ceiling I put up in the living room.

BIFF: I'm leaving early tomorrow.

HAPPY: He's going to see Bill Oliver, Pop.

WILLY [*interestedly*]: Oliver? For what?

BIFF [*with reserve, but trying; trying*]: He always said he'd stake me. I'd like to go into business, so maybe I can take him up on it.

LINDA: Isn't that wonderful?

WILLY: Don't interrupt. What's wonderful about it? There's fifty men in the City of New York who'd stake him. [*To Biff.*] Sporting goods?

BIFF: I guess so. I know something about it and . . .

WILLY: He knows something about it! You know sporting goods better than Spalding, for God's sake! How much is he giving you?

BIFF: I don't know, I didn't even see him yet, but . . .

WILLY: Then what're you talkin' about?

BIFF [*getting angry*]: Well, all I said was I'm gonna see him, that's all!

WILLY [*turning away*]: Ah, you're counting your chickens again.

BIFF [*starting left for the stairs*]: Oh, Jesus, I'm going to sleep!

WILLY [*calling after him*]: Don't curse in this house!

BIFF [*turning*]: Since when did you get so clean?

HAPPY [*trying to stop them*]: Wait a . . .

WILLY: Don't use that language to me! I won't have it!

HAPPY [*grabbing Biff, shouts*]: Wait a minute! I got an idea. I got a fea-sible idea. Come here, Biff, let's talk this over now, let's talk some sense here. When I was down in Florida last time, I thought of a great idea to sell sporting goods. It just came back to me. You and I, Biff—we have a line, the Loman Line. We train a couple of weeks, and put on a couple of exhibitions, see?

WILLY: That's an idea!

HAPPY: Wait! We form two basketball teams, see? Two water-polo teams. We play each other. It's a million dollars' worth of publicity. Two brothers, see? The Loman Brothers. Displays in the Royal Palms—all the hotels. And banners over the ring and the basketball court: "Loman Brothers." Baby, we could sell sporting goods!

WILLY: That is a one-million-dollar idea!

LINDA: Marvelous!

BIFF: I'm in great shape as far as that's concerned.

HAPPY: And the beauty of it is, Biff, it wouldn't be like a business. We'd be out playin' ball again.

BIFF [*enthused*]: Yeah, that's . . .

WILLY: Million-dollar . . .

HAPPY: And you wouldn't get fed up with it, Biff. It'd be the family again. There'd be the old honor, and comradeship, and if you wanted to go off for a swim or somethin'—well, you'd do it! Without some smart cooky gettin' up ahead of you!

WILLY: Lick the world! You guys together could absolutely lick the civilized world.

BIFF: I'll see Oliver tomorrow. Hap, if we could work that out . . .

LINDA: Maybe things are beginning to . . .

WILLY [*widely enthused, to Linda*]: Stop interrupting! [*To Biff.*] But don't wear a sport jacket and slacks when you see Oliver.

BIFF: No, I'll . . .

WILLY: A business suit, and talk as little as possible, and don't crack any jokes.

BIFF: He did like me. Always liked me.

LINDA: He loved you!

WILLY [*to Linda*]: Will you stop! [*To Biff.*] Walk in very serious. You are not applying for a boy's job. Money is to pass. Be quiet, fine, and serious. Everybody likes a kidder, but nobody lends him money.

HAPPY: I'll try to get some myself, Biff. I'm sure I can.

WILLY: I see great things for you kids, I think your troubles are over. But remember, start big and you'll end big. Ask for fifteen. How much you gonna ask for?

BIFF: Gee, I don't know . . .

WILLY: And don't say "Gee." "Gee" is a boy's word. A man walking in for fifteen thousand dollars does not say "Gee!"

BIFF: Ten, I think, would be top though.

WILLY: Don't be so modest. You always started too low. Walk in with a big laugh. Don't look worried. Start off with a couple of your good stories to lighten things up. It's not what you say, it's how you say it—because personality always wins the day.

LINDA: Oliver always thought the highest of him . . .

WILLY: Will you let me talk?

BIFF: Don't yell at her, Pop, will ya?

WILLY [angrily]:   I was talking, wasn't I?

BIFF: I don't like you yelling at her all the time, and I'm tellin' you, that's all.

WILLY: What're you, takin' over this house?

LINDA: Willy . . .

WILLY [turning to her]:   Don't take his side all the time, goddammit!

BIFF [furiously]:   Stop yelling at her!

WILLY [suddenly pulling on his cheek, beaten down, guilt ridden]:   Give my best to Bill Oliver—he may remember me. [He exits through the living room doorway.]

LINDA [her voice subdued]:   What'd you have to start that for? [Biff turns away.] You see how sweet he was as soon as you talked hopefully? [She goes over to Biff.] Come up and say good night to him. Don't let him go to bed that way.

HAPPY: Come on, Biff, let's buck him up.

LINDA: Please, dear. Just say good night. It takes so little to make him happy. Come. [She goes through the living room doorway, calling upstairs from within the living room.] Your pajamas are hanging in the bathroom, Willy!

HAPPY [looking toward where Linda went out]:   What a woman! They broke the mold when they made her. You know that, Biff?

BIFF: He's off salary. My God, working on commission!

HAPPY: Well, let's face it: he's no hot-shot selling man. Except that sometimes, you have to admit, he's a sweet personality.

BIFF [deciding]:   Lend me ten bucks, will ya? I want to buy some new ties.

HAPPY: I'll take you to a place I know. Beautiful stuff. Wear one of my striped shirts tomorrow.

BIFF: She got gray. Mom got awful old. Gee, I'm gonna go in to Oliver tomorrow and knock him for a . . .

HAPPY: Come on up. Tell that to Dad. Let's give him a whirl. Come on.

BIFF [*steamed up*]: You know, with ten thousand bucks, boy!

HAPPY [*as they go into the living room*]: That's the talk, Biff, that's the first time I've heard the old confidence out of you! [*From within the living room, fading off*] You're gonna live with me, kid, and any babe you want just say the word . . . [*The last lines are hardly heard. They are mounting the stairs to their parents' bedroom.*]

LINDA [*entering her bedroom and addressing Willy, who is in the bathroom. She is straightening the bed for him*]: Can you do anything about the shower? It drips.

WILLY [*from the bathroom*]: All of a sudden everything falls to pieces. Goddam plumbing, oughta be sued, those people. I hardly finished putting it in and the thing . . . [*His words rumble off.*]

LINDA: I'm just wondering if Oliver will remember him. You think he might?

WILLY [*coming out of the bathroom in his pajamas*]: Remember him? What's the matter with you, you crazy? If he'd've stayed with Oliver he'd be on top by now! Wait'll Oliver gets a look at him. You don't know the average caliber any more. The average young man today—[*he is getting into bed*]—is got a caliber of zero. Greatest thing in the world for him was to bum around.

Biff and Happy enter the bedroom. Slight pause.

WILLY [*stops short, looking at Biff*]: Glad to hear it, boy.

HAPPY: He wanted to say good night to you, sport.

WILLY [*to Biff*]: Yeah. Knock him dead, boy. What'd you want to tell me?

BIFF: Just take it easy, Pop. Good night. [*He turns to go.*]

WILLY [*unable to resist*]: And if anything falls off the desk while you're talking to him—like a package or something—don't you pick it up. They have office boys for that.

LINDA: I'll make a big breakfast . . .

WILLY: Will you let me finish? [*To Biff.*] Tell him you were in the business in the West. Not farm work.

BIFF: All right, Dad.

LINDA: I think everything . . .

WILLY [*going right through her speech*]: And don't undersell yourself. No less than fifteen thousand dollars.

BIFF [*unable to bear him*]:   Okay. Good night, Mom. [*He starts moving.*]

WILLY: Because you got a greatness in you, Biff, remember that. You got all kinds of greatness . . . [*He lies back, exhausted. Biff walks out.*]

LINDA [*calling after Biff*]:   Sleep well, darling!

HAPPY: I'm gonna get married, Mom. I wanted to tell you.

LINDA: Go to sleep, dear.

HAPPY [*going*]:   I just wanted to tell you.

WILLY: Keep up the good work. [*Happy exits.*] God . . . remember that Ebbets Field game? The championship of the city?

LINDA: Just rest. Should I sing to you?

WILLY: Yeah. Sing to me. [*Linda hums a soft lullaby.*] When that team came out—he was the tallest, remember?

LINDA: Oh, yes. And in gold.

Biff enters the darkened kitchen, takes a cigarette, and leaves the house. He comes downstage into a golden pool of light. He smokes, staring at the night.

WILLY: Like a young god. Hercules—something like that. And the sun, the sun all around him. Remember how he waved to me? Right up from the field, with the representatives of three colleges standing by? And the buyers I brought, and the cheers when he came out—Loman, Loman, Loman! God Almighty, he'll be great yet. A star like that, magnificent, can never really fade away!

The light on Willy is fading. The gas heater begins to glow through the kitchen wall, near the stairs, a blue flame beneath red coils.

LINDA [*timidly*]:   Willy dear, what has he got against you?

WILLY: I'm so tired. Don't talk any more.

Biff slowly returns to the kitchen. He stops, stares toward the heater.

LINDA: Will you ask Howard to let you work in New York?

WILLY: First thing in the morning. Everything'll be all right.

Biff reaches behind the heater and draws out a length of rubber tubing. He is horrified and turns his head toward Willy's room, still dimly lit, from which the strains of Linda's desperate but monotonous humming rise.

WILLY [*staring through the window into the moonlight*]:   Gee, look at the moon moving between the buildings! [*Biff wraps the tubing around his hand and quickly goes up the stairs.*]

Act II

Scene: Music is heard, gay and bright. The curtain rises as the music fades away. Willy, in shirt sleeves, is sitting at the kitchen table, sipping coffee, his hat in his lap. Linda is filling his cup when she can.

WILLY: Wonderful coffee. Meal in itself.

LINDA: Can I make you some eggs?

WILLY: No. Take a breath.

LINDA: You look so rested, dear.

WILLY: I slept like a dead one. First time in months. Imagine, sleeping till ten on a Tuesday morning. Boys left nice and early, heh?

LINDA: They were out of here by eight o'clock.

WILLY: Good work!

LINDA: It was so thrilling to see them leaving together. I can't get over the shaving lotion in this house!

WILLY [*smiling*]: Mmm . . .

LINDA: Biff was very changed this morning. His whole attitude seemed to be hopeful. He couldn't wait to get downtown to see Oliver.

WILLY: He's heading for a change. There's no question, there simply are certain men that take longer to get—solidified. How did he dress?

LINDA: His blue suit. He's so handsome in that suit. He could be a— anything in that suit!

Willy gets up from the table. Linda holds his jacket for him.

WILLY: There's no question, no question at all. Gee, on the way home tonight I'd like to buy some seeds.

LINDA [*laughing*]: That'd be wonderful. But not enough sun gets back there. Nothing'll grow any more.

WILLY: You wait, kid, before it's all over we're gonna get a little place out in the country, and I'll raise some vegetables, a couple of chickens . . .

LINDA: You'll do it yet, dear.

Willy walks out of his jacket. Linda follows him.

WILLY: And they'll get married, and come for a weekend. I'd build a little guest house. 'Cause I got so many fine tools, all I'd need would be a little lumber and some peace of mind.

LINDA [*joyfully*]: I sewed the lining . . .

WILLY: I could build two guest houses, so they'd both come. Did he decide how much he's going to ask Oliver for?

LINDA [*getting him into the jacket*]:   He didn't mention it, but I imagine ten or fifteen thousand. You going to talk to Howard today?

WILLY: Yeah. I'll put it to him straight and simple. He'll just have to take me off the road.

LINDA: And Willy, don't forget to ask for a little advance, because we've got the insurance premium. It's the grace period now.

WILLY: That's a hundred . . . ?

LINDA: A hundred and eight, sixty-eight. Because we're a little short again.

WILLY: Why are we short?

LINDA: Well, you had the motor job on the car . . .

WILLY: That goddam Studebaker!

LINDA: And you got one more payment on the refrigerator . . .

WILLY: But it just broke again!

LINDA: Well, it's old, dear.

WILLY: I told you we should've bought a well-advertised machine. Charley bought a General Electric and it's twenty years old and it's still good, that son-of-a-bitch.

LINDA: But, Willy . . .

WILLY: Whoever heard of a Hastings refrigerator? Once in my life I would like to own something outright before it's broken! I'm always in a race with the junkyard! I just finished paying for the car and it's on its last legs. The refrigerator consumes belts like a goddam maniac. They time those things. They time them so when you finally paid for them, they're used up.

LINDA [*buttoning up his jacket as he unbuttons it*]:   All told, about two hundred dollars would carry us, dear. But that includes the last payment on the mortgage. After this payment, Willy, the house belongs to us.

WILLY: It's twenty-five years!

LINDA: Biff was nine years old when we bought it.

WILLY: Well, that's a great thing. To weather a twenty-five year mortgage is . . .

LINDA: It's an accomplishment.

WILLY: All the cement, the lumber, the reconstruction I put in this house! There ain't a crack to be found in it any more.

LINDA: Well, it served its purpose.

WILLY: What purpose? Some stranger'll come along, move in, and that's that. If only Biff would take this house, and raise a family . . . [*He starts to go.*] Good-by, I'm late.

LINDA [*suddenly remembering*]: Oh, I forgot! You're supposed to meet them for dinner.

WILLY: Me?

LINDA: At Frank's Chop House on Forty-eighth near Sixth Avenue.

WILLY: Is that so! How about you?

LINDA: No, just the three of you. They're gonna blow you to a big meal!

WILLY: Don't say! Who thought of that?

LINDA: Biff came to me this morning, Willy, and he said, "Tell Dad, we want to blow him to a big meal." Be there six o'clock. You and your two boys are going to have dinner.

WILLY: Gee whiz! That's really somethin'. I'm gonna knock Howard for a loop, kid. I'll get an advance, and I'll come home with a New York job. Goddammit, now I'm gonna do it!

LINDA: Oh, that's the spirit, Willy!

WILLY: I will never get behind a wheel the rest of my life!

LINDA: It's changing, Willy, I can feel it changing!

WILLY: Beyond a question. G'by, I'm late. [*He starts to go again.*]

LINDA [*calling after him as she runs to the kitchen table for a handkerchief*]: You got your glasses?

WILLY [*feels for them, then comes back in*]: Yeah, yeah, got my glasses.

LINDA [*giving him the handkerchief*]: And a handkerchief.

WILLY: Yeah, handkerchief.

LINDA: And your saccharine?

WILLY: Yeah, my saccharine.

LINDA: Be careful on the subway stairs.

She kisses him, and a silk stocking is seen hanging from her hand. Willy notices it.

WILLY: Will you stop mending stockings? At least while I'm in the house. It gets me nervous. I can't tell you. Please.

Linda hides the stocking in her hand as she follows Willy across the forestage in front of the house.

LINDA: Remember, Frank's Chop House.

WILLY [*passing the apron*]: Maybe beets would grow out there.

ARTHUR MILLER

392

LINDA [*laughing*]:   But you tried so many times.

WILLY: Yeah. Well, don't work hard today. [*He disappears around the right corner of the house.*]

LINDA: Be careful!

As Willy vanishes, Linda waves to him. Suddenly the phone rings. She runs across the stage and into the kitchen and lifts it.

LINDA: Hello? Oh, Biff! I'm so glad you called, I just . . . Yes, sure, I just told him. Yes, he'll be there for dinner at six o'clock, I didn't forget. Listen, I was just dying to tell you. You know that little rubber pipe I told you about? That he connected to the gas heater? I finally decided to go down the cellar this morning and take it away and destroy it. But it's gone! Imagine? He took it away himself, it isn't there! [*She listens.*] When? Oh, then you took it. Oh—nothing, it's just that I'd hoped he'd taken it away himself. Oh, I'm not worried, darling, because this morning he left in such high spirits, it was like the old days! I'm not afraid any more. Did Mr. Oliver see you? . . . Well, you wait there then. And make a nice impression on him, darling. Just don't perspire too much before you see him. And have a nice time with Dad. He may have big news too! . . . That's right, a New York job. And be sweet to him tonight, dear. Be loving to him. Because he's only a little boat looking for a harbor. [*She is trembling with sorrow and joy.*] Oh, that's wonderful, Biff, you'll save his life. Thanks, darling. Just put your arm around him when he comes into the restaurant. Give him a smile. That's the boy . . . Good-by, dear. . . . You got your comb? . . . That's fine. Good-by, Biff dear.

In the middle of her speech, Howard Wagner, thirty-six, wheels in a small typewriter table on which is a wire-recording machine and proceeds to plug it in. This is on the left forestage. Light slowly fades on Linda as it rises on Howard. Howard is intent on threading the machine and only glances over his shoulder as Willy appears.

WILLY: Pst! Pst!

HOWARD: Hello, Willy, come in.

WILLY: Like to have a little talk with you, Howard.

HOWARD: Sorry to keep you waiting. I'll be with you in a minute.

WILLY: What's that, Howard?

HOWARD: Didn't you ever see one of these? Wire recorder.

WILLY: Oh. Can we talk a minute?

HOWARD: Records things. Just got delivery yesterday. Been driving me crazy, the most terrific machine I ever saw in my life. I was up all night with it.

WILLY: What do you do with it?

HOWARD: I bought it for dictation, but you can do anything with it. Listen to this. I had it home last night. Listen to what I picked up. The first one is my daughter. Get this. [*He flicks the switch and "Roll Out the Barrel" is heard being whistled.*] Listen to that kid whistle.

WILLY: That is lifelike, isn't it?

HOWARD: Seven years old. Get that tone.

WILLY: Ts, ts. Like to ask a little favor if you . . .

The whistling breaks off, and the voice of Howard's daughter is heard.

HIS DAUGHTER: "Now you, Daddy."

HOWARD: She's crazy for me! [*Again the same song is whistled.*] That's me! Ha! [*He winks.*]

WILLY: You're very good!

The whistling breaks off again. The machine runs silent for a moment.

HOWARD: Sh! Get this now, this is my son.

HIS SON: "The capital of Alabama is Montgomery; the capital of Arizona is Phoenix; the capital of Arkansas is Little Rock; the capital of California is Sacramento . . . " [*and on, and on.*]

HOWARD [*holding up five fingers*]:   Five years old, Willy!

WILLY: He'll make an announcer some day!

HIS SON [*continuing*]:   "The capital . . . "

HOWARD: Get that—alphabetical order! [*The machine breaks off suddenly.*] Wait a minute. The maid kicked the plug out.

WILLY: It certainly is a . . .

HOWARD: Sh, for God's sake!

HIS SON: "It's nine o'clock, Bulova watch time. So I have to go to sleep."

WILLY: That really is . . .

HOWARD: Wait a minute! The next is my wife.

They wait.

ARTHUR MILLER

HOWARD'S VOICE: "Go on, say something." [*Pause.*] "Well, you gonna talk?"

HIS WIFE: "I can't think of anything."

HOWARD'S VOICE: "Well, talk—it's turning."

HIS WIFE [*shyly, beaten*]:   "Hello." [*Silence.*] "Oh, Howard, I can't talk into this . . . "

HOWARD [*snapping the machine off*]:   That was my wife.

WILLY: That is a wonderful machine. Can we . . .

HOWARD: I tell you, Willy, I'm gonna take my camera, and my bandsaw, and all my hobbies, and out they go. This is the most fascinating relaxation I ever found.

WILLY: I think I'll get one myself.

HOWARD: Sure, they're only a hundred and a half. You can't do without it. Supposing you wanna hear Jack Benny, see? But you can't be at home at that hour. So you tell the maid to turn the radio on when Jack Benny comes on, and this automatically goes on with the radio . . .

WILLY: And when you come home you . . .

HOWARD: You can come home twelve o'clock, one o'clock, any time you like, and you get yourself a Coke and sit yourself down, throw the switch, and there's Jack Benny's program in the middle of the night!

WILLY: I'm definitely going to get one. Because lots of times I'm on the road, and I think to myself, what I must be missing on the radio!

HOWARD: Don't you have a radio in the car?

WILLY: Well, yeah, but who ever thinks of turning it on?

HOWARD: Say, aren't you supposed to be in Boston?

WILLY: That's what I want to talk to you about, Howard. You got a minute? [*He draws a chair in from the wing.*]

HOWARD: What happened? What're you doing here?

WILLY: Well . . .

HOWARD: You didn't crack up again, did you?

WILLY: Oh, no. No . . .

HOWARD: Geez, you had me worried there for a minute. What's the trouble?

WILLY: Well, tell you the truth, Howard. I've come to the decision that I'd rather not travel any more.

HOWARD: Not travel! Well, what'll you do?

WILLY: Remember, Christmas time, when you had the party here? You said you'd try to think of some spot for me here in town.

HOWARD: With us?

WILLY: Well, sure.

HOWARD: Oh, yeah, yeah. I remember. Well, I couldn't think of anything for you, Willy.

WILLY: I tell ya, Howard. The kids are all grown up, y'know. I don't need much any more. If I could take home—well, sixty-five dollars a week, I could swing it.

HOWARD: Yeah, but Willy, see I . . .

WILLY: I tell ya why, Howard. Speaking frankly and between the two of us, y'know—I'm just a little tired.

HOWARD: Oh, I could understand that, Willy. But you're a road man, Willy, and we do a road business. We've only got a half-dozen salesmen on the floor here.

WILLY: God knows, Howard. I never asked a favor of any man. But I was with the firm when your father used to carry you in here in his arms.

HOWARD: I know that, Willy, but . . .

WILLY: Your father came to me the day you were born and asked me what I thought of the name Howard, may he rest in peace.

HOWARD: I appreciate that, Willy, but there just is no spot here for you. If I had a spot I'd slam you right in, but I just don't have a single solitary spot.

He looks for his lighter. Willy has picked it up and gives it to him. Pause.

WILLY [*with increasing anger*]:   Howard, all I need to set my table is fifty dollars a week.

HOWARD: But where am I going to put you, kid?

WILLY: Look, it isn't a question of whether I can sell merchandise, is it?

HOWARD: No, but it's business, kid, and everybody's gotta pull his own weight.

WILLY [*desperately*]:   Just let me tell you a story, Howard . . .

HOWARD: 'Cause you gotta admit, business is business.

WILLY [*angrily*]:   Business is definitely business, but just listen for a minute. You don't understand this. When I was a boy—eighteen, nineteen—I was already on the road. And there was a question in my mind as to whether selling had a future for me. Because in those days I had a yearning to go to Alaska. See, there were three gold strikes in one month in Alaska, and I felt like going out. Just for the ride, you might say.

HOWARD [*barely interested*]: Don't say.

WILLY: Oh, yeah, my father lived many years in Alaska. He was an adventurous man. We've got quite a little streak of self-reliance in our family. I thought I'd go out with my older brother and try to locate him, and maybe settle in the North with the old man. And I was almost decided to go, when I met a salesman in the Parker House. His name was Dave Singleman. And he was eighty-four years old, and he'd drummed merchandise in thirty-one states. And old Dave, he'd go up to his room, y'understand, put on his green velvet slippers—I'll never forget—and pick up his phone and call the buyers, and without ever leaving his room, at the age of eighty-four, he made his living. And when I saw that, I realized that selling was the greatest career a man could want. 'Cause what could be more satisfying than to be able to go, at the age of eight-four, into twenty or thirty different cities, and pick up a phone, and be remembered and loved and helped by so many different people? Do you know? when he died—and by the way he died the death of a salesman, in his green velvet slippers in the smoker of the New York, New Haven and Hartford, going into Boston—when he died, hundreds of salesmen and buyers were at his funeral. Things were sad on a lotta trains for months after that. [*He stands up, Howard has not looked at him.*] In those days there was personality in it, Howard. There was respect, and comradeship, and gratitude in it. Today, it's all cut and dried, and there's no chance for bringing friendship to bear—or personality. You see what I mean? They don't know me any more.

HOWARD [*moving away, to the right*]: That's just the thing, Willy.

WILLY: If I had forty dollars a week—that's all I'd need. Forty dollars, Howard.

HOWARD: Kid, I can't take blood from a stone, I . . .

WILLY [*desperation is on him now*]: Howard, the year Al Smith was nominated, your father came to me and . . .

HOWARD [*starting to go off*]: I've got to see some people, kid.

WILLY [*stopping him*]: I'm talking about your father! There were promises made across this desk! You mustn't tell me you've got people to see—I put thirty-four years into this firm, Howard, and now I can't pay my insurance! You can't eat the orange and throw the peel away—a man is not a piece of fruit! [*After a pause.*] Now pay attention. Your father—in 1928 I had a big year. I averaged a hundred and seventy dollars a week in commissions.

HOWARD [*impatiently*]:   Now, Willy, you never averaged . . .

WILLY [*banging his hand on the desk*]:   I averaged a hundred and seventy dollars a week in the year of 1928! And your father came to me—or rather, I was in the office here—it was right over this desk—and he put his hand on my shoulder . . .

HOWARD [*getting up*]:   You'll have to excuse me, Willy, I gotta see some people. Pull yourself together. [*Going out.*] I'll be back in a little while.

[*On Howard's exit, the light on his chair grows very bright and strange.*]

WILLY: Pull myself together! What the hell did I say to him? My God, I was yelling at him! How could I? [*Willy breaks off, staring at the light, which occupies the chair, animating it. He approaches this chair, standing across the desk from it.*] Frank, Frank, don't you remember what you told me that time? How you put your hand on my shoulder, and Frank . . . [*He leans on the desk and as he speaks the dead man's name he accidentally switches on the recorder, and instantly—*]

HOWARD'S SON: " . . . of New York is Albany. The capital of Ohio is Cincinnati, the capital of Rhode Island is . . . " [*The recitation continues.*]

WILLY [*leaping away with fright, shouting*]:   Ha! Howard! Howard! Howard!

HOWARD [*rushing in*]:   What happened?

WILLY [*pointing at the machine, which continues nasally, childishly, with the capital cities*]:   Shut it off! Shut it off!

HOWARD [*pulling the plug out*]:   Look, Willy . . .

WILLY [*pressing his hands to his eyes*]:   I gotta get myself some coffee. I'll get some coffee . . .

Willy starts to walk out. Howard stops him.

HOWARD [*rolling up the cord*]:   Willy, look . . .

WILLY: I'll go to Boston.

HOWARD: Willy, you can't go to Boston for us.

WILLY: Why can't I go?

HOWARD: I don't want you to represent us. I've been meaning to tell you for a long time now.

WILLY: Howard, are you firing me?

HOWARD: I think you need a good long rest, Willy.

WILLY: Howard . . .

HOWARD: And when you feel better, come back, and we'll see if we can work something out.

WILLY: But I gotta earn money, Howard. I'm in no position to . . .

HOWARD: Where are your sons? Why don't your sons give you a hand?

WILLY: They're working on a very big deal.

HOWARD: This is no time for false pride, Willy. You go to your sons and you tell them that you're tired. You've got two great boys, haven't you?

WILLY: Oh, no question, no question, but in the meantime . . .

HOWARD: Then that's that, heh?

WILLY: All right, I'll go to Boston tomorrow.

HOWARD: No, no.

WILLY: I can't throw myself on my sons. I'm not a cripple!

HOWARD: Look, kid, I'm busy this morning.

WILLY [*grasping Howard's arm*]: Howard, you've got to let me go to Boston!

HOWARD [*hard, keeping himself under control*]: I've got a line of people to see this morning. Sit down, take five minutes, and pull yourself together, and then go home, will ya? I need the office, Willy. [*He starts to go, turns, remembering the recorder, starts to push off the table holding the recorder.*] Oh, yeah. Whenever you can this week, stop by and drop off the samples. You'll feel better, Willy, and then come back and we'll talk. Pull yourself together, kid, there's people outside.

Howard exits, pushing the table off left. Willy stares into space, exhausted. Now the music is heard—Ben's music—first distantly, then closer, closer. As Willy speaks, Ben enters from the right. He carries valise and umbrella.

WILLY: Oh, Ben, how did you do it? What is the answer? Did you wind up the Alaska deal already?

BEN: Doesn't take much time if you know what you're doing. Just a short business trip. Boarding ship in an hour. Wanted to say good-by.

WILLY: Ben, I've got to talk to you.

BEN [*glancing at his watch*]: Haven't the time, William.

WILLY [*crossing the apron to Ben*]: Ben, nothing's working out. I don't know what to do.

BEN: Now, look here, William. I've bought timberland in Alaska and I need a man to look after things for me.

WILLY: God, timberland! Me and my boys in those grand outdoors!

BEN: You've a new continent at your doorstep, William. Get out of these cities, they're full of talk and time payments and courts of law. Screw on your fists and you can fight for a fortune up there.

WILLY: Yes, yes! Linda, Linda!

Linda enters as of old, with the wash.

LINDA: Oh, you're back?

BEN: I haven't much time.

WILLY: No, wait! Linda, he's got a proposition for me in Alaska.

LINDA: But you've got . . . [*To Ben.*] He's got a beautiful job here.

WILLY: But in Alaska, kid, I could . . .

LINDA: You're doing well enough, Willy!

BEN [*to Linda*]:   Enough for what, my dear?

LINDA [*frightened of Ben and angry at him*]:   Don't say those things to him! Enough to be happy right here, right now. [*To Willy, while Ben laughs.*] Why must everybody conquer the world? You're well liked, and the boys love you, and someday—[*To Ben*]—why, old man Wagner told him just the other day that if he keeps it up he'll be a member of the firm, didn't he, Willy?

WILLY: Sure, sure. I am building something with this firm, Ben, and if a man is building something he must be on the right track, mustn't he?

BEN: What are you building? Lay your hand on it. Where is it?

WILLY [*hesitantly*]:   That's true, Linda, there's nothing.

LINDA: Why? [*To Ben.*] There's a man eighty-four years old . . .

WILLY: That's right, Ben, that's right. When I look at that man I say, what is there to worry about?

BEN: Bah!

WILLY: It's true, Ben. All he has to do is go into any city, pick up the phone, and he's making his living and you know why?

BEN [*picking up his valise*]:   I've got to go.

WILLY [*holding BEN back*]:   Look at this boy!

Biff, in his high school sweater, enters carrying suitcase. Happy carries Biff's shoulder guards, gold helmet, and football pants.

WILLY: Without a penny to his name, three great universities are begging for him, and from there the sky's the limit, because it's not what you do, Ben. It's who you know and the smile on your face! It's contacts, Ben, contacts! The whole wealth of Alaska passes over the lunch table at the Commodore Hotel, and that's the wonder, the wonder of this country, that a man can end with diamonds here on the basis of being liked! [*He turns to Biff.*] And that's why when you get out on that field today it's important. Because thousands of people will be rooting for you and loving you. [*To Ben, who has again begun to leave.*] And Ben! when he walks into a business office his name will sound out like a bell and all the doors will open to him! I've seen it, Ben, I've seen it a thousand times! You can't feel it with your hand like timber, but it's there!

BEN: Good-by, William.

WILLY: Ben, am I right? Don't you think I'm right? I value your advice.

BEN: There's a new continent at your doorstep, William. You could walk out rich. Rich! [*He is gone.*]

WILLY: We'll do it here, Ben! You hear me? We're gonna do it here!

Young Bernard rushes in. The gay music of the Boys is heard.

BERNARD: Oh, gee, I was afraid you left already!

WILLY: Why? What time is it?

BERNARD: It's half-past one!

WILLY: Well, come on, everybody! Ebbets Field next stop! Where's the pennants? [*He rushes through the wall-line of the kitchen and out into the living room.*]

LINDA [*to Biff*]: Did you pack fresh underwear?

BIFF [*who has been limbering up*]: I want to go!

BERNARD: Biff, I'm carrying your helmet, ain't I?

HAPPY: No, I'm carrying the helmet.

BERNARD: Oh, Biff, you promised me.

HAPPY: I'm carrying the helmet.

BERNARD: How am I going to get in the locker room?

LINDA: Let him carry the shoulder guards. [*She puts her coat and hat on in the kitchen.*]

BERNARD: Can I, Biff? 'Cause I told everybody I'm going to be in the locker room.

HAPPY: In Ebbets Field it's the clubhouse.

BERNARD: I meant the clubhouse. Biff!

HAPPY: Biff!

BIFF [*grandly, after a slight pause*]: Let him carry the shoulder guards.

HAPPY [*as he gives Bernard the shoulder guards*]: Stay close to us now.

Willy rushes in with the pennants.

WILLY [handing them out]:   Everybody wave when Biff comes out on the field. [Happy and Bernard run off.] You set now, boy?

The music has died away.

BIFF: Ready to go, Pop. Every muscle is ready.

WILLY [at the edge of the apron]:   You realize what this means?

BIFF: That's right, Pop.

WILLY [feeling Biff's muscles]:   You're comin' home this afternoon captain of the All-Scholastic Championship Team of the City of New York.

BIFF: I got it, Pop. And remember, pal, when I take off my helmet, that touchdown is for you.

WILLY: Let's go! [He is starting out, with his arm around Biff, when Charley enters, as of old, in knickers.] I got no room for you, Charley.

CHARLEY: Room? For what?

WILLY: In the car.

CHARLEY: You goin' for a ride? I wanted to shoot some casino.

WILLY [furiously]:   Casino! [Incredulously.] Don't you realize what to-day is?

LINDA: Oh, he knows, Willy. He's just kidding you.

WILLY: That's nothing to kid about!

CHARLEY: No, Linda, what's goin' on?

LINDA: He's playing in Ebbets Field.

CHARLEY: Baseball in this weather?

WILLY: Don't talk to him. Come on, come on! [He is pushing them out.]

CHARLEY: Wait a minute, didn't you hear the news?

WILLY: What?

CHARLEY: Don't you listen to the radio? Ebbets Field just blew up.

WILLY: You go to hell! [Charley laughs. Pushing them out.] Come on, come on! We're late.

CHARLEY [as they go]:   Knock a homer, Biff, knock a homer!

WILLY [the last to leave, turning to Charley]:   I don't think that was funny, Charley. This is the greatest day of his life.

CHARLEY: Willy, when are you going to grow up?

WILLY: Yeah, heh? When this game is over, Charley, you'll be laughing out of the other side of your face. They'll be calling him another Red Grange. Twenty-five thousand a year.

CHARLEY [kidding]:   Is that so?

WILLY: Yeah, that's so.

CHARLEY: Well, then, I'm sorry, Willy. But tell me something.

WILLY: What?

CHARLEY: Who is Red Grange?

WILLY: Put up your hands. Goddam you, put up your hands!

Charley, chuckling, shakes his head and walks away, around the left corner of the stage. Willy follows him. The music rises to a mocking frenzy.

WILLY: Who the hell do you think you are, better than everybody else? You don't know everything, you big, ignorant, stupid . . . Put up your hands!

Light rises, on the right side of the forestage, on a small table in the reception room of Charley's office. Traffic sounds are heard. Bernard, now mature, sits whistling to himself. A pair of tennis rackets and an old overnight bag are on the floor beside him.

WILLY [*offstage*]: What are you walking away for? Don't walk away! If you're going to say something say it to my face! I know you laugh at me behind my back. You'll laugh out of the other side of your goddam face after this game. Touchdown! Touchdown! Eighty thousand people! Touchdown! Right between the goal posts.

Bernard is a quiet, earnest, but self-assured young man. Willy's voice is coming from right upstage now. Bernard lowers his feet off the table and listens. Jenny, his father's secretary, enters.

JENNY [*distressed*]: Say, Bernard, will you go out in the hall?

BERNARD: What is that noise? Who is it?

JENNY: Mr. Loman. He just got off the elevator.

BERNARD [*getting up*]: Who's he arguing with?

JENNY: Nobody. There's nobody with him. I can't deal with him any more, and your father gets all upset every time he comes. I've got a lot of typing to do, and your father's waiting to sign it. Will you see him?

WILLY [*entering*]: Touchdown! Touch—[*He sees Jenny.*] Jenny, Jenny, good to see you. How're ya? Workin'? Or still honest?

JENNY: Fine. How've you been feeling?

WILLY: Not much any more, Jenny. Ha, ha! [*He is surprised to see the rackets.*]

BERNARD: Hello, Uncle Willy.

WILLY [*almost shocked*]: Bernard! Well, look who's here! [*He comes quickly, guiltily, to Bernard and warmly shakes his hand.*]

BERNARD: How are you? Good to see you.

WILLY: What are you doing here?

BERNARD: Oh, just stopped by to see Pop. Get off my feet till my train leaves. I'm going to Washington in a few minutes.

WILLY: Is he in?

BERNARD: Yes, he's in his office with the accountant. Sit down.

WILLY [*sitting down*]: What're you going to do in Washington?

BERNARD: Oh, just a case I've got there, Willy.

WILLY: That so? [*Indicating the rackets.*] You going to play tennis there?

BERNARD: I'm staying with a friend who's got a court.

WILLY: Don't say. His own tennis court. Must be fine people, I bet.

BERNARD: They are, very nice. Dad tells me Biff's in town.

WILLY [*with a big smile*]: Yeah, Biff's in. Working on a very big deal, Bernard.

BERNARD: What's Biff doing?

WILLY: Well, he's been doing very big things in the West. But he decided to establish himself here. Very big. We're having dinner. Did I hear your wife had a boy?

BERNARD: That's right. Our second.

WILLY: Two boys! What do you know!

BERNARD: What kind of a deal has Biff got?

WILLY: Well, Bill Oliver—very big sporting-goods man—he wants Biff very badly. Called him in from the West. Long distance, carte blanche, special deliveries. Your friends have their own private tennis court?

BERNARD: You still with the old firm, Willy?

WILLY [*after a pause*]: I'm—I'm overjoyed to see how you made the grade, Bernard, overjoyed. It's an encouraging thing to see a young man really—really . . . Looks very good for Biff—very . . . [*He breaks off, then.*] Bernard . . . [*He is so full of emotion, he breaks off again.*]

BERNARD: What is it, Willy?

WILLY [*small and alone*]: What—what's the secret?

BERNARD: What secret?

WILLY: How—how did you? Why didn't he ever catch on?

BERNARD: I wouldn't know that, Willy.

WILLY [*confidentially, desperately*]: You were his friend, his boyhood friend. There's something I don't understand about it. His life ended after that Ebbets Field game. From the age of seventeen nothing good ever happened to him.

BERNARD: He never trained himself for anything.

WILLY: But he did, he did. After high school he took so many correspondence courses. Radio mechanics; television; God knows what,
and never made the slightest mark.

BERNARD [*taking off his glasses*]:   Willy, do you want to talk candidly?

WILLY [*rising, faces Bernard*]:   I regard you as a very brilliant man,
Bernard. I value your advice.

BERNARD: Oh, the hell with the advice, Willy. I couldn't advise you.
There's just one thing I've always wanted to ask you. When he was
supposed to graduate, and the math teacher flunked him . . .

WILLY: Oh, that son-of-a-bitch ruined his life.

BERNARD: Yeah, but, Willy, all he had to do was go to summer school
and make up that subject.

WILLY: That's right, that's right.

BERNARD: Did you tell him not to go to summer school?

WILLY: Me? I begged him to go. I ordered him to go!

BERNARD: Then why wouldn't he go?

WILLY: Why? Why! Bernard, that question has been trailing me like a
ghost for the last fifteen years. He flunked the subject, and laid
down and died like a hammer hit him!

BERNARD: Take it easy, kid.

WILLY: Let me talk to you—I got nobody to talk to. Bernard, Bernard,
was it my fault? Y'see? It keeps going around in my mind, maybe
I did something to him. I got nothing to give him.

BERNARD: Don't take it so hard.

WILLY: Why did he lay down? What is the story there? You were his
friend!

BERNARD: Willy, I remember, it was June, and our grades came out.
And he'd flunked math.

WILLY: That son-of-a-bitch!

BERNARD: No, it wasn't right then. Biff just got very angry, I remember, and he was ready to enroll in summer school.

WILLY [*surprised*]:   He was?

BERNARD: He wasn't beaten by it at all. But then, Willy, he disappeared
from the block for almost a month. And I got the idea that he'd gone
up to New England to see you. Did he have a talk with you then?

Willy stares in silence.

BERNARD: Willy?

WILLY [*with a strong edge of resentment in his voice*]: Yeah, he came to Boston. What about it?

BERNARD: Well, just that when he came back—I'll never forget this, it always mystifies me. Because I'd thought so well of Biff, even though he'd always taken advantage of me. I loved him, Willy, y'know? And he came back after that month and took his sneakers—remember those sneakers with "University of Virginia" printed on them? He was so proud of those, wore them every day. And he took them down in the cellar, and burned them up in the furnace. We had a fist fight. It lasted at least half an hour. Just the two of us, punching each other down the cellar, and crying right through it. I've often thought of how strange it was that I knew he'd given up his life. What happened in Boston, Willy?

Willy looks at him as at an intruder.

BERNARD: I just bring it up because you asked me.

WILLY [*angrily*]: Nothing. What do you mean, "What happened?" What's that got to do with anything?

BERNARD: Well, don't get sore.

WILLY: What are you trying to do, blame it on me? If a boy lays down is that my fault?

BERNARD: Now, Willy, don't get . . .

WILLY: Well, don't—don't talk to me that way! What does that mean, "What happened?"

Charley enters. He is in his vest, and he carries a bottle of bourbon.

CHARLEY: Hey, you're going to miss that train. [*He waves the bottle.*]

BERNARD: Yeah, I'm going. [*He takes the bottle.*] Thanks, Pop. [*He picks up his rackets and bag.*] Good-by, Willy, and don't worry about it. You know, "If at first you don't succeed . . ."

WILLY: Yes, I believe in that.

BERNARD: But sometimes, Willy, it's better for a man just to walk away.

WILLY: Walk away?

BERNARD: That's right.

WILLY: But if you can't walk away?

BERNARD [*after a slight pause*]: I guess that's when it's tough. [*Extending his hand.*] Good-by, Willy.

WILLY [*shaking Bernard's hand*]: Good-by, boy.

CHARLEY [*an arm on Bernard's shoulder*]: How do you like this kid? Gonna argue a case in front of the Supreme Court.

BERNARD [*protesting*]: Pop!

WILLY [*genuinely shocked, pained, and happy*]: No! The Supreme Court!

BERNARD: I gotta run. 'By, Dad!

CHARLEY: Knock 'em dead, Bernard!

Bernard goes off.

WILLY [*as Charley takes out his wallet*]: The Supreme Court! And he didn't even mention it!

CHARLEY [*counting out money on the desk*]: He don't have to—he's gonna do it.

WILLY: And you never told him what to do, did you? You never took any interest in him.

CHARLEY: My salvation is that I never took any interest in anything. There's some money—fifty dollars. I got an accountant inside.

WILLY: Charley, look . . . [*with difficulty.*] I got my insurance to pay. If you can manage it—I need a hundred and ten dollars.

Charley doesn't reply for a moment; merely stops moving.

WILLY: I'd draw it from my bank but Linda would know, and I . . .

CHARLEY: Sit down, Willy.

WILLY [*moving toward the chair*]: I'm keeping an account of everything, remember. I'll pay every penny back. [*He sits.*]

CHARLEY: Now listen to me, Willy.

WILLY: I want you to know I appreciate . . .

CHARLEY [*sitting down on the table*]: Willy, what're you doin'? What the hell is going on in your head?

WILLY: Why? I'm simply . . .

CHARLEY: I offered you a job. You make fifty dollars a week. And I won't send you on the road.

WILLY: I've got a job.

CHARLEY: Without pay? What kind of a job is a job without pay? [*He rises.*] Now, look, kid, enough is enough. I'm no genius but I know when I'm being insulted.

WILLY: Insulted!

CHARLEY: Why don't you want to work for me?

WILLY: What's the matter with you? I've got a job.

CHARLEY: Then what're you walkin' in here every week for?

WILLY [*getting up*]: Well, if you don't want me to walk in here . . .

CHARLEY: I'm offering you a job.

WILLY: I don't want your goddam job!

ARTHUR MILLER

408

CHARLEY: When the hell are you going to grow up?

WILLY [*furiously*]: You big ignoramus, if you say that to me again I'll rap you one! I don't care how big you are! [*He's ready to fight.*]

Pause.

CHARLEY [*kindly, going to him*]: How much do you need, Willy?

WILLY: Charley, I'm strapped. I'm strapped. I don't know what to do. I was just fired.

CHARLEY: Howard fired you?

WILLY: That snotnose. Imagine that? I named him. I named him Howard.

CHARLEY: Willy, when're you gonna realize that them things don't mean anything? You named him Howard, but you can't sell that. The only thing you got in this world is what you can sell. And the funny thing is that you're a salesman, and you don't know that.

WILLY: I've always tried to think otherwise, I guess. I always felt that if a man was impressive, and well liked, that nothing . . .

CHARLEY: Why must everybody like you? Who liked J. P. Morgan? Was he impressive? In a Turkish bath he'd look like a butcher. But with his pockets on he was very well liked. Now listen, Willy, I know you don't like me, and nobody can say I'm in love with you, but I'll give you a job because—just for the hell of it, put it that way. Now what do you say?

WILLY: I—I just can't work for you, Charley.

CHARLEY: What're you, jealous of me?

WILLY: I can't work for you, that's all, don't ask me why.

CHARLEY [*angered, takes out more bills*]: You been jealous of me all your life, you damned fool! Here, pay your insurance. [*He puts the money in Willy's hand.*]

WILLY: I'm keeping strict accounts.

CHARLEY: I've got some work to do. Take care of yourself. And pay your insurance.

WILLY [*moving to the right*]: Funny, y'know? After all the highways, and the trains, and the appointments, and the years, you end up worth more dead than alive.

CHARLEY: Willy, nobody's worth nothin' dead. [*After a slight pause.*] Did you hear what I said?

Willy stands still, dreaming.

CHARLEY: Willy!

WILLY: Apologize to Bernard for me when you see him. I didn't mean to argue with him. He's a fine boy. They're all fine boys, and they'll end up big—all of them. Someday they'll all play tennis together. Wish me luck, Charley. He saw Bill Oliver today.

CHARLEY: Good luck.

WILLY [*on the verge of tears*]: Charley, you're the only friend I got. Isn't that a remarkable thing? [*He goes out.*]

CHARLEY: Jesus!

Charley stares after him a moment and follows. All light blacks out. Suddenly raucous music is heard, and a red glow rises behind the screen at right. Stanley, a young waiter, appears, carrying a table, followed by Happy, who is carrying two chairs.

STANLEY [*putting the table down*]: That's all right, Mr. Loman, I can handle it myself. [*He turns and takes the chairs from Happy and places them at the table.*]

HAPPY [*glancing around*]: Oh, this is better.

STANLEY: Sure, in the front there you're in the middle of all kinds of noise. Whenever you got a party, Mr. Loman, you just tell me and I'll put you back here. Y'know, there's a lotta people they don't like it private, because when they go out they like to see a lotta action around them because they're sick and tired to stay in the house by theirself. But I know you, you ain't from Hackensack. You know what I mean?

HAPPY [*sitting down*]: So how's it coming, Stanley?

STANLEY: Ah, it's a dog life. I only wish during the war they'd a took me in the Army. I coulda been dead by now.

HAPPY: My brother's back, Stanley.

STANLEY: Oh, he come back, heh? From the Far West.

HAPPY: Yeah, big cattle man, my brother, so treat him right. And my father's coming too.

STANLEY: Oh, your father too!

HAPPY: You got a couple of nice lobsters?

STANLEY: Hundred per cent, big.

HAPPY: I want them with the claws.

STANLEY: Don't worry, I don't give you no mice. [*Happy laughs.*] How about some wine? It'll put a head on the meal.

HAPPY: No. You remember, Stanley, that recipe I brought you from overseas? With the champagne in it?

ARTHUR MILLER

STANLEY: Oh, yeah, sure. I still got it tacked up yet in the kitchen. But that'll have to cost a buck apiece anyways.

HAPPY: That's all right.

STANLEY: What'd you, hit a number or somethin'?

HAPPY: No, it's a little celebration. My brother is—I think he pulled off a big deal today. I think we're going into business together.

STANLEY: Great! That's the best for you. Because a family business, you know what I mean?—that's the best.

HAPPY: That's what I think.

STANLEY: 'Cause what's the difference? Somebody steals? It's in the family. Know what I mean? [*Sotto voce.*] Like this bartender here. The boss is goin' crazy what kinda leak he's got in the cash register. You put it in but it don't come out.

HAPPY [*raising his head*]: Sh!

STANLEY: What?

HAPPY: You notice I wasn't lookin' right or left, was I?

STANLEY: No.

HAPPY: And my eyes are closed.

STANLEY: So what's the . . . ?

HAPPY: Strudel's comin'.

STANLEY [*catching on, looks around*]: Ah, no, there's no . . .

He breaks off as a furred, lavishly dressed Girl enters and sits at the next table. Both follow her with their eyes.

STANLEY: Geez, how'd ya know?

HAPPY: I got radar or something. [*Staring directly at her profile.*] Oooooooo . . . Stanley.

STANLEY: I think that's for you, Mr. Loman.

HAPPY: Look at that mouth. Oh, God. And the binoculars.

STANLEY: Geez, you got a life, Mr. Loman.

HAPPY: Wait on her.

STANLEY [*going to the Girl's table*]: Would you like a menu, ma'am?

GIRL: I'm expecting someone, but I'd like a . . .

HAPPY: Why don't you bring her—excuse me, miss, do you mind? I sell champagne, and I'd like you to try my brand. Bring her a champagne, Stanley.

GIRL: That's awfully nice of you.

HAPPY: Don't mention it. It's all company money. [*He laughs.*]

GIRL: That's a charming product to be selling, isn't it?

HAPPY: Oh, gets to be like everything else. Selling is selling, y'know.

GIRL: I suppose.

HAPPY: You don't happen to sell, do you?

GIRL: No, I don't sell.

HAPPY: Would you object to a compliment from a stranger? You ought to be on a magazine cover.

GIRL [looking at him a little archly]: I have been.

Stanley comes in with a glass of champagne.

HAPPY: What'd I say before, Stanley? You see? She's a cover girl.

STANLEY: Oh, I could see, I could see.

HAPPY [to the Girl]: What magazine?

GIRL: Oh, a lot of them. [She takes the drink.] Thank you.

HAPPY: You know what they say in France, don't you? "Champagne is the drink of the complexion"—Hya, Biff!

Biff has entered and sits with Happy.

BIFF: Hello, kid. Sorry I'm late.

HAPPY: I just got here. Uh, Miss . . . ?

GIRL: Forsythe.

HAPPY: Miss Forsythe, this is my brother.

BIFF: Is Dad here?

HAPPY: His name is Biff. You might've heard of him. Great football player.

GIRL: Really? What team?

HAPPY: Are you familiar with football?

GIRL: No, I'm afraid I'm not.

HAPPY: Biff is quarterback with the New York Giants.

GIRL: Well, that is nice, isn't it? [She drinks.]

HAPPY: Good health.

GIRL: I'm happy to meet you.

HAPPY: That's my name. Hap. It's really Harold, but at West Point they called me Happy.

GIRL [now really impressed]: Oh, I see. How do you do? [She turns her profile.]

BIFF: Isn't Dad coming?

HAPPY: You want her?

BIFF: Oh, I could never make that.

HAPPY: I remember the time that idea would never come into your head. Where's the old confidence, Biff?

BIFF: I just saw Oliver . . .

HAPPY: Wait a minute. I've got to see that old confidence again. Do you want her? She's on call.

BIFF: Oh, no. [*He turns to look at the Girl.*]

HAPPY: I'm telling you. Watch this. [*Turning to the Girl.*] Honey? [*She turns to him.*] Are you busy?

GIRL: Well, I am . . . but I could make a phone call.

HAPPY: Do that, will you, honey? And see if you can get a friend. We'll be here for a while. Biff is one of the greatest football players in the country.

GIRL [*standing up*]: Well, I'm certainly happy to meet you.

HAPPY: Come back soon.

GIRL: I'll try.

HAPPY: Don't try, honey, try hard.

The Girl exits. Stanley follows, shaking his head in bewildered admiration.

HAPPY: Isn't that a shame now? A beautiful girl like that? That's why I can't get married. There's not a good woman in a thousand. New York is loaded with them, kid!

BIFF: Hap, look . . .

HAPPY: I told you she was on call!

BIFF [*strangely unnerved*]: Cut it out, will ya? I want to say something to you.

HAPPY: Did you see Oliver?

BIFF: I saw him all right. Now look, I want to tell Dad a couple of things and I want you to help me.

HAPPY: What? Is he going to back you?

BIFF: Are you crazy? You're out of your goddam head, you know that?

HAPPY: Why? What happened?

BIFF [*breathlessly*]: I did a terrible thing today, Hap. It's been the strangest day I ever went through. I'm all numb, I swear.

HAPPY: You mean he wouldn't see you?

BIFF: Well, I waited six hours for him, see? All day. Kept sending my name in. Even tried to date his secretary so she'd get me to him, but no soap.

HAPPY: Because you're not showin' the old confidence, Biff. He remembered you, didn't he?

BIFF [*stopping Happy with a gesture*]: Finally, about five o'clock, he comes out. Didn't remember who I was or anything. I felt like such an idiot, Hap.

HAPPY: Did you tell him my Florida idea?

BIFF: He walked away. I saw him for one minute. I got so mad I could've torn the walls down! How the hell did I ever get the idea I was a salesman there? I even believed myself that I'd been a salesman for him! And then he gave me one look and—I realized what a ridiculous lie my whole life has been! We've been talking in a dream for fifteen years. I was a shipping clerk.

HAPPY: What'd you do?

BIFF [*with great tension and wonder*]: Well, he left, see. And the secretary went out. I was all alone in the waiting room. I don't know what came over me, Hap. The next thing I know I'm in his office—paneled walls, everything. I can't explain it. I—Hap. I took his fountain pen.

HAPPY: Geez, did he catch you?

BIFF: I ran out. I ran down all eleven flights. I ran and ran and ran.

HAPPY: That was an awful dumb—what'd you do that for?

BIFF [*agonized*]: I don't know, I just—wanted to take something, I don't know. You gotta help me, Hap. I'm gonna tell Pop.

HAPPY: You crazy? What for?

BIFF: Hap, he's got to understand that I'm not the man somebody lends that kind of money to. He thinks I've been spiting him all these years and it's eating him up.

HAPPY: That's just it. You tell him something nice.

BIFF: I can't.

HAPPY: Say you got a lunch date with Oliver tomorrow.

BIFF: So what do I do tomorrow?

HAPPY: You leave the house tomorrow and come back at night and say Oliver is thinking it over. And he thinks it over for a couple of weeks, and gradually it fades away and nobody's the worse.

BIFF: But it'll go on forever!

HAPPY: Dad is never so happy as when he's looking forward to something!

Willy enters.

HAPPY: Hello, scout!

WILLY: Gee, I haven't been here in years!

Stanley has followed Willy in and sets a chair for him. Stanley starts off but Happy stops him.

HAPPY: Stanley!

Stanley stands by, waiting for an order.

BIFF [*going to Willy with guilt, as to an invalid*]: Sit down, Pop. You want a drink?

WILLY: Sure, I don't mind.

BIFF: Let's get a load on.

WILLY: You look worried.

BIFF: N-no. [*To Stanley.*] Scotch all around. Make it doubles.

STANLEY: Doubles, right. [*He goes.*]

WILLY: You had a couple already, didn't you?

BIFF: Just a couple, yeah.

WILLY: Well, what happened, boy? [*Nodding affirmatively, with a smile.*] Everything go all right?

BIFF [*takes a breath, then reaches out and grasps Willy's hand*]: Pal . . . [*He is smiling bravely, and Willy is smiling too.*] I had an experience today.

HAPPY: Terrific, Pop.

WILLY: That so? What happened?

BIFF [*high, slightly alcoholic, above the earth*]: I'm going to tell you everything from first to last. It's been a strange day. [*Silence. He looks around, composes himself as best he can, but his breath keeps breaking the rhythm of his voice.*] I had to wait quite a while for him, and . . .

WILLY: Oliver?

BIFF: Yeah, Oliver. All day, as a matter of cold fact. And a lot of—instances—facts, Pop, facts about my life came back to me. Who was it, Pop? Who ever said I was a salesman with Oliver?

WILLY: Well, you were.

BIFF: No, Dad, I was a shipping clerk.

WILLY: But you were practically . . .

BIFF [*with determination*]: Dad, I don't know who said it first, but I was never a salesman for Bill Oliver.

WILLY: What're you talking about?

BIFF: Let's hold on to the facts tonight, Pop. We're not going to get anywhere bullin' around. I was a shipping clerk.

WILLY [*angrily*]: All right, now listen to me . . .

BIFF: Why don't you let me finish?

WILLY: I'm not interested in stories about the past or any crap of that kind because the woods are burning, boys, you understand? There's a big blaze going on all around. I was fired today.

BIFF [*shocked*]: How could you be?

WILLY: I was fired, and I'm looking for a little good news to tell your mother, because the woman has waited and the woman has suffered. The gist of it is that I haven't got a story left in my head, Biff. So don't give me a lecture about facts and aspects. I am not interested. Now what've you got to say to me?

Stanley enters with three drinks. They wait until he leaves.

WILLY: Did you see Oliver?

BIFF: Jesus, Dad!

WILLY: You mean you didn't go up there?

HAPPY: Sure he went up there.

BIFF: I did. I—saw him. How could they fire you?

WILLY [*on the edge of his chair*]: What kind of a welcome did he give you?

BIFF: He won't even let you work on commission?

WILLY: I'm out! [*Driving.*] So tell me, he gave you a warm welcome?

HAPPY: Sure, Pop, sure!

BIFF [*driven*]: Well, it was kind of . . .

WILLY: I was wondering if he'd remember you. [*To Happy.*] Imagine, man doesn't see him for ten, twelve years and gives him that kind of a welcome!

HAPPY: Damn right!

BIFF [*trying to return to the offensive*]: Pop, look . . .

WILLY: You know why he remembered you, don't you? Because you impressed him in those days.

BIFF: Let's talk quietly and get this down to the facts, huh?

WILLY [*as though Biff had been interrupting*]: Well, what happened? It's great news, Biff. Did he take you into his office or'd you talk in the waiting room?

BIFF: Well, he came in, see, and . . .

WILLY [*with a big smile*]: What'd he say? Betcha he threw his arm around you.

BIFF: Well, he kinda . . .

WILLY: He's a fine man. [*To Happy.*] Very hard man to see, y'know.

HAPPY [*agreeing*]: Oh, I know.

WILLY [*to Biff*]: Is that where you had the drinks?

BIFF: Yeah, he gave me a couple of—no, no!

HAPPY [*cutting in*]: He told him my Florida idea.

WILLY: Don't interrupt. [*To Biff.*] How'd he react to the Florida idea?

BIFF: Dad, will you give me a minute to explain?

WILLY: I've been waiting for you to explain since I sat down here! What happened? He took you into his office and what?

BIFF: Well—I talked. And—and he listened, see.

WILLY: Famous for the way he listens, y'know. What was his answer?

BIFF: His answer was—[*He breaks off, suddenly angry.*] Dad, you're not letting me tell you what I want to tell you!

WILLY [*accusing, angered*]: You didn't see him, did you?

BIFF: I did see him!

WILLY: What'd you insult him or something? You insulted him, didn't you?

BIFF: Listen, will you let me out of it, will you just let me out of it!

HAPPY: What the hell!

WILLY: Tell me what happened!

BIFF [*to Happy*]: I can't talk to him!

A single trumpet note jars the ear. The light of green leaves stains the house, which holds the air of night and a dream. Young Bernard enters and knocks on the door of the house.

YOUNG BERNARD [*frantically*]: Mrs. Loman, Mrs. Loman!

HAPPY: Tell him what happened!

BIFF [*to Happy.*]: Shut up and leave me alone!

WILLY: No, no! You had to go and flunk math!

BIFF: What math? What're you talking about?

YOUNG BERNARD: Mrs. Loman, Mrs. Loman!

Linda appears in the house, as of old.

WILLY [*wildly*]: Math, math, math!

BIFF: Take it easy, Pop!

YOUNG BERNARD: Mrs. Loman!

WILLY [*furiously*]: If you hadn't flunked you'd've been set by now!

BIFF: Now, look, I'm gonna tell you what happened, and you're going to listen to me.

YOUNG BERNARD: Mrs. Loman!

BIFF: I waited six hours . . .

HAPPY: What the hell are you saying?

BIFF: I kept sending in my name but he wouldn't see me. So finally he . . . [*He continues unheard as light fades low on the restaurant.*]

YOUNG BERNARD: Biff flunked math!

LINDA: No!

YOUNG BERNARD: Birnbaum flunked him! They won't graduate him!

LINDA: But they have to. He's gotta go to the university. Where is he? Biff! Biff!

YOUNG BERNARD: No, he left. He went to Grand Central.

LINDA: Grand—You mean he went to Boston!

YOUNG BERNARD: Is Uncle Willy in Boston?

LINDA: Oh, maybe Willy can talk to the teacher. Oh, the poor, poor boy!

Light on house area snaps out.

BIFF [*at the table, now audible, holding up a gold fountain pen*]: . . . so I'm washed up with Oliver, you understand? Are you listening to me?

WILLY [*at a loss*]: Yeah, sure. If you hadn't flunked . . .

BIFF: Flunked what? What're you talking about?

WILLY: Don't blame everything on me! I didn't flunk math—you did! What pen?

HAPPY: That was awful dumb, Biff, a pen like that is worth—

WILLY [*seeing the pen for the first time*]: You took Oliver's pen?

BIFF [*weakening*]: Dad, I just explained it to you.

WILLY: You stole Bill Oliver's fountain pen!

BIFF: I didn't exactly steal it! That's just what I've been explaining to you!

HAPPY: He had it in his hand and just then Oliver walked in, so he got nervous and stuck it in his pocket!

WILLY: My God, Biff!

BIFF: I never intended to do it, Dad!

OPERATOR'S VOICE: Standish Arms, good evening!

WILLY [*shouting*]: I'm not in my room!

BIFF [*frightened*]: Dad, what's the matter? [*He and Happy stand up.*]

OPERATOR: Ringing Mr. Loman for you!

WILLY: I'm not there, stop it!

BIFF [*horrified, gets down on one knee before Willy*]: Dad, I'll make good, I'll make good. [*Willy tries to get to his feet. Biff holds him down.*] Sit down now.

WILLY: No, you're no good, you're no good for anything.

BIFF: I am, Dad, I'll find something else, you understand? Now don't worry about anything. [*He holds up Willy's face.*] Talk to me, Dad.

OPERATOR: Mr. Loman does not answer. Shall I page him?

WILLY [*attempting to stand, as though to rush and silence the Operator*]: No, no, no!

HAPPY: He'll strike something, Pop.

WILLY: No, no . . .

BIFF [*desperately, standing over Willy*]: Pop, listen! Listen to me! I'm telling you something good. Oliver talked to his partner about the Florida idea. You listening? He—he talked to his partner, and he came to me . . . I'm going to be all right, you hear? Dad, listen to me, he said it was just a question of the amount!

WILLY: Then you . . . got it?

HAPPY: He's gonna be terrific, Pop!

WILLY [*trying to stand*]: Then you got it, haven't you? You got it! You got it!

BIFF [*agonized, holds Willy down*]: No, no. Look, Pop. I'm supposed to have lunch with them tomorrow. I'm just telling you this so you'll know that I can still make an impression, Pop. And I'll make good somewhere, but I can't go tomorrow, see.

WILLY: Why not? You simply . . .

BIFF: But the pen, Pop!

WILLY: You give it to him and tell him it was an oversight!

HAPPY: Sure, have lunch tomorrow!

BIFF: I can't say that . . .

WILLY: You were doing a crossword puzzle and accidentally used his pen!

BIFF: Listen, kid, I took those balls years ago, now I walk in with his fountain pen? That clinches it, don't you see? I can't face him like that! I'll try elsewhere.

PAGE'S VOICE: Paging Mr. Loman!

WILLY: Don't you want to be anything?

BIFF: Pop, how can I go back?

WILLY: You don't want to be anything, is that what's behind it?

BIFF [*now angry at Willy for not crediting his sympathy*]: Don't take it that way! You think it was easy walking into that office after what I'd done to him? A team of horses couldn't have dragged me back to Bill Oliver!

WILLY: Then why'd you go?

BIFF: Why did I go? Why did I go! Look at you! Look at what's become of you!

Off left, The Woman laughs.

WILLY: Biff, you're going to go to that lunch tomorrow, or . . .

BIFF: I can't go. I've got no appointment!

HAPPY: Biff, for . . . !

WILLY: Are you spiting me?

BIFF: Don't take it that way! Goddammit!

WILLY [*strikes Biff and falters away from the table*]:   You rotten little louse! Are you spiting me?

THE WOMAN: Someone's at the door, Willy!

BIFF: I'm no good, can't you see what I am?

HAPPY [*separating them*]:   Hey, you're in a restaurant! Now cut it out, both of you! [*The girls enter.*] Hello, girls, sit down.

The Woman laughs, off left.

MISS FORSYTHE: I guess we might as well. This is Letta.

THE WOMAN: Willy, are you going to wake up?

BIFF [*ignoring Willy*]:   How're ya, miss, sit down. What do you drink?

MISS FORSYTHE: Letta might not be able to stay long.

LETTA: I gotta get up very early tomorrow. I got jury duty. I'm so excited! Were you fellows ever on a jury?

BIFF: No, but I been in front of them! [*The girls laugh.*] This is my father.

LETTA: Isn't he cute? Sit down with us, Pop.

HAPPY: Sit him down, Biff!

BIFF [*going to him*]:   Come on, slugger, drink us under the table. To hell with it! Come on, sit down, pal.

On Biff's last insistence, Willy is about to sit.

THE WOMAN [*now urgently*]:   Willy, are you going to answer the door!

The Woman's call pulls Willy back. He starts right, befuddled.

BIFF: Hey, where are you going?

WILLY: Open the door.

BIFF: The door?

WILLY: The washroom . . . the door . . . where's the door?

BIFF [*leading Willy to the left*]:   Just go straight down.

Willy moves left.

THE WOMAN: Willy, Willy, are you going to get up, get up, get up, get up?

Willy exits left.

LETTA: I think it's sweet you bring your daddy along.

MISS FORSYTHE: Oh, he isn't really your father!

BIFF [*at left, turning to her resentfully*]:   Miss Forsythe, you've just seen a prince walk by. A fine, troubled prince. A hardworking, unappreciated prince. A pal, you understand? A good companion. Always for his boys.

LETTA: That's so sweet.

HAPPY: Well, girls, what's the program? We're wasting time. Come on, Biff. Gather round. Where would you like to go?

BIFF: Why don't you do something for him?

HAPPY: Me!

BIFF: Don't you give a damn for him, Hap?

HAPPY: What're you talking about? I'm the one who . . .

BIFF: I sense it, you don't give a good goddam about him. [*He takes the rolled-up hose from his pocket and puts it on the table in front of Happy.*] Look what I found in the cellar, for Christ's sake. How can you bear to let it go on?

HAPPY: Me? Who goes away? Who runs off and . . .

BIFF: Yeah, but he doesn't mean anything to you. You could help him—I can't! Don't you understand what I'm talking about? He's going to kill himself, don't you know that?

HAPPY: Don't know it! Me!

BIFF: Hap, help him! Jesus . . . help him . . . Help me, help me, I can't bear to look at his face! [*Ready to weep, he hurries out, up right.*]

HAPPY [*starting after him*]:   Where are you going?

MISS FORSYTHE: What's he so mad about?

HAPPY: Come on, girls, we'll catch up with him.

MISS FORSYTHE [*as Happy pushes her out*]:   Say, I don't like that temper of his!

HAPPY: He's just a little overstrung, he'll be all right!

WILLY [*off left, as The Woman laughs*]:   Don't answer! Don't answer!

LETTA: Don't you want to tell your father . . .

HAPPY: No, that's not my father. He's just a guy. Come on, we'll catch Biff, and, honey, we're going to paint this town! Stanley, where's the check! Hey, Stanley!

They exit. Stanley looks toward left.

STANLEY [*calling to Happy indignantly*]:   Mr. Loman! Mr. Loman!

Stanley picks up a chair and follows them off. Knocking is heard off left. The Woman enters, laughing. Willy follows her. She is in a black slip; he is buttoning his shirt. Raw, sensuous music accompanies their speech:

WILLY: Will you stop laughing? Will you stop?

THE WOMAN: Aren't you going to answer the door? He'll wake the whole hotel.

WILLY: I'm not expecting anybody.

THE WOMAN: Whyn't you have another drink, honey, and stop being so damn self-centered?

WILLY: I'm so lonely.

THE WOMAN: You know you ruined me, Willy? From now on, whenever you come to the office, I'll see that you go right through to the buyers. No waiting at my desk anymore, Willy. You ruined me.

WILLY: That's nice of you to say that.

THE WOMAN: Gee, you are self-centered! Why so sad? You are the saddest, self-centeredest soul I ever did see-saw. [*She laughs. He kisses her.*] Come on inside, drummer boy. It's silly to be dressing in the middle of the night. [*As knocking is heard.*] Aren't you going to answer the door?

WILLY: They're knocking on the wrong door.

THE WOMAN: But I felt the knocking. And he heard us talking in here. Maybe the hotel's on fire!

WILLY [*his terror rising*]: It's a mistake.

THE WOMAN: Then tell him to go away!

WILLY: There's nobody there.

THE WOMAN: It's getting on my nerves, Willy. There's somebody standing out there and it's getting on my nerves!

WILLY [*pushing her away from him*]: All right, stay in the bathroom here, and don't come out. I think there's a law in Massachusetts about it, so don't come out. It may be that new room clerk. He looked very mean. So don't come out. It's a mistake, there's no fire.

The knocking is heard again. He takes a few steps away from her, and she vanishes into the wing. The light follows him, and now he is facing Young Biff, who carries a suitcase. Biff steps toward him. The music is gone.

BIFF: Why didn't you answer?

WILLY: Biff! What are you doing in Boston?

BIFF: Why didn't you answer? I've been knocking for five minutes, I called you on the phone . . .

ARTHUR MILLER

WILLY: I just heard you. I was in the bathroom and had the door shut. Did anything happen home?

BIFF: Dad—I let you down.

WILLY: What do you mean?

BIFF: Dad . . .

WILLY: Biffo, what's this about? [*Putting his arm around Biff.*] Come on, let's go downstairs and get you a malted.

BIFF: Dad, I flunked math.

WILLY: Not for the term?

BIFF: The term. I haven't got enough credits to graduate.

WILLY: You mean to say Bernard wouldn't give you the answers?

BIFF: He did, he tried, but I only got a sixty-one.

WILLY: And they wouldn't give you four points?

BIFF: Birnbaum refused absolutely. I begged him, Pop, but he won't give me those points. You gotta talk to him before they close the school. Because if he saw the kind of man you are, and you just talked to him in your way, I'm sure he'd come through for me. The class came right before practice, see, and I didn't go enough. Would you talk to him? He'd like you, Pop. You know the way you could talk.

WILLY: You're on. We'll drive right back.

BIFF: Oh, Dad, good work! I'm sure he'll change it for you!

WILLY: Go downstairs and tell the clerk I'm checkin' out. Go right down.

BIFF: Yes, sir! See, the reason he hates me, Pop—one day he was late for class so I got up at the blackboard and imitated him. I crossed my eyes and talked with a lithp.

WILLY [*laughing*]: You did? The kids like it?

BIFF: They nearly died laughing!

WILLY: Yeah? What'd you do?

BIFF: The thquare root of thixty twee is . . . [*Willy bursts out laughing; Biff joins.*] And in the middle of it he walked in!

Willy laughs and The Woman joins in offstage.

WILLY [*without hesitation*]: Hurry downstairs and . . .

BIFF: Somebody in there?

WILLY: No, that was next door.

The Woman laughs offstage.

BIFF: Somebody got in your bathroom!

WILLY: No, it's the next room, there's a party . . .

THE WOMAN [*enters, laughing; she lisps this*]:   Can I come in? There's something in the bathtub, Willy, and it's moving!

Willy looks at Biff; who is staring open-mouthed and horrified at The Woman.

WILLY: Ah—you better go back to your room. They must be finished painting by now. They're painting her room so I let her take a shower here. Go back, go back . . . [*He pushes her.*]

THE WOMAN [*resisting*]:   But I've got to get dressed, Willy, I can't . . .

WILLY: Get out of here! Go back, go back . . . [*Suddenly striving for the ordinary.*] This is Miss Francis, Biff, she's a buyer. They're painting her room. Go back, Miss Francis, go back . . .

THE WOMAN: But my clothes, I can't go out naked in the hall!

WILLY [*pushing her offstage*]:   Get outa here! Go back, go back!

Biff slowly sits down on his suitcase as the argument continues offstage.

THE WOMAN: Where's my stockings? You promised me stockings, Willy!

WILLY: I have no stockings here!

THE WOMAN: You had two boxes of size nine sheers for me, and I want them!

WILLY: Here, for God's sake, will you get outa here!

THE WOMAN [*enters holding a box of stockings*]:   I just hope there's nobody in the hall. That's all I hope. [*To Biff.*] Are you football or baseball?

BIFF: Football.

THE WOMAN [*angry, humiliated*]:   That's me too. G'night. [*She snatches her clothes from Willy, and walks out.*]

WILLY [*after a pause*]:   Well, better get going. I want to get to the school first thing in the morning. Get my suits out of the closet. I'll get my valise. [*Biff doesn't move.*] What's the matter! [*Biff remains motionless, tears falling.*] She's a buyer. Buys for J. H. Simmons. She lives down the hall—they're painting. You don't imagine—[*He breaks off. After a pause.*] Now listen, pal, she's just a buyer. She sells merchandise in her room and they have to keep it looking just so . . . [*Pause. Assuming command.*] All right, get my suits. [*Biff doesn't move.*] Now stop crying and do as I say. I gave you an order. Biff, I gave you an order!

Is that what you do when I give you an order? How dare you cry! [*Putting his arm around Biff.*] Now look, Biff, when you grow up you'll understand about these things. You mustn't—you mustn't overemphasize a thing like this. I'll see Birnbaum first thing in the morning.

BIFF: Never mind.

WILLY [*getting down beside Biff*]: Never mind! He's going to give you those points. I'll see to it.

BIFF: He wouldn't listen to you.

WILLY: He certainly will listen to me. You need those points for the U. of Virginia.

BIFF: I'm not going there.

WILLY: Heh? If I can't get him to change that mark you'll make it up in summer school. You've got all summer to . . .

BIFF [*his weeping breaking from him*]: Dad . . .

WILLY [*infected by it*]: Oh, my boy . . .

BIFF: Dad . . .

WILLY: She's nothing to me, Biff. I was lonely, I was terribly lonely.

BIFF: You—you gave her Mama's stockings! [*His tears break through and he rises to go.*]

WILLY [*grabbing for Biff*]: I gave you an order!

BIFF: Don't touch me, you—liar!

WILLY: Apologize for that!

BIFF: You fake! You phony little fake! You fake! [*Overcome, he turns quickly and weeping fully goes out with his suitcase. Willy is left on the floor on his knees.*]

WILLY: I gave you an order! Biff, come back here or I'll beat you! Come back here! I'll whip you!

Stanley comes quickly in from the right and stands in front of Willy.

WILLY [*shouts at Stanley*]: I gave you an order . . .

STANLEY: Hey, let's pick it up, pick it up, Mr. Loman. [*He helps Willy to his feet.*] Your boys left with the chippies. They said they'll see you home.

A second waiter watches some distance away.

WILLY: But we were supposed to have dinner together.

Music is heard, Willy's theme.

STANLEY: Can you make it?

WILLY: I'll—sure, I can make it. [*Suddenly concerned about his clothes.*] Do I—I look all right?

STANLEY: Sure, you look all right. [*He flicks a speck off Willy's lapel.*]

WILLY: Here—here's a dollar.

STANLEY: Oh, your son paid me. It's all right.

WILLY [*putting it in Stanley's hand*]:   No, take it. You're a good boy.

STANLEY: Oh, no, you don't have to . . .

WILLY: Here—here's some more, I don't need it any more. [*After a slight pause.*] Tell me—is there a seed store in the neighborhood?

STANLEY: Seeds? You mean like to plant?

As Willy turns, Stanley slips the money back into his jacket pocket.

WILLY: Yes. Carrots, peas . . .

STANLEY: Well, there's hardware stores on Sixth Avenue, but it may be too late now.

WILLY [*anxiously*]:   Oh, I'd better hurry. I've got to get some seeds. [*He starts off to the right.*] I've got to get some seeds, right away. Nothing's planted. I don't have a thing in the ground.

Willy hurries out as the light goes down. Stanley moves over to the right after him, watches him off. The other waiter has been staring at Willy.

STANLEY [*to the waiter*]:   Well, whatta you looking at?

The waiter picks up the chairs and moves off right. Stanley takes the table and follows him. The light fades on this area. There is a long pause, the sound of the flute coming over. The light gradually rises on the kitchen, which is empty. Happy appears at the door of the house, followed by Biff. Happy is carrying a large bunch of long-stemmed roses. He enters the kitchen, looks around for Linda. Not seeing her, he turns to Biff, who is just outside the house door, and makes a gesture with his hands, indicating "Not here, I guess." He looks into the living room and freezes. Inside, Linda, unseen, is seated, Willy's coat on her lap. She rises ominously and quietly and moves toward Happy, who backs up into the kitchen, afraid.

HAPPY: Hey, what're you doing up? [*Linda says nothing but moves toward him implacably.*] Where's Pop? [*He keeps backing to the right, and now Linda is in full view in the doorway to the living room.*] Is he sleeping?

LINDA: Where were you?

HAPPY [*trying to laugh it off*]: We met two girls, Mom, very fine types. Here, we brought you some flowers. [*Offering them to her.*] Put them in your room, Ma.

She knocks them to the floor at Biff's feet. He has now come inside and closed the door behind him. She stares at Biff, silent.

HAPPY: Now what'd you do that for? Mom, I want you to have some flowers . . .

LINDA [*cutting Happy off, violently to Biff*]: Don't you care whether he lives or dies?

HAPPY [*going to the stairs*]: Come upstairs, Biff.

BIFF [*with a flare of disgust, to Happy*]: Go away from me! [*To Linda.*] What do you mean, lives or dies? Nobody's dying around here, pal.

LINDA: Get out of my sight! Get out of here!

BIFF: I wanna see the boss.

LINDA: You're not going near him!

BIFF: Where is he? [*He moves into the living room and Linda follows.*]

LINDA [*shouting after Biff*]: You invite him for dinner. He looks forward to it all day—[*Biff appears in his parents' bedroom, looks around, and exits*]—and then you desert him there. There's no stranger you'd do that to!

HAPPY: Why? He had a swell time with us. Listen, when I—[*Linda comes back into the kitchen*]—desert him I hope I don't outlive the day!

LINDA: Get out of here!

HAPPY: Now look, Mom . . .

LINDA: Did you have to go to women tonight? You and your lousy rotten whores!

Biff re-enters the kitchen.

HAPPY: Mom, all we did was follow Biff around trying to cheer him up! [*To Biff.*] Boy, what a night you gave me!

LINDA: Get out of here, both of you, and don't come back! I don't want you tormenting him any more. Go on now, get your things together! [*To Biff.*] You can sleep in his apartment. [*She starts to pick up the flowers and stops herself.*] Pick up this stuff, I'm not your maid any more. Pick it up, you bum, you!

Happy turns his back to her in refusal. Biff slowly moves over and gets down on his knees, picking up the flowers.

LINDA: You're a pair of animals! Not one, not another living soul would have had the cruelty to walk out on that man in a restaurant!

BIFF [not looking at her]:   Is that what he said?

LINDA: He didn't have to say anything. He was so humiliated he nearly limped when he came in.

HAPPY: But, Mom, he had a great time with us . . .

BIFF [cutting him off violently]:   Shut up!

Without another word, Happy goes upstairs.

LINDA: You! You didn't even go in to see if he was all right!

BIFF [still on the floor in front of Linda, the flowers in his hand; with self-loathing]:   No. Didn't. Didn't do a damned thing. How do you like that, heh? Left him babbling in a toilet.

LINDA: You louse. You . . .

BIFF: Now you hit it on the nose! [He gets up, throws the flowers in the wastebasket.] The scum of the earth, and you're looking at him!

LINDA: Get out of here!

BIFF: I gotta talk to the boss, Mom. Where is he?

LINDA: You're not going near him. Get out of this house!

BIFF [with absolute assurance, determination]:   No. We're gonna have an abrupt conversation, him and me.

LINDA: You're not talking to him.

Hammering is heard from outside the house, off right. Biff turns toward the noise.

LINDA [suddenly pleading]:   Will you please leave him alone?

BIFF: What's he doing out there?

LINDA: He's planting the garden!

BIFF [quietly]:   Now? Oh, my God!

Biff moves outside, Linda following. The light dies down on them and comes up on the center of the apron as Willy walks into it. He is carrying a flashlight, a hoe, and a handful of seed packets. He raps the top of the hoe sharply to fix it firmly, and then moves to the left, measuring off the distance with his foot. He holds the flashlight to look at the seed packets, reading off the instructions. He is in the blue of night.

WILLY: Carrots . . . quarter-inch apart. Rows . . . one-foot rows. [He measures it off.] One foot. [He puts down a package and measures off.]

Beets. [*He puts down another package and measures again.*] Lettuce. [*He reads the package, puts it down.*] One foot—[*He breaks off as Ben appears at the right and moves slowly down to him.*] What a proposition, ts, ts. Terrific, terrific. 'Cause she's suffered, Ben, the woman has suffered. You understand me? A man can't go out the way he came in, Ben, a man has got to add up to something. You can't, you can't—[*Ben moves toward him as though to interrupt.*] You gotta consider now. Don't answer so quick. Remember, it's a guaranteed twenty-thousand-dollar proposition. Now look, Ben, I want you to go through the ins and outs of this thing with me. I've got nobody to talk to, Ben, and the woman has suffered, you hear me?

BEN [*standing still, considering*]: What's the proposition?

WILLY: It's twenty thousand dollars on the barrelhead. Guaranteed, gilt-edged, you understand?

BEN: You don't want to make a fool of yourself. They might not honor the policy.

WILLY: How can they dare refuse? Didn't I work like a coolie to meet every premium on the nose? And now they don't pay off? Impossible!

BEN: It's called a cowardly thing, William.

WILLY: Why? Does it take more guts to stand here the rest of my life ringing up a zero?

BEN [*yielding*]: That's a point, William. [*He moves, thinking, turns.*] And twenty thousand—that is something one can feel with the hand, it is there.

WILLY [*now assured, with rising power*]: Oh, Ben, that's the whole beauty of it! I see it like a diamond, shining in the dark, hard and rough, that I can pick up and touch in my hand. Not like—like an appointment! This would not be another damned-fool appointment, Ben, and it changes all the aspects. Because he thinks I'm nothing, see, and so he spites me. But the funeral . . . [*Straightening up.*] Ben, that funeral will be massive! They'll come from Maine, Massachusetts, Vermont, New Hampshire! All the old-timers with the strange license plates—that boy will be thunderstruck, Ben, because he never realized—I am known! Rhode Island, New York, New Jersey—I am known, Ben, and he'll see it with his eyes once and for all. He'll see what I am, Ben! He's in for a shock, that boy!

BEN [*coming down to the edge of the garden*]: He'll call you a coward.

WILLY [*suddenly fearful*]: No, that would be terrible.

BEN: Yes. And a damned fool.

WILLY: No, no, he mustn't, I won't have that! [*He is broken and desperate.*]

BEN: He'll hate you, William.

The gay music of the Boys is heard.

WILLY: Oh, Ben, how do we get back to all the great times? Used to be so full of light, and comradeship, the sleigh-riding in winter, and the ruddiness on his cheeks. And always some kind of good news coming up, always something nice coming up ahead. And never even let me carry the valises in the house, and simonizing, simonizing that little red car! Why, why can't I give him something and not have him hate me?

BEN: Let me think about it. [*He glances at his watch.*] I still have a little time. Remarkable proposition, but you've got to be sure you're not making a fool of yourself.

Ben drifts off upstage and goes out of sight. Biff comes down from the left.

WILLY [*suddenly conscious of Biff, turns and looks up at him, then begins picking up the packages of seeds in confusion*]: Where the hell is that seed? [*Indignantly.*] You can't see nothing out here! They boxed in the whole goddam neighborhood!

BIFF: There are people all around here. Don't you realize that?

WILLY: I'm busy. Don't bother me.

BIFF [*taking the hoe from Willy*]: I'm saying good-by to you, Pop. [*Willy looks at him, silent, unable to move.*] I'm not coming back any more.

WILLY: You're not going to see Oliver tomorrow?

BIFF: I've got no appointment, Dad.

WILLY: He put his arm around you, and you've got no appointment?

BIFF: Pop, get this now, will you? Everytime I've left it's been a—fight that sent me out of here. Today I realized something about myself and I tried to explain it to you and I—I think I'm just not smart enough to make any sense out of it for you. To hell with whose fault it is or anything like that. [*He takes Willy's arm.*] Let's just wrap it up, heh? Come on in, we'll tell Mom. [*He gently tries to pull Willy to left.*]

WILLY [*frozen, immobile, with guilt in his voice*]: No, I don't want to see her.

BIFF: Come on! [*He pulls again, and Willy tries to pull away.*]

WILLY [*highly nervous*]: No, no, I don't want to see her.

BIFF [*tries to look into Willy's face, as if to find the answer there*]:   Why don't you want to see her?

WILLY [*more harshly now*]:   Don't bother me, will you?

BIFF: What do you mean, you don't want to see her? You don't want them calling you yellow, do you? This isn't your fault; it's me, I'm a bum. Now come inside! [*Willy strains to get away.*] Did you hear what I said to you?

Willy pulls away and quickly goes by himself into the house. Biff follows.

LINDA [*to Willy*]:   Did you plant, dear?

BIFF [*at the door, to Linda*]:   All right, we had it out. I'm going and I'm not writing any more.

LINDA [*going to Willy in the kitchen*]:   I think that's the best way, dear. 'Cause there's no use drawing it out, you'll just never get along.

Willy doesn't respond.

BIFF: People ask where I am and what I'm doing, you don't know, and you don't care. That way it'll be off your mind and you can start brightening up again. All right? That clears it, doesn't it? [*Willy is silent, and Biff goes to him.*] You gonna wish me luck, scout? [*He extends his hand.*] What do you say?

LINDA: Shake his hand, Willy.

WILLY [*turning to her, seething with hurt*]:   There's no necessity—to mention the pen at all, y'know.

BIFF [*gently*]:   I've got no appointment, Dad.

WILLY [*erupting fiercely*]:   He put his arm around . . . ?

BIFF: Dad, you're never going to see what I am, so what's the use of arguing? If I strike oil I'll send you a check. Meantime forget I'm alive.

WILLY [*to Linda*]:   Spite, see?

BIFF: Shake hands, Dad.

WILLY: Not my hand.

BIFF: I was hoping not to go this way.

WILLY: Well, this is the way you're going. Good-by.

Biff looks at him a moment, then turns sharply and goes to the stairs.

WILLY [*stops him with*]:   May you rot in hell if you leave this house!

BIFF [*turning*]:   Exactly what is it that you want from me?

WILLY: I want you to know, on the train, in the mountains, in the valleys, wherever you go, that you cut down your life for spite!

BIFF: No, no.

WILLY: Spite, spite, is the word of your undoing! And when you're down and out, remember what did it. When you're rotting somewhere beside the railroad tracks, remember, and don't you dare blame it on me!

BIFF: I'm not blaming it on you!

WILLY: I won't take the rap for this, you hear?

Happy comes down the stairs and stands on the bottom step, watching.

BIFF: That's just what I'm telling you!

WILLY [*sinking into a chair at a table, with full accusation*]:   You're trying to put a knife in me—don't think I don't know what you're doing!

BIFF: All right, phony! Then let's lay it on the line. [*He whips the rubber tube out of his pocket and puts it on the table.*]

HAPPY: You crazy . . .

LINDA: Biff! [*She moves to grab the hose, but Biff holds it down with his hand.*]

BIFF: Leave it there! Don't move it!

WILLY [*not looking at it*]:   What is that?

BIFF: You know goddam well what that is.

WILLY [*caged, wanting to escape*]:   I never saw that.

BIFF: You saw it. The mice didn't bring it into the cellar! What is this supposed to do, make a hero out of you? This supposed to make me sorry for you?

WILLY: Never heard of it.

BIFF: There'll be no pity for you, you hear it? No pity!

WILLY [*to Linda*]:   You hear the spite!

BIFF: No, you're going to hear the truth—what you are and what I am!

LINDA: Stop it!

WILLY: Spite!

HAPPY [*coming down toward Biff*]:   You cut it now!

BIFF [*to Happy*]:   The man don't know who we are! The man is gonna know! [*To Willy.*] We never told the truth for ten minutes in this house!

HAPPY: We always told the truth!

BIFF [*turning on him*]:   You big blow, are you the assistant buyer?
You're one of the two assistants to the assistant, aren't you?

HAPPY: Well, I'm practically . . .

BIFF: You're practically full of it! We all are! and I'm through with it.
[*To Willy.*] Now hear this, Willy, this is me.

WILLY: I know you!

BIFF: You know why I had no address for three months? I stole a suit
in Kansas City and I was in jail. [*To Linda, who is sobbing.*] Stop crying. I'm through with it.

Linda turns away from them, her hands covering her face.

WILLY: I suppose that's my fault!

BIFF: I stole myself out of every good job since high school!

WILLY: And whose fault is that?

BIFF: And I never got anywhere because you blew me so full of hot
air I could never stand taking orders from anybody! That's whose
fault it is!

WILLY: I hear that!

LINDA: Don't, Biff!

BIFF: It's goddam time you heard that! I had to be boss big shot in
two weeks, and I'm through with it!

WILLY: Then hang yourself! For spite, hang yourself!

BIFF: No! Nobody's hanging himself, Willy! I ran down eleven flights
with a pen in my hand today. And suddenly I stopped, you hear me?
And in the middle of that office building, do you hear this? I
stopped in the middle of that building and I saw—the sky. I saw the
things that I love in this world. The work and the food and time to
sit and smoke. And I looked at the pen and said to myself, what the
hell am I grabbing this for? Why am I trying to become what I don't
want to be? What am I doing in an office, making a contemptuous,
begging fool of myself, when all I want is out there, waiting for me
the minute I say I know who I am! Why can't I say that, Willy? [*He
tries to make Willy face him, but Willy pulls away and moves to the left.*]

WILLY [*with hatred, threateningly*]:   The door of your life is wide open!

BIFF: Pop! I'm a dime a dozen, and so are you!

WILLY [*turning on him now in an uncontrolled outburst*]:   I am not a
dime a dozen! I am Willy Loman, and you are Biff Loman!

*Biff starts for Willy, but is blocked by Happy. In his fury, Biff
seems on the verge of attacking his father.*

BIFF: I am not a leader of men, Willy, and neither are you. You were never anything but a hard-working drummer who landed in the ash can like all the rest of them! I'm one dollar an hour, Willy! I tried seven states and couldn't raise it. A buck an hour! Do you gather my meaning? I'm not bringing home any prizes any more, and you're going to stop waiting for me to bring them home!

WILLY [*directly to Biff*]: You vengeful, spiteful mutt!

Biff breaks from Happy. Willy, in fright, starts up the stairs. Biff grabs him.

BIFF [*at the peak of his fury*]: Pop! I'm nothing! I'm nothing, Pop. Can't you understand that? There's no spite in it any more. I'm just what I am, that's all.

Biff's fury has spent itself and he breaks down, sobbing, holding on to Willy, who dumbly fumbles for Biff's face.

WILLY [*astonished*]: What're you doing? What're you doing? [*To Linda.*] Why is he crying?

BIFF [*crying, broken*]: Will you let me go, for Christ's sake? Will you take that phony dream and burn it before something happens? [*Struggling to contain himself, he pulls away and moves to the stairs.*] I'll go in the morning. Put him—put him to bed. [*Exhausted, Biff moves up the stairs to his room.*]

WILLY [*after a long pause, astonished, elevated*]: Isn't that—isn't that remarkable? Biff—he likes me!

LINDA: He loves you, Willy!

HAPPY [*deeply moved*]: Always did, Pop.

WILLY: Oh, Biff! [*Staring wildly.*] He cried! Cried to me. [*He is choking with his love, and now cries out his promise.*] That boy—that boy is going to be magnificent!

Ben appears in the light just outside the kitchen.

BEN: Yes, outstanding, with twenty thousand behind him.

LINDA [*sensing the racing of his mind, fearfully, carefully*]: Now come to bed, Willy. It's all settled now.

WILLY [*finding it difficult not to rush out of the house*]: Yes, we'll sleep. Come on. Go to sleep, Hap.

BEN: And it does take a great kind of a man to crack the jungle.

In accents of dread, Ben's idyllic music starts up.

HAPPY [*his arm around Linda*]:   I'm getting married, Pop, don't forget it. I'm changing everything. I'm gonna run that department before the year is up. You'll see, Mom. [*He kisses her.*]

BEN: The jungle is dark but full of diamonds, Willy.

Willy turns, moves, listening to Ben.

LINDA: Be good. You're both good boys, just act that way, that's all.

HAPPY: 'Night, Pop. [*He goes upstairs.*]

LINDA [*to Willy*]:   Come, dear.

BEN [*with greater force*]:   One must go in to fetch a diamond out.

WILLY [*to Linda, as he moves slowly along the edge of the kitchen, toward the door*]:   I just want to get settled down, Linda. Let me sit alone for a little.

LINDA [*almost uttering her fear*]:   I want you upstairs.

WILLY [*taking her in his arms*]:   In a few minutes, Linda. I couldn't sleep right now. Go on, you look awful tired. [*He kisses her.*]

BEN: Not like an appointment at all. A diamond is rough and hard to the touch.

WILLY: Go on now. I'll be right up.

LINDA: I think this is the only way, Willy.

WILLY: Sure, it's the best thing.

BEN: Best thing!

WILLY: The only way. Everything is gonna be—go on, kid, get to bed. You look so tired.

LINDA: Come right up.

WILLY: Two minutes.

Linda goes into the living room, then reappears in her bedroom. Willy moves just outside the kitchen door.

WILLY: Loves me. [*Wonderingly.*] Always loved me. Isn't that a remarkable thing? Ben, he'll worship me for it!

BEN [*with promise*]:   It's dark there, but full of diamonds.

WILLY: Can you imagine that magnificence with twenty thousand dollars in his pocket?

LINDA [*calling from her room*]:   Willy! Come up!

WILLY [*calling into the kitchen*]:   Yes! Yes. Coming! It's very smart, you realize that, don't you, sweetheart? Even Ben sees it. I gotta go, baby. 'By! 'By! [*Going over to Ben, almost dancing.*] Imagine? When the mail comes he'll be ahead of Bernard again!

BEN: A perfect proposition all around.

WILLY: Did you see how he cried to me? Oh, if I could kiss him, Ben!

BEN: Time, William, time!

WILLY: Oh, Ben, I always knew one way or another we were gonna make it, Biff and I.

BEN [looking at his watch]: The boat. We'll be late. [He moves slowly off into the darkness.]

WILLY [elegiacally, turning to the house]: Now when you kick off, boy, I want a seventy-yard boot, and get right down the field under the ball, and when you hit, hit low and hit hard, because it's important, boy. [He swings around and faces the audience.] There's all kinds of important people in the stands, and the first thing you know . . . [Suddenly realizing he is alone.] Ben! Ben, where do I . . . ? [He makes a sudden movement of search.] Ben, how do I . . . ?

LINDA [calling]: Willy, you coming up?

WILLY [uttering a gasp of fear, whirling about as if to quiet her]: Sh! [He turns around as if to find his way; sounds, faces, voices, seem to be swarming in upon him and he flicks at them, crying.] Sh! Sh! [Suddenly music, faint and high, stops him. It rises in intensity, almost to an unbearable scream. He goes up and down on his toes, and rushes off around the house.] Shhh!

LINDA: Willy?

There is no answer. Linda waits. Biff gets up off his bed. He is still in his clothes. Happy sits up. Biff stands listening.

LINDA [with real fear]: Willy, answer me! Willy!

There is the sound of a car starting and moving away at full speed.

LINDA: No!

BIFF [rushing down the stairs]: Pop!

As the car speeds off the music crashes down in a frenzy of sound, which becomes the soft pulsation of a single cello string. Biff slowly returns to his bedroom. He and Happy gravely don their jackets. Linda slowly walks out of her room. The music has developed into a dead march. The leaves of day are appearing over everything. Charley and Bernard, somberly dressed, appear and knock on the kitchen door. Biff and Happy slowly descend the stairs to the kitchen as Charley and Bernard enter. All stop a moment when Linda, in clothes of mourning, bearing a little bunch of roses, comes through *the draped doorway into the kitchen. She goes to Charley and takes his arm. Now all move toward the audience, through the wall-line of the kitchen. At the limit of the apron, Linda lays down the flowers, kneels, and sits back on her heels. All stare down at the grave.*

Requiem

CHARLEY: It's getting dark, Linda.

Linda doesn't react. She stares at the grave.

BIFF: How about it, Mom? Better get some rest, heh? They'll be closing the gate soon.

Linda makes no move. Pause.

HAPPY [*deeply angered*]:   He had no right to do that. There was no necessity for it. We would've helped him.

CHARLEY [*grunting*]:   Hmmm.

BIFF: Come along, Mom.

LINDA: Why didn't anybody come?

CHARLEY: It was a very nice funeral.

LINDA: But where are all the people he knew? Maybe they blame him.

CHARLEY: Naa. It's a rough world, Linda. They wouldn't blame him.

LINDA: I can't understand it. At this time especially. First time in thirty-five years we were just about free and clear. He only needed a little salary. He was even finished with the dentist.

CHARLEY: No man only needs a little salary.

LINDA: I can't understand it.

BIFF: There were a lot of nice days. When he'd come home from a trip; or on Sundays, making the stoop; finishing the cellar; putting on the new porch; when he built the extra bathroom; and put up the garage. You know something, Charley, there's more of him in that front stoop than in all the sales he ever made.

CHARLEY: Yeah. He was a happy man with a batch of cement.

LINDA: He was so wonderful with his hands.

BIFF: He had the wrong dreams. All, all, wrong.

HAPPY [*almost ready to fight Biff*]:   Don't say that!

BIFF: He never knew who he was.

CHARLEY [*stopping Happy's movement and reply; to Biff*]:   Nobody dast blame this man. You don't understand: Willy was a salesman. And for a salesman, there is no rock bottom to the life. He don't put a bolt to a nut, he don't tell you the law or give you medicine.

He's a man way out there in the blue, riding on a smile and a shoeshine. And when they start not smiling back—that's an earthquake. And then you get yourself a couple of spots on your hat, and you're finished. Nobody dast blame this man. A salesman is got to dream, boy. It comes with the territory.

BIFF: Charley, the man didn't know who he was.

HAPPY [*infuriated*]: Don't say that!

BIFF: Why don't you come with me, Happy?

HAPPY: I'm not licked that easily. I'm staying right in this city, and I'm gonna beat this racket! [*He looks at Biff, his chin set.*] The Loman Brothers!

BIFF: I know who I am, kid.

HAPPY: All right, boy. I'm gonna show you and everybody else that Willy Loman did not die in vain. He had a good dream. It's the only dream you can have—to come out number-one man. He fought it out here, and this is where I'm gonna win it for him.

BIFF [*with a hopeless glance at Happy, bends toward his mother*]: Let's go, Mom.

LINDA: I'll be with you in a minute. Go on, Charley. [*He hesitates.*] I want to, just for a minute. I never had a chance to say good-by.

Charley moves away, followed by Happy. Biff remains a slight distance up and left of Linda. She sits there, summoning herself. The flute begins, not far away, playing behind her speech.

LINDA: Forgive me, dear. I can't cry. I don't know what it is, but I can't cry. I don't understand it. Why did you ever do that? Help me, Willy, I can't cry. It seems to me that you're just on another trip. I keep expecting you. Willy, dear, I can't cry. Why did you do it? I search and search and I search, and I can't understand it, Willy. I made the last payment on the house today. Today, dear. And there'll be nobody home. [*A sob rises in her throat.*] We're free and clear. [*Sobbing mournfully, released.*] We're free. [*Biff comes slowly toward her.*] We're free . . . We're free . . .

Biff lifts her to her feet and moves out up right with her in his arms. Linda sobs quietly. Bernard and Charley come together and follow them, followed by Happy. Only the music of the flute is left on the darkening stage as over the house the hard towers of the apartment buildings rise into sharp focus and the curtain falls.

—1949

Edward Albee began his career as the author of one-act plays that were per-
formed off-Broadway and in Europe. The Zoo Story *was first produced in*
Berlin on a double bill with another one-act play by Samuel Beckett, and Al-
bee was immediately recognized as one of the earliest American playwrights
associated with the theater of the absurd. Albee first came to the attention of
mainstream audiences with the 1962 Broadway production of the full-length
Who's Afraid of Virginia Woolf?, *which was later made into a successful*
film by Mike Nichols, starring Elizabeth Taylor and Richard Burton. Since
*then, Albee's work has been frequently performed, and three plays—*A Delicate Balance *(1966),* Seascape *(1975), and* Three Tall Women *(1994)—have*
won Pulitzer Prizes. In 1996, Albee was a Kennedy Center Honoree and was
awarded a National Medal of the Arts. Now in his 80s, Albee continues
teaching at the University of Houston's Edward Albee New Playwrights
Workshop and has recently won a Tony Award for best play for The Goat, or
Who Is Sylvia? *(2002).* Who's Afraid of Virginia Woolf *was successfully re-*
vived on Broadway in 2005, starring Kathleen Turner.

EDWARD ALBEE

438

The Sandbox

Characters

The Young Man, *25, a good-looking, well-built boy in a bathing suit*
Mommy, *55, a well-dressed, imposing woman*
Daddy, *60, a small man; gray, thin*
Grandma, *86, a tiny, wizened woman with bright eyes*
The Musician, *no particular age, but young would be nice*

Note: When, in the course of the play, Mommy and Daddy call each other by
these names, there should be no suggestion of regionalism. These names are
of empty affection and point up the pre-senility and vacuity of their children.

Scene: *A bare stage, with only the following: Near the footlights, far stage-*
right, two simple chairs set side by side, facing the audience; near the foot-
lights, far stage-left, a chair facing stage-right with a music stand before it;
farther back, and stage-center, slightly elevated and raked, a large child's
sandbox with a toy pail and shovel; the background is the sky, which alters
from brightest day to deepest night.

At the beginning, it is brightest day, the Young Man is alone on stage, to
the rear of the sandbox, and to one side. He is doing calisthenics; he does

calisthenics until quite at the very end of the play. These calisthenics, employing the arms only, should suggest the beating and fluttering of wings. The Young Man is, after all, the Angel of Death.

Mommy and Daddy enter from the stage-left, Mommy first.

MOMMY [*motioning to Daddy*]:   Well, here we are; this is the beach.

DADDY [*whining*]:   I'm cold.

MOMMY [*dismissing him with a little laugh*]:   Don't be silly; it's as warm as toast. Look at that nice young man over there: *he* doesn't think it's cold. [*Waves to the Young Man.*] Hello.

YOUNG MAN [*with an endearing smile*]:   Hi!

MOMMY [*looking about*]:   This will do perfectly . . . don't you think so, Daddy? There's sand there . . . and the water beyond. What do you think, Daddy?

DADDY [*vaguely*]:   Whatever you say, Mommy.

MOMMY [*with the same little laugh*]:   Well, of course . . . whatever I say. Then, it's settled, is it?

DADDY [*shrugs*]:   She's your mother, not mine.

MOMMY: I know she's my mother. What do you take me for? [*A pause.*] All right, now; let's get on with it. [*She shouts into the wings, stage-left.*] You! Out there! You can come in now.

The Musician enters, seats himself in the chair, stage-left, places music on the music stand, is ready to play. Mommy nods approvingly.

MOMMY: Very nice; very nice. Are you ready, Daddy? Let's go get Grandma.

DADDY: Whatever you say, Mommy.

MOMMY [*leading the way out, stage-left*]:   Of course, whatever I say. [*To the Musician.*] You can begin now.

The Musician begins playing; Mommy and Daddy exit; the Musician, all the while playing nods to the Young Man.

YOUNG MAN [*with the same endearing smile*]:   Hi!

After a moment, Mommy and Daddy re-enter, carrying Grandma. She is borne in by their hands under her armpits; she is quite rigid; her legs are drawn up; her feet do not touch the ground; the expression on her ancient face is that of puzzlement and fear.

DADDY: Where do we put her?

MOMMY [*the same little laugh*]:   Wherever I say, of course. Let me see . . . well . . . all right, over there . . . in the sandbox. [*Pause.*] Well, what are you waiting for Daddy? . . . The sandbox!

Together they carry Grandma over to the sandbox and more or less dump her in.

GRANDMA [*righting herself to a sitting position; her voice a cross between a baby's laugh and cry*]:   Ahhhhhh! Graaaaa!
DADDY [*dusting himself*]:   What do we do now?
MOMMY [*to the Musician*]:   You can stop now. [*The Musician stops.*] [*Back to Daddy.*] What do you mean, what do we do now? We go over there and sit down, of course. [*To the Young Man.*] Hello there.
YOUNG MAN [*again smiling*]:   Hi!

Mommy and Daddy move to the chairs, stage-right, and sit down. A pause.

GRANDMA [*same as before*]:   Ahhhhhh! Ahhaaaaaa! Graaaaaa!
DADDY: Do you think . . . do you think she's . . . comfortable?
MOMMY [*impatiently*]:   How would I know?
DADDY [*pause*]:   What do we do now?
MOMMY [*as if remembering*]:   We . . . wait. We . . . sit here . . . and we wait . . . that's what we do.
DADDY [*after a pause*]:   Shall we talk to each other?
MOMMY [*with that little laugh; picking something off her dress*]:   Well, you can talk, if you want to . . . if you can think of anything to say . . . if you can think of anything *new*.
DADDY [*thinks*]:   No . . . I suppose not.
MOMMY [*with a triumphant laugh*]:   Of course not!
GRANDMA [*banging the toy shovel against the pail*]:   Haaaaaa! Ah-haaaaaa!
MOMMY [*out over the audience*]:   Be quiet, Grandma . . . just be quiet, and wait.

Grandma throws a shovelful of sand at Mommy.

MOMMY [*still out over the audience*]:   She's throwing sand at me! You stop that, Grandma; you stop throwing sand at Mommy! [*To Daddy.*] She's throwing sand at me.

Daddy looks around at Grandma, who screams at him.

GRANDMA: GRAAAAAA!

EDWARD ALBEE

MOMMY: Don't look at her. Just . . . sit here . . . be very still . . . and
wait. [*To the Musician.*] You . . . uh . . . you go ahead and do whatever it is you do.

*The Musician plays. Mommy and Daddy are fixed, staring out
beyond the audience. Grandma looks at them, looks at the Musician, looks at the sandbox, throws down the shovel.*

GRANDMA: Ah-haaaaaa! Graaaaaa! [*Looks for reaction; gets none.*]
Now . . . [*directly to the audience.*] Honestly! What a way to treat an
old woman! Drag her out of the house . . . stick her in a car . . .
bring her out here from the city . . . dump her in a pile of sand . . .
and leave her here to set. I'm eighty-six years old! I was married
when I was seventeen. To a farmer. He died when I was thirty. [*To
the Musician.*] Will you stop that, please?

The Musician stops playing.

I'm a feeble old woman . . . how do you expect anybody to hear
me over that peep! peep! peep! [*To herself.*] There's no respect
around here. [*To the Young Man.*] There's no respect around
here!

YOUNG MAN [*same smile*]:   Hi!

GRANDMA [*after a pause, a mild double-take, continues, to the audience*]:
My husband died when I was thirty [*indicates Mommy*], and I had to
raise that big cow over there all by my lonesome. You can imagine
what *that* was like. Lordy! [*To the Young Man.*] Where'd they get *you*?

YOUNG MAN: Oh . . . I've been around for a while.

GRANDMA: I'll bet you have! Heh, heh, heh. Will you look at you!

YOUNG MAN [*flexing his muscles*]:   Isn't that something? [*Continues his
calisthenics.*]

GRANDMA: Boy, oh boy; I'll say. Pretty good.

YOUNG MAN [*sweetly*]:   I'll say.

GRANDMA: Where ya from?

YOUNG MAN: Southern California.

GRANDMA [*nodding*]:   Figgers, figgers. What's your name, honey?

YOUNG MAN: I don't know . . .

GRANDMA [*to the audience*]:   Bright, too!

YOUNG MAN: I mean . . . I mean, they haven't given me one yet . . .
the studio . . .

GRANDMA: [*giving him the once-over*].   You don't say . . . you don't say.
Well . . . uh, I've got to talk some more . . . don't you go 'way.

YOUNG MAN: Oh, no.

GRANDMA [*turning her attention back to the audience*]:   Fine; fine. [*Then, once more, back to the Young Man.*] You're . . . you're an actor, hunh?

YOUNG MAN [*beaming*]:   Yes. I am.

GRANDMA [*to the audience again; shrugs*]:   I'm smart that way. *Anyhow,* I had to raise . . . that over there all by my lonesome; and what's next to her there . . . that's what she married. Rich? I tell you . . . money, money, money. They took me off the *farm* . . . which was real decent of them . . . and they moved me into the big town house with *them* . . . fixed a nice place for me under the stove . . . gave me an army blanket . . . and my own dish . . . my very own dish! So, what have I got to complain about? Nothing, of course, I'm not complaining. [*She looks up at the sky, shouts to someone offstage.*] Shouldn't it be getting dark now, dear?

The lights dim; night comes on. The Musician begins to play; it becomes deepest night. There are spots on all the players, including the Young Man, who is, of course, continuing his calisthenics.

DADDY [*stirring*]:   It's nighttime.

MOMMY: Shhhh. Be still . . . wait.

DADDY [*whining*]:   It's so hot.

MOMMY: Shhhhhh. Be still . . . wait.

GRANDMA [*to herself*]:   That's better. Night. [*To the Musician.*] Honey, do you play all through this part?

The Musician nods.

Well, keep it nice and soft; that's a good boy.

The Musician nods again; plays softly.

That's nice.

There is an off-stage rumble.

DADDY [*starting*]:   What was that?

MOMMY [*beginning to weep*]:   It was nothing.

DADDY: It was . . . it was . . . thunder . . . or a wave breaking . . . or something.

MOMMY: [*whispering, through her tears*]:   It was an off-stage rumble . . . and you know what *that* means . . .

DADDY: I forget. . . .

MOMMY [*barely able to talk*]: It means the time has come for poor Grandma . . . and I can't bear it!

DADDY: [*vacantly*]: I . . . I suppose you've got to be brave.

GRANDMA [*mocking*]: That's right, kid; be brave. You'll bear up; you'll get over it.

Another off-stage rumble . . . louder.

MOMMY: Ohhhhhhhhhh . . . poor Grandma . . . poor Grandma. . . .

GRANDMA [*to Mommy*]: I'm fine! I'm all right! It hasn't happened yet!

A violent off-stage rumble. All the lights go out, save the spot on the Young Man; the Musician stops playing.

MOMMY: Ohhhhhhhhhh. . . . Ohhhhhhhhhh. . . .

Silence.

GRANDMA: Don't put the lights up yet . . . I'm not ready; I'm not quite ready. [*Silence.*] All right, dear . . . I'm about done.

The lights come up again, to brightest day; the Musician begins to play. Grandma is discovered, still in the sandbox, lying on her side, propped up on an elbow, half covered, busily shoveling sand over herself.

GRANDMA [*muttering*]: I don't know how I'm supposed to do anything with this goddam toy shovel. . . .

DADDY: Mommy! It's daylight!

MOMMY [*brightly*]: So it is! Well! Our long night is over. We must put away our tears, take off our mourning . . . and face the future. It's our duty.

GRANDMA [*still shoveling; mimicking*]: . . . take off our mourning . . . face the future. . . . Lordy!

Mommy and Daddy rise, stretch. Mommy waves to the young man.

YOUNG MAN [*with that smile*]: Hi!

Grandma plays dead. [!] Mommy and Daddy go over to look at her; she is a little more than half buried in the sand; the toy shovel is in her hands, which are crossed on her breast.

MOMMY [*before the sandbox; shaking her head*]: Lovely! It's . . . it's hard to be sad . . . she looks . . . so happy. [*With pride and conviction.*] It pays to do things well. [*To the Musician.*] All right, you can stop now, if you want to. I mean, stay around for a swim, or something; it's all right with us. [*She sighs heavily.*] Well, Daddy . . . off we go.

DADDY: Brave Mommy!

MOMMY: Brave Daddy!

They exit, stage-left.

GRANDMA [*after they leave; lying quite still*]: It pays to do things well. . . . Boy, oh boy! [*She tries to sit up*] . . . well, kids . . . [*but she finds she can't*] . . . I . . . I can't get up, I . . . I can't move. . . .

The Young Man stops his calisthenics, nods to the Musician, walks over to Grandma, kneels down by the sandbox.

GRANDMA: I . . . can't move. . . .

YOUNG MAN: Shhhhh . . . be very still. . . .

GRANDMA: I . . . I can't move. . . .

YOUNG MAN: Uh . . . ma'am; I . . . I have a line here.

GRANDMA: Oh, I'm sorry, sweetie; you go right ahead.

YOUNG MAN: I am . . . uh . . .

GRANDMA: Take your time, dear.

YOUNG MAN [*prepares; delivers the line like a real amateur*]: I am the Angel of Death. I am . . . uh . . . I am come for you.

GRANDMA: What . . . wha . . . [*Then, with resignation.*] . . . ohhhh . . . ohhhh, I see.

The Young Man bends over, kisses Grandma gently on the forehead.

GRANDMA [*her eyes closed, her hands folded on her breast again, the shovel between her hands, a sweet smile on her face*]: Well . . . that was very nice, dear . . .

YOUNG MAN [*still kneeling*]: Shhhhhh . . . be still. . . .

GRANDMA: What I mean was . . . you did that very well, dear. . . .

YOUNG MAN [*blushing*]: . . . oh . . .

GRANDMA: No; I mean it. You've got that . . . you've got a quality.

YOUNG MAN [*with his endearing smile*]: Oh . . . thank you; thank you very much . . . ma'am.

GRANDMA [*slowly; softly—as the Young Man puts his hands on top of Grandma's*]: You're . . . you're welcome . . . dear.

Tableau. The Musician continues to play as the curtain slowly comes down.

Curtain

ATHOL FUGARD ■ (b. 1932)

Athol Fugard was born in Middelburg, Cape Province, South Africa, and was educated at the University of Cape Town. Growing up during the period of South African apartheid, Fugard both resisted and participated in the segregationist policies of the government, even insisting, at one point, that the family servants call him Master Harold (his given first name) and, in a moment of anger, spitting on one with whom he had been especially close. As he later said to an interviewer, "I think at a fairly early age I became suspicious of what the system was trying to do to me. . . . I became conscious of what attitudes it was trying to implant in me and what prejudices it was trying to pass on to me." Fugard founded the first important black theatrical company in South Africa, and he gained early prominence in his native country by his exploration of racial issues. While Fugard does not consider himself a political writer, his depictions of the interplay of black and white lives made him a controversial figure as a critic of apartheid. "Master Harold". . . and the boys is clearly an autobiographical work, for Fugard's father was a wounded war veteran, and his mother helped to support the family by running a tea room. After leaving college to travel to the Far East as a crew member of a tramp steamer, Fugard at first attempted to write novels but soon turned to the theater. Fugard began to produce his plays in the mid-1950s, and the New York production of The Blood Knot in 1964 established his American reputation. "Master Harold" . . . and the boys was first produced in New Haven, Connecticut, in 1982 and soon enjoyed a successful Broadway run. Since the end of the apartheid era, Fugard has continued to write plays and autobiographical memoirs. He has often been mentioned as a possible recipient of the Nobel Prize.

"Master Harold" . . . and the boys

Characters

Hally

Sam

Willie

Scene: The St. George's Park Tea Room on a wet and windy Port Elizabeth afternoon.

Tables and chairs have been cleared and are stacked on one side except for one which stands apart with a single chair. On this table a knife, fork, spoon and side plate in anticipation of a simple meal, together with a pile of comic books.

Other elements: a serving counter with a few stale cakes under glass and a not very impressive display of sweets, cigarettes and cool drinks, etc.; a few cardboard advertising handouts—Cadbury's Chocolate, Coca-Cola—and a blackboard on which an untrained hand has chalked up the prices of Tea, Coffee, Scones, Milkshakes—all flavors—and Cool Drinks; a few sad ferns in pots; a telephone; an old-style jukebox.

There is an entrance on one side and an exit into a kitchen on the other.

Leaning on the solitary table, his head cupped in one hand as he pages through one of the comic books, is Sam. A black man in his mid-forties. He wears the white coat of a waiter. Behind him on his knees, mopping down the floor with a bucket of water and a rag, is Willie. Also black and about the same age as Sam. He has his sleeves and trousers rolled up.

The year: 1950

WILLIE [*Singing as he works*]:
"She was scandalizin' my name,
She took my money
She called me honey
But she was scandalizin' my name.
Called it love but was playin' a game . . ."

He gets up and moves the bucket. Stands thinking for a moment, then, raising his arms to hold an imaginary partner, he launches into an intricate ballroom dance step. Although a mildly comic figure, he reveals a reasonable degree of accomplishment.

Hey, Sam.

Sam, absorbed in the comic book, does not respond.

Hey, Boet Sam!

Sam looks up.

I'm getting it. The quickstep. Look now and tell me. [*He repeats the step*] Well?

SAM [*Encouragingly*]:   Show me again.

WILLIE: Okay, count for me.

SAM: Ready?

WILLIE: Ready.

SAM: Five, six, seven, eight . . . [*Willie starts to dance*] A-n-d one two three four . . . and one two three four . . . [*Ad libbing as Willie dances*] Your shoulders, Willie . . . your shoulders! Don't look down! Look happy, Willie! Relax, Willie!

WILLIE [*Desperate but still dancing*]: I am relax.

SAM: No, you're not.

WILLIE [*He falters*]: Ag no man, Sam! Mustn't talk. You make me make mistakes.

SAM: But you're too stiff.

WILLIE: Yesterday I'm not straight . . . today I'm too stiff!

SAM: Well, you are. You asked me and I'm telling you.

WILLIE: Where?

SAM: Everywhere. Try to glide through it.

WILLIE: Glide?

SAM: Ja, make it smooth. And give it more style. It must look like you're enjoying yourself.

WILLIE [*Emphatically*]: I wasn't.

SAM: Exactly.

WILLIE: How can I enjoy myself? Not straight, too stiff and now it's also glide, give it more style, make it smooth. . . . Haai! Is hard to remember all those things, Boet Sam.

SAM: That's your trouble. You're trying too hard.

WILLIE: I try hard because it *is* hard.

SAM: But don't let me see it. The secret is to make it look easy. Ballroom must look happy, Willie, not like hard work. It must . . . Ja! . . . it must look like romance.

WILLIE: Now another one! What's romance?

SAM: Love story with happy ending. A handsome man in tails, and in his arms, smiling at him, a beautiful lady in evening dress!

WILLIE: Fred Astaire, Ginger Rogers.

SAM: You got it. Tapdance or ballroom, it's the same. Romance. In two weeks' time when the judges look at you and Hilda, they must see a man and a woman who are dancing their way to a happy ending. What I saw was you holding her like you were frightened she was going to run away.

WILLIE: Ja! Because that is what she wants to do! I got no romance left for Hilda anymore, Boet Sam.

SAM: Then pretend. When you put your arms around Hilda, imagine she is Ginger Rogers.

WILLIE: With no teeth? You try.

SAM: Well, just remember, there's only two weeks left.

WILLIE: I know, I know! [*To the jukebox*] I do it better with music. You got sixpence for Sarah Vaughan?

SAM: That's a slow foxtrot. You're practicing the quick-step.

WILLIE: I'll practice slow foxtrot.

SAM [*Shaking his head*]: It's your turn to put money in the jukebox.

WILLIE: I only got bus fare to go home. [*He returns disconsolately to his work*] Love story and happy ending! She's doing it all right, Boet Sam, but is not me she's giving happy endings. Fuckin' whore! Three nights now she doesn't come practice. I wind up gramophone, I get record ready and I sit and wait. What happens? Nothing. Ten o'clock I start dancing with my pillow. You try and practice romance by yourself, Boet Sam. Struesgod, she doesn't come tonight I take back my dress and ballroom shoes and I find me new partner. Size twenty-six. Shoes size seven. And now she's also making trouble for me with the baby again. Reports me to Child Wellfed, that I'm not giving her money. She lies! Every week I am giving her money for milk. And how do I know is my baby? Only his hair looks like me. She's fucking around all the time I turn my back. Hilda Samuels is a bitch! [*Pause*] Hey, Sam!

SAM: Ja.

WILLIE: You listening?

SAM: Ja.

WILLIE: So what you say?

SAM: About Hilda?

WILLIE: Ja.

SAM: When did you last give her a hiding?

WILLIE [*Reluctantly*]: Sunday night.

SAM: And today is Thursday.

WILLIE [*He knows what's coming*]: Okay.

SAM: Hiding on Sunday night, then Monday, Tuesday and Wednesday she doesn't come to practice . . . and you are asking me why?

WILLIE: I said okay, Boet Sam!

SAM: You hit her too much. One day she's going to leave you for good.

WILLIE: So? She makes me the hell-in too much.

SAM [*Emphasizing his point*]: *Too* much and *too* hard. You had the same trouble with Eunice.

WILLIE: Because she also make the hell-in, Boet Sam. She never got the steps right. Even the waltz.

SAM: Beating her up every time she makes a mistake in the waltz?
[*Shaking his head*] No, Willie! That takes the pleasure out of ballroom dancing.

WILLIE: Hilda is not too bad with the waltz, Boet Sam. Is the quick-
step where the trouble starts.

SAM [*Teasing him gently*]:   How's your pillow with the quickstep?

WILLIE [*Ignoring the tease*]:   Good! And why? Because it got no legs.
That's her trouble. She can't move them quick enough, Boet Sam. I
start the record and before halfway Count Basie is already winning.
Only time we catch up with him is when gramophone runs down.

Sam laughs.

Haaikona, Boet Sam, is not funny.

SAM [*Snapping his fingers*]:   I got it! Give her a handicap.

WILLIE: What's that?

SAM: Give her a ten-second start and then let Count Basie go. Then I
put my money on her. Hot favorite in the Ballroom Stakes: Hilda
Samuels ridden by Willie Malopo.

WILLIE [*Turning away*]:   I'm not talking to you no more.

SAM [*Relenting*]:   Sorry, Willie . . .

WILLIE: It's finish between us.

SAM: Okay, okay . . . I'll stop.

WILLIE: You can also fuck off.

SAM: Willie, listen! I want to help you!

WILLIE: No more jokes?

SAM: I promise.

WILLIE: Okay. Help me.

SAM [*His turn to hold an imaginary partner*]:   Look and learn. Feet together. Back straight. Body relaxed. Right hand placed gently in
the small of her back and wait for the music. Don't start worrying
about making mistakes or the judges or the other competitors. It's
just you, Hilda and the music, and you're going to have a good
time. What Count Basie do you play?

WILLIE: "You the cream in my coffee, you the salt in my stew."

SAM: Right. Give it to me in strict tempo.

WILLIE: Ready?

SAM: Ready.

WILLIE: A-n-d . . . [*Singing*]
"You the cream in my coffee.
You the salt in my stew.

You will always be my necessity.
I'd be lost without
    you. . . ." [*etc.*]

Sam launches into the quickstep. He is obviously a much more accomplished dancer than Willie. Hally enters. A seventeen-year-old white boy. Wet raincoat and school case. He stops and watches Sam. The demonstration comes to an end with a flourish. Applause from Hally and Willie.

HALLY: Bravo! No question about it. First place goes to Mr. Sam Semela.

WILLIE [*In total agreement*]:   You was gliding with style, Boet Sam.

HALLY [*Cheerfully*]:   How's it, chaps?

SAM: Okay, Hally.

WILLIE [*Springing to attention like a soldier and saluting*]:   At your service, Master Harold!

HALLY: Not long to the big event, hey!

SAM: Two weeks.

HALLY: You nervous?

SAM: No.

HALLY: Think you stand a chance?

SAM: Let's just say I'm ready to go out there and dance.

HALLY: It looked like it. What about you, Willie?

Willie groans.

What's the matter?

SAM: He's got leg trouble.

HALLY [*Innocently*]:   Oh, sorry to hear that, Willie.

WILLIE: Boet Sam! You promised. [*Willie returns to his work*]

Hally deposits his school case and takes off his raincoat. His clothes are a little neglected and untidy: black blazer with school badge, gray flannel trousers in need of an ironing, khaki shirt and tie, black shoes. Sam has fetched a towel for Hally to dry his hair.

HALLY: God, what a lousy bloody day. It's coming down cats and dogs out there. Bad for business, chaps . . . [*Conspiratorial whisper*] . . . but it also means we're in for a nice quiet afternoon.

SAM: You can speak loud. Your Mom's not here.

HALLY: Out shopping?

SAM: No. The hospital.

HALLY: But it's Thursday. There's no visiting on Thursday afternoons. Is my Dad okay?

SAM: Sounds like it. In fact, I think he's going home.

HALLY [*Stopped short by Sam's remark*]: What do you mean?

SAM: The hospital phoned.

HALLY: To say what?

SAM: I don't know. I just heard your Mom talking.

HALLY: So what makes you say he's going home?

SAM: It sounded as if they were telling her to come and fetch him.

Hally thinks about what Sam has said for a few seconds.

HALLY: When did she leave?

SAM: About an hour ago. She said she would phone you. Want to eat?

Hally doesn't respond.

Hally, want your lunch?

HALLY: I suppose so. [*His mood has changed*] What's on the menu? . . . as if I don't know.

SAM: Soup, followed by meat pie and gravy.

HALLY: Today's?

SAM: No.

HALLY: And the soup?

SAM: Nourishing pea soup.

HALLY: Just the soup. [*The pile of comic books on the table*] And these?

SAM: For your Dad. Mr. Kempston brought them.

HALLY: You haven't been reading them, have you?

SAM: Just looking.

HALLY [*Examining the comics*]: Jungle Jim . . . Batman and Robin . . . Tarzan . . . God, what rubbish! Mental pollution. Take them away.

Sam exits waltzing into the kitchen. Hally turns to Willie.

HALLY: Did you hear my Mom talking on the telephone, Willie?

WILLIE: No, Master Hally. I was at the back.

HALLY: And she didn't say anything to you before she left?

WILLIE: She said I must clean the floors.

HALLY: I mean about my Dad.

WILLIE: She didn't say nothing to me about him, Master Hally.

HALLY [*With conviction*]: No! It can't be. They said he needed at least another three weeks of treatment. Sam's definitely made a mistake.

[*Rummages through his school case, finds a book and settles down at the table to read*] So, Willie!

WILLIE: Yes, Master Hally! Schooling okay today?

HALLY: Yes, okay. . . . [*He thinks about it*] . . . No, not really. Ag, what's the difference? I don't care. And Sam says you've got problems.

WILLIE: Big problems.

HALLY: Which leg is sore?

Willie groans.

Both legs.

WILLIE: There is nothing wrong with my legs. Sam is just making jokes.

HALLY: So then you *will* be in the competition.

WILLIE: Only if I can find me a partner.

HALLY: But what about Hilda?

SAM [*Returning with a bowl of soup*]: She's the one who's got trouble with her legs.

HALLY: What sort of trouble, Willie?

SAM: From the way he describes it, I think the lady has gone a bit lame.

HALLY: Good God! Have you taken her to see a doctor?

SAM: I think a vet would be better.

HALLY: What do you mean?

SAM: What do you call it again when a racehorse goes very fast?

HALLY: Gallop?

SAM: That's it!

WILLIE: Boet Sam!

HALLY: "A gallop down the homestretch to the winning post." But what's that got to do with Hilda?

SAM: Count Basie always gets there first.

Willie lets fly with his slop rag. It misses Sam and hits Hally.

HALLY [*Furious*]: For Christ's sake, Willie! What the hell do you think you're doing!

WILLIE: Sorry, Master Hally, but it's him. . . .

HALLY: Act your bloody age! [*Hurls the rag back at Willie*] Cut out the nonsense now and get on with your work. And you too, Sam. Stop fooling around.

Sam moves away.

No. Hang on. I haven't finished! Tell me exactly what my Mom said.

SAM: I have. "When Hally comes, tell him I've gone to the hospital and I'll phone him."

HALLY: She didn't say anything about taking my Dad home?

SAM: No. It's just that when she was talking on the phone . . .

HALLY [*Interrupting him*]: No, Sam. They can't be discharging him. She would have said so if they were. In any case, we saw him last night and he wasn't in good shape at all. Staff nurse even said there was talk about taking more X-rays. And now suddenly today he's better? If anything, it sounds more like a bad turn to me . . . which I sincerely hope it isn't. Hang on . . . how long ago did you say she left?

SAM: Just before two . . . [*His wrist watch*] . . . hour and a half.

HALLY: I know how to settle it. [*Behind the counter to the telephone. Talking as he dials*] Let's give her ten minutes to get to the hospital, ten minutes to load him up, another ten, at the most, to get home and another ten to get him inside. Forty minutes. They should have been home for at least half an hour already. [*Pause—he waits with the receiver to his ear*] No reply, chaps. And you know why? Because she's at his bedside in hospital helping him pull through a bad turn. You definitely heard wrong.

SAM: Okay.

As far as Hally is concerned, the matter is settled. He returns to his table, sits down and divides his attention between the book and his soup. Sam is at his school case and picks up a textbook.

Modern Graded Mathematics for Standards Nine and Ten. [*Opens it at random and laughs at something he sees*] Who is this supposed to be?

HALLY: Old fart-face Prentice.

SAM: Teacher?

HALLY: Thinks he is. And believe me, that is not a bad likeness.

SAM: Has he seen it?

HALLY: Yes.

SAM: What did he say?

HALLY: Tried to be clever, as usual. Said I was no Leonardo da Vinci and that bad art had to be punished. So, six of the best, and his are bloody good.

SAM: On your bum?

HALLY: Where else? The days when I got them on my hands are gone forever, Sam.

SAM: With your trousers down!

HALLY: No. He's not quite that barbaric.

SAM: That's the way they do it in jail.

HALLY [*Flicker of morbid interest*]:   Really?

SAM: Ja. When the magistrate sentences you to "strokes with a light cane."

HALLY: Go on.

SAM: They make you lie down on a bench. One policeman pulls down your trousers and holds your ankles, another one pulls your shirt over your head and holds your arms . . .

HALLY: Thank you! That's enough.

SAM: . . . and the one that gives you the strokes talks to you gently and for a long time between each one. [*He laughs*]

HALLY: I've heard enough, Sam! Jesus! It's a bloody awful world when you come to think of it. People can be real bastards.

SAM: That's the way it is, Hally.

HALLY: It doesn't *have* to be that way. There is something called progress, you know. We don't exactly burn people at the stake anymore.

SAM: Like Joan of Arc.

HALLY: Correct. If she was captured today, she'd be given a fair trial.

SAM: And then the death sentence.

HALLY [*A world-weary sigh*]:   I know, I know! I oscillate between hope and despair for this world as well, Sam. But things will change, you wait and see. One day somebody is going to get up and give history a kick up the backside and get it going again.

SAM: Like who?

HALLY [*After thought*]:   They're called social reformers. Every age, Sam, has got its social reformer. My history book is full of them.

SAM: So where's ours?

HALLY: Good question. And I hate to say it, but the answer is: I don't know. Maybe he hasn't even been born yet. Or is still only a babe in arms at his mother's breast. God, what a thought.

SAM: So we just go on waiting.

HALLY: Ja, looks like it. [*Back to his soup and the book*]

SAM [*Reading from the textbook*]:   "Introduction: In some mathematical problems only the magnitude . . ." [*He mispronounces the word "magnitude"*]

HALLY [*Correcting him without looking up*]:   Magnitude.

SAM: What's it mean?

HALLY: How big it is. The size of the thing.

SAM [*Reading*]:   ". . . magnitude of the quantities is of importance. In other problems we need to know whether these quantities are negative or positive. For example, whether there is a debit or credit bank balance . . ."

HALLY: Whether you're broke or not.

SAM: ". . . whether the temperature is above or below Zero . . ."

HALLY: Naught degrees. Cheerful state of affairs! No cash and you're freezing to death. Mathematics won't get you out of that one.

SAM: "All these quantities are called . . ." [*Spelling the word*] . . . s-c-a-l . . .

HALLY: Scalars.

SAM: Scalars! [*Shaking his head with a laugh*] You understand all that?

HALLY [*Turning a page*]:   No. And I don't intend to try.

SAM: So what happens when the exams come?

HALLY: Failing a maths exam isn't the end of the world, Sam. How many times have I told you that examination results don't measure intelligence?

SAM: I would say about as many times as you've failed one of them.

HALLY [*Mirthlessly*]:   Ha, ha, ha.

SAM [*Simultaneously*]:   Ha, ha, ha.

HALLY: Just remember Winston Churchill didn't do particularly well at school.

SAM: You've also told me that one many times.

HALLY: Well, it just so happens to be the truth.

SAM [*Enjoying the word*]:   Magnitude! Magnitude! Show me how to use it.

HALLY [*After thought*]:   An intrepid social reformer will not be daunted by the magnitude of the task he has undertaken.

SAM [*Impressed*]:   Couple of jaw-breakers in there!

HALLY: I gave you three for the price of one. Intrepid, daunted and magnitude. I did that once in an exam. Put five of the words I had to explain in one sentence. It was half a page long.

SAM: Well, I'll put my money on you in the English exam.

HALLY: Piece of cake. Eighty percent without even trying.

SAM [*Another textbook from Hally's case*]:   And history?

HALLY: So-so. I'll scrape through. In the fifties if I'm lucky.

SAM: You didn't do too badly last year.

ATHOL FUGARD

HALLY: Because we had World War One. That at least had some action. You try to find that in the South African Parliamentary system.

SAM [*Reading from the history textbook*]:   "Napoleon and the principle of equality." Hey! This sounds interesting. "After concluding peace with Britain in 1802, Napoleon used a brief period of calm to in-sti-tute . . ."

HALLY: Introduce.

SAM: ". . . many reforms. Napoleon regarded all people as equal be-fore the law and wanted them to have equal opportunities for advancement. All ves-ti-ges of the feu-dal system with its oppression of the poor were abolished." Vestiges, feudal system and abolished. I'm all right on oppression.

HALLY: I'm thinking. He swept away . . . abolished . . . the last re-mains . . . vestiges . . . of the bad old days . . . feudal system.

SAM: Ha! There's the social reformer we're waiting for. He sounds like a man of some magnitude.

HALLY: I'm not so sure about that. It's a damn good title for a book, though. A man of magnitude!

SAM: He sounds pretty big to me, Hally.

HALLY: Don't confuse historical significance with greatness. But maybe I'm being a bit prejudiced. Have a look in there and you'll see he's two chapters long. And hell! . . . has he only got dates, Sam, all of which you've got to remember! This campaign and that campaign, and then, because of all the fighting, the next thing is we get Peace Treaties all over the place. And what's the end of the story? Battle of Waterloo, which he loses. Wasn't worth it. No, I don't know about him as a man of magnitude.

SAM: Then who would you say was?

HALLY: To answer that, we need a definition of greatness, and I suppose that would be somebody who . . . somebody who benefited all mankind.

SAM: Right. But like who?

HALLY [*He speaks with total conviction*]:   Charles Darwin. Remember him? That big book from the library. *The Origin of the Species*.

SAM   Him?

HALLY: Yes. For his Theory of Evolution.

SAM: You didn't finish it.

HALLY: I ran out of time. I didn't finish it because my two weeks was up. But I'm going to take it out again after I've digested what I read. It's safe. I've hidden it away in the Theology section. Nobody ever goes in there. And anyway who are you to talk? You hardly even looked at it.

SAM: I tried. I looked at the chapters in the beginning and I saw one called "The Struggle for an Existence." Ah ha, I thought. At last! But what did I get? Something called the mistletoe which needs the apple tree and there's too many seeds and all are going to die except one . . . ! No, Hally.

HALLY [*Intellectually outraged*]:   What do you mean, No! The poor man had to start somewhere. For God's sake, Sam, he revolutionized science. Now we know.

SAM: What?

HALLY: Where we come from and what it all means.

SAM: And that's a benefit to mankind? Anyway, I still don't believe it.

HALLY: God, you're impossible. I showed it to you in black and white.

SAM: Doesn't mean I got to believe it.

HALLY: It's the likes of you that kept the Inquisition in business. It's called bigotry. Anyway, that's my man of magnitude. Charles Darwin! Who's yours?

SAM [*Without hesitation*]:   Abraham Lincoln.

HALLY: I might have guessed as much. Don't get sentimental, Sam. You've never been a slave, you know. And anyway we freed your ancestors here in South Africa long before the Americans. But if you want to thank somebody on their behalf, do it to Mr. William Wilberforce. Come on. Try again. I want a real genius. [*Now enjoying himself, and so is Sam. Hally goes behind the counter and helps himself to a chocolate*]

SAM: William Shakespeare.

HALLY [*No enthusiasm*]:   Oh. So you're also one of them, are you? You're basing that opinion on only one play, you know. You've only read my *Julius Caesar* and even I don't understand half of what they're talking about. They should do what they did with the old Bible: bring the language up to date.

SAM: That's all you've got. It's also the only one *you've* read.

HALLY: I know. I admit it. That's why I suggest we reserve our judgment until we've checked up on a few others. I've got a feeling, though, that by the end of this year one is going to be enough for me, and I can give you the names of twenty-nine other chaps in the Standard Nine class of the Port Elizabeth Technical College who feel the same. But if you want him, you can have him. My turn now. [*Pacing*] This is a damned good exercise, you know! It started off looking like a simple question and here it's got us really probing into the intellectual heritage of our civilization.

SAM: So who is it going to be?

HALLY: My next man . . . and he gets the title on two scores: social reform and literary genius . . . is Leo Nikolaevich Tolstoy.

SAM: That Russian.

HALLY: Correct. Remember the picture of him I showed you?

SAM: With the long beard.

HALLY [*Trying to look like Tolstoy*]:   And those burning, visionary eyes. My God, the face of a social prophet if ever I saw one! And remember my words when I showed it to you? Here's a *man*, Sam!

SAM: Those were words, Hally.

HALLY: Not many intellectuals are prepared to shovel manure with the peasants and then go home and write a "little book" called *War and Peace*. Incidentally, Sam, he was somebody else who, to quote, ". . . did not distinguish himself scholastically."

SAM: Meaning?

HALLY: He was also no good at school.

SAM: Like you and Winston Churchill.

HALLY [*Mirthlessly*]:   Ha, ha, ha.

SAM [*Simultaneously*]:   Ha, ha, ha.

HALLY: Don't get clever, Sam. That man freed his serfs of his own free will.

SAM: No argument. He was a somebody, all right. I accept him.

HALLY: I'm sure Count Tolstoy will be very pleased to hear that. Your turn. Shoot. [*Another chocolate from behind the counter*] I'm waiting, Sam.

SAM: I've got him.

HALLY: Good. Submit your candidate for examination.

SAM: Jesus.

HALLY [*Stopped dead in his tracks*]:   Who?

SAM: Jesus Christ.

HALLY: Oh, come on, Sam!

SAM: The Messiah.

HALLY: Ja, but still . . . No, Sam. Don't let's get started on religion. We'll just spend the whole afternoon arguing again. Suppose I turn around and say Mohammed?

ATHOL FUGARD

SAM: All right.

HALLY: You can't have them both on the same list!

SAM: Why not? You like Mohammed, I like Jesus.

HALLY: I *don't* like Mohammed. I never have. I was merely being hypothetical. As far as I'm concerned, the Koran is as bad as the Bible. No. Religion is out! I'm not going to waste my time again arguing with you about the existence of God. You know perfectly well I'm an atheist . . . and I've got homework to do.

SAM: Okay, I take him back.

HALLY: You've got time for one more name.

SAM [*After thought*]:   I've got one I know we'll agree on. A simple straightforward great Man of Magnitude . . . and no arguments. And *he* really *did* benefit all mankind.

HALLY: I wonder. After your last contribution I'm beginning to doubt whether anything in the way of an intellectual agreement is possible between the two of us. Who is he?

SAM: Guess.

HALLY: Socrates? Alexandre Dumas? Karl Marx? Dostoevsky? Nietzsche?

Sam shakes his head after each name.

Give me a clue.

SAM: The letter P is important . . .

HALLY: Plato!

SAM: . . . and his name begins with an F.

HALLY: I've got it. Freud and Psychology.

SAM: No. I didn't understand him.

HALLY: That makes two of us.

SAM: Think of mouldy apricot jam.

HALLY [*After a delighted laugh*]:   Penicillin and Sir Alexander Fleming! And the title of the book: *The Microbe Hunters*. [*Delighted*] Splendid, Sam! Splendid. For once we are in total agreement. The major breakthrough in medical science in the Twentieth Century. If it wasn't for him, we might have lost the Second World War. It's deeply gratifying, Sam, to know that I haven't been wasting my time in talking to you. [*Strutting around proudly*] Tolstoy may have educated his peasants, but I've educated you.

SAM: Standard Four to Standard Nine.

HALLY: Have we been at it as long as that?

SAM: Yep. And my first lesson was geography.

HALLY [*Intrigued*]: Really? I don't remember.

SAM: My room there at the back of the old Jubilee Boarding House. I had just started working for your Mom. Little boy in short trousers walks in one afternoon and asks me seriously: "Sam, do you want to see South Africa?" Hey man! Sure I wanted to see South Africa!

HALLY: Was that me?

SAM: . . . So the next thing I'm looking at a map you had just done for homework. It was your first one and you were very proud of yourself.

HALLY: Go on.

SAM: Then came my first lesson. "Repeat after me, Sam: Gold in the Transvaal, mealies in the Free State, sugar in Natal and grapes in the Cape." I still know it!

HALLY: Well, I'll be buggered. So that's how it all started.

SAM: And your next map was one with all the rivers and the mountains they came from. The Orange, the Vaal, the Limpopo, the Zambezi . . .

HALLY: You've got a phenomenal memory!

SAM: You should be grateful. That is why you started passing your exams. You tried to be better than me.

They laugh together. Willie is attracted by the laughter and joins them.

HALLY: The old Jubilee Boarding House. Sixteen rooms with board and lodging, rent in advance and one week's notice. I haven't thought about it for donkey's years . . . and I don't think that's an accident. God, was I glad when we sold it and moved out. Those years are not remembered as the happiest ones of an unhappy childhood.

WILLIE [*Knocking on the table and trying to imitate a woman's voice*]: "Hally, are you there?"

HALLY: Who's that supposed to be?

WILLIE: "What you doing in there, Hally? Come out at once!"

HALLY [*To Sam*]: What's he talking about?

SAM: Don't you remember?

WILLIE: "Sam, Willie . . . is he in there with you boys?"

SAM: Hiding away in our room when your mother was looking for you.

HALLY [*Another good laugh*]: Of course! I used to crawl and hide under your bed! But finish the story, Willie. Then what used to happen?

You chaps would give the game away by telling her I was in there with you. So much for friendship.

SAM: We couldn't lie to her. She knew.

HALLY: Which meant I got another rowing for hanging around the "servants' quarters." I think I spent more time in there with you chaps than anywhere else in that dump. And do you blame me? Nothing but bloody misery wherever you went. Somebody was always complaining about the food, or my mother was having a fight with Micky Nash because she'd caught her with a petty officer in her room. Maud Meiring was another one. Remember those two? They were prostitutes, you know. Soldiers and sailors from the troopships. Bottom fell out of the business when the war ended. God, the flotsam and jetsam that life washed up on our shores! No joking, if it wasn't for your room, I would have been the first certified ten-year-old in medical history. Ja, the memories are coming back now. Walking home from school and thinking: "What can I do this afternoon?" Try out a few ideas, but sooner or later I'd end up in there with you fellows. I bet you I could still find my way to your room with my eyes closed. [*He does exactly that*]. Down the corridor . . . telephone on the right, which my Mom keeps locked because somebody is using it on the sly and not paying . . . past the kitchen and unappetizing cooking smells . . . around the corner into the backyard, hold my breath again because there are more smells coming when I pass your lavatory, then into that little passageway, first door on the right and into your room. How's that?

SAM: Good. But, as usual, you forgot to knock.

HALLY: Like that time I barged in and caught you and Cynthia . . . at it. Remember? God, was I embarrassed! I didn't know what was going on at first.

SAM: Ja, that taught you a lesson.

HALLY: And about a lot more than knocking on doors, I'll have you know, and I don't mean geography either. Hell, Sam, couldn't you have waited until it was dark?

SAM: No.

HALLY: Was it that urgent?

SAM: Yes, and if you don't believe me, wait until your time comes.

HALLY: No, thank you. I am not interested in girls. [*Back to his memories . . . Using a few chairs he recreates the room as he lists the items*] A gray little room with a cold cement floor. Your bed against that wall . . . and I now know why the mattress sags so much! . . . Willie's bed . . . it's propped up on bricks because one leg is broken . . . that wobbly little table with the washbasin and jug of water . . . Yes! . . . stuck to the wall above it are some pin-up pictures from magazines. Joe Louis . . .

WILLIE: Brown Bomber. World Title. [*Boxing pose*] Three rounds and knockout.

HALLY: Against who?

SAM: Max Schmeling.

HALLY: Correct. I can also remember Fred Astaire and Ginger Rogers, and Rita Hayworth in a bathing costume which always made me hot and bothered when I looked at it. Under Willie's bed is an old suitcase with all his clothes in a mess, which is why I never hide there. Your things are neat and tidy in a trunk next to your bed, and on it there is a picture of you and Cynthia in your ballroom clothes, your first silver cup for third place in a competition and an old radio which doesn't work anymore. Have I left out anything?

SAM: No.

HALLY: Right, so much for the stage directions. Now the characters. [*Sam and Willie move to their appropriate positions in the bedroom*] Willie is in bed, under his blankets with his clothes on, complaining nonstop about something, but we can't make out a word of what he's saying because he's got his head under the blankets as well. You're on your bed trimming your toenails with a knife—not a very edifying sight—and as for me . . . What am I doing?

SAM: You're sitting on the floor giving Willie a lecture about being a good loser while you get the checker board and pieces ready for a game. Then you go to Willie's bed, pull off the blankets and make him play with you first because you know you're going to win, and that gives you the second game with me.

HALLY: And you certainly were a bad loser, Willie!

WILLIE: Haai!

HALLY: Wasn't he, Sam? And so slow! A game with you almost took the whole afternoon. Thank God I gave up trying to teach you how to play chess.

WILLIE: You and Sam cheated.

HALLY: I never saw Sam cheat, and mine were mostly the mistakes of youth.

WILLIE: Then how is it you two was always winning?

HALLY: Have you ever considered the possibility, Willie, that it was because we were better than you?

WILLIE: Every time better?

HALLY: Not every time. There were occasions when we deliberately let you win a game so that you would stop sulking and go on playing with us. Sam used to wink at me when you weren't looking to show me it was time to let you win.

WILLIE: So then you two didn't play fair.

HALLY: It was for your benefit, Mr. Malopo, which is more than being fair. It was an act of self-sacrifice. [*To Sam*] But you know what my best memory is, don't you?

SAM: No.

HALLY: Come on, guess. If your memory is so good, you must remember it as well.

SAM: We got up to a lot of tricks in there, Hally.

HALLY: This one was special, Sam.

SAM: I'm listening.

HALLY: It started off looking like another of those useless nothing-to-do afternoons. I'd already been down to Main Street looking for adventure, but nothing had happened. I didn't feel like climbing trees in the Donkin Park or pretending I was a private eye and following a stranger . . . so as usual: See what's cooking in Sam's room. This time it was you on the floor. You had two thin pieces of wood and you were smoothing them down with a knife. It didn't look particularly interesting, but when I asked you what you were doing, you just said, "Wait and see, Hally. Wait . . . and see" . . . in that secret sort of way of yours, so I knew there was a surprise coming. You teased me, you bugger, by being deliberately slow and not answering my questions!

Sam laughs.

And whistling while you worked away! God, it was infuriating! I could have brained you! It was only when you tied them together in a cross and put that down on the brown paper that I realized what you were doing. "Sam is making a kite?" And when I asked you and you said "Yes" . . . ! [*Shaking his head with disbelief*] The sheer audacity of it took my breath away. I mean, seriously, what the hell does a black man know about flying a kite? I'll be honest with you, Sam, I had no hopes for it. If you think I was excited and happy, you got another guess coming. In fact, I was shit-scared that we were going to make fools of ourselves. When we left the boarding house to go up onto the hill, I was praying quietly that there wouldn't be any other kids around to laugh at us.

SAM [*Enjoying the memory as much as Hally*]:   Ja, I could see that.

HALLY: I made it obvious, did I?

SAM: Ja. You refused to carry it.

HALLY: Do you blame me? Can you remember what the poor thing looked like? Tomato-box wood and brown paper! Flour and water for glue! Two of my mother's old stockings for a tail, and then all those bits and pieces of string you made me tie together so that we could fly it! Hell, no, that was now only asking for a miracle to happen.

SAM: Then the big argument when I told you to hold the string and run with it when I let go.

HALLY: I was prepared to run, all right, but straight back to the boarding house.

SAM [*Knowing what's coming*]:   So what happened?

HALLY: Come on, Sam, you remember as well as I do.

SAM: I want to hear it from you.

Hally pauses. He wants to be as accurate as possible.

HALLY: You went a little distance from me down the hill, you held it up ready to let it go. . . . "This is it," I thought. "Like everything else in my life, here comes another fiasco." Then you shouted, "Go, Hally!" and I started to run. [*Another pause*] I don't know how to describe it, Sam. Ja! The miracle happened! I was running, waiting for it to crash to the ground, but instead suddenly there was something alive behind me at the end of the string, tugging at it as if it wanted to be free. I looked back . . . [*Shakes his head*] . . . I still can't believe my eyes. It was flying! Looping around and trying to climb even higher into the sky. You shouted to me to let it have more string. I did, until there was none left and I was just holding that piece of wood we had tied it to. You came up and joined me. You were laughing.

SAM: So were you. And shouting, "It works, Sam! We've done it!"

HALLY: And we had! I was so proud of us! It was the most splendid thing I had ever seen. I wished there were hundreds of kids around to watch us. The part that scared me, though, was when you showed me how to make it dive down to the ground and then just when it was on the point of crashing, swoop up again!

SAM: You didn't want to try yourself.

HALLY: Of course not! I would have been suicidal if anything had happened to it. Watching you do it made me nervous enough. I was quite happy just to see it up there with its tail fluttering behind it. You left me after that, didn't you? You explained how to get it down, we tied it to the bench so that I could sit and watch it, and you went away. I wanted you to stay, you know. I was a little scared of having to look after it by myself.

SAM [*Quietly*]:   I had work to do, Hally.

HALLY: It was sort of sad bringing it down, Sam. And it looked sad again when it was lying there on the ground. Like something that had lost its soul. Just tomato-box wood, brown paper and two of my mother's old stockings! But, hell, I'll never forget that first moment when I saw it up there. I had a stiff neck the next day from looking up so much.

Sam laughs. Hally turns to him with a question he never thought of asking before.

Why did you make that kite, Sam?

SAM [*Evenly*]:   I can't remember.

HALLY: Truly?

SAM: Too long ago, Hally.

HALLY: Ja, I suppose it was. It's time for another one, you know.

SAM: Why do you say that?

HALLY: Because it feels like that. Wouldn't be a good day to fly it, though.

SAM: No. You can't fly kites on rainy days.

HALLY   [*He studies Sam. Their memories have made him conscious of the man's presence in his life*]:   How old are you, Sam?

SAM: Two score and five.

HALLY: Strange, isn't it?

SAM: What?

HALLY: Me and you.

SAM: What's strange about it?

HALLY: Little white boy in short trousers and a black man old enough to be his father flying a kite. It's not every day you see that.

SAM: But why strange? Because the one is white and the other black?

HALLY: I don't know. Would have been just as strange, I suppose, if it had been me and my Dad . . . cripple man and a little boy! Nope!

There's no chance of me flying a kite without it being strange. [*Simple statement of fact—no self-pity*] There's a nice little short story there. "The Kite-Flyers." But we'd have to find a twist in the ending.

SAM: Twist?

HALLY: Yes. Something unexpected. The way it ended with us was too straightforward . . . me on the bench and you going back to work. There's no drama in that.

WILLIE: And me?

HALLY: You?

WILLIE: Yes me.

HALLY: You want to get into the story as well, do you? I got it! Change the title: "Afternoons in Sam's Room" . . . expand it and tell all the stories. It's on its way to being a novel. Our days in the old Jubilee. Sad in a way that they're over. I almost wish we were still in that little room.

SAM: We're still together.

HALLY: That's true. It's just that life felt the right size in there . . . not too big and not too small. Wasn't so hard to work up a bit of courage. It's got so bloody complicated since then.

The telephone rings. Sam answers it.

SAM: St. George's Park Tea Room . . . Hello, Madam . . . Yes, Madam, he's here. . . . Hally, it's your mother.

HALLY: Where is she phoning from?

SAM: Sounds like the hospital. It's a public telephone.

HALLY [*Relieved*]: You see! I told you. [*The telephone*] Hello, Mom . . . Yes . . . Yes no fine. Everything's under control here. How's things with poor old Dad? . . . Has he had a bad turn? . . . What? . . . Oh, God! . . . Yes, Sam told me, but I was sure he'd made a mistake. But what's this all about, Mom? He didn't look at all good last night. How can he get better so quickly? . . . Then very obviously you must say no. Be firm with him. You're the boss. . . . You know what it's going to be like if he comes home. . . . Well then, don't blame me when I fail my exams at the end of the year. . . . Yes! How am I expected to be fresh for school when I spend half the night massaging his gammy leg? . . . So am I! . . . So tell him a white lie. Say Dr. Colley wants more X-rays of his stump. Or bribe him. We'll sneak in double tots of brandy in future. . . . What? . . . Order him to get back into bed at once! If he's going to behave like a child, treat him like one. . . . All right, Mom! I was just trying to . . . I'm sorry. . . . I said I'm sorry. . . . Quick, give me your number. I'll phone you back. [*He hangs up and waits a few seconds*] Here we go again! [*He dials*] I'm sorry, Mom. . . . Okay . . . But now listen to me carefully. All it needs is for you to put your foot down. Don't take no for an answer. . . . Did you hear me? And whatever you do, don't discuss it with him. . . . Because I'm frightened you'll give in to him. . . . Yes, Sam gave me lunch. . . . I ate all of it! . . . No, Mom not a soul. It's still raining here. . . . Right, I'll tell them. I'll just do some homework and then lock up. . . . But remember now, Mom. Don't listen to anything he says. And phone me back and let me know what happens. . . . Okay. Bye, Mom. [*He hangs up. The men are staring at him*] My Mom says that when you're finished with the floors you must do the windows. [*Pause*] Don't misunderstand me, chaps. All I want is for him to get better. And if he was, I'd be the first person to say: "Bring him home." But he's not, and we can't give him the medical care and attention he needs at home. That's what hospitals are there for. [*Brusquely*] So don't just stand there! Get on with it!

Sam clears Hally's table.

You heard right. My Dad wants to go home.

SAM: Is he better?

HALLY [*Sharply*]:   No! How the hell can he be better when last night he was groaning with pain? This is not an age of miracles!

SAM: Then he should stay in hospital.

HALLY [*Seething with irritation and frustration*]:   Tell me something I don't know, Sam. What the hell do you think I was saying to my Mom? All I can say is fuck-it-all.

SAM: I'm sure he'll listen to your Mom.

HALLY: You don't know what she's up against. He's already packed his shaving kit and pajamas and is sitting on his bed with his crutches, dressed and ready to go. I know him when he gets in that mood. If she tries to reason with him, we've had it. She's no match for him when it comes to a battle of words. He'll tie her up in knots. [*Trying to hide his true feelings*]

SAM: I suppose it gets lonely for him in there.

HALLY: With all the patients and nurses around? Regular visits from the Salvation Army? Balls! It's ten times worse for him at home. I'm at school and my mother is here in the business all day.

SAM: He's at least got you at night.

HALLY [*Before he can stop himself*]: And we've got him! Please! I don't want to talk about it anymore. [*Unpacks his school case, slamming down books on the table*] Life is just a plain bloody mess, that's all. And people are fools.

SAM: Come on, Hally.

HALLY: Yes, they are! They bloody well deserve what they get.

SAM: Then don't complain.

HALLY: Don't try to be clever, Sam. It doesn't suit you. Anybody who thinks there's nothing wrong with this world needs to have his head examined. Just when things are going along all right, without fail someone or something will come along and spoil everything. Somebody should write that down as a fundamental law of the Universe. The principle of perpetual disappointment. If there is a God who created this world, he should scrap it and try again.

SAM: All right, Hally, all right. What you got for homework?

HALLY: Bullshit, as usual. [*Opens an exercise book and reads*] "Write five hundred words describing an annual event of cultural or historical significance."

SAM: That should be easy enough for you.

HALLY: And also plain bloody boring. You know what he wants, don't you? One of their useless old ceremonies. The commemoration of the landing of the 1820 Settlers, or if it's going to be culture, Carols by Candlelight every Christmas.

SAM: It's an impressive sight. Make a good description, Hally. All those candles glowing in the dark and the people singing hymns.

HALLY: And it's called religious hysteria. [*Intense irritation*] Please, Sam! Just leave me alone and let me get on with it. I'm not in the mood for games this afternoon. And remember my Mom's orders . . . you're to help Willie with the windows. Come on now, I don't want any more nonsense in here.

SAM: Okay, Hally, okay.

Hally settles down to his homework; determined preparations . . . pen, ruler, exercise book, dictionary, another cake . . . all of which will lead to nothing.

Sam waltzes over to Willie and starts to replace tables and chairs. He practices a ballroom step while doing so. Willie watches. When Sam is finished, Willie tries.

Good! But just a little bit quicker on the turn and only move in to her after she's crossed over. What about this one?

Another step. When Sam is finished, Willie again has a go.

Much better. See what happens when you just relax and enjoy yourself? Remember that in two weeks' time and you'll be all right.

WILLIE: But I haven't got partner, Boet Sam.

SAM: Maybe Hilda will turn up tonight.

WILLIE: No, Boet Sam. [*Reluctantly*] I gave her a good hiding.

SAM: You mean a bad one.

WILLIE: Good bad one.

SAM: Then you mustn't complain either. Now you pay the price for losing your temper.

WILLIE: I also pay two pounds ten shilling entrance fee.

SAM: They'll refund you if you withdraw now.

WILLIE [*Appalled*]:   You mean, don't dance?

SAM: Yes.

WILLIE: No! I wait too long and I practice too hard. If I find me new partner, you think I can be ready in two weeks? I ask Madam for my leave now and we practice every day.

SAM: Quickstep non-stop for two weeks. World record, Willie, but you'll be mad at the end.

WILLIE: No jokes, Boet Sam.

SAM: I'm not joking.

WILLIE: So then what?

SAM: Find Hilda. Say you're sorry and promise you won't beat her again.

WILLIE: No.

SAM: Then withdraw. Try again next year.

WILLIE: No.

SAM: Then I give up.

WILLIE: Haaikona, Boet Sam, you can't.

SAM: What do you mean, I can't? I'm telling you: I give up.

WILLIE [*Adamant*]:   No! [*Accusingly*] It was you who start me ballroom dancing.

SAM: So?

WILLIE: Before that I use to be happy. And is you and Miriam who bring me to Hilda and say here's partner for you.

SAM: What are you saying, Willie?

WILLIE: You!

SAM: But me what? To blame?

WILLIE: Yes.

SAM: Willie . . . ? [Bursts into laughter]

WILLIE: And now all you do is make jokes at me. You wait. When Miriam leaves you is my turn to laugh. Ha! Ha! Ha!

SAM [He can't take Willie seriously any longer]: She can leave me tonight! I know what to do. [Bowing before an imaginary partner] May I have the pleasure? [He dances and sings]

"Just a fellow with his pillow . . .

Dancin' like a willow . . .

In an autumn breeze . . ."

WILLIE: There you go again!

Sam goes on dancing and singing.

Boet Sam!

SAM: There's the answer to your problem! Judges' announcement in two weeks' time: "Ladies and gentlemen, the winner in the open section . . . Mr. Willie Malopo and his pillow!"

This is too much for a now really angry Willie. He goes for Sam, but the latter is too quick for him and puts Hally's table between the two of them.

HALLY [Exploding]: For Christ's sake, you two!

WILLIE [Still trying to get at Sam]: I donner you, Sam! Struesgod!

SAM [Still laughing]: Sorry, Willie . . . Sorry . . .

HALLY: Sam! Willie! [Grabs his ruler and gives Willie a vicious whack on the bum] How the hell am I supposed to concentrate with the two of you behaving like bloody children!

WILLIE: Hit him too!

HALLY: Shut up, Willie.

WILLIE: He started jokes again.

HALLY: Get back to your work. You too, Sam. [His ruler] Do you want another one, Willie?

Sam and Willie return to their work. Hally uses the opportunity to escape from his unsuccessful attempt at homework. He struts around like a little despot, ruler in hand, giving vent to his anger and frustration.

Suppose a customer had walked in then? Or the Park Superinten-
dent. And seen the two of you behaving like a pair of hooligans.
That would have been the end of my mother's license, you know.
And your jobs! Well, this is the end of it. From now on there will
be no more of your ballroom nonsense in here. This is a business
establishment, not a bloody New Brighton dancing school. I've
been far too lenient with the two of you. [*Behind the counter for a
green cool drink and a dollop of ice cream. He keeps up his tirade as he
prepares it*] But what really makes me bitter is that I allow you
chaps a little freedom in here when business is bad and what do
you do with it? The foxtrot! Specially you, Sam. There's more to
life than trotting around a dance floor and I thought at least you
knew it.

SAM: It's a harmless pleasure, Hally. It doesn't hurt anybody.

HALLY: It's also a rather simple one, you know.

SAM: You reckon so? Have you ever tried?

HALLY: Of course not.

SAM: Why don't you? Now.

HALLY: What do you mean? Me dance?

SAM: Yes. I'll show you a simple step—the waltz—then you try it.

HALLY: What will that prove?

SAM: That it might not be as easy as you think.

HALLY: I didn't say it was easy. I said it was simple—like in simple-
minded, meaning mentally retarded. You can't exactly say it chal-
lenges the intellect.

SAM: It does other things.

HALLY: Such as?

SAM: Make people happy.

HALLY [*The glass in his hand*]:   So do American cream sodas with ice
cream. For God's sake, Sam, you're not asking me to take ballroom
dancing serious, are you?

SAM: Yes.

HALLY [*Sigh of defeat*]:   Oh, well, so much for trying to give you a decent education. I've obviously achieved nothing.

SAM: You still haven't told me what's wrong with admiring something that's beautiful and then trying to do it yourself.

HALLY: Nothing. But we happen to be talking about a foxtrot, not a
thing of beauty.

SAM: But that is just what I'm saying. If you were to see two champions doing, two masters of the art . . . !

HALLY: Oh, God, I give up. So now it's also art!

SAM: Ja.

HALLY: There's a limit, Sam. Don't confuse art and entertainment.

SAM: So then what is art?

HALLY: You want a definition?

SAM: Ja.

HALLY [*He realizes he has got to be careful. He gives the matter a lot of thought before answering*]: Philosophers have been trying to do that for centuries. What is Art? What is Life? But basically I suppose it's . . . the giving of meaning to matter.

SAM: Nothing to do with beautiful?

HALLY: It goes beyond that. It's the giving of form to the formless.

SAM: Ja, well, maybe it's not art, then. But I still say it's beautiful.

HALLY: I'm sure the word you mean to use is entertaining.

SAM [*Adamant*]: No. Beautiful. And if you want proof, come along to the Centenary Hall in New Brighton in two weeks' time.

The mention of the Centenary Hall draws Willie over to them.

HALLY: What for? I've seen the two of you prancing around in here often enough.

SAM [*He laughs*]: This isn't the real thing, Hally. We're just playing around in here.

HALLY: So? I can use my imagination.

SAM: And what do you get?

HALLY: A lot of people dancing around and having a so-called good time.

SAM: That all?

HALLY: Well, basically it is that, surely.

SAM: No, it isn't. Your imagination hasn't helped you at all. There's a lot more to it than that. We're getting ready for the championships, Hally, not just another dance. There's going to be a lot of people, all right, and they're going to have a good time, but they'll only be spectators, sitting around and watching. It's just the competitors out there on the dance floor. Party decorations and fancy lights all around the walls! The ladies in beautiful evening dresses!

HALLY: My mother's got one of those, Sam, and, quite frankly, it's an embarrassment every time she wears it.

SAM [*Undeterred*]:   Your imagination left out the excitement.

Hally scoffs.

Oh, yes. The finalists are not going to be out there just to have a good time. One of those couples will be the 1950 Eastern Province Champions. And your imagination left out the music.

WILLIE: Mr. Elijah Gladman Guzana and his Orchestral Jazzonions.

SAM: The sound of the big band, Hally. Trombone, trumpet, tenor and alto sax. And then, finally, your imagination also left out the climax of the evening when the dancing is finished, the judges have stopped whispering among themselves and the Master of Ceremonies collects their scorecards and goes up onto the stage to announce the winners.

HALLY: All right. So you make it sound like a bit of a do. It's an occasion. Satisfied?

SAM [*Victory*]:   So you admit that!

HALLY: Emotionally yes, intellectually no.

SAM: Well, I don't know what you mean by that, all I'm telling you is that it is going to be *the* event of the year in New Brighton. It's been sold out for two weeks already. There's only standing room left. We've got competitors coming from Kingwilliamstown, East London, Port Alfred.

Hally starts pacing thoughtfully.

HALLY: Tell me a bit more.

SAM: I thought you weren't interested . . . intellectually.

HALLY [*Mysteriously*]:   I've got my reasons.

SAM: What do you want to know?

HALLY: It takes place every year?

SAM: Yes. But only every third year in New Brighton. It's East London's turn to have the championships next year.

HALLY: Which, I suppose, makes it an even more significant event.

SAM: Ah ha! We're getting somewhere. Our "occasion" is now a "significant event."

HALLY: I wonder.

SAM: What?

HALLY: I wonder if I would get away with it.

SAM: But what?

HALLY [*To the table and his exercise book*]:   "Write five hundred words describing an annual event of cultural or historical significance."

Would I be stretching poetic license a little too far if I called your ballroom championships a cultural event?

SAM: You mean . . . ?

HALLY: You think we could get five hundred words out of it, Sam?

SAM: Victor Sylvester has written a whole book on ballroom dancing.

WILLIE: You going to write about it, Master Hally?

HALLY: Yes, gentlemen, that is precisely what I am considering doing. Old Doc Bromely—he's my English teacher—is going to argue with me, of course. He doesn't like natives. But I'll point out to him that in strict anthropological terms the culture of a primitive black society includes its dancing and singing. To put my thesis in a nutshell: The war-dance has been replaced by the waltz. But it still amounts to the same thing: the release of primitive emotions through movement. Shall we give it a go?

SAM: I'm ready.

WILLIE: Me also.

HALLY: Ha! This will teach the old bugger a lesson. [*Decision taken*] Right. Let's get ourselves organized. [*This means another cake on the table. He sits*] I think you've given me enough general atmosphere, Sam, but to build the tension and suspense I need facts. [*Pencil poised*]

WILLIE: Give him facts, Boet Sam.

HALLY: What you called the climax . . . how many finalists?

SAM: Six couples.

HALLY [*Making notes*]:   Go on. Give me the picture.

SAM: Spectators seated right around the hall. [*Willie becomes a spectator*]

HALLY: . . . and it's a full house.

SAM: At one end, on the stage, Gladman and his Orchestral Jazzonions. At the other end is a long table with the three judges. The six finalists go onto the dance floor and take up their positions. When they are ready and the spectators have settled down, the Master of Ceremonies goes to the microphone. To start with, he makes some jokes to get the people laughing . . .

HALLY: Good touch! [*As he writes*] ". . . creating a relaxed atmosphere which will change to one of tension and drama as the climax is approached."

SAM [*Onto a chair to act out the M.C.*]:   "Ladies and gentlemen, we come now to the great moment you have all been waiting for this evening . . . . The finals of the 1950 Eastern Province Open Ballroom

Dancing Championships. But first let me introduce the finalists! Mr. and Mrs. Welcome Tchabalala from Kingwilliamstown . . ."

WILLIE [He applauds after every name]:   Is when the people clap their hands and whistle and make a lot of noise, Master Hally.

SAM: "Mr. Mulligan Njikelane and Miss Nomhle Nkonyeni of Grahamstown; Mr. and Mrs. Norman Nchinga from Port Alfred; Mr. Fats Bokolane and Miss Dina Plaatjies from East London; Mr. Sipho Dugu and Mrs. Mable Magada from Peddie; and from New Brighton our very own Mr. Willie Malopo and Miss Hilda Samuels."

Willie can't believe his ears. He abandons his role as spectator and scrambles into position as a finalist.

WILLIE: Relaxed and ready to romance!

SAM: The applause dies down. When everybody is silent, Gladman lifts up his sax, nods at the Orchestral Jazzonions . . .

WILLIE: Play the jukebox please, Boet Sam!

SAM: I also only got bus fare, Willie.

HALLY: Hold it, everybody. [*Heads for the cash register behind the counter*] How much is in the till, Sam?

SAM: Three shillings. Hally . . . your Mom counted it before she left.

Hally hesitates.

HALLY: Sorry, Willie. You know how she carried on the last time I did it. We'll just have to pool our combined imaginations and hope for the best. [*Returns to the table*] Back to work. How are the points scored, Sam?

SAM: Maximum of ten points each for individual style, deportment, rhythm and general appearance.

WILLIE: Must I start?

HALLY: Hold it for a second, Willie. And penalties?

SAM: For what?

HALLY: For doing something wrong. Say you stumble or bump into somebody . . . do they take off any points?

SAM [*Aghast*]:   Hally . . . !

HALLY: When you're dancing. If you and your partner collide into another couple.

Hally can get no further. Sam has collapsed with laughter. He explains to Willie.

SAM: If me and Miriam bump into you and Hilda . . .

Willie joins him in another good laugh.

Hally, Hally . . . !

HALLY [*Perplexed*]:   Why? What did I say?

SAM: There's no collisions out there, Hally. Nobody trips or stumbles or bumps into anybody else. That's what that moment is all about. To be one of those finalists on that dance floor is like . . . like being in a dream about a world in which accidents don't happen.

HALLY [*Genuinely moved by Sam's image*]:   Jesus, Sam! That's beautiful!

WILLIE [*Can endure waiting no longer*]:   I'm starting! [*Willie dances while Sam talks*]

SAM: Of course it is. That's what I've been trying to say to you all afternoon. And it's beautiful because that is what we want life to be like. But instead, like you said, Hally, we're bumping into each other all the time. Look at the three of us this afternoon: I've bumped into Willie, the two of us have bumped into you, you've bumped into your mother, she bumping into your Dad. . . . None of us knows the steps and there's no music playing. And it doesn't stop with us. The whole world is doing it all the time. Open a newspaper and what do you read? America has bumped into Russia, England is bumping into India, rich man bumps into poor man. Those are big collisions, Hally. They make for a lot of bruises. People get hurt in all that bumping, and we're sick and tired of it now. It's been going on for too long. Are we never going to get it right? . . . Learn to dance life like champions instead of always being just a bunch of beginners at it?

HALLY [*Deep and sincere admiration of the man*]:   You've got a vision, Sam!

SAM: Not just me. What I'm saying to you is that everybody's got it. That's why there's only standing room left for the Centenary Hall in two weeks' time. For as long as the music lasts, we are going to see six couples get it right, the way we want life to be.

HALLY: But is that the best we can do, Sam . . . watch six finalists dreaming about the way it should be?

SAM: I don't know. But it starts with that. Without the dream we won't know what we're going for. And anyway I reckon there are a few people who have got past just dreaming about it and are trying for something real. Remember that thing we read once in the paper about the Mahatma Gandhi? Going without food to stop those riots in India?

HALLY: You're right. He certainly was trying to teach people to get the steps right.

SAM: And the Pope.

HALLY: Yes, he's another one. Our old General Smuts as well, you know. He's also out there dancing. You know, Sam, when you come to think of it, that's what the United Nations boils down to . . . a dancing school for politicians!

SAM: And let's hope they learn.

HALLY [*A little surge of hope*]: You're right. We mustn't despair. Maybe there's some hope for mankind after all. Keep it up, Willie. [*Back to his table with determination*] This is a lot bigger than I thought. So what have we got? Yes, our title: "A World Without Collisions."

SAM: That sounds good! "A World Without Collisions."

HALLY: Subtitle: "Global Politics on the Dance Floor." No. A bit too heavy, hey? What about "Ballroom Dancing as a Political Vision"?

The telephone rings. Sam answers it.

SAM: St. George's Park Tea Room . . . Yes, Madam . . . Hally, it's your Mom.

HALLY [*Back to reality*]: Oh, God, yes! I'd forgotten all about that. Shit! Remember my words, Sam? Just when you're enjoying yourself, someone or something will come along and wreck everything.

SAM: You haven't heard what she's got to say yet.

HALLY: Public telephone?

SAM: No.

HALLY: Does she sound happy or unhappy?

SAM: I couldn't tell. [*Pause*] She's waiting, Hally.

HALLY [*To the telephone*]: Hello, Mom . . . No, everything is okay here. Just doing my homework. . . . What's your news? . . . You've what? . . . [*Pause. He takes the receiver away from his ear for a few seconds. In the course of Hally's telephone conversation, Sam and Willie discretely position the stacked tables and chairs. Hally places the receiver back to his ear*] Yes, I'm still here. Oh, well, I give up now. Why did you do it, Mom? . . . Well, I just hope you know what you've let us in for. . . . [*Loudly*] I said I hope you know what you've let us in for! It's the end of the peace and quiet we've been having. [*Softly*] Where is he? [*Normal voice*] He can't hear us from in there. But for God's sake, Mom, what happened? I told you to be firm with him. . . . Then you and the nurses should have held him down, taken his crutches away. . . . I know only too well he's my father! . . . I'm not being disrespectful, but I'm sick and tired of emptying stinking chamberpots full of phlegm and piss. . . . Yes, I do! When you're not there, he asks *me* to do it. . . . If you really want to know the truth, that's why I've got no appetite for my food. . . . Yes! There's a lot of things you don't know about. For your information, I still haven't got that science textbook I need. And you know why? He borrowed the money you gave me for it. . . . Because I didn't want to start another fight between you two. . . . He says that every time. . . . All right, Mom! [*Viciously*] Then just remember to start hiding your bag away again, because he'll be at your purse before long for money for booze. And when he's well enough to come down here, you better keep an eye on the till as well, because that is also going to develop a leak. . . . Then don't complain to me when he starts his old tricks. . . . Yes, you do. I get it from you on one side and from him on the other, and it makes life hell for me. I'm not going to be the peacemaker anymore. I'm warning you now: when the two of you start fighting again, I'm leaving home. . . . Mom, if you start crying, I'm going to put down the receiver. . . . Okay . . . [*Lowering his voice to a vicious whisper*] Okay, Mom. I heard you. [*Desperate*] No. . . . Because I don't want to. I'll see him when I get home! Mom! . . . [*Pause. When he speaks again, his tone changes completely. It is not simply pretense. We sense a genuine emotional conflict*] Welcome home, chum! . . . What's that? . . . Don't be silly, Dad. You being home is just about the best news in the world. . . . I bet you are. Bloody depressing there with everybody going on about their ailments, hey! . . . How you feeling? . . . Good . . . Here as well, pal. Coming down cats and dogs. . . . That's right. Just the day for a kip and a toss in your old Uncle Ned. . . . Everything's just hunky-dory on my side, Dad. . . . Well, to start with, there's a nice pile of comics for you on the counter. . . . Yes, old Kemple brought them in. *Batman and Robin, Submariner* . . . just your cup of tea . . . I will. . . . Yes, we'll spin a few yarns tonight. . . . Okay, chum, see you in a little while. . . . No, I promise. I'll come straight home. . . . [*Pause—his mother comes back on the phone*] Mom? Okay. I'll lock up now. . . . What? . . . Oh, the brandy . . . Yes, I'll remember! . . . I'll put it in my suitcase now, for God's sake. I know well enough what will happen if he doesn't get it. . . . [*Places a bottle of brandy on the counter*] I *was* kind to him, Mom. I didn't say anything nasty! . . . All right. Bye. [*End of telephone conversation. A desolate Hally doesn't move. A strained silence*]

SAM [*Quietly*]:   That sounded like a bad bump, Hally.

HALLY [*Having a hard time controlling his emotions. He speaks carefully*]: Mind your own business, Sam.

SAM: Sorry. I wasn't trying to interfere. Shall we carry on? Hally? [*He indicates the exercise book. No response from Hally*]

WILLIE [*Also trying*]:   Tell him about when they give out the cups, Boet Sam.

SAM: Ja! That's another big moment. The presentation of the cups after the winners have been announced. You've got to put that in.

Still no response from Hally.

WILLIE: A big silver one, Master Hally, called floating trophy for the champions.

SAM: We always invite some big-shot personality to hand them over. Guest of honor this year is going to be His Holiness Bishop Jabulani of the All African Free Zionist Church.

Hally gets up abruptly, goes to his table and tears up the page he was writing on.

HALLY: So much for a bloody world without collisions.

SAM: Too bad. It was on its way to being a good composition.

HALLY: Let's stop bullshitting ourselves, Sam.

SAM: Have we been doing that?

HALLY: Yes! That's what all our talk about a decent world has been . . . just so much bullshit.

SAM: We did say it was still only a dream.

HALLY: And a bloody useless one at that. Life's a fuck-up and it's never going to change.

SAM: Ja, maybe that's true.

HALLY: There's no maybe about it. It's a blunt and brutal fact. All we've done this afternoon is waste our time.

SAM: Not if we'd got your homework done.

HALLY: I don't give a shit about my homework, so, for Christ's sake, just shut up about it. [*Slamming books viciously into his school case*] Hurry up now and finish your work. I want to lock up and get out of here. [*Pause*] And then go where? Home-sweet-fucking-home. Jesus, I hate that word.

Hally goes to the counter to put the brandy bottle and comics in his school case. After a moment's hesitation, he smashes the bottle of brandy. He abandons all further attempts to hide his feelings. Sam and Willie work away as unobtrusively as possible.

Do you want to know what is really wrong with your lovely little dream, Sam? It's not just that we are all bad dancers. That does happen to be perfectly true, but there's more to it than just that. You left out the cripples.

SAM: Hally!

HALLY [*Now totally reckless*]:   Ja! Can't leave them out, Sam. That's why we always end up on our backsides on the dance floor. They're also out there dancing . . . like a bunch of broken spiders trying to do the quick-step! [*An ugly attempt at laughter*] When you come to think of it, it's a bloody comical sight. I mean, it's bad enough on two legs . . . but one and a pair of crutches! Hell, no, Sam. That's guaranteed to turn that dance floor into a shambles. Why you shaking your head? Picture it, man. For once this afternoon let's use our imaginations sensibly.

SAM: Be careful, Hally.

HALLY: Of what? The truth? I seem to be the only one around here who is prepared to face it. We've had the pretty dream, it's time now to wake up and have a good long look at the way things really are. Nobody knows the steps, there's no music, the cripples are also out there tripping up everybody and trying to get into the act, and it's all called the All-Comers-How-to-Make-a-Fuckup-of-Life Championships. [*Another ugly laugh*] Hang on, Sam! The best bit is still coming. Do you know what the winner's trophy is? A beautiful big chamber-pot with roses on the side, and it's full to the brim with piss. And guess who I think is going to be this year's winner.

SAM [*Almost shouting*]:   Stop now!

HALLY [*Suddenly appalled by how far he has gone*]:   Why?

SAM: Hally? It's your father you're talking about.

HALLY: So?

SAM: Do you know what you've been saying?

Hally can't answer. He is rigid with shame. Sam speaks to him sternly.

No, Hally, you mustn't do it. Take back those words and ask for forgiveness! It's a terrible sin for a son to mock his father with jokes like that. You'll be punished if you carry on. Your father is your father, even if he is a . . . cripple man.

WILLIE: Yes, Master Hally. Is true what Sam say.

SAM: I understand how you are feeling, Hally, but even so . . .

HALLY: No, you don't!

SAM: I think I do.

HALLY: And I'm telling you you don't. Nobody does. [*Speaking carefully as his shame turns to rage at Sam*] It's your turn to be careful, Sam. Very careful! You're treading on dangerous ground. Leave me and my father alone.

SAM: I'm not the one who's been saying things about him.

HALLY: What goes on between me and my Dad is none of your business!

SAM: Then don't tell me about it. If that's all you've got to say about him, I don't want to hear.

For a moment Hally is at loss for a response.

HALLY: Just get on with your bloody work and shut up.

SAM: Swearing at me won't help you.

HALLY: Yes, it does! Mind your own fucking business and shut up!

SAM: Okay. If that's the way you want it, I'll stop trying.

He turns away. This infuriates Hally even more.

HALLY: Good. Because what you've been trying to do is meddle in something you know nothing about. All that concerns you in here, Sam, is to try and do what you get paid for—keep the place clean and serve the customers. In plain words, just get on with your job. My mother is right. She's always warning me about allowing you to get too familiar. Well, this time you've gone too far. It's going to stop right now.

No response from Sam.

You're only a servant in here, and don't forget it.

Still no response. Hally is trying hard to get one.

And as far as my father is concerned, all you need to remember is that he is your boss.

SAM [*Needled at last*]: No, he isn't. I get paid by your mother.

HALLY: Don't argue with me, Sam!

SAM: Then don't say he's my boss.

HALLY: He's a white man and that's good enough for you.

SAM: I'll try to forget you said that.

HALLY: Don't! Because you won't be doing me a favor if you do. I'm telling you to remember it.

A pause. Sam pulls himself together and makes one last effort.

SAM: Hally, Hally . . . ! Come on now. Let's stop before it's too late. You're right. We *are* on dangerous ground. If we're not careful, somebody is going to get hurt.

HALLY: It won't be me.

SAM: Don't be so sure.

HALLY: I don't know what you're talking about, Sam.

SAM: Yes, you do.

HALLY [*Furious*]: Jesus, I wish you would stop trying to tell me what I do and what I don't know.

Sam gives up. He turns to Willie.

SAM: Let's finish up.

HALLY: Don't turn your back on me! I haven't finished talking.

He grabs Sam by the arm and tries to make him turn around. Sam reacts with a flash of anger.

SAM: Don't do that, Hally! [*Facing the boy*] All right, I'm listening. Well? What do you want to say to me?

HALLY [*Pause as Hally looks for something to say*]: To begin with, why don't you also start calling me Master Harold, like Willie.

SAM: Do you mean that?

HALLY: Why the hell do you think I said it?

SAM: And if I don't?

HALLY: You might just lose your job.

SAM [*Quietly and very carefully*]: If you make me say it once, I'll never call you anything else again.

HALLY: So? [*The boy confronts the man*] Is that meant to be a threat?

SAM: Just telling you what will happen if you make me do that. You must decide what it means to you.

HALLY: Well, I have. It's good news. Because that is exactly what Master Harold wants from now on. Think of it as a little lesson in respect, Sam, that's long overdue, and I hope you remember it as well as you do your geography. I can tell you now that somebody who will be glad to hear I've finally given it to you will be my Dad. Yes! He agrees with my Mom. He's always going on about it as well. "You must teach the boys to show you more respect, my son."

SAM: So now you can stop complaining about going home. Everybody is going to be happy tonight.

HALLY: That's perfectly correct. You see, you mustn't get the wrong idea about me and my Dad, Sam. We also have our good times together. Some bloody good laughs. He's got a marvelous sense of humor. Want to know what our favorite joke is? He gives out a big groan, you see, and says: "It's not fair, is it, Hally?" Then I have to ask: "What, chum?" And then he says: "A nigger's arse" . . . and we both have a good laugh.

The men stare at him with disbelief.

What's the matter, Willie? Don't you catch the joke? You always were a bit slow on the uptake. It's what is called a pun. You see, fair means both light in color and to be just and decent. [*He turns to Sam*] I thought *you* would catch it, Sam.

SAM: Oh ja, I catch it all right.

HALLY: But it doesn't appeal to your sense of humor.

SAM: Do you really laugh?

HALLY: Of course.

SAM: To please him? Make him feel good?

HALLY: No, for heaven's sake! I laugh because I think it's a bloody good joke.

SAM: You're really trying hard to be ugly, aren't you? And why drag poor old Willie into it? He's done nothing to you except show you the respect you want so badly. That's also not being fair, you know . . . and I mean just or decent.

WILLIE: It's all right, Sam. Leave it now.

SAM: It's me you're after. You should just have said "Sam's arse" . . . because that's the one you're trying to kick. Anyway, how do you know it's not fair? You've never seen it. Do you want to? [*He drops his trousers and underpants and presents his backside for Hally's inspection*] Have a good look. A real Basuto arse . . . which is about as nigger as they can come. Satisfied? [*Trousers up*] Now you can make your Dad even happier when you go home tonight. Tell him I showed you my arse and he is quite right. It's not fair. And if it will give him an even better laugh next time, I'll also let *him* have a look. Come, Willie, let's finish up and go.

Sam and Willie start to tidy up the tea room. Hally doesn't move. He waits for a moment when Sam passes him.

HALLY [*Quietly*]:   Sam . . .

Sam stops and looks expectantly at the boy. Hally spits in his face. A long and heartfelt groan from Willie. For a few seconds Sam doesn't move.

SAM [*Taking out a handkerchief and wiping his face*]:   It's all right, Willie.

To Hally.

Ja, well, you've done it . . . Master Harold. Yes, I'll start calling you that from now on. It won't be difficult anymore. You've hurt yourself, Master Harold. I saw it coming. I warned you, but you wouldn't listen. You've just hurt yourself *bad*. And you're a coward, Master Harold. The face you should be spitting in is your father's . . . but you used mine, because you think you're safe inside your fair skin . . . and this time I don't mean just or decent. [*Pause, then moving violently towards Hally*] Should I hit him, Willie?

WILLIE [*Stopping Sam*]:   No, Boet Sam.

SAM [*Violently*]:   Why not?

WILLIE: It won't help, Boet Sam.

SAM: I don't want to help! I want to hurt him.

WILLIE: You also hurt yourself.

SAM: And if he had done it to you, Willie?

WILLIE: Me? Spit at me like I was a dog? [*A thought that had not occurred to him before. He looks at Hally*] Ja. Then I want to hit him. I want to hit him hard!

A dangerous few seconds as the men stand staring at the boy. Willie turns away, shaking his head.

But maybe all I do is go cry at the back. He's little boy, Boet Sam. Little *white* boy. Long trousers now, but he's still little boy.

SAM [*His violence ebbing away into defeat as quickly as it flooded*]: You're right. So go on, then: groan again, Willie. You do it better than me. [*To Hally*] You don't know all of what you've just done . . . Master Harold. It's not just that you've made me feel dirtier than

ATHOL FUGARD

I've ever been in my life . . . I mean, how do I wash off yours and your father's filth? . . . I've also failed. A long time ago I promised myself I was going to try and do something, but you've just shown me . . . Master Harold . . . that I've failed. [*Pause*] I've also got a memory of a little white boy when he was still wearing short trousers and a black man, but they're not flying a kite. It was the old Jubilee days, after dinner one night. I was in my room. You came in and just stood against the wall, looking down at the ground, and only after I'd asked you what you wanted, what was wrong, I don't know how many times, did you speak and even then so softly I almost didn't hear you. "Sam, please help me to go and fetch my Dad." Remember? He was dead drunk on the floor of the Central Hotel Bar. They'd phoned for your Mom, but you were the only one at home. And do you remember how we did it? You went in first by yourself to ask permission for me to go into the bar. Then I loaded him onto my back like a baby and carried him back to the boarding house with you following behind carrying his crutches. [*Shaking his head as he remembers*] A crowded Main Street with all the people watching a little white boy following his drunk father on a nigger's back! I felt for that little boy . . . Master Harold. I felt for him. After that we still had to clean him up, remember? He'd messed in his trousers, so we had to clean him up and get him into bed.

HALLY [*Great pain*]:   I love him, Sam.

SAM: I know you do. That's why I tried to stop you from saying these things about him. It would have been so simple if you could have just despised him for being a weak man. But he's your father. You love him and you're ashamed of him. You're ashamed of so much! . . . And now that's going to include yourself. That was the promise I made to myself: to try and stop that happening. [*Pause*] After we got him to bed you came back with me to my room and sat in a corner and carried on just looking down at the ground. And for days after that! You hadn't done anything wrong, but you went around as if you owed the world an apology for being alive. I didn't like seeing that! That's not the way a boy grows up to be a man!. . . But the one person who should have been teaching you what that means was the cause of your shame. If you really want to know, that's why I made you that kite. I wanted you to look up, be proud of something, of yourself . . . [*Bitter smile at the memory*] . . . and you certainly were that when I left you with it up there on the hill. Oh, ja . . . something else! . . . If you ever do write it as a short story, there *was* a twist in our ending. I couldn't sit down there and stay with you. It was a "Whites Only" bench. You were too young, too excited to notice then. But not anymore. If you're not careful . . . Master Harold . . . you're going to be sitting up there by yourself for a long time to come, and there won't be a kite in the sky. [*Sam has got nothing more to say. He exits into the kitchen, taking off his waiter's jacket*]

WILLIE: Is bad. Is all all bad in here now.

HALLY [*Books into his school case, raincoat on*]: Willie . . . [*It is difficult to speak*] Will you lock up for me and look after the keys?

WILLIE: Okay.

Sam returns. Hally goes behind the counter and collects the few coins in the cash register. As he starts to leave . . .

SAM: Don't forget the comic books.

Hally returns to the counter and puts them in his case. He starts to leave again.

SAM [*To the retreating back of the boy*]: Stop . . . Hally . . .

Hally stops, but doesn't turn to face him.

Hally . . . I've got no right to tell you what being a man means if I don't behave like one myself, and I'm not doing so well at that this afternoon. Should we try again, Hally?

HALLY: Try what?

SAM: Fly another kite, I suppose. It worked once, and this time I need it as much as you do.

HALLY: It's still raining, Sam. You can't fly kites on rainy days, remember.

SAM: So what do we do? Hope for better weather tomorrow?

HALLY [*Helpless gesture*]: I don't know. I don't know anything anymore.

SAM: You sure of that, Hally? Because it would be pretty hopeless if that was true. It would mean nothing has been learnt in here this afternoon, and there was a hell of a lot of teaching going on . . . one way or the other. But anyway, I don't believe you. I reckon

ATHOL FUGARD

486

there's one thing you know. You don't *have* to sit up there by yourself. You know what that bench means now, and you can leave it any time you choose. All you've got to do is stand up and walk away from it.

Hally leaves. Willie goes up quietly to Sam.

WILLIE: Is okay, Boet Sam. You see. Is . . . [*He can't find any better words*] . . . is going to be okay tomorrow. [*Changing his tone*] Hey, Boet Sam! [*He is trying hard*] You right. I think about it and you right. Tonight I find Hilda and say sorry. And make promise I won't beat her no more. You hear me, Boet Sam?

SAM: I hear you, Willie.

WILLIE: And when we practice I relax and romance with her from beginning to end. Non-stop! You watch! Two weeks' time: "First prize for promising newcomers: Mr. Willie Malopo and Miss Hilda Samuels." [*Sudden impulse*] To hell with it! I walk home. [*He goes to the jukebox, puts in a coin and selects a record. The machine comes to life in the gray twilight, blushing its way through a spectrum of soft, romantic colors*] How did you say it, Boet Sam? Let's dream. [*Willie sways with the music and gestures for Sam to dance*]

Sarah Vaughan sings.

"Little man you're crying,
I know why you're blue,
Someone took your kiddy car away;
Better go to sleep now,
Little man you've had a busy day." [*etc. etc.*]
You lead. I follow.

The men dance together.

"Johnny won your marbles,
Tell you what we'll do;
Dad will get you new ones right away;
Better go to sleep now,
Little man you've had a busy day."

—1982

August Wilson, whose birth name was Frederick August Kittel, was born in Pittsburgh's predominantly African-American Hill District, the setting of many of his plays. The child of a mixed-race marriage, he grew up fatherless and credits his real education in life and, incidentally, in language to the older men in his neighborhood, whose distinctive voices echo memorably in his plays. A school dropout at fifteen after a teacher unjustly accused him of plagiarism, he joined in the Black Power movement of the 1960s, eventually founding the Black Horizon on the Hill, an African-American theater company. Wilson admits to having had little confidence in his own ability to write dialogue during his early career, and his first publications were poems. A move to St. Paul, Minnesota, led to work with the Minneapolis Playwrights' Center. After his return to Pittsburgh he wrote Jitney *and* Fullerton Street, *which were staged by regional theaters. His career hit full stride with the successful debut of* Ma Rainey's Black Bottom *(1984), which was first produced at the Yale Repertory Theater and later moved to Broadway.* Joe Turner's Come and Gone *(1986) was his next success, and* Fences *(1987) and* The Piano Lesson *(1990) both won Pulitzer Prizes and other major awards, establishing Wilson as the most prominent African-American dramatist. In most of Wilson's plays a historical theme is prominent, as Wilson attempts to piece together the circumstances that led African Americans to northern cities, depicting how they remain united and sometimes divided by a common cultural heritage that transcends even the ties of friendship and family. But to these social concerns Wilson brings a long training in the theater and a poet's love of language. As he said to an interviewer in 1991, "[Poetry] is the bedrock of my playwriting. . . . The idea of metaphor is a very large idea in my plays and something that I find lacking in most contemporary plays. I think I write the kinds of plays that I do because I have twenty-six years of writing poetry underneath all of that."* Two Trains Running *(1992),* Seven Guitars *(1995), and* King Hedley II *(2001) are recent plays.*

The Piano Lesson

Characters

Doaker
Boy Willie
Lymon
Berniece

Maretha
Avery
Wining Boy
Grace

Scene: *The action of the play takes place in the kitchen and parlor of the house where Doaker Charles lives with his niece, Berniece, and her eleven-year-old daughter, Maretha. The house is sparsely furnished, and although there is evidence of a woman's touch, there is a lack of warmth and vigor. Berniece and Maretha occupy the upstairs rooms. Doaker's room is prominent and opens onto the kitchen. Dominating the parlor is an old upright piano. On the legs of the piano, carved in the manner of African sculpture, are mask-like figures resembling totems. The carvings are rendered with a grace and power of invention that lifts them out of the realm of craftsmanship and into the realm of art. At left is a staircase leading to the upstairs.*

Act I

Scene I

The lights come up on the Charles household. It is five o'clock in the morning. The dawn is beginning to announce itself, but there is something in the air that belongs to the night. A stillness that is a portent, a gathering, a coming together of something akin to a storm. There is a loud knock at the door.

BOY WILLIE: [*Off stage, calling.*] Hey, Doaker . . . Doaker! [*He knocks again and calls.*]
Hey, Doaker! Hey, Berniece! Berniece!

Doaker enters from his room. He is a tall, thin man of forty-seven, with severe features, who has for all intents and purposes retired from the world though he works full-time as a railroad cook.

DOAKER: Who is it?
BOY WILLIE: Open the door, nigger! It's me . . . Boy Willie!
DOAKER: Who?
BOY WILLIE: Boy Willie! Open the door!

Doaker opens the door and Boy Willie and Lymon enter. Boy Willie is thirty years old. He has an infectious grin and a boyishness that is apt for his name. He is brash and impulsive, talkative and somewhat crude in speech and manner. Lymon is twenty-nine. Boy Willie's partner, he talks little, and then with a straightforwardness that is often disarming.

DOAKER: What you doing up here?

BOY WILLIE: I told you, Lymon. Lymon talking about you might be sleep. This is Lymon. You remember Lymon Jackson from down home? This my Uncle Doaker.

DOAKER: What you doing up here? I couldn't figure out who that was. I thought you was still down in Mississippi.

BOY WILLIE: Me and Lymon selling watermelons. We got a truck out there. Got a whole truckload of watermelons. We brought them up here to sell. Where's Berniece?

Calls.

AUGUST WILSON

490

Hey, Berniece!

DOAKER: Berniece up there sleep.

BOY WILLIE: Well, let her get up.

Calls.

Hey, Berniece!

DOAKER: She got to go to work in the morning.

BOY WILLIE: Well she can get up and say hi. It's been three years since I seen her.

Calls.

Hey, Berniece! It's me . . . Boy Willie.

DOAKER: Berniece don't like all that hollering now. She got to work in the morning.

BOY WILLIE: She can go on back to bed. Me and Lymon been riding two days in that truck . . . the least she can do is get up and say hi.

DOAKER: [*Looking out the window.*] Where you all get that truck from?

BOY WILLIE: It's Lymon's. I told him let's get a load of watermelons and bring them up here.

LYMON: Boy Willie say he going back, but I'm gonna stay. See what it's like up here.

BOY WILLIE: You gonna carry me down there first.

LYMON: I told you I ain't going back down there and take a chance on that truck breaking down again. You can take the train. Hey, tell him Doaker, he can take the train back. After we sell them watermelons he have enough money he can buy him a whole railroad car.

DOAKER: You got all them watermelons stacked up there no wonder the truck broke down. I'm surprised you made it this far with a load like that. Where you break down at?

BOY WILLIE: We broke down three times! It took us two and a half days to get here. It's a good thing we picked them watermelons fresh.

LYMON: We broke down twice in West Virginia. The first time was just as soon as we got out of Sunflower. About forty miles out she broke down. We got it going and got all the way to West Virginia before she broke down again.

BOY WILLIE: We had to walk about five miles for some water.

LYMON: It got a hole in the radiator but it runs pretty good. You have to pump the brakes sometime before they catch. Boy Willie have his door open and be ready to jump when that happens.

BOY WILLIE: Lymon think that's funny. I told the nigger I give him ten dollars to get the brakes fixed. But he thinks that funny.

LYMON: They don't need fixing. All you got to do is pump them till they catch.

Berniece enters on the stairs. Thirty-five years old, with an eleven-year-old daughter, she is still in mourning for her husband after three years.

BERNIECE: What you doing all that hollering for?

BOY WILLIE: Hey, Berniece. Doaker said you was sleep. I said at least you could get up and say hi.

BERNIECE: It's five o'clock in the morning and you come in here with all this noise. You can't come like normal folks. You got to bring all that noise with you.

BOY WILLIE: Hell, I ain't done nothing but come in and say hi. I ain't got in the house good.

BERNIECE: That's what I'm talking about. You start all that hollering and carry on as soon as you hit the door.

BOY WILLIE: Aw hell, woman, I was glad to see Doaker. You ain't had to come down if you didn't want to. I come eighteen hundred miles to see my sister I figure she might want to get up and say hi. Other than that you can go back upstairs. What you got, Doaker? Where your bottle? Me and Lymon want a drink.

To Berniece.

This is Lymon. You remember Lymon Jackson from down home.

LYMON: How you doing, Berniece. You look just like I thought you looked.

BERNIECE: Why you all got to come in hollering and carrying on? Waking the neighbors with all that noise.

BOY WILLIE: They can come over and join the party. We fixing to have a party. Doaker, where your bottle? Me and Lymon celebrating. The Ghosts of the Yellow Dog got Sutter.

BERNIECE: Say what?

BOY WILLIE: Ask Lymon, they found him the next morning. Say he drowned in his well.

DOAKER: When this happen, Boy Willie?

BOY WILLIE: About three weeks ago. Me and Lymon was over in Stoner County when we heard about it. We laughed. We thought it was funny. A great big old three-hundred-and-forty-pound man gonna fall down his well.

LYMON: It remind me of Humpty Dumpty.

BOY WILLIE: Everybody say the Ghosts of the Yellow Dog pushed him.

BERNIECE: I don't want to hear that nonsense. Somebody down there pushing them people in their wells.

DOAKER: What was you and Lymon doing over in Stoner County?

BOY WILLIE: We was down there working. Lymon got some people down there.

LYMON: My cousin got some land down there. We was helping him.

BOY WILLIE: Got near about a hundred acres. He got it set up real nice. Me and Lymon was down there chopping down trees. We was using Lymon's truck to haul the wood. Me and Lymon used to haul wood all around them parts.

To Berniece.

Me and Lymon got a truckload of watermelons out there.

Berniece crosses to the window to the parlor.

Doaker, where your bottle? I know you got a bottle stuck up in your room. Come on, me and Lymon want a drink.

Doaker exits into his room.

BERNIECE: Where you all get that truck from?

AUGUST WILSON

492

BOY WILLIE: I told you it's Lymon's.

BERNIECE: Where you get the truck from, Lymon?

LYMON: I bought it.

BERNIECE: Where he get that truck from, Boy Willie?

BOY WILLIE: He told you he bought it. Bought it for a hundred and twenty dollars. I can't say where he got that hundred and twenty dollars from . . . but he bought that old piece of truck from Henry Porter. [*To* LYMON.] Where you get that hundred and twenty dollars from, nigger?

LYMON: I got it like you get yours. I know how to take care of money.

Doaker brings a bottle and sets it on the table.

BOY WILLIE: Aw hell, Doaker got some of that good whiskey. Don't give Lymon none of that. he ain't used to good whiskey. He liable to get sick.

LYMON: I done had good whiskey before.

BOY WILLIE: Lymon bought that truck so he have him a place to sleep. He down there wasn't doing no work or nothing. Sheriff looking for him. He bought that truck to keep away from the sheriff. Got Stovall looking for him too. He down there sleeping in that truck ducking and dodging both of them. I told him come on let's go up and see my sister.

BERNIECE: What the sheriff looking for you for, Lymon?

BOY WILLIE: The man don't want you to know all his business. He's my company. He ain't asking you no questions.

LYMON: It wasn't nothing. It was just a misunderstanding.

BERNIECE: He in my house. You say the sheriff looking for him, I wanna know what he looking for him for. Otherwise you all can go back out there and be where nobody don't have to ask you nothing.

LYMON: It was just a misunderstanding. Sometimes me and the sheriff we don't think alike. So we just got crossed on each other.

BERNIECE: Might be looking for him about that truck. He might have stole that truck.

BOY WILLIE: We ain't stole no truck, woman. I told you Lymon bought it.

DOAKER: Boy Willie and Lymon got more sense than to ride all the way up here in a stolen truck with a load of watermelons. Now they might have stole them watermelons, but I don't believe they stole that truck.

BOY WILLIE: You don't even know the man good and you calling him a thief. And we ain't stole them watermelons either. Them old man Pitterford's watermelons. He give me and Lymon all we could load for ten dollars.

DOAKER: No Wonder you got them stacked up out there. You must have five hundred watermelons stacked up out there.

BERNIECE: Boy Willie, when you and Lymon planning on going back?

BOY WILLIE: Lymon say he staying. As soon as we sell them watermelons I'm going on back.

BERNIECE: [*Starts to exit up the stairs.*] That's what you need to do. And you need to do it quick. Come in here disrupting the house. I don't want all that loud carrying on around here. I'm surprised you ain't woke Maretha up.

BOY WILLIE: I was fixing to get her now.

Calls.

Hey, Maretha!

DOAKER: Berniece don't like all that hollering now.

BERNIECE: Don't you wake that child up!

BOY WILLIE: You going up there . . . wake her up and tell her her uncle's here. I ain't seen her in three years. Wake her up and send her down here. She can go back to bed.

BERNIECE: I ain't waking that child up . . . and don't you be making all that noise. You and Lymon need to sell them watermelons and go on back.

Berniece exits up the stairs.

BOY WILLIE: I see Berniece still try to be stuck up.

DOAKER: Berniece alright. She don't want you making all that noise. Maretha up there sleep. Let her sleep until she get up. She can see you then.

BOY WILLIE: I ain't thinking about Berniece. You hear from Wining Boy? You know Cleotha died?

DOAKER: Yeah, I heard that. He come by here about a year ago. Had a whole sack of money. He stayed here about two weeks. Ain't offered nothing. Berniece asked him for three dollars to buy some food and he got mad and left.

LYMON: Who's Wining Boy?

BOY WILLIE: That's my uncle. That's Doaker's brother. You heard me talk about Wining Boy. He play piano. He done made some records and everything. He still doing that, Doaker?

DOAKER: He made one or two records a long time ago. That's the only ones I ever known him to make. If you let him tell it he a big recording star.

BOY WILLIE: He stopped down home about two years ago. That's what I hear. I don't know. Me and Lymon was up on Parchman Farm doing them three years.

DOAKER: He don't never stay in one place. Now, he been here about eight months ago. Back in the winter. Now, you subject not to see him for another two years. It's liable to be that long before he stop by.

BOY WILLIE: If he had a whole sack of money you liable never to see him. You ain't gonna see him until he get broke. Just as soon as that sack of money is gone you look up and he be on your doorstep.

LYMON: [*Noticing the piano.*] Is that the piano?

BOY WILLIE: Yeah . . . look here, Lymon. See how it got all those carvings on it. See, that's what I was talking about. See how it's carved up real nice and polished and everything? You never find you another piano like that.

LYMON: Yeah, that look real nice.

BOY WILLIE: I told you. See how it's polished? My mama used to polish it every day. See all them pictures carved on it? That's what I was talking about. You can get a nice price for that piano.

LYMON: That's all Boy Willie talked about the whole trip up here. I got tired of hearing him talk about the piano.

BOY WILLIE: All you want to talk about is women. You ought to hear this nigger, Doaker. Talking about all the women he gonna get when he get up here. He ain't had none down there but he gonna get a hundred when he get up here.

DOAKER: How your people doing down there, Lymon?

LYMON: They alright. They still there. I come up here to see what it's like up here. Boy Willie trying to get me to go back and farm with him.

BOY WILLIE: Sutter's brother selling the land. He say he gonna sell it to me. That's why I come up here. I got one part of it. Sell them watermelons and get me another part. Get Berniece to sell that piano and I'll have the third part.

DOAKER: Berniece ain't gonna sell that piano.

BOY WILLIE: I'm gonna talk to her. When she see I got a chance to get Sutter's land she'll come around.

DOAKER: You can put that thought out your mind. Berniece ain't gonna sell that piano.

BOY WILLIE: I'm gonna talk to her. She been playing on it?

DOAKER: You know she won't touch that piano. I ain't never known her to touch it since Mama Ola died. That's over seven years now. She say it got blood on it. She got Maretha playing on it though. Say Maretha can go on and do everything she can't do. Got her in an extra school down at the Irene Kaufman Settlement House. She want Maretha to grow up and be a schoolteacher. Say she good enough she can teach on the piano.

BOY WILLIE: Maretha don't need to be playing on no piano. She can play on the guitar.

DOAKER: How much land Sutter got left?

BOY WILLIE: Got a hundred acres. Good land. He done sold it piece by piece, he kept the good part for himself. Now he got to give that up. His brother come down from Chicago for the funeral . . . he up there in Chicago got some kind of business with soda fountain equipment. He anxious to sell the land, Doaker. He don't want to be bothered with it. He called me to him and said cause of how long our families done known each other and how we been good friends and all, say he wanted to sell the land to me. Say he'd rather see me with it than Jim Stovall. Told me he'd let me have it for two thousand dollars cash money. He don't know I found out the most Stovall would give him for it was fifteen hundred dollars. He trying to get that extra five hundred out of me telling me he doing me a favor. I thanked him just as nice. Told him what a good man Sutter was and how he had my sympathy and all. Told him to give me two weeks. He said he'd wait on me. That's why I come up here. Sell them watermelons. Get Berniece to sell that piano. Put them two parts with the part I done saved. Walk in there. Tip my hat. Lay my money down on the table. Get my deed and walk on out. This time I get to keep all the cotton. Hire me some men to work it for me. Gin my cotton. Get my seed. And I'll see you again next year. Might even plant some tobacco or some oats.

DOAKER: You gonna have a hard time trying to get Berniece to sell that piano. You know Avery Brown from down there don't you? He up here now. He followed Berniece up here trying to get her to marry him after Crawley got killed. He been up here about two years. He call himself a preacher now.

BOY WILLIE: I know Avery. I know him from when he used to work on the Willshaw place. Lymon know him too.

DOAKER: He after Berniece to marry him. She keep telling him no but he won't give up. He keep pressing her on it.

BOY WILLIE: Avery think all white men is bigshots. He don't know there some white men ain't got as much as he got.

DOAKER: He supposed to come past here this morning. Berniece going down to the bank with him to see if he can get a loan to start his church. That's why I know Berniece ain't gonna sell that piano. He tried to get her to sell it to help him start his church. Sent the man around and everything.

BOY WILLIE: What man?

DOAKER: Some white fellow was going around to all the colored people's houses looking to buy up musical instruments. He'd buy anything. Drums. Guitars. Harmonicas. Pianos. Avery sent him past here. He looked at the piano and got excited. Offered her a nice price. She turned him down and got on Avery for sending him past. The man kept on her about two weeks. He seen where she wasn't gonna sell it, he gave her his number and told her if she ever wanted to sell it to call him first. Say he'd go one better than what anybody else would give her for it.

BOY WILLIE: How much he offer her for it?

DOAKER: Now you know me. She didn't say and I didn't ask. I just know it was a nice price.

LYMON: All you got to do is find out who he is and tell him somebody else wanna buy it from you. Tell him you can't make up your mind who to sell it to, and if he like Doaker say, he'll give you anything you want for it.

BOY WILLIE: That's what I'm gonna do. I'm gonna find out who he is from Avery.

DOAKER: It ain't gonna do you no good. Berniece ain't gonna sell that piano.

BOY WILLIE: She ain't got to sell it. I'm gonna sell it. I own just as much of it as she does.

BERNIECE: [Offstage, hollers.] Doaker! Go on get away. Doaker!

DOAKER: [Calling.] Berniece?

Doaker and Boy Willie rush to the stairs, Boy Willie runs up the stairs, passing Berniece as she enters, running.

DOAKER: Berniece, what's the matter? You alright? What's the matter?

Berniece tries to catch her breath. She is unable to speak.

DOAKER: That's alright. Take your time. You alright. What's the matter?

He calls.

Hey, Boy Willie?

BOY WILLIE: [*Offstage.*] Ain't nobody up here.

BERNIECE: Sutter . . . Sutter's standing at the top of the steps.

DOAKER: [*Calls.*] Boy Willie!

Lymon crosses to the stairs and looks up. Boy Willie enters from the stairs.

BOY WILLIE: Hey Doaker, what's wrong with her? Berniece, what's wrong? Who was you talking to?

DOAKER: She say she seen Sutter's ghost standing at the top of the stairs.

BOY WILLIE: Seen what? Sutter? She ain't seen no Sutter.

BERNIECE: He was standing right up there.

BOY WILLIE: [*Entering on the stairs.*] That's all in Berniece's head. Ain't nobody up there. Go on up there, Doaker.

DOAKER: I'll take your word for it. Berniece talking about what she seen. She say Sutter's ghost standing at the top of the steps. She ain't just make all that up.

BOY WILLIE: She up there dreaming. She ain't seen no ghost.

LYMON: You want a glass of water, Berniece? Get her a glass of water, Boy Willie.

BOY WILLIE: She don't need no water. She ain't seen nothing. Go on up there and look. Ain't nobody up there but Maretha.

DOAKER: Let Berniece tell it.

BOY WILLIE: I ain't stopping her from telling it.

DOAKER: What happened, Berniece?

BERNIECE: I come out my room to come back down here and Sutter was standing there in the hall.

BOY WILLIE: What he look like?

BERNIECE: He look like Sutter. He look like he always look.

BOY WILLIE: Sutter couldn't find his way from Big Sandy to Little Sandy. How he gonna find his way all the way up here to Pittsburgh? Sutter ain't never even heard of Pittsburgh.

DOAKER: Go on, Berniece.

BERNIECE: Just standing there with the blue suit on.

BOY WILLIE: The man ain't never left Marlin County when he was living . . . and he's gonna come all the way up here now that he's dead?

DOAKER: Let her finish. I want to hear what she got to say.

BOY WILLIE: I'll tell you this. If Berniece had seen him like she think she seen him she'd still be running.

DOAKER: Go on, Berniece. Don't pay Boy Willie no mind.

BERNIECE: He was standing there . . . had his hand on top of his head. Look like he might have thought if he took his hand down his head might have fallen off.

LYMON: Did he have on a hat?

BERNIECE: Just had on that blue suit . . . I told him to go away and he just stood there looking at me . . . calling Boy Willie's name.

BOY WILLIE: What he calling my name for?

BERNIECE: I believe you pushed him in the well.

BOY WILLIE: Now what kind of sense that make? You telling me I'm gonna go out there and hide in the weeds with all them dogs and things he got around there . . . I'm gonna hide and wait till I catch him looking down his well just right . . . then I'm gonna run over and push him in. A great big old three-hundred-and-forty-pound man.

BERNIECE: Well, what he calling your name for?

BOY WILLIE: He bending over looking down his well, woman . . . how he know who pushed him? It could have been anybody. Where was you when Sutter fell in his well? Where was Doaker? Me and Lymon was over in Stoner County. Tell her, Lymon. The Ghosts of the Yellow Dog got Sutter. That's what happened to him.

BERNIECE: You can talk all that Ghosts of the Yellow Dog stuff if you want. I know better.

LYMON: The Ghosts of the Yellow Dog pushed him. That's what the people say. They found him in his well and all the people say it must be the Ghosts of the Yellow Dog. Just like all them other men.

BOY WILLIE: Come talking about he looking for me. What he come all the way up here for? If he looking for me all he got to do is wait. He could have saved himself a trip if he looking for me. That ain't nothing but in Berniece's head. Ain't no telling what she liable to come up with next.

AUGUST WILSON

BERNIECE: Boy Willie, I want you and Lymon to go ahead and leave my house. Just go on somewhere. You don't do nothing but bring trouble with you everywhere you go. If it wasn't for you Crawley would still be alive.

BOY WILLIE: Crawley what? I ain't had nothing to do with Crawley getting killed. Crawley three time seven. He had his own mind.

BERNIECE: Just go on and leave. Let Sutter go somewhere else looking for you.

BOY WILLIE: I'm leaving. Soon as we sell them watermelons. Other than that I ain't going nowhere. Hell, I just got here. Talking about Sutter looking for me. Sutter was looking for that piano. That's what he was looking for. He had to die to find out where that piano was at . . . If I was you I'd get rid of it. That's the way to get rid of Sutter's ghost. Get rid of that piano.

BERNIECE: I want you and Lymon to go on and take all this confusion out of my house!

BOY WILLIE: Hey, tell her, Doaker. What kind of sense that make? I told you, Lymon, as soon as Berniece see me she was gonna start something. Didn't I tell you that? Now she done made up that story about Sutter just so she could tell me to leave her house. Well, hell, I ain't going nowhere till I sell them watermelons.

BERNIECE: Well why don't you go out there and sell them! Sell them and go on back!

BOY WILLIE: We waiting till the people get up.

LYMON: Boy Willie say if you get out there too early and wake the people up they get mad at you and won't buy nothing from you.

DOAKER: You won't be waiting long. You done let the sun catch up with you. This the time everybody be getting up around here.

BERNIECE: Come on, Doaker, walk up here with me. Let me get Maretha up and get her started. I got to get ready myself. Boy Willie, just go on out there and sell them watermelons and you and Lymon leave my house.

Berniece and Doaker exit up the stairs.

BOY WILLIE: [*Calling after them.*] If you see Sutter up there . . . tell him I'm down here waiting on him.

LYMON: What if she see him again?

BOY WILLIE: That's all in her head. There ain't no ghost up there.

Calls.

Hey, Doaker . . . I told you ain't nothing up there.

LYMON: I'm glad he didn't say he was looking for me.

BOY WILLIE: I wish I would see Sutter's ghost. Give me a chance to put a whupping on him.

LYMON: You ought to stay up here with me. You be down there working his land . . . he might come looking for you all the time.

BOY WILLIE: I ain't thinking about Sutter. And I ain't thinking about staying up here. You stay up here. I'm going back and get Sutter's land. You think you ain't got to work up here. You think this the land of milk and honey. But I ain't scared of work. I'm going back and farm every acre of that land.

Doaker enters from the stairs.

I told you there ain't nothing up there, Doaker. Berniece dreaming all that.

DOAKER: I believe Berniece seen something. Berniece level-headed. She ain't just made all that up. She say Sutter had on a suit. I don't believe she ever seen Sutter in a suit. I believe that's what he was buried in, and that's what Berniece saw.

BOY WILLIE: Well, let her keep on seeing him then. As long as he don't mess with me.

Doaker starts to cook his breakfast.

I heard about you, Doaker. They say you got all the women looking out for you down home. They be looking to see you coming. Say you got a different one every two weeks. Say they be fighting one another for you to stay with them.

To Lymon.

Look at him, Lymon. He know it's true.

DOAKER: I ain't thinking about no women. They never get me tied up with them. After Coreen I ain't got no use for them. I stay up on Jack Slattery's place when I be down there. All them women want is somebody with a steady payday.

BOY WILLIE: That ain't what I hear. I hear every two weeks the women all put on their dresses and line up at the railroad station.

DOAKER: I don't get down there but once a month. I used to go down there every two weeks but they keep switching me around. They keep switching all the fellows around.

BOY WILLIE: Doaker can't turn that railroad loose. He was working the railroad when I was walking around crying for sugartit. My mama used to brag on him.

DOAKER: I'm cooking now, but I used to line track. I pieced together the Yellow Dog stitch by stitch. Rail by rail. Line track all up around there. I lined track all up around Sunflower and Clarksdale. Wining Boy worked with me. He helped put in some of that track. He'd work it for six months and quit. Go back to playing piano and gambling.

BOY WILLIE: How long you been with the railroad now?

DOAKER: Twenty-seven years. Now, I'll tell you something about the railroad. What I done learned after twenty-seven years. See, you got North. You got West. You look over here you got South. Over there you got East. Now, you can start from anywhere. Don't care where you at. You got to go one of them four ways. And whichever way you decide to go they got a railroad that will take you there. Now, that's something simple. You think anybody would be able to understand that. But you'd be surprised how many people trying to go North get on a train going West. They think the train's supposed to go where they going rather than where it's going.

Now, why people going? Their sister's sick. They leaving before they kill somebody . . . and they sitting across from somebody who's leaving to keep from getting killed. They leaving cause they can't get satisfied. They going to meet someone. I wish I had a dollar for every time that someone wasn't at the station to meet them. I done seen that a lot. In between the time they sent the telegram and the time the person get there . . . they done forgot all about them.

They got so many trains out there they have a hard time keeping them from running into each other. Got trains going every whichaway. Got people on all of them. Somebody going where somebody just left. If everybody stay in one place I believe this would be a better world. Now what I done learned after twenty-seven years of railroading is this . . . if the train stays on the track . . . it's going to get where it's going. It might not be where you going. If it ain't then all you got to do is sit and wait cause the train's coming back to get you. The train don't never stop. It'll come back every time. Now I'll tell you another thing . . .

BOY WILLIE: What you cooking over there, Doaker? Me and Lymon's hungry.

DOAKER: Go on down there to Wylie and Kirkpatrick to Eddie's restaurant. Coffee cost a nickel and you can get two eggs, sausage, and grits for fifteen cents. He even give you a biscuit with it.

BOY WILLIE: That look good what you got. Give me a little piece of that grilled bread.

DOAKER: Here . . . go on take the whole piece.

BOY WILLIE: Here you go, Lymon . . . you want a piece?

He gives Lymon a piece of toast. Maretha enters from the stairs.

BOY WILLIE: Hey, sugar. Come here and give me a hug. Come on give Uncle Boy Willie a hug. Don't be shy. Look at her, Doaker. She done got bigger. Ain't she got big?

DOAKER: Yeah, she getting up there.

BOY WILLIE: How you doing, sugar?

MARETHA: Fine.

BOY WILLIE: You was just a little old thing last time I seen you. You remember me, don't you? This your Uncle Boy Willie from down South. That there's Lymon. He my friend. We come up here to sell watermelons. You like watermelons?

Maretha nods.

We got a whole truckload out front. You can have as many as you want. What you been doing?

MARETHA: Nothing.

BOY WILLIE: Don't be shy now. Look at you getting all big. How old is you?

MARETHA: Eleven. I'm gonna be twelve soon.

BOY WILLIE: You like it up here? You like the North?

MARETHA: It's alright.

BOY WILLIE: That there's Lymon. Did you say hi to Lymon?

MARETHA: Hi.

LYMON: How you doing? You look just like your mama. I remember you when you was wearing diapers.

BOY WILLIE: You gonna come down South and see me? Uncle Boy Willie gonna get him a farm. Gonna get a great big old farm. Come down there and I'll teach you how to ride a mule. Teach you how to kill a chicken, too.

MARETHA: I seen my mama do that.

BOY WILLIE: Ain't nothing to it. You just grab him by his neck and twist it. Get you a real good grip and then you just wring his neck and throw him in the pot. Cook him up. Then you got some good eating. What you like to eat? What kind of food you like?

MARETHA: I like everything . . . except I don't like no black-eyed peas.

BOY WILLIE: Uncle Doaker tell me your mama got you playing that piano. Come on play something for me.

Boy Willie crosses over to the piano followed by Maretha.

Show me what you can do. Come on now. Here . . . Uncle Boy Willie give you a dime . . . show me what you can do. Don't be bashful now. That dime say you can't be bashful.

Maretha plays. It is something any beginner first learns.

Here, let me show you something.

Boy Willie sits and plays a simple boogie-woogie.

See that? See what I'm doing? That's what you call the boogie-woogie. See now . . . you can get up and dance to that. That's how good it sound. It sound like you wanna dance. You can dance to that. It'll hold you up. Whatever kind of dance you wanna do you can dance to that right there. See that? See how it go? Ain't nothing to it. Go on you do it.

MARETHA: I got to read it on the paper.

BOY WILLIE: You don't need no paper. Go on. Do just like that there.

BERNIECE: Maretha! You get up here and get ready to go so you be on time. Ain't no need you trying to take advantage of company.

MARETHA: I got to go.

BOY WILLIE: Uncle Boy Willie gonna get you a guitar. Let Uncle Doaker teach you how to play that. You don't need to read no paper to play the guitar. Your mama told you about that piano? You know how them pictures got on there?

MARETHA: She say it just always been like that since she got it.

BOY WILLIE: You hear that, Doaker? And you sitting up here in the house with Berniece.

DOAKER: I ain't got nothing to do with that. I don't get in the way of Berniece's raising her.

BOY WILLIE: You tell your mama to tell you about that piano. You ask her how them pictures got on there. If she don't tell you I'll tell you.

BERNIECE: Maretha!

MARETHA: I got to get ready to go.

BOY WILLIE: She getting big, Doaker. You remember her, Lymon?

LYMON: She used to be real little.

There is a knock on the door. Doaker goes to answer it. Avery enters. Thirty-eight years old, honest and ambitious, he has taken to the city like a fish to water, finding in it opportunities for growth and advancement that did not exist for him in the rural South. He is dressed in a suit and tie with a gold cross around his neck. He carries a small Bible.

DOAKER: Hey, Avery, come on in. Berniece upstairs.

BOY WILLIE: Look at him . . . look at him . . . he don't know what to say. He wasn't expecting to see me.

AVERY: Hey, Boy Willie. What you doing up here?

BOY WILLIE: Look at him, Lymon.

AVERY: Is that Lymon? Lymon Jackson?

BOY WILLIE: Yeah, you know Lymon.

DOAKER: Berniece be ready in a minute, Avery.

BOY WILLIE: Doaker say you a preacher now. What . . . we supposed to call you Reverend? You used to be plain old Avery. When you get to be a preacher, nigger?

LYMON: Avery say he gonna be a preacher so he don't have to work.

BOY WILLIE: I remember when you was down there on the Willshaw place planting cotton. You wasn't thinking about no Reverend then.

AVERY: That must be your truck out there. I saw that truck with them watermelons, I was trying to figure out what it was doing in front of the house.

BOY WILLIE: Yeah, me and Lymon selling watermelons. That's Lymon's truck.

DOAKER: Berniece say you all going down to the bank.

AVERY: Yeah, they give me a half day off work. I got an appointment to talk to the bank about getting a loan to start my church.

BOY WILLIE: Lymon say preachers don't have to work. Where you working at, nigger?

DOAKER: Avery got him one of them good jobs. He working at one of them skyscrapers downtown.

AVERY: I'm working down there at the Gulf Building running an elevator. Got a pension and everything. They even give you a turkey on Thanksgiving.

LYMON: How you know the rope ain't gonna break? Ain't you scared the rope's gonna break?

AVERY: That's steel. They got steel cables hold it up. It take a whole lot of breaking to break that steel. Naw, I ain't worried about nothing like that. It ain't nothing but a little old elevator. Now, I wouldn't get in none of them airplanes. You couldn't pay me to do nothing like that.

LYMON: That be fun. I'd rather do that than ride in one of them elevators.

BOY WILLIE: How many of them watermelons you wanna buy?

AVERY: I thought you was gonna give me one seeing as how you got a whole truck full.

BOY WILLIE: You can get one, get two. I'll give you two for a dollar.

AVERY: I can't eat but one. How much are they?

BOY WILLIE: Aw, nigger, you know I'll give you a watermelon. Go on, take as many as you want. Just leave some for me and Lymon to sell.

AVERY: I don't want but one.

BOY WILLIE: How you get to be a preacher, Avery? I might want to be a preacher one day. Have everybody call me Reverend Boy Willie.

AVERY: It come to me in a dream. God called me and told me he wanted me to be a shepherd for his flock. That's what I'm gonna call my church . . . The Good Shepherd Church of God in Christ.

DOAKER: Tell him what you told me. Tell him about the three hobos.

AVERY: Boy Willie don't want to hear all that.

LYMON: I do. Lots a people say your dreams can come true.

AVERY: Naw. You don't want to hear all that.

DOAKER: Go on. I told him you was a preacher. He didn't want to believe me. Tell him about the three hobos.

AVERY: Well, it come to me in a dream. See . . . I was sitting out in this railroad yard watching the trains go by. The train stopped and these three hobos got off. They told me they had come from Nazareth and was on their way to Jerusalem. They had three candles. They gave me one and told me to light it . . . but to be careful that it didn't go out. Next thing I knew I was standing in front of this house. Something told me to go knock on the door. This old woman opened the door and said they had been waiting on me. Then she led me into this room. It was a big room and it was full of all kinds of different people. They looked like anybody else except they all had sheep heads and was making noise like sheep make. I heard somebody call my name. I looked around and there was these same three hobos. They told me to take off my clothes and they give me a blue robe with gold thread. They washed my feet and combed my hair. Then they showed me these three doors and told me to pick one.

I went through one of them doors and that flame leapt off that candle and it seemed like my whole head caught fire. I looked around and there was four or five other men standing there with these same blue robes on. Then we heard a voice tell us to look out across this valley. We looked out and saw the valley was full of wolves. The voice told us that these sheep people that I had seen in the other room had to go over to the other side of this valley and somebody had to take them. Then I heard another voice say, "Who shall I send?" Next thing I knew I said, "Here I am. Send me." That's when I met Jesus. He say, "If you go, I'll go with you." Something told me to say, "Come on. Let's go." That's when I woke up. My head still felt like it was on fire . . . but I had a peace about myself that was hard to explain. I knew right then that I had been filled with the Holy Ghost and called to be a servant of the Lord. It took me a while before I could accept that. But then a lot of little ways God showed me that it was true. So I became a preacher.

LYMON: I see why you gonna call it the Good Shepherd Church. You dreaming about them sheep people. I can see that easy.

BOY WILLIE: Doaker say you sent some white man past the house to look at that piano. Say he was going around to all the colored people's houses looking to buy up musical instruments.

AVERY: Yeah, but Berniece didn't want to sell that piano. After she told me about it . . . I could see why she didn't want to sell it.

BOY WILLIE: What's this man's name?

AVERY: Oh, that's a while back now. I done forgot his name. He give Berniece a card with his name and telephone number on it, but I believe she throwed it away.

Berniece and Maretha enter from the stairs.

BERNIECE: Maretha, run back upstairs and get my pocketbook. And wipe that hair grease off your forehead. Go ahead, hurry up.

Maretha exits up the stairs.

How you doing, Avery? You done got all dressed up. You look nice. Boy Willie, I thought you and Lymon was going to sell them watermelons.

BOY WILLIE: Lymon done got sleepy. We liable to get some sleep first.

LYMON: I ain't sleepy.

DOAKER: As many watermelons as you got stacked up on that truck out there, you ought to have been gone.

BOY WILLIE: We gonna go in a minute. We going.

BERNIECE: Doaker. I'm gonna stop down there on Logan Street. You want anything?

DOAKER: You can pick up some ham hocks if you going down there. See if you can get the smoked ones. If they ain't got that get the fresh ones. Don't get the ones that got all that fat under the skin. Look for the long ones. They nice and lean.

He gives her a dollar.

Don't get the short ones lessen they smoked. If you got to get the fresh ones make sure that they the long ones. If they ain't got them smoked then go ahead and get the short ones.

Pause.

You may as well get some turnip greens while you down there. I got some buttermilk . . . if you pickup some cornmeal I'll make me some cornbread and cook up them turnip greens.

Maretha enters from the stairs.

MARETHA: We gonna take the streetcar?

BERNIECE: Me and Avery gonna drop you off at the settlement house. You mind them people down there. Don't be going down there showing your color. Boy Willie, I done told you what to do. I'll see you later, Doaker.

AVERY: I'll be seeing you again, Boy Willie.

BOY WILLIE: Hey, Berniece . . . what's the name of that man Avery sent past say he want to buy the piano?

BERNIECE: I knew it. I knew it when I first seen you. I knew you was up to something.

BOY WILLIE: Sutter's brother say he selling the land to me. He waiting on me now. Told me he'd give me two weeks. I got one part. Sell them watermelons get me another part. Then we can sell that piano and I'll have the third part.

BERNIECE: I ain't selling that piano, Boy Willie. If that's why you come up here you can just forget about it.

To Doaker.

Doaker, I'll see you later. Boy Willie ain't nothing but a whole lot of mouth. I ain't paying him no mind. If he come up here thinking he gonna sell that piano then he done come up here for nothing.

Berniece, Avery, and Maretha exit the front door.

BOY WILLIE: Hey, Lymon! You ready to go sell these watermelons.

Boy Willie and Lymon start to exit. At the door Boy Willie turns to Doaker.

Hey, Doaker . . . if Berniece don't want to sell that piano . . . I'm gonna cut it in half and go on and sell my half.

Boy Willie and Lymon exit.

The lights go down on the scene.

Scene II

The lights come up on the kitchen. It is three days later. Wining Boy sits at the kitchen table. There is a half-empty pint bottle on the table. Doaker busies himself washing pots. Wining Boy is fifty-six years old. Doaker's older brother, he tries to present the image of a successful musician and gambler, but his music, his clothes, and even his manner of presentation are old. He is a man who looking back over his life continues to live it with an odd mixture of zest and sorrow.

WINING BOY: So the Ghosts of the Yellow Dog got Sutter. That just go to show you I believe I always lived right. They say every dog gonna have his day and time it go around it sure come back to you. I done seen that a thousand times. I know the truth of that. But I'll tell you outright . . . if I see Sutter's ghost I'll be on the first thing I find that got wheels on it.

Doaker enters from his room.

DOAKER: Wining Boy!
WINING BOY: And I'll tell you another thing . . . Berniece ain't gonna sell that piano.
DOAKER: That's what she told him. He say he gonna cut it in half and go on and sell his half. They been around here three days trying to

sell them watermelons. They trying to get out to where the white folks live but the truck keep breaking down. They go a block or two and it break down again. They trying to get out to Squirrel Hill and can't get around the corner. He say soon as he can get that truck empty to where he can set the piano up in there he gonna take it out of here and go sell it.

WINING BOY: What about them boys Sutter got? How come they ain't farming that land?

DOAKER: One of them going to school. He left down there and come North to school. The other one ain't got as much sense as that frying pan over yonder. That is the dumbest white man I ever seen. He'd stand in the river and watch it rise till it drown him.

WINING BOY: Other than seeing Sutter's ghost how's Berniece doing?

DOAKER: She doing alright. She still got Crawley on her mind. He been dead three years but she still holding on to him. She need to go out here and let one of these fellows grab a whole handful of whatever she got. She act like it done got precious.

WINING BOY: They always told me any fish will bite if you got good bait.

DOAKER: She stuck up on it. She think it's better than she is. I believe she messing around with Avery. They got something going. He a preacher now. If you let him tell it the Holy Ghost sat on his head and heaven opened up with thunder and lightning and God was calling his name. Told him to go out and preach and tend to his flock. That's what he gonna call his church. The Good Shepherd Church.

WINING BOY: They had that joker down in Spear walking around talking about he Jesus Christ. He gonna live the life of Christ. Went through the Last Supper and everything. Rented him a mule on Palm Sunday and rode through the town. Did everything . . . talking about he Christ. He did everything until they got up to that crucifixion part. Got up to that part and told everybody to go home and quit pretending. He got up to the crucifixion part and changed his mind. Had a whole bunch of folks come down there to see him get nailed to the cross. I don't know who's the worse fool. Him or them. Had all them folks come down there . . . even carried the cross up this little hill. People standing around waiting to see him get nailed to the cross and he stop everything and preach a little sermon and told everybody to go home. Had enough nerve to tell them to come to church on Easter Sunday to celebrate his resurrection.

DOAKER: I'm surprised Avery ain't thought about that. He trying every little thing to get him a congregation together. They meeting over at his house till he get him a church.

WINING BOY: Ain't nothing wrong with being a preacher. You got the preacher on one hand and the gambler on the other. Sometimes there ain't too much difference in them.

DOAKER: How long you been in Kansas City?

WINING BOY: Since I left here. I got tied up with some old gal down there.

Pause.

You know Cleotha died.

DOAKER: Yeah, I heard that last time I was down there. I was sorry to hear that.

WINING BOY: One of her friends wrote and told me. I got the letter right here.

He takes the letter out of his pocket.

I was down in Kansas City and she wrote and told me Cleotha had died. Name of Willa Bryant. She say she know cousin Rupert.

He opens the letter and reads.

Dear Wining Boy: I am writing this letter to let you know Miss Cleotha Holman passed on Saturday the first of May she departed this world in the loving arms of her sister Miss Alberta Samuels. I know you would want to know this and am writing as a friend of Cleotha. There have been many hardships since last you seen her but she survived them all and to the end was a good woman whom I hope have God's grace and is in His Paradise. Your cousin Rupert Bates is my friend also and he give me your address and I pray this reaches you about Cleotha. Miss Willa Bryant. A friend.

He folds the letter and returns it to his pocket.

They was nailing her coffin shut by the time I heard about it. I never knew she was sick. I believe it was that yellow jaundice. That's what killed her mama.

DOAKER: Cleotha wasn't but forty-some

WINING BOY: She was forty-six. I got ten years on her. I met her when she was sixteen. You remember I used to run around there. Couldn't nothing keep me still. Much as I loved Cleotha I loved to ramble.

Couldn't nothing keep me still. We got married and we used to fight about it all the time. Then one day she asked me to leave. Told me she loved me before I left. Told me, Wining Boy, you got a home as long as I got mine. And I believe in my heart I always felt that and that kept me safe.

DOAKER: Cleotha always did have a nice way about her.

WINING BOY: Man that woman was something. I used to thank the Lord. Many a night I sat up and looked out over my life. Said, well, I had Cleotha. When it didn't look like there was nothing else for me, I said, thank God, at least I had that. If ever I go anywhere in this life I done known a good woman. And that used to hold me till the next morning.

Pause.

What you got? Give me a little nip. I know you got something stuck up in your room.

DOAKER: I ain't seen you walk in here and put nothing on the table. You done sat there and drank up your whiskey. Now you talking about what you got.

WINING BOY: I got plenty money. Give me a little nip.

Doaker carries a glass into his room and returns with it half-filled. He sets it on the table in front of Wining Boy.

WINING BOY: You hear from Coreen?

DOAKER: She up in New York. I let her go from my mind.

WINING BOY: She was something back then. She wasn't too pretty but she had a way of looking at you made you know there was a whole lot of woman there. You got married and snatched her out from under us and we all got mad at you.

DOAKER: She up in New York City. That's what I hear.

The door opens and Boy Willie and Lymon enter.

BOY WILLIE: Aw hell . . . look here! We was just talking about you. Doaker say you left out of here with a whole sack of money. I told him we wasn't going see you till you got broke.

WINING BOY: What you mean broke? I got a whole pocketful of money.

DOAKER: Did you all get that truck fixed?

BOY WILLIE: We got it running and got halfway out there on Centre and it broke down again. Lymon went out there and messed it

AUGUST WILSON

up some more. Fellow told us we got to wait till tomorrow to get it fixed. Say he have it running like new. Lymon going back down there and sleep in the truck so the people don't take the watermelons.

LYMON: Lymon nothing. You go down there and sleep in it.

BOY WILLIE: You was sleeping in it down home, nigger! I don't know nothing about sleeping in no truck.

LYMON: I ain't sleeping in no truck.

BOY WILLIE: They can take all the watermelons. I don't care. Wining Boy, where you coming from? Where you been?

WINING BOY: I been down in Kansas City.

BOY WILLIE: You remember Lymon? Lymon Jackson.

WINING BOY: Yeah, I used to know his daddy.

BOY WILLIE: Doaker say you don't never leave no address with nobody. Say he got to depend on your whim. See when it strike you to pay a visit.

WINING BOY: I got four or five addresses.

BOY WILLIE: Doaker say Berniece asked you for three dollars and you got mad and left.

WINING BOY: Berniece try and rule over you too much for me. That's why I left. It wasn't about no three dollars.

BOY WILLIE: Where you getting all these sacks of money from? I need to be with you. Doaker say you had a whole sack of money . . . turn some of it loose.

WINING BOY: I was just fixing to ask you for five dollars.

BOY WILLIE: I ain't got no money. I'm trying to get some. Doaker tell you about Sutter? The Ghosts of the Yellow Dog got him about three weeks ago. Berniece done seen his ghost and everything. He right upstairs.

Calls.

Hey Sutter! Wining Boy's here. Come on, get a drink!

WINING BOY: How many that make the Ghosts of the Yellow Dog done got?

BOY WILLIE: Must be about nine or ten, eleven or twelve. I don't know.

DOAKER: You got Ed Saunders. Howard Peterson. Charlie Webb.

WINING BOY: Robert Smith. That fellow that shot Becky's boy . . . say he was stealing peaches . . .

DOAKER: You talking about Bob Mallory.

BOY WILLIE: Berniece say she don't believe all that about the Ghosts of the Yellow Dog.

WINING BOY: She ain't got to believe. You go ask them white folks in Sunflower County if they believe. You go ask Sutter if he believe. I don't care if Berniece believe or not. I done been to where the Southern cross the Yellow Dog and called out their names. They talk back to you, too.

LYMON: What they sound like? The wind or something?

BOY WILLIE: You done been there for real, Wining Boy?

WINING BOY: Nineteen thirty. July of nineteen thirty I stood right there on that spot. It didn't look like nothing was going right in my life. I said everything can't go wrong all the time . . . let me go down there and call on the Ghosts of the Yellow Dog, see if they can help me. I went down there and right there where them two railroads cross each other . . . I stood right there on that spot and called out their names. They talk back to you, too.

LYMON: People say you can ask them questions. They talk to you like that?

WINING BOY: A lot of things you got to find out on your own. I can't say how they talked to nobody else. But to me it just filled me up in a strange sort of way to be standing there on that spot. I didn't want to leave. It felt like the longer I stood there the bigger I got. I seen the train coming and it seem like I was bigger than the train. I started not to move. But something told me to go ahead and get on out the way. The train passed and I started to go back up there and stand some more. But something told me not to do it. I walked away from there feeling like a king. Went on and had a stroke of luck that run on for three years. So I don't care if Berniece believe or not. Berniece ain't got to believe. I know cause I been there. Now Doaker'll tell you about the Ghosts of the Yellow Dog.

DOAKER: I don't try and talk that stuff with Berniece. Avery got her all tied up in that church. She just think it's a whole lot of nonsense.

BOY WILLIE: Berniece don't believe in nothing. She just think she believe. She believe in anything if it's convenient for her to believe. But when that convenience run out then she ain't got nothing to stand on.

WINING BOY: Let's not get on Berniece now. Doaker tell me you talking about selling that piano.

BOY WILLIE: Yeah . . . hey, Doaker, I got the name of that man Avery was talking about. The man what's fixing the truck gave me his name. Everybody know him. Say he buy up anything you can make music with. I got his name and his telephone number. Hey, Wining Boy, Sutter's brother say he selling the land to me. I got one part. Sell them watermelons get me the second part. Then . . . soon as I get them watermelons out that truck I'm gonna take and sell that piano and get the third part.

DOAKER: That land ain't worth nothing no more. The smart white man's up here in these cities. He cut the land loose and step back and watch you and the dumb white man argue over it.

WINING BOY: How you know Sutter's brother ain't sold it already? You talking about selling the piano and the man's liable to sold the land two or three times.

BOY WILLIE: He say he waiting on me. He say he give me two weeks. That's two weeks from Friday. Say if I ain't back by then he might gonna sell it to somebody else. He say he wanna see me with it.

WINING BOY: You know as well as I know the man gonna sell the land to the first one walk up and hand him the money.

BOY WILLIE: That's just who I'm gonna be. Look, you ain't gotta know he waiting on me. I know. Okay. I know what the man told me. Stoval already done tried to buy the land from him and he told him no. The man say he waiting on me . . . he waiting on me. Hey, Doaker . . . . give me a drink. I see Wining Boy got his glass.

Doaker exists into his room.

Wining Boy, what you doing in Kansas City? What they got down there?

LYMON: I hear they got some nice-looking women in Kansas City. I sure like to go down there and find out.

WINING BOY: Man, the women down there is something else.

Doaker enters with a bottle of whiskey. He sets it on the table with some glasses.

DOAKER: You wanna sit up here and drink up my whiskey, leave a dollar on the table when you get up.

BOY WILLIE: You ain't doing nothing but showing your hospitality. I know we ain't got to pay for your hospitality.

WINING BOY: Doaker say they had you and Lymon down on the Parchman Farm. Had you on my old stomping grounds.

BOY WILLIE: Me and Lymon was down there hauling wood for Jim Miller and keeping us a little bit to sell. Some white fellows tried to run us off of it. That's when Crawley got killed. They put me and Lymon in the penitentiary.

LYMON: They ambushed us right there where that road dip down and around that bend in the creek. Crawley tried to fight them. Me and Boy Willie got away but the sheriff got us. Say we was stealing wood. They shot me in my stomach.

BOY WILLIE: They looking for Lymon down there now. They rounded him up and put him in jail for not working.

LYMON: Fined me a hundred dollars. Mr. Stovall come and paid my hundred dollars and the judge say I got to work for him to pay him back his hundred dollars. I told them I'd rather take my thirty days but they wouldn't let me do that.

BOY WILLIE: As soon as Stovall turned his back, Lymon was gone. He down there living in that truck dodging the sheriff and Stovall. He got both of them looking for him. So I brought him up here.

LYMON: I told Boy Willie I'm gonna stay up here. I ain't going back with him.

BOY WILLIE: Ain't nobody twisting your arm to make you go back. You can do what you want to do.

WINING BOY: I'll go back with you. I'm on my way down there. You gonna take the train? I'm gonna take the train.

LYMON: They treat you better up here.

BOY WILLIE: I ain't worried about nobody mistreating me. They treat you like you let them treat you. They mistreat me I mistreat them right back. Ain't no difference in me and the white man.

WINING BOY: Ain't no difference as far as how somebody supposed to treat you. I agree with that. But I'll tell you the difference between the colored man and the white man. Alright. Now you take and eat some berries. They taste real good to you. So you say I'm gonna go out and get me a whole pot of these berries and cook them up to make a pie or whatever. But you ain't looked to see them berries is sitting in the white fellow's yard. Ain't got no fence around them. You figure anybody want something they'd fence it in. Alright. Now the white man come along and say that's my land. Therefore everything that grow on it belong to me. He tell the sheriff, "I want you to put this nigger in jail as a warning to all the other niggers. Otherwise first thing you know these niggers have everything that belong to us."

BOY WILLIE: I'd come back at night and haul off his whole patch while he was sleep.

AUGUST WILSON

WINING BOY: Alright. Now Mr. So and So, he sell the land to you. And he come to you and say, "John, you own the land. It's all yours now. But them is my berries. And come time to pick them I'm gonna send my boys over. You got the land . . . but them berries, I'm gonna keep them. They mine." And he go and fix it with the law that them is his berries. Now that's the difference between the colored man and the white man. The colored man can't fix nothing with the law.

BOY WILLIE: I don't go by what the law say. The law's liable to say anything. I go by if it's right or not. It don't matter to me what the law say. I take and look at it for myself.

LYMON: That's why you gonna end up back down there on the Parchman Farm.

BOY WILLIE: I ain't thinking about no Parchman Farm. You liable to go back before me.

LYMON: They work you too hard down there. All that weeding and hoeing and chopping down trees. I didn't like all that.

WINING BOY: You ain't got to like your job on Parchman. Hey, tell him, Doaker, the only one got to like his job is the waterboy.

DOAKER: If he don't like his job he need to set that bucket down.

BOY WILLIE: That's what they told Lymon. They had Lymon on water and everybody got mad at him cause he was lazy.

LYMON: That water was heavy.

BOY WILLIE: They had Lymon down there singing:

Sings.

O Lord Berta Berta O Lord gal oh-ah
O Lord Berta Berta O Lord gal well

[Lymon *and* Wining Boy *join in.*]

Go 'head marry don't you wait on me oh-ah
Go 'head marry don't you wait on me well
Might not want you when I go free oh-ah
Might not want you when I go free well

BOY WILLIE: Come on, Doaker. Doaker know this one.

As Doaker joins in the men stamp and clap to keep time. They sing in harmony with great fervor and style.

O Lord Berta Berta O Lord gal oh-ah
O Lord Berta Berta O Lord gal well

Raise them up higher, let them drop on down oh-ah
Raise them up higher, let them drop on down well
Don't know the difference when the sun go down oh-ah
Don't know the difference when the sun go down well

Berta in Meridan and she living at ease oh-ah
Berta in Meridan and she living at ease well
I'm on old Parchman, got to work or leave oh-ah
I'm on old Parchman, got to work or leave well

O Alberta, Berta, O Lord gal oh-ah
O Alberta, Berta, O Lord gal well

When you marry, don't marry no farming man oh-ah
When you marry, don't marry no farming man well
Everyday Monday, hoe handle in your hand oh-ah
Everyday Monday, hoe handle in your hand well

When you marry, marry a railroad man, oh-ah
When you marry, marry a railroad man, well
Everyday Sunday, dollar in your hand oh-ah
Everyday Sunday, dollar in your hand well

O Alberta, Berta, O Lord gal oh-ah
O Alberta, Berta, O Lord gal well

BOY WILLIE: Doaker like that part. He like that railroad part.

LYMON: Doaker sound like Tangleye. He can't sing a lick.

BOY WILLIE: Hey, Doaker, they still talk about you down on Parchman. They ask me, "You Doaker Boy's nephew?" I say, "Yeah, me and him is family." They treated me alright soon as I told them that. say, "Yeah, he my uncle."

DOAKER: I don't never want to see none of them niggers no more.

BOY WILLIE: I don't want to see them either. Hey, Wining Boy, come on play some piano. You a piano player, play some piano. Lymon wanna hear you.

WINING BOY: I give that piano up. That was the best thing that ever happened to me, getting rid of that piano. That piano got so big and I'm carrying it around on my back. I don't wish that on no-body. See, you think it's all fun being a recording star. Got to carrying that piano around and man did I get slow. Got just like mo-lasses. The world just slipping by me and I'm walking around with that piano. Alright. Now, there ain't but so many places you can go.

Only so many road wide enough for you and that piano. And that piano get heavier and heavier. Go to a place and they find out you play piano, the first thing they want to do is give you a drink, find you a piano, and sit you right down. And that's where you gonna be for the next eight hours. They ain't gonna let you get up! Now, the first three or four years of that is fun. You can't get enough whiskey and you can't get enough women and you don't never get tired of playing that piano. But that only last so long. You look up one day and you hate the whiskey, and you hate the women, and you hate the piano. But that's all you got. You can't do nothing else. All you know how to do is play that piano. Now, who am I? Am I me? Or am I the piano player? Sometime it seem like the only thing to do is shoot the piano player cause he the cause of all the trouble I'm having.

DOAKER: What you gonna do when your troubles get like mine?

LYMON: If I knew how to play it, I'd play it. That's a nice piano.

BOY WILLIE: Whoever playing better play quick. Sutter's brother say he waiting on me. I sell them watermelons. Get Berniece to sell that piano. Put them two parts with the part I done saved . . .

WINING BOY: Berniece ain't gonna sell that piano. I don't see why you don't know that.

BOY WILLIE: What she gonna do with it? She ain't doing nothing but letting it sit up there and rot. That piano ain't doing nobody no good.

LYMON: That's a nice piano. If I had it I'd sell it. Unless I knew how to play like Wining Boy. You can get a nice price for that piano.

DOAKER: Now I'm gonna tell you something, Lymon don't know this . . . but I'm gonna tell you why me and Wining Boy say Berniece ain't gonna sell that piano.

BOY WILLIE: She ain't got to sell it! I'm gonna sell it! Berniece ain't got no more rights to that piano than I do.

DOAKER: I'm talking to the man . . . let me talk to the man. See, now . . . to understand why we say that . . . to understand about that piano . . . you got to go back to slavery time. See, our family was owned by a fellow named Robert Sutter. That was Sutter's grandfather. Alright. The piano was owned by a fellow named Joel Nolander. He was one of the Nolander brothers from down in Georgia. It was coming up on Sutter's wedding anniversary and he was looking to buy his wife . . . Miss Ophelia was her name . . . he was looking to buy her an anniversary present. Only thing with him . . . he ain't had no money. But he had some niggers. So he asked Mr. Nolander to see if maybe he could trade off some of his niggers for that piano. Told him he would give him one and a half niggers for it. That's the way he told him. Say he could have one full grown and one half grown. Mr. Nolander agreed only he say he had to pick them. He didn't want Sutter to give him just any old nigger. He say he wanted to have the pick of the litter. So Sutter lined up his niggers and Mr. Nolander looked them over and out of the whole bunch he picked my grandmother . . . her name was Berniece . . . same like Berniece . . . and he picked my daddy when he wasn't nothing but a little boy nine years old. They made the trade off and Miss Ophelia was so happy with that piano that it got to be just about all she would do was play on that piano.

WINING BOY: Just get up in the morning, get all dressed up and sit down and play on that piano.

DOAKER: Alright. Time go along. Time go along. Miss Ophelia got to missing my grandmother . . . the way she would cook and clean the house and talk to her and what not. And she missed having my daddy around the house to fetch things for her. So she asked to see if maybe she could trade back that piano and get her niggers back. Mr. Nolander said no. Said a deal was a deal. Him and Sutter had a big falling out about it and Miss Ophelia took sick to the bed. Wouldn't get out of the bed in the morning. She just lay there. The doctor said she was wasting away.

WINING BOY: That's when Sutter called our granddaddy up to the house.

DOAKER: Now, our granddaddy's name was Boy Willie. That's who Boy Willie's named after . . . only they called him Willie Boy. Now, he was a worker of wood. He could make you anything you wanted out of wood. He'd make you a desk. A table. A lamp. Anything you wanted. Them white fellows around there used to come up to Mr. Sutter and get him to make all kinds of things for them. Then they'd pay Mr. Sutter a nice price. See, everything my granddaddy made Mr. Sutter owned cause he owned him. That's why when Mr. Nolander offered to buy him to keep the family together Mr. Sutter wouldn't sell him. Told Mr. Nolander he didn't have enough money to buy him. Now . . . am I telling it right, Wining Boy?

WINING BOY: You telling it.

DOAKER: Sutter called him up to the house and told him to carve my grandmother and my daddy's picture on the piano for Miss Ophelia. And he took and carved this . . .

Doaker crosses over to the piano.

See that right there? That's my grandmother, Berniece. She looked just like that. And he put a picture of my daddy when he wasn't nothing but a little boy the way he remembered him. He made them up out of his memory. Only thing . . . he didn't stop there. He carved all this. He got a picture of his mama . . . Mama Esther . . . and his daddy, Boy Charles.

WINING BOY: That was the first Boy Charles.

DOAKER: Then he put on the side here all kinds of things. See that? That's when him and Mama Berniece got married. They called it jumping the broom. That's how you got married in them days. Then he got here when my daddy was born . . . and here he got Mama Esther's funeral . . . and down here he got Mr. Nolander taking Mama Berniece and my daddy away down to his place in Georgia. He got all kinds of things what happened with our family. When Mr. Sutter seen the piano with all them carvings on it he got mad. He didn't ask for all that. But see . . . there wasn't nothing he could do about it. When Miss Ophelia seen it . . . she got excited. Now she had her piano and her niggers too. She took back to playing it and played on it right up till the day she died. Alright . . . now see, our brother Boy Charles . . . that's Berniece and Boy Willie's daddy . . . he was the oldest of us three boys. He's dead now. But he would have been fifty-seven if he had lived. He died in 1911 when he was thirty-one years old. Boy Charles used to talk about that piano all the time. He never could get it off his mind. Two or three months go by and he be talking about it again. He be talking about taking it out of Sutter's house. Say it was the story of our whole family and as long as Sutter had it . . . he had us. Say we was still in slavery. Me and wining Boy tried to talk him out of it but it wouldn't do any good. Soon as he quiet down about it he'd start up again. We seen where he wasn't gonna get it off his mind . . . so, on the Fourth of July, 1911 . . . when Sutter was at the picnic what the county give every year . . . me and Wining Boy went on down there with him and took that piano out of Sutter's house. We put it on a wagon and me and Wining Boy carried it over into the next county with Mama Ola's people. Boy Charles decided to stay around there and wait until Sutter got home to make it look like business as usual.

Now, I don't know what happened when Sutter came home and found that piano gone. But somebody went up to Boy Charles's house and set it on fire. But he wasn't in there. He must have seen them coming cause he went down and caught the 3:57 Yellow Dog. He didn't know they was gonna come down and stop the train. Stopped the train and found Boy Charles in the boxcar with four of them hobos. Must have got mad when they couldn't find the piano cause they set the boxcar afire and killed everybody. Now, nobody know who done that. Some people say it was Sutter cause it was his piano. Some people say it was Sheriff Carter. Some people say it was Robert Smith and Ed Saunders. But don't nobody know for sure. It was about two months after that that Ed Saunders fell down his well. Just upped and fell down his well for no reason. People say it was the ghost of them men who burned up in the boxcar that pushed him in his well. They started calling them the Ghosts of the Yellow Dog. Now, that's how all that got started and that's why we say Berniece ain't gonna sell that piano. Cause her daddy died over it.

BOY WILLIE: All that's in the past. If my daddy had seen where he could have traded that piano in for some land of his own, it wouldn't be sitting up here now. He spent his whole life farming on somebody else's land. I ain't gonna do that. See, he couldn't do no better. When he come along he ain't had nothing he could build on. His daddy ain't had nothing to give him. The only thing my daddy had to give me was that piano. And he died over giving me that. I ain't gonna let it sit up there and rot without trying to do something with it. If Berniece can't see that, then I'm gonna go ahead and sell my half. And you and Wining Boy know I'm right.

DOAKER: Ain't nobody said nothing about who's right and who's wrong. I was just telling the man about the piano. I was telling him why we say Berniece ain't gonna sell it.

LYMON: Yeah, I can see why you say that now. I told Boy Willie he ought to stay up here with me.

BOY WILLIE: You stay! I'm going back! That's what I'm gonna do with my life! Why I got to come up here and learn to do something I don't know how to do when I already know how to farm? You stay up here and make your own way if that's what you want to do. I'm going back and live my life the way I want to live it.

Wining Boy gets up and crosses to the piano.

WINING BOY: Let's see what we got here. I ain't played on this thing for a while.

DOAKER: You can stop telling that. You was playing on it the last time you was through here. We couldn't get you off of it. Go on and play something.

Wining Boy sits down at the piano and plays and sings. The song is one which has put many dimes and quarters in his pocket, long ago, in dimly remembered towns and way stations. He plays badly, without hesitation, and sings in a forceful voice.

WINING BOY: *Singing.*

I am a rambling gambling man
I gambled in many towns
I rambled this wide world over
I rambled this world around
I had my ups and downs in life
And bitter times I saw
But I never knew what misery was
Till I lit on old Arkansas.

I started out one morning
To meet that early train
He said, "You better work for me
I have some land to drain.
I'll give you fifty cents a day,
Your washing, board and all
And you shall be a different man
In the state of Arkansas."

I worked six months for the rascal
Joe Herrin was his name
He fed me old corn dodgers
They was hard as any rock
My tooth is all got loosened
And my knees begin to knock
That was the kind of hash I got
In the state of Arkansas.

Traveling man
I've traveled all around this world

Traveling man
I've traveled from land to land
Traveling man
I've traveled all around this world
Well it ain't no use
writing no news
I'm a traveling man.

The door opens and Berniece enters with Maretha.

BERNIECE: Is that . . . Lord, I know that ain't Wining Boy sitting there.

WINING BOY: Hey, Berniece.

BERNIECE: You all had this planned. You and Boy Willie had this planned.

WINING BOY: I didn't know he was gonna be here. I'm on my way down home. I stopped by to see you and Doaker first.

DOAKER: I told the nigger he left out of here with that sack of money, we thought we might never see him again. Boy Willie say he wasn't gonna see him till he got broke. I looked up and seen him sitting on the doorstep asking for two dollars. Look at him laughing. He know it's the truth.

BERNIECE: Boy Willie, I didn't see that truck out there. I thought you was out selling watermelons.

BOY WILLIE: We done sold them all. Sold the truck too.

BERNIECE: I don't want to go through none of your stuff. I done told you to go back where you belong.

BOY WILLIE: I was just teasing you, woman. You can't take no teasing?

BERNIECE: Wining Boy, when you get here?

WINING BOY: A little while ago. I took the train from Kansas City.

BERNIECE: Let me go upstairs and change and then I'll cook you something to eat.

BOY WILLIE: You ain't cooked me nothing when I come.

BERNIECE: Boy Willie, go on and leave me alone. Come on, Maretha, get up here and change your clothes before you get them dirty.

Berniece exits up the stairs, followed by Maretha.

WINING BOY: Maretha sure getting big, ain't she, Doaker. And just as pretty as she want to be. I didn't know Crawley had it in him.

Boy Willie crosses to the piano.

BOY WILLIE: Hey, Lymon . . . get up on the other side of this piano and let me see something.

WINING BOY: Boy Willie, what is you doing?

BOY WILLIE: I'm seeing how heavy this piano is. Get up over there, Lymon.

WINING BOY: Go on and leave that piano alone. You ain't taking that piano out of here and selling it.

BOY WILLIE: Just as soon as I get them watermelons out that truck.

WINING BOY: Well, I got something to say about that.

BOY WILLIE: This my daddy's piano.

WINING BOY: He ain't took it by himself. Me and Doaker helped him.

BOY WILLIE: He died by himself. Where was you and Doaker at then? Don't come telling me nothing about this piano. This is me and Berniece's piano. Am I right, Doaker?

DOAKER: Yeah, you right.

BOY WILLIE: Let's see if we can lift it up, Lymon. Get a good grip on it and pick it up on your end. Ready? Lift!

As they start to move the piano, the sound of Sutter's Ghost is heard. Doaker is the only one to hear it. With difficulty they move the piano a little bit so it is out of place.

BOY WILLIE: What you think?

LYMON: It's heavy . . . but you can move it. Only it ain't gonna be easy.

BOY WILLIE: It wasn't that heavy to me. Okay, let's put it back.

The sound of Sutter's Ghost is heard again. They all hear it as Berniece enters on the stairs.

BERNIECE: Boy Willie . . . you gonna play around with me one too many times. And then God's gonna bless you and West is gonna dress you. Now set that piano back over there. I done told you a hundred times I ain't selling that piano.

BOY WILLIE: I'm trying to get me some land, woman. I need that piano to get me some money so I can buy Sutter's land.

BERNIECE: Money can't buy what that piano cost. You can't sell your soul for money. It won't go with the buyer. It'll shrivel and shrink to know that you ain't taken on to it. But it won't go with the buyer.

BOY WILLIE: I ain't talking about all that, woman. I ain't talking about selling my soul. I'm talking about trading that piece of wood for some land. Get something under your feet. Land the only thing

God ain't making no more of. You can always get you another piano. I'm talking about some land. What you get something out the ground from. That's what I'm talking about. You can't do nothing with that piano but sit up there and look at it.

BERNIECE: That's just what I'm gonna do. Wining Boy, you want me to fry you some pork chops?

BOY WILLIE: Now, I'm gonna tell you the way I see it. The only thing that make that piano worth something is them carvings Papa Willie Boy put on there. That's what make it worth something. That was my great-granddaddy. Papa Boy Charles brought that piano into the house. Now, I'm supposed to build on what they left me. You can't do nothing with that piano sitting up here in the house. That's just like if I let them watermelons sit out there and rot. I'd be a fool. Alright now, if you say to me, Boy Willie, I'm using that piano. I give out lessons on it and that help me make my rent or whatever. Then that be something else. I'd have to go on and say, well, Berniece using that piano. She building on it. Let her go on and use it. I got to find another way to get Sutter's land. But Doaker say you ain't touched that piano the whole time it's been up here. So why you wanna stand in my way? See, you just looking at the sentimental value. See, that's good. That's alright. I take my hat off whenever somebody say my daddy's name. But I ain't gonna be no fool about no sentimental value. You can sit up here and look at the piano for the next hundred years and it's just gonna be a piano. You can't make more than that. Now I want to get Sutter's land with that piano. I get Sutter's land and I can go down and cash in the crop and get my seed. As long as I got the land and the seed then I'm alright. I can always get me a little something else. Cause that land give back to you. I can make me another crop and cash that in. I still got the land and the seed. But that piano don't put out nothing else. You ain't got nothing working for you. Now, the kind of man my daddy was he would have understood that. I'm sorry you can't see it that way. But that's why I'm gonna take that piano out of here and sell it.

BERNIECE: You ain't taking that piano out of my house.

She crosses to the piano.

Look at this piano. Look at it. Mama Ola polished this piano with her tears for seventeen years. For seventeen years she rubbed on it till her hands bled. Then she rubbed the blood in . . . mixed it up with the rest of the blood on it. Every day that God breathed life into her body she rubbed and cleaned and polished and prayed over it. "Play something for me, Berniece. Play something for me, Berniece." Every day. "I cleaned it up for you, play something for me, Berniece." You always talking about your daddy but you ain't never stopped to look at what his foolishness cost your mama. Seventeen years' worth of cold nights and an empty bed. For what? For a piano? For a piece of wood? To get even with somebody? I look at you and you're all the same. You, Papa Boy Charles, Wining Boy, Doaker, Crawley . . . you're all alike. All this thieving and killing and thieving and killing. And what it ever lead to? More killing and more thieving. I ain't never seen it come to nothing. People getting burned up. People getting shot. People falling down their wells. It don't never stop.

DOAKER: Come on now, Berniece, ain't no need in getting upset.

BOY WILLIE: I done a little bit of stealing here and there, but I ain't never killed nobody. I can't be speaking for nobody else. You all got to speak for yourself, but I ain't never killed nobody.

BERNIECE: You killed Crawley just as sure as if you pulled the trigger.

BOY WILLIE: See, that's ignorant. That's downright foolish for you to say something like that. You ain't doing nothing but showing your ignorance. If the nigger was here I'd whup his ass for getting me and Lymon shot at.

BERNIECE: Crawley ain't knew about the wood.

BOY WILLIE: We told the man about the wood. Ask Lymon. He knew all about the wood. He seen we was sneaking it. Why else we gonna be out there at night? Don't come telling me Crawley ain't knew about the wood. Them fellows come up on us and Crawley tried to bully them. Me and Lymon seen the sheriff with them and give in. Wasn't no sense in getting killed over fifty dollars' worth of wood.

BERNIECE: Crawley ain't knew you stole that wood.

BOY WILLIE: We ain't stole no wood. Me and Lymon was hauling wood for Jim Miller and keeping us a little bit on the side. We dumped our little bit down there by the creek till we had enough to make a load. Some fellows seen us and we figured we better get it before they did. We come up there and got Crawley to help us load it. Figured we'd cut him in. Crawley trying to keep the wolf from his door . . . we was trying to help him.

LYMON: Me and Boy Willie told him about the wood. We told him some fellows might be trying to beat us to it. He say let me go back and get my thirty-eight. That's what caused all the trouble.

BOY WILLIE: If Crawley ain't had the gun he'd be alive today.

LYMON: We had it about half loaded when they come up on us. We seen the sheriff with them and we tried to get away. We ducked around near the bend in the creek . . . but they was down there too. Boy Willie say let's give in. But Crawley pulled out his gun and started shooting. That's when they started shooting back.

BERNIECE: All I know is Crawley would be alive if you hadn't come up there and got him.

BOY WILLIE: I ain't had nothing to do with Crawley getting killed. That was his own fault.

BERNIECE: Crawley's dead and in the ground and you still walking around here eating. That's all I know. He went off to load some wood with you and ain't never come back.

BOY WILLIE: I told you, woman . . . I ain't had nothing to do with . . .

BERNIECE: He ain't here, is he? He ain't here!

Berniece hits Boy Willie.

I said he ain't here. Is he?

Berniece continues to hit Boy Willie, who doesn't move to defend himself, other than back up and turning his head so that most of the blows fall on his chest and arms.

DOAKER: [*Grabbing Berniece:*] Come on, Berniece . . . let it go, it ain't his fault.

BERNIECE: He ain't here, is he? Is he?

BOY WILLIE: I told you I ain't responsible for Crawley.

BERNIECE: He ain't here.

BOY WILLIE: Come on now, Berniece . . . don't' do this now. Doaker get her. I ain't had nothing to do with Crawley.

BERNIECE: You come up there and got him!

BOY WILLIE: I done told you now. Doaker, get her. I ain't playing.

DOAKER: Come on, Berniece.

Maretha is heard screaming upstairs. It is a scream of stark terror.

MARETHA: Mama! . . . Mama!

The lights go down to black. End of Act One.

AUGUST WILSON

Act II

Scene I

The lights come up on the kitchen. It is the following morning. Doaker is ironing the pants to his uniform. He has a pot cooking on the stove at the same time. He is singing a song. The song provides him with the rhythm for his work and he moves about the kitchen with the ease born of many years as a railroad cook.

DOAKER:

> *Gonna leave Jackson Mississippi*
> *and go to Memphis*
> *and double back to Jackson*
> *Come on down to Hattiesburg*
> *Change cars on the Y.D.*
> *coming through the territory to*
> *Meridian*
> *and Meridian to Greenville*
> *and Greenville to Memphis*
> *I'm on my way and I know where*
>
> *Change cars on the Katy*
> *Leaving Jackson*
> *and going through Clarksdale*
> *Hello Winona!*
> *Courtland!*
> *Bateville!*
> *Como!*
> *Senitobia!*
> *Lewisberg!*
> *Sunflower!*
> *Glendora!*
> *Sharkey!*
> *And double back to Jackson*
> *Hello Greenwood*
> *I'm on my way Memphis*
> *Clarksdale*
> *Moorhead*
> *Indianola*
> *Can a highball pass through?*

Highball on through sir
Grand Carson!
Thirty First Street Depot
Fourth Street Depot
Memphis!

Wining Boy enters carrying a suit of clothes.

DOAKER: I thought you took that suit to the pawnshop?

WINING BOY: I went down there and the man tell me the suit is too old. Look at this suit. This is one hundred percent silk! How a silk suit gonna get too old? I know what it was he just didn't want to give me five dollars for it. Best he wanna give me is three dollars. I figure a silk suit is worth five dollars all over the world. I wasn't gonna part with it for no three dollars so I brought it back.

DOAKER: They got another pawnshop up on Wylie.

WINING BOY: I carried it up there. He say he don't take no clothes. Only thing he take is guns and radios. Maybe a guitar or two. Where's Berniece?

DOAKER: Berniece still at work. Boy Willie went down there to meet Lymon this morning. I guess they got that truck fixed, they been out there all day and ain't come back yet. Maretha scared to sleep up there now. Berniece don't know, but I seen Sutter before she did.

WINING BOY: Say what?

DOAKER: About three weeks ago. I had just come back from down there. Sutter couldn't have been dead more than three days. He was sitting over there at the piano. I come out to go to work . . . and he was sitting right there. Had his hand on top of his head just like Berniece said. I believe he broke his neck when he fell in the well. I kept quiet about it. I didn't see no reason to upset Berniece.

WINING BOY: Did he say anything? Did he say he was looking for Boy Willie?

DOAKER: He was just sitting there. He ain't said nothing. I went on out the door and left him sitting there. I figure as long as he was on the other side of the room everything be alright. I don't know what I would have done if he had started walking toward me.

WINING BOY: Berniece say he was calling Boy Willie's name.

DOAKER: I ain't heard him say nothing. He was just sitting there when I seen him. But I don't believe Boy Willie pushed him in the well. Sutter here cause of that piano. I heard him playing on it one time. I thought it was Berniece but then she don't play that kind of music. I come out here and ain't seen nobody, but them piano keys was moving a mile a minute. Berniece need to go on and get rid of if. It ain't done nothing but cause trouble.

WINING BOY: I agree with Berniece. Boy Charles ain't took it to give it back. He took it cause he figure he had more right to it than Sutter did. If Sutter can't understand that . . . then that's just the way that go. Sutter dead and in the ground . . . don't care where his ghost is. He can hover around and play on the piano all he want. I want to see him carry it out the house. That's what I want to see. What time Berniece get home? I don't see how I let her get away from me this morning.

DOAKER: You up there sleep. Berniece leave out of here early in the morning. She out there in Squirrel Hill cleaning house for some bigshot down there at the steel mill. They don't like you to come late. You come late they won't give you your carfare. What kind of business you got with Berniece?

WINING BOY: My business. I ain't asked you what kind of business you got.

DOAKER: Berniece ain't got no money. If that's why you was trying to catch her. She having a hard enough time trying to get by as it is. If she go ahead and marry Avery . . . he working every day . . . she go ahead and marry him they could do alright for themselves. But as it stands she ain't got no money.

WINING BOY: Well, let me have five dollars.

DOAKER: I just give you a dollar before you left out of here. You ain't gonna take my five dollars out there and gamble and drink it up.

WINING BOY: Aw, nigger, give me five dollars. I'll give it back to you.

DOAKER: You wasn't looking to give me five dollars when you had that sack of money. You wasn't looking to throw nothing my way. Now you wanna come in here and borrow five dollars. If you going back with Boy Willie you need to be trying to figure out how you gonna get train fare.

WINING BOY: That's why I need the five dollars. If I had five dollars I could get me some money.

Doaker goes into his pocket.

Make it seven.

DOAKER: You take this five dollars . . . and you bring my money back here too.

*Boy Willie and Lymon enter. They are happy and excited. They have
money in all of their pockets and are anxious to count it.*

DOAKER: How'd you do out there?

BOY WILLIE: They was lining up for them.

LYMON: Me and Boy Willie couldn't sell them fast enough. Time we
got one sold we'd sell another.

BOY WILLIE: I seen what was happening and told Lymon to up the
price on them.

LYMON: Boy Willie say charge them a quarter more. They didn't care.
A couple of people give me a dollar and told me to keep the
change.

BOY WILLIE: One fellow bought five. I say now what he gonna do with
five watermelons? He can't eat them all. I sold him the five and
asked him did he want to buy five more.

LYMON: I ain't never seen nobody snatch a dollar fast as Boy Willie.

BOY WILLIE: One lady asked me say, "Is they sweet?" I told her say,
"Lady, where we grow these watermelons we put sugar in the
ground." You know, she believed me. Talking about she had never
heard of that before. Lymon was laughing his head off. I told her,
"Oh, yeah, we put the sugar right in the ground with the seed." She
say, "Well, give me another one." Them white folks is something
else . . . ain't they, Lymon?

LYMON: Soon as you holler watermelons they come right out their
door. Then they go and get their neighbors. Look like they having
a contest to see who can buy the most.

WINING BOY: I got something for Lymon.

*Wining Boy goes to get his suit. Boy Willie and Lymon continue
to count their money.*

BOY WILLIE: I know you got more than that. You ain't sold all them
watermelons for that little bit of money.

LYMON: I'm still looking. That ain't all you got either. Where's all them
quarters?

BOY WILLIE: You let me worry about the quarters. Just put the money
on the table.

WINING BOY: [*Entering with his suit.*] Look here, Lymon . . . see this?
Look at his eyes getting big. He ain't never seen a suit like this.
This is one hundred percent silk. Go ahead . . . put it on. See if it
fit you.

Lymon tries the suit coat on.

Look at that. Feel it. That's one hundred percent genuine silk. I got that in Chicago. You can't get clothes like that nowhere but New York and Chicago. You can't get clothes like that in Pittsburgh. These folks in Pittsburgh ain't never seen clothes like that.

LYMON: This is nice, feel real nice and smooth.

WINING BOY: That's a fifty-five-dollar suit. That's the kind of suit the bigshots wear. You need a pistol and a pocketful of money to wear that suit. I'll let you have it for three dollars. The women will fall out their windows they see you in a suit like that. Give me three dollars and go on and wear it down the street and get you a woman.

BOY WILLIE: That looks nice, Lymon. Put the pants on. Let me see it with the pants.

Lymon begins to try on the pants.

WINING BOY: Look at that . . . see how it fits you? Give me three dollars and go on and take it. Look at that, Doaker . . . don't he look nice?

DOAKER: Yeah . . . that's a nice suit.

WINING BOY: Got a shirt to go with it. Cost you an extra dollar. Four dollars you got the whole deal.

LYMON: How this look, Boy Willie?

BOY WILLIE: That look nice . . . if you like that kind of thing. I don't like them dress-up kind of clothes. If you like it, look real nice.

WINING BOY: That's the kind of suit you need for up here in the North.

LYMON: Four dollars for everything? The suit and the shirt?

WINING BOY: That's cheap. I should be charging you twenty dollars. I give you a break cause you a homeboy. That's the only way I let you have it for four dollars.

LYMON: [*Going into his pocket.*] Okay . . . here go the four dollars.

WINING BOY: You got some shoes? What size you wear?

LYMON: Size nine.

WINING BOY: That's what size I got! Size nine. I let you have them for three dollars.

LYMON: Where they at? Let me see them.

WINING BOY: They real nice shoes, too. Got a nice tip to them. Got pointy toe just like you want.

Wining Boy goes to get his shoes.

LYMON: Come on, Boy Willie, let's go out tonight. I wanna see what it looks like up here. Maybe we go to a picture show. Hey, Doaker, they got picture shows up here?

DOAKER: The Rhumba Theater. Right down there on Fullerton Street. Can't miss it. Got the speakers outside on the sidewalk. You can hear it a block away. Boy Willie know where it's at.

Doaker exits into his room.

LYMON: Let's go to the picture show, Boy Willie. Let's go find some women.

BOY WILLIE: Hey, Lymon, how many of them watermelons would you say we got left? We got just under a half a load . . . right?

LYMON: About that much. Maybe a little more.

BOY WILLIE: You think that piano will fit up in there?

LYMON: If we stack them watermelons you can sit it up in the front there.

BOY WILLIE: I'm gonna call that man tomorrow.

WINING BOY: [*Returns with his shoes.*] Here you go . . . size nine. Put them on. Cost you three dollars. That's a Florsheim shoe. That's the kind Staggerlee wore.

LYMON: [*Trying on the shoes.*] You sure these size nine?

WINING BOY: You can look at my feet and see we wear the same size. Man, you put on that suit and them shoes and you got something there. You ready for whatever's out there. But is they ready for you? With them shoes on you be the King of the Walk. Have everybody stop to look at your shoes. Wishing they had a pair. I'll give you a break. Go on and take them for two dollars.

Lymon pays Wining Boy two dollars.

LYMON: Come on, Boy Willie . . . let's go find some women. I'm gonna go upstairs and get ready. I'll be ready to go in a minute. Ain't you gonna get dressed?

BOY WILLIE: I'm gonna wear what I got on. I ain't dressing up for these city niggers.

Lymon exits up the stairs.

That's all Lymon think about is women.

WINING BOY: His daddy was the same way. I used to run around with him. I know his mama too. Two strokes back and I would have been his daddy! His daddy's dead now . . . but I got the nigger out of jail one time. They was fixing to name him Daniel and walk him through the Lion's Den. He got in a tussle with one of them white fellows and the sheriff lit on him like white on rice. That's how the whole thing come about between me and Lymon's mama. She knew me and his daddy used to run together and he got in jail and she went down there and took the sheriff a hundred dollars. Don't get me to lying about where she got it from. I don't know. The sheriff *looked at that hundred dollars and turned his nose up.* Told her, say, "That ain't gonna do him no good. You got to put another hundred on top of that." She come up *there and got me where I was playing at this saloon* . . . said she had all but fifty dollars and asked me if I could help. Now the way I figured it . . . without that fifty dollars the sheriff was gonna turn him over to Parchman. The sheriff turn him over to Parchman it be three years before anybody see him again. Now I'm gonna say it right . . . I will give anybody fifty dollars to keep them out of jail for three years. I give her the fifty dollars and she told me to come over to the house. I ain't asked her. I figure if she was nice enough to invite me I ought to go. I ain't had to say a word. She invited me over just as nice. Say, "Why don't you come over to the house?" She ain't had to say nothing else. Them words rolled off her tongue just as nice. I went on down there and sat about three hours. Started to leave and changed my mind. She grabbed hold to me and say, "Baby, it's all night long." That was one of the shortest nights I have ever spent on this earth! I could have used another eight hours. Lymon's daddy didn't even say nothing to me when he got out. He just looked at me funny. He had a good notion something had happened between me an' her. L. D. Jackson. That was one bad-luck nigger. Got killed at some dance. Fellow walked in and shot him thinking he was somebody else.

Doaker enters from his room.

Hey, Doaker, you remember L. D. Jackson?

DOAKER: That's Lymon's daddy. That was one bad-luck nigger.

BOY WILLIE: Look like you ready to railroad some.

DOAKER: Yeah, I got to make that run.

Lymon enters from the stairs. He is dressed in his new suit and shoes, to which he has added a cheap straw hat.

LYMON: How I look?

WINING BOY: You look like a million dollars. Don't he look good, Doaker? Come on, let's play some cards. You wanna play some cards?

BOY WILLIE: We ain't gonna play no cards with you. Me and Lymon gonna find some women. Hey, Lymon, don't play no cards with Wining Boy. He'll take all your money.

WINING BOY: [to Lymon.] You got a magic suit there. You can get you a woman easy with that suit . . . but you got to know the magic words. You know the magic words to get you a woman?

LYMON: I just talk to them to see if I like them and they like me.

WINING BOY: You just walk right up to them and say, "If you got the harbor I got the ship." If that don't work ask them if you can put them in your pocket. The first thing they gonna say is, "It's too small." That's when you look them dead in the eye and say, "Baby, ain't nothing small about me." If that don't work then you move on to another one. Am I telling him right, Doaker?

DOAKER: That man don't need you to tell him nothing about no women. These women these days ain't gonna fall for that kind of stuff. You got to buy them a present. That's what they looking for these days.

BOY WILLIE: Come on, I'm ready. You ready, Lymon? Come on, let's go find some women.

WINING BOY: Here, let me walk out with you. I wanna see the women fall out their window when they see Lymon.

They all exit and the lights go down on the scene.

Scene II

The lights come up on the kitchen. It is late evening of the same day. Berniece has set a tub for her bath in the kitchen. She is heating up water on the stove. There is a knock at the door.

BERNIECE: Who is it?

AVERY: It's me, Avery.

Berniece opens the door and lets him in.

BERNIECE: Avery, come on in. I was just fixing to take my bath.

AVERY: Where Boy Willie? I see that truck out there almost empty. They done sold almost all them watermelons.

BERNIECE: They was gone when I come home. I don't know where they went off to. Boy Willie around here about to drive me crazy.

AVERY: They sell them watermelons . . . he'll be gone soon.

BERNIECE: What Mr. Cohen say about letting you have the place?

AVERY: He say he'll let me have it for thirty dollars a month. I talked him out of thirty-five and he say he'll let me have it for thirty.

BERNIECE: That's a nice spot next to Benny Diamond's store.

AVERY: Berniece . . . I be at home and I get to thinking you up here an' I'm down there. I get to thinking how that look to have a preacher that ain't married. It makes for a better congregation if the preacher was settled down and married.

BERNIECE: Avery . . . not now. I was fixing to take my bath.

AVERY: You know how I feel about you, Berniece. Now . . . I done got the place from Mr. Cohen. I get the money from the bank and I can fix it up real nice. They give me a ten cents a hour raise down there on the job . . . now Berniece, I ain't got much in the way of comforts. I got a hole in my pockets near about as far as money is concerned. I ain't never found no way through life to a woman I care about like I care about you. I need that. I need somebody on my bond side. I need a woman that fits in my hand.

BERNIECE: Avery, I ain't ready to get married now.

AVERY: You too young a woman to close up, Berniece.

BERNIECE: I ain't said nothing about closing up. I got a lot of woman left in me.

AVERY: Where's it at? When's the last time you looked at it?

BERNIECE: [Stunned by his remark.] That's a nasty thing to say. And you call yourself a preacher.

AVERY: Anytime I get anywhere near you . . . you push me away.

BERNIECE: I got enough on my hands with Maretha. I got enough people to love and take care of.

AVERY: Who you got to love you? Can't nobody get close enough to you. Doaker can't half say nothing to you. You jump all over Boy Willie. Who you got to love you, Berniece?

BERNIECE: You trying to tell me a woman can't be nothing without a man. But you alright, huh? You can just walk out of here without me—without a woman—and still be a man. that's alright. Ain't nobody gonna ask you, "Avery, who you got to love you?" That's alright for you. But everybody gonna be worried about Berniece. "How Berniece gonna take care of herself? How she gonna raise that child without a man? Wonder what she do with herself. How she gonna live like that?" Everybody got all kinds of questions for Berniece. Everybody telling me I can't be a woman unless I got a man. Well, you tell me, Avery—you know—how much woman am I?

AVERY: It wasn't me, Berniece. You can't blame me for nobody else. I'll own up to my own shortcomings. But you can't blame me for Crawley or nobody else.

BERNIECE: I ain't blaming nobody for nothing. I'm just stating the facts.

AVERY: How long you gonna carry Crawley with you, Berniece? It's been over three years. At some point you got to let go and go on. Life's got all kinds of twists and turns. That don't mean you stop living. That don't mean you cut yourself off from life. You can't go through life carrying Crawley's ghost with you. Crawley's been dead three years. Three years, Berniece.

BERNIECE: I know how long Crawley's been dead. You ain't got to tell me that. I just ain't ready to get married right now.

AVERY: What is you ready for, Berniece? You just gonna drift along from day to day. Life is more than making it from one day to another. You gonna look up one day and it's all gonna be past you. Life's gonna be gone out of your hands—there won't be enough to make nothing with. I'm standing here now, Berniece—but I don't know how much longer I'm gonna be standing here waiting on you.

BERNIECE: Avery, I told you . . . when you get your church we'll sit down and talk about this. I got too many other things to deal with right now. Boy Willie and the piano . . . and Sutter's ghost. I thought I might have been seeing things, but Maretha done seen Sutter's ghost, too.

AVERY: When this happen, Berniece?

BERNIECE: Right after I came home yesterday. Me and Boy Willie was arguing about the piano and Sutter's ghost was standing at the top of the stairs. Maretha scared to sleep up there now. Maybe if you bless the house he'll go away.

AVERY: I don't know, Berniece. I don't know if I should fool around with something like that.

BERNIECE: I can't have Maretha scared to go to sleep up there. Seem like if you bless the house he would go away.

AVERY: You might have to be a special kind of preacher to do something like that.

BERNIECE: I keep telling myself when Boy Willie leave he'll go on and leave with him. I believe Boy Willie pushed him in the well.

AVERY: That's been going on down there a long time. The Ghosts of the Yellow Dog been pushing people in their wells long before Boy Willie got grown.

BERNIECE: Somebody down there pushing them people in their wells. They ain't just upped and fell. Ain't no wind pushed nobody in their well.

AVERY: Oh, I don't know. God works in mysterious ways.

BERNIECE: He ain't pushed nobody in their wells.

AVERY: He caused it to happen. God is the Great Causer. He can do anything. He parted the Red Sea. He say I will smite my enemies. Reverend Thompson used to preach on the Ghosts of the Yellow Dog as the hand of God.

BERNIECE: I don't care who preached what. Somebody down there pushing them people in their wells. Somebody like Boy Willie. I can see him doing something like that. You ain't gonna tell me that Sutter just upped and fell in his well. I believe Boy Willie pushed him so he could get his land.

AVERY: What Doaker say about Boy Willie selling the piano?

BERNIECE: Doaker don't want no part of that piano. He ain't never wanted no part of it. He blames himself for not staying behind with Papa Boy Charles. He washed his hands of that piano a long time ago. He didn't want me to bring it up here—but I wasn't gonna leave it down there.

AVERY: Well, it seems to me somebody ought to be able to talk to Boy Willie.

BERNIECE: You can't talk to Boy Willie. He been that way all his life. Mama Ola had her hands full trying to talk to him. He don't listen to nobody. He just like my daddy. He get his mind fixed on something and can't nobody turn him from it.

AVERY: You ought to start a choir at the church. Maybe if he seen you was doing something with it—if you told him you was gonna put it in my church—maybe he'd see it different. You ought to put it down in the church and start a choir. The Bible say, "Make a joyful noise unto the Lord." Maybe if Boy Willie see you was doing something with it he'd see it different.

BERNIECE: I done told you I don't play on that piano. Ain't no need in you to keep talking this choir stuff. When my mama died I shut the top on that piano and I ain't never opened it since. I was only playing it for her. When my daddy died seem like all her life went into that piano. She used to have me playing on it . . . had Miss Eula come in and teach me . . . say when I played it she could hear my daddy talking to her. I used to think them pictures came alive and walked through the house. Sometime late at night I could hear my mama talking to them. I said that wasn't gonna happen to me. I don't play that piano cause I don't want to wake them spirits. They never be walking around in this house.

AVERY: You got to put all that behind you, Berniece.

BERNIECE: I got Maretha playing on it. She don't know nothing about it. Let her go on and be a schoolteacher or something. She don't have to carry all of that with her. She got a chance I didn't have. I ain't gonna burden her with that piano.

AVERY: You got to put all of that behind you, Berniece. That's the same thing like Crawley. Everybody got stones in their passway. You got to step over them or walk around them. You picking them up and carrying them with you. All you got to do is set them down by the side of the road. You ain't got to carry them with you. You can walk over there right now and play that piano. You can walk over there right now and God will walk over there with you. Right now you can set that sack of stones down by the side of the road and walk away from it. You don't have to carry it with you. You can do it right now.

Avery crosses over to the piano and raises the lid.

Come on, Berniece . . . set it down and walk away from it. Come on, play "Old Ship of Zion." Walk over here and claim it as an instrument of the Lord. You can walk over here right now and make it into a celebration.

Berniece moves toward the piano.

BERNIECE: Avery . . . I done told you I don't want to play that piano. Now or no other time.

AVERY: The Bible say, "The Lord is my refuge . . . and my strength!" With the strength of God you can put the past behind you, Berniece. With the strength of God you can do anything! God got a bright tomorrow. God don't ask what you done . . . God ask what you gonna do. The strength of God can move mountains! God's got a bright tomorrow for you . . . all you got to do is walk over here and claim it.

BERNIECE: Avery, just go on and let me finish my bath. I'll see you tomorrow.

AVERY: Okay, Berniece. I'm gonna go home. I'm gonna go home and read up on my Bible. And tomorrow . . . if the good Lord give me strength tomorrow . . . I'm gonna come by and bless the house . . . and show you the power of the Lord.

Avery crosses to the door.

It's gonna be alright, Berniece. God say he will soothe the troubled waters. I'll come by tomorrow and bless the house.

The lights go down to black.

Scene III

Several hours later. The house is dark. Berniece has retired for the night. Boy Willie enters the darkened house with Grace.

BOY WILLIE: Come on in. This my sister's house. My sister live here. Come on, I ain't gonna bite you.

GRACE: Put some light on. I can't see.

BOY WILLIE: You don't need to see nothing, baby. This here is all you need to see. All you need to do is see me. If you can't see me you can feel me in the dark. How's that, sugar?

He attempts to kiss her.

GRACE: Go on now . . . wait!

BOY WILLIE: Just give me one little old kiss.

GRACE: [*Pushing him away.*] Come on, now. Where I'm gonna sleep at?

BOY WILLIE: We got to sleep out here on the couch. Come on, my sister don't mind. Lymon come back he just got to sleep on the floor. He run off with Dolly somewhere he better stay there. Come on, sugar.

GRACE: Wait now . . . you ain't told me nothing about no couch. I thought you had a bed. Both of us can't sleep on that little old couch.

BOY WILLIE: It don't make no difference. We can sleep on the floor. Let Lymon sleep on the couch.

GRACE: You ain't told me nothing about no couch.

BOY WILLIE: What difference it make? You just wanna be with me.

GRACE: I don't want to be with you on no couch. Ain't you got no bed?

BOY WILLIE: You don't need no bed, woman. My granddaddy used to take women on the backs of horses. What you need a bed for? You just want to be with me.

GRACE: You sure is country. I didn't know you was this country.

BOY WILLIE: There's a lot of things you don't know about me. Come on, let me show you what this country boy can do.

GRACE: Let's go to my place. I got a room with a bed if Leroy don't come back there.

BOY WILLIE: Who's Leroy? You ain't said nothing about no Leroy.

GRACE: He used to be my man. He ain't coming back. He gone off with some other gal.

BOY WILLIE: You let him have your key?

GRACE: He ain't coming back.

BOY WILLIE: Did you let him have your key?

GRACE: He got a key but he ain't coming back. He took off with some other gal.

BOY WILLIE: I don't wanna go nowhere he might come. Let's stay here. Come on, sugar.

He pulls her over to the couch.

Let me heist your hood and check your oil. See if your battery needs charged.

He pulls her to him. They kiss and tug at each other's clothing. In their anxiety they knock over a lamp.

BERNIECE: Who's that . . . Wining Boy?

BOY WILLIE: It's me . . . Boy Willie. Go on back to sleep. Everything's alright.

To Grace.

That's my sister. Everything's alright, Berniece. Go on back to sleep.

BERNIECE: What you doing down there? What you done knocked over?

BOY WILLIE: It wasn't nothing. Everything's alright. Go on back to sleep.

To Grace.

That's my sister. We alright. She gone back to sleep.

They begin to kiss. Berniece enters from the stairs dressed in a nightgown. She cuts on the light.

BERNIECE: Boy Willie, what you doing down here?

BOY WILLIE: It was just that there lamp. It ain't broke. It's okay. Everything's alright. Go on back to bed.

AUGUST WILSON

BERNIECE: Boy Willie, I don't allow that in my house. You gonna have to take your company someplace else.

BOY WILLIE: It's alright. We ain't doing nothing. We just sitting here talking. This here is Grace. That's my sister Berniece.

BERNIECE: You know I don't allow that kind of stuff in my house.

BOY WILLIE: Allow what? We just sitting here talking.

BERNIECE: Well, your company gonna have to leave. Come back and talk in the morning.

BOY WILLIE: Go on back upstairs now.

BERNIECE: I got an eleven-year-old girl upstairs. I can't allow that around here.

BOY WILLIE: Ain't nobody said nothing about that. I told you we just talking.

GRACE: Come on . . . let's go to my place. Ain't nobody got to tell me to leave but once.

BOY WILLIE: You ain't got to be like that, Berniece.

BERNIECE: I'm sorry, Miss. But he know I don't allow that in here.

GRACE: You ain't got to tell me but once. I don't stay nowhere I ain't wanted.

BOY WILLIE: I don't know why you want to embarrass me in front of my company.

GRACE: Come on, take me home.

BERNIECE: Go on, Boy Willie. Just go on with your company.

Boy Willie and Grace exit. Berniece puts the light on in the kitchen and puts on the teakettle. Presently there is a knock at the door. Berniece goes to answer it. Berniece opens the door. Lymon enters.

LYMON: How you doing, Berniece? I thought you'd be asleep. Boy Willie been back here?

BERNIECE: He just left out of here a minute ago.

LYMON: I went out to see a picture show and never got there. We always end up doing something else. I was with this woman she just wanted to drink up all my money. So I left her there and came back looking for Boy Willie.

BERNIECE: You just missed him. He just left out of here.

LYMON: They got some nice-looking women in this city. I'm gonna like it up here real good. I like seeing them with their dresses on. Got them high heels. I like that. Make them look like they real precious. Boy Willie met a real nice one today. I wish I had met her before he did.

BERNIECE: He come by here with some woman a little while ago. I told him to go on and take all that out of my house.

LYMON: What she look like, the woman he was with? Was she a brown-skinned woman about this high? Nice and healthy? Got nice hips on her?

BERNIECE: She had on a red dress.

LYMON: That's her! That's Grace. She real nice. Laugh a lot. Lot of fun to be with. She don't be trying to put on. Some of these woman act like they the Queen of Sheba. I don't like them kind. Grace ain't like that. She real nice with herself.

BERNIECE: I don't know what she was like. He come in here all drunk knocking over the lamp, and making all kind of noise. I told them to take that somewhere else. I can't really say what she was like.

LYMON: She real nice. I seen her before he did. I was trying not to act like I seen her. I wanted to look at her a while before I said something. She seen me when I come into the saloon. I tried to act like I didn't see her. Time I looked around Boy Willie was talking to her. She was talking to him kept looking at me. That's when her friend Dolly came. I asked her if she wanted to go to the picture show. She told me to buy her a drink while she thought about it. Next thing I knew she done had three drinks talking about she too tired to go. I bought her another drink, then I left. Boy Willie was gone and I thought he might have come back here. Doaker gone, huh? He say he had to make a trip.

BERNIECE: Yeah, he gone on his trip. This is when I can usually get me some peace and quiet, Maretha asleep.

LYMON: She look just like you. Got them big eyes. I remember her when she was in diapers.

BERNIECE: Time just keep on. It go on with or without you. She going on twelve.

LYMON: She sure is pretty. I like kids.

BERNIECE: Boy Willie say you staying . . . what you gonna do up here in this big city? You thought about that?

LYMON: They never get me back down there. The sheriff looking for me. All because they gonna try and make me work for somebody when I don't want to. They gonna try and make me work for Stovall when he don't pay nothing. It ain't like that up here. Up here you more or less do what you want to. I figure I find me a job and try to get set up and then see what the year brings. I tried to do that two or three times down there ... but it never would work out. I was always in the wrong place.

BERNIECE: This ain't a bad city once you get to know your way around.

LYMON: Up here is different. I'm gonna get me a job unloading box-cars or something. One fellow told me say he know a place. I'm gonna go over there with him next week. Me and Boy Willie finish selling them watermelons I'll have enough money to hold me for a while. But I'm gonna go over there and see what kind of jobs they have.

BERNIECE: You shouldn't have too much trouble finding a job. It's all in how you present yourself. See now, Boy Willie couldn't get no job up here. Somebody hire him they got a pack of trouble on their hands. Soon as they find that out they fire him. He don't want to do nothing unless he do it his way.

LYMON: I know. I told him let's go to the picture show first and see if there was any women down there. They might get tired of sitting at home and walk down to the picture show. He say he wanna look around first. We never did get down there. We tried a couple of places and then we went to this saloon where he met Grace. I tried to meet her before he did but he beat me to her. We left Wining Boy sitting down there running his mouth. He told me if I wear this suit I'd find me a woman. He was almost right.

BERNIECE: You don't need to be out there in them saloons. Ain't no telling what you liable to run into out there. This one liable to cut you as quick as that one shoot you. You don't need to be out there. You start out that fast life you can't keep it up. It makes you old quick. I don't know what them women out there be thinking about.

LYMON: Mostly they be lonely and looking for somebody to spend the night with them. Sometimes it matters who it is and sometimes it don't. I used to be the same way. Now it got to matter. That's why I'm here now. Dolly liable not to even recognize me if she sees me again. I don't like women like that. I like my women to be with me in a nice and easy way. That way we can both enjoy ourselves. The way I see it we the only two people like us in the world. We got to see how we fit together. A woman that don't want to take the time to do that I don't bother with. Used to. Used to bother with all of them. Then I woke up one time with this woman and I didn't know who she was. She was the prettiest woman I had ever seen in my life. I spent the whole night with her and didn't even know it. I had never taken the time to look at her. I guess she kinda knew I ain't never really looked at her. She must have known that cause she ain't wanted to see me no more. If she had wanted to see me I believe we might have got married. How come you ain't married? It seem like to me you would be married. I remember Avery from down home. I used to call him plain old Avery. Now he Reverend Avery. That's kinda funny about him becoming a preacher. I like when he told about how that come to him in a dream about them sheep people and them hobos. Nothing ever come to me in a dream like that. I just dream about women. Can't never seem to find the right one.

BERNIECE: She out there somewhere. You just got to get yourself ready to meet her. That's what I'm trying to do. Avery's alright. I ain't really got nobody in mind.

LYMON: I get me a job and a little place and get set up to where I can make a woman comfortable I might get married. Avery's nice. You ought to go ahead and get married. You be a preacher's wife you won't have to work. I hate living by myself. I didn't want to be no strain on my mama so I left home when I was about sixteen. Everything I tried seem like it just didn't work out. Now I'm trying this.

BERNIECE: You keep trying it'll work out for you.

LYMON: You ever go down there to the picture show?

BERNIECE: I don't go in for all that.

LYMON: Ain't nothing wrong with it. It ain't like gambling and sinning. I went to one down in Jackson once. It was fun.

BERNIECE: I just stay home most of the time. Take care of Maretha.

LYMON: It's getting kind of late. I don't know where Boy Willie went off to. He's liable not to come back. I'm gonna take off these shoes. My feet hurt. Was you in bed? I don't mean to be keeping you up.

BERNIECE: You ain't keeping me up. I couldn't sleep after that Boy Willie woke me up.

LYMON: You got on that nightgown. I likes women when they wear them fancy nightclothes and all. It makes their skin look real pretty.

BERNIECE: I got this at the five-and-ten-cents store. It ain't so fancy.

LYMON: I don't too often get to see a woman dressed like that.

There is a long pause. Lymon takes off his suit coat.

Well, I'm gonna sleep here on the couch. I'm supposed to sleep on the floor but I don't reckon Boy Willie's coming back tonight. Wining Boy sold me this suit. Told me it was a magic suit. I'm gonna put it on again tomorrow. Maybe it bring me a woman like he say.

He goes into his coat pocket and takes out a small bottle of perfume.

I almost forgot I had this. Some man sold me this for a dollar. Say it come from Paris. This is the same kind of perfume the Queen of France wear. That's what he told me. I don't know if it's true or not. I smelled it. It smelled good to me. Here . . . smell it see if you like it. I was gonna give it to Dolly. But I didn't like her too much.

BERNIECE: [*Takes the bottle.*] It smells nice.

LYMON: I was gonna give it to Dolly if she had went to the picture with me. Go on, you take it.

BERNIECE: I can't take it. Here . . . go on you keep it. You'll find somebody to give it to.

LYMON: I wanna give it to you. Make you smell nice.

He takes the bottle and puts perfume behind Berniece's ear.

They tell me you supposed to put it right here behind your ear. Say if you put it there you smell nice all day.

Berniece stiffens at his touch. Lymon bends down to smell her.

There . . . you smell real good now.

He kisses her neck.

You smell real good for Lymon.

He kisses her again. Berniece returns the kiss, then breaks the embrace and crosses to the stairs. She turns and they look silently at each other. Lymon hands her the bottle of perfume. Berniece exits up the stairs. Lymon picks up his suit coat and strokes it lovingly with the full knowledge that it is indeed a magic suit. The lights go down on the scene.

Scene IV

It is late the next morning. The lights come up on the parlor. Lymon is asleep on the sofa. Boy Willie enters the front door.

BOY WILLIE: Hey, Lymon! Lymon, come on get up.

LYMON: Leave me alone.

BOY WILLIE: Come on, get up, nigger! Wake up, Lymon.

LYMON: What you want?

BOY WILLIE: Come on, let's go. I done called the man about the piano.

LYMON: What piano?

BOY WILLIE: [*Dumps Lymon on the floor.*] Come on, get up!

LYMON: Why you leave, I looked around and you was gone.

BOY WILLIE: I come back here with Grace, then I went looking for you. I figured you'd be with Dolly.

LYMON: She just want to drink and spend up your money. I come on back here looking for you to see if you wanted to go to the picture show.

BOY WILLIE: I been up at Grace's house. Some nigger named Leroy come by but I had a chair up against the door. He got mad when he couldn't get in. He went off somewhere and I got out of there before he could come back. Berniece got mad when we came here.

LYMON: She say you was knocking over the lamp busting up the place.

BOY WILLIE: That was Grace doing all that.

LYMON: Wining Boy seen Sutter's ghost last night.

BOY WILLIE: Wining Boy's liable to see anything. I'm surprised he found the right house. Come on, I done called the man about the piano.

LYMON: What he say?

BOY WILLIE: He say to bring it on out. I told him I was calling for my sister, Miss Berniece Charles. I told him some man wanted to buy it for eleven hundred dollars and asked him if he would go any better. He said yeah, he would give me eleven hundred and fifty dollars for it if it was the same piano. I described it to him again and he told me to bring it out.

LYMON: Why didn't you tell him to come and pick it up?

BOY WILLIE: I didn't want to have no problem with Berniece. This way we just take it on out there and it be out the way. He want to charge twenty-five dollars to pick it up.

LYMON: You should have told him the man was gonna give you twelve hundred for it.

BOY WILLIE: I figure I was taking a chance with that eleven hundred. If I had told him twelve hundred he might have run off. Now I wish I had told him twelve-fifty. It's hard to figure out white folks sometimes.

LYMON: You might have been able to tell him anything. White folks got a lot of money.

BOY WILLIE: Come on, let's get it loaded before Berniece come back. Get that end over there. All you got to do is pick it up on that side. Don't worry about this side. You wanna stretch you' back for a minute?

LYMON: I'm ready.

BOY WILLIE: Get a real good grip on it now.

The sound of Sutter's Ghost is heard. They do not hear it.

LYMON: I got this end. You get that end.

BOY WILLIE: Wait till I say ready now. Alright. You got it good? You got a grip on it?

LYMON: Yeah, I got it. You lift up on that end.

BOY WILLIE: Ready? Lift!

The piano will not budge.

LYMON: Man, this piano is heavy! It's gonna take more than me and you to move this piano.

BOY WILLIE: We can do it. Come on—we did it before.

LYMON: Nigger—you crazy! That piano weighs five hundred pounds!

BOY WILLIE: I got three hundred pounds of it! I know you can carry two hundred pounds! You be lifting them cotton sacks! Come on lift this piano!

They try to move the piano again without success.

LYMON: It's stuck. Something holding it.

BOY WILLIE: How the piano gonna be stuck? We just moved it. Slide you' end out.

LYMON: Naw—we gonna need two or three more people. How this big old piano get in the house?

BOY WILLIE: I don't know how it got in the house. I know how it's going out though! You get on this end. I'll carry three hundred and fifty pounds of it. All you got to do is slide your end out. Ready?

They switch sides and try again without success. Doaker enters from his room as they try to push and shove it.

LYMON: Hey, Doaker . . . how this piano get in the house?

DOAKER: Boy Willie, what you doing?

BOY WILLIE: I'm carrying this piano out the house. What it look like I'm doing? Come on, Lymon, let's try again.

DOAKER: Go on let the piano sit there till Berniece come home.

BOY WILLIE: You ain't got nothing to do with this, Doaker. This my business.

DOAKER: This is my house, nigger! I ain't gonna let you or nobody else carry nothing out of it. You ain't gonna carry nothing out of here without my permission!

BOY WILLIE: This is my piano. I don't need your permission to carry my belongings out of your house. This is mine. This ain't got nothing to do with you.

DOAKER: I say leave it over there till Berniece come home. She got part of it too. Leave it set there till you see what she say.

BOY WILLIE: I don't care what Berniece say. Come on, Lymon. I got this side.

DOAKER: Go on and cut it half in two if you want to. Just leave Berniece's half sitting over there. I can't tell you what to do with your piano. But I can't let you take her half out of here.

BOY WILLIE: Go on, Doaker. You ain't got nothing to do with this. I don't want you starting nothing now. Just go on and leave me alone. Come on, Lymon. I got this end.

Doaker goes into his room. Boy Willie and Lymon prepare to move the piano.

LYMON: How we gonna get it in the truck?

BOY WILLIE: Don't worry about how we gonna get it on the truck. You got to get it out the house first.

LYMON: It's gonna take more than me and you to move this piano.

BOY WILLIE: Just lift up on that end, nigger!

Doaker comes to the doorway of his room and stands.

DOAKER: [*Quietly with authority.*] Leave that piano set over there till Berniece come back. I don't care what you do with it then. But you gonna leave it sit over there right now.

BOY WILLIE: Alright . . . I'm gonna tell you this, Doaker. I'm going out of here . . . I'm gonna get me some rope . . . find me a plank and some wheels . . . and I'm coming back. Then I'm gonna carry that

piano out of here . . . sell it and give Berniece half the money. See
. . . now that's what I'm gonna do. And you . . . or nobody else is
gonna stop me. Come on, Lymon . . . let's go get some rope and
stuff. I'll be back, Doaker.

Boy Willie and Lymon exit. The lights go down on the scene.

Scene V

*The lights come up. Boy Willie sits on the sofa, screwing casters on a wooden
plank. Maretha is sitting on the piano stool. Doaker sits at the table playing
solitaire.*

BOY WILLIE: [*To Maretha.*] Then after that them white folks down
around there started falling down their wells. You ever seen a well?
A well got a wall around it. It's hard to fall down a well. You got to
be leaning way over. Couldn't nobody figure out too much what
was making these fellows fall down their well . . . so everybody
says the Ghosts of the Yellow Dog must have pushed them. That's
what everybody called them four men what got burned up in the
boxcar.

MARETHA: Why they call them that?

BOY WILLIE: Cause the Yazoo Delta railroad got yellow boxcars. Sometime the way the whistle blow sound like an old dog howling so
the people call it the Yellow Dog.

MARETHA: Anybody ever see the Ghosts?

BOY WILLIE: I told you they like the wind. Can you see the wind?

MARETHA: No.

BOY WILLIE: They like the wind you can't see them. But sometimes
you be in trouble they might be around to help you. They say if
you go where the Southern cross the Yellow Dog . . . you go to
where them two railroads cross each other . . . and call out their
names . . . they say they talk back to you. I don't know, I ain't never
done that. But Uncle Wining Boy he say he been down there and
talked to them. You have to ask him about that part.

Berniece has entered from the front door.

BERNIECE: Maretha, you go on and get ready for me to do your hair.

Maretha crosses to the steps.

Boy Willie, I done told you to leave my house.

To Maretha.

Go on, Maretha.

Maretha is hesitant about going up the stairs.

BOY WILLIE: Don't be scared. Here, I'll go up there with you. If we see Sutter's ghost I'll put a whupping on him. Come on, Uncle Boy Willie going with you.

Boy Willie and Maretha exit up the stairs.

BERNIECE: Doaker—what is going on here?

DOAKER: I come home and him and Lymon was moving the piano. I told them to leave it over there till you got home. He went out and got that board and them wheels. He say he gonna take that piano out of here and ain't nobody gonna stop him.

BERNIECE: I ain't playing with Boy Willie. I got Crawley's gun upstairs. He don't know but I'm through with it. Where Lymon go?

DOAKER: Boy Willie sent him for some rope just before you come in.

BERNIECE: I ain't studying Boy Willie or Lymon—or the rope. Boy Willie ain't taking that piano out this house. That's all there is to it.

Boy Willie and Maretha enter on the stairs. Maretha carries a hot comb and a can of hair grease. Boy Willie crosses over and continues to screw the wheels on the board.

MARETHA: Mama, all the hair grease is gone. There ain't but this little bit left.

BERNIECE: [*Gives her a dollar.*] Here . . . run across the street and get another can. You come straight back, too. Don't you be playing around out there. And watch the cars. Be careful when you cross the street.

Maretha exits out the front door.

Boy Willie, I done told you to leave my house.

BOY WILLIE: I ain't in you' house. I'm in Doaker's house. If he ask me to leave then I'll go on and leave. But consider me done left your part.

BERNIECE: Doaker, tell him to leave. Tell him to go on.

DOAKER: Boy Willie ain't done nothing for me to put him out of the house. I told you if you can't get along just go on and don't have nothing to do with each other.

BOY WILLIE: I ain't thinking about Berniece.

He gets up and draws a line across the floor with his foot.

There! Now I'm out of your part of the house. Consider me done left your part. Soon as Lymon come back with that rope. I'm gonna take that piano out of here and sell it.

BERNIECE: You ain't gonna touch that piano.

BOY WILLIE: Carry it out of here just as big and bold. Do like my daddy would have done come time to get Sutter's land.

BERNIECE: I got something to make you leave it over there.

BOY WILLIE: It's got to come better than this thirty-two-twenty.

DOAKER: Why don't you stop all that! Boy Willie, go on and leave her alone. You know how Berniece get. Why you wanna sit there and pick with her?

BOY WILLIE: I ain't picking with her. I told her the truth. She the one talking about what she got. I just told her what she better have.

BERNIECE: That's alright, Doaker. Leave him alone.

BOY WILLIE: She trying to scare me. Hell, I ain't scared of dying. I look around and see people dying every day. You got to die to make room for somebody else. I had a dog that died. Wasn't nothing but a puppy. I picked it up and put it in a bag and carried it up there to Reverend C. L. Thompson's church. I carried it up there and prayed and asked Jesus to make it live like he did the man in the Bible. I prayed real hard. Knelt down and everything. Say ask in Jesus' name. Well, I must have called Jesus' name two hundred times. I called his name till my mouth got sore. I got up and looked in the bag and the dog still dead. It ain't moved a muscle! I say, "Well, ain't nothing precious." And then I went out and killed me a cat. That's when I discovered the power of death. See, a nigger that ain't afraid to die is the worse kind of nigger for the white man. He can't hold that power over you. That's what I learned when I killed that cat. I got the power of death too. I can command him. I can call him up. The white man don't like to see that. He don't like for you to stand up and look him square in the eye and say, "I got it too." Then he got to deal with you square up.

BERNIECE: That's why I don't talk to him, Doaker. You try and talk to him and that's the only kind of stuff that comes out his mouth.

DOAKER: You say Avery went home to get his Bible?

BOY WILLIE: What Avery gonna do? Avery can't do nothing with me. I wish Avery would say something to me about this piano.

DOAKER: Berniece ain't said about that. Avery went home to get his Bible. He coming by to bless the house see if he can get rid of Sutter's ghost.

BOY WILLIE: Ain't nothing but a house full of ghosts down there at the church. What Avery look like chasing away somebody's ghost?

Maretha enters the front door.

BERNIECE: Light that stove and set that comb over there to get hot. Get something to put around your shoulders.

BOY WILLIE: The Bible say an eye for an eye, a tooth for a tooth, and a life for a life. Tit for tat. But you and Avery don't want to believe that. You gonna pass up that part and pretend it ain't in there. Everything else you gonna agree with. But if you gonna agree with part of it you got to agree with all of it. You can't do nothing halfway. You gonna go at the Bible halfway. You gonna act like that part ain't in there. But you pull out the Bible and open it and see what it say. Ask Avery. He a preacher. He'll tell you it's in there. He the Good Shepherd. Unless he gonna shepherd you to heaven with half the Bible.

BERNIECE: Maretha, bring me that comb. Make sure it's hot.

Maretha brings the comb. Berniece begins to do her hair.

BOY WILLIE: I will say this for Avery. He done figured out a path to go through life. I don't agree with it. But he done fixed it so he can go right through it real smooth. Hell, he liable to end up with a million dollars that he done got from selling bread and wine.

MARETHA: OWWWWWW!

BERNIECE: Be still, Maretha. If you was a boy I wouldn't be going through this.

BOY WILLIE: Don't you tell that girl that. Why you wanna tell her that?

BERNIECE: You ain't got nothing to do with this child.

BOY WILLIE: Telling her you wished she was a boy. How's that gonna make her feel?

BERNIECE: Boy Willie, go on and leave me alone.

DOAKER: Why don't you leave her alone? What you got to pick with her for? Why don't you go on out and see what's out there in the streets? Have something to tell the fellows down home.

BOY WILLIE: I'm waiting on Lymon to get back with that truck. Why don't you go on out and see what's out there in the streets? You ain't got to work tomorrow. Talking about me . . . why don't you go out there? It's Friday night.

DOAKER: I got to stay around here and keep you all from killing one another.

BOY WILLIE: You ain't got to worry about me. I'm gonna be here just as long as it takes Lymon to get back here with that truck. You ought to be talking to Berniece. Sitting up there telling Maretha she wished she was a boy. What kind of thing is that to tell a child? If you want to tell her something tell her about that piano. You ain't even told her about that piano. Like that's something to be ashamed of. Like she supposed to go off and hide somewhere about that piano. You ought to mark down on the calendar the day that Papa Boy Charles brought that piano into the house. You ought to mark that day down and draw a circle around it . . . and every year when it come up throw a party. Have a celebration. If you did that she wouldn't have no problem in life. She could walk around here with her head held high. I'm talking about a big party!

Invite everybody! Mark that day down with a special meaning. That way she know where she at in the world. You got her going out here thinking she wrong in the world. Like there ain't no part of it belong to her.

BERNIECE: Let me take care of my child. When you get one of your own then you can teach it what you want to teach it.

Doaker exits into his room.

BOY WILLIE: What I want to bring a child into this world for? Why I wanna bring somebody else into all this for? I'll tell you this . . . If I was Rockefeller I'd have forty or fifty. I'd make one every day. Cause they gonna start out in life with all the advantages. I ain't got no advantages to offer nobody. Many is the time I looked at my daddy and seen him staring off at his hands. I got a little older I know what he was thinking. He sitting there saying, "I got these big old hands but what I'm gonna do with them? Best I can do is make a fifty-acre crop for Mr. Stovall. Got these big old hands capable of doing anything. I can take and build something with these hands. But where's the tools? All I got is these hands. Unless I go out here and kill me somebody and take what they got . . . it's a long row to hoe for me to get something of my own. So what I'm gonna do with these big old hands? What would you do?"

See now . . . if he had his own land he wouldn't have felt that way. If he had something under his feet that belonged to him he could stand up taller. That's what I'm talking about. Hell, the land is there for everybody. All you got to do is figure out how to get you a piece. Ain't no mystery to life. You just got to go out and meet it square on. If you got a piece of land you'll find everything else fall right into place. You can stand right up next to the white man and talk about the price of cotton . . . the weather, and anything else you want to talk about. If you teach that girl that she living at the bottom of life, she's gonna grow up and hate you.

BERNIECE: I'm gonna teach her the truth. That's just where she living. Only she ain't got to stay there.

To Maretha.

Turn you' head over to the other side.

BOY WILLIE: This might be your bottom but it ain't mine. I'm living at the top of life. I ain't gonna just take my life and throw it away at the bottom. I'm in the world like everybody else. The way I see it everybody else got to come up a little taste to be where I am.

BERNIECE: You right at the bottom with the rest of us.

BOY WILLIE: I'll tell you this . . . and ain't a living soul can put a come back on it. If you believe that's where you at then you gonna act that way. If you act that way then that's where you gonna be. It's as simple as that. Ain't no mystery to life. I don't know how you come to believe that stuff. Crawley didn't think like that. He wasn't living at the bottom of life. Papa Boy Charles and Mama Ola wasn't living at the bottom of life. You ain't never heard them say nothing like that. They would have taken a strap to you if they heard you say something like that.

Doaker enters from his room.

Hey, Doaker . . . Berniece say the colored folks is living at the bottom of life. I tried to tell her if she think that . . . that's where she gonna be. You think you living at the bottom of life? Is that how you see yourself?

DOAKER: I'm just living the best way I know how. I ain't thinking about no top or no bottom.

BOY WILLIE: That's what I tried to tell Berniece. I don't know where she got that from. That sound like something Avery would say. Avery think cause the white man give him a turkey for Thanksgiving that makes him better than everybody else. That's gonna raise him out of the bottom of life. I don't need nobody to give me a turkey. I can get my own turkey. All you have to do is get out my way. I'll get me two or three turkeys.

BERNIECE: You can't even get a chicken let alone two or three turkeys. Talking about get out your way. Ain't nobody in your way.

To Maretha.

Straighten your head, Maretha! Don't be bending down like that. Hold your head up!

To Boy Willie.

All you got going for you is talk. You' whole life that's all you ever had going for you.

BOY WILLIE: See now . . . I'll tell you something about me. I done strung along and strung along. Going this way and that. Whatever way would lead me to a moment of peace. That's all I want. To be as easy with everything. But I wasn't born to that. I was born to a time of fire.

The world ain't wanted no part of me. I could see that since I was about seven. The world say it's better off without me. See, Berniece accept that. She trying to come up to where she can prove something to the world. Hell, the world a better place cause of me. I don't see it like Berniece. I got a heart that beats here and it beats just as loud as the next fellow's. Don't care if he black or white. Sometime it beats louder. When it beats louder, then everybody can hear it. Some people get scared of that. Like Berniece. Some people get scared to hear a nigger's heart beating. They think you ought to lay low with that heart. Make it beat quiet and go along with everything the way it is. But my mama ain't birthed me for nothing. So what I got to do? I got to mark my passing on the road. Just like you write on a tree, "Boy Willie was here."

That's all I'm trying to do with that piano. Trying to put my mark on the road. Like my daddy done. My heart say for me to sell that piano and get me some land so I can make a life for myself to live in my own way. Other than that I ain't thinking about nothing Berniece got to say.

There is a knock at the door. Boy Willie crosses to it and yanks it open thinking it is Lymon. Avery enters. He carries a Bible.

BOY WILLIE: Where you been, nigger? Aw . . . I thought you was Lymon. Hey, Berniece, look who's here.

BERNIECE: Come on in, Avery. Don't you pay Boy Willie no mind.

BOY WILLIE: Hey . . . Hey, Avery . . . tell me this . . . can you get to heaven with half the Bible?

BERNIECE: Boy Willie . . . I done told you to leave me alone.

BOY WILLIE: I just ask the man a question. He can answer. He don't need you to speak for him. Avery . . . if you only believe on half the Bible and don't want to accept the other half . . . you think God let you in heaven? Or do you got to have the whole Bible? Tell Berniece . . . if you only believe in part of it . . . when you see God he gonna ask you why you ain't believed in the other part . . . then he gonna send you straight to Hell.

AVERY: You got to be born again. Jesus say unless a man be born again he cannot come unto the Father and who so ever heareth my words and believeth them not shall be cast into a fiery pit.

BOY WILLIE: That's what I was trying to tell Berniece. You got to believe in it all. You can't go at nothing halfway. She think she going to heaven with half the Bible.

To Berniece.

You hear that . . . Jesus say you got to believe in it all.

BERNIECE: You keep messing with me.

BOY WILLIE: I ain't thinking about you.

DOAKER: Come on in, Avery, and have a seat. Don't pay neither one of them no mind. They been arguing all day.

BERNIECE: Come on in, Avery.

AVERY: How's everybody in here?

BERNIECE: Here, set this comb back over there on that stove.

To Avery.

Don't pay Boy Willie no mind. He been around here bothering me since I come home from work.

BOY WILLIE: Boy Willie ain't bothering you. Boy Willie ain't bothering nobody. I'm just waiting on Lymon to get back. I ain't thinking about you. You heard the man say I was right and you still don't want to believe it. You just wanna go and make up anythin'. Well there's Avery . . . there's the preacher . . . go on and ask him.

AVERY: Berniece believe in the Bible. She been baptized.

BOY WILLIE: What about that part that say an eye for an eye a tooth for a tooth and a life for a life? Ain't that in there?

DOAKER: What they say down there at the bank, Avery?

AVERY: Oh, they talked to me real nice. I told Berniece . . . they say maybe they let me borrow the money. They done talked to my boss down at work and everything.

DOAKER: That's what I told Berniece. You working every day you ought to be able to borrow some money.

AVERY: I'm getting more people in my congregation every day. Berniece says she gonna be the Deaconess. I get me my church I can get married and settled down. That's what I told Berniece.

DOAKER: That be nice. You all ought to go ahead and get married. Berniece don't need to be by herself. I tell her that all the time.

BERNIECE: I ain't said nothing about getting married. I said I was thinking about it.

DOAKER: Avery get him his church you all can make it nice.

To Avery.

Berniece said you was coming by to bless the house.

AVERY: Yeah, I done read up on my Bible. She asked me to come by and see if I can get rid of Sutter's ghost.

BOY WILLIE: Ain't no ghost in this house. That's all in Berniece's head. Go on up there and see if you see him. I'll give you a hundred dollars if you see him. That's all in her imagination.

DOAKER: Well, let her find that out then. If Avery blessing the house is gonna make her feel better . . . what you got to do with it?

AVERY: Berniece say Maretha seen him too. I don't know, but I found a part in the Bible to bless the house. If he is here then that ought to make him go.

BOY WILLIE: You worse than Berniece believing all that stuff. Talking about . . . if he here. Go on up there and find out. I been up there I ain't seen him. If you reading from that Bible gonna make him leave out of Berniece imagination, well, you might be right. But if you talking about . . .

DOAKER: Boy Willie, why don't you just be quiet? Getting all up in the man's business. This ain't got nothing to do with you. Let him go ahead and do what he gonna do.

BOY WILLIE: I ain't stopping him. Avery ain't got no power to do nothing.

AVERY: Oh, I ain't got no power. God got the power! God got power over everything in His creation. God can do anything. God say, "As I commandeth so it shall be." God said, "Let there be light," and there was light. He made the world in six days and rested on the seventh. God's got a wonderful power. He got power over life and death. Jesus raised Lazareth from the dead. They was getting ready to bury him and Jesus told him say, "Rise up and walk." He got up and walked and the people made great rejoicing at the power of God. I ain't worried about him chasing away a little old ghost!

There is a knock at the door. Boy Willie goes to answer it. Lymon enters carrying a coil of rope.

BOY WILLIE: Where you been? I been waiting on you and you run off somewhere.

LYMON: I ran into Grace. I stopped and bought her drink. She say she gonna go to the picture show with me.

BOY WILLIE: I ain't thinking about no Grace nothing.

LYMON: Hi, Berniece.

BOY WILLIE: Give me that rope and get up on this side of the piano.

DOAKER: Boy Willie, don't start nothing now. Leave the piano alone.

BOY WILLIE: Get that board there, Lymon. Stay out of this, Doaker.

Berniece exits up the stairs.

DOAKER: You just can't take the piano. How you gonna take the piano? Berniece ain't said nothing about selling that piano.

BOY WILLIE: She ain't got to say nothing. Come on, Lymon. We got to lift one end at a time up on the board. You got to watch so that the board don't slide up under there.

LYMON: What we gonna do with the rope?

BOY WILLIE: Let me worry about the rope. You just get up on this side over here with me.

Berniece enters from the stairs. She has her hand in her pocket where she has Crawley's gun.

AVERY: Boy Willie . . . Berniece . . . why don't you all sit down and talk this out now?

BERNIECE: Ain't nothing to talk out.

BOY WILLIE: I'm through talking to Berniece. You can talk to Berniece till you get blue in the face, and it don't make no difference. Get up on that side, Lymon. Throw that rope around there and tie it to the leg.

LYMON: Wait a minute . . . wait a minute, Boy Willie. Berniece got to say. Hey, Berniece . . . did you tell Boy Willie he could take this piano?

BERNIECE: Boy Willie ain't taking nothing out of my house but himself. Now you let him go ahead and try.

BOY WILLIE: Come on, Lymon, get up on this side with me.

Lymon stands undecided.

Come on, nigger! What you standing there for?

LYMON: Maybe Berniece is right, Boy Willie. Maybe you shouldn't sell it.

AVERY: You all ought to sit down and talk it out. See if you can come to an agreement.

DOAKER: That's what I been trying to tell them. Seem like one of them ought to respect the other one's wishes.

BERNIECE: I wish Boy Willie would go on and leave my house. That's what I wish. Now, he can respect that. Cause he's leaving here one way or another.

BOY WILLIE: What you mean one way or another? What's that supposed to mean? I ain't scared of no gun.

DOAKER: Come on, Berniece, leave him alone with that.

BOY WILLIE: I don't care what Berniece say. I'm selling my half. I can't help it if her half got to go along with it. It ain't like I'm trying to cheat her out of her half. Come on, Lymon.

LYMON: Berniece . . . I got to do this . . . Boy Willie say he gonna give you half of the money . . . say he want to get Sutter's land.

BERNIECE: Go on, Lymon. Just go on . . . I done told Boy Willie what to do.

BOY WILLIE: Here, Lymon . . . put that rope up over there.

LYMON: Boy Willie, you sure you want to do this? The way I figure it . . . I might be wrong . . . but I figure she gonna shoot you first.

BOY WILLIE: She just gonna have to shoot me.

BERNIECE: Maretha, get on out the way. Get her out the way, Doaker.

DOAKER: Go on, do what your mama told you.

BERNIECE: Put her in your room.

Maretha exits to Doaker's room. Boy Willie and Lymon try to lift the piano. The door opens and Wining Boy enters. He has been drinking.

WINING BOY: Man, these niggers around here! I stopped down there at Seefus . . . . These folks standing around talking about Patchneck Red's coming. They jumping back and getting off the sidewalk talking about Patchneck Red this and Patchneck Red that. Come to find out . . . you know who they was talking about? Old John D. from up around Tyler! Used to run around with Otis Smith. He got everybody scared of him. Calling him Patchneck Red. They don't know I whupped the nigger's head in one time.

BOY WILLIE: Just make sure that board don't slide, Lymon.

LYMON: I got this side. You watch that side.

WINING BOY: Hey, Boy Willie, what you got? I know you got a pint stuck up in your coat.

BOY WILLIE: Wining Boy, get out the way!

WINING BOY: Hey, Doaker. What you got? Gimme a drink. I want a drink.

DOAKER: It look like you had enough of whatever it was. Come talking about "What you got?" You ought to be trying to find somewhere to lay down.

WINING BOY: I ain't worried about no place to lay down. I can always find me a place to lay down in Berniece's house. Ain't that right, Berniece?

BERNIECE: Wining Boy, sit down somewhere. You been out there drinking all day. Come in here smelling like an old polecat. Sit on down there, you don't need nothing to drink.

DOAKER: You know Berniece don't like all that drinking.

WINING BOY: I ain't disrespecting Berniece. Berniece, am I disrespecting you? I'm just trying to be nice. I been with strangers all day and they treated me like family. I come in here to family and you treat me like a stranger. I don't need your whiskey. I can buy my own. I wanted your company, not your whiskey.

DOAKER: Nigger, why don't you go upstairs and lay down? You don't need nothing to drink.

WINING BOY: I ain't thinking about no laying down. Me and Boy Willie fixing to party. Ain't that right, Boy Willie? Tell him. I'm fixing to play me some piano. Watch this.

Wining Boy sits down at the piano.

BOY WILLIE: Come on, Wining Boy! Me and Lymon fixing to move the piano.

WINING BOY: Wait a minute . . . wait a minute. This a song I wrote for Cleotha. I wrote this song in memory of Cleotha.

He begins to play and sing.

Hey little woman what's the matter with you now
Had a storm last night and blowed the line all down

Tell me how long
Is I got to wait
Can I get it now
Or must I hesitate

It takes a hesitating stocking in her hesitating shoe
It takes a hesitating woman wanna sing the blues

Tell me how long
Is I got to wait
Can I kiss you now
Or must I hesitate.

BOY WILLIE: Come on, Wining Boy, get up! Get up, Wining Boy! Me and Lymon's fixing to move the piano.

WINING BOY: Naw . . . Naw . . . you ain't gonna move this piano!

BOY WILLIE: Get out the way, Wining Boy.

Wining Boy, his back to the piano, spreads his arms out over the piano.

WINING BOY: You ain't taking this piano out the house. You got to take me with it!

BOY WILLIE: Get on out the way, Wining Boy! Doaker get him!

There is a knock on the door.

BERNIECE: I got him, Doaker. Come on, Wining Boy. I done told Boy Willie he ain't taking the piano.

Berniece tries to take Wining Boy away from the piano.

WINING BOY: He got to take me with it!

Doaker goes to answer the door. Grace enters.

GRACE: Is Lymon here?

DOAKER: Lymon.

WINING BOY: He ain't taking that piano.

BERNIECE: I ain't gonna let him take it.

GRACE: I thought you was coming back. I ain't gonna sit in that truck all day.

LYMON: I told you I was coming back.

GRACE: [*Sees Boy Willie.*] Oh, hi, Boy Willie. Lymon told me you was gone back down South.

LYMON: I said he was going back. I didn't say he had left already.

GRACE: That's what you told me.

BERNIECE: Lymon, you got to take your company someplace else.

LYMON: Berniece, this is Grace. That there is Berniece. That's Boy Willie's sister.

GRACE: Nice to meet you.

To Lymon.

I ain't gonna sit out in that truck all day. You told me you was gonna take me to the movie.

LYMON: I told you I had something to do first. You supposed to wait on me.

BERNIECE: Lymon, just go on and leave. Take Grace or whoever with you. Just go on get out my house.

BOY WILLIE: You gonna help me move this piano first, nigger!

LYMON: [*To Grace.*] I got to help Boy Willie move the piano first.

Everybody but Grace suddenly senses Sutter's presence.

GRACE: I ain't waiting on you. Told me you was coming right back. Now you got to move a piano. You just like all the other men.

Grace now senses something.

Something ain't right here. I knew I shouldn't have come back up in this house.

Grace exits.

LYMON: Hey, Grace! I'll be right back, Boy Willie.

BOY WILLIE: Where you going, nigger?

LYMON: I'll be back. I got to take Grace home.

BOY WILLIE: Come on, let's move the piano first!

LYMON: I got to take Grace home. I told you I'll be back.

Lymon exits. Boy Willie exits and calls after him.

BOY WILLIE: Come on, Lymon! Hey . . . Lymon! Lymon . . . come on!

Again, the presence of Sutter is felt.

WINING BOY: Hey, Doaker, did you feel that? Hey, Berniece . . . did you get cold? Hey, Doaker . . .

DOAKER: What you calling me for?

WINING BOY: I believe that's Sutter.

DOAKER: Well, let him stay up there. As long as he don't mess with me.

BERNIECE: Avery, go on and bless the house.

DOAKER: You need to bless that piano. That's what you need to bless. It ain't done nothing but cause trouble. If you gonna bless anything go on and bless that.

WINING BOY: Hey, Doaker, if he gonna bless something let him bless everything. The kitchen . . . the upstairs. Go on and bless it all.

BOY WILLIE: Ain't no ghost in this house. He need to bless Berniece's head. That's what he need to bless.

AVERY: Seem like that piano's causing all the trouble. I can bless that. Berniece, put me some water in that bottle.

Avery takes a small bottle from his pocket and hands it to Berniece, who goes into the kitchen to get water. Avery takes a candle from his pocket and lights it. He gives it to Berniece as she gives him the water.

Hold this candle. Whatever you do make sure it don't go out.

    O Holy Father we gather here this evening in the Holy Name to cast out the spirit of one James Sutter. May this vial of water be empowered with thy spirit. May each drop of it be a weapon and a shield against the presence of all evil and may it be a cleansing and blessing of this humble abode.

    Just as Our Father taught us how to pray so He say, "I will prepare a table for you in the midst of mine enemies," and in His hands we place ourselves to come unto his presence. Where there is Good so shall it cause Evil to scatter to the Four Winds.

He throws water at the piano at each commandment.

AVERY: Get thee behind me, Satan! Get thee behind the face of Righteousness as we Glorify His Holy Name! Get thee behind the Hammer of Truth that breaketh down the Wall of Falsehood! Father. Father. Praise. Praise. We ask in Jesus' name and call forth the power of the Holy Spirit as it is written. . . .

He opens the Bible and reads from it.

I will sprinkle clean water upon thee and ye shall be clean.

BOY WILLIE: All this old preaching stuff. Hell, just tell him to leave.

Avery continues reading throughout Boy Willie's outburst.

AVERY: I will sprinkle clean water upon you and you shall be clean: from all your uncleanliness, and from all your idols, will I cleanse you. A new heart also will I give you, and a new spirit will I put within you: and I will take out of your flesh the heart of stone, and I will give you a heart of flesh. And I will put my spirit within you, and cause you to walk in my statutes, and ye shall keep my judgments, and do them.

Boy Willie grabs a pot of water from the stove and begins to fling it around the room.

BOY WILLIE: Hey Sutter! Sutter! Get your ass out this house! Sutter! Come on and get some of this water! You done drowned in the well, come on and get some more of this water!

Boy Willie is working himself into a frenzy as he runs around the room throwing water and calling Sutter's name. Avery continues reading.

BOY WILLIE: Come on, Sutter!

He starts up the stairs.

Come on, get some water! Come on, Sutter!

The sound of Sutter's Ghost is heard. As Boy Willie approaches the steps he is suddenly thrown back by the unseen force, which is choking him. As he struggles he frees himself, then dashes up the stairs.

BOY WILLIE: Come on, Sutter!

AVERY: [*Continuing.*] A new heart also will I give you and a new spirit will I put within you: and I will take out of your flesh the heart of stone, and I will give you a heart of flesh. And I will put my spirit within you, and cause you to walk in my statutes, and ye shall keep my judgments, and do them.

There are loud sounds heard from upstairs as Boy Willie begins to wrestle with Sutter's Ghost. It is a life-and-death struggle fraught with perils and faultless terror. Boy Willie is thrown down the stairs. Avery is stunned into silence. Boy Willie picks himself up and dashes back upstairs.

AVERY: Berniece, I can't do it.

There are more sounds heard from upstairs. Doaker and Wining Boy stare at one another in stunned disbelief. It is in this moment, from somewhere old, that Berniece realizes what she must do. She crosses to the piano. She begins to play. The song is found piece by piece. It is an old urge to song that is both a commandment and a plea. With each repetition it gains in strength. It is intended as an exorcism and a dressing for battle. A rustle of wind blowing across two continents.

BERNIECE: [*Singing.*]

I want you to help me
I want you to help me
I want you to help me
I want you to help me
I want you to help me
I want you to help me
Mama Berniece
I want you to help me
Mama Esther
I want you to help me
Papa Boy Charles
I want you to help me
Mama Ola
I want you to help me

I want you to help me
I want you to help me
I want you to help me
I want you to help me
I want you to help me
I want you to help me
I want you to help me
I want you to help me

The sound of a train approaching is heard. The noise upstairs subsides.

BOY WILLIE: Come on, Sutter! Come back, Sutter!

Berniece begins to chant:

BERNIECE:

> *Thank you.*
> *Thank you.*
> *Thank you.*

> *A calm comes over the house. Maretha enters from Doaker's room. Boy Willie enters on the stairs. He pauses a moment to watch Berniece at the piano.*

BERNIECE:

> *Thank you.*
> *Thank you.*

BOY WILLIE: Wining Boy, you ready to go back down home? Hey, Doaker, what time the train leave?

DOAKER: You still got time to make it.

> *Maretha crosses and embraces Boy Willie.*

BOY WILLIE: Hey Berniece . . . if you and Maretha don't keep playing on that piano . . . ain't no telling . . . me and Sutter both liable to be back.

> *He exits.*

BERNIECE: Thank you.

> *The lights go down to black.*

DAVID IVES ■ (b. 1950)

David Ives grew up on Chicago's South Side, the son of working-class par-
ents, and wrote his first play at the age of nine: "But then I realized you had
to have a copy of the script for each person in the play, so that was the end of
it." Impressed by theatrical productions he saw in his teens, Ives entered North-
western University and after graduation attended Yale Drama School. After
several attempts to become a "serious writer" he decided to "aspire to silliness
on a daily basis" and began creating the short comic plays on which his repu-
tation rests. An evening of six one-act comedies, All in the Timing, *had a*
successful off-Broadway production in 1994, running over two years. In 1996
it was the most performed contemporary play in the nation, and Sure Thing,
its signature piece, remains popular, especially with student drama groups. A
second collection of one acts, Mere Mortals, *had a successful run at Primary*
Stages in 1997, and a third collection, Lives of Saints, *was produced in 1999.*
A number of his collections—including All in the Timing *(1995),* Time Flies
(2001), and Polish Joke and Other Plays *(2004)—have been published. Ives's*
comedic skills range from a hilarious parody of David Mamet's plays (pre-
sented at an event honoring Mamet) to his witty revision of a legendary char-
acter in the full-length Don Juan in Chicago *(1995). His short plays, in many*
cases, hinge on brilliant theatrical conceits; in Mayflies, *a boy mayfly and girl*
mayfly must meet, court, and consummate their relationship before their one
day of adult life ends. Sure Thing, *a piece that plays witty tricks with time,*
resembles a scene in the Bill Murray film Groundhog Day, *the script of*
which was written some years after Ives's play. Recently Ives has published a
children's novel and has been working on stage adaptations of the Disney
film The Little Mermaid *and* Batman: The Musical. *In an article titled*
"Why I Shouldn't Write Plays," Ives notes, among other reasons, "All reviews
should carry a Surgeon General's warning. The good ones turn your head, the
bad ones break your heart."

Sure Thing

Characters

Betty
Bill

Scene: *A café.*

Betty, a woman in her late twenties, is reading at a café table. An empty
chair is opposite her. Bill, same age, enters.

BILL: Excuse me. Is this chair taken?

BETTY: Excuse me?

BILL: Is this taken?

BETTY: Yes it is.

BILL: Oh. Sorry.

BETTY: Sure thing.

A bell rings softly.

BILL: Excuse me. Is this chair taken?

BETTY: Excuse me?

BILL: Is this taken?

BETTY: No, but I'm expecting somebody in a minute.

BILL: Oh. Thanks anyway.

BETTY: Sure thing.

A bell rings softly.

BILL: Excuse me. Is this chair taken?

BETTY: No, but I'm expecting somebody very shortly.

BILL: Would you mind if I sit here till he or she or it comes?

BETTY [*glances at her watch*]:   They do seem to be pretty late. . . .

BILL: You never know who you might be turning down.

BETTY: Sorry. Nice try, though.

BILL: Sure thing.

Bell.

Is this seat taken?

BETTY: No it's not.

BILL: Would you mind if I sit here?

BETTY: Yes I would.

BILL: Oh.

Bell.

Is this chair taken?

BETTY: No it's not.

BILL: Would you mind if I sit here?

BETTY: No. Go ahead.

BILL: Thanks. [*He sits. She continues reading.*] Everyplace else seems to
be taken.

BETTY: Mm-hm.

BILL: Great place.

DAVID IVES

BETTY: Mm-hm.

BILL: What's the book?

BETTY: I just wanted to read in quiet, if you don't mind.

BILL: No. Sure thing.

Bell.

BILL: Everyplace else seems to be taken.

BETTY: Mm-hm.

BILL: Great place for reading.

BETTY: Yes, I like it.

BILL: What's the book?

BETTY: *The Sound and the Fury.*

BILL: Oh. Hemingway.

Bell.

What's the book?

BETTY: *The Sound and the Fury.*

BILL: Oh. Faulkner.

BETTY: Have you read it?

BILL: Not . . . actually. I've sure read *about* it, though. It's supposed to be great.

BETTY: It is great.

BILL: I hear it's great. [*Small pause.*] Waiter?

Bell.

What's the book?

BETTY: *The Sound and the Fury.*

BILL: Oh. Faulkner.

BETTY: Have you read it?

BILL: I'm a Mets fan, myself.

Bell.

BETTY: Have you read it?

BILL: Yeah, I read it in college.

BETTY: Where was college?

BILL: I went to Oral Roberts University.

Bell.

BETTY: Where was college?

BILL: I was lying. I never really went to college. I just like to party.

Bell.

BETTY: Where was college?

BILL: Harvard.

BETTY: Do you like Faulkner?

BILL: I love Faulkner. I spent a whole winter reading him once.

BETTY: I've just started.

BILL: I was so excited after ten pages that I went out and bought everything else he wrote. One of the greatest reading experiences of my life. I mean, all that incredible psychological understanding. Page after page of gorgeous prose. His profound grasp of the mystery of time and human existence. The smells of the earth . . . What do you think?

BETTY: I think it's pretty boring.

Bell.

BILL: What's the book?

BETTY: *The Sound and the Fury.*

BILL: Oh! Faulkner!

BETTY: Do you like Faulkner?

BILL: I love Faulkner.

BETTY: He's incredible.

BILL: I spent a whole winter reading him once.

BETTY: I was so excited after ten pages that I went out and bought everything else he wrote.

BILL: All that incredible psychological understanding.

BETTY: And the prose is so gorgeous.

BILL: And the way he's grasped the mystery of time—

BETTY: —and human existence. I can't believe I've waited this long to read him.

BILL: You never know. You might not have liked him before.

BETTY: That's true.

BILL: You might not have been ready for him. You have to hit these things at the right moment or it's no good.

BETTY: That's happened to me.

BILL: It's all in the timing. [*Small pause.*] My name's Bill, by the way.

BETTY: I'm Betty.

BILL: Hi.

BETTY: Hi. [*Small pause.*]

BILL: Yes I thought reading Faulkner was . . . a great experience.

BETTY: Yes. [*Small pause.*]

BILL: *The Sound and the Fury* . . . [*Another small pause.*]

BETTY: Well. Onwards and upwards. [*She goes back to her book.*]

BILL: Waiter—?

Bell.

You have to hit these things at the right moment or it's no good.

BETTY: That's happened to me.

BILL: It's all in the timing. My name's Bill, by the way.

BETTY: I'm Betty.

BILL: Hi.

BETTY: Hi.

BILL: Do you come in here a lot?

BETTY: Actually I'm just in town for two days from Pakistan.

BILL: Oh. Pakistan.

Bell.

My name's Bill, by the way.

BETTY: I'm Betty.

BILL: Hi.

BETTY: Hi.

BILL: Do you come in here a lot?

BETTY: Every once in a while. Do you?

BILL: Not so much anymore. Not as much as I used to. Before my nervous breakdown.

Bell.

Do you come in here a lot?

BETTY: Why are you asking?

BILL: Just interested.

BETTY: Are you really interested, or do you just want to pick me up?

BILL: No, I'm really interested.

BETTY: Why would you be interested in whether I come in here a lot?

BILL: I'm just . . . getting acquainted.

BETTY: Maybe you're only interested for the sake of making small talk long enough to ask me back to your place to listen to some music, or because you've just rented this great tape for your VCR, or because you've got some terrific unknown Django Reinhardt record, only all you really want to do is fuck—which you won't do very well—after which you'll go into the bathroom and pee very loudly, then pad into the kitchen and get yourself a beer from the refrigerator without asking me whether I'd like anything, and then you'll proceed to lie back down beside me and confess that you've got a girlfriend named Stephanie who's away at medical school in Belgium for a year, and that you've been involved with her—*off and on*—in what you'll call a very "intricate" relationship, for the past *seven YEARS*. None of which *interests* me, mister!

BILL: Okay.

Bell.

Do you come in here a lot?

BETTY: Every other day, I think.

BILL: I come in here quite a lot and I don't remember seeing you.

BETTY: I guess we must be on different schedules.

BILL: Missed connections.

BETTY: Yes. Different time zones.

BILL: Amazing how you can live right next door to somebody in this town and never even know it.

BETTY: I know.

BILL: City life.

BETTY: It's crazy.

BILL: We probably pass each other in the street every day. Right in front of this place, probably.

BETTY: Yep.

BILL [*looks around*]: Well the waiters here sure seem to be in some different time zone. I can't seem to locate one anywhere. . . . Waiter! [*He looks back.*] So what do you—[*He sees that she's gone back to her book.*]

BETTY: I beg pardon?

BILL: Nothing. Sorry.

Bell.

BETTY: I guess we must be on different schedules.

BILL: Missed connections.

BETTY: Yes. Different time zones.

BILL: Amazing how you can live right next door to somebody in this town and never even know it.

BETTY: I know.

BILL: City life.

BETTY: It's crazy.

BILL: You weren't waiting for somebody when I came in, were you?

BETTY: Actually I was.

BILL: Oh. Boyfriend?

BETTY: Sort of.

BILL: What's a sort-of boyfriend?

BETTY: My husband.

BILL: Ah-ha.

Bell.

You weren't waiting for somebody when I came in, were you?

BETTY: Actually I was.

BILL: Oh. Boyfriend?

BETTY: Sort of.

BILL: What's a sort-of boyfriend?

BETTY: We were meeting here to break up.

BILL: Mm-hm . . .

Bell.

What's a sort-of boyfriend?

BETTY: My lover. Here she comes right now!

Bell.

BILL: You weren't waiting for somebody when I came in, were you?

BETTY: No, just reading.

BILL: Sort of a sad occupation for a Friday night, isn't it? Reading here, all by yourself?

BETTY: Do you think so?

BILL: Well sure. I mean, what's a good-looking woman like you doing out alone on a Friday night?

BETTY: Trying to keep away from lines like that.

BILL: No, listen—

Bell.

You weren't waiting for somebody when I came in, were you?

BETTY: No, just reading.

BILL: Sort of a sad occupation for a Friday night, isn't it? Reading here all by yourself?

BETTY: I guess it is, in a way.

BILL: What's a good-looking woman like you doing out alone on a Friday night anyway? No offense, but . . .

BETTY: I'm out alone on a Friday night for the first time in a very long time.

BILL: Oh.

BETTY: You see, I just recently ended a relationship.

BILL: Oh.

BETTY: Of rather long standing.

BILL: I'm sorry. [*Small pause.*] Well listen, since reading by yourself *is* such a sad occupation for a Friday night, would you like to go elsewhere?

BETTY: No . . .

BILL: Do something else?

BETTY: No thanks.

BILL: I was headed out to the movies in a while anyway.

BETTY: I don't think so.

BILL: Big chance to let Faulkner catch his breath. All those long sentences get him pretty tired.

BETTY: Thanks anyway.

BILL: Okay.

BETTY: I appreciate the invitation.

BILL: Sure thing.

Bell.

You weren't waiting for somebody when I came in, were you?

BETTY: No, just reading.

BILL: Sort of a sad occupation for a Friday night, isn't it? Reading here all by yourself?

BETTY: I guess I was trying to think of it as existentially romantic. You know—cappuccino, great literature, rainy night . . .

BILL: That only works in Paris. We *could* hop the late plane to Paris. Get on a Concorde. Find a café . . .

BETTY: I'm a little short on plane fare tonight.

BILL: Darn it, so am I.

BETTY: To tell you the truth, I was headed to the movies after I finished this section. Would you like to come along? Since you can't locate a waiter?

BILL: That's a very nice offer, but . . .

BETTY: Uh-huh. Girlfriend?

BILL: Two, actually. One of them's pregnant, and Stephanie—

Bell.

BETTY: Girlfriend?

BILL: No, I don't have a girlfriend. Not if you mean the castrating bitch I dumped last night.

Bell.

BETTY: Girlfriend?

BILL: Sort of. Sort of.

BETTY: What's a sort-of girlfriend?

BILL: My mother.

Bell.

I just ended a relationship, actually.

BETTY: Oh.

BILL: Of rather long standing.

BETTY: I'm sorry to hear it.

BILL: This is my first night out alone in a long time. I feel a little bit at sea, to tell you the truth.

BETTY: So you didn't stop to talk because you're a Moonie, or you have some weird political affiliation—?

BILL: Nope. Straight-down-the-ticket Republican.

Bell.

Straight-down-the-ticket Democrat.

Bell.

Can I tell you something about politics?

Bell.

I like to think of myself as a citizen of the universe.

Bell.

I'm unaffiliated.

BETTY: That's a relief. So am I.

BILL: I vote my beliefs.

BETTY: Labels are not important.

BILL: Labels are not important, exactly. Take me, for example. I mean, what does it matter if I had a two-point at—

Bell.

three-point at—

Bell.

four-point at college? Or if I did come from Pittsburgh—

Bell.

Cleveland—

Bell.

Westchester County?

BETTY: Sure.

BILL: I believe that a man is what he is.

Bell.

A person is what he is.

Bell.

A person is . . . what they are.

BETTY: I think so too.

BILL: So what if I admire Trotsky?

Bell.

So what if I once had a total-body liposuction?

Bell.

So what if I don't have a penis?

Bell.

So what if I spent a year in the Peace Corps? I was acting on my convictions.

BETTY: Sure.

BILL: You just can't hang a sign on a person.

BETTY: Absolutely. I'll bet you're a Scorpio.

Many bells ring.

Listen, I was headed to the movies after I finished this section. Would you like to come along?

BILL: That sounds like fun. What's playing?

BETTY: A couple of the really early Woody Allen movies.

BILL: Oh.

BETTY: You don't like Woody Allen?

BILL: Sure. I like Woody Allen.

BETTY: But you're not crazy about Woody Allen.

BILL: Those early ones kind of get on my nerves.
BETTY: Uh-huh.

Bell.

BILL: Y'know I was headed to the—
BETTY [*simultaneously*]: I was thinking about—
BILL: I'm sorry.
BETTY: No, go ahead.
BILL: I was going to say that I was headed to the movies in a little while, and . . .
BETTY: So was I.
BILL: The Woody Allen festival?
BETTY: Just up the street.
BILL: Do you like the early ones?
BETTY: I think anybody who doesn't ought to be run off the planet.
BILL: How many times have you seen *Bananas*?
BETTY: Eight times.
BILL: Twelve. So are you still interested? [*Long pause.*]
BETTY: Do you like Entenmann's crumb cake . . . ?
BILL: Last night I went out at two in the morning to get one. Did you have an Etch-a-Sketch as a child?
BETTY: Yes! And do you like Brussels sprouts? [*Pause.*]
BILL: No, I think they're disgusting.
BETTY: They *are* disgusting!
BILL: Do you still believe in marriage in spite of current sentiments against it?
BETTY: Yes.
BILL: And children?
BETTY: Three of them.
BILL: Two girls and a boy.
BETTY: Harvard, Vassar, and Brown.
BILL: And will you love me?
BETTY: Yes.
BILL: And cherish me forever?
BETTY: Yes.
BILL: Do you still want to go to the movies?
BETTY: Sure thing.
BILL AND BETTY [*together*]: Waiter!

Blackout   —1988

Milcha Sanchez-Scott was born in Bali of Indonesian and Colombian parents. She attended school in England and moved to California in her teens. Following college at the University of San Diego, she had her first plays produced in the early 1980s. The Cuban Swimmer, first performed in 1984, displays elements of the "magic realism" practiced in fiction by Colombian Nobel–prize winner Gabriel García Márquez. Her most successful full-length play is Roosters *(1987), which was made into a 1995 film starring Edward James Olmos.*

The Cuban Swimmer

Characters

Margarita Suárez, *the swimmer*
Eduardo Suárez, *her father, the coach*
Simón Suárez, *her brother*
Aída Suárez, *the mother*
Abuela, *her grandmother*
Voice of Mel Munson
Voice of Mary Beth White
Voice of Radio Operator

Scene: *The Pacific Ocean between San Pedro and Catalina Island.*

Time: *Summer.*

Live conga drums can be used to punctuate the action of the play.

Scene I

Pacific Ocean. Midday. On the horizon, in perspective, a small boat enters upstage left, crosses to upstage right, and exits. Pause. Lower on the horizon, the same boat, in larger perspective, enters upstage right, crosses and exits upstage left. Blackout.

Scene II

Pacific Ocean. Midday. The swimmer, Margarita Suárez, is swimming. On the boat following behind her are her father, Eduardo Suárez, holding a megaphone, and Simón, her brother, sitting on top of the cabin with his shirt off, punk sunglasses on, binoculars hanging on his chest.

EDUARDO: [*Leaning forward, shouting in time to Margarita's swimming.*] *Uno, dos, uno, dos. Y uno, dos* . . . keep your shoulders parallel to the water.

SIMÓN: I'm gonna take these glasses off and look straight into the sun.

EDUARDO: [*Through megaphone.*] *Muy bien, muy bien* . . . but punch those arms in, baby.

SIMÓN: [*Looking directly at the sun through binoculars.*] Come on, come on, zap me. Show me something. [*He looks behind at the shoreline and ahead at the sea.*] Stop! Stop, Papi! Stop!

Aída Suárez and Abuela, the swimmer's mother and grand-mother, enter running from the back of the boat.

AÍDA AND ABUELA: *Qué? Qué es?*

AÍDA: *Es un* shark?

EDUARDO: Eh?

ABUELA: *Que es un* shark *dicen?*

Eduardo blows whistle. Margarita looks up at the boat.

SIMÓN: No, *Papi*, no shark, no shark. We've reached the halfway mark.

ABUELA: [*Looking into the water.*] *A dónde está?*

AÍDA: It's not in the water.

ABUELA: Oh, no? Oh, no?

AÍDA: No! *A poco* do you think they're gonna have signs in the water to say you are halfway to Santa Catalina? No. It's done very scientific. *A ver, hijo,* explain it to your grandma.

SIMÓN: Well, you see, Abuela—[*He points behind.*] There's San Pedro. [*He points ahead.*] And there's Santa Catalina. Looks halfway to me.

Abuela shakes her head and is looking back and forth, trying to make the decision, when suddenly the sound of a helicopter is heard.

ABUELA: [*Looking up.*] Virgencita de la Caridad del Cobre. *Qué es eso?*

Sound of helicopter gets closer. Margarita looks up.

MARGARITA: *Papi, Papi!*

A small commotion on the boat, with Everybody pointing at the helicopter above. Shadows of the helicopter fall on the boat. Simón looks up at it through binoculars.

Papi—qué es? What is it?

EDUARDO: [*Through megaphone.*] Uh . . . uh . . . uh, *un momentico . . . mi hija.* . . . Your *papi*'s got everything under control, understand? Uh . . . you just keep stroking. And stay . . . uh . . . close to the boat.

SIMÓN: Wow, *Papi!* We're on TV, man! Holy Christ, we're all over the fucking U.S.A.! It's Mel Munson and Mary Beth White!

AÍDA: *Por Dios!* Simón, don't swear. And put on your shirt.

Aída fluffs her hair, puts on her sunglasses and waves to the heli-copter. Simón leans over the side of the boat and yells to Margarita.

SIMÓN: Yo, Margo! You're on TV, man.

EDUARDO: Leave your sister alone. Turn on the radio.

MARGARITA: *Papi! Qué está pasando?*

ABUELA: *Que es la televisión dicen?* [*She shakes her head.*] *Porque como yo no puedo ver nada sin mis espejuelos.*

Abuela rummages through the boat, looking for her glasses. Voices of Mel Munson and Mary Beth White are heard over the boat's radio.

MEL'S VOICE: As we take a closer look at the gallant crew of *La Havana* . . . and there . . . yes, there she is . . . the little Cuban swimmer from Long Beach, California, nineteen-year-old Margarita Suárez. The unknown swimmer is our Cinderella entry . . . a bundle of tenacity, battling her way through the choppy, murky waters of the cold Pacific to reach the Island of Romance . . . Santa Catalina . . . where should she be the first to arrive, two thousand dollars and a gold cup will be waiting for her.

AÍDA: Doesn't even cover our expenses.

ABUELA: *Qué dice?*

EDUARDO: Shhhh!

MARY BETH'S VOICE: This is really a family effort, Mel, and—

MEL'S VOICE: Indeed it is. Her trainer, her coach, her mentor, is her father, Eduardo Suárez. Not a swimmer himself, it says here, Mr. Suárez is head usher of the Holy Name Society and the owner-operator of Suárez Treasures of the Sea and Salvage Yard. I guess it's one of those places—

MARY BETH'S VOICE: If I might interject a fact here, Mel, assisting in this swim is Mrs. Suárez, who is a former Miss Cuba.

MEL'S VOICE: And a beautiful woman in her own right. Let's try and get a closer look.

Helicopter sound gets louder. Margarita, frightened, looks up again.

MARGARITA: *Papi!*

EDUARDO: [*Through megaphone.*] *Mi hija,* don't get nervous . . . it's the press. I'm handling it.

AÍDA: I see how you're handling it.

EDUARDO: [*Through megaphone.*] Do you hear? Everything is under control. Get back into your rhythm. Keep your elbows high and kick and kick and kick and kick . . .

ABUELA [*Finds her glasses and puts them on.*]: *Ay sí, es la televisión . . .* [*She points to helicopter.*] *Qué lindo mira . . .* [*She fluffs her hair, gives a big wave.*] *Aló América! Viva mi Margarita, viva todo los Cubanos en los Estados Unidos!*

AÍDA: *Ay por Dios,* Cecilia, the man didn't come all this way in his helicopter to look at you jumping up and down, making a fool of yourself.

ABUELA: I don't care. I'm proud.

AÍDA: He can't understand you anyway.

ABUELA: *Viva . . .* [*She stops.*] Simón, *cómo se dice viva?*

SIMÓN: Hurray.

ABUELA: Hurray for *mi Margarita y* for all the Cubans living *en* the United States, *y un abrazo . . .* Simón, *abrazo . . .*

SIMÓN: A big hug.

ABUELA: *Sí,* a big hug to all my friends in Miami, Long Beach, Union City, except for my son Carlos, who lives in New York in sin! He lives . . . [*She crosses herself.*] in Brooklyn with a Puerto Rican woman in sin! *No decente . . .*

SIMÓN: Decent.

ABUELA: Carlos, *no decente.* This family, *decente.*

AÍDA: Cecilia, *por Dios.*

MEL'S VOICE: Look at that enthusiasm. The whole family has turned out to cheer little Margarita on to victory! I hope they won't be too disappointed.

MARY BETH'S VOICE: She seems to be making good time, Mel.

MEL'S VOICE: Yes, it takes all kinds to make a race. And it's a testimonial to the all-encompassing fairness . . . the greatness of this, the Wrigley Invitational Women's Swim to Catalina, where among all the professionals there is still room for the amateurs . . . like these, the simple people we see below us on the ragtag *La Havana,* taking their long-shot chance to victory. *Vaya con Dios!*

Helicopter sound fading as family, including Margarita, watch silently. Static as Simón turns radio off. Eduardo walks to bow of boat, looks out on the horizon.

EDUARDO: [*To himself.*] Amateurs.

AÍDA: Eduardo, that person insulted us. Did you hear, Eduardo? That he called us a simple people in a ragtag boat? Did you hear . . . ?

ABUELA [*Clenching her fist at departing helicopter.*]:   Mal-Rayo los parta!

SIMÓN: [*Same gesture.*] Asshole!

Aída follows Eduardo as he goes to side of boat and stares at Margarita.

AÍDA: This person comes in his helicopter to insult your wife, your family, your daughter . . .

MARGARITA [*Pops her head out of the water.*]:   Papi?

AÍDA: Do you hear me, Eduardo? I am not simple.

ABUELA: Sí.

AÍDA: I am complicated.

ABUELA: Sí, demasiada complicada.

AÍDA: Me and my family are not so simple.

SIMÓN: Mom, the guy's an asshole.

ABUELA [*Shaking her fist at helicopter.*]:   Asshole!

AÍDA: If my daughter was simple, she would not be in that water swimming.

MARGARITA: Simple? Papi . . . ?

AÍDA: Ahora, Eduardo, this is what I want you to do. When we get to Santa Catalina, I want you to call the TV station and demand an apology.

EDUARDO: Cállete mujer! Aquí mando yo. I will decide what is to be done.

MARGARITA: Papi, tell me what's going on.

EDUARDO: Do you understand what I am saying to you, Aída?

SIMÓN [*Leaning over side of boat, to Margarita.*]:   Yo Margo! You know that Mel Munson guy on TV? He called you a simple amateur and said you didn't have a chance.

ABUELA [*Leaning directly behind Simón.*]:   Mi hija, insultó a la familia. Desgraciado!

AÍDA [*Leaning in behind Abuela.*]:   He called us peasants! And your father is not doing anything about it. He just knows how to yell at me.

EDUARDO [*Through megaphone.*]:   Shut up! All of you! Do you want to break her concentration? Is that what you are after? Eh?

MILCHA SANCHEZ-SCOTT

Abuela, Aída, and Simón shrink back. Eduardo paces before them.

Swimming is rhythm and concentration. You win a race *aquí.* [*Pointing to his head.*] Now . . . [*To Simón.*] you, take care of the boat, Aída *y Mama* . . . do something. Anything. Something practical.

Abuela and Aída get on knees and pray in Spanish.

Hija, give it everything, eh? . . . *por la familia. Uno* . . . *dos.* . . . You must win.

Simón goes into cabin. The prayers continue as lights change to indicate bright sunlight, later in the afternoon.

Scene III

Tableau for a couple of beats. Eduardo on bow with timer in one hand as he counts strokes per minute. Simón is in the cabin steering, wearing his sunglasses, baseball cap on backward. Abuela and Aída are at the side of the boat, heads down, hands folded, still muttering prayers in Spanish.

AÍDA AND ABUELA: [*Crossing themselves.*] *En el nombre del Padre, del Hijo y del Espíritu Santo amén.*

EDUARDO: [*Through megaphone.*] You're stroking seventy-two!

SIMÓN: [*Singing.*] Mama's stroking, Mama's stroking seventy-two. . . .

EDUARDO: [*Through megaphone.*] You comfortable with it?

SIMÓN: [*Singing.*] Seventy-two, seventy-two, seventy-two for you.

AÍDA: [*Looking at the heavens.*] Ay, Eduardo, *ven acá,* we should be grateful that *Nuestro Señor* gave us such a beautiful day.

ABUELA: [*Crosses herself.*] *Sí, gracias a Dios.*

EDUARDO: She's stroking seventy-two, with no problem [*He throws a kiss to the sky.*] It's a beautiful day to win.

AÍDA: *Qué hermoso!* So clear and bright. Not a cloud in the sky. *Mira! Mira!* Even rainbows on the water . . . a sign from God.

SIMÓN: [*Singing.*] Rainbows on the water . . . you in my arms . . .

ABUELA AND EDUARDO: [*Looking the wrong way.*] *Dónde?*

AÍDA: [*Pointing toward Margarita.*] There, dancing in front of margarita, leading her on . . .

EDUARDO: Rainbows on . . . *Ay coño!* It's an oil slick! You . . . you . . . [*To Simón.*] Stop the boat. [*Runs to bow, yelling.*] Margarita! Margarita!

On the next stroke, Margarita comes up all covered in black oil.

MARGARITA: *Papi! Papi . . . !*

Everybody goes to the side and stares at Margarita, who stares back. Eduardo freezes.

AÍDA: *Apúrate,* Eduardo, move . . . what's wrong with you . . . *no me oíste,* get my daughter out of the water.

EDUARDO: [*Softly.*] We can't touch her. If we touch her, she's disqualified.

AÍDA: But I'm her mother.

EDUARDO: Not even by her own mother. Especially by her own mother. . . . You always want the rules to be different for you, you always want to be the exception. [*To Simón.*] And you . . . you didn't see it, eh? You were playing again?

SIMÓN: *Papi,* I was watching . . .

AÍDA: [*Interrupting.*] *Pues,* do something Eduardo. You are the big coach, the monitor.

SIMÓN: Mentor! Mentor!

EDUARDO: How can a person think around you? [*He walks off to bow, puts head in hands.*]

ABUELA: [*Looking over side.*] *Mira como todos los* little birds are dead. [*She crosses herself.*]

AÍDA: Their little wings are glued to their sides.

SIMÓN: Christ, this is like the La Brea tar pits.

AÍDA: They can't move their little wings.

ABUELA: *Esa niña tiene que moverse.*

SIMÓN: Yeah, Margo, you gotta move, man.

Abuela and Simón gesture for Margarita to move. Aída gestures for her to swim.

ABUELA: *Anda niña, muévete.*

AÍDA: Swim, *hija,* swim or the *aceite* will stick to your wings.

MARGARITA: *Papi?*

ABUELA: [*Taking megaphone.*] Your *papi* say "move it!"

Margarita with difficulty starts moving.

ABUELA, AÍDA AND SIMÓN [*Laboriously counting.*]: *Uno, dos . . . uno, dos . . . anda . . . uno, dos.*

EDUARDO: [*Running to take megaphone from Abuela.*] *Uno, dos . . .*

Simón races into cabin and starts the engine. Abuela, Aída and Eduardo count together.

SIMÓN: [*Looking ahead.*] *Papi,* it's over there!

EDUARDO: Eh?

SIMÓN: [*Pointing ahead and to the right.*] It's getting clearer over there.

EDUARDO: [*Through megaphone.*] Now pay attention to me. Go to the right.

Simón, Abuela, Aída and Eduardo all lean over side. They point ahead and to the right, except Abuela, who points to the left.

FAMILY: [*Shouting together.*] Para yá! Para yá!

Lights go down on boat. A special light on Margarita, swimming through the oil, and on Abuela, watching her.

ABUELA: *Sangre de mi sangre,* you will be another to save us. En Bolondron, where your great-grandmother Luz Suárez was born, they say one day it rained blood. All the people, they run into their houses. They cry, they pray, *pero* your great-grandmother Luz she had cojones like a man. She run outside. She look straight at the sky. She shake her fist. And she say to the evil one, "*Mira . . .* [*Beating her chest.*] coño, Diablo, aquí estoy si me quieres.*" And she open her mouth, and she drunk the blood.

Blackout.

Scene IV

Lights up on boat. Aída and Eduardo are on deck watching Margarita swim. We hear the gentle, rhythmic lap, lap, lap of the water, then the sound of inhaling and exhaling as Margarita's breathing becomes louder. Then Margarita's heartbeat is heard, with the lapping of the water and the breathing under it. These sounds continue beneath the dialogue to the end of the scene.

AÍDA: *Dios mío.* Look how she moves through the water. . . .

EDUARDO: You see, it's very simple. It is a matter of concentration.

AÍDA: The first time I put her in water she came to life, she grew before my eyes. She moved, she smiled, she loved it more than me. She didn't want my breast any longer. She wanted the water.

EDUARDO: And of course, the rhythm. The rhythm takes away the pain and helps the concentration.

Pause. Aída and Eduardo watch Margarita.

AÍDA: Is that my child or a seal. . . .

MILCHA SANCHEZ-SCOTT

EDUARDO: Ah, a seal, the reason for that is that she's keeping her arms very close to her body. She cups her hands, and then she reaches and digs, reaches and digs.

AÍDA: To think that a daughter of mine. . . .

EDUARDO: It's the training, the hours in the water. I used to tie weights around her little wrists and ankles.

AÍDA: A spirit, an ocean spirit, must have entered my body when I was carrying her.

EDUARDO: [*To Margarita.*] Your stroke is slowing down.

Pause. We hear Margarita's heartbeat with the breathing under, faster now.

AÍDA: Eduardo, that night, the night on the boat . . .

EDUARDO: Ah, the night on the boat again . . . the moon was . . .

AÍDA: The moon was full. We were coming to America. . . . *Qué romantico.*

Heartbeat and breathing continue.

EDUARDO: We were cold, afraid, with no money, and on top of everything, you were hysterical, yelling at me, tearing at me with your nails. [*Opens his shirt, points to the base of his neck.*] Look, I still bear the scars . . . telling me that I didn't know what I was doing . . . saying that we were going to die. . . .

AÍDA: You took me, you stole me from my home . . . you didn't give me a chance to prepare. You just said we have to go now, now! Now, you said. You didn't let me take anything. I left everything behind. . . . I left everything behind.

EDUARDO: Saying that I wasn't good enough, that your father didn't raise you so that I could drown you in the sea.

AÍDA: You didn't let me say even a good-bye. You took me, you stole me, you tore me from my home.

EDUARDO: I took you so we could be married.

AÍDA: That was in Miami. But that night on the boat, Eduardo. . . . We were not married, that night on the boat.

EDUARDO: *No pasó nada!* Once and for all get it out of your head, it was cold, you hated me, and we were afraid. . . .

AÍDA: *Mentiroso!*

EDUARDO: A man can't do it when he is afraid.

AÍDA: Liar! You did it very well.

EDUARDO: I did?

AÍDA: *Sí.* Gentle. You were so gentle and then strong . . . my passion
for you so deep. Standing next to you . . . I would ache . . . looking
at your hands I would forget to breathe, you were irresistible.

EDUARDO: I was?

AÍDA: You took me into your arms, you touched my face with your
fingertips . . . you kissed my eyes . . . *la esquina de la boca y* . . .

EDUARDO: *Sí, Sí,* and then . . .

AÍDA: I look at your face on top of mine, and I see the lights of Havana
in your eyes. That's when you seduced me.

EDUARDO: Shhh, they're gonna hear you.

Lights go down. Special on Aída.

AÍDA: That was the night. A woman doesn't forget those things . . . and
later that night was the dream . . . the dream of a big country with
fields of fertile land and big, giant things growing. And there by a
green, slimy pond I found a giant pea pod and when I opened it, it
was full of little, tiny baby frogs.

*Aída crosses herself as she watches Margarita. We hear louder
breathing and heartbeat.*

MARGARITA: Santa Teresa. Little Flower of God, pray for me. San
Martín de Porres, pray for me. Santa Rosa de Lima, *Virgencita de la
Caridad del Cobre,* pray for me. . . . Mother pray for me.

Scene V

*Loud howling of wind is heard, as lights change to indicate unstable
weather, fog, and mist. Family on deck, braced and huddled against the
wind. Simón is at the helm.*

AÍDA: *Ay Dios mío, qué viento.*

EDUARDO: [*Through megaphone.*] Don't drift out . . . that wind is pushing you out. [*To Simón.*] You! Slow down. Can't you see your sister
is drifting out?

SIMÓN: It's the wind, *Papi.*

AÍDA: Baby, don't go so far. . . .

ABUELA: [*To heaven.*] *Ay Gran Poder de Dios, quita este maldito viento.*

SIMÓN: Margo! Margo! Stay close to the boat.

EDUARDO: Dig in. Dig in hard . . . .Reach down from your guts and
dig in.

ABUELA: [*To heaven.*] *Ay Virgen de la Caridad del Cobre, por lo más tú quieres a pararla.*

AÍDA: [*Putting her hand out, reaching for Margarita.*] Baby, don't go far.

Abuela crosses herself. Action freezes. Lights get dimmer, special on Margarita. She keeps swimming, stops, starts again, stops, then, finally exhausted, stops altogether. The boat stops moving.

EDUARDO: What's going on here? Why are we stopping?

SIMÓN: *Papi,* she's not moving! *Yo* Margo!

The family all run to the side.

EDUARDO: *Hija!* . . . *Hijita!* You're tired, eh?

AÍDA: *Por supuesto* she's tired. I like to see you get in the water, waving your arms and legs from San Pedro to Santa Catalina. A person isn't a machine, a person has to rest.

SIMÓN: *Yo, Mama!* Cool out, it ain't fucking brain surgery.

EDUARDO: [*To Simón.*] Shut up, you. [*Louder to Margarita.*] I guess your mother's right for once, huh? . . . I guess you had to stop, eh? . . . Give your brother, the idiot . . . a chance to catch up with you.

SIMÓN: [*Clowning like Mortimer Snerd.*] Dum dee dum dee dum ooops, ah shucks . . .

EDUARDO: I don't think he's Cuban.

SIMÓN: [*Like Ricky Ricardo.*] *Oye,* Lucy! I'm home! Ba ba lu!

EDUARDO: [*Joins in clowning, grabbing Simón in a headlock.*] What am I gonna do with this idiot, eh? I don't understand this idiot. He's not like us, Margarita. [*Laughing.*] You think if we put him into your bathing suit with a cap on his head . . . [*He laughs hysterically.*] You think anyone would know . . . huh? Do you think anyone would know? [*Laughs.*]

SIMÓN: [*Vamping.*] *Ay, mi amor.* Anybody looking for tits would know.

Eduardo slaps Simón across the face, knocking him down. Aída runs to Simón's aid. Abuela holds Eduardo back.

MARGARITA: *Mía culpa! Mía culpa!*

ABUELA: *Qué dices hija?*

MARGARITA: *Papi,* it's my fault, it's all my fault. . . . I'm so cold, I can't move. . . . I put my face in the water . . . and I hear them whispering . . . laughing at me. . . .

AÍDA: Who is laughing at you?

MARGARITA: The fish are all biting me . . . they hate me . . . they whisper about me. She can't swim, they say. She can't glide. She has no grace. . . . Yellowtails, bonita, tuna, man-o'-war, snub-nose sharks, *los baracudas* . . . they all hate me . . . only the dolphins care . . . and sometimes I hear the whales crying . . . she is lost, she is dead. I'm so numb, I can't feel. *Papi! Papi!* Am I dead?

EDUARDO: *Vamos,* baby, punch those arms in. Come on . . . do you hear me?

MARGARITA: *Papi . . . Papi . . .* forgive me. . . .

All is silent on the boat. Eduardo drops his megaphone, his head bent down in dejection. Abuela, Aída, Simón, all leaning over the side of the boat. Simón slowly walks away.

AÍDA: *Mi hija, qué tienes?*

SIMÓN: Oh, Christ, don't make her say it. Please don't make her say it.

ABUELA: Say what? *Qué cosa?*

SIMÓN: She wants to quit, can't you see she's had enough?

ABUELA: *Mira, para eso. Esta niña* is turning blue.

AÍDA: *Oyeme, mi hija.* Do you want to come out of the water?

MARGARITA: *Papi?*

SIMÓN: [*To Eduardo.*] She won't come out until *you* tell her.

AÍDA: Eduardo . . . answer your daughter.

EDUARDO: *Le dije* to concentrate . . . concentrate on your rhythm. Then the rhythm would carry her . . . ay, it's a beautiful thing, Aída. It's like yoga, like meditation, the mind over matter . . . the mind controlling the body . . . that's how the great things in the world have been done. I wish you . . . I wish my wife could understand.

MARGARITA: *Papi?*

SIMÓN: [*To Margarita.*] Forget him.

AÍDA: [*Imploring.*] Eduardo, *por favor.*

EDUARDO: [*Walking in circles.*] Why didn't you let her concentrate? Don't you understand, the concentration, the rhythm is everything. But no, you wouldn't listen. [*Screaming to the ocean.*] Goddamn Cubans, why, God, why do you make us go everywhere with our families? [*He goes to back of boat.*]

AÍDA: [*Opening her arms.*] Mi hija, ven, come to *Mami*. [*Rocking.*] Your *mami* knows.

Abuela has taken the training bottle, puts it in a net. She and Simón lower it to Margarita.

SIMÓN: Take this. Drink it. [*As Margarita drinks, Abuela crosses herself.*]
ABUELA: *Sangre de mi sangre.*

> *Music comes up softly. Margarita drinks, gives the bottle back, stretches out her arms, as if on a cross. Floats on her back. She begins a graceful backstroke. Lights fade on boat as special lights come up on Margarita. She stops. Slowly turns over and starts to swim, gradually picking up speed. Suddenly as if in pain she stops, tries again, then stops in pain again. She becomes disoriented and falls to the bottom of the sea. Special on Margarita at the bottom of the sea.*

MARGARITA: *Ya no puedo* . . . I can't. . . . A person isn't a machine . . . *es mi culpa* . . . Father forgive me . . . *Papi! Papi!* One, two. *Uno, dos.* [*Pause.*] *Papi! A dónde estás?* [*Pause.*] One, two, one, two. *Papi! Ay, Papi!* Where are you . . . ? Don't leave me. . . . Why don't you answer me? [*Pause. She starts to swim, slowly.*] *Uno, dos, uno, dos.* Dig in, dig in. [*Stops swimming.*] *Por favor, Papi!* [*Starts to swim again.*] One, two, one, two. Kick from your hip, kick from your hip. [*Stops swimming. Starts to cry.*] Oh God, please. . . . [*Pause.*] Hail Mary, full of grace . . . dig in, dig in . . . the Lord is with thee. . . . [*She swims to the rhythm of her Hail Mary.*] Hail Mary, full of grace . . . dig in, dig in . . . the Lord is with thee . . . dig in, dig in. . . . Blessed art thou among women. . . . *Mami*, it hurts. You let go of my hand. I'm lost. . . . And blessed is the fruit of thy womb, now and at the hour of our death. Amen. I don't want to die, I don't want to die.

> *Margarita is still swimming. Blackout. She is gone.*

Scene VI

Lights up on boat, we hear radio static. There is a heavy mist. On deck we see only black outline of Abuela with shawl over her head. We hear the voices of Eduardo, Aída, and Radio Operator.

EDUARDO'S VOICE: *La Havana!* Coming from San Pedro. Over.
RADIO OPERATOR'S VOICE: Right, DT6-6, you say you've lost a swimmer.
AÍDA'S VOICE: Our child, our only daughter . . . listen to me. Her name is Margarita Inez Suárez, she is wearing a black one-piece bathing suit cut high in the legs with a white racing stripe down the sides, a white bathing cap with goggles and her whole body covered with a . . . with a . . .

EDUARDO'S VOICE: With lanolin and paraffin.

AÍDA'S VOICE: *Sí . . . con lanolin and paraffin.*

More radio static. Special on Simón, on the edge of the boat.

SIMÓN: Margo! Yo Margo! [*Pause.*] Man don't do this. [*Pause.*] Come on. . . . Come on. . . . [*Pause.*] God, why does everything have to be so hard? [*Pause.*] Stupid. You know you're not supposed to die for this. Stupid. It's his dream and he can't even swim. [*Pause.*] Punch those arms in. Come home. Come home. I'm your little brother. Don't forget what Mama said. You're not supposed to leave me behind. *Vamos, Margarita,* take your little brother, hold his hand tight when you cross the street. He's so little. [*Pause.*] Oh Christ, give us a sign. . . . I know! I know! Margo, I'll send you a message . . . like mental telepathy. I'll hold my breath, close my eyes, and I'll bring you home. [*He takes a deep breath; a few beats.*] This time I'll beep . . . I'll send out sonar signals like a dolphin. [*He imitates dolphin sounds.*]

The sound of real dolphins takes over from Simón, then fades into sound of Abuela saying the Hail Mary in Spanish, as full lights come up slowly.

Scene VII

Eduardo coming out of cabin, sobbing, Aída holding him. Simón anxiously scanning the horizon. Abuela looking calmly ahead.

EDUARDO: *Es mi culpa, sí, es mi culpa.* [*He hits his chest.*]

AÍDA: *Ya, ya viejo.* . . . it was my sin . . . I left my home.

EDUARDO: Forgive me, forgive me. I've lost our daughter, our sister, our granddaughter, *mi carne, mi sangre, mis ilusiones.* [*To heaven.*] *Dios mío,* take me . . . take me, I say . . . Goddammit, take me!

SIMÓN: I'm going in.

AÍDA AND EDUARDO: No!

EDUARDO [*Grabbing and holding Simón, speaking to heaven*]: God, take me, not my children. They are my dreams, my illusions . . . and not this one, this one is my mystery . . . he has my secret dreams. In him are the parts of me I cannot see.

Eduardo embraces Simón. Radio static becomes louder.

AÍDA: I . . . I think I see her.

SIMÓN: No, it's just a seal.

ABUELA [*Looking out with binoculars.*]:   *Mi nietacita, dónde estás?* [*She feels her heart.*] I don't feel the knife in my heart . . . my little fish is not lost.

Radio crackles with static. As lights dim on boat, Voices of Mel and Mary Beth are heard over the radio.

MEL'S VOICE: Tragedy has marred the face of the Wrigley Invitational Women's Race to Catalina. The Cuban swimmer, little Margarita Suárez, has reportedly been lost at sea. Coast Guard and divers are looking for her as we speak. Yet in spite of this tragedy the race must go on because . . .

MARY BETH'S VOICE: [*Interrupting loudly.*] Mel!

MEL'S VOICE: [*Startled.*] What!

MARY BETH'S VOICE: Ah . . . excuse me, Mel . . . we have a winner. We've just received word from Catalina that one of the swimmers is just fifty yards from the breakers . . . it's, oh, it's . . . Margarita Suárez!

Special on family in cabin listening to radio.

MEL'S VOICE: What? I thought she died!

Special on Margarita, taking off bathing cap, trophy in hand, walking on the water.

MARY BETH'S VOICE: Ahh . . . unless . . . unless this is a tragic . . . No . . . there she is, Mel. Margarita Suárez! The only one in the race wearing a black bathing suit cut high in the legs with a racing stripe down the side.

Family cheering, embracing.

SIMÓN: [*Screaming.*]Way to go, Margo!

MEL'S VOICE: This is indeed a miracle! It's a resurrection! Margarita Suárez, with a flotilla of boats to meet her, is now walking on the waters, through the breakers . . . onto the beach, with crowds of people cheering her on. What a jubilation! This is a miracle!

Sound of crowds cheering. Lights and cheering sounds fade.

Blackout.

—1984

Born in Bogalusa, Louisiana, Arlene Hutton took a degree in theater at Rollins College and did graduate work in acting at the Asolo Conservatory at Florida State University. The Nibroc Trilogy, *which comprises* Last Train to Nibroc, See Rock City, *and* Gulf View Drive, *has been performed internationally and has garnered many awards.* I Dream Before I Take the Stand *was first produced in 1995 and was collected in* Best American Short Plays. *From 2005 to 2008 Hutton served as Tennessee Williams Fellow in Playwriting at the University of the South. The Los Angeles Times noted, "Had Arlene Hutton been around during Broadway's golden age, her finely wrought plays might rank with those of William Inge or Horton Foote. Among postmodern dramatists, Hutton stands apart, relying on traditional techniques in an era where such values grow ever rarer."*

I Dream Before I Take the Stand

Characters

She: *a petite woman*
He: *a man, probably a lawyer*

Scene: *A chair.*

Time: *Right now*

Casting Note: *The man is age 25–50, the woman 20–50, both of any race. The woman should be petite in height or very slim if taller, but the specific hair color lines may be changed with the author's permission.*

Lights up on a petite woman sitting in a chair. It is possible that the lights begin the play full and soft, narrowing very slowly throughout, so that by the end of the play only a narrow spot is focused on the woman, like an interrogation room. The man, a lawyer, walks around her throughout, at first in the full circle of light, later appearing in and out of the focused light. Perhaps by the end of the play, the light has narrowed on the woman, and the man is barely seen. There are many ways to present this play. But the pauses are a part of the dialogue.

SHE: I was walking through the park.
HE: Why were you in the park?
SHE: I was on my way to work.
HE: Do you have to walk through the park to get to work?

SHE: No.

HE: Do you always walk through the park to work?

SHE: No.

HE: Why did you walk through the park that day?

SHE: It was a beautiful day. I like to walk to work through the park when the weather's good.

Pause.

HE: Were you in a hurry?

SHE: I was on my way to work.

HE: Were you late?

SHE: No, I would have been on time.

HE: Were you strolling or walking fast?

SHE: I always walk fairly quickly.

HE: Why? The park is not safe?

SHE: I guess not.

HE: Yet you walk through it to get to work.

SHE: There are lots of people around.

HE: But you walk quickly through the park.

SHE: Yes.

Pause.

HE: How do you walk?

SHE: Which way?

HE: Do you swing your arms?

SHE: I don't know.

HE: Were you carrying anything?

SHE: Just my purse.

HE: So your arms were free to swing along as you walked.

SHE: Maybe.

HE: Or maybe you walk with them folded.

SHE: I don't know what you mean.

HE: Perhaps you fold your arms. [*He demonstrates.*]

SHE: Maybe.

HE: So sometimes you swing your arms and sometimes you fold them.

SHE: I guess.

HE: What else would you do with them?

SHE: I guess you're right.

Pause.

HE: So you were walking through the park that day on your way to work.

SHE: Yes. I already said that.

Pause.

HE: What were you wearing?

SHE: A skirt and a top.

HE: What color was the skirt?

SHE: It was a print.

HE: What color?

SHE: Black and red.

HE: And the top?

SHE: What?

HE: What color was the top?

SHE: Black.

HE: Just black?

SHE: It had a little red flower on it.

HE: The fabric?

SHE: No. A decoration.

HE: Where?

SHE: In the center of the neckline.

HE: A rose.

SHE: I guess. It was tiny.

HE: It was in the fabric?

SHE: No. It was a small ribbon.

HE: Like the little flowers on lingerie.

SHE: Like that.

HE: How sweet. [*A pause.*] Were you wearing jewelry?

SHE: No. Just a watch.

HE: An expensive watch?

SHE: No.

HE: An expensive *looking* watch?

SHE: No. Just a Timex.

HE: So that you could hurry through the park to be at work on time.

SHE: Of course.

HE: No other jewelry?

SHE: No.

HE: Why not?

SHE: I don't wear jewelry in the park.

HE: Why not?

SHE: I don't want to attract attention.

HE: You don't want to get mugged.

SHE: Right.

Pause.

HE: Your hair is up today. Were you wearing it that way in the park?

SHE: No. I was wearing it down.

HE: Why?

SHE: It probably wasn't quite dry.

HE: You go out with wet hair? Why?

SHE: In nice weather.

HE: Why?

SHE: It feels good.

HE: And you color your hair.

SHE: Yes.

HE: And why is that?

SHE: I like it.

HE: Why? What is your natural color?

SHE: Like this when I was in college.

HE: But now?

SHE: I don't know.

HE: You don't know what color your hair is?

SHE: It's been a while—

HE: What color do you think it is?

SHE: I imagine it's sort of a dirty blond with a little gray. [*Note: "dirty blond" can be "mousy brown," depending on the hair color of the actress. "With a little gray" can be omitted.*]

HE: But you don't really know.

SHE: Not really.

HE: [*Optional pause.*] Do you think you are more attractive with colored hair?

SHE: I don't know.

HE: Then why do you color it?

SHE: I guess so.

HE: What?

SHE: I guess I think I'm—

HE: So you color your hair to be more attractive.

SHE: I guess.

HE: But your fingernails are not painted.

SHE: No.

HE: Do you sometimes paint your fingernails?

SHE: Sometimes I wear nail polish.

HE: Were your fingernails painted that day?

SHE: I think so.

HE: What nail color did you use?

SHE: A pink polish.

HE: Not red.

SHE: No. Just pink.

HE: Why?

SHE: To match my makeup.

HE: You were wearing makeup?

SHE: Yes.

HE: Do you always wear makeup to the park?

SHE: No.

HE: They why were you wearing it that day?

SHE: I was on my way to work.

HE: What sort of makeup were you wearing?

SHE: What brand?

HE: Which items of makeup had you put on? Lipstick?

SHE: Yes.

HE: What color?

SHE: The actual name?

HE: What color would *you* call the lipstick you wore?

SHE: A sort of peach, maybe, with a darker—

HE: You were wearing two colors on your lips?

SHE: Well, yes.

HE: How does one do that?

SHE: It's a lip liner with a brush and then a tube lipstick.

HE: You outline your lips before you put on your lipstick.

SHE: Yes. It's—

HE: You add definition to your lips.

SHE: Sort of.

HE: To emphasize them. You emphasize your lips.

SHE: It's just the way you put on makeup.

Possibly a pause.

HE: What other makeup were you wearing?

ARLENE HUTTON

SHE: A little powder.

HE: Why?

SHE: So my nose wouldn't be shiny.

HE: And why would it?

SHE: It was a fairly warm day.

HE: You might have perspired a little.

SHE: Maybe.

HE: And was there color on your cheeks?

SHE: Yes. I use a little blush.

HE: Color on the eyes?

SHE: Eyeliner. Maybe a little eye shadow.

HE: Mascara.

SHE: No.

HE: Are you sure?

SHE: Yes. I don't use mascara.

HE: Why not?

SHE: It bothers my contact lenses.

HE: Were you wearing contact lenses in the park?

SHE: Yes.

HE: You weren't wearing glasses?

SHE: No.

HE: But you are wearing glasses now.

SHE: Sometimes I wear contact lenses.

HE: You were wearing contact lenses in the park.

SHE: I already said that.

HE: Your hair was down and you were wearing makeup and contact lenses.

SHE: I already said that.

HE: Your hair was down and you were wearing makeup and contact lenses.

SHE: Yes.

A pause.

HE: Were you wearing perfume?

SHE: Cologne.

HE: Do you always wear perfume?

SHE: Cologne. I was wearing cologne.

HE: Do you always wear cologne?

SHE: Usually.

HE: In the park?

SHE: To work.

HE: And it was a warm day.

SHE: Yes. But what does that—

HE: You were walking through the park on your way to work dressed in your skirt and top. Your hair was down and you were wearing makeup and perfume.

SHE: Cologne.

A long pause. She has won this round, and he must regroup.

HE: You were walking through the park.

SHE: Yes.

HE: You passed a man sitting on a bench.

SHE: [*After a slight pause.*] There were lots of people sitting on benches.

HE: You passed many people.

SHE: Yes.

HE: The park was crowded.

SHE: No.

HE: The park was not empty.

SHE: No. But there were a lot of people.

HE: Did you see anyone you knew?

SHE: No.

HE: No neighbors or friends or familiar faces?

SHE: No.

HE: You walked past the people sitting on benches.

SHE: Yes.

HE: There was a man sitting on a bench by himself.

SHE: I didn't notice he was alone.

HE: He spoke to you.

SHE: Yes.

HE: You spoke to him.

SHE: No.

HE: He spoke to you.

SHE: Yes.

HE: What did he say?

SHE: He just said hello.

HE: And what did you do?

SHE: I nodded to him and kept on walking.

HE: Did you know him?

SHE: No.

HE: Had you ever seen him before?

SHE: No.

HE: He was a stranger.

SHE: Yes.

HE: Yet you nodded at him. Did you smile as you nodded?

SHE: Yes.

HE: Why?

SHE: It was a beautiful day. I was just passing by and he said hello.

HE: Do you always acknowledge comments from strangers on the street?

SHE: Not always.

HE: Then why did you acknowledge this man?

SHE: It was such a nice day. And I don't like to be rude.

HE: So this stranger said hello and you smiled and nodded.

SHE: That's right.

HE: Did you speak to other people sitting on the benches?

SHE: No.

HE: Did you speak to anyone else in the park?

SHE: No.

HE: Why not?

SHE: No one else spoke to me.

HE: But when a strange man said hello you smiled and nodded at him.

SHE: Yes. There were lots of people—

HE: Did you stop to smile and nod?

SHE: What?

HE: Did you stop still in front of the man to smile at him?

SHE: No. I kept walking.

HE: Why didn't you stop?

SHE: I didn't think about it. It was just a casual hello. I just kept walking. It was nothing.

HE: Not really. [*Pause.*] What were you wearing?

SHE: What?

HE: What were you wearing?

SHE: I told you.

HE: You have to answer. What were you wearing?

SHE: A skirt and a top.

HE: To go to work?

SHE: I had a jacket in the office.

HE: What kind of skirt?

SHE: A printed one.

HE: A red and black print.

SHE: Yes.

HE: Was it long or short?

SHE: What?

HE: The skirt. Was it below your knees?

SHE: No.

HE: It came above your knees.

SHE: Yes.

HE: It was tight. It clung to your body?

SHE: No. It was gathered. A full skirt.

HE: So it might have moved when you walked.

SHE: I don't know.

HE: What was the fabric?

SHE: Chiffon.

HE: Chiffon is a sheer fabric.

SHE: It was lined.

HE: What was the lining?

SHE: The lining was chiffon, too.

HE: So you were wearing a see-through miniskirt.

SHE: No.

HE: Describe the blouse.

SHE: What?

HE: You were wearing a top.

SHE: Yes. A T-shirt.

HE: A knit top.

SHE: Yes.

HE: Did it have sleeves?

SHE: No. It was sleeveless.

HE: A tank top. It was tight.

SHE: No.

HE: It fitted closely on your body. What color was it?

SHE: I already told you.

HE: What color was it?

SHE: [*An outburst.*] Black.

HE: With a little red flower. [*Possibly a pause.*] Were you wearing underwear?

SHE: [*Surprised at this question.*] Yes.

HE: Were you wearing a slip?

SHE: No.

HE: Why not?

SHE: It was warm out. And the skirt was lined.

HE: Were you wearing pantyhose?

SHE: No.

HE: Your legs were bare.

SHE: Yes.

HE: No socks?

SHE: I told you. I was wearing sandals.

HE: For the office?

SHE: I keep stockings and pumps in my desk.

HE: Along with a jacket.

SHE: Yes.

HE: You walk through the park half naked and cover up for the office.

SHE: [*After a pause.*] It's air-conditioned.

HE: What?

SHE: The office. It's air-conditioned. It gets cold.

HE: But the park was hot.

SHE: Yes.

HE: So you don't wear much clothing. Were your legs shaved?

SHE: Yes.

HE: Why do you shave your legs?

SHE: I just do.

HE: It looks better.

SHE: Yes.

HE: So you weren't wearing panty hose.

SHE: I already said that.

HE: No stockings at all.

SHE: I was wearing sandals.

HE: Were you wearing a bra?

SHE: What?

HE: Were you wearing a bra?

SHE: Yes.

HE: What size?

SHE: Thirty-four.

HE: Thirty-four what?

SHE: Just thirty-four.

HE: What cup size are you?

SHE: Um, uh, B or C.

HE: You don't know?

SHE: It depends on the bra. What brand.

HE: What was the cup size of the bra you had on that day?

SHE: It didn't have a cup size. It was just a thirty four.

HE: Why didn't it have a cup size? Don't most bras have a cup size?

SHE: It wasn't sized that way. It didn't have an underwire.

HE: So it was an elastic sort of bra.

SHE: I don't know. Maybe.

A slight pause.

HE: How tall are you?

SHE: Five foot three.

HE: You are considered a petite woman, then.

SHE: I guess so.

HE: But thirty-four B or C is a fairly large bra size for a small woman.

SHE: It's average.

HE: Not for a petite woman. You wouldn't say your breasts were small.

SHE: My . . .

HE: Your breasts. They are not small breasts.

SHE: I don't know.

HE: You don't know you have large breasts?

SHE: They're average.

HE: Do you always wear a bra?

SHE: When?

HE: When you walk through the park, do you always wear a bra?

SHE: Yes.

HE: Why?

SHE: I feel more comfortable.

HE: Because you have large breasts.

SHE: [*No answer.*]

HE: You would not say that you have small breasts.

SHE: No . . .

HE: You have a large bust. But you were wearing a tank top.

SHE: It was hot.

HE: You were wearing a tight T-shirt. How wide were the straps on your tank top?

SHE: I don't know.

HE: Wide enough to cover the bra straps?

SHE: Well, yes.

HE: You were carrying a purse.

SHE: Yes.

HE: What kind?

SHE: A small leather one.

HE: You were carrying it in your hand.

SHE: No.

HE: It had a strap.

SHE: Yes.

HE: How were you carrying your purse?

SHE: On my shoulder. The strap was on my shoulder.

HE: Could it cause your tank top strap to shift?

SHE: What?

HE: The strap on your tank top. Could your purse strap have caused it to shift?

SHE: I guess.

HE: Revealing your bra strap.

SHE: Maybe.

HE: So your bra straps could have been showing as you walked through the park.

SHE: I don't know.

Pause.

HE: What color was your underwear?

SHE: What does it matter?

HE: What color was your underwear?

SHE: [*Overlapping.*] Black.

HE: The bra or the panties?

SHE: Both.

HE: They matched?

SHE: Yes.

HE: Did they have lace?

SHE: Yes.

HE: You were wearing a black lacy bra and panties?

SHE: That's right.

HE: Why not white or beige?

SHE: To match the tank top and skirt.

HE: Why? Did you expect anyone to see your underwear that day?

SHE: What?

HE: [*Doesn't answer.*]

SHE: No.

HE: Did you have a date with a boyfriend later?

SHE: No.

HE: Then why did it have to match?

SHE: What?

HE: The underwear. The bra and panties

SHE: In case it . . . in case the tank strap . . .

HE: So you expected the bra strap to be seen.

SHE: Not necessarily.

HE: But you thought it might.

SHE: I didn't really think about it. It's just what I put on that morning.

HE: Black lacy underwear is considered sexy.

SHE: I guess.

HE: It is sexier than white or beige.

SHE: I guess so.

HE: Black is considered a sexy color. So is red.

SHE: I don't know.

HE: Your skirt was black and red. Your top was black with a little red ribbon flower on it. Your bra and panties were black.

SHE: That's right.

HE: So why were you wearing sexy underwear if no one was to see it?

SHE: I just like it.

HE: Why?

SHE: It makes me feel . . .

HE: Sexier.

SHE: Prettier.

HE: More sensual.

SHE: More feminine.

HE: You walked through the park wearing sexy underwear and revealing clothes and you smiled and nodded at a man you did not know.

SHE: No.

HE: No?

SHE: Not like that.

HE: You walked through the park.

SHE: Yes.

HE: You were wearing black lacy underwear.

SHE: Yes.

HE: You were wearing a tight tank top and a see-through skirt.

SHE: I . . .

HE: You nodded at a strange man.

SHE: Okay.

HE: You smiled at him.

SHE: Okay.

HE: Your bra strap had slipped, and you felt sexy.

SHE: No.

HE: It was a hot day.

SHE: Yes.

HE: Your legs were bare. Your thighs were warm.

SHE: No.

HE: The weather was warm.

SHE: Yes.

HE: You were walking quickly.

SHE: Yes.

HE: You worked up a sweat.

SHE: I don't know.

HE: It is likely you were perspiring.

SHE: I guess.

HE: Your clothes were clinging to you.

SHE: No.

HE: You were moist with sweat and the chiffon lining of your skirt was clinging to your legs as you walked. Your knit top was damp and clung closely to your body.

SHE: That's not right.

HE: It was a hot day. You were walking quickly. You were perspiring.

SHE: [No answer.]

HE: Your clothes were warm and sticky. The shape of your body was revealed. Have your breasts been artificially enlarged?

SHE: No.

HE: Or reduced?

SHE: No.

HE: They have not been altered in any way.

SHE: No.

HE: So your breasts are not, shall we say, unnaturally firm.

SHE: I guess not.

HE: And your bra had no underwire.

SHE: We've been through that.

HE: So your breasts had little support.

SHE: I was wearing a bra.

HE: You were walking quickly.

SHE: Yes.

HE: Your breasts were bouncing.

SHE: I don't know.

HE: Your strap might have slipped. Your breasts had no support.

SHE: I was wearing a bra.

HE: You were swinging your arms.

SHE: You said that.

HE: You were either swinging your arms or your arms were folded holding up your breasts.

SHE: I don't know.

HE: Tank tops are low cut.

SHE: It wasn't really—

HE: You folded your arms under your breasts to show your cleavage.

SHE: No.

HE: Might you have folded your arms?

SHE: Not to—

HE: Is it possible you folded your arms?

SHE: Maybe.

HE: Or you were swinging your arms?

SHE: No.

HE: You were walking quickly.

SHE: Yes. To—

HE: Then you were swinging your arms.

SHE: I don't know.

HE: You were swaying your hips.

SHE: No.

HE: You were swinging your arms and your breasts were bouncing.

SHE: No.

HE: Your large breasts were bouncing and your strap was showing.

SHE: No.

HE: If you were walking at a fast pace your breasts would bounce and your hips sway.

SHE: I didn't think about it.

HE: That's right.

Pause.

HE: What size panties?

SHE: What?

HE: What size were your panties?

SHE: Medium, I guess.

HE: You don't know?

SHE: I don't remember.

HE: What size panties do you usually buy?

SHE: Medium or small. It depends.

HE: On what?

SHE: On what's on sale, the style, I don't know.

HE: What style?

SHE: I don't know what you mean.

HE: What style were those panties? Bikini panties?

SHE: That's right.

HE: Why?

SHE: Why what?

HE: Why were you wearing bikini panties?

SHE: They matched the bra.

HE: Wouldn't a looser fitting panty be more comfortable?

SHE: Not really.

HE: Bikini panties allow your thighs to touch each other.

SHE: Stop it.

HE: It was a very hot day. You walked quickly through the park wearing sexy clothes with your breasts bouncing and your thighs damp and you smiled and nodded at a stranger.

SHE: That's not it.

HE: You were walking through the park.

SHE: Yes.

HE: It was a hot day.

SHE: Yes.

HE: You smiled at stranger. And he followed you.

SHE: I didn't know.

HE: What?

SHE: I didn't know that he had followed me.

HE: When did you notice that he followed you?

ARLENE HUTTON

SHE: When he grabbed me.

HE: Not before?

SHE: He grabbed me from behind. I didn't see him.

HE: You didn't turn when you heard someone behind you?

SHE: There was loud music. I didn't hear anything.

HE: The music was so loud you didn't hear someone behind you?

SHE: There was a machine . . .

HE: A lawnmower?

SHE: Louder. An edger. There was loud music and loud noise. I didn't hear him.

HE: You went into the park.

SHE: To walk to work.

HE: You were wearing suggestive clothing.

SHE: No.

HE: You signaled to a man.

SHE: No.

HE: You enticed him.

SHE: No.

HE: You led him on.

SHE: No.

HE: You acknowledged him.

SHE: [*No answer.*]

HE: You smiled at him.

SHE: Yes.

The lights are beginning to dim, leaving an ever-brightening single spot focused in the woman's eyes, like an interrogation room. Perhaps the man fades into the background during the rest of the play. Or maybe not.

HE: [*He verbally rapes her.*] You left your glasses off. Your dyed hair was bobbing in the breeze. You had painted nails and wore rouge. Your body was scented. You were wearing a revealing outfit, you were feeling sexy in your dainty black lacy undies and your tight shirt and your sheer skirt, and you were shaking your breasts and rolling your hips at this man.

SHE: [*Quite possibly a scream.*] No!

A very long pause.

HE: Start at the beginning.

SHE: What?

HE: Start at the beginning.

SHE: I was walking through the park.

HE: And?

SHE: It was a nice day. [*Pause.*] It was a nice day.

Blackout. End of play.

—1995

acknowledgments

Edward Albee. *The Sandbox* by Edward Albee. Copyright © 1959, renewed 1987 by Edward Albee. All rights reserved. Reprinted by permission of William Morris Agency, Inc. on behalf of the author.

CAUTION: Professionals and amateurs are hereby warned that *The Sandbox* is subject to a royalty. It is fully protected under the copyright laws of the United States of America and of all countries covered by the International Copyright Union (including the Dominion of Canada and the rest of the British Commonwealth), the Berne Convention, the Pan-American Copyright Convention and the Universal Copyright Convention, as well as all countries with which the United States has reciprocal copyright relations. All rights, including professional/amateur stage rights, motion picture, recitation, lecturing, public reading, radio broadcasting, television, video or sound recording, all other forms of mechanical or electronic reproduction, such as CD-ROM, CD-I, information storage and retrieval systems and photocopying, and the rights of translation into foreign languages, are strictly reserved. Particular emphasis is laid upon the matter of readings, permission for which must be secured from the Author's agent in writing. Inquiries concerning rights should be addressed to William Morris Agency, Inc., 1325 Avenue of the Americas, New York, NY 10019, Attn: Eric Lupfer.

Athol Fugard. *Master Harold and the Boys* by Athol Fugard. Copyright © 1982 by Athol Fugard. Reprinted by permission of William Morris Agency, Inc. on behalf of the author.

CAUTION: Professionals and amateurs are hereby warned that *Master Harold and the Boys* is subject to a royalty. It is fully protected under the copyright laws of the United States of America and of all countries covered by the International Copyright Union (including the Dominion of Canada and the rest of the British Commonwealth), the Berne Convention, the Pan-American Copyright Convention and the Universal Copyright Convention, as well as all countries with which the United States has reciprocal copyright relations. All rights, including professional/amateur stage rights, motion picture, recitation, lecturing, public reading, radio broadcasting, television, video or sound recording, all other forms of mechanical or electronic reproduction, such as CD-ROM, CD-I, information storage and retrieval systems and photocopying, and the rights of translation into foreign languages, are strictly reserved. Particular emphasis is laid upon the matter of readings, permission for which must be secured from the Author's agent in writing. Inquiries concerning rights should be addressed to William Morris Agency, Inc., 1325 Avenue of the Americas, New York, NY 10019, Attn: Eric Lupfer.

Arlene Hutton. *I Dream Before I Take the Stand.* Copyright © 2003 by Arlene Hutton. All rights reserved. Reprinted by permission of the author. Written permission is required for live or recorded performance of any sort. For amateur and stock performances please contact Playscripts.com. All other inquiries should be sent to the author's agent, Pat McLaughlin,

Beacon Artists Agency, 120 E. 56th Street, Suite 540, New York, New York 10022.

Henrik Ibsen. From *An Enemy of the People* by Henrik Ibsen, adapted by Arthur Miller, copyright 1951, © renewed 1979. Used by permission of Viking Penguin, a division of Penguin Group (USA) Inc.

David Ives. "Sure Thing" from *All in the Timing* by David Ives, copyright © 1989, 1990, 1992 by David Ives. Used by permission of Vintage Books, a division of Random House, Inc.

Arthur Miller. From *Death of a Salesman* by Arthur Miller, copyright 1949, renewed © 1977 by Arthur Miller. Used by permission of Viking Penguin, a division of Penguin Group (USA) Inc.

Sanchez-Scott, Milcha. *The Cuban Swimmer* by Milcha Sanchez-Scott, copyright © 1984, 1988 by Milcha Sanchez-Scott. All rights reserved. Reprinted by permission of William Morris Agency, LLC on behalf of the Author.

CAUTION: Professionals and amateurs are hereby warned that *The Cuban Swimmer* is subject to a royalty. It is fully protected under the copyright laws of the United States of America and of all countries covered by the International Copyright Union (including the Dominion of Canada and the rest of the British Commonwealth), the Berne Convention, the Pan-American Copyright Convention and the Universal Copyright Convention as well as all countries with which the United States has reciprocal copyright relations. All rights, including professional/amateur stage rights, motion picture, recitation, lecturing, public reading, radio broadcasting, television, video or sound recording, all other forms of mechanical or electronic reproduction, such as CD-ROM, CD-I, information storage and retrieval systems and photocopying, and the rights of translation into foreign languages, are strictly reserved. Particular emphasis is laid upon the matter of readings, permission for which must be secured from the Author's agent in writing. Inquiries concerning rights should be addressed to William Morris Agency, Inc., 1325 Avenue of the Americas, New York, NY 10019, Attn: Eric Lupfer.

Originally produced in New York City by INTAR Hispanic American Arts Center.

William Shakespeare. Notes to "Othello" from *The Complete Works of Shakespeare* 4th ed. by David Bevington. Copyright © 1992 by HarperCollins Publishers. Reprinted by permission of Pearson Education, Inc.

Sophocles. "Antigone," by Sophocles, from *Three Theban Plays* by Sophocles, translated by Robert Fagles, copyright © 1982 by Robert Fagles. Used by permission of Viking Penguin, a division of Penguin Group (USA) Inc.

Tennessee Williams. "The Glass Menagerie" by Tennessee Williams. Copyright © 1945 The University of the South. Reprinted by permission of Georges Borchardt, Inc. for the Estate of Tennessee Williams.

August Wilson. From *The Piano Lesson* by August Wilson, copyright © 1988, 1990 by August Wilson. Used by permission of Dutton Signet, a division of Penguin Group (USA) Inc.

index of critical terms